ENVIRONMENTAL CONTROL SYSTEMS

heating cooling lighting

ENVIRONMENTAL CONTROL SYSTEMS
heating cooling lighting

Fuller Moore

McGraw-Hill, Inc.

New York   St. Louis   San Francisco   Auckland   Bogotá   Caracas   Lisbon   London   Madrid   Mexico
Milan   Montreal   New Delhi   Paris   San Juan   Singapore   Sydney   Tokyo   Toronto

ENVIRONMENTAL CONTROL SYSTEMS:
HEATING COOLING LIGHTING

3 4 5 6 7 8 9   QPD   QPD   9 0 9 8 7

Quebecor Printing/Dubuque was printer and binder.

ISBN 0-07-042889-1

The designer and illustrator was Fuller Moore; the editor was B. J. Clark; the production supervisor was Louise Karam.

Library of Congress Catalog Card Number: 92-61312

TABLE OF CONTENTS

cover: Patoka Interpretive Nature Center, Birdseye, Indiana, Fuller Moore, Architect.

PREFACE

The goal of this book is to introduce the concepts of controlling the thermal and luminous environment in buildings. I've written from an architect's viewpoint with the comfort of the occupant as the central design determinant.

I've always felt that basic physical concepts must be thoroughly understood and internalized in order to intelligently apply environmental control issues. To this end, I've relied extensively on conceptual diagrams and analogies to help the reader develop an intuitive understanding of how heating, cooling, and lighting affect people and the design of buildings.

I've strongly emphasized passive approaches for two reasons. First, because they have such a direct effect on the design of the building envelope (especially in the placement and design of windows). Second, for reasons of comfort and energy-efficiency, passive systems should be considered as primary strategies and mechanical/electrical systems treated as supplemental.

Beginning with an introduction to the basic physical principles (heat transfer and photometry), human response (thermal and visual comfort), and design response to site and climate, both passive systems (solar heating, cooling, and daylighting) and mechanical systems (HVAC and electric lighting) are covered. They are presented conceptually and illustrated extensively using diagrams and case study buildings. Throughout the book, I've tried to emphasize the relationship of the concepts and calculations to the design of both large- and small-scale buildings.

While the book was written from a conceptual point of view, I've also stressed the importance of basic quantitative procedures through the use of worksheet calculations or graphic design tools; formulas are kept to a minimum. Finally, as study aids, I have included questions and a summary of terms at the end of each chapter.

Actually, the final decision as to what to include in this book was made only after considerable debate among my editor, reviewers, and myself. Options included passive systems exclusively, passive systems plus mechanical/electrical, and a comprehensive treatment that would add related technologies: elevators, plumbing, electricity, and fire suppression. The final decision (after surveying numerous faculty at other schools) was to go with passive systems plus mechanical/electrical, with the possibility of a second volume which would cover the related technologies.

Acknowledgments

In looking back over the manuscript, I'm struck by how little original material that I have contributed...and how indebted I am to others on whose work I have so heavily drawn. I've tried to be thorough in my citations, but somehow their brevity and formality fail to adequately represent the importance of their contributions and my appreciation for the opportunity to include them.

Perhaps even more important are my teachers, students, and colleagues who have helped me to form the values and priorities that underlie my own teaching and practice and, inevitably, this book. The Society of Buildings Science Educators has been a major source of inspiration and energy, and many members have contributed to the planning and content of this book: Erv Bales, Cris Benton, Dale Bentrup, Gail Brager, Harvey Bryan, Virginia Cartwright, Robert Chaing, Jeff Cook, Bruce Haglund, Scott Johnston, Norbert Lechner, Russ Leslie, David Lord, Joel Loveland, Murray Milne, Fatih Rifki to name a few.

I am especially grateful to several people who have contributed parts of the text: Harrison Fraker (for his chapter on the formal implications of passive design), Donald Watson (for his section on the history of the passive solar movement), the firm of Burt Hill Kosar Rittelman (for the excerpts on the DOE Commercial Buildings Program), Doug Balcomb and Los Alamos National Laboratory Group Q-11 (for the excerpts and figures on the LCR calculations), and David Lord (for his wonderful collection of solar quotes which I used at the beginning of several chapters).

Fred Morgan, Doug Balcomb, and Rob Pena reviewed the manuscript and I am particularly grateful for their thoroughness and numerous thoughtful comments.

My greatest debt is to John Reynolds who, in addition to being a most thorough manuscript reviewer, has been a source of inspiration, support, and advice as far back as 1969 when I began teaching ECS with him at Oregon (yes, I am a member of the Oregon ECS conspiracy). John, thanks for everything.

— Fuller Moore

INTRODUCTION:

ARCHITECTURE AND ENERGY

"PREINDUSTRIAL" ARCHITECTURE

Prior to the 1800s, architecture was characterized by abundant resources and limited technology. Architects had to utilize the building envelope as the principal mediator between exterior and interior environmental conditions. The building envelope was the principal means of controlling the thermal environment, with the fireplace providing supplemental heat. Architects simply could not afford to ignore the existing conditions of the site and, by necessity, depended on the building envelope to admit light and control other environmental variables. Illumination was principally daylighting and determined by climate, window size and placement, and activity location. Supplemental illumination was in the form of candles and oil lamps, and activities requiring illumination were primarily limited to daytime hours.

"INDUSTRIAL" ARCHITECTURE

The industrial revolution changed all of that. With the innovations developed during that period, designers were offered the means to free their buildings from the constraints that had forever determined their form. The temptation was too great. Designers eagerly took the bait and the direction of architecture was fundamentally and drastically changed.

Previously (with the notable exception of gothic church architecture), bearing–wall construction was the most widely used vertical support system. Exterior masonry walls were thick, massive, and relatively continuous in order to support the weight of the entire structure above. The development of the structural frame and the availability of economical, high–strength steel members allowed the building to be economically supported solely by columns. The exterior wall became supported by the frame at each floor. Its role was reduced to that of a skin to exclude wind and water, and its thickness and mass were reduced to minimize the weight on the columns. The larger openings permitted by the structural frame were filled by great windows, utilizing the newly available larger glass sizes. The advantage of increased access to daylight illumination around the perimeter of the building was accompanied by the potential for increased glare, winter heat loss, and summer solar gain.

The thermal qualities of the more massive construction were lost, and this function replaced by mechanical heating and cooling systems. The invention of the gas mantel, then the incandescent lamp, and later the fluorescent lamp, allowed buildings to have greater depth. These devices replaced windows and skylights as primary sources of illumination. No longer was lighting dependent on proximity to the exterior. Previously the width of the building plan was limited to a maximum of about 80 ft so that no location was more than 40 ft from exterior illumination. Greater building depth was previously also restricted by the necessity of natural ventilation. The invention of forced ventilation, and later air conditioning, changed that. Operable windows became unnecessary, and, in fact, even interfered with mechanical operation. It is important to recognize that it was the twin developments of the fluorescent lamp and mechanical air conditioning that made the deep, lower–ceilinged office building possible. Either development alone would not have sufficed (Banham, 1969).

The structural frame and the elevator allowed buildings to exceed the height limitations previously imposed by bearing walls and stairs. The sanitary requirements of the higher buildings were adequately served by recent developments in water pumps, central plumbing, and waste treatment systems.

As transportation systems developed during this period (first rail and later truck), construction materials were no longer economically limited to those available locally. Mechanical cranes and excavation equipment minimized the design constraints of natural site topography.

The effects of these changes in building technology became first evident in larger buildings, where the costs of engineering, toolup, and custom fabrication of equipment could be justified. Later, as a result of mass production, many of these developments were utilized in smaller buildings and residences.

THE MODERN MOVEMENT

The pioneers of the modern movement, reacting to the ornamental excesses of the late Renaissance period, used the freedom allowed by the technical developments of the industrial revolution to explore new building forms.

Some architects (notably Frank Lloyd Wright, Le Corbusier, and Alvar Aalto), retained many of the historic principles of site orientation, natural ventilation, and daylight illumination while selectively incorporating the new technology as a *means* in the process of building design.

Others, ignoring climate, used the new building technology as the *end*, directly generating the building form. This latter movement became dominant early in the twentieth century during the rebuilding of post–World War I Europe. Because the components were mass–produced in a variety of distant locations, and because they allowed (even encouraged) the ignoring of the influence of climate and customs, this "International" style reflected none of the localized elements characteristic of traditional architecture. The movement quickly spread to the United States, partially due to the immigration of several of the leading European proponents (Walter Gropius, Eliel Saarinen, and Mies van der Rohe) who established successful practices and began teaching and writing. The resulting simple geometric building forms were also influenced by the contemporary cubist and de Stijl movements in painting and sculpture, and as a reaction to the overornamentation of the classical–revival architecture of the previous century. In general, the International style became

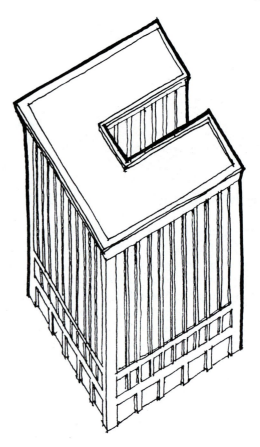

Figure 2: Wainwright Building showing notch for access to daylight and ventilation (Louis Sullivan, architect). *(After Ternoey et al., 1985.)*

widely accepted in America once the students of these early advocates graduated and entered the profession. As the interrelationships of these technical developments became established and matured, there emerged an identifiable, industrially based, energy–dependent architectural style that fundamentally differed from previous shelter–oriented styles.

Economy of structure, space, ornament, labor, and construction cost were characteristic of the new International style. This concern for economy did not extend to energy. To the contrary, virtually every technical development that characterized the movement was possible only through a greater use of energy in every phase of the life of the building, including component manufacturing, transportation, construction, and particularly operation. Consider the electric lamp, the structural frame, the lightweight envelope materials (especially aluminum), the large glass areas, waterproofing materials, the elevator, and

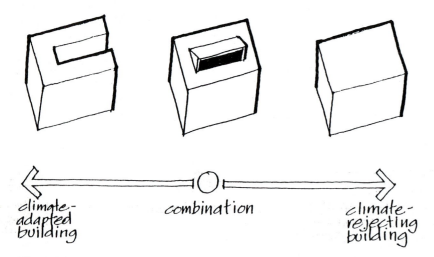

Figure 1: Continuum of building climatic response: from (a) climate-responsive, through combination, to (c) climate-rejecting. *(Suggested by Steve Hogg, after Ternoey et al., 1985.)*

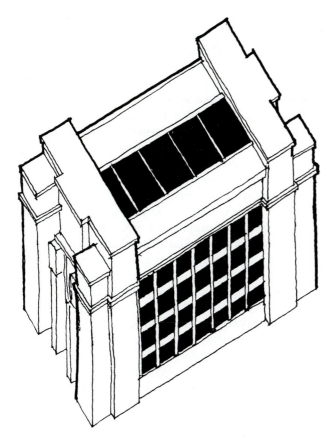

Figure 3: Larkin Building (Frank Lloyd Wright, architect). *(After Ternoey et al., 1985.)*

the electronic sound amplification and communication systems. In every case, increased energy usage was the price of these developments that freed architecture from the constraints of climate and site.

RESPONSE TO CLIMATE

Commercial building design solutions may be characterized as a continuum between two extremes (climate–adaptive and climate–rejecting buildings); this range can be illustrated with a discussion of three representative buildings (Toerney, et al., 1985).

The Wainwright Building, designed by Louis Sullivan in 1890, is an example of a climate–adaptive building. The familiar frontal elevation of this building shows it as a solid block form, similar to modern office buildings. In plan, however, the building is deeply notched to provide access to daylight and

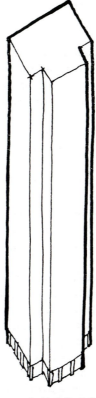

Figure 4: Seagram's Building (Mies van der Rohe and Philip Johnson, architects). *(After Ternoey et al., 1985.)*

natural ventilation. In addition, high ceilings provided for circulation of air and distribution of daylight. The envelope was extensively punctured with operable windows. The U–shaped plan represents a design trade–off between increased surface area (for daylight and ventilation) and the associated increased heat loss. Infilling the U–shape would have provided a more efficient envelope (less relative surface area) for heating purposes, but would have made lighting and cooling more difficult. Such trade–offs are typical of buildings which utilize both natural and conventional energy sources.

The Larkin Building (Buffalo, New York), designed by Frank Lloyd Wright in 1904, is an example from the middle of this continuum. In response to air pollution from nearby railyards, it was one of the first "sealed" buildings, using evaporative cooling and filtration to provide "air conditioning." Actually, by modern definitions, the Larkin Building cannot be considered truly air conditioned because humidity was not controlled (Banham, 1966). Like the Wainwright Building, most office space in the Larkin Building was bilaterally daylit by exterior windows and a top–glazed atrium. The continuous skylight greatly reduced the thermal perimeter of the building and minimized the problems associated with the large surface area of the Wainwright notch. Like the Wainwright, the Larkin Building required high ceilings and additional volume due to the atrium: the use of natural energies demands a larger building box.

The Seagram Building, designed by Mies van der Rohe in 1958, represents the extreme in climate–rejecting large office building design. Utilizing complete artificial environmental control, the building was free to become much deeper than buildings of the past. The center of the building is 70 ft from the nearest window, four times greater than the Wainwright or Larkin buildings. Without the need for daylight and natural ventilation, the ceilings were lowered to house lighting fixtures and mechanical distribution systems. This reduced the volume necessary to heat, light, and cool. More important, the surface–to–volume ratio was reduced (0.33 for the Seagram's Building, 0.88 for the Larkin Building).

The effect of architectural practice

The new direction of architecture was not alone in encouraging energy–intensive solutions. The very way in which architecture was practiced changed organizationally in a way that fostered energy–intensive solutions. Prior to the industrial revolution, building technology was relatively uncomplicated. The architect was sufficiently knowledgeable in all major technical areas to make overall design decisions in a holistic and integrated way. By contrast, the technology of the modern movement developed so rapidly and was so complex, that it became impossible for a single individual to be sufficiently knowledgeable to make conceptual design decisions in the areas of mechanical, electrical, and structural systems.

Specialists emerged in each technical area, and the architect became dependent on them during the critical conceptual design phase. The architect lost the capacity to evaluate the various technical choices independently in terms of their effect on the overall design.

As specialists established independent consulting firms, design decisions have become even more fragmented and integration more difficult. For example, the thermal implications of a certain type of wall construction might not be appreciated by an architect with a limited understanding of heat transfer and the energy and equipment costs associated with this design decision. With the architect's rationale for the choice of this type of construction obscure to the consulting mechanical engineer, his or her primary concern is the provision of a heating and cooling system adequately large to maintain thermal comfort. Under such an organizational arrangement, there is no incentive for the consulting engineer to integrate his or her efforts with those of the architect in order to reduce equipment size or energy usage. To the contrary, not only does such coordination require considerably greater effort, but it is discouraged by currently prevailing contractual arrangements between architects and consultants under which the consultant's fees are a percentage of the cost of equipment specified.

"POSTINDUSTRIAL" ARCHITECTURE

As long as energy was abundant and cheap, the excesses of the International style were of little concern. Predictions and evidence of the consequences of the prevailing direction of architecture (depletion of nonrenewable energy resources and ecological implications) were largely ignored by archi-

tects and clients alike. The inertia of these attitudes is considerable. The architectural profession and the construction industry (including trade union jurisdictions) have evolved and flourished in an era that favored specialization and compartmentalization at the expense of energy consumption.

The oil embargo of 1973 was a rude awakening. The combination of the pocketbook impact of escalating energy costs (with no evidence of a long–term solution) and the personal indignity of waiting in long gasoline lines began to accomplish what environmental concerns could not. Namely, an awakening of professional and public consciousness to the energy (and economic) consequences that the modern movement had wrought.

Ironically, the oil prices, set artificially high by the monopoly enjoyed by the Organization of Petroleum–Exporting Countries (OPEC) during the 1970s, spurred high levels of production. Many oil–producing countries borrowed heavily to build the increased production capacity as well as to begin many capital–intensive domestic improvement programs (schools, infrastructure, port development, etc.). The heavy debt incurred by these countries was based on expectations of continued high oil prices. Yet oil prices fell in the early eighties and have remained relatively stable since. Debt–ridden oil–producing countries have been forced to high production levels and have ended up competing with one another for available demand. With this, OPEC has effectively lost the ability to control production and, in turn, prices. As a result, a temporary surplus of oil is available on the world market and prices remain stable. Yet, with the increased supply, consumption remains high and available reserves are being depleted at an accelerated rate. Known oil reserves remain finite and the long–term energy–supply situation remains bleak.

Most professional, industrial, financial, and client decision makers were educated prior to the oil embargo in a protechnology, energy–abundant era. It is relatively easy for the client and lending institutions to change their posture to one supportive of energy conservation; it requires only a look beyond construction costs and visual aspects to life–cycle cost–benefit analyses.

For the architect, the task is more formidable and requires the rethinking of previously accepted design methods and strategies. It requires acquisition of the fundamental technical knowledge necessary to reclaim the lost role of an integrative designer.

ENERGY REQUIRED FOR BUILDING CONSTRUCTION

The study of buildings and energy use is usually devoted to a consideration of the energy required to operate buildings. This is understandable since it represents approximately 33 percent of all national energy use. However, the amount of energy required to build, alter, and maintain buildings is frequently overlooked. The University of Illinois Center for Advanced Computation estimates this "capital" building energy represents 6.25 percent of all energy use in the United States (Stein and Serber, 1979).

Direct energy use on the construction site is the largest single energy user in the building industry, accounting for 15 percent of the 6.25 percent total, or almost 1 percent of all national energy. It almost entirely consists of refined petroleum products — gasoline, diesel fuel, kerosene, heating fuels, and asphalt and road oils. In general, wood frame construction has low amount of energy embodied in construction in comparison with concrete and steel systems most commonly associated with commercial construction. And concrete structural systems embody only slightly more than half of the energy than that of standard steel construction.

THE PASSIVE SOLAR MOVEMENT
by Donald Watson (1989)

Beginning in the early 1930s, Chicago architects Fred and William Keck began a decade–long investigation of south–facing windows in residences that became the first to be called "solar houses." During this same period, two internationally reknowned modern architects, Walter Gropius and Marcel Breuer, both applied climatic analysis as major design determinants, as evidenced by generous south–facing and properly shaded windows. Frank Lloyd Wright in his Usonian house designs in Wisconsin and simultaneously in his design of Taliesin West in Arizona, all executed in the late 1930s, ingeniously and appropriately applied climatic design elements to diverse and contrasting climates, giving ample testimony that climatic principles underlie a mastery of architecture, regardless of style.

In 1947, as part of an effort to market their newly developed Thermopane insulating glass, the Libbey–Owens–Ford company commissioned leading architects to design low–cost "solar houses" for each of the then–48 states. The list of architects included such notables as Hugh Stubbins, Edward Stone, Louis Kahn, Alden B. Dow, John Lloyd Wright, George Keck, Henry Kamphoefner, O'Neil Ford, Paul Thiry, Pietro Belluschi, and Harwell Hamilton Harris. The results were published in a widely circulated book, *Your Solar Home* (Simon, 1947). This book did much to publicize "solar" homes (predominately south–facing insulated glass with overhangs).

Climate data suitable for building design were first defined in a series of articles published in *House Beautiful* magazine (1949–1951) and subsequently as *Bulletins of the American Institute of Architects* under the editorial leadership of James Marston Fitch and Paul Siple (AIA, 1949–1952). In this effort, the climatic data of a dozen areas of the United States were detailed, with corresponding design recommendations. (More recently, the AIA Research Corporation, 1979, published similar but more detailed design guidelines for each of sixteen climatic regions in the United States.) Concurrently, *House Beautiful* ran popular magazine articles promoting features such as window shading and white reflective roofs for warm climates, and earth–sheltering and solar orientation for cool climates.

In the post–World War II years in the United States, research at schools of architecture, notably the Texas A&M Experiment Station (founded by W. S. Caudill) and the Princeton Architectural Laboratory (founded by Victor and Adalar Olgyay), established full–scale laboratories to test wind, daylighting, and solar effects in buildings. However, by the late 1950s, at the very point that bioclimatic design was widely promulgated in professional and popular housing literature, advances in heat–resistant glazings and in mechanical heating and air conditioning were developed, allowing architects to ignore climate, if at the cost of energy efficiency and thermal comfort. The era of "air conditioning" had begun. The Equitable Savings and Loan Building (1948, Portland, Oregon) was the first fully sealed and air–conditioned office building in the United States, and used double–paned green–tinted glass (Cook, 1982). In 1952, the Lever House was the first modern skyscraper in New York City to use the newly developed heat–absorbing tinted glass as a means to reduce undesired solar gain. Shortly thereafter, the same glass was specified in the United Nations Building, instead of the sun–shades proposed by architectural consultants Le Corbusier and Oscar Niemeyer. These two buildings, rather than the earlier work of Wright, Gropius, and Breuer, established the style of all–glass–faced modern buildings that was to dominate contemporary architecture for the ensuing decades.

The term *bioclimatic approach to architectural regionalism* was first proposed by Victor and Adalar Olgyay (1953); it recognized that architectural design begins with the physiological aspects of human comfort. In the mid–1970s, the term *passive solar design* came into popular use to describe similar but more limited applications of solar energy. However, the Olgyay term is nonetheless more comprehensive, since it includes all climatic impacts and places human well–being as central to the conception of building design.

From the 1950s to 1970s, significant research in climatic design continued elsewhere in the world, primarily out of the need to design buildings for hot climates in the developing countries, some still in their late colonial periods. Givoni (1969) and Koenigsberger, et al. (1974) authored important professional texts in building climatology that continued the tradition established by Olgyay and Olgyay. They developed techniques by which practicing architects could translate climatic data into specific design. This work became the research basis for the "rediscovery" of bioclimatic design, prompted by the 1973 OPEC oil embargo, which abruptly brought energy costs to the public consciousness. Energy conservation in buildings became a part of the overall effort to develop renewable energy in national energy policy. The initial response to oil shortages was to promote solar heating, first in *active* solar heating based on technologies developed by Hottel and others at MIT and soon thereafter as passive solar heating. Both active and passive concepts were first used by individual designers and homebuilders in the United States who were willing and able to be experimental. Much of the early experimentation in passive solar heating was done in the southwest, particularly in New Mexico. Pioneers such as Peter van Dresser, Steve Baer, Wayne and Susan Nichols, and David Wright sparked a regional interest in these techniques through local meetings which in turn spread to support a series of national conferences beginning in Albuquerque in 1976. These proceedings (Passive Division of American Solar Energy Society, 1975 through 1991) record the development of solar heating in the United States.

Currently, more than energy shortages and energy efficiency per se compel the continued research and professional interest in low–energy architectural design. Regional and global environmental concerns have led to a "systems" view of building and environment, based on a biological view of environmental health and resource conservation. The role of fossil fuel use in contributing to global environmental degradation is a more recent concern worldwide. This enlarged conception of environmental architecture includes the building's impact on air and water quality, water conservation, and planting and vegetation.

This bioclimatic research and design spans more than five decades. During this time, the emphasis has changed according to perceived public concerns. Viewed as a continuous development, it can be seen that the idea of bioclimatic design, first articulated by the Olgyay brothers in the early 1950s, has developed into a mature and coherent body of building research.

1

HEAT TRANSFER

The Hymn to the Sun

Your light illumines the highways and byways.
The very fish in the water cavort before you,
And your beams strike to the very depths of the ocean.

Your rays provide nutriment for the fields,
And when you smile, they flourish,
And become fruitful for you.

– Akhenaton

HEAT AND TEMPERATURE

Heat and temperature are terms which are often confused. Heat is the energy of vibrating molecules in a substance. Temperature is the measure of the average vibrating energy in each of the molecules of a substance. Temperature, then, is a measure of the concentration of heat within a substance.

Virtually all earthly substances have heat by virtue of the fact that their molecules are in motion. By definition, "absolute zero" (–459.69°F, –273.15°C, or 0°K) is the temperature at which all molecular motion stops. The faster the molecular vibration, the higher the temperature.

From day-to-day experience, most people are familiar with temperature (as measured in degrees Fahrenheit or Celsius). Less familiar is the measure of heat: the *British thermal unit* (or Btu) or *calorie*. A Btu is defined as the amount of heat required to raise the temperature of one pound of water one Fahrenheit degree. A wooden kitchen match releases about one Btu when burned.

It is frequently (and erroneously) assumed that a high temperature means that a substance contains more heat. Consider the following example. Two containers of water (Fig 1.1) begin at the same temperature. One contains 1 lb of water and is heated 2°F (i.e., 2 Btu are added). Another contains three pounds of water and is heated 1°F (i.e., 3 Btu are added). The second contains more heat, but the first is a higher temperature because the heat was concentrated in a smaller amount of water.

Heat always flows from warmer to cooler substances. If there is no temperature difference, there can be no heat transfer. For example, consider several objects near one another in a room, all at different temperatures. Those that are warm will become cooler and those that are cool will become warmer until all reach a common temperature. This equalizing of temperature is caused by three types of heat transfer: conduction, radiation, and convection.

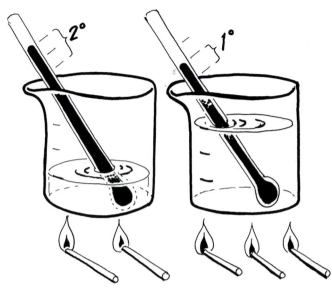

Figure 1.1: Two containers of water begin at the same temperature. One contains one pound of water and is heated 2°F (i.e., 2 Btu are added). Another contains three pounds of water and is heated 1°F (i.e., 3 Btu are added). The second contains more heat, but the first is a higher temperature because the heat is concentrated in a smaller mass.

In special circumstances, where moisture (liquid water or gaseous water vapor) is involved, heat can be transferred by phase change (evaporation and condensation).

CONDUCTION

Conduction is the transfer of vibrating energy between adjacent molecules. The transfer is always from the warmer region (faster vibration) to the cooler region (slower vibration). The transfer occurs equally readily in any direction (up, down, sideways) and is independent of gravity.

A familiar demonstration of conduction transfer is holding a metal spoon in a bowl of hot soup; it quickly becomes hot to the touch. The heat enters the spoon where it is immersed in soup, and is transmitted along its length to the fingers. The hot soup causes the molecules in the heated end of the spoon to vibrate more rapidly. These faster (warmer) spoon molecules collide with adjacent slower (cooler) spoon molecules and cause them to move faster. These, in turn, cause their cooler neighbors to speed up, setting up a chain reaction, and effecting a flow of heat by conduction from the warmer soup to the cooler fingers. But the total amount of heat in this simplified soup–spoon–

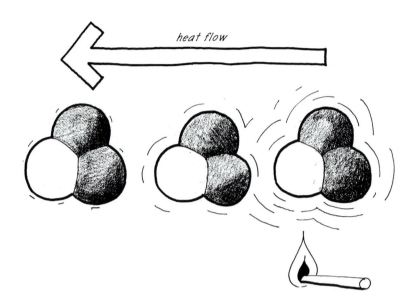

Figure 1.2: Heat transfer by conduction.

hand system remains the same; the soup is cooled as it gives up thermal energy to the spoon. The spoon is cooled as it warms the hand. Eventually all three elements stabilize at a common temperature and no further heat transfer occurs.

How readily a substance conducts heat depends on its molecular structure. For substances common to the architectural environment, it is a general rule that the denser the material, the more readily it will conduct heat. Metals (aluminum, steel, copper) are excellent conductors. Concrete and masonry materials are also good conductors; solid wood, less so.

Air (and other common gases) are especially poor conductors and thus good insulators. Porous materials (such as wool, fiberglass insulation, and rigid foams) which contain a large number of small airspaces are good insulators and are often used in building construction to reduce heat loss or gain.

Because conduction depends on the transfer of vibrating energy between adjacent molecules, no conduction can occur in the absence of molecules (i.e., a vacuum). This is why a Thermos bottle, with the near–vacuum space between two layers of glass, is so effective in keeping liquids hot or cold. However, because of the structural problems in withstanding the pressure of the surrounding atmosphere, vacuum materials are rarely used in buildings.

MEASURING CONDUCTION

The ability to conduct heat is dependent on several factors:

- The conducting ability of the material itself (generally, the greater the density and the less air entrained, the more heat conducted).

- The temperature difference (the greater the difference on each side of the material, the more heat conducted).

- Its thickness (how far through the substance the heat is flowing — the less the thickness, the more heat conducted).

- Its exposed area (the greater the area of the substance exposed to the temperature difference, the more heat conducted).

- The duration of exposure (the longer the exposure, the more heat conducted).

Thermal conductivity (k) is the heat transferred by conduction through a substance of a given thickness in a given time when a given temperature

difference is applied to a given area. It is the basic measure of conduction heat transfer of a substance. The units are Btu–inches per square foot per degree F temperature difference per hour or (Btu•in.)/(ft^2•hr•°F). For example, concrete has a conductivity of 12.0 (Fig. 1.3) meaning that if one square foot of concrete one inch thick is exposed to a constant temperature difference of

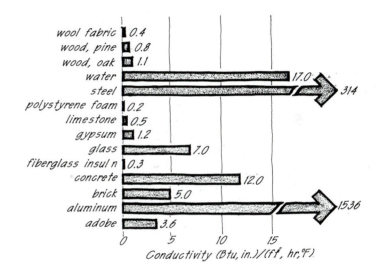

Figure 1.4: Conductivity of some building materials. (*Note*: the "conductivity" value for water takes into account the heat transfer effects of internal convection.)

1.0 Btu between the two sides, then 12 Btu will be conducted in one hour. *Thermal resistivity (r)* is the reciprocal of conductivity.

Thermal conductance (C) is the heat transferred by conduction through a substance of a particular thickness per unit of time when a given temperature difference is applied to a unit area; the units are Btu per square foot per degree F temperature difference per hour or Btu/(ft^2• hr•°F).

Conductance is similar to *conductivity* but it is the measurement for a particular thickness; the units are Btu/(hr•ft^2•°F). For example, a 3–in. thickness of concrete has a conductance of 4.0 (calculated by dividing the conductivity *k* by the thickness 3) meaning that if 1 ft^2 of concrete 3 in. thick is exposed to a constant temperature difference of 1.0 Btu between the two sides, then 4 Btu will be conducted through in one hour. Because many building components may have variable characteristics (i.e., variable area of hollow concrete masonry units), tables of the measured conductances of variety of building components are available and typically used for calculating heat loss through the building envelope.

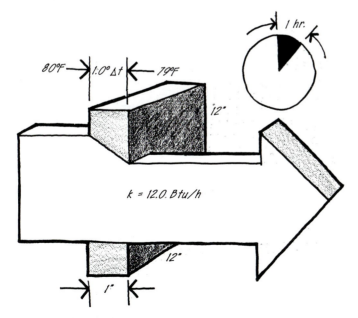

Figure 1.3: Thermal conductivity of concrete.

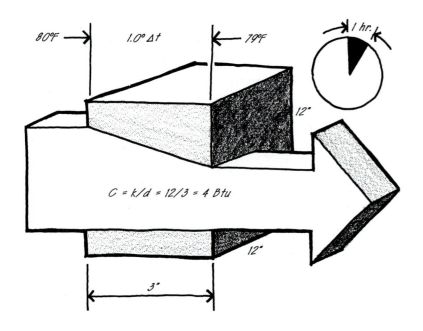

$$C = k/d = 12/3 = 4\ Btu$$

Figure 1.5: Calculating the thermal conductance C through a 3-in. thickness of concrete.

Thermal resistance (R, or more popularly, R–value) is the reciprocal of thermal conductance ($1/C$); the units are hour–ft^2–degree F per Btu [(hr•ft^2•°F)/ Btu]. It is a more familiar unit for measuring and designating the insulating performance of building components. The greater the R–value, the greater the insulating value. It is a particularly convenient unit for calculating the insulating ability of a composite construction assembly because the resistances of each of the components can be simply summed to determine the resistance for the entire assembly.

The R–value of the 3–in. concrete slab example is 0.25 (the reciprocal of the conductance C, or 1/4). If a layer of 2 in. of rigid urethane foam insulation (R 12.5) were added to the concrete, then the R would be 12.75. If the concrete–foam sandwich was a vertical wall, then add the insulating effects of an air film inside (R 0.68) and outside (R 0.17 — smaller due to probable effects of wind outdoors), creating an R–value of 13.6 for the entire wall assembly.

Unfortunately, the units of resistance (hr•ft^2•°F/Btu) are intuitively meaningless (and seldom used in practice). And, while R is a convenient unit

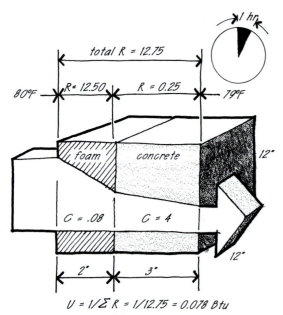

$$U = 1/\Sigma R = 1/12.75 = 0.078\ Btu$$

Figure 1.6: Calculating the thermal resistance R through an insulated wall assembly.

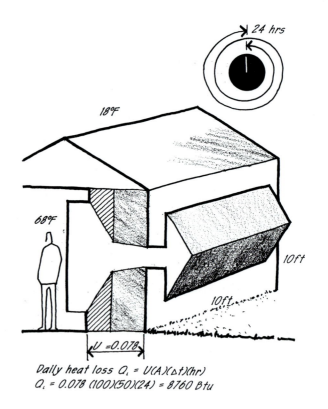

Daily heat loss $Q_t = U(A)(\Delta t)(hr)$
$Q_t = 0.078\ (100)(50)(24) = 8760\ Btu$

Figure 1.7: Calculation of daily heat loss through an insulated concrete wall.

to quantify the insulating ability of a wall assembly, it does not directly express the heat conducted through the wall.

THERMAL TRANSMITTANCE

Thermal transmittance (U) is the unit measure of the heat transferred through a building assembly per unit of time per unit of area and is reciprocal of the total R–value. The units of thermal transmittance U are (like conductance C) Btu/(hr•ft^2•°F). Note, however, that while component R-values can be summed to determine the R for a total assembly, conductances C cannot be summed to determine the transmittance U. Instead, take the reciprocals of the component conductances C to determine the component R–values. Then sum the R–values to find a total resistance R for the entire assembly, and finally take the reciprocal of the total R to determine the thermal transmittance U.

In our example, it would be *incorrect* to try to sum the conductances C of the components directly [i.e., outside air film (C 5.9) + concrete (C 4.0) + urethane foam (C 0.08) + inside air film (C 5.9) is *not* the same as total C of 15.88]. Instead, sum the resistance R–values [outside air (R 0.17) + concrete (R 0.25) + urethane foam (R 12.5) + inside air (R 0.68)] to determine the composite resistance R = 13.6. Then the total thermal transmittance U = 1/total R = 0.073 Btu/(hr•ft^2•°F). If the total wall area was 100 ft^2, the average daily outside air temperature is 18°F, and the inside air temperature was maintained at 68°F, then the building would lose 8760 Btu during a 24–hour period (0.073 U–value x 100 ft^2 x 50°F x 24 hrs).

Because of the difficulty in calculating the separate effects of radiation and convection heat transfer, virtually all published values of conductance (C), resistance (R), and transmission (U) include the total heat transferred in the material by all means (conduction, radiation, and convection).

THERMAL STORAGE

The above method of calculating heat loss by conduction presumes a constant temperature difference over a long period of time. While this ideal seldom occurs in reality, the method is still reliable if comparatively little heat is stored in the building materials. This is typically the case if the building structure is comparatively light in weight (e.g., wood, steel, glass). However, more massive materials (e.g., concrete, brick) store significant amounts of heat and are slow to warm up and cool down. The thermal storage capacity of the building envelope can significantly affect its thermal performance.

SPECIFIC HEAT

By definition, water is able to "store" one Btu per pound for each degree Fahrenheit temperature rise. *Specific heat* is a measure of the ability of a material to store heat, and is defined as the Btus required to raise the temperature of one pound of a substance one Fahrenheit degree; the units are

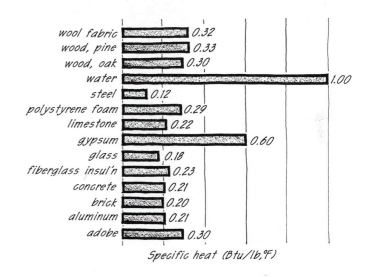

Figure 1.8: Specific heat of some common building materials.

Btu/lb•°F. Water, with a specific heat (by definition) of 1.0, is the standard against which all other materials are measured.

A relatively small amount of water absorbs a great deal of heat for a correspondingly small rise in temperature. Similarly, water takes a long time to cool down. This has practical architectural design implications in two areas: climate and solar heat storage.

If water did not have such a high heat storage capacity, northern Europe would be as cold as the northeastern regions of Canada, because both regions are at the same latitude and get about the same amount of annual solar radiation. But the Gulf Stream absorbs heat in the warm Caribbean and holds its heat long enough to reach the North Atlantic off the coast of Europe where it cools, releasing its heat to the prevailing westerly winds which carry the heat over northern Europe.

Because of the great thermal inertia of water (slow to heat or cool), building sites near large bodies of water experience significantly less daily and annual temperature fluctuation than comparable landlocked regions. This explains

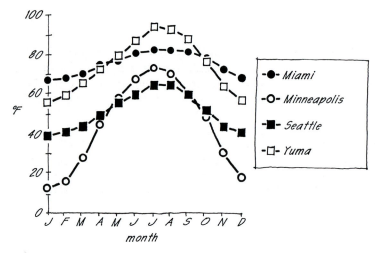

Figure 1.9: Mean daily temperatures by months for Yuma, Arizona; Miami, Florida; Minneapolis, Minnesota; and Seattle, Washington. Notice that the temperatures in coastal cities vary less due to the thermal storage of the nearby water mass.

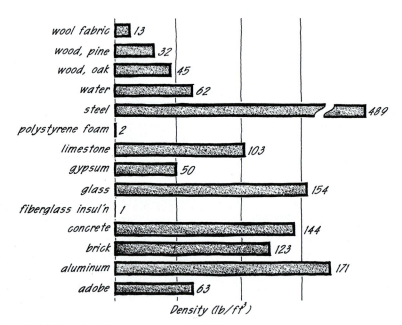

Figure 1.10: Density of some common building materials.

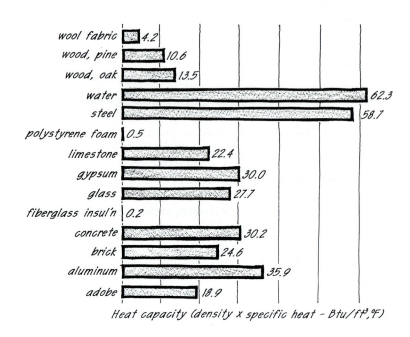

Figure 1.11: Heat capacity [density x specific heat — Btu/(ft^3•°F)] of some common building materials.

At the building scale, if the outside temperature is comparatively constant, the thermal storage characteristics of the building materials have little effect on the building's interior temperatures. However, if there are major daily temperature swings, the choice of materials with a high thermal storage capacity can help stabilize interior temperatures. *Specific heat*, by itself, is an inadequate indicator of the suitability of a building material for thermal storage because it does not take into account the volume required for the process. *Heat capacity* is a better measure because it takes into account the amount of heat that can be stored per unit of volume; it is the product of *density* (lb/ft^3) and *specific heat*. The units of heat capacity are Btu/ft^3•°F.

But even heat capacity fails to take into account the need for transferring the heat away from the surface of the material and spreading it throughout the internal mass. If the heat is not conducted readily to the core of the material, then the surface overheats while the heat capacity of the cool core is underutilized. Conductance, then, is the third essential ingredient in measuring the suitability of a material for storing heat in a building. *Thermal storage capacity* is the product of density, specific heat, and conductivity; its units are Btu^2/(h•ft^4•°F^2).

the relatively constant temperatures of peninsula cities (like Miami) or island cities (like Honolulu).

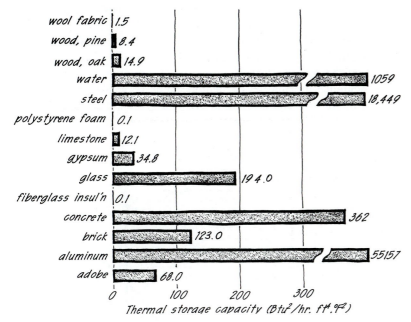

Figure 1.12: Thermal storage capacity (density x specific heat x conductivity — Btu²/h•ft⁴•°F²) of some common building materials. (*Note*: The "conductivity" value for water takes into account the heat transfer effects of internal convection.)

RADIATION

Thermal radiation is the transfer of heat (molecular vibrating energy) by electromagnetic waves. When molecules on the surface of a substance vibrate, they give off (emit) radiant energy in the form of electromagnetic radiation. Thermal radiation is one type of electromagnetic radiation. Like conduction, energy is transferred from a warmer substance to a cooler substance. Unlike conduction, no molecular medium is required. In fact, radiation occurs most readily in a complete vacuum.

The vibrating motion of the surface molecules of a substance create electromagnetic (or radiation) waves which travel away from the surface at the speed of light. (Actually the quantum theory of light recognizes that light travels in tiny packets of radiation called photons that exhibit a strange mixture of wave and particle properties. However, for architectural applications, the simpler concept of radiation as waves suffices and will be used here.)

The vibration of the surface molecules is slowed when their thermal energy is converted into wave (radiant) energy. These waves travel until they strike a surface and are absorbed. The molecules on the receiving surface absorb some of the radiant energy and convert it to heat energy, increasing their vibration,

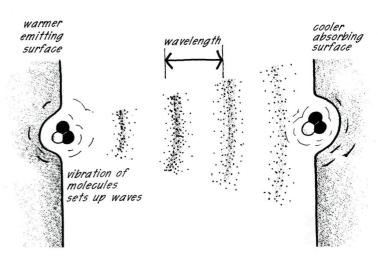

Figure 1.13: Radiant energy transfer between two surface molecules.

and raising in temperature. Because radiation travels in a straight line, it is necessary that both surfaces (the emitting and the absorbing) have a line–of–sight relationship to one another.

All substances radiate energy in all directions as a function (of the fourth power) of the absolute surface temperature. Thus, even a cool surface radiates energy to a warmer surface. However, this cooler surface receives from the warm surface even more energy. Therefore, the *net* radiant energy transfer is always from a warmer surface to a cooler surface. Like conduction, radiation is independent of gravity and occurs equally in all directions.

The temperature of a surface not only determines the quantity of radiation emitted, it also determines the length (frequency) of the radiation waves. Each surface molecule vibration initiates a wave. Because radiation travels at a constant speed (that of light, 186,000 miles per second), the vibrating speed of the molecule determines the frequency (length) of this wave. The fastest (warmest) molecules emit the shortest wavelengths. For example, the relatively hot surface of the sun emits radiation in comparatively short wavelengths (between 0.4 and 4.0 microns; one micron = 0.000001 meter). Building surface molecules vibrate slower, emitting longer wavelengths (between 8 and 50 microns).

MEASUREMENT OF RADIATION

Radiant flux is the time rate of flow of radiant energy, and the units are Btu/(h•ft²). For example, a surface oriented perpendicular (normal) to the sun would typically receive about 250 Btu/(h•ft²) on a clear day in an urban

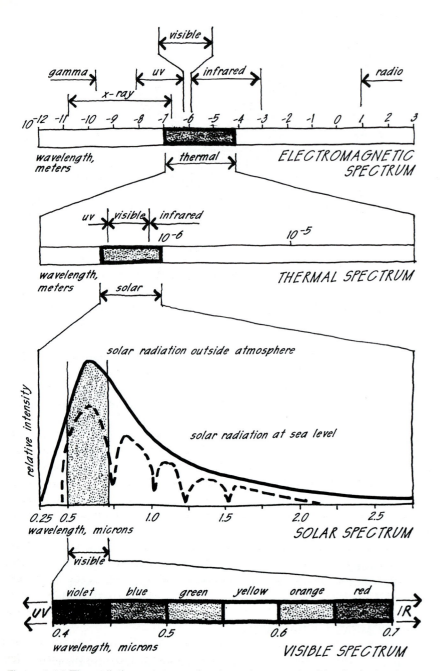

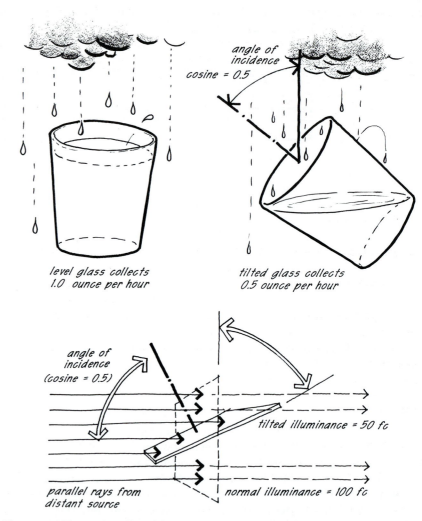

environment. The solar flux just outside the earth's atmosphere (the extraterrestrial solar constant) is 429.2 Btu/(h•ft^2).

If the receiving surface is tilted relative to the radiation source, the radiant flux is distributed over a larger area and its density or concentration is reduced as a result of the *cosine effect*. The amount of reduction is the cosine of the angle of incidence (normal or perpendicular is 0° angle of incidence). For example, if the normal radiant flux is 275 Btu/(h•ft^2), a surface tilted at 60° (i.e., cosine 60° = 0.5) will receive 137.5 Btu/(h•ft^2).

Figure 1.14: The radiation spectrum, showing enlargements of the thermal, solar, and visible spectrums. *(Reproduced from Moore, 1985, by permission.)*

Figure 1.15: The cosine effect: (a) water glass analogy, and (b) radiation striking a tilted surface. *(Reproduced from Moore, 1985, by permission.)*

THE VISIBLE, NEAR–IR, AND FAR–IR SPECTRAL REGIONS

Central to an understanding of radiation behavior in buildings is a recognition that there are three regions of the radiation spectrum of particular interest to the designer. These may be characterized as the *visible*, *near–IR*, and *far–IR* regions of the spectrum. The visible region is that part of the total solar spectrum that is visible to the eye and thus useful for lighting (0.4 to 0.7 microns). The near–IR region is the invisible portion of the solar spectrum (0.7 to 4.0 microns). The small solar ultraviolet (solar–UV) region (0.3 to 0.4 microns) is also invisible but architecturally significant only for its effect on the fading of interior finishes and plant growth. The far–IR region is the invisible portion of the spectrum emitted from warm room and other terrestrial surfaces (greater than 8 to 50 microns). The distinction between the near–IR and far–IR regions is particularly important architecturally because of the different behavior of glazing materials in these regions.

Radiation (in either of these regions) that is transmitted or reflected retains similar wavelength characteristics. However, absorbed radiation is converted to heat which is then conducted, convected, or reradiated. This reradiation occurs only in the far–IR region and should thus not be confused with transmitted or reflected radiation.

OPTICAL PROPERTIES

When radiant energy strikes a surface, any combination of three things can occur. It can be absorbed and converted into thermal energy, warming the receiving surface, it can be reflected back out away from the substance, whereby no heating occurs, or, if the material is transparent to the radiation wavelengths involved, it can be transmitted. The measures involved (absorptance, reflectance, and transmittance) are unitless between 0.0 and 1.0; the sum of the three for any substance must equal 1.0. In other words, the quantity of incident radiation must always equal the sum of the radiation absorbed, reflected, and transmitted.

EMISSIVITY

Emissivity is the measure of the ability of a surface to emit radiation at a given surface temperature; the range of unitless values is 0.0 (no emittance possible) to 1.0 (ideal maximum — a "black body"). At any given temperature (i.e., within any given region of the radiation spectrum), a surface's emissivity is exactly equal to its absorptance (Kirchhoff's law). Most common building materials are good far–IR absorbers and are, therefore, good emitters (far–IR emittance > 0.9).

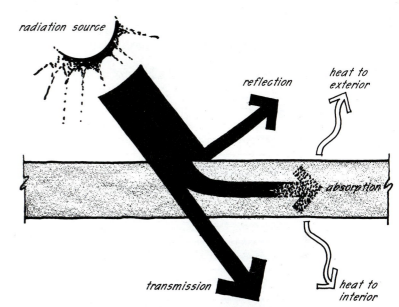

Figure 1.16: Absorption, reflection, and transmission of radiation striking a semitransparent material. *(Reproduced from Moore, 1985, by permission.)*

Polished metallic surfaces, however, are typically poor far–IR absorbers (good reflectors) and are correspondingly poor emitters. In other words, metallic surfaces reflect far–IR well (difficult to heat by surrounding warmer surfaces), but once warm tend to hold heat well (reluctant to give off heat by radiation).

To illustrate this important principle, consider an experiment where two identical aluminum cans are filled with hot water. The surface of one can is painted white and the other is polished aluminum. Both are then placed inside of separate cardboard boxes. The inside and outside of each box is white cardboard. The water in the polished can will cool more slowly because its surface emittance is lower than its painted counterpart (and far–IR radiation heat loss is reduced).

Now add a third can of water and another box. The new can is painted white, but the inside of the new box is covered with aluminum foil. When the experiment is repeated, the third can will also cool off slowly (at about the same rate as the polished metal can in the painted box) because the far–IR radiant transfer between the new can and box is reduced — this time because of the high far–IR reflectivity of the foil box.

The combination of a polished metal can and foil–lined box contributes little to the overall heat retention capabilities over a single metal surface (on either the can or the box). Most of the radiant transfer is eliminated by one low–emittance surface. The remaining heat transfer is by conduction (through direct contact between the bottom of the can and the supporting surface) and by convection (due to air circulation within the box).

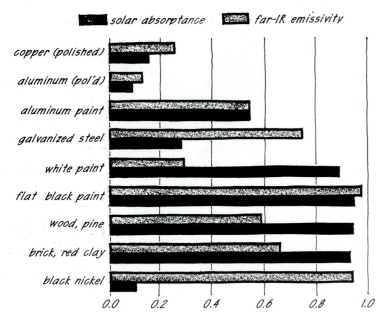

Figure 1.17: Optical properties of some common opaque materials.

However, adding a foil surface to the *outside* of the box further reduces heat loss by reducing radiant transfer from the box exterior and the surrounding cooler room surfaces.

If the inside of the water can were either polished metal or painted white, heat loss would not be affected because the heat transferred between the water and the can is by conduction only.

These experiments demonstrate that having a low far–IR–emittance surface on at least one side of an airspace can effectively reduce radiant transfer. A similar low far–IR–emittance surface sandwiched between two other solid substances has little effect because transfer is by conduction only. This principle has direct application in building construction. Foil–faced wall materials (such as fiberglass batt insulation or gypsum wallboard) significantly reduce heat transfer through the wall if (and only if) the foil is positioned adjacent to an airspace. Foils are less effective on room wall surfaces (and virtually ineffective on outdoor wall surfaces) because convection transfer due to air motion predominates.

The *visible* and *near–IR* absorptance of building materials is closely related to surface color (darker = greater absorptance). But these materials (being much cooler than the sun) emit only in the *far–IR* region, and for that reason

their emittance for these lower temperatures is the only value of interest. As seen above, nonmetallic surfaces are good emitters; metallic ones are not.

From this information, it can be concluded that dark surfaces make good solar absorbers (and quickly heat up), light–colored surfaces reflect solar heat (and stay cool), and warm polished–metal objects hold their heat, while warm painted objects cool off quickly. The ideal surface for a solar collector is one that is both black (to absorb most visible and near–IR) and metallic (to minimize cooling by radiation). While such selective surfaces do not occur naturally, they have been developed for use on solar collectors.

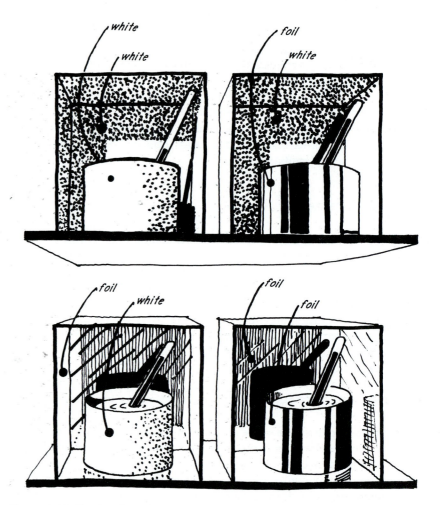

Figure 1.18: Section through example boxes — the painted can emits more far–IR radiation (and cools off quicker) than the polished metal can.

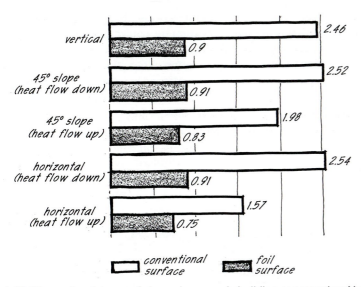

Figure 1.19: Thermal resistance of plane air spaces in building construction. Notice the effect of a low-emissivity foil added to one side of the air space. *(Based on ASHRAE, 1985, data.)*

THE GREENHOUSE EFFECT

On a clear day, the atmosphere of the earth is comparatively transparent to solar radiation (especially in the visible and near–IR regions). After passing through the atmosphere, the solar radiation strikes some terrestrial surface and is either reflected (about 20 percent) or absorbed (about 80 percent). Reflected solar radiation is transmitted back out of the atmosphere as easily as it came in. But the radiation absorbed is converted to heat, warming the absorbing surface.

The atmosphere is comparatively more opaque to the longer *far–IR* radiation emitted from solar–warmed earth surfaces. It becomes a radiation "blanket" preventing the radiation of the earth's heat to outer space. This effect is responsible for the comparatively warm and stable thermal environment of the atmosphere.

The amount of moisture in the air has a profound effect on the greenhouse effect. Humid climates have comparatively stable daily air temperatures, while desert regions experience great daily air temperature swings due to the ease of radiating heat out through a clear, dry atmosphere to outer space.

The greenhouse effect is also present in some building materials. Glazings (the transparent component in windows and skylights) are used in buildings for a variety of radiation–control purposes including admitting light, admitting solar heat, allowing view in and out, and blocking or allowing radiant heat losses from the interior. In addition to radiation control, glazings are used as a barrier to convection. (Glazing materials have a relatively high conductance and do not contribute directly to reducing conductive losses.) While other materials are equally effective in controlling convection, glazings are unique in their capability to control radiation. Because of the importance of windows and skylights in buildings, it is important to the designer to have a conceptual understanding of their important and unique optical properties. Glazing materials and their optical properties are considered in detail in Chapter 19.

CONVECTION

As a substance is heated, its molecules vibrate faster and faster. As a general rule, in response to this greater activity, the molecules separate themselves further and further apart. This results in an expansion of the substance. Solids and liquids increase in volume. Liquids and gases become less dense and thus more buoyant than nearby cooler fluids. *Convection* is the transfer of heat by a moving fluid medium (e.g., air or water). Technically, convection is a form of radiation and conduction in combination with the motion of the fluid but, for the purposes of understanding heat transfer in the architectural environment, it will be considered a separate mode of heat transfer.

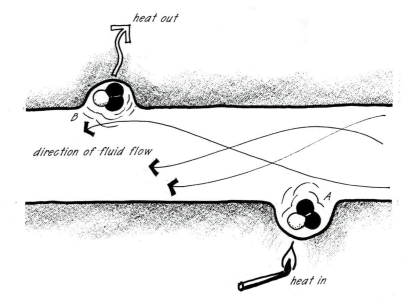

Figure 1.20: Heat transfer from *A* to *B* by conduction.

Consider the transfer of heat between two points, warmer *A* and cooler *B*. The moving fluid is warmed by conduction and radiation as it comes in contact with point *A*. This heat then diffuses to other parts of the fluid stream by conduction and physical mixing. When the moving fluid reaches point *B*, heat is again transferred by conduction and radiation.

An essential difference between conduction and convection is the type of molecular movement. In conduction, molecules do not change location, but instead transfer energy from one molecule to the next in a vibrating "domino" effect. In convection, the energy is transferred by the physical relocation of the molecules as the fluid moves.

NATURAL CONVECTION

The fluid motion required for convection transfer can be caused by temperature-induced buoyancy differences of the fluid within the system. This is *natural* convection (also known as thermosiphoning or thermal circulation). When a fluid is heated, the movement of its molecules increases, and they

move further apart, making the fluid less dense. If upper portions of the fluid are cooler than other lower portions, then the cooler (denser) fluid will displace the warmer, more buoyant fluid, which will rise. Because natural convection is gravity–dependent, the general direction of heat flow will always be upward.

Thermal circulation can be *closed–loop* (as in a thermosiphoning solar hot water heater) if the path of the fluid is confined. By limiting the circulation to a linear path, the behavior of such closed–loop systems is comparatively simple and easy to predict. But thermal circulation can also be *free* (as in a room with one warm wall and an opposite cool wall). Without boundaries to direct the flow in a linear direction, turbulent convection currents mix air throughout the room in complex patterns that are difficult to predict.

Figure 1.22: Open or free convection circulation.

FORCED CONVECTION

The fluid motion required for convection can also be caused by an external force (e.g., fan, pump, or wind). This is *forced convection*. Because forced convection does not depend on gravity and buoyancy, heat flow can occur in any direction.

Air is the convective medium of greatest interest in building envelopes, although there are a few convective applications for water (for example, the internal mixing in passive solar thermal storage tanks).

Convection heat transfer is basically a function of three factors: (1) the temperature difference between the warm and cool regions, (2) the volumetric rate of fluid flow, and (3) the specific heat and density of the transfer fluid. If the rate of flow and the specific heat and density are held constant (typical of

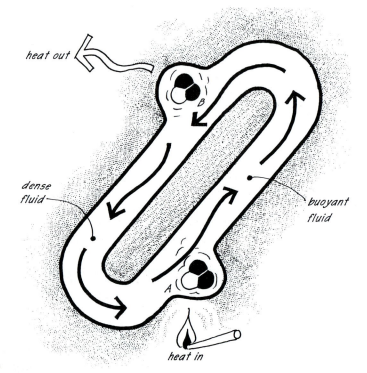

Figure 1.21: Closed-loop thermosiphoning heat transfer.

fan– and pump–operated forced–convection systems), then convection heat transfer is dependent only on temperature difference (as is conduction).

In natural convection systems (which are more typically found in the building envelope), however, the rate of flow is not constant, but is itself dependent on temperature differences to create the buoyant forces. Thus, as temperature differences increase, the rate of fluid flow increases nonlinearly. This is further complicated by the frictional resistance to compressible fluid flow (which is a nonlinear function of fluid velocity and path smoothness). In free conditions (such as a room) where even the path of flow is variable, accurate calculation of convective flow is impractical, if not impossible.

INFILTRATION

Infiltration is the accidental leakage of outside air into the building. It is a major source of convective heat transfer through the envelope, and thus of particular interest to the designer. Infiltration is a combination of forced and natural convection.

Forced infiltration is primarily due to exterior wind conditions. As wind flows around and over a building, exterior air pressures become greater on windward surfaces and less on leeward surfaces. Outside air flows into the building through windward openings (e.g., cracks, doors, windows), and inside air flows out through leeward openings. The heat transfer due to wind–induced infiltration is a function of inside–outside temperature difference and the volumetric rate of airflow (which is a complex function of windspeed, aerodynamic shape of the building, and amount and location of openings).

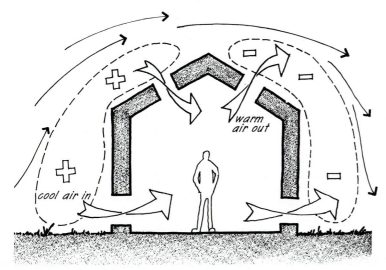

Figure 1.23: Wind-forced infiltration (winter).

Stack–effect infiltration is a form of natural convection due to temperature–related differences in the buoyancy of inside and outside air. It is most pronounced in the winter as warm inside air rises to escape through openings in the upper regions of the building, and is replaced by cool outside air drawn in through openings around the base of the building. It is dependent on temperature differences and the rate of volumetric flow. As with other types of natural convection, the rate of volumetric flow is also dependent on temperature differences. Thus, as temperature differences increase, natural convection infiltration transfer increases at an accelerated rate.

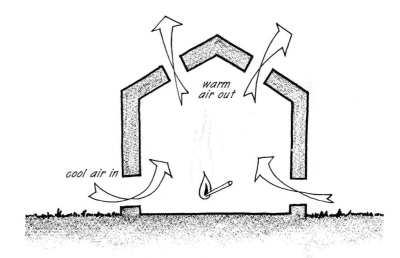

Figure 1.24: Stack-effect infiltration (winter).

PHASE CHANGE

When a material changes state or phase (e.g., going from liquid to gas) a large amount of heat must be absorbed (or released) in order to make the transition. Because water–to–vapor phase change is common in an architectural environment and because its thermal behavior is unique, it will be considered here as a type of heat transfer distinct from conduction, radiation, and convection.

DRY–BULB TEMPERATURE

If the air in a room were completely dry, its thermal properties could be described using a conventional thermometer to measure its *dry-bulb temperature*. In real environments, this state virtually never exists; there is always some moisture present in the form of water vapor. The amount of moisture in the air has a significant effect on thermal comfort, especially in warmer environments.

SENSIBLE HEAT, LATENT HEAT, AND ENTHALPY

Sensible heat is the "dry" heat in the air related to dry–bulb temperature. Heat added to that air from the glowing coil of an electric cooking range is an example of sensible heat.

Latent heat is the "wet" heat released into the air as water changes from liquid to vapor by evaporation or boiling. Water vapor added to the air as a result of a tea kettle boiling on the stove is an example of latent heat. The process is reversible, as latent heat is released when moisture is condensed out of the air.

Enthalpy is the sum of the sensible and latent heat in the air; it is sometimes called *total heat*.

The units for sensible heat, latent heat, and enthalpy are all the same: Btu/lb of dry air.

WET–BULB TEMPERATURE

One measure of the effect of moisture in an air–vapor mixture is *wet–bulb temperature*. It is measured using a thermometer with a wetted bulb moving rapidly through the air in order to promote evaporation. If the air is relatively dry, evaporation is rapid, resulting in a cooling of the thermometer bulb and a measured temperature substantially lower than the dry–bulb temperature. This difference (between corresponding dry– and wet–bulb temperatures) is the *wet–bulb depression*. Similarly, if the air is moisture–laden, wet bulb evaporation will be minimal, and the wet–bulb depression will be small.

PSYCHROMETRY

HUMIDITY RATIO

The relationship between dry–bulb air temperature and water vapor present in the air can be described graphically with a *psychrometric* (a.k.a. "psych") chart. The psych chart is constructed by plotting a dry–bulb temperature of the air on the horizontal scale and a scale of the humidity ratio of the air on the vertical axis. *Humidity ratio* is the ratio of weight of moisture to the weight of dry air in the air–vapor mixture.

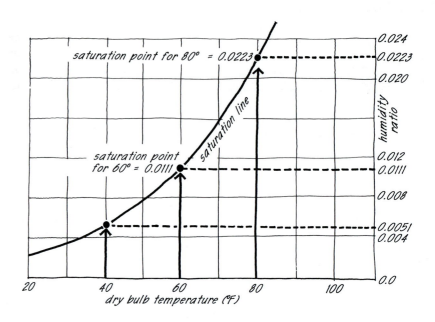

Figure 1.25: Construction of the psychrometric chart: air saturation as a function of temperature.

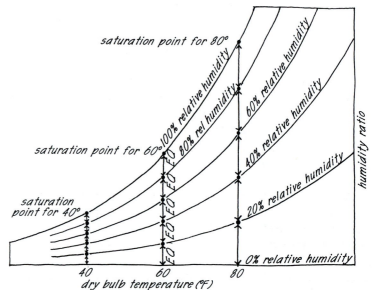

Figure 1.26: Construction of the psychrometric chart: relative humidity curves created by dividing vertical dry-bulb temperature lines into equal parts below the saturation line.

SATURATION

For any air temperature, there is a maximum humidity ratio that can be held at that temperature (recall that the capacity of air for moisture increases with air temperature). This is the *saturation point* of air. This critical saturation humidity ratio can be plotted for each temperature to form the *saturation line*.

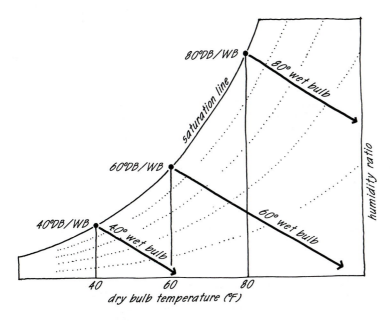

Figure 1.27: Construction of the psychrometric chart: At saturation, wet-bulb temperature equals dry-bulb temperature; to maintain constant wet-bulb temperature, the humidity ratio must be lowered while dry-bulb temperature increases. Constant wet-bulb lines extend down and to the right from the saturation line origin.

RELATIVE HUMIDITY

Relative humidity is the humidity ratio of the air expressed as percent of saturation point for that temperature. For example, the humidity ratio of the air in a room is measured to be 0.0111 and the dry–bulb (DB) temperature to be 80°F. The saturation point for 80°F (DB) is 0.0222; therefore, the relative humidity ratio is 50 percent.

Relative humidity curves (lines of constant relative humidity) can be plotted by simply dividing each of the vertical temperature lines into equal parts between the bottom of the chart (0 humidity ratio) and the saturation point.

WET–BULB TEMPERATURE LINES

Wet–bulb temperature lines can be plotted on the psych chart. If the air is saturated, no evaporation occurs and the wet- and dry–bulb temperatures are equal. On the chart, this occurs where the vertical dry–bulb temperature lines intersect the saturation line. In order for the wet–bulb temperature to remain constant as dry–bulb temperature increases, the humidity ratio must be lowered. As a result, constant wet–bulb lines extend diagonally down and to the right from the saturation line origin. Because these relationships (between dry–bulb, wet–bulb, and humidity ratio) are both constant and linear, the lines are straight and parallel.

ENTHALPY

Wet–bulb temperature is a direct indicator of enthalpy (the sum of sensible and latent heat) in the air. It was noted earlier that when evaporation occurs, the air gains latent heat and releases a corresponding amount of sensible heat (i.e., the dry–bulb temperature decreases as humidity ratio increases), and the enthalpy remains constant. When constant–enthalpy evaporation occurs, the conditions of the air as plotted on the psych chart move down and to the right

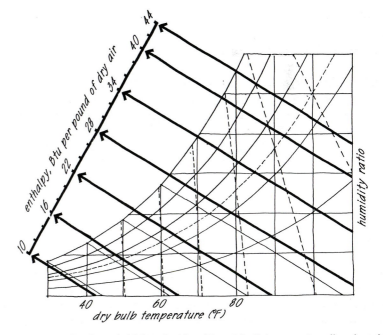

Figure 1.28: Enthalpy lines (which coincide with wet-bulb temperature lines) projected to the enthalpy scale outside of the chart.

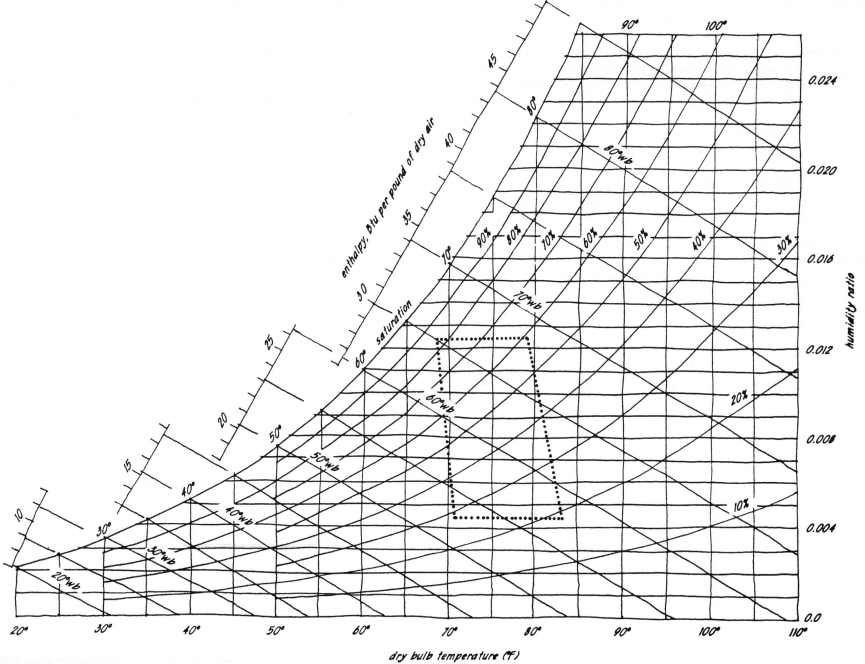

Figure 1.29: Completed psychrometric chart.

along the wet–bulb lines. And conversely, when constant–enthalpy condensation occurs, the conditions of the air as plotted on the psych chart move up and to the left along the wet–bulb lines.

The units of enthalpy are Btu/lb of dry air. Because the constant–enthalpy lines and the constant wet–bulb lines coincide on the chart, to prevent confusion, the enthalpy lines are extended beyond the saturation–line limits of the chart where the enthalpy scale is plotted.

MEASURING LATENT AND SENSIBLE HEAT

Any vertical–only movement on the psych chart (which corresponds to a change in the humidity ratio) represents a change in latent heat which can be measured on the enthalpy scale. For example, assume that the initial condition of a body of air is 100°F DB and a humidity ratio of 0.0132. The corresponding enthalpy can be read on the chart as 38.6 Btu/lb dry air. If the humidity ratio is lowered to 0.0023 while the dry–bulb temperature is held constant, then the new enthalpy is 26.7 Btu/lb dry air and the enthalpy change is –11.9. Because this change is solely due to removing moisture, there is no change in sensible heat, and all of the heat removed from the air is latent (i.e., 11.9 Btu/lb dry air).

Conversely, any horizontal–only movement on the chart (which corresponds to a change in the dry–bulb temperature) represents a change in sensible heat which can be measured on the enthalpy scale. For example, assume that the initial condition of a body of air is again 100°F DB and a humidity ratio of 0.0132; the corresponding enthalpy is again 38.6 Btu/lb dry air. If the dry–bulb temperature is lowered from 100°F to 70°F while the humidity ratio is held constant, then the new enthalpy is 31.2 Btu/lb dry air and the enthalpy change is -7.4. Because this change is solely due to changing the dry–bulb temperature, then there is no change in latent heat, and all of the heat removed from the air is sensible (i.e., 7.4 Btu/lb dry air).

Diagonal movement, being a combination of both vertical and horizontal movement, signals change in both latent and sensible heat. For example, once again assume that the initial condition is 100°F DB and a humidity ratio of 0.0132; the corresponding enthalpy is once again 38.6 Btu/lb dry air. If the dry–bulb temperature is lowered to 70°F *and* the humidity ratio is lowered to 0.0023, the new enthalpy is 19.3 Btu/lb dry air (i.e., a change of 019.3 Btu/lb). This diagonal movement can be broken down into separate vertical and horizontal movements in order to determine the latent (–11.9) and sensible (–7.4) components.

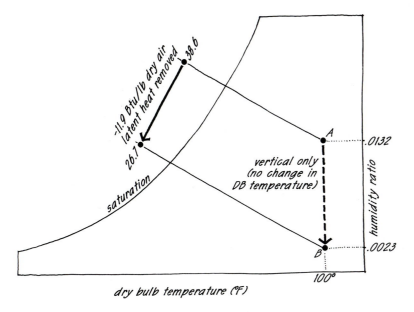

Figure 1.30: Determining change in enthalpy and latent heat due solely to changing moisture (vertical-only movement on the chart).

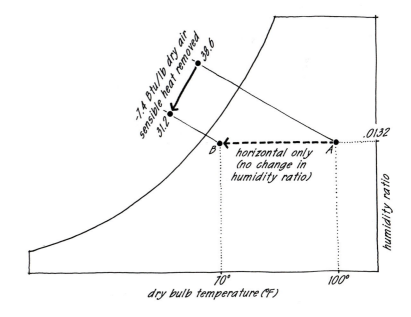

Figure 1.31: Determining change in enthalpy and sensible heat due solely to changing dry-bulb temperature (horizontal-only movement on the chart).

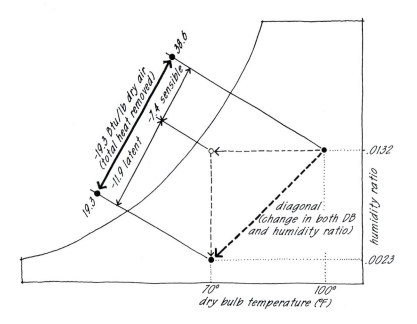

Figure 1.32: Determining changes in enthalpy and latent and sensible heat due to simultaneous change in humidity ratio and dry-bulb temperature (diagonal movement on the chart).

While this change is the result of a single diagonal movement on the chart, to determine what portion of the change is sensible and what portion latent, plot the change in two stages: horizontal and vertical displacement. In this manner, the enthalpy change due solely to dry–bulb temperature change (i.e., the horizontal displacement) can be determined separately from that due solely to the change in humidity ratio (the vertical displacement).

EVAPORATIVE COOLING

Evaporation is a constant–enthalpy process that occurs when latent heat (moisture) is added to the air while the same amount of sensible heat is removed as the dry–bulb temperature is lowered. This can be a practical and effective cooling process whenever the humidity ratio of the initial condition is low, allowing considerable diagonal movement along the constant–enthalpy/ constant–wet–bulb line before "running into" the saturation line — by definition, the limit of evaporation.

DESICCANT DEHUMIDIFICATION

Desiccation is the reverse of evaporation and occurs when sensible heat (dry–bulb temperature) is added as the same amount of latent heat (moisture) is removed from the air. The process of desiccating moist air usually involves

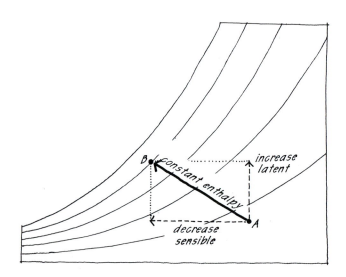

Figure 1.33: Evaporative cooling, a constant-enthalpy process achieved by exchanging latent and sensible heat, occurs along the wet-bulb/enthalpy lines.

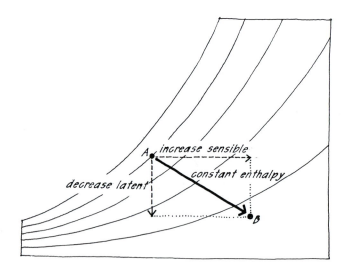

Figure 1.34: Desiccant dehumidification — a constant-enthalpy process achieved by exchanging latent and sensible heat.

a chemical drying agent (e.g., calcium chloride) and, while it is suitable for controlling the humidity in a confined space (such as an instrument case), it is of limited practical application in buildings.

CONDENSATION

When moist air is cooled, molecules vibrate slower and get closer together. The air's capacity to hold moisture is diminished, and eventually *condensation* occurs. Condensation is the process of changing vapor into liquid by extracting heat. This occurs when sensible heat is removed (dry–bulb temperature lowered) while the humidity ratio is held constant.

DEW POINT

A common example of this sensible cooling occurs when warm moist air in a room comes in contact with a cool window surface. If the temperature of the surface is cool enough (and the dry–bulb air temperature is lowered as it comes in contact), the limit of the capacity of the air to hold moisture will be reached. This is the critical point at which condensation occurs as the excess moisture released by the air forms on the cool surface, and by definition, occurs along the saturation (100 percent relative humidity) line. *Dew point* is this critical temperature at which condensation occurs as the dry bulb temperature of moist air is lowered.

Because the dew point and the saturation point both occur along the saturation line on the psych chart, they are often confused. The difference is that the saturation point is related to a particular dry–bulb temperature (indicating the amount of moisture that air at that temperature can hold), while dew point is related to a particular humidity ratio (indicating the temperature at which air with that amount of moisture will begin condensing).

If the air continues to cool after the dew point is reached, moisture will be released as condensation occurs. On the psych chart, this process will continue along the saturation line, lowering the dry–bulb temperature while lowering the humidity ratio. Condensation is the most common method of removing moisture in the architectural environment. In an architectural environment, mechanical refrigeration is usually necessary to reach temperatures well below the dew point to significantly lower the humidity ratio.

REHEATING

Unfortunately, after being cooled to the dew–point temperature and beyond to effect condensation (and reduce the humidity ratio), air is left at 100 percent relative humidity. In order to lower the relative humidity, it is necessary to add sensible heat while holding the moisture (latent heat). As the air is reheated to temperatures above the dew point, it moves horizontally to

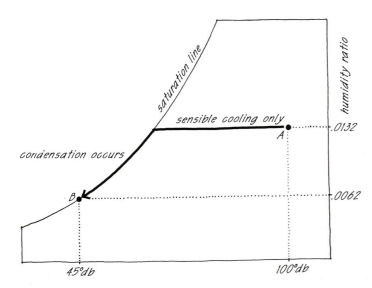

Figure 1.35: Dehumidification is achieved by cooling the air below the dew point temperature causing condensation.

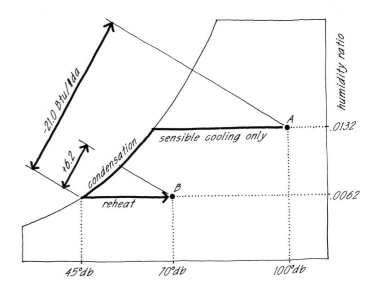

Figure 1.36: Mechanical cooling typically involves cooling air below dew point until the desired humidity ratio is achieved, and then reheating the air to achieve the desired dry-bulb air temperature.

the right on the psych chart. This very roundabout process (of cooling to condense moisture out of the air and reheating) is the only way possible to achieve lower temperatures while holding the relative humidity constant. It is not possible to move directly along the relative humidity curves on the chart. The process requires mechanical refrigeration equipment and a considerable expenditure of energy to accomplish.

SUMMARY OF TERMS

Heat — the energy of vibrating molecules in a substance.

Temperature — the measure of the average vibrating energy in each of the molecules of a substance; a measure of the *concentration of heat* within a substance.

"Absolute zero" — the Kelvin–scale temperature at which all molecular motion stops (–459.69°F, –273.15°C).

Btu (British thermal unit) — the amount of heat required to raise the temperature of one pound of water one Fahrenheit degree.

Conduction — the transfer of vibrating (thermal) energy between adjacent molecules.

Thermal conductivity (k) — the heat transferred by conduction through a substance of a unit thickness in a unit time when a given temperature difference as applied to a unit area; the units customarily used are Btu–inches per square foot per degree F temperature difference per hour (Btu•in.)/(ft²•hr•°F).

Thermal conductance (C) — the heat transferred by conduction through a substance of a particular thickness per unit of time when a given temperature difference as applied to a unit area; the units are Btu/(h•ft²•°F).

Thermal resistance (R or R–value) — the reciprocal of thermal conductance (1/C); the units are (h•ft²•°F)/Btu.

Thermal transmittance (U) — the unit measure of the heat transferred through a building assembly per unit of time per unit of area; the units are Btu/(h•ft²•°F).

Specific heat — the quantity of heat required to raise the temperature one unit of mass one degree of temperature; units are Btu/(lb•°F).

Density — mass per unit volume; units are lb/ft³.

Heat capacity — the product of density and specific heat; units are Btu/(ft³•°F).

Thermal storage capacity — the product of density, specific heat, and conductivity; units are Btu²/(h•ft⁴•°F²).

Thermal radiation — the transfer of heat (or molecular vibrating energy) by electromagnetic waves.

Transmission — the passage of radiant energy through a substance.

Transmittance — the ratio of radiation transmitted through a substance to the radiation striking its surface; range is 0.0 to 1.0.

Absorption — the process of converting radiation into heat when it strikes or passes through a substance.

Absorptance — the ratio of radiation absorbed by a substance to the radiation striking its surface; range is 0.0 to 1.0.

Reflection — the process whereby, after striking a surface, radiation leaves the surface on the incident side.

Reflectance — the ratio of radiation reflected by a substance to the radiation striking its surface; range is 0.0 to 1.0.

Visible radiation — thermal radiation in the solar spectral region to which the human eye is sensitive (between 0.4 and 0.7 microns).

Near–IR radiation — thermal radiation in the solar spectral region too long to be perceived by the human eye (between 0.7 and 4 microns).

Far–IR radiation — thermal radiation emitted from building surfaces (less than 150°F or 65°C; 8 to 50 microns).

Emissivity — the measure of the ability of a surface to emit radiation at a given surface temperature; the range of unitless values is 0.0 (no emittance possible) to 1.0 (ideal maximum).

Specular — clear (transmission) or mirrorlike (reflection).

Diffuse — opalescent (transmission) or matte (reflection) so that radiation is redistributed in many directions.

Convection — the transfer of heat by a moving fluid medium (e.g., air or water). *Natural convection* is circulation caused by temperature–induced buoyancy differences of the fluid within the system. *Forced convection* is the circulation of a fluid caused by an external force (e.g., fan, pump, or wind).

Infiltration — the accidental leakage of outside air into the building. *Forced infiltration* is caused by wind. *Stack–effect infiltration* is due to temperature–related differences in the buoyancy of inside and outside air.

Dry–bulb temperature — air temperature measured using a conventional thermometer.

Sensible heat — the "dry" heat in the air related to dry–bulb temperature; units are Btu/lb of dry air.

Wet–bulb temperature — the temperature of air measured using a thermometer with a wetted bulb moving rapidly through the air in order to promote evaporation.

Latent heat — the "wet" heat released into the air as water changes from liquid to vapor by evaporation or boiling; units are Btu/lb of dry air.

Enthalpy — the sum of the sensible and latent heat in the air; total heat; units are Btu/lb of dry air.

Humidity ratio — the ratio of weight of moisture to the weight of dry air in the air–vapor mixture.

Saturation point — maximum humidity ratio that can be held at a given temperature. *Saturation line* on the psychrometric chart is defined by the saturation points for all dry–bulb temperatures.

Relative humidity — the humidity ratio of the air expressed as percent of saturation point for that temperature.

Evaporative cooling — a constant–enthalpy process whereby latent heat is added while the same amount of sensible heat is removed from the air.

Condensation — the process of changing vapor into liquid by extracting heat.

Dew point — the temperature at which condensation occurs as the dry–bulb temperature of moist air is lowered.

STUDY QUESTIONS

1. Distinguish between temperature and heat.

2. San Francisco is warmer in winter than Washington, D.C. Why is it cooler in the summer?

3. If you survey a site for a client on a cold day using a steel measuring tape, will the measurement be larger or smaller than they actually are?

4. Wood is a better insulator than glass. Explain why fiberglass is commonly used as a building insulating material.

5. Why will a nail inserted in a potato decrease the baking time?

6. Explain why a covering of snow protects crops from damage on a suddenly cold day.

7. Since all objects are absorbing energy from their surroundings, why doesn't the temperature of all bodies continually increase?

8. Why is whitewash sometimes applied to greenhouses in the summer?

9. Explain why, in the winter, "drafts" develop in rooms with large windows (but not cracks to the outside).

10. Why is evaporation a cooling process?

11. Differentiate between evaporation and boiling.

12. Explain the difference between sensible heat, latent heat, and enthalpy.

13. Why can warmer air hold a greater amount of water vapor?

14. Distinguish between saturation point and dew point.

2

THERMAL COMFORT

Thermal qualities — warm, cool, humid, breezy, radiant, cozy — are important experiential qualities of a space. They not only influence what people choose to do there, but how they feel about a space. For example, the fireplace was traditionally the center of family life. "Its dancing light, smoky smells, and warm crackling created an ambiance that made a house more a home. And the traditions around the hearth stretched back through the ages, connecting each house to deep cultural roots" (Heschong, 1979).

Life can exist only within a small range of temperatures — generally between the freezing and boiling points of water. Each species has definite limits and thrives only within a narrow range. Many have ways of extending their range. Deciduous trees reduce their exposure to severe cold or drought by dropping their leaves. Cold-blooded animals and some mammals reduce their life processes (breathing, metabolism, blood circulation) and go into hibernation. They seek a thermally protected shelter (like an underground nest) and become dormant in order to conserve energy to survive the most severe winter conditions.

Most mammals, and especially humans, maintain constant deep body temperature — a process known as *homeostasis*. To do this, it is necessary to exactly balance the total heat exchange of the body so that the amount lost to the surrounding environment equals the amount gained. This process is regulated by the hypothalamus. If the deep body temperature varies by even a few degrees, sickness (and ultimately death) will follow.

METABOLISM

The primary way that the human body gains heat is through metabolism — the conversion of chemical energy (food) into mechanical energy (activity) and thermal energy (heat). In general, the greater the activity, the greater the rate of metabolism; in other words, the faster that food is converted into work and heat. Therefore, the greater the level of activity, the more heat that must be dissipated from the body in order to maintain that constant body temperature.

The siesta is one traditional regional response to temperature. In hot climates, most daily activity takes place in the relative cool of the morning, and everyone slows down in the hot afternoon. This ensures that people's metabolism (and heat generation) is minimized during the hottest part of the day.

BODILY HEAT TRANSFER

Because the deep body temperature must be maintained constant, the heat generated by metabolism must be released to the surrounding environment by the skin surface and respiration. This is done by a combination of convection, radiation, conduction, and evaporation.

CONVECTION

The skin is cooled by convection as surrounding cooler air flows across the skin's surface. The greater the temperature difference (cooler the air), the greater the transfer. As the air temperature increases, convection cooling is reduced. As air temperatures exceed skin temperature, the body actually begins to gain heat from the environment. The rate of convective heat loss is also affected by the speed of the air movement across the skin's surface. This is the "wind chill factor" referred to in weather reports. One of the functions of winter clothing is to provide a barrier to the wind, trapping body-warmed air near the skin and preventing its rapid replacement by the moving surrounding cool air.

Similarly, breathing causes additional convective transfer (dry respiration heat loss) as surrounding cool air is drawn into the lungs, warmed, and exhaled.

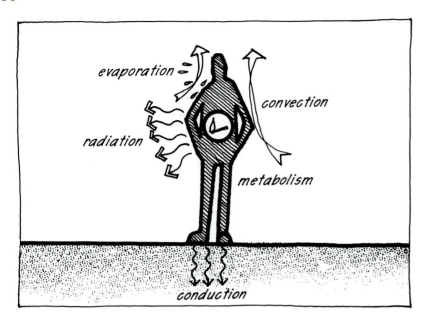

Figure 2.1: Maintaining the thermal balance by equalizing heat gain (due primarily to metabolic heat generation) and heat losses (by convection, radiation, conduction, and evaporation).

RADIATION

The skin also loses heat surrounding exposed surfaces by radiation. Because radiation only travels in a straight line, only surfaces "visible" to the skin are affected. *Mean radiant temperature* (MRT) is a useful concept for understanding the role of surrounding surface temperatures in affecting the radiative heat loss from the body. MRT can be defined as the angular-size-weighted average temperature of surrounding surfaces. In other words, the larger that a surface appears to the skin, the greater effect its temperature will have on the radiation from (and to) the skin. A large warm surface far away might have the same effect as a smaller but nearer surface of the same temperature. Small-sized surfaces (such as the sun seen from the earth) which are very hot can significantly affect radiative comfort environment; the effect is immediately noticeable as one moves from shade into direct sunlight.

It is important to recognize that MRT is completely independent of air temperature; the two have entirely different effects on bodily heat loss. For example, if the body is sufficiently exposed to radiant heat sources (such as the sun or a radiant heater), it will be comfortable at lower air temperatures than would otherwise be possible.

Operative temperature takes into account the effects of both air and surface temperature (essentially an average of the air temperature and MRT) and is better than either measure alone in assessing the effects of the thermal environment on comfort. It is measured by globe thermometer (typically a black metal toilet float with ordinary air temperature thermometer inserted into the interior). However, because it fails to take into account the effects of humidity on comfort, operative temperature is not a widely used indicator.

EVAPORATION

A third way that the body loses heat to the surrounding environment is through evaporation. As surrounding surface and air temperatures increase (or as activity increases) it becomes increasingly difficult for the body to maintain its thermal balance solely by convection and radiation. As skin temperature increases, perspiration increases, and the skin is cooled by evaporation. The rate of evaporation is dependent on both the relative humidity and velocity of surrounding air. As relative humidity increases, the rate of evaporation decreases; at 100 percent relative humidity no evaporation occurs and cooling by evaporation ceases. Conversely, as air movement increases, the rate of evaporation increases and cooling is increased.

In addition, water vapor diffuses through the skin in a physiological process independent of perspiration (Fanger, 1982). However, because the skin-cooling effects are similar, it will be considered here as part of the perspiration cooling process.

The body also loses some latent heat as part of the respiration process (dry air inhaled, moist air exhaled). Like skin evaporation, latent respiration decreases as relative humidity increases; it is, of course, unaffected by surrounding air movement.

CONDUCTION

Under certain circumstances, conduction can be a major source of bodily heat loss. For example, if the body is immersed in cold water following a boating capsize, the combined conductive/convective heat loss is so rapid that hypothermia and death can occur in a short period of time. One need only to stand on a tile surface to appreciate that touching a cool, conductive surface can produce a strong sensory experience. However, in normal architectural environments, the area of contact with hot or cold surfaces is limited. Their total effect on bodily heat loss is minimal and will be ignored here.

PHYSIOLOGICAL ADAPTATION TO THERMAL STRESS

In order to regulate its heat loss from (or gain to) the surrounding environment, the human body automatically activates a variety of physiological changes.

When surrounding air and surface temperatures are around 75°F, thermal comfort exists, and blood flow is primarily through relatively deep veins and little heat is transferred from blood to the skin.

As air and surrounding surface temperatures rise, the superficial veins (particularly in the extremities) begin to dilate, and a greater proportion of the blood is circulated near the skin causing the skin temperature to rise, increasing heat transfer by radiation and convection to the surrounding environment.

When this dilation reaches the maximum, the skin temperature becomes relatively uniform throughout the body. At this point (98.6°F surrounding temperature) no additional heat can be dissipated by radiation and convection, and evaporation becomes the only remaining means.

However, the sweating mechanism tends to fatigue with time, and the rate will decrease after several hours of exposure, partially due to the consumption of bodily fluids (Stein, et. al, 1986).

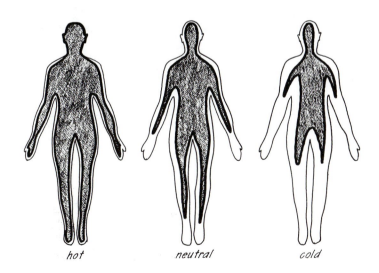

Figure 2.2: Blood migration in response to warm and cold environments. The "core" (shaded) area and the shell of the body; the core is maintained at a relatively constant temperature. The shell varies in temperature depending on external conditions. *(After Edholm, 1978.)*

Conversely, in cold environments, the body attempts to minimize heat loss. One of its most important strategies is "thermal zoning" (or blood migration): the physiological process strives to maintain the deep body temperature of vital organs as the first priority, taking precedence over less-vital (arms, legs) and least-vital (fingers, toes) extremities. To do this, deep veins dilate while superficial veins (particularly in the extremities) constrict. In addition, at and below comfort conditions, perspiration pores constrict, minimizing the heat lost by evaporation.

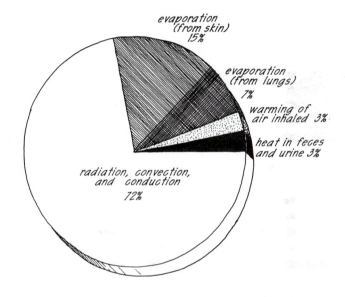

Figure 2.3: Proportions of bodily heat loss at 70°F. *(After Stein et al., 1986.)*

Unlike many other animals, humans cannot adjust the insulating quality of their skin by fluffing up fur or feathers. "Goose bumps" are thought to be obsolete symptoms of skin's unsuccessful attempt to duplicate this temperature response.

Finally, as temperatures continue to drop and variation in blood flow can no longer compensate adequately, deep tissue temperature drops and involuntary physical activity (shivering) increases metabolism and internal heat production. This is an attempt to prevent further drop in body temperature.

ACCLIMATIZATION

As environmental temperatures stabilize at a higher or lower level, the more permanent constriction or dilation of vessels causes the body to respond by changing the total volume of blood (variation as much as 20 percent, with greater volume required for warmer conditions). This adjustment requires four or more days to accomplish and is the major factor in determining the general acclimatization of the body (Lind and Bass, 1963). There is also an effect on sweating ability — after prolonged exposure to high temperatures, the maximum sweating rate increases over a period of several weeks (Eichna et al., 1950).

THERMAL COMFORT

Thermal comfort is a subjective state of satisfaction that varies with the individual and a number of circumstantial factors. ASHRAE (1989) has defined it as "that condition of mind in which satisfaction is expressed with the thermal environment." Because of the importance of maintaining a pleasant thermal environment in buildings, considerable empirical research has been done in efforts to establish the range of conditions that satisfies a majority of people. But, beyond the ideal conditions of comfort that the research identifies, some variation may be not only acceptable, but desirable. Lisa Heschong (1979) writes:

The steady-state approach to the thermal environment assumes that any degree of thermal stress is undesirable. A constant temperature is maintained in order to save people from the effort and the distraction of adjusting to different conditions. And yet, in spite of the extra effort required to adjust to thermal stimuli, people definitely seem to enjoy a range to temperatures. Indeed, they frequently seek out an extreme thermal environment for recreation or vacations. This must explain in large part the love of the Finns for their saunas and the Japanese for their scalding hot baths. Americans flock to beaches in the summer to bake in the sun and travel great distances in the winter to ski on frosty mountain slopes. People relish the very hotness or coldness of these places.

We should note that all of these places of thermal extremes have their opposites close at hand. The Finns make a practice of jumping from the sauna into a snowbank or a cold lake. At the beach, after baking in the hot sun, there is the cold ocean to swim in. The skier freezes on the slope, knowing all the while that the lodge waits down below with a roaring fire and some warming libation. There are probably two reasons for having the extremes right next to each other. The first is physiological: the availability of extremes ensures that we can move from one to the other to maintain a thermal balance. This gives us the safety to enjoy fully both extremes. We can be greatly overheated for a while and then be chilled to the bone, all without affecting our health.

There are six primary factors that affect thermal comfort. *Air temperature, humidity, surface temperature,* and *air motion* are environmental conditions affected by decisions by the architect. *Activity* and *clothing* are comfort factors determined by the occupant. Each of these has a unique combination of effects on the way that the body transfers heat.

ENVIRONMENTAL CONDITIONS

Air temperature only affects bodily heat transfer by convection. It is most important at temperatures in and below the comfort range where the temperature difference with the skin is significant. Humidity only affects bodily heat loss by evaporation. It is most important at higher air and surface temperatures where the effectiveness of radiation and convection are reduced (due to the low temperature difference between the skin and surrounding air and surfaces).

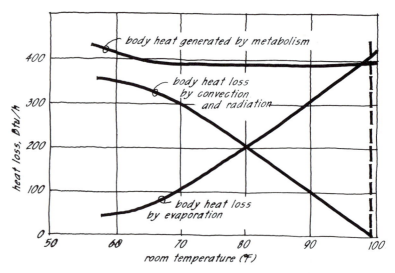

Figure 2.4: At lower temperatures heat loss by convection and radiation dominate, but above 80°F air and surface temperature evaporation begins to dominate. *(After Flynn and Segil, 1970.)*

EFFECTIVE TEMPERATURE

One of the most widely used measures of the thermal environment is *effective temperature* (ET). It takes into account the combined effects of air temperature and humidity on comfort. Lines of constant ET can be plotted on a psych chart to show the lines of equal comfort conditions (assuming that MRT and air movement are constant). Notice that each ET line slopes from lower right to upper left, and crosses the corresponding dry-bulb air temperature line at the 50 percent relative humidity line. This is a result of the fact that as humidity increases, the air temperature of equal comfort (for the greatest number of people) decreases. Also note that, at lower temperatures, the ET lines are nearly vertical because humidity has a comparatively small effect on comfort. As temperatures increase, the effect of humidity on comfort becomes more significant and the ET lines become more sloped. This reflects the physiological response of the body to depend increasingly on evaporation to lose heat as ambient air (and surface) temperatures increase. "Humiture" is one of several popularly used equivalents of ET and is frequently used by broadcast meteorologists to describe summer comfort conditions in weather reports.

COMFORT ZONES

The most widely accepted standard of thermal comfort is that defined by ASHRAE. Winter and summer conditions are shown, reflecting the insulating effect of the different seasonal clothing customarily worn indoors (equivalent of light slacks and short-sleeve shirt in the summer, and heavy slacks and long-sleeve shirt in the winter).

While comfort depends on a variety of other factors (including air movement, MRT, activity, and clothing), all comfort zone envelopes are bounded by an upper limit of 0.012 humidity ratio (level at which mildew becomes a problem) and a lower limit of 0.0043 (level at which respiratory discomfort, such as coughs and nosebleeds, due to excessively dry air is expected). They are bounded on the side limits by sloping ET lines (air temperature corrected for the effect of humidity on comfort).

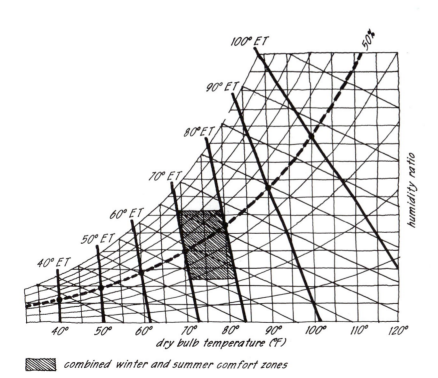

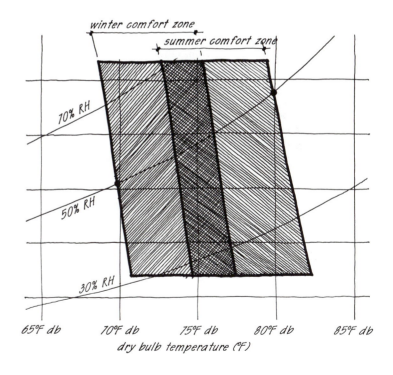

Figure 2.5: Effective temperature lines on a psychrometric chart. *(Redrawn from ASHRAE, 1989, by permission.)*

Figure 2.6: Winter and summer comfort zones, for light activity in typical seasonal clothing (winter 0.9 clo, summer 0.5 clo), with minimal air movement (less than 0.15 m/s winter and 0.25 m/s summer), and where dry-bulb air temperature and mean radiant temperature are equal. *(Reproduced from ASHRAE, 1981, by permission.)*

Surface temperature

The temperature of surrounding surfaces (measured by MRT) affects the ability of the body to lose heat by radiation. Because radiation heat loss increases with the difference in temperature between the skin and surrounding surfaces, it becomes most important at lower temperatures (winter). In most buildings, surface temperatures are nearly identical to air temperature. However, when the two are different, there can be dramatic effects on thermal comfort. The effect of lower air temperature on thermal comfort can be compensated by a rise in the MRT.

For example, exposure to a radiant source (such as sunlight through a window or a wall warmed by the sun) allows one to be comfortable in lower air temperatures. Conversely, exposure to a large, unusually cool surface (such as a large window in the winter) requires the compensation of higher air temperature in order to maintain comfort. Radiant heating (warming the body rather than the air) or cooling are effective comfort strategies where it is impractical to condition the air (for example, in outdoor or very large interior locations). Because of the radiant contribution of the sun, south-facing windows become a valuable passive solar winter heating strategy. Similarly, shielding the building (and especially its glass) with overhangs and trees is a primary defensive design strategy in hot climates.

Air movement

Convection heat loss increases with air movement because the warmer air adjacent to the skin is more rapidly displaced by cooler air than would normally occur in still air conditions. Convection heat loss is most important when the air-skin temperature difference is greatest (during colder seasons). This effect is so substantial that air temperature alone is an insufficient measure of outdoor winter conditions. The "wind chill factor" reported by meteorologists is the calm-wind temperature that would produce the same bodily heat loss as the actual combination of windspeed and air temperature. Note that the wind chill effect does not imply that surfaces can be cooled below the air temperature. It reflects the fact that wind accelerates the rate of bodily heat loss by convection, so that the skin surface is cooling faster toward the ambient air temperature.

Evaporative heat loss is also affected by air motion. Evaporation rate (and thus skin cooling) increases with air motion as saturated air near the skin is displaced by drier ambient air. This primarily affects thermal comfort in warmer air temperatures when active sweating occurs. Because of this, the comfort zone can be extended to include higher dry-bulb air temperatures as air motion increases. This extension is limited by occupants' tolerance of high air velocities. Traditional standards of comfort (ASHRAE, 1889, for example)

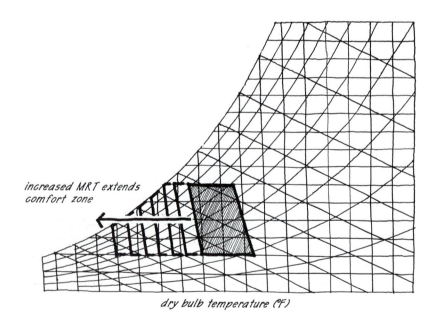

dry bulb temperature (°F)

Figure 2.7: Effect of mean radiant temperature on comfort zones. *(After Arends et al., 1980, modified to current ASHRAE comfort zone.)*

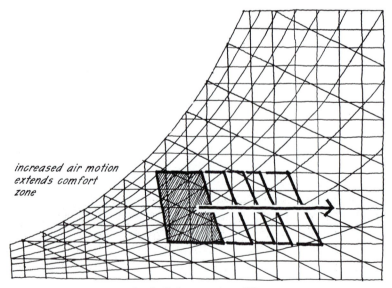

dry bulb temperature (°F)

Figure 2.8: Effect of air motion on the summer comfort zone. *(After Arends et al., 1980, modified to current ASHRAE comfort zone.)*

set limits on the maximum tolerable air velocity, thus effectively limiting the amount that the comfort zone can be extended by air motion alone. As interest in building energy conservation has increased, these conservative limits are being challenged by research indicating that occupants tolerate air velocities higher than previously believed possible (Arends et al., 1980). This means that under certain conditions, simply increasing air motion can be an effective cooling alternative to mechanical air conditioning.

Humidity (again)

Recall that, under calm air motion and standard MRT conditions, the top and bottom boundaries of the comfort zone are determined by humidity ratios of 0.012 and 0.0043, respectively. These top and bottom limits are unchanged even when the zone is extended by either changes in air motion or MRT (ASHRAE, 1989). Other researchers have recommended less conservative comfort limits, arguing that as air motion increases, most people remain comfortable even at *even higher* relative humidities. This indicates, for example, that comfort may be achieved over a much wider range of air temperature and humidity conditions than present standards recognize, simply by increasing air motion without the necessity of mechanical air conditioning.

OCCUPANT FACTORS

While the above environmental factors (air temperature, humidity, surface temperature, and air movement) are affected by design decisions, clothing and activity are comfort factors that are determined by the occupant and are typically beyond the control of the designer. However, because these affect thermal comfort, they have an indirect effect on design decisions.

Clothing

While humans lack the feathers or fur that provides thermal protection to other warm-blooded animals, they have developed the ability to cloth themselves. Clothing serves as an insulating layer surrounding the body. It affects heat transfer by convection (by creating a layer of trapped, insulating air), by radiation (body heat is radiated to clothing instead of surrounding external surfaces), and by evaporation (air motion across the skin is reduced, and, depending on the fabric, perspiration may be trapped on the skin or wicked away). Clo is a quantitative measure (first proposed by Gagge et. al, 1941) of the total thermal resistance from the skin to the outer surface of the clothed body; 0 clo is totally nude and 4.0 is the practical maximum while still providing for basic bodily movement. As clo levels increase, the comfort zone is extended to lower effective temperatures.

Table 2.1: Clo Values for Various Men's Clothing Ensembles

Clothing Ensemble	clo value
Nude	0
Shorts	0.1
Tropical clothing: shorts, open-neck short-sleeved shirt, light socks and sandals	0.3 - 0.4
Light summer clothing: long light-weight trousers, open-neck short-sleeved shirt	0.5
Light working clothing: athletic shorts, wool socks, open-neck short-sleeved cotton shirt, long cotton trousers	0.6
Light outdoor sportswear: T-shirt, cotton shirt, cotton undershorts, cotton trousers, cotton socks, shoes, and single-ply, light-weight poplin jacket	0.7
Typical business suit	1.0
Typical business suit with cotton topcoat (or heavy wool suit without topcoat)	1.5
U.S. Army standard cold-wet uniform: cotton-wool undershirt and undershorts, wool/nylon flannel shirt, wind-resistant, water-repellent trousers and field coat, cloth mohair and wool coat, and wool socks	1.5 - 2.0
Heavy wool pile ensemble: (Polar weather suit)	3.0 - 4.0

(Reproduced from Fanger, 1982, by permission.)

The effect of clothing on comfort changes with activity level. For example, an increase in clothing from 0 clo (nude) to 1.5 clo will decrease the necessary ambient temperature by 8°C for a sedentary person, but by 19°C for a person of high activity (Fanger, 1982). Even a sedentary person in polar clothes will prefer an ambient temperature as high as 8°C.

ACTIVITY

As noted earlier in this chapter, as activity increases, metabolic heat generation increases. The rate of metabolism is measured in metabolic or *met* units. One met = 18.4 $Btu/h \cdot ft^2$; it is the total energy per unit of surface area generated by a normal seated adult at rest; the total heat for a normal adult is about 400 Btu/h. One's metabolic rate increases with the level of physical activity, up to a maximum of about 2000 Btu/h for sustained activity.

The increased metabolic heat generated by higher levels of activity must be dissipated to the environment in order to maintain constant body temperature. To maintain comfort at higher levels of activity, the other conditions that affect comfort must adjust to increase the rate of heat dissipation. Lower air or surface temperature, lower humidity, greater air motion, or less clothing would all tend to compensate for the effects of higher activity.

Table 2.2: Typical Metabolic Heat Generation for Various Activities

Activity	Btu/h•ft²	Typical adult male	Met
Sleeping	13	250	0.7
Seated	18	350	1.0
Standing, relaxed	22	450	1.2
Walking, 3 mph	50	1000	2.7
Housecleaning	55	1080	3.0
Ditchdigging	80	1600	4.3
Athletics	100	2000	5.4

(Reproduced from ASHRAE, 1989, by permission.)

Other factors

The above six factors are the primary determinants of thermal comfort. Other factors have little or no effect.

Nationality — Once acclimatized, there are no significant differences among different nationalities in preferred comfort conditions and no seasonal variations exist (Fanger, 1982).

Age — Age has little effect on people's preferred thermal environment. The lower metabolism of older people is compensated by a lower evaporative loss (Collins and Hoinville, 1980). However, older people often set the thermostat in their home higher than younger people; this may be a result of the lower activity of elderly people, who are sedentary for a greater part of the day.

Gender — Men and women prefer almost the same thermal environments. The slightly lower metabolic rate of women is offset by their slightly lower skin temperature and evaporative loss. Women normally wear lighter clothing and therefore prefer slightly higher ambient temperatures to compensate (Fanger and Langkilde, 1975; Fanger, 1982; Nevins et al., 1966).

Body build — It is popularly assumed that obese people prefer a cooler environment than thin people. Under strenuous exercise, obese people generate more metabolic heat and need cooler conditions to dissipate it. However, under sedentary conditions, obese and thin people prefer the same thermal environment (Fanger 1982).

Alcohol — Alcohol consumption does not increase metabolic heat production (metabolic rate); however, it does create an illusion of warmth and causes skin vasodilation (increasing heat loss). Thus the practice of drinking alcohol to "warm up" on a cold day has, in fact, the detrimental effect of upsetting the normal physiological protection of reducing blood flow to the skin to conserve heat loss. This accelerates the effects of bodily heat loss and hypothermia (Fanger, 1982).

Color — There is no physiological or psychological effects due to the color of the environment (Fanger, 1982).

Crowding — Crowding does not have a direct effect on thermal comfort (Rohles et al., 1966). However, lower air temperatures are necessary to offset the inherently higher mean radiant temperatures caused by the surrounding bodies (Yaglou and Drinker, 1928).

SUMMARY OF TERMS

Homeostasis — the physiological process of maintaining a constant deep-body temperature.

Hypothalamus — that portion of the brain that regulates body temperature.

Metabolism — the bodily process that converts chemical energy (food) into mechanical energy (activity) and thermal energy (heat).

Mean radiant temperature (MRT) — conceptually, the angular-size-weighted average temperature of surrounding surfaces.

Operative temperature — an average of the dry-bulb air temperature and MRT; measured with a globe thermometer.

Effective temperature (ET) — a measure of the thermal environment that takes into account the combined effects of air temperature and humidity on comfort.

Thermal comfort — a condition of mind in which satisfaction is expressed with the thermal environment.

Wind chill factor — the calm-wind temperature that would produce the same bodily heat loss as the actual combination of windspeed and air temperature.

Clo — a quantitative measure of the total thermal resistance from the skin to the outer surface of the clothed body; 0 clo is totally nude and 4.0 is the practical maximum while still providing for basic bodily movement.

STUDY QUESTIONS

1. Describe how the human body adapts to a cold environment in order to maintain its constant temperature.

2. Describe how the human body adapts to a hot environment in order to maintain its constant temperature.

3. In a cold environment, drinking alcohol gives a warming sensation. Explain why this is a dangerous practice and can lead to hypothermia.

4. Why does the human body lose most of its heat by radiation and convection at low temperatures, and by evaporation at higher temperatures?

5. What are the primary factors that affect thermal comfort?

6. Which of these are affected by architectural design decisions and which are determined solely by the individual?

7. Why are effective temperature lines on the psych chart nearly vertical at lower db temperatures, but become increasingly sloped at higher temperatures?

8. If the surfaces of a room are of different temperatures (for example, a large, cold window surface in the winter), explain how the mean radiant temperature varies at different places in the room.

9. Why are there different comfort zones on the psych chart for winter and summer?

CLIMATE AND SHELTER

The first American house built in war-time Java completely bewildered natives there. Instead of building walls of local bamboo, which is closely spaced to keep out rain while admitting light and air, the white man put up solid walls to keep out light and air, and then cut windows in the walls to admit the light and air. Next, he put glass panes in the windows to admit light but keep out the air. Then, he covered the panes with blinds and curtains to keep out the light too.

— Ken Kerr (1978)

Climate has an obvious and direct effect on the thermal environment. While the combinations of the various daily climatic variables (air temperature, sunshine, humidity, wind speed and direction, and precipitation) are endless, the design of buildings is concerned principally with two types of generalized climatic data.

First, in designing the building envelope, the primary concern is with the *average daily* high and low conditions [air temperature, insolation (incident solar radiation), humidity, and wind] that can be expected to occur in a representative month of each season (usually January, April, July, October). These long-term averages are important to the building designer because they determine the comparative importance that should be given to various building design strategies. For example, in determining the appropriate wall insulation thickness, it is more important to know the average daily low temperatures in the winter months than it is to know the extreme low temperature that might occur only once or twice a year.

On the other hand, it is necessary to consider *probable temperature extremes* in designing supplemental mechanical equipment. Actually even for this purpose, record temperatures are not used for these extremes; instead, the high and low temperatures that could be reasonably expected to occur (i.e.,

exceeded only a small percent of the time — 2.5 percent is the widely accepted design standard) are the limits that are typically used in sizing supplemental heating and air conditioning equipment.

To make the most efficient and cost-effective use of building resources, design the building envelope (a long-term strategy) for the seasonal average conditions that can be expected, and assume that short-term strategies (heating appliances and clothing) will be used to supplement the performance of the building envelope under extreme conditions.

The variation of the daily air temperature depends on the condition of the atmosphere. On clear days, a large amount of incoming radiation and a free path for outgoing radiation produce a wide daily temperature range. On an overcast day, both incoming and outgoing radiation are restricted and the temperature variation is less. Even invisible moisture in the air, in the form of humidity, has a pronounced effect on the transparency of the air to radiation. This greenhouse effect is responsible for certain parts of the incoming solar radiation spectrum being absorbed by water vapor. More significantly, water vapor is even more opaque to longer-wavelength outgoing radiation and retards the nighttime radiant cooling of the earth surfaces.

This is the reason that desert regions heat up so much during the day but cool off (by radiation to the clear sky) rapidly at night. And similarly why humid regions have so little daily temperature variation — night radiation to the clear night sky is minimized by the relatively opaque water vapor in the air. Thus the presence (or lack) of humidity in a region has a profound effect on the temperature ranges and thus the overall climate of the region.

VISUALIZING CLIMATE

The two most important climatic considerations are air temperature and humidity. To aid in visualizing these characteristics in relation to comfort conditions, it is helpful to plot them on the psychrometric chart. This immediately reveals the portion of a typical year that will be comfortable, and when some type of heating and cooling will be required. Appendix D shows climatic, design, and solar performance data for a representative city in each

of the 16 distinct climatic regions in the United States (see U.S. Department of Commerce, 1978, for data for other locations).

While average temperature and humidity data are available for each hour of every month, for design purposes these can be simplified to the daily average high and low conditions for each of four representative months (January, April, July, and October — representing the hottest and coldest months and two intermediate months). For a typical day, a plot of the hourly dry-bulb temperature and humidity combinations forms a long, flat loop. These monthly loops can be further simplified into a single line connecting two points: the high temperature-low humidity point and the low temperature-high humidity point for each month.

Notice that each line is relatively level, with a decrease in relative humidity as the temperature increases. Actually, there is a small but predictable increase in absolute humidity as temperature increases. Why is this? One would expect the moisture content in the air to remain constant throughout the day. The explanation is that as the sun rises and warms plant and ground

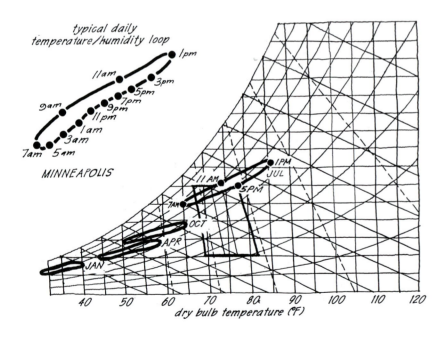

Figure 3.1: Monthly temperature and humidity loops for Minneapolis. Each loop represents the temperature and relative humidity conditions for a typical day for that month. Notice that as temperature rises, the relative humidity drops; the minimum relative humidity usually coincides with the maximum dry-bulb air temperature and vice versa.

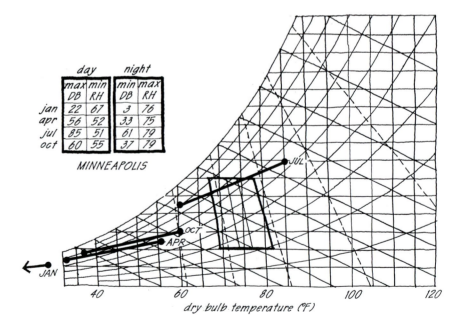

Figure 3.2: Using a line to represent monthly temperature and humidity loops for Minneapolis. Each line connects the maximum temperature-minimum relative humidity and the minimum temperature-maximum relative humidity for each representative month, using data from U.S. Department of Commerce (1978) or a similar source.

surfaces above the air temperature, moisture is released into the air, and the process reverses at night as plant and ground surfaces cool down below air temperature by radiation to the clear night sky.

CLIMATE AND INDIGENOUS HOUSING

In its most fundamental form, housing (indeed all building) is shelter — a system of components designed to mediate the existing environment (which is less than satisfactory in some way) into a comfortable and satisfactory environment. Historically, shelter has been built to reduce the range of local climatic variations; to avoid some of the heat of the sun in hot climates, to conserve heat in cold climates, to welcome the breezes when they can provide desired cooling, and to avoid winds when they serve to compound the problems of an already cold environment, to admit light in sufficient amounts for task lighting and to keep out excessive or unnecessary light.

Indigenous structures are valuable subjects for study because of their ingenious use of available materials and technology to produce houses which provide a remarkably high degree of thermal comfort in sometimes hostile environments. These forms should not be duplicated blindly, but instead should be analyzed for their thermal principles and construction efficiency, and their lessons applied to contemporary materials and methods of construction and cultural needs.

It should be noted that many forces other than climate also affect the design of indigenous housing. The culture and means of subsistence determines whether the shelter will be permanent, mobile, seasonal, or temporary. If the culture is a hunting one like the original inhabitants of the great plains of North America, or a herding one like the nomads of the Asiatic steppes, the architecture will tend to be demountable and mobile. But it will not be expendable because suitable building materials are not readily available in those regions. The structurally brilliant invention of the tent — lightweight and composed of small, transportable members — is easily dismantled, packed, transported, and reerected (Fitch and Branch, 1960).

CLIMATIC REGIONS

For the purposes of illustrating climatic principles found in indigenous shelter, five climates will be discussed: cold (where the winter is the dominant season and concerns for conserving heat predominate all other concerns), temperate (where approximately equally severe winter and summer conditions are separated by mild transitional seasons), hot/arid (where very high summer temperatures with great fluctuation predominate with dry conditions throughout

the year), warm/humid (where warm stable conditions predominate with high humidity throughout the year), and hot regions with seasonable humidity (where hot temperatures dominate, but part of the year is humid with stable temperatures and part of the year is arid with great temperature variation). This latter climatic zone is not found in North America, but is common to parts of Asia (particularly India) and Africa (Nigeria, for example).

Figure 3.3: Four major climatic zones of North America. *(After Olgyay, 1963.)*

COLD REGION

The climate of Minneapolis, Minnesota (Fig. 3.2), typifies the cold region. It is characterized by severely cold winters, cool springs, mild summers, and long autumns. The severity of this climate suggests that cold temperature and wind conditions alone dictate the building siting, form, organization, and wall and window construction. So severe are the winter conditions that designing for all other conditions (sun, summer breezes, and humidity) are subordinated to the demands of the cold. Winter temperatures drop well below freezing for months at a time and are often combined with sustained winds of 10 mph and more (AIA Research Corporation, 1978)

Cold region: biological response

Cats are an excellent example of behavioral response to temperature. On a cold day, a cat will curl up not only to minimize its total exposed surface area to the air but to shield its stomach (which has a comparatively thin fur). As the temperature rises, the cat will uncurl, stretch out, and in a truly warm environment, may lie on its back or side to deliberately expose its relatively warm stomach area, all in order to cool off.

Hibernation is an effective means of surviving severe winter conditions. Black bears are particularly efficient hibernators (although they have a relatively high body temperature) and are able to sleep for months without eating, drinking, urinating or defecating. Hibernators with lower body temperatures (woodchucks, chipmunks, ground squirrels) must awaken every few days, raise their temperature to 94°F, move around in their burrow and urinate. Bears have low surface-to-mass ratio so heat is lost very slowly. They can maintain a deep-body temperature of 88°F (within 12° of summertime temperature). Their main insulation is thick winter fur, which has double the insulating value of summer fur. The fur is thickest on back of the neck and sides, and thinnest on muzzle, legs, and underside. The hibernating bear sleeps in a curled-up position with its nose near its tail. This position minimizes its surface area and reduces heat loss from the thinly furred areas. For extra insulation, they sleep on a nest of leaves, grass, and other material that they rake into the den (Rogers, 1981).

In addition to hibernation, polar bears exhibit another remarkable climatic response. Recent research has revealed that the "white" fur of these bears is not really white, but a pigmentless structure with a core of such low density that it is nearly hollow. In other words, the white appearance of the fur is caused by internal reflection in the individual hairs. This is similar to the whitish appearance associated with ice which derives from light reflections off of many internal surfaces. Various special photographic films have revealed that the polar bear was absorbing energy in the ultraviolet range. Did this mean that that the low-density core of the the fur was acting as a "light pipe," efficiently transmitting solar energy into the skin through internal reflections? A mathematical model of the optical properties of the polar bear hair has shown this to be a possibility (Hansen, 1981).

Birds "mini-hibernate" at night allowing their body temperature to drop about 20°F when exposed to night air temperature of 32°F; this results in a

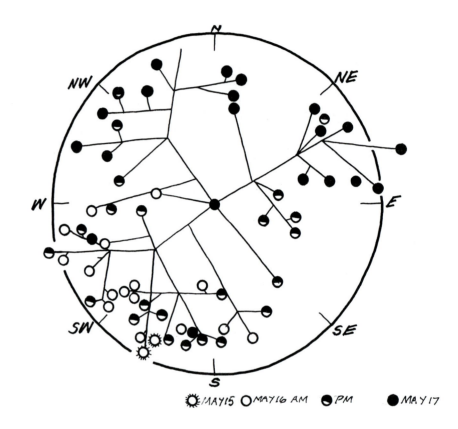

Figure 3.4: Effect of sunlight on the blooming sequence of a fifteen-year-old pine tree standing in open at Ebserwald in May 1937. *(After Geiger, 1950.)*

savings of about a fourth of the energy required to maintain normal temperatures.

An alternative to hibernating is to increase heat generation by increasing activity in the form of shivering. In an experiment, Carey and Marsh (1981) found that goldfinches, by shivering, were able to elevate their metabolic heat production to over five times the normal level and maintain a difference of 198°F between the body and the –94°F ambient air temperature. Staying warm is particularly difficult for small birds (such as goldfinches) weighing less than about 30 g due to their large surface-to-mass ratio, less feather insulation thickness, and because larger birds can endure shivering for longer periods of time than smaller ones.

In general, in cold climates, plant forms tend to be compact with thick leaves to a maximum of volume for a minimum surface area. Coniferous plants are most abundant and satisfy this geometry. The pine needle is a representative example with its slightly flattened cylindrical shape which provides the tree with a successful passive defense against cold, drought, and winds.

However, some cold climate plants are more active and actually utilize the sun specifically for heating to modify their thermal environment. Some plants are heliotropic (sun-following) to maximize their exposure to the radiant warmth of the sun (the familiar sunflower, for example). Others utilize their geometry to concentrate solar collection. For example, the reflective white petals on certain flowers reflect sunlight toward the center of the plant. The snow trilium is able to maintain its center at a temperature 14 to 18°F above ambient in this manner; the temperature returns to ambient when the plant is shaded. In a similar manner, arctic poppies effectively increase the degree-days available for growth by 25 percent due to passive solar heating. Insects bask on the leaves of these poppies, developing surface temperatures as much as 32°F above ambient. This accelerates the development of pollen and seeds and aids the survival and speed of reproduction of visiting insects (Knutson, 1981).

Cold region: traditional clothing

Eskimos developed traditional clothing as well-suited to the arctic winter climate as the igloo. A complete winter outfit consisted of an inner parka worn with the hair against the body, an outer parka worn fur-out, inner and outer pants in the same manner, fur stockings, boots, and mittens. The entire outfit weighed just above 10 lb. It was loose and airy enough to avoid sweating, yet warm enough to permit a hunter to stand for many hours in -50°C temperature and high winds. The tightness of the bottom of the parka could be adjusted to regulate ventilation in response to the level of activity — in severely cold climates it is important to prevent sweating which may wet the clothing and reduce its insulating effectiveness. For the same reason, outer clothing layers which may be covered with snow are always taken off before entering the heated igloo and left in a cold, dry outer chamber where they would not thaw (Bruemmer, 1981).

Feathers and down are also desirable natural materials for cold weather clothing, provided that they can be protected from mechanical abrasion. Both trap air in small compartments, thus reducing conductive heat transfer. The finer the fiber, the smaller the compartments and the greater the insulating value. Feathers and down differ markedly in structure. Feathers are two-dimensional with vanes emerging on the opposite sides of each quill. Down, on the other hand, is three-dimensional. This is the reason that feathers tend to pack and compress, while down tends to remain fluffed up, maintaining its air pockets and insulating quality.

Wool, among the traditional fibers used for cold weather clothing, has many desirable characteristics. Fine wools, with a fiber width of only 17 microns, present a large surface area, trapping air. In addition wool fibers possess a naturally wavy structure, or crimp, that serves several useful purposes. Crimped fibers interlock readily so that they hold together when twisted into yarns. Furthermore, the crimp yields a strong, not easily matted yarn without much twist — just what is needed to produce a porous, low-density structure for thermal insulation (Hansen, 1981).

Cold region: traditional building response

The indigenous dwellings of this climatic region used predominantly "barrier-rich" envelopes characterized by minimum surface area, minimum openings, and maximum insulation. The Eskimo *igloo* is a model of sheltering efficiency. Its excellent performance is a function of both form and material. The dome shape offers the minimum surface area for heat loss while providing an aerodynamic shape to deflect the arctic winds. The vaulted construction is structurally stable and takes advantage of the surprisingly great compressive strength of compacted snow blocks. The shell is composed of snow blocks (about 18 in. high, 36 in. long, and 6 in. thick) laid in one continuous, in-sloping spiral. The insulating value of the shell is further improved by a glaze of ice that the heat from an oil lamp and the bodies of the occupants

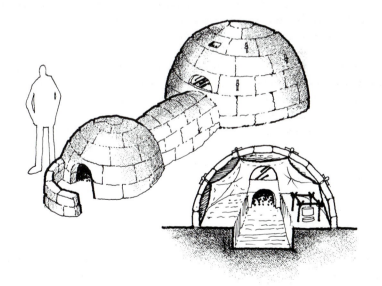

Figure 3.5: Eskimo igloo, with section showing draped animal skin insulation. *(Redrawn from "Primative architecture and climate," by Fitch and Branch. Copyright © 1960 by Scientific American, Inc. All rights reserved.)*

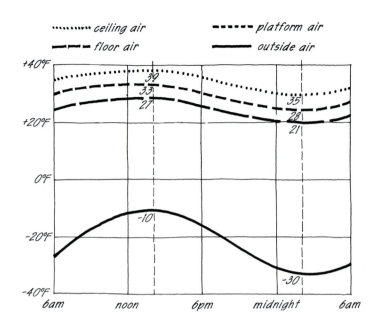

Figure 3.6: Igloo temperatures may run as much as 65°F higher than outside air temperatures using only a small oil lamp and occupant body heat. *(Redrawn from "Primative architecture and climate," by Fitch and Branch. Copyright © 1960 by Scientific American, Inc. All rights reserved.)*

Figure 3.7: The summer house of the Nunamiut Eskimos follows the form of the igloo but is constructed using sticks covered with slabs of turf. *(Redrawn from "Primative architecture and climate," by Fitch and Branch. Copyright © 1960 by Scientific American, Inc. All rights reserved.)*

automatically add to the interior. A draped liner of skins and furs can be added to the interior of more permanent structures to add an insulating layer of dead air. With the liner in place, it is possible to raise the uppermost air temperature to 40°F without melting the dome.

Ventilation is minimal, consisting of a small opening near the top of the dome. A model of construction efficiency, the snow blocks are cut from a trench which, in turn, becomes the lowest floor level of the completed structure creating a pool of cold air below the warmer, occupied sleeping and sitting ledge above. More elaborate igloos have an entrance "vestibule" vault, with a curved outside wall to deflect the wind.

The igloo encloses a volume that is most effectively heated by the radiant heat afforded by a couple of kudliks (lamps carved of soapstone with wicks of moss and grass and fueled by seal or whale oil). Finally, the igloo melts every spring, the world's first self-demolishing house — a feature whose value designers are just now (after Pruett-Igoe) beginning to appreciate.

In the Pacific northwest, indigenous houses, such as those of the Haida tribe, were larger and more permanent. But like the igloo, these structures had a small surface-to-volume ratio with a minimum of openings. The large

communal houses were constructed with thick timber walls. A shallow-sloped post-and-beam roof construction supported the heavy snow buildup which provided thermal insulation. Often, several of these "long houses" were arranged side by side with only a narrow separation space. These passage spaces were enclosed in the winter to further minimize the exposed exterior. Heating and lighting were primarily by the plentiful wood supplies available locally.

TEMPERATE REGION

The climate of New York, New York typifies the temperate region. The summers are hot and humid, and the winters are cold. In much of the region, the topography is generally flat, allowing cold winter winds to come in from the northwest and cool summer breezes to flow in from the southwest. The four seasons are almost equally long, with the spring and fall being quite comfortable provided that shade and ventilation are available (AIA Research Corporation, 1978).

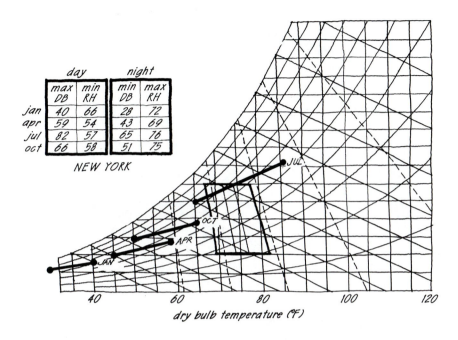

Figure 3.8: Typical temperate climate — New York, New York. Daily temperature and humidity ranges for January, April, July, and October. *(Data from U.S. Department of Commerce, 1978.)*

Temperate region: biological response

Most furbearing animals in this region respond to the change in seasons by altering the thickness and density of their coat. In the northern habitats, beavers build lodges, a half-submerged beehive-shaped structure, for winter protection. The lodge is made of interlaced branches plastered with mud and situated on some type of solid foundation — usually a submerged tree or small natural island. The sticks are piled on top of the foundation to make a dome, and an air shaft is formed by the loose mat of sticks in the center which are not covered with mud. The large and well-insulated chamber inside the lodge is reached from underwater entrances below the ice level. It is formed by the beavers tunneling into the solid mass of sticks and gnawing off the branches as they progress. In cold winters, additional layers of sticks and mud are added to the exterior for greater insulation (Hancocks, 1973).

Deciduous trees and plants are common to temperate regions and have the remarkable ability to spread large, broad leaves during the spring and mild summer. The shape is flat to assure maximum exposure to the sun. In the fall, the tree enters a state of dormancy (similar to animal hibernation) and its

leaves dry out and drop off to minimize surface area exposure during the coldest month. This seasonal response of deciduous foliage coincides with the solar needs of buildings. The leafless winter form allows warming sunlight to pass and strike a building. In the spring, the foliage fills in at almost exactly the time when protection from solar overheating is needed; in the fall, the leaves drop just when solar heating becomes beneficial.

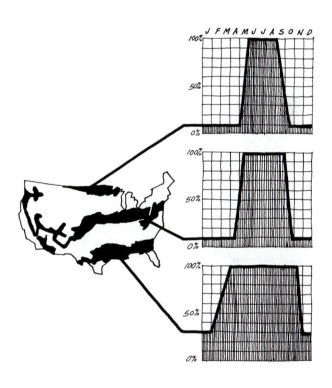

Figure 3.9: Shading period of typical deciduous hardwood trees in the temperate region of North America. *(After Olgyay, 1963.)*

Temperate region: traditional clothing

Like plants and animals, the characteristic response of clothing to temperate climates is its adaptability. In response to rapid temperature changes on a daily and seasonal basis, clothing in this region has always been layered, allowing addition and subtraction depending on temperature and level of activity. Beyond this, garments are comparatively sophisticated in their ability to be opened or restricted depending on conditions and circumstances.

Temperate region: traditional building response

Because of the wide range of seasonal temperatures that characterize this temperate region, indigenous building envelopes (like clothing and plants) are quite sophisticated in their ability to open and close, adapting to the changeable conditions. The envelopes are "switch-rich" in that they utilize a variety of components that can be switched from a closed to an open configuration, rejecting or admitting outside conditions. In addition, because many of the natives of this climate were hunter-gatherers, the shelters had to be portable, adding to their complexity.

Figure 3.11: Mongolian yurt, with collapsible "pantograph" side walls, and felt mat covering. *(Redrawn from "Primative architecture and climate," by Fitch and Branch. Copyright © 1960 by Scientific American, Inc. All rights reserved.)*

The North American *tipi* is a wonderful example of this primitive sophistication. Like all tents, it is a tension structure that uses a minimum material to cover a large volume. Comfortable, roomy, and well ventilated, it was well suited for the roving life these people led in following the migratory buffalo herds. They are warm in winter and cool in summer, easy to pitch, and, because of its conical shape, able to withstand heavy winds or driving rain.

The tipi is erected by first positioning a tripod of three (in some cases, four) primary tapered wood poles. Against these are leaned additional secondary poles arranged in a conical shape. This is covered with a membrane of sewn buffalo skins (canvas fabric in more recent years) cut in a semicircular shape. Two large flaps at the top provide an opening for smoke. This can be adjusted (and even closed tightly) depending on the needs of temperature and wind direction. In cold weather, an inner liner can be added to create a dead air space or allow limited ventilation required for smoke exhaustion while shielding the occupant from direct drafts. A door covering provided additional protection from the cold, and under severe conditions, a windbreak of dead branches could be erected around the perimeter. In the summer, the perimeter of the tipi could be rolled up to allow maximum ventilation.

The Mongolian *yurt* is the most sophisticated of the nomadic structures. Its walls are formed in a circle by a set of collapsible "pantograph-type" lightweight willow panels with a single entry door. These panels are very light and compact when closed, but quickly open up into sizable wall panels the

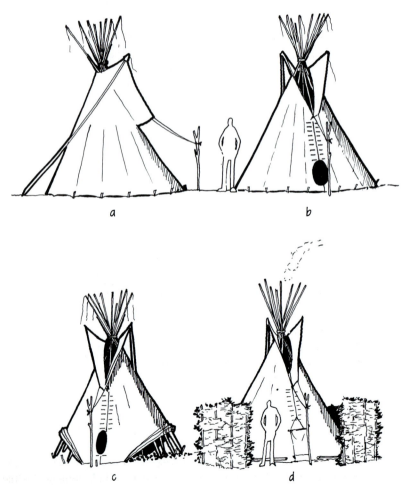

Figure 3.10: North American Indian tipi (a) side, and (b) front view; configured for (c) hot weather, and (d) cold weather. *(After Laubin and Laubin, 1977.)*

height of a person. The roof is either a dome or conical structure composed of radial beams spanning from the outside wall to a center compression ring which is left open for smoke and ventilation. Finally the frame is covered with one or more layers of thick felt mats and held in place with a pattern of ropes. A yurt can be erected in half an hour. In the winter, up to eight layers of felt are used, providing a comfortable environment in conditions down to -40°F in heavy wind. In the summer, one layer of felt and one layer of canvas is used. The sides may be rolled up to provide ventilation on the rare warm day (Rapoport, 1969).

HOT-ARID REGION

The climate of Phoenix, Arizona, typifies the hot-arid region. Located in the desert region that spans California, Arizona, and Nevada, the climate is characterized by extremely hot summers and moderately cold winters. The cold season lasts from November until March or April, with January temperature

minimums in the thirties and maximums in the sixties. A small amount of precipitation (less than 4 in. per year) occurs during the winter. The summers are extremely hot and arid, with a great temperature variation between day and night. This is a result of the clear skies (it is the sunniest region in North America with over 85 percent annual possible sunshine) and low humidity (driest in North America) which allow intense sunshine during the day and rapid night radiation back to the clear night sky (AIA Research Corporation, 1978).

Hot-arid region: biological response

In this climate, many animals have adopted underground habitats for shelter from the temperature extremes of this climate. Some, such as the wombat, burrow very deep (up to 100 ft) but even the small burrows of the kangaroo rat of Arizona considerably reduce the impact of the desert — while the daytime surface temperature rises to 160°F, the temperature at the end of the rat's burrow only a half a meter long was reduced to 90°F. Furthermore, humidity was maintained at four to five times that of outside air. The kangaroo rat stays in the cool and humid burrows during the most unfavorable daytime

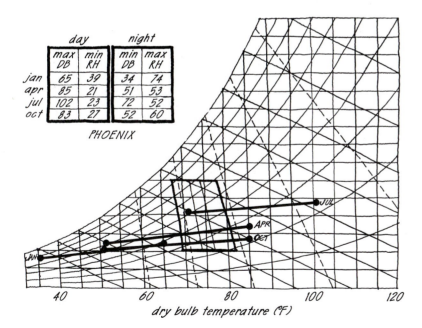

	day		night	
	max DB	min RH	min DB	max RH
jan	65	39	34	74
apr	85	21	51	53
jul	102	23	72	52
oct	83	27	52	60

PHOENIX

dry bulb temperature (°F)

Figure 3.12: Typical hot-arid climate — Phoenix, Arizona. Daily temperature and humidity ranges for January, April, July, and October. (Data from U.S. Department of Commerce, 1978.)

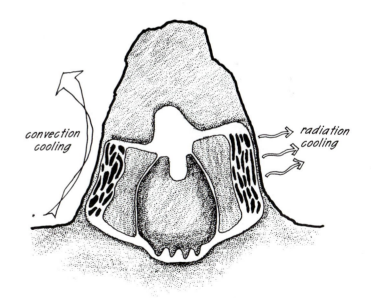

Figure 3.13: The *Macrotermes* termite mound controls the temperature and oxygen supply in the nest by a system of convection currents. Heat conducts through the thin walls and is dissipated by radiation and convection. Fresh oxygen is absorbed from the exterior through a system of capillary ducts. (After Hancocks, 1973.)

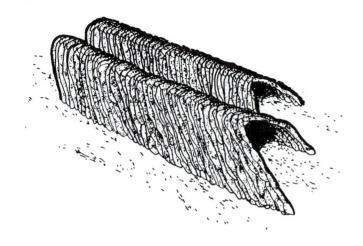

Figure 3.14: Long, vaulted shells of mud built by the solitary mud-dauber wasp. Each is subdivided into separate compartments containing an egg and stocked with paralyzed spiders as future provisions for its young. Notice that the vaulted shells are formed in sloping layers. *(After Hancocks, 1973.)*

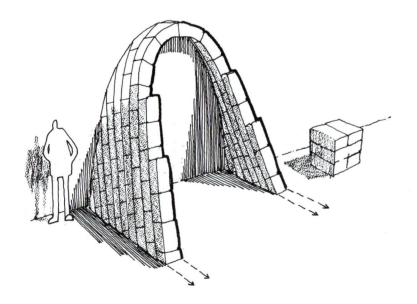

Figure 3.15: Construction of masonry vaults without forms. The inclined face of the courses give support of succeeding courses. *(After Fathy, 1973.)*

hours and emerges at night. Like many desert animals they are small and can move at speed from one shelter to another. Their long legs keep their body clear of the hot sand.

Some termite colonies have very sophisticated humidity control mechanisms, especially in desert areas where over 90 percent relative humidity is required. Hancocks (1973) has found that the construction of the nest walls assists in the control of humidity, especially with a mound nest where the dense material of the structure prevents evaporation; also it is covered with a cemented layer of sand and clay impervious to moisture. Water vapor in the nest tends to be trapped by the intricate layout of the galleries. In some instances the walls of the nest are constructed in such a way that favorable temperatures are guaranteed.

Hot-arid region: traditional clothing

In this severe climate, the principle clothing strategy is to defend against high temperatures and solar heat gain. The flowing robes of desert nomads cover almost the entire body. There seems to be no agreement on color; some wear white robes to reflect the sun, while others prefer less transparent black to minimize solar transmittance through the fabric. In the very hottest regions, wool is the surprising fabric of choice because of its insulating qualities (remember that air temperature can be well above that of the body) and the natural kinkyness of its fibers which touches the body in a minimum of places and does not wick moisture away from the skin as rapidly as cotton. Perspiration evaporates rapidly regardless of clothing and needs to be minimized (by clothing the entire body) to prevent rapid dehydration.

Hot-arid region: traditional building response

The indigenous shelters of this region appear in many ways like those of the cold region. Both share such severe and inhospitable conditions that the envelopes are "barrier-rich." Like the cold region, a compact geometry and thick insulation were used to minimize heat transfer. Thick adobe construction or underground construction was used to (1) *delay* the effects of high afternoon outside temperatures until the cool of the evening, and (2) to *reduce the interior temperature swings.* Because of the high daytime air temperatures and the intense sunshine, window and door openings are kept to a minimum, although these were often opened in the evening to introduce the cool night air. Courtyards form a mini-oasis to induce convective airflow and promote evaporative cooling. Flat roofs were used to accommodate a thick layer of earth to delay the impact of the intense midday sun.

The Bedouin tent, still in use today, is a beautifully refined tensile structure that answers needs of the desert nomad of the Arabian peninsula. It is mobile and eminently adaptable to the conditions of the desert. It can be dismantled, rolled up, and loaded on a camel in less than one hour. In a climate of extreme temperature fluctuations, it furnishes shelter, shade, warmth, or cooling drafts of air as required. It is woven of black goat hair and is almost completely opaque to sunlight. Even though it also absorbs (and the surface is heated by) the solar radiation, the opacity of the black and the insulating quality of the wool makes these black tents cooler than comparable white fabrics (which transmit as much as 40 percent of the solar radiation). The tent side cloths can be easily shifted according to the wind and sun direction. Similar tents are used by nomads of the north African deserts (Grundfeld, 1975).

While lightweight and minimal materials contribute to the portability essential to the nomad, this very lightness prevents taking advantage of one of the most important resources of this climate — the dramatic temperature swings that occur from day to night. While daytime temperatures often exceed 120°F, night temperatures may drop substantially to around 60°F. The average of these — 90°F — is a moderate (if warm) condition that is entirely acceptable. Massive construction (such as adobe) can slowly absorb and release heat and can approach this average throughout the day — even drop below it with ventilative cooling.

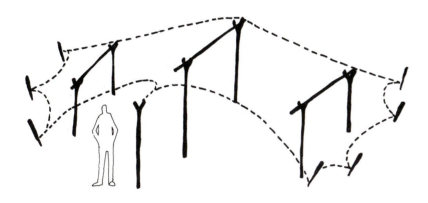

Figure 3.16: Diagram of desert tent structure. *(After Rudofsky, 1964.)*

The most familiar example of indigenous shelter using massive construction is the Pueblo dwelling of the southwestern United States. It is a communal house, often multistory. The primary building material is sun-dried mud brick (adobe) usually reinforced with straw, and often "plastered" with a smooth layer of mud. The walls are quite thick (16 to 30 in.); this provides tremendous thermal storage capacity to take advantage of the large daily temperature

swings. Window openings were few and deeply recessed to protect the interior from the heat and glare of the intense midday sun. Each successive story was set back to provide terraces on the roofs of the story below. These setbacks were oriented so that the stepped profile faced south.

The roof structure consisted of round, closely spaced wooden beams, with small branch infill. On the top of this was built up a thick layer of earth which provided thermal benefits similar to the walls. Exterior ladders provided access to the upper levels. In general, interior rooms maintained the most stable temperatures and were used for storage, while perimeter rooms, having the advantage of better access to light and ventilation, were used for living.

Figure 3.17: Acoma pueblo, New Mexico, looking northeast. *(Reproduced from Knowles, 1974, by permission.)*

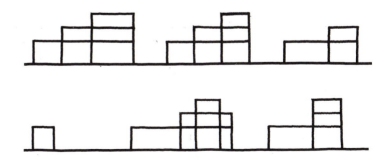

Figure 3.18: Acoma Pueblo, New Mexico. Typical sections show the critical spacing between rows of three- and two-story houses to ensure solar access. *(Redrawn from Knowles, 1974, by permission.)*

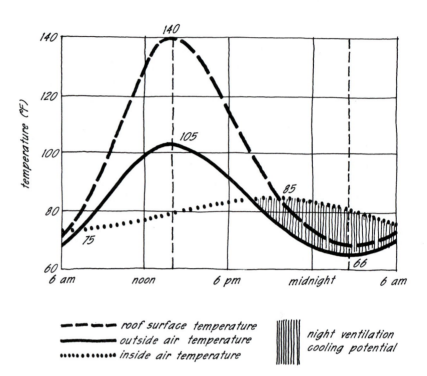

Figure 3.19: Cutaway drawing showing construction of adobe Pueblo dwelling. *(Redrawn from "Primative architecture and climate," by Fitch and Branch. Copyright © 1960 by Scientific American, Inc. All rights reserved.)*

Figure 3.20: Temperatures in and around an adobe dwelling. Notice that while the average inside and outside temperature are about equal, the maximum interior temperature occurs about 10 p.m. — about eight hours after the outside peak. By this time the outside temperature has actually dropped below the inside and the window can be opened for ventilative cooling. Notice that the outside temperature swing is about 40°F wile the interior is only about 10°F. Finally, the shaded area shows the cooling effect of night ventilation. The thermal qualities of this primitive construction system are impressive indeed. *(Redrawn from "Primative architecture and climate," by Fitch and Branch. Copyright © 1960 by Scientific American, Inc. All rights reserved.)*

One Pueblo structure, the "Longhouse" at Mesa Verde, Colorado, makes an even greater utilization of sunlight to maintain comfort throughout the year. Located in a south-facing recess eroded naturally into a sandstone cliff, the structure was constructed over the period between 1100 and 1500 A.D. Built of the stone and clay available on the site, the form of the structure consists of many rooms arranged so that the roofs of some act as terraces for others above, gradually stepping back up under the shallow cave. This arrangement provides the building and the surrounding cliff a maximum exposure to the low winter sun and its solar heating effect. Furthermore, the "brow" of the cave projected just far enough to provide shade from the higher summer sun, without obstructing the winter sun.

In desert climates, such as found in Saudi Arabia, urban settlements were usually densely packed with common-wall adobe construction and courtyards to provide self-shading and minimal exposure to the sun. Settlements were so dense that they appear to be one solid layer or "poche" of building pierced only by courtyards and meandering streets.

The dense geometry and massive adobe construction of the middle eastern courtyard house mediates harsh desert temperatures in two ways. First, the drastic daily outside air temperature swings of 35°F are reduced to about 10°F. Second, the effect of the temperature is delayed several hours as it travels through the thick adobe, so that the hottest temperatures on the interior are delayed until night — when the outside temperatures are lowest. The courtyard acts as a lightwell as well as an airshaft, bringing both daylight and ventilation to the rooms around it. It induces a particularly beneficial thermal effect in this climate that is just now beginning to be understood and appreciated.

Figure 3.21: Longhouse Pueblo at Mesa Verde, Colorado. *(Reproduced from Knowles, 1974, by permission.)*

Talib (1984) has described how the courtyard functions in three phases. During the first phase, the cool night air descends into the courtyard and fills the surrounding rooms. Walls, floors, columns, roofs, ceilings, even furniture are cooled at night and remain so until late afternoon. In addition the courtyard loses heat rapidly by radiation to the clear night sky; it is often used for sleeping during the summer.

During the second phase, at midday, the sun strikes the courtyard floor directly. Some of the cool air begins to rise and also leaks out of the surrounding rooms. This induces convection currents which may afford further comfort. The courtyard now begins to act as a chimney during this time when the outside temperatures are highest. The thick adobe walls and roof do not permit the external heat to immediately penetrate to the interior — the time delay for this wall thickness is as much as 12 hours.

During the third phase, the courtyard floor and the inside of the house get warmer and further convection currents are set up by late afternoon. Most of the cool air trapped within the rooms spills out by sunset. During the late afternoon the street, courtyard, and building are further protected by shadows of adjacent structures. As the sun sets in the desert, the air temperature falls rapidly as the courtyard begins to radiate rapidly to the clear night sky. Cool air begins to descend into the courtyard, completing the cycle.

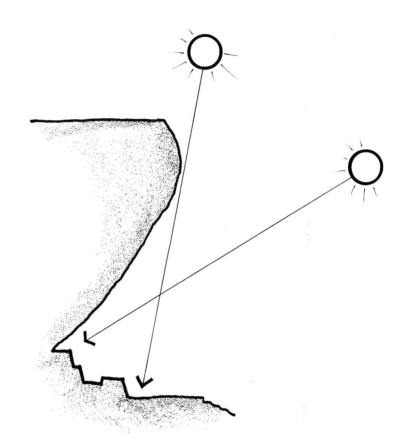

Figure 3.22: Longhouse Pueblo. Buildings were placed inside the cave in such a way that their vertical stone walls and horizontal terraces received great benefit from the low winter sun while being protected during the summer by shadow cast from the upper edge of the cave opening and by the high summer altitude of the sun. *(Reproduced from Knowles, 1974, by permission.)*

The ultimate in thermal mass is underground construction. The house has the advantage of the remarkable thermal stability underground where, at depths of about 20 ft, the soil temperature virtually stabilizes at the average annual air temperature of the region. One example of a highly developed underground settlement is found in China in the loess belt. Loess is compacted silt that has been transported and deposited by the wind. Because it is both soft and porous (about 45 percent air), it can easily be carved into habitable shelters. In the Honnan, Shansi, Shensi, and Kansu provinces more than 10 million people inhabit these underground dwellings carved out of loess

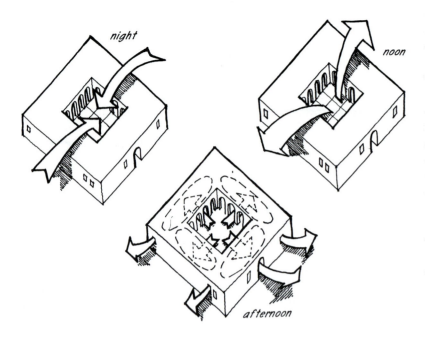

Figure 3.23: Diagrammatic explanation of the three thermal phases of a courtyard. *(Reproduced from Talib, 1984, by permission.)*

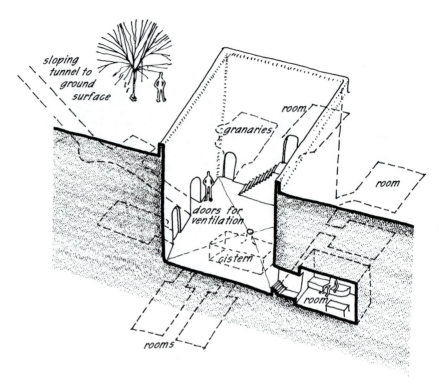

Figure 3.24: Cutaway view of typical Matmata dwelling, Sahara. *(After Rapoport, 1969.)*

(Rudofsky, 1964). A similar underground settlement is found in Matmata, Tunisia. Here the soil is similar to the loess of China, the climate is hot and dry, and the structures are free from dampness throughout the year. The houses occupy an area of about 100 by 100 ft, including the center courtyard and the rooms surrounding it. In addition to the stable temperatures afforded underground, these dwellings offer protection from the dusty winds of the Sahara.

WARM-HUMID REGION

> *We first spread a parasol to throw shadow in the earth and in the shadow we put together a house.*
>
> — *Tanizaki.*

The climate of Miami, Florida typifies this hot-humid region. It is characterized by high humidity and warm summer temperatures. Day to night temperature swings during the summer are insignificant because of the extensive humidity and cloud cover which prevents surfaces from reradiation to the night sky. Early morning summer temperatures, however, can drop to 75°F so that extensive ventilation, bringing this somewhat cooler air into the building, can offset the higher temperatures of the late morning and afternoon. Very mild winters, on the other hand, make for a short heating season. Substantial sunshine is available throughout the year, and can be a source of winter heating if care is taken to ensure that it does not also cause overheating during the summer (AIA Research Corporation, 1978).

Warm-humid region: biological response

Temperature in beehives is critical to maintaining the wax honeycomb structure and egg incubation. It is controlled by ventilation in a community effort. Operating in teams distributed around the hive, "house" bees fan their wings to divert air currents in the most advantageous directions. The temperature in the hive can fall below 15°C and the bees will remain active, but

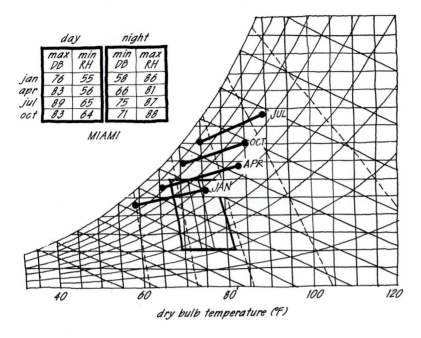

	day		night	
	max DB	min RH	min DB	max RH
jan	76	55	58	86
apr	83	56	66	81
jul	89	65	75	87
oct	83	64	71	88

MIAMI

dry bulb temperature (°F)

Figure 3.25: Typical hot-humid climate — Miami, Florda. Daily temperature and humidity ranges for January, April, July, and October. *(Data from U.S. Department of Commerce, 1978.)*

In rainforest environments, with abundant shade available, a minimal covering of clothing consistent with cultural customs is traditional. In locations more exposed to direct sunlight, loose-fitting cotton clothing is used for protection from the sun while allowing maximum ventilation.

Warm-humid region: traditional building response

In this climate, where the need for shelter from the sun and rain predominates, the roof becomes the dominant structural and formal element: steeply sloping to shed torrential rains, opaque to solar radiation, with a maximum of insulation (in the form of trapped air), and large overhangs to protect the inhabitants against slanting sun and blowing rain. The floor is often raised on stilts for better exposure to cool breezes, escaping the earth-warmed ground layer of air, while providing protection from snakes, rats, and crawling insects.

In coastal regions, the presence of the large body of water effects tremendous thermal inertia on the thermal environment, greatly reducing both daily and annual temperature variation. Under these near-constant temperature conditions, the stabilizing thermal effect of massive masonry conduction is of little advantage; the walls are usually minimized to provide free airflow. However, contrary to popular belief, masonry construction is not

the optimum temperature required at the brood nest must not fluctuate more than one or two degrees from 35°C and this has to be maintained irrespective of external conditions. Extreme heat is particularly distressing to the bees and in hot weather hundreds of workers are co-opted as temporary house bees to drive air current though the hive with furiously buzzing wings. Humidity is also controlled within the hive; in the brood area it is maintained between 35 and 45 percent. Excess water vapor tends to be removed by normal ventilation but in hot, dry conditions humidification is accomplished by workers who bring water back to the hive in their crops and droplets are smeared over the combs. As this evaporates, it helps to chill the air and increases the humidity ratio (Hancocks, 1973).

Warm-humid region: traditional clothing

The traditional clothing response is to provide maximum ventilation to encourage evaporation of perspiration — the only means of dissipating bodily heat at these high ambient temperatures. In addition, shade from clothing is desirable in locations where shade is not readily available from trees.

Figure 3.26: Seminole house is an open post-and-beam construction with a gable roof of thatch. *(Redrawn from "Primative architecture and climate," by Fitch and Branch. Copyright © 1960 by Scientific American, Inc. All rights reserved.)*

Figure 3.27: Simple dome hut of Banbuti Pygmies is a woven frame of twigs covered with large leaves. *(Redrawn from "Primative architecture and climate," by Fitch and Branch. Copyright © 1960 by Scientific American, Inc. All rights reserved.)*

Figure 3.28: The design of this Ma'dan house (Iraq), built of 20 ft tall local reeds, has remained unchanged for 6,000 years. The sides can be raised to maximize ventilation. *(After Grundfeld, 1975.)*

a thermal liability in humid climates, even in the most stable temperature conditions. In more inland humid regions there is usually sufficient daily temperature variation to make masonry construction advantageous, provided it can be incorporated without obstructing cooling breezes.

The predominant materials are vegetable fibers of all sorts: saplings, bamboo, vines, shredded fronds and grasses. In the historical absence of iron tools, the cutting and fitting of timbers in the tradition of carpentry is totally missing. Instead the structures are assembled using the skills of basketry and weaving.

The Ma'dan, or "marsh Arabs," who live in Iraq at the mouths of the Tigris and Euphrates, build the airiest of homes with the only material available — giant swamp reeds which grow twenty feet high. Massive bundles of these reeds are set into the ground 18 to 20 ft apart and the ends are bent over to form arches. These arches, set about 4 ft on center, form the ribs of a barrel vault which is then infilled with overlapping layers of reed matting. The matting on the sides can be opened or closed as weather dictates. The largest of these, the *mudhifs* (guest house), are 20 ft wide and 120 ft long. The reeds, being hollow wooden tubes, are efficient structurally, having a high strength-to-

weight ratio. Furthermore, the air trapped inside and between the reeds serves as a good insulator, reducing the solar impact of the sun on the roof.

HOT-WITH-SEASONAL-HUMIDITY REGION

This climate is a combination of the previous two. For a portion of the year it is hot and arid (similar to Phoenix), with its characteristic very hot days, cool nights, minimal rainfall, and low humidity. For the remainder of the year — the rainy season — it is warm to hot and humid (similar to Miami) with relatively constant daily temperatures, high rainfall (virtually daily), and high humidity. This climate is not found in North America, but is typical of parts of southern Asia and Africa.

Hot-with-seasonal-humidity region: traditional building response

Indigenous buildings of this regions are characterized by a combination of thermal mass (usually adobe) with protection for rain, usually in the form of sloping, thatched roofs with sufficient overhang to provide rain and sun protection for the adobe walls. Double roofs are particularly suited to hot climates with seasonal humidity because they offer moisture protection and shading while providing the benefits of thermal mass. They can be found in several locations throughout the world, including among the Massa tribe in the Cameroons, on the Bauchi plateau of Nigeria, and in Orissa, India, as well as the double walls of New Caledonia. The double roof has five consequences:

1. *The thatch sheds water and protects the mud in the rainy season.*

2. *The thatch shades the mud roof from the direct sun, reducing heat buildup and hence the heating up of the dwelling. It also reduces the thermal expansion and contraction of the mud, which prolongs its life.*

3. *The airspace provides important additional insulation during midday, while the heat capacity of the mud delays the effects of the daytime temperatures.*

4. *The slope of the roof induces a convective airflow in the airspace, allowing the warm air to rise and escape near the ridge and be replaced by cooler air near the eave.*

5. *The thermal mass of the mud conserves the heat for cooler nights, and the hatch helps it conserve that heat for a longer portion of the night by reducing heat loss to the clear night sky.*

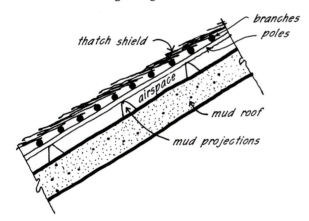

Figure 3.29: Section of double roof in Orissa, India. *(After Rapoport, 1969.)*

Certain tribes of Natal in South Africa build a hut whose light wooden frame is sheathed in woven fiber mats. The weave contracts in dry weather, permitting the movement of air through its small openings; in wet weather, the fibers expand to close the openings creating a nearly watertight membrane. In the Khosian tribe of South Africa these mats are detachable and can be moved from wall to wall according to wind direction (Fitch and Branch, 1960).

CONCLUSIONS

Contemporary architecture continues to respond to climate with a minimum number of mass-produced design solutions. In general, the typical house (or skyscraper) responds with only one type of wall and one type of roof. They are thermally suited for a climate such as Detroit, yet they are employed indiscriminately across the United States in climates as diverse as those of Scotland, the Sahara, the Russian steppes, and the subtropics of Central America. The basic inefficiency of this process is masked by relatively low energy costs and the availability of efficient mechanical equipment to heat, cool, and ventilate buildings. Contemporary architecture would be greatly enriched, both aesthetically and operationally, by a careful analysis of the climatic response of primitive architecture and a more thoughtful application of these fundamental principles (although not necessarily the actual materials or methods) to contemporary buildings (Fitch and Branch, 1960).

STUDY QUESTIONS

1. When analyzing climatic data for a building site, why are average daily high and low conditions important in designing the building envelope? Why are probable temperature extremes important?

2. Why do desert regions experience such variation in daily temperature while humid regions are comparatively stable?

3. Shivering is an involuntary response of the body to very cold temperature. Explain how shivering helps the body cope with these extreme conditions.

4. Describe the construction and thermal characteristics of an igloo.

5. Explain how adobe construction modifies the effects of the extreme temperatures characteristic of hot-arid climates in two ways to create a comfortable interior.

6. Why isn't ventilation cooling usually a good strategy in hot-arid regions?

7. Under what conditions can ventilation in hot, arid regions be advantageous?

8. Some desert cultures have adopted dark clothing while others use white robes. What are the thermal advantages of each?

MICROCLIMATE,

SITE PLANNING, AND DEVELOPMENT

*The fundamental tenet of energy-conscious site planning
is that the climate can be modified using the natural features
of the site, thus reducing or in some cases eliminating the need
for artificial conditioning.*

— Layne Ridley (1990)

Climatic factors affect the way that buildings use energy and the comfort of their occupants. By understanding both the general climate of the region and the way that this is modified by the unique physical features of the site to form the microclimate, it is possible to design both the landscape and the building envelope to save energy and increase comfort. Natural features such as earth forms, vegetation, and water can be used to uniquely affect the temperature, sun, humidity, and wind conditions of each site.

Generally speaking, climate can be considered at two scales: macro (regional scale, hundreds of square miles in area) and micro (site scale).

TEMPERATURE

TEMPERATURE MACROCLIMATE

Normal daily maximum and minimum temperatures for each month for cities representing the 16 climatic regions of the United States are shown in Appendix D. Data for other cities can be found in the literature (for example,

U.S. Department of Commerce, 1978). These data are valuable in order to understand thermal trends and large-scale tendencies, but it is important to recognize the limitations of this information.

TEMPERATURE MICROCLIMATE

At the building site scale, many factors serve to modify these "undisturbed" conditions which meteorological stations strive to record. For example, the wide climatological variation that can occur over a single project site is demonstrated in the late winter with melting snow-cover patterns, and in early spring when north sides of hills may be frozen and brown while south slopes are already green with new vegetation. Plants are sensitive indicators of favorable temperatures, a fact known to most farmers, who prefer southern slopes for vineyards or orchards (Geiger, 1950).

Altitude

Air temperature decreases with altitude; as a rule of thumb the temperature will drop about 1°F for each 330-ft rise in summer, and for each 400-ft rise in winter (this is known as the adiabatic lapse rate). Even small differences in terrain can effect major differences in the temperature of the site. Cool air is heavier than warm, and at night the outgoing radiation causes a cold-air layer to form near the ground. While it tends to flow like a liquid toward the lowest elevations (more about this in a later section), on the slopes of valleys the thermal behavior is more complex.

Proximity to water

The stabilizing influence of large bodies of water on temperature variation is considerable. They raise winter temperature minimums and lower summer maximums. For example, in the Great Lakes region, this effect raises the mean January temperature about 5°F and lowers the summer high temperature a similar amount.

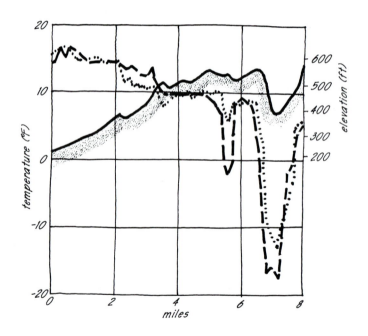

Figure 4.1: Effect of land formation and distance from large body of water on temperature distribution — section in Toronto showing temperature varying with elevation and distance from Lake Ontario recorded on a clear February evening at midnight. *(After Middleton and Millar, 1936.)*

In one instance, the air temperatures were measured at shore locations adjacent to Lake Ontario on a clear night. Temperature gradually decreased as the distance from the lake increased. Seven miles from the lake, a valley

caused the formation of a "cold pool." The temperature dropped about 7°F during the first 6 mi; it dropped abruptly another 25°F in the last mile as the terrain sloped down almost 200 ft into the valley.

Soil depth

The mass of the earth is a virtually infinite thermal storage medium. The soil delays and reduces the variation of surface temperature conditions. Daily fluctuations are lost after only a few inches of depth, while the temperature virtually stabilizes at the average annual surface temperature at depths below 20 ft.

Figure 4.2: Comparison of the effects of plants and paving on ground temperatures: (a) seasonal variation, (b) daily variation. *(Reproduced from Robinette, 1977, by permission.)*

Ground cover

The character of the ground cover of the site can have a pronounced effect on temperatures. Natural vegetation tends to moderate extreme temperatures. Plant and grassy ground covers reduce temperatures by absorption of insolation and evaporative cooling. On sunny summer days, the air temperatures over grass surfaces are 10 to 14°F cooler than over exposed soil. Temperatures under a tree at midday are often 5°F lower than in comparable unshaded areas.

Conversely, synthetic surfaces tend to elevate temperatures, because the materials are usually both thermally absorptive and conductive. Asphalt paving temperatures typically elevate 25°F over air temperatures. Cities are warmer than surrounding suburbs: 8°F during a summer day and 11°F at night (Landsberg, 1959).

Urban heat island

Landsberg (1981) provides this description of London in 1812 by Luke Howard:

> *London was this day involved, for several hours, in palpable darkness. The ships, offices, etc. were necessarily lighted up; but the streets not being lighted as a night, it required no small care in the passenger to find his way and avoid accidents. The sky, where any light pervaded it, showed the aspect of bronze. Such is, occasionally, the effect of the accumulation of smoke between two opposite gentle currents, or by means of a misty calm. I am informed that the fuliginous cloud was visible, in this instance, for a distance of forty miles. Were it not for the extreme mobility of the atmosphere, this volcano of a thousand mouths would, in winter, be scarcely habitable.*

In general, urban development raises the ambient air temperatures higher than a comparable rural environment. Known as the *urban heat island* effect, the paved surfaces and walls not only rise to a higher temperature during the day, they store some of the insolation for a longer time before releasing it after sunset to its air environment. This effect is exacerbated by the lack of evaporation in the cities. Insolation that is used in the country in the morning to evaporate dew, precipitation on plants, and frost is directly absorbed by the building materials. Urban evapotranspiration is also sharply reduced because of the reduced plant cover. The rapid runoff after precipitation essentially eliminates water storage in and evaporation from the soil.

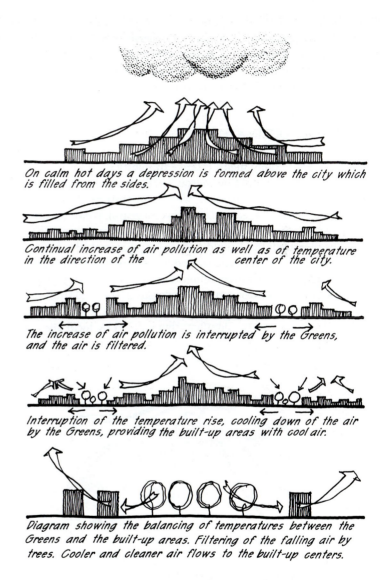

On calm hot days a depression is formed above the city which is filled from the sides.

Continual increase of air pollution as well as of temperature in the direction of the center of the city.

The increase of air pollution is interrupted by the Greens, and the air is filtered.

Interruption of the temperature rise, cooling down of the air by the Greens, providing the built-up areas with cool air.

Diagram showing the balancing of temperatures between the Greens and the built-up areas. Filtering of the falling air by trees. Cooler and cleaner air flows to the built-up centers.

Figure 4.3: Convective air circulation due to "urban heat island" effect and the mitigation of this effect through the use of parks and greenspaces. *(Redrawn from Robinette, 1977, by permission.)*

HUMIDITY

Humidity is an important site resource for two reasons. First, it affects comfort directly by controlling the rate of perspiration evaporation and thus the ability of the body to dissipate heat at higher ambient temperatures. Second, it affects the ability of the earth to receive insolation (cloud cover has a major effect and humidity a minor effect on the transparency of the atmosphere to solar radiation) and to reradiate heat from warm terrestrial surfaces to the night sky (the temperature of deep space is effectively absolute zero).

HUMIDITY MACROCLIMATE

Although normal daily mean relative humidity data for each month are available (U.S. Department of Commerce, 1978, for example) it is important to relate the daily humidity variation with temperature. When considering normal data (that is, data averaged over several years), it can be assumed that the highest relative humidity occurs when the daily temperature is lowest and vice versa. The mean relative humidity data for representative cities in each of the sixteen climatic regions in the United States are provided in Appendix D. These describe the humidity macroclimate of the major climatic regions of the country. These are valuable in order to understand thermal trends and large-scale tendencies, but it is important to recognize the limitations of this information. Humidity can be significantly modified by local site conditions.

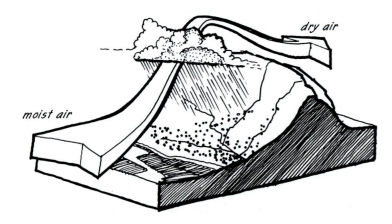

Figure 4.4: Warm moisture-laden air cools adiabatically as it rises against coastal mountains. When the air is cooled to the dew point, moisture condenses as precipitation. Most of this occurs on the windward side, producing a rain-forest microclimate. On the leeward side, the air rewarms as it drops to lower altitudes and the relative humidity lowers to produce a dry arid region. *(Reproduced from Robinette, 1977, by permission.)*

HUMIDITY MICROCLIMATE

Altitude affects air temperature; as air rises, its volume increases, and its temperature decreases at a rate of 1°C per 100 m (about 0.55°F per 100 ft) difference in altitude. This is known as the *adiabatic lapse rate* because the temperature change occurs without the change in the heat contained in the air. If the temperature of the rising air drops below the dew point, then

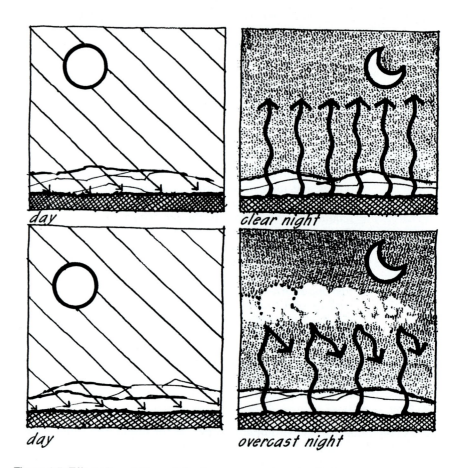

Figure 4.5: Effect of humidity and cloud cover on nocturnal radiation cooling. *(Redrawn from Robinette, 1977, by permission.)*

condensation will occur in the form of precipitation. This often occurs as prevailing winds force air up and over coastal mountain ranges.

Humidity, precipitation, and vegetation

As plants affect temperature, insolation, and wind, they also affect humidity in the atmosphere. In understanding the effects of plant material on humidity, the role of the plant in the water cycle must be clearly understood. The trees in the forest act not only as interceptors of precipitation, but also as "water pumps" bringing moisture out of the soil and transpiring it back into the atmosphere. Water is essential for the growth of plants, but at the same time moisture moves through the leaves, branches, trunks, and roots of the plant in its passage between the soil and atmosphere.

Plants also affect precipitation on the site. Some precipitation that falls on a plant does not reach the ground, either evaporating into the atmosphere or being absorbed by the plant. Some studies have found that only 60 percent of the rain falling on a pine forest canopy reaches the ground, and 80 percent of the rain falling on a hardwood forest reaches the ground. The reason for the difference is that pine needles have a greater number of sharp angles and trap water droplets in their numerous cavities, while the smooth deciduous leaf sheds water more readily.

Urban humidity

Several factors affect the humidity in urban areas. One is the nature of surface materials. Impermeable areas — roofs and pavements — are everywhere. These are designed to carry off all precipitation as rapidly as possible and convert it into runoff. In inner cities, there is little if any vegetation left and thus evapotranspiration is radically reduced. On the other hand, in cities, there are many combustion processes (including automobiles and furnaces) that have water vapor as one of the end products. In addition, many industrial processes release steam and evaporate vast amounts of cooling water. Power plants are a prime example. Overall, however, the preponderance of evidence indicates that, near ground level, the relative humidity in urban areas is lower than in comparable rural and suburban areas. A comparison of the relative humidities measured at two urban airports (La Guardia in New York and Midway in Chicago) with two comparable nearby suburban airports (Kennedy and O'Hare) supports this.

At higher altitudes above the city, however, clouds are more likely to form than over comparable surrounding rural areas. This is caused by both the increased convection associated with the heat island and by the enormous production of hygroscopic condensation nuclei. In general, this effect holds true throughout the year. The former effect is more likely to produce urban clouds in the summer, while the latter is more apt to cause early condensation at inversion layers in the higher winter humidities.

SOLAR RADIATION

SOLAR RADIATION MACROCLIMATE

The total amount of sunlight — *direct* or beam (direct from the sun), *diffuse* (refracted by the humidity and dust in the atmosphere), and *reflected* (reflected

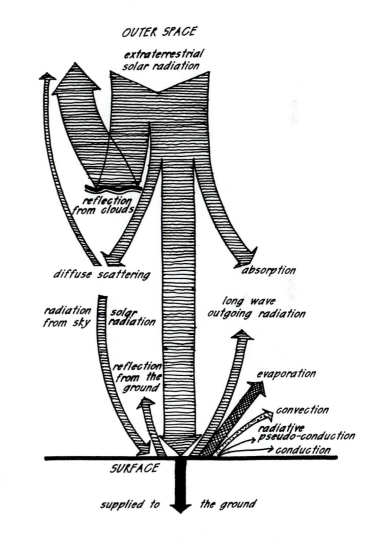

Figure 4.6: Typical daytime solar radiation exchange, summer. The width of the arrows correspond to the transferred heat amounts. *(After Geiger, 1950.)*

from clouds) — is called incident solar radiation or *insolation*. It is the heat energy measured in Btu•h/ft^2 or langleys/h. Three types of local solar availability data are useful to designers as a preliminary indicator of the potential of sunshine as a heating resource (or a cooling problem). These are mean daily solar radiation (by month and annually, in langleys), mean percentage of possible sunshine (by month and annually), and mean total hours of sunshine (by month and annually). Maps of the United States showing these data are available (for example, U.S. Department of Commerce, 1978).

More specialized data intended for the estimation of annual passive solar heating performance will be presented in Chapter 11; data for estimating the instantaneous heat gain due to insolation will be presented in Chapter 5.

SOLAR RADIATION MICROCLIMATE

The quantity of solar radiation has a dominant effect on the temperature microclimate of the site as well as the overall climate of the region. South-facing slopes receive sunlight more perpendicular to the ground surface than does level terrrain. Because of this cosine effect, south-facing slopes experience the warming effects of the sun that duplicate the seasonal progression similar to a comparable level site several hundred miles to the south. Conversely, because sunlight strikes north slopes at a more oblique angle, these locations are similar in climate to much more northerly locations, with shorter growing seasons and more prolonged snow cover.

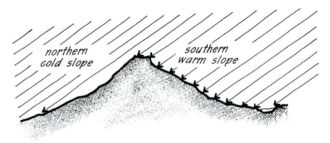

Figure 4.8: Effect of topography on solar radiation and temperature. Because of the cosine effect, south-facing slopes receive a greater concentration of insolation than north slopes, resulting in a higher ground temperature and extended growing season. *(Reproduced from Robinette, 1977, by permission.)*

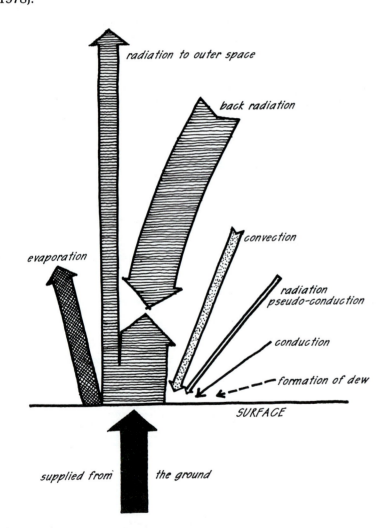

Figure 4.7: Typical nighttime radiation exchange, summer. *(After Geiger, 1950.)*

WIND

As noted in previous chapters, air movement has a significant effect on thermal comfort, both during cool periods (accelerating bodily heat loss by convection in the form of the wind chill effect) and during warm periods (increasing perspiration evaporation, which becomes the primary means of maintaining comfort at higher temperatures).

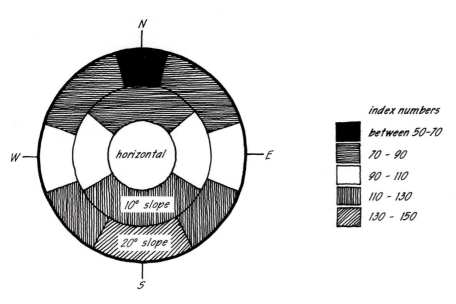

Figure 4.9: Diagrammatic site plan of a hill showing the total radiation effect on 10 and 20° slopes facing in different directions in the New York-New Jersey area (110 index number means that the total annual insolation on the hill surface is equal to 110 percent of that received on a comparable level site). *(After Olgyay, 1963.)*

WIND MACROCLIMATE

Three types of wind availability data are of interest to the designer. Prevailing direction and mean speed for a representative month of each season are used in selecting the appropriate landscape and building design strategies. Surface wind roses show the percentage of time during these representative months that the wind comes from different directions and are therefore an indicator of the reliability of the prevailing direction during those months; they are used to evaluate the appropriateness on unidirectional vs. multidirectional seasonal strategies. Examples of climatic maps showing these data are included in Appendix C; see U.S. Department of Commerce (1978) for additional data.

In general, strong winter winds suggest strategies which reduce building infiltration heat loss — tighter construction and shielding (by adjacent plants, landforms, or adjacent buildings) from predominant winter winds. In the summer, knowledge of the direction and velocity of available cooling breezes is important in encouraging ventilation through the building by utilizing the design of landscape, windows, and interior partitions.

WIND MICROCLIMATE

Small differences in terrain can create remarkably large modification of the wind microclimate. An understanding of the basic principles behind these localized effects is essential to the design of landscapes that effectively defend against winter wind or utilize summer breezes.

Convective airflow

As noted earlier in this chapter, cool air is heavier than warm air, and at night the outgoing radiation causes a cold-air layer to form near the ground surface. The cold air behaves like a liquid, flowing toward the lowest points. This settles in the lowest areas to form cool air "pools." Accordingly, vertical obstructions that impede this flow offset the distribution of the nocturnal temperatures by dam action. This same phenomenon is enhanced when a large volume of cold air is involved, as in valleys. This flow reverses the following morning, as surfaces warm up.

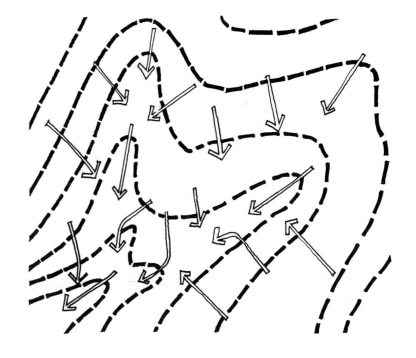

Figure 4.10: Example of convection topographic analysis; note that convective breeze flow is indicated by arrows and are generally perpendicular to contours — downslope at night (upslope in the morning). Cool "puddles" are found in low areas, while "thermal" belts are halfway up the slope.

body of water must be large (the size of the Great Lakes for example) and sky conditions must be clear (for both daytime solar heating and night radiative cooling of the land surface).

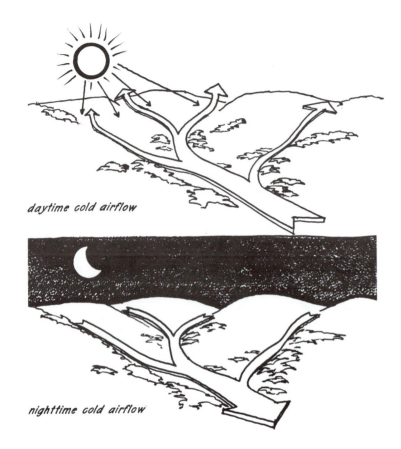

Figure 4.11: Cold air behaves like a liquid, flowing toward the lowest points early in the evening, and reverses the following morning as the sun begins to warm the terrain. *(Redrawn from Robinette, 1977, by permission.)*

Figure 4.12: Diurnal air movements near a large body of water. *(Redrawn from Robinette, 1977, by permission.)*

Terrain friction

Wind speeds are generally higher above the ground, where they are not influenced by the friction of ground obstructions. The larger the obstructions, the greater the height necessary to reach undisturbed flow. In general, urban areas reduce surface windspeed more than comparable rural areas and affect the wind at greater heights. The reasons include the greater mechanical friction of urban obstructions, but also may be influenced by the greater vertical convection currents found over the warmer city.

Windbreaks

Plants, particularly if in full foliage, are obstructions to wind. As a rule of thumb, there is a major reduction in wind velocity up to five times the height of the obstruction, and the flow is turbulent (direction is unpredictable). There is some reduction in velocity as far out as 10 times the tree height for single trees. Dense rows of trees are even more effective in providing shelter. For example, wind velocity may be reduced by 50 percent for a distance downwind from 10 to 20 times the height of such dense shelterbelts. Wind is also affected on the windward side of the obstruction, but only one-third as far as to leeward (Robinette, 1977).

The sea-breeze effect

As also noted earlier, large water bodies are more stable in temperature than adjacent land surfaces (as a result of the higher specific heat of water). During the day, the sun heats up the land surface quickly to a temperature higher than the adjacent water. The air over the land is warmed in turn, and begins to rise. Cooler air is drawn in from over the water to replace it, resulting in a predictable daytime onshore breeze. At night, as the land surface cools off rapidly (by radiation to the clear night sky) to a temperature lower than the water, the cycle reverses, and an offshore breeze continues until dawn. For this effect to be reliable (usually overpowering the prevailing weather system), the

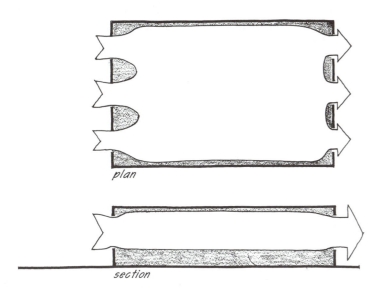

Figure 4.13: The natural airflow pattern through the building test model with no planting. *(After White, 1953.)*

Figure 4.15: Effect on ventilation of a medium hedge located parallel to the windward windows at different distances. *(After White, 1953.)*

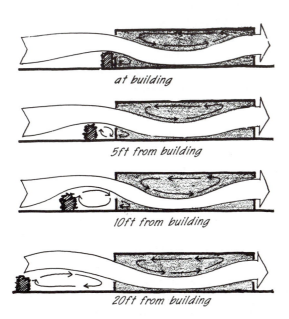

Figure 4.14: Effect on ventilation of a low hedge (less than 3 ft high) located parallel to the windward windows at different distances. *(After White, 1953.)*

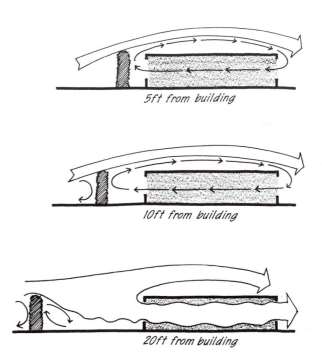

Figure 4.16: Effect on ventilation of a high hedge located parallel to the windward windows at different distances. *(After White, 1953.)*

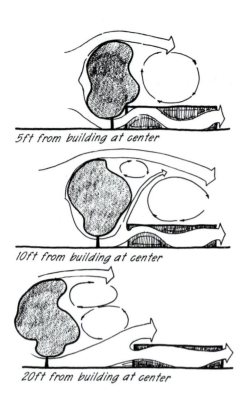

5ft from building at center

10ft from building at center

20ft from building at center

Figure 4.17: Effect on ventilation of a 30-ft tree on the windward side at different distances. *(After White, 1953.)*

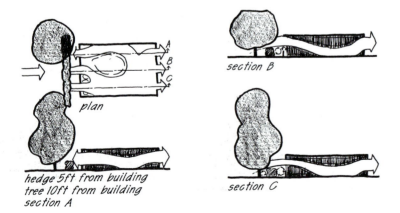

plan

section B

section C

hedge 5ft from building
tree 10ft from building
section A

Figure 4.18: Effect on ventilation of a hedge-tree combination; notice that the direction of interior airflow actually reverses behind the tree. *(After White, 1953.)*

Channeling breezes

White's (1953) classic study of the effects of the placement of plants adjacent to buildings to enhance ventilative cooling concluded that:

1. Planting can materially affect the movement of air through and about buildings.

2. Depending on the way it is used, planting may either augment or reduce the natural airflow through the building.

3. Planting may cause actual change of direction of airflow within the building.

4. Planting on the lee side of buildings has little or no effect on the movement through the building, unless it is in such a position that it obstructs the outlet openings.

Because prevailing winds may change direction seasonally (see seasonal maps showing prevailing wind direction in Appendix C), plants should be the type best suited for controlling winds from all directions. For example, a dense coniferous windbreak on the northwest side of a structure may protect it from harsh winter winds from that direction, yet may direct summer breezes around and through it. Not only may the wind be slowed or deflected for preserving warmth, it may also enhance the cooling effect by actually accelerating and channeling the breeze though and around the house.

OPTIMUM SITE LOCATIONS

Olgyay (1963) has described the optimum building site on a hill in each of the four major climates. In cold climates, where heat conservation is the main objective, build on a south-southeast slope about halfway up the slope to provide exposure to the sun, recognizing the need for morning warmup, while providing protection from the northwest winter winds which prevail in most of the colder regions of the U.S.

In temperate climates, where the needs of both warm and cool seasons must be balanced, build on a south-southeast slope about halfway up the slope, slightly further east than that recommended for cold climates. This provides exposure to the sun, recognizing the need for morning warmup, while providing protection from the northwest winds which prevail in most of the colder regions of the U.S. in the winter. The midslope location provides protection from the high-speed winds as they are accelerated over the peak, while avoiding the effect of cool air "puddling" at the lowest elevations at night.

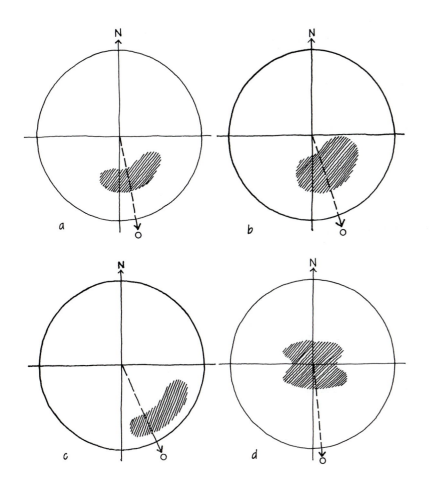

Figure 4.19: Schematic site plans of a hill showing desirable site locations in four climates: (a) cold, (b) temperate, (c) hot arid, and (d) warm humid. *(After Olgyay, 1963.)*

Because conditions are not as severe as those found in a cold climate, the exact placement is less critical and a wider range of slope steepness, exposure, and solar orientation is suitable.

The optimum site location for hot-arid climates, where the desirability of heat loss overrules the demand of the cool periods, is the lower hillside benefiting from cool airflow provided arrangements are made to avoid the flow during underheated times by "dam" action. Wind effects are of relatively small importance. The large daily temperature swing makes the easterly exposure desirable for daily heat balance. In a large portion of the year afternoon shade is required; accordingly sites with east-southeast exposure are preferred in this region.

The optimum building location for warm-humid climates, where air movement is the main objective, is at the top of a hill or ridge. Offset the building from the prevailing wind direction, but expose it to the high-air-stream areas near the crest of a hill, or high elevations on the windward side of a hill. Southern and northern slopes are desirable because wall exposure to the sun is minimized (sun is at a very altitude angle at midday) compared with the east and especially west exposures (where the sun is lower and strikes walls more directly). However, because shading can be accomplished in other ways, exposure to cooling breezes is the dominant priority.

NEWPORT WEST: MICROCLIMATE CASE STUDY

The following case study of a housing project in Ann Arbor, Michigan by Johnson, Johnson, and Roy, Architects demonstrates how effective use of climatic site analysis and landscape and architectural design can combine to effectively use the resources of the site and microclimate to create a pleasant and comfortable environment while conserving energy for heating and cooling (Robinette, 1977).

Glacial action shaped the topography of the site and the slopes are the expression of the terminal glacial moraines. The slopes are generally oriented to the east and south, facing into the morning and afternoon sun angles throughout the year.

The predominant soil on the site is a moist, heavy clay. Potential site development difficulties which might be expected to occur as a result of this soil condition (such as cold, wet basements in housing units) are essentially eliminated through several site factors which counter the effects of the heavy soils. The excellent natural drainage characteristics of the site assure efficient removal of surface water, so soils, at least on the slopes, are not waterlogged. The slope orientation to the warmth of the east and southeast sun exposure somewhat alleviates the tendency to cold soils. Also, the 15 to 25 percent slopes extending the length of the entire site are ideal for two-level slope construction, allowing many of the housing units to be constructed with exposed basements on the downslope side, facing the warm morning sun.

The valley floor, which parallels the toe of the primary slope, is an ideal dividing line and transitional zone between the housing community and the nature preserve. The low wetland valley, with an abundant variety of both flora and fauna, provides a natural air and surface water flow from higher elevations to tributary drainage swales. These swales are linked to the preserved wetland valley at intervals through the entire length of the site; the valley then connects to the expansive Huron River valley three quarters of a mile to the northeast.

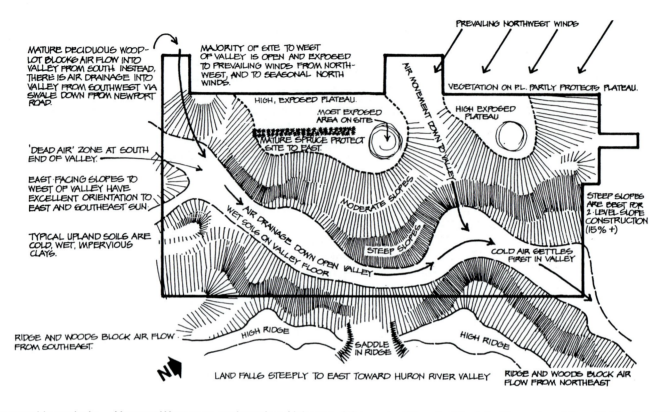

MATURE DECIDUOUS WOOD-LOT BLOCKS AIR FLOW INTO VALLEY FROM SOUTH. INSTEAD, THERE IS AIR DRAINAGE INTO VALLEY FROM SOUTHWEST VIA SWALE DOWN FROM NEWPORT ROAD.

MAJORITY OF SITE TO WEST OF VALLEY IS OPEN AND EXPOSED TO PREVAILING WINDS FROM NORTH-WEST, AND TO SEASONAL NORTH WINDS.

PREVAILING NORTHWEST WINDS

AIR MOVEMENT DOWN VALLEY

VEGETATION ON P.L. PARTLY PROTECTS PLATEAU.

HIGH, EXPOSED PLATEAU.

HIGH EXPOSED PLATEAU

MOST EXPOSED AREA ON SITE

MATURE SPRUCE PROTECT SITE TO EAST.

'DEAD AIR' ZONE AT SOUTH END OF VALLEY.

EAST-FACING SLOPES TO WEST OF VALLEY HAVE EXCELLENT ORIENTATION TO EAST AND SOUTHEAST SUN.

MODERATE SLOPES

STEEP SLOPES ARE BEST FOR 1-LEVEL SLOPE CONSTRUCTION (15% +)

TYPICAL UPLAND SOILS ARE COLD, WET, IMPERVIOUS CLAYS.

AIR DRAINAGE DOWN OPEN VALLEY
WET SOILS ON VALLEY FLOOR

STEEP SLOPES

COLD AIR SETTLES FIRST IN VALLEY

RIDGE AND WOODS BLOCK AIR FLOW FROM SOUTHEAST.

N

HIGH RIDGE

SADDLE IN RIDGE

HIGH RIDGE

RIDGE AND WOODS BLOCK AIR FLOW FROM NORTHEAST

LAND FALLS STEEPLY TO EAST TOWARD HURON RIVER VALLEY

Figure 4.20: Topographic analysis — Newport West case study project (Johnson, Johnson and Roy, Architects). *(Reproduced from Robinette, 1977, by permission.)*

The existing natural drainage system was preserved as a permanent open space in order to maximize these natural functions. The small exposed hilltop to the west edge of the site was planned to modify the force of the prevailing westerly and northwesterly winds by several means: arrangement of buffer-type plant materials, orientation of windows on buildings within the clusters, interior building use arrangement, and adequate insulation in those facades oriented to the harshest exposures.

The impressive woodland image of the site has been preserved by locating almost all of the housing units on the open, unexposed slopes. One woodland pocket next to the valley was opened up to improve airflow and sun exposure. Other than this one small zone, nearly all of the vegetation was preserved, including the meadows of native herbaceous plants with scattered native hawthorn. A long double row of mature 80-ft-high Norway spruce was preserved on the ridge line of the plateau, providing an excellent barrier from

prevailing westerlies (an extremely harsh wind that extends the cool season and amplifies the cold during the winter months).

The housing units are arranged in a series of clusters adapting to the microphysiography of the site, forming pockets of microclimates which optimize available solar energy and provide protective buffers from the cold, windy, north exposures. The resulting sunpockets function as comfortable outdoor areas during the cool spring and autumn days, where exotic plants of more temperate climates can survive.

Large window areas, oriented to the optimum southeast sun, serve as auxiliary heat sources during the autumn, winter, and spring. They enable more rapid heating of the units in the morning by receiving the low early southeast sun. A tendency to an uncomfortable degree of solar heat buildup in summer is reduced by the location of large deciduous trees in position to diffuse the hot southwest summer sun from the south and west building

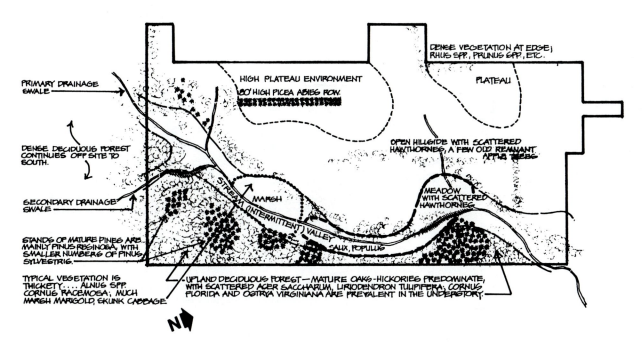

Figure 4.21: Vegetation analysis — Newport West case study project. *(Reproduced from Robinette, 1977, by permission.)*

facades; the east facades are kept open, receiving the comfortable morning sun and shaded by the buildings from heat of southwest afternoon exposure.

SITE DESIGN GUIDELINES

Robinette (1977) has suggested the following site design guidelines for improving the microclimate of a site.

TEMPERATURE

In order to make a site *warmer*:

1. Emphasize and utilize all of the maximum solar exposures on a particular site.

2. Provide for paved areas and rock or masonry surfaces on south-facing slopes or surfaces.

3. Provide vegetational outdoor canopies to reduce outgoing radiation at night.

4. Provide, allow for, or retain "sun pockets" which are potentially on a site or already in existence.

5. Provide for windbreaks and cold airflow diverters either with vegetation, walls, fences, or the building itself.

6. Provide paved areas and terraces on the south side of the building and remove shading devices during the day.

7. Use heat-retaining structural materials such as concrete and masonry.

8. Remove shade or shading devices from the south and west sides of a structure when they would block sunlight during the cooler months.

9. Locate outdoor terraces, used in the afternoon, on the south or southwest sides of the building.

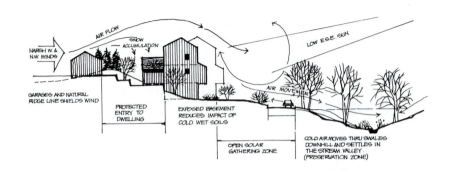

Figure 4.22: Site section — Newport West case study project. *(Reproduced from Robinette, 1977, by permission.)*

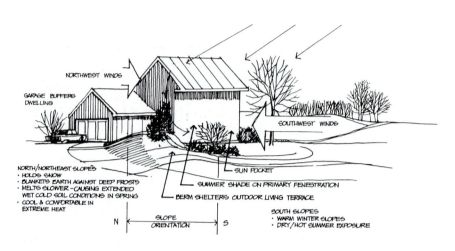

Figure 4.24: Detailed response to wind and sun — Newport West case study project. *(Reproduced from Robinette, 1977, by permission.)*

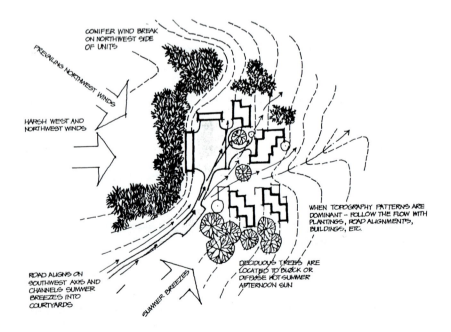

Figure 4.23: Site plan detail — Newport West case study project. *(Reproduced from Robinette, 1977, by permission.)*

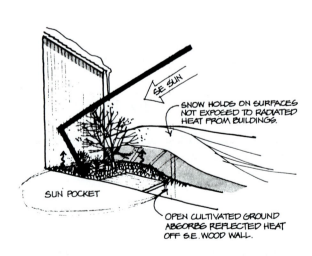

Figure 4.25: Sunpockets — Newport West case study project. *(Reproduced from Robinette, 1977, by permission.)*

In order to make a site *cooler*:

1. Make extensive use of shade trees as an overhead canopy.

2. Use vines, either on an overhead trellis or canopy or on south- and west-facing walls.

3. Use overhangs, trellises, arbors, or canopies where possible (this makes the area cooler in the daytime and yet warmer at night since it limits the release of radiation to the cool night sky).

4. Use ground covers or turf on earth surfaces rather than paving.

5. Prune lower branches of tall trees and remove or thin lower trees and shrubs to improve and increase air circulation.

6. Provide for evaporative cooling from sprinkler, fountains, and pools and locate activities downwind of these elements.

7. Use areas on the north and east of the building for outdoor activities.

8. Remove windbreaks which would limit airflow of prevailing breezes during the warmer months.

HUMIDITY

In order to make a site more *humid*:

1. Allow standing water to remain on the site and limit drainage to the minimum.

2. Encourage or increase overhead planting which slows evaporation and adds moisture through transpiration from the plants.

3. Add fountains, pools, sprinklers, and waterfalls which increase the moisture in the air. Even the sound of water will increase the sensation of coolness and humidity.

4. Use turf or ground cover on all surfaces where possible rather than paving.

5. Use relatively low windbreaks, below four ft high, to preserve moisture transpired by turf or ground cover.

6. Use natural wood chip or peat mulch under all plantings.

In order to make a site *drier*:

1. Maximize solar radiation exposure on the site and reduce shading devices.

2. Maximize the airflow and ventilation across the site.

3. Provide an efficient water drainage system for groundwater and for storm drainage.

4. Pave all horizontal ground surfaces.

5. Reduce planting, especially ground covers and turf.

6. Eliminate all water bodies, pools, and fountains.

WIND

In order to make a site less *windy*:

1. Use extensive windbreaks (plants, landforms, structures).

2. Use outdoor living areas which are semienclosed either by the building or landscape elements.

3. Do not prune or thin lower branches on tall trees or under-story vegetation in heavily wooded areas.

4. Locate outdoor activities in areas protected by natural windbreaks.

5. Excavate and place activities partly below ground level in order to use the earth to block binds and to require lower additional windbreaks.

In order to *increase* the wind flow and the cooling effect of the wind on the site:

1. Remove all obstructions to prevailing and otherwise predictable warm season breezes.

2. Use plants and landforms to funnel and accelerate warm season breezes.

3. Prune all lower branches of taller trees.

4. Curtail and limit all low plant growth between 1 ft and 10 ft high which would obstruct wind flow.

5. Locate outdoor activities in areas which have the maximum exposure to cooling breezes.

6. Build decks or platforms on the areas of the site most exposed to breezes.

7. Locate evening activities in cool air "puddles" or in sloped valleys to take advantage of convection drainage airflow.

SOLAR ACCESS AND LAND USE REGULATION

In the late seventies and early eighties, state and local legislation concerned with encouraging the use of solar energy was adopted at an unprecedented rate. The measures varied widely. Incentives were written into property, income, and sales tax codes, modifications were made in building codes and utility rate structures, and programs were established for loans, grants, demonstration projects, and training. But the most widely used controls were legal changes to land use policy, including solar access protection. These were efforts to build energy consciousness into standard development practice at the most fundamental level (Ridley, 1990).

The wide range of possible controls include: modifying traditional zoning tools, mandating local planning boards to include an energy conservation element in their master plans, subdivision and site plan review ordinances, solar envelope zoning, zoning incentives, mandated local energy impact statements, vesting of solar collector rights by local recording, and and easements.

SOLAR ENVELOPE

If a building site is to utilize the sun for heating, it is essential that its access to the sun not be blocked by structures on adjacent properties. Similarly, to assure sun to adjacent sites, the structure to be built should be designed so that its shadow does not extend onto neighboring sites during critical times of the day and year. Knowles (1974) has developed a methodology for determining the maximum buildable envelope that would prevent shading adjacent sites during the most critical periods of insolation. For square sites, the result is a simple pyramidal shape describing the maximum allowable volume.

As public appreciation of the value of sunlight exposure increases (for economic, comfort, and aesthetic reasons), it is likely that zoning regulations will be changed to reflect the importance of this resource. A number of communities have enacted "solar access" legislation, and others are likely to follow. Both Knowles and Berry (1980) have summarized the legal and policy issues of such zoning legislation.

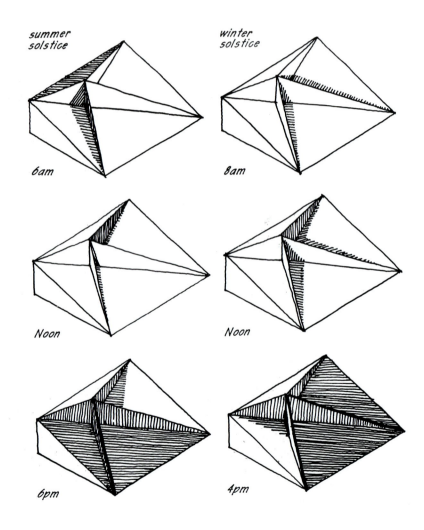

Figure 4.26: The solar envelope is a representation of the maximum buildable volume (while preserving solar access on adjacent sites during specified times) using a clocklike arrangement of vertical planes to study different building configurations within the pyramid of volume allowed. *(Redrawn from Knowles, 1974, by permission.)*

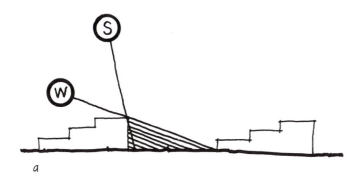

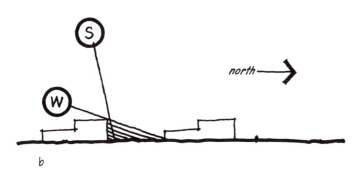

Figure 4.27: Acoma Pueblo, New Mexico. Typical sections show the critical spacing between rows of (a) three- and (b) two-story houses to ensure solar access. *(Redrawn from Knowles, 1974, by permission.)*

SUBDIVISIONS

Subdivisions have been (and continue to be) a major means of new residential development. They are the most favorable scale on which careful site planning can affect the overall energy performance of a community. Most successful subdivisions are *planned unit developments* (PUDs) which offer a number of energy-related advantages. The two most important are *density transfer* and *district integration*. Density transfer is the use of units per acre for overall development instead of rigid lot size requirements to control density; this permits flexible clustering of housing units. District integration combines single-family and multifamily housing with commercial and recreational uses and allows land uses to be more accessible to each other (Ridley, 1990).

The development of new subdivisions is also a level where local governments can exercise basic controls that address the most important issues of energy-efficient site design. Strategies can address: street orientation (to the extent that streets in the subdivision can be oriented to run east-west, the lots in the subdivision will be able to use a north-south orientation to allow maximum solar access), reducing street widths and coordinating streets with bike and pedestrian paths, slope orientation (requiring maximum use of south- and east-facing slopes will permit use of natural solar exposure), vegetation (requiring maximum retention of natural tree cover, as well as landscaping and shrubbery, can create natural shelter from winds while providing shade in the summer), building energy use (allowing cluster housing, mixing of single- and multifamily units, and higher density can reduce the energy needed in each housing unit), and services (proper planning of road patterns and service access to make possible less paving, shorter sewer and power lines, and less outside lighting can result in small expenditures for embodied energy as well as lower per unit infrastructure costs).

Even with these provisions, if new housing developments are located ever further from city centers, their energy savings might be more than offset by the additional transportation energy involved. While a typical, well-insulated, efficient passive solar house might reduce energy requirements by up to 70 percent (for a typical savings of 21 million Btu per year), if even one person in the household commuted 30 mi to work, the added transportation energy would equal more than six times that saved due to energy-efficient construction. The Urban Land Institute (1980) concluded that "the form and density of housing, the land use patterns and the resulting transportation systems have a much greater potential for energy savings than any solar application. If our community scale development is rational, residential solar applications need provide little more than marginal improvements."

SUMMARY OF TERMS

Cool air drainage — a local nocturnal breeze resulting from dense cool air flowing like water down hillsides and "downstream" in the valleys to finally collect as cool pools in terrain depressions.

Wind chill factor — the still-air equivalent temperature that will produce comparable bodily heat loss to the combination of wind-induced convective cooling and air temperature.

Wind shadow — the area to leeward of an obstruction in which wind velocity is significantly reduced. As a rule of thumb, wind shadows extend five times the height of a dense obstruction.

Sea-breeze effect — a local diurnal wind occurrence near large bodies of water resulting from the temperature difference of land and water surfaces.

Urban heat island effect — a tendency for ambient temperatures to be higher in urban areas than in adjacent rural areas.

Density transfer — the use of housing-units-per-acre for overall subdivision development (instead of rigid lot size requirements) to control density; this permits flexible clustering of housing units.

District integration — a strategy for planning energy-efficient subdivisions that combines single-family and multifamily housing with commercial and recreational uses and allows land uses to be more accessible to each other.

Solar envelopes and bulk plane zoning — a strategy for insuring solar access that utilizes a maximum buildable volume as defined by an envelope consisting of one or more planes at the top, which slope at different angles.

STUDY QUESTIONS

1. Explain how variations in the direction of the slope of a site affect its microclimate.

2. Explain why valleys typically experience cool breezes at night even when no prevailing wind exists.

3. Explain the "urban heat island" effect.

4. What site design strategies can be used to make a site warmer in a cool climate?

5. What site design strategies can be used to make a site cooler in a warm climate?

6. Explain why the rainfall on the west slope of the coastal mountain range in Oregon is much greater than on the eastern slope.

7. Why is humidity in urban areas typically lower than nearby rural areas?

8. What site design strategies can be used to make a site more humid in an arid climate?

9. Discuss some of the controls that local governments can use to promote energy-efficient site design in new subdivision developments.

5

SOLAR GEOMETRY AND SHADING

. . . In the darkness of the room she was able to thread a needle and sew a buttonhole and she knew when the milk was about to boil. She knew with so much certainty the location of everything that she herself forgot that she was blind at times.

Sometimes unforeseen accidents would happen. One afternoon when Amaranta was embroidering on the porch with the begonias Ursula bumped into her.

"For heaven's sake," Amaranta protested, "Watch where you're going."

"It's your fault," Ursula said. "You're not sitting where you're supposed to."

She was sure of it. But that day she began to realize something that no one else had noticed and it was that with the passage of the year the sun imperceptibly changed position and those who sat on the porch had to change their position little by little without being aware of it. From then on Ursula had only to remember the date in order to know exactly where Amaranta was sitting.

- Marquez, G. G., (1970)

If the sun is to be utilized in a proposed building for either heating or lighting, it is necessary to determine its availability on the site. Surrounding objects such as other buildings, trees, and landforms all act as solar obstructions by blocking either direct sunlight or portions of the sky as visible from the building location. Because of its potential effect on heating, cooling, and illumination, and because of its directionality, the position of the sun is of particular interest to the designer.

SOLAR GEOMETRY

The position of the sun in the sky can be described by its *altitude* angle (vertical angle above the horizon) and its *azimuth* angle (horizontal angle east or west of south).

Solar azimuth and altitude are a function of site latitude, day of the year, and solar time of day. While azimuth and altitude angles can be determined

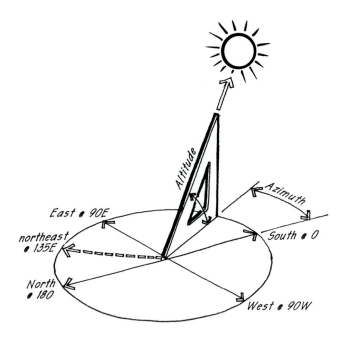

Figure 5.1: Solar azimuth and altitude angles. *Azimuth* angles are measured in each direction from south (for example, northeast = 135° E). *Altitude* angles are measured vertically from the horizon. *(Reproduced from Moore, 1985, by permission.)*

by a formula or from tables in standard reference books (ASHRAE, 1987, for example) these numerical values are not directly usable in the architectural design process. Instead, two graphic methods are particularly applicable in daylighting, passive solar, shading, and reflector design. These are the sundial and sun path diagrams.

SUNDIAL

The sundial is a diagram of the locations of the shadow of the tip of a gnomon (vertical pointer) cast on a horizontal plane. It is constructed using polar coordinates where the gnomon is assumed at the center. The polar angles are the azimuth angles and the distance from the center out to the end of the shadow (radius) is equal to the tangent of the height of the pointer. Since the sundial is flat, the shadows of low sun angles become long, and sunrise and sunset positions cannot be accommodated. In practical use this limitation is not serious and is offset by the simplicity and flexibility of the method.

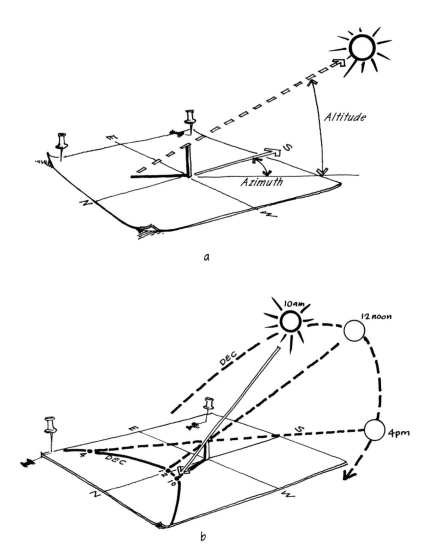

Figure 5.2: (a) Shadow location on a sundial at 2 p.m. December 21, and (b) shadow path for December 21, 40° N latitude. *(Reproduced from Moore, 1985, by permission.)*

A complete set of sundials for northern latitudes 28° through 56° is provided in Appendix A. (Sundials for comparable southern latitudes are mirror images of these with the compass arrow being north instead of south.) The 4° latitude increments provide sufficient accuracy for most building design applications.

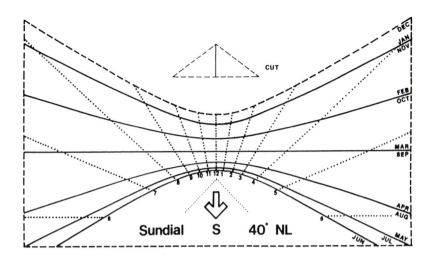

Figure 5.3: Completed sundial for 40° N. latitude. *(Reproduced from Moore, 1985, by permission.)*

Preliminary solar obstruction survey

There are numerous commercial devices available for the purpose of determining solar obstructions to the site. The sundial allows a quick and accurate identification of those obstructions during the critical December period. Make a copy of the sundial for the latitude nearest the site. Cut out the pointer. Glue the copy of the sundial on a piece of stiff flat board. Cut along the outside dotted "cut" line. Fold the pointer and glue it where shown on the sundial so that the folded edge is vertical. Next, where each of the "hour lines" meet the curved edge of the dial (i.e., the December sun path), place a black mark on the edge of the mounting board. The sundial is now complete. When the base is horizontal and oriented toward true south, a line from any time point on the dial to the tip of the pointer will point to the position of the sun at that time and date. Conversely, the time points on the dial show the location of the shadow of pointer at that time.

At the site, hold the sundial horizontal and oriented south. (A camera tripod can be used by cutting a small hole in the sundial to receive the mounting screw.) With the eye slightly below (and to the north of) the sundial, sight over the curved edge so that the top of the pointer is just visible and aligned with an hour mark previously made on the curved edge. This line of site corresponds to the sun's location on December 21 at that time. If an obstruction is in that line of site, then that will obscure the December sun at that time. By moving the eye along the curved edge in alignment with the pointer, all December solar obstructions can be identified.

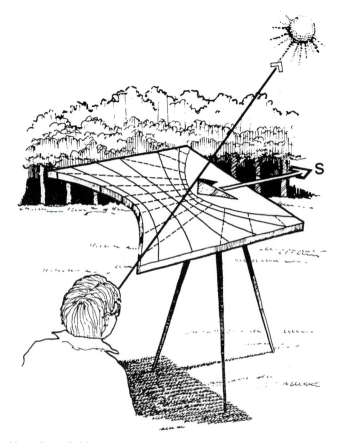

Figure 5.4: Use of sundial for preliminary obstruction survey. The sundial is level and oriented south. Sight from below from north edge, over pointer, to December sun location. *(Reproduced from Moore, 1985, by permission.)*

This same sundial can be used for model studies later in the design process. Attach the sundial to the model base, oriented toward south on the model. In direct sunlight, tilt the model base so that the shadow of the pointer touches the time and month of interest. The resulting shadows allow detailed study of overhang shading, site shading by the building, and sunlight penetration throughout the year.

If direct sunlight is not available, the sundial can be used with a distant incandescent lamp. An alternative to studying cast shadows directly is to view (or photograph) the model under diffuse light from the sun's position by using the sundial on the model base as a "sighting" device. With the eye (camera) in the sun's location, all visible surfaces would be sunlit. Conversely, all hidden surfaces would be in shadow.

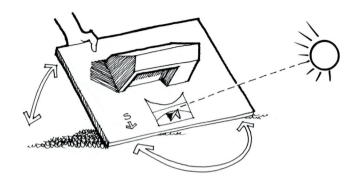

Figure 5.5: Seasonal shadow studies on a building model using the sundial. Attach the sundial to the model (oriented level and south relative to the model). Using direct sunlight (or another distant, point-source of light), tilt the model until the shadow of the pointer touches the time to be studied. The model shadows will accurately represent the building shadows at that time. *(Reproduced from Moore, 1985, by permission.)*

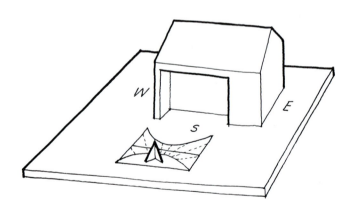

Figure 5.6: Viewing (photographing) the model from the sun's position, using the sundial as a sighting device. All visible surfaces receive direct sunlight. All others are in shade. Viewing distance should be large (relative to model size) to minimize perspective distortion. *(Reproduced from Moore, 1985, by permission.)*

Site shadow analysis

A valuable site analysis tool is a site plan showing the shadows of solar obstructions. A shadow plan is prepared over a site plan with topographic contours (with the location and height of all potential obstructions shown). Because solar radiation is minimal when altitude angles are below 10°, it is recommended that shadows be plotted only for hours when the sun is above

10°. Differentiate between obstructions that are permanent (for example, buildings, landforms, evergreen trees) and those that are seasonal (deciduous trees).

Using the sundial base for the latitude nearest that of the site, note the December hours that fall within the 10° altitude circle. For example, at 40° latitude these hours include 9 a.m. to 3 p.m. standard time (10 a.m. to 4 p.m. daylight savings time).

On a tracing overlay, draw a line from the pointer base straight to the December 3 p.m. point, then trace along the curved December line from 3 p.m. to 9 a.m., then a straight line back to the pointer. Next, measure the height of the pointer at the scale of the site plan. For example, if this is 15 ft, then the traced outline represents the area path of the shadow of a 15-ft-tall vertical pole on a flat site. Enlarge or reduce this shape proportionally for other heights.

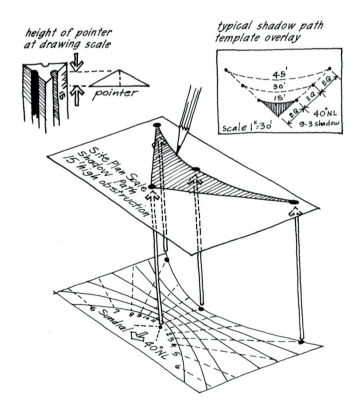

Figure 5.7: Construction of a site shadow template overlay. *(Reproduced from Moore, 1985, by permission.)*

On sloped terrain, change the shadow length to compensate for differences in contours between the obstruction and the end of the shadow.

For daylighting or solar collection purposes, ground shading is not as critical as window shading. Therefore, deduct 6 ft from the height of all obstructions to define areas subject to shading 6 ft above the existing grade. Using the outline as a template, sketch the shadows on a tracing over the site plan. Similar templates and site overlays may be prepared for March/September and June.

Sun path diagrams

As discussed previously, the path of the sun across the sky can be visualized as paths traced on the overhead sky dome. In order to be useful in the design process, this three-dimensional representation must be projected into two dimensions. One method is based on a plan projection of the sky dome. The plan is constructed so that altitude angles are projected as equal

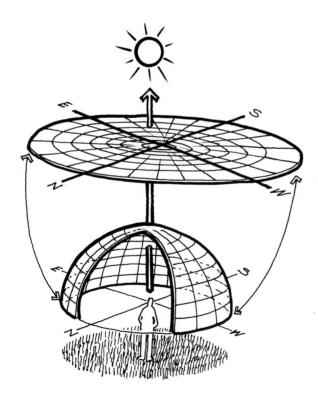

Figure 5.8: Sky dome, with equidistant plan projection showing azimuth and altitude coordinates. *(Reproduced from Moore, 1985, by permission.)*

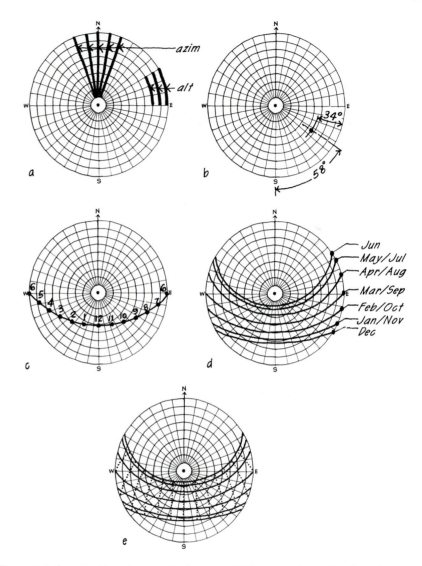

Figure 5.9: Construction of sun path diagrams. All times are true solar time; however, local standard time is sufficiently accurate for design applications. (a) The coordinates of the sun chart represent the altitude (radial angles) and azimuth (concentric rings) angles of the sky dome. (b) The sun's position for 9 a.m. March 21, 40° N latitude (58° E azimuth, 34° altitude). (c) Plotting the sun's position for various hours on a particular day results in the sun path for that day. (d) Plotting the sun path for the 21st day of each month provides monthly sun paths. Note that except for June 21 and December 21, each sun path is the path for two months. For example, the sun paths for March 21 and September 21 are identical. (e) Dotted lines indicate the sun's position at a particular hour throughout the year. *(Reproduced from Moore, 1985, by permission.)*

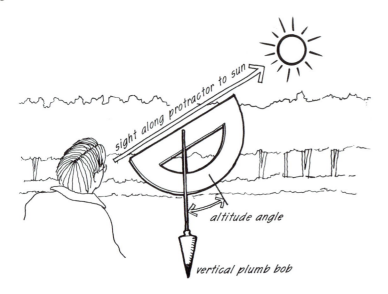

Figure 5.10: Using a protractor and plumb bob to measure altitude angles.

distances in plan (to avoid foreshortened distortion near the horizon). This equidistant plan projection is the basis for two widely used methods. Olgyay and Olgyay (1957) present a detailed method of shading device analysis using this plan projection. Because of its widespread professional use, the format of the Libbey-Owens-Ford (LOF) *Sun Angle Calculator* (1974) will be used for the methodology and charts presented in this chapter. A complete set of sun path charts for northern latitudes 24 through 52° is provided in Appendix A. (Charts for comparable southern latitudes are mirror images of these, with the north and south designations reversed.) Charts for other latitudes can be constructed from local solar angle data.

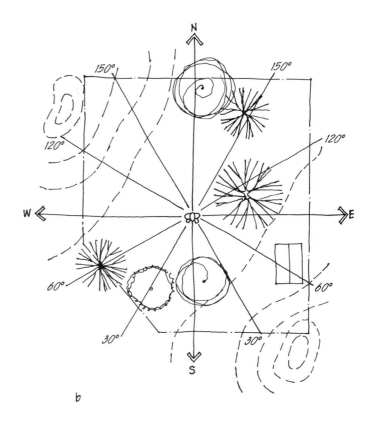

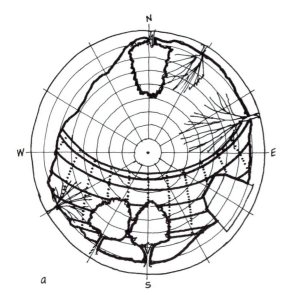

Figure 5.11: Charting site obstructions from a specific location: (a) obstruction diagram, and (b) site plan. Plot the obstructions as follows: (1) aiming the level true south, determine the altitude (angle above the horizon) of the skyline. Plot this point on the sun chart above 0° true south, (2) similarly, find and record the altitudes of skyline for each 10° azimuth both east and west of south, (3) plot these readings for the respective azimuth angles on the sky chart and connect them, (4) for isolated tall objects that block the sun such as tall evergreen trees, find both the bearing angle and the altitude for each object and record them at the appropriate point on the chart, and (5) finally, plot the deciduous trees in the skyline with a dotted line because they will block the sun during spring through fall and let most of the sun pass through when their leaves are gone in late fall through early spring.

Solar site survey

In order to utilize sunlight it is necessary to survey the site for solar access. The sun path diagram can be used to plot a profile of all solar obstructions surrounding the site. This provides a graphic representation of obstructions at all sun angles, and forms the basis for later calculation of illuminance at window locations (due to beam, sky, and/or ground component), shading and reflector device design, and interior illuminance due to the sky component. In order to measure altitude angles at the site, a surveyor's transit is desirable. However, because a high degree of accuracy is unnecessary for preliminary design purposes, a simple protractor with a plumb bob can be substituted. In addition, a magnetic compass for measuring azimuth angles is required.

SUN PROTECTION

Protection from radiant solar gain is an important strategy in any overheated climate. Without shading, building surfaces absorb insolation, raising that surface temperature well above that of ambient air and adding to the cooling load due to air temperature and humidity. For most opaque building surfaces, the amount of insolation that is absorbed as heat is dependent on the surface absorptivity; in general, the lighter the color of the surface, the less heat absorbed. It is preferable, however, to intercept the insolation before it strikes the surface, in effect shielding the building from the sun. Trees are particularly effective at shading the building when the sun is at low angles — for example, in the morning on the east side in the summer, or on the west side in the afternoon. At higher angles, roof overhangs are more effective — for example, on south walls in the middle part of the day.

For the very reasons that windows are effective passive solar heaters in the winter, they are especially problematic in the summer. Unlike opaque wall and roof surfaces, glass transmits as much as 85 percent of the incident solar radiation instantaneously. To minimize this unwanted gain, it is necessary to protect windows from the direct sun by a combination of orientation and shading.

SHADING COEFFICIENT

The *shading coefficient (SC)* is a widely used index of the effective solar rejection performance of fenestration (combination of the exterior shading component, glazing, and interior controls such as drapes or blinds). It is defined as the ratio of the solar heat gain through a glazing system under a specific set of conditions to the solar gain through a single layer of double-strength sheet glass under the same conditions. Most glazing manufacturer's publish shading coefficient data in their technical literature; where this glazing is used in conjunction with other fenestration components (such as drapery), the final SC is the product of the two.

Shading coefficients are particularly useful as a single-value factor for determining average solar heat gain throughout the day when it is impractical to take into account the effects of solar incidence angle and the three-dimensional geometry of the fenestration.

Table 5.1: Typical Shading Coefficients (SC)

Fenestration	SC	Fenestration	SC
regular DS single glass	1.00	white venetian blind full down	0.55
inside dark shade half down	0.90	light gray drapery closed	0.47
regular double glass	0.85	light-reflecting film on glass	varies
inside medium shade half down	0.81	inside white shade full down	0.40
inside dark shade full down	0.81	off-white drapery closed	0.40
regular triple glass	0.75	outside vert fins on E and W	0.30
inside light shade full down	0.70	horizontal overhang on south	0.25
1/4" heat absorbing glass	0.66	tree providing heavy shade	0.25
dark gray drapery closed	0.58	outside dark canvas awning	0.15
tree providing light shade	0.55	outside adjustable louvers	0.15

TYPES OF SHADING DEVICES

In most passive systems some form of shading is required to avoid overheating during the summer. Shading devices can be placed on either the inside or the outside of the window.

If placed on the exterior, the device will intercept direct solar radiation before it passes through the glazing. This is the preferred location because glass is opaque to the far-IR radiation that is reradiated from interior surfaces. Interior shading devices should be as light in color as possible to reflect solar heat back out through the glass before it is absorbed and reradiated in the far-IR spectrum. Interior shades have the advantage of being both less expensive and easier to adjust than exterior alternatives.

In general, horizontal overhangs are best for south-facing windows. By encouraging air movement across the glazing, open, vertical-slatted trellises are slightly more effective than solid overhangs in reducing cooling requirements.

East and west exposures are particularly problematic; summer morning and afternoon sun altitude angles are so low that overhangs are seldom effective. The best alternative for these orientations is deciduous trees that can shade while minimizing the obstruction of view. Egg-crate designs are also effective on east and west exposures. To design an effective egg-crate shading device, angle the vertical fins and horizontal louvers so that they are aimed at the location of the 10 a.m. (or 2 p.m. in the west) December sun's position. Then adjust the depth of the louvers as necessary to just barely cutoff the sun in the June position at the same times.

Shallow vertical louvers are sufficient to shield north windows from late afternoon summer sun.

SIZING SOUTH-FACING OVERHANGS

The formula for determining the noon solar altitude angle for the *summer* solstice is:

$$\alpha_{summer} = (90° - latitude) + 23.5°$$

The noon solar altitude angle for the *winter* solstice is:

$$\alpha_{winter} = (90° - latitude) - 23.5°$$

On a section through the window, extend a line from the bottom of the window up and away from the building at the noon summer sun altitude angle. Any overhang touching this line will provide complete summer shading. (For this to be literally true, the overhang would have to extend well beyond the sides of the windows to prevent sunlight from reaching the window from under the ends of the overhang in the morning and afternoon; in practice, if the overhang is only as wide as the window, any sunlight reaching the window under the ends of the overhang is at such an oblique angle as to contribute minimal summer heat gain.) Next, from the top of the window, extend a line up and out at the winter noon sun angle. As long as the overhang is at or above this line, full sunlight throughout the day of December 21 is assured. Finally, the outer bottom edge of the overhang is properly located exactly at the

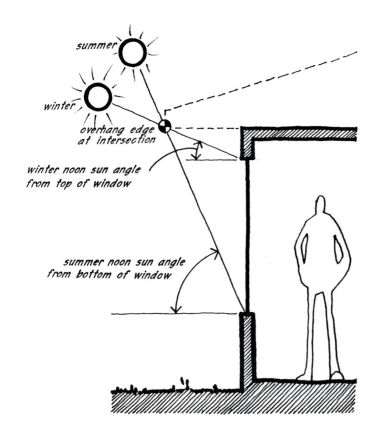

Figure 5.12: Calculating an overhang above a south-facing window.

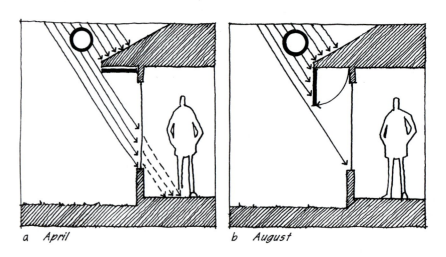

Figure 5.13: A two-position overhang allows solar heating in the spring — April, for example (a), while providing needed shading in the summer — August, for example (b), when the sun path is identical.

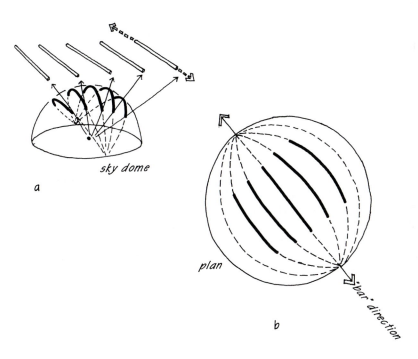

Figure 5.14: Plan projection of horizontal edges (profiles) (a) on sky dome, and (b) in plan. *(Reproduced from Moore, 1985, by permission.)*

intersection of these two lines assuring complete shading at noon on June 21 and full sun exposure on December 21.

A problem inherent in any *fixed* overhang is its inability to respond to seasonal lag. The warmest period of the summer occurs in early August about 5 or 6 weeks after the summer solstice (June 21 when the sun is highest in the sky). A fixed overhang designed to provide complete shading only on June 21 (as the above method does) allows unwanted sunlight to enter the window when the daily temperatures are warmest five weeks later. Conversely, designing to provide complete shading during the warmest period (in early August) also results in similar complete shading from mid-May when solar heat may still be desirable. One solution is an adjustable overhang (such as a two-position overhang or an awning) that provides deeper shading after the solstice than before. Another is a "living awning" — a trellis with deciduous vines which are bare during the spring but have dense foliage during the summer when the solar position is the same (such as those used on the Emerald People's Utility District headquarters building in Eugene, Oregon (see Fig. 23.12).

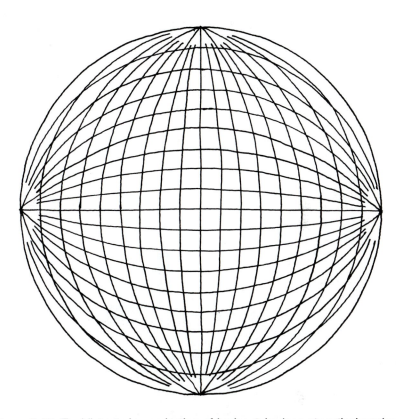

Figure 5.15: Equidistant plan projection of horizontal edges at vertical angles (10° increments). *(Reproduced from Moore, 1985, by permission.)*

DETAILED SHADING ANALYSIS

The above method is only applicable for south-facing windows. For other orientations, a more detailed analysis is required. The sun path diagrams introduced earlier can be used to determine the seasonal shading of glass; this is important for both thermal analysis and daylight penetration into the building. A complete set of sun path diagrams is available in Appendix A.

Using the equidistant plan projection format, it is possible to construct a *mask* diagram that defines that portion of the sky that is blocked by obstructions such as building shading devices (such as overhangs, vertical fins, "egg-crates," and awnings) as well as site obstructions (such as buildings, hills, and trees). When used together with the sun path chart, the hours of direct sun penetration (and shading) can be determined (Moore, 1985)

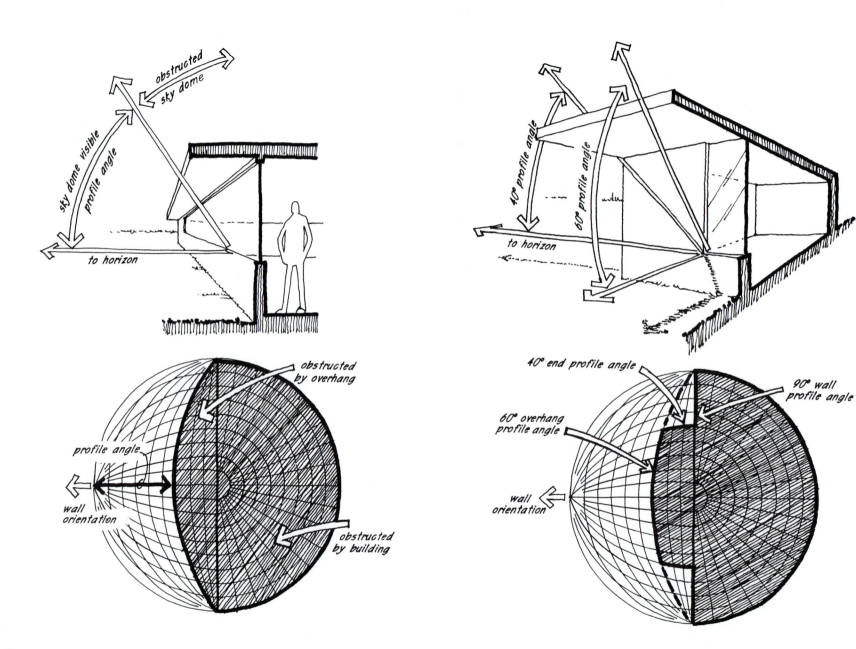

Figure 5.16: Obstruction mask of a long overhang with a 60° profile angle (measured from window sill). *(Reproduced from Moore, 1985, by permission.)*

Figure 5.17: Modified obstruction mask for a short overhang. *(Reproduced from Moore, 1985, by permission.)*

Horizontal edges

To visualize the geometry of this mask, imagine a series of parallel horizontal overhead "bars" as viewed from a reference point on the ground. If these bars are projected as lines on the sky dome, they would form an "orange segment" pattern, with the lines converging to a point on the horizon in the direction of the bars. This pattern projects in plan as a series of converging curved lines (except for the trace of a bar directly overhead, which projects as a straight line through the center).

This chart can be used to construct a mask showing the portion of the sky dome obscured by a long horizontal overhang from a window. The critical angle is the *profile* (or vertical shading, or "cutoff") angle. None of the sky above this angle is visible from any point on the window.

If the overhang extends a certain length to each side of the window, the mask should be modified to show the sky dome "visible" under each end. Because each end of the overhang is also horizontal (though perpendicular to the window opening), the same profile angle chart can be used to further define the mask.

In a similar manner, a mask can be constructed for a long sloped skylight. The relevant profile angle defines the part of the sky visible from the opening.

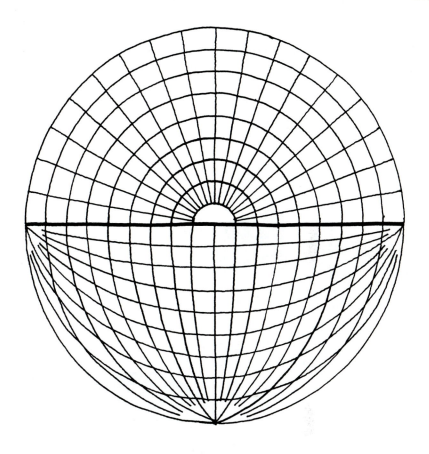

Figure 5.19: Combination chart for vertical and horizontal masks. *(Reproduced from Moore, 1985, by permission.)*

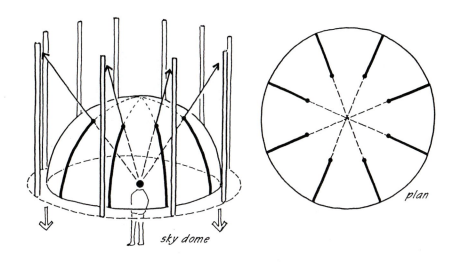

Figure 5.18: Plan projection of vertical bar traces on sky dome. *(Reproduced from Moore, 1985, by permission.)*

Vertical edges

Next, imagine a series of tall vertical "bars" arranged in a circle. If these bars are projected as lines on the sky dome, they would also trace an "orange segment" pattern, but the lines would converge at the top of the sky dome (e.g., at the zenith). This pattern projects in plan as a series of straight lines radiating out from the center.

This chart can be used to construct a mask showing the portion of the sky dome obscured by a vertical side fin from a given reference location. The critical angle is the horizontal cutoff angle. None of the sky beyond this angle is visible from any point on the window.

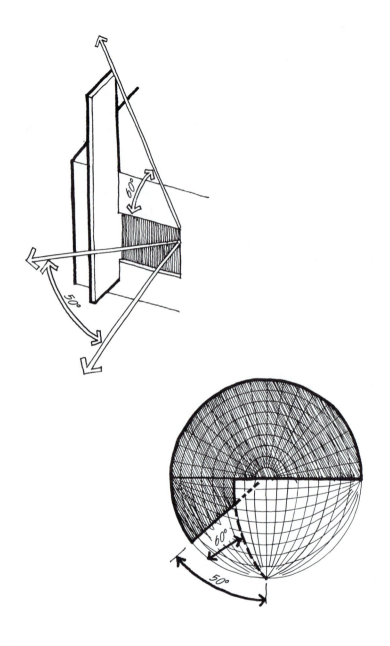

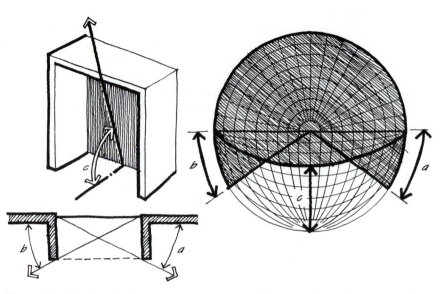

Figure 5.21: Glazing shading mask for overhang with vertical fins. *(Reproduced from Moore, 1985, by permission.)*

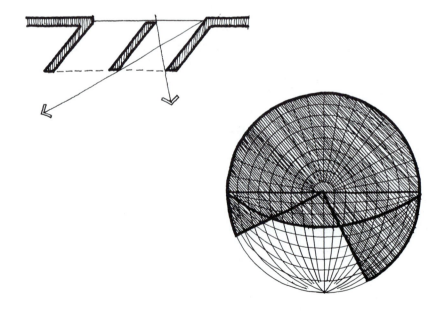

Figure 5.20: Glazing shading mask for vertical fin. *(Reproduced from Moore, 1985, by permission.)*

Figure 5.22: Glazing shading mask for vertical louvers (plan). *(Reproduced from Moore, 1985, by permission.)*

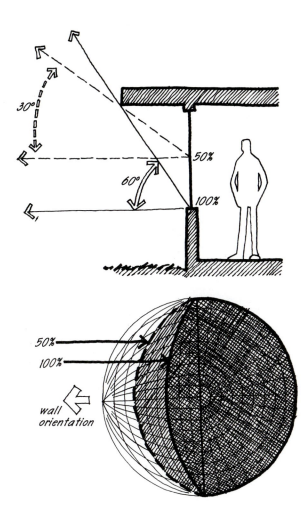

Figure 5.23: Glazing shading mask for horizontal overhang. For 100 percent shading, profile angles are taken from outer edge of glazing; for 50 percent shading, this angle is taken from center of glazing. *(Reproduced from Moore, 1985, by permission.)*

It should be noted that the obstruction mask itself is dependent only on the building configuration and not dependent on compass orientation or latitude (e.g., a given overhang geometry has only one obstruction mass regardless of wall direction or site location). Moreover, angular geometry (not physical size) determines an obstruction mask. A single large overhang and a series of small blind louvers with the same cutoff angles will generate the same mask.

Shading analysis

While an obstruction mask is not dependent on orientation, it was constructed using the same coordinate system as the sun path charts. Because of this, the mask can be overlaid on the appropriate chart to determine the times of shading or sunlight penetration. The mask is rotated so that its orientation arrow points to the correct compass direction on the sun chart. Those times on the sun chart visible through the unshaded portions of the mask indicate sun exposure.

SUMMARY OF TERMS

Azimuth — the horizontal angular position of an object in the sky (or above the horizon) measured east or west of south (northeast = 135°E; southwest = 45°W; south = 0°; north = 180°).

Altitude — the vertical angular position of an object in the sky above the horizon (= 0°; vertical or zenith = 90°).

Zenith — directly overhead; 90° altitude angle.

Sundial — a latitude-specific device for orienting a building model relative to a distant light source for the purpose of predicting the effect of sun angles on the building at various times of the year. Also, a primitive device for telling time of day based on shadows from the sun. Sundials for U.S. latitudes are included in Appendix A.

Solar envelope — the maximum buildable volume that will ensure that shadows from the project building do not extend onto adjacent properties during specified hours.

Sunpath diagram — a latitude-specific equidistant plan projection of the paths of the sun on different days of the year traced across the sky dome; useful for determining the solar azimuth and altitude angles at different times for a particular latitude. Sun path diagrams for U.S. latitudes are included in Appendix A.

Solar site survey — the azimuth and altitude of key points on the skyline surrounding a potential building site are measured (using a surveying transit, for example) and plotted on the polar coordinates of a sun path diagram (Appendix D) for that latitude. This plot reveals the times during the year when sunlight will be able to reach the reference location.

Profile angle — the vertical shading angle of an overhang; the profile angle is equal to the solar azimuth angle when the solar azimuth is perpendicular to the building wall.

Shading coefficient, SC — the ratio of the solar heat gain through a fenestration system under a specific set of conditions to the solar gain through a single light of double-strength sheet glass under the same conditions.

Fenestration — a glazed opening (such as a window or skylight) including any devices in the immediate proximity of the opening that affect light distribution (such as baffles, louvers, draperies, overhangs, light shelves, jambs, sills, and other light-diffusing components).

STUDY QUESTIONS

1. On the equinox, the sun rises exactly in the east at 6 a.m. and sets exactly in the west at 6 p.m. regardless of latitude. Explain why this is true.

2. Using the sun path diagram for 40°N latitude, determine the solar azimuth and altitude for 9 a.m., noon, and 3 p.m. on December 21, March 21, and June 21.

3. What is a *shading coefficient* and how is it used?

4. Calculate the outer edge location of fixed south-facing overhang for 36°N latitude and draw a section showing how it works with summer and winter noon sun angles.

6

CONSERVATION

Conservation strategies for reducing energy for heating and cooling buildings fall into four categories: winter defensive strategies (reducing transmission heat loss, reducing infiltration heat loss, reducing annual temperature swings), winter offensive strategies (increase winter solar heat gain), summer defensive strategies (reduce solar heat gain, reduce conductive heat gain, reduce infiltration heat gain, reduce humidity gain, reduce daily temperature swings, reduce annual temperature swings), and summer offensive strategies (increase ventilation, increase evaporative cooling).

GUIDELINES FOR ENERGY-EFFICIENT HOUSES

While each of these strategies may be desirable to some degree in every location in the United States at some time of the year, differences in climate make it important to concentrate on the most important regional strategies in order to generate cost-effective design solutions for small buildings (such as residences). A study by the AIA Research Corporation (1978) identified 16 distinct climatic regions in the United States and not only identified those strategies important to each region but also prioritized them. It is important to note that these guidelines are intended only for small buildings (such as houses) that are dominated by envelope loads; commercial-type buildings which are dominated by internal loads (such as lighting, equipment, and people) have energy-use patterns that are too complex to be resolved by such simplified guidelines.

The following are specific design responses to the overall energy conservation strategies (AIA Research Corporation, 1978):

To reduce winter and summer transmission heat loss: use compact and multistory floor plans to minimize exposed surface area; use common walls between adjacent structures; insulate walls, floors, and especially ceilings well; provide windows with high thermal resistance (low-emissivity — "low-e" — glass and low-conductance frames, or movable insulation); locate unoccu-

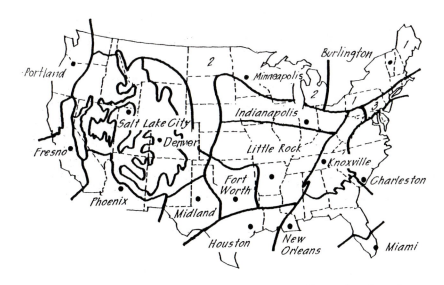

Figure 6.1: General climatic regions of the United States. These climatic regions are defined by NOAA weather data based on heating and cooling needs, solar radiation in the 50 to 60°F range, wind availability in a 75 to 85°F range, daily temperature ranges, and relative humidity. *(After A.I.A. Research Corporation, 1978.)*

pied areas (such as closets) on exterior walls to provide an insulating buffer zone around occupied areas.

To reduce winter and summer infiltration heat loss: create a wind barrier by planting coniferous windbreaks on the windward side of the building; locate an unheated structure (such as a garage) on the windward side; cluster buildings to provide mutual wind protection; seal leaks in the envelope by caulking and weatherstripping. Use snow fences and wind screens to prevent snow from piling up in entries; shelter entries from winds with overhangs and

CLIMATIC REGION

CONSERVATION STRATEGY	Burlington VT	Minneapolis MN	Indianapolis IN	Salt Lake City UT	Denver CO	Portland OR	Fresno CA	Charleston SC	Little Rock AR	Knoxville TN	Phoenix AZ	Midland TX	Fort Worth TX	New Orleans LA	Houston TX	Miami FL
Reduce winter transmission heat loss	1	1	1	3	1	1	2	1	1	1	5	4			7	
Reduce winter infiltration heat loss	2	2	2	2	3	3	7	5	4	5		5	4	6	5	4
Increase winter solar heat gain	3	3	3	1	2	2	1	3	2	4	6	2	2	5	6	
Reduce summer solar heat gain	4	5	5	6			4	4	5		2	3	3	2	3	1
Reduce summer transmission heat gain		4									1	4			1	5
Reduce summer infiltration heat gain		4									1					5
Reduce summer humidity gain								6	6	6				4	4	3
Reduce daily temperature swings		4		4	3					2	4	4	5	3		
Reduce annual temperature swings	5	1	4	3	4						4	4	5	3	1	
Increase summer ventilation cooling		6	6	5			6	2	3	3	7	6	1	1	2	2
Increase summer evaporative cooling			4				3				3	1	6			
Increase summer radiative cooling											3	7	6			

Figure 6.2: Priorities for energy conservation strategies for houses for 16 climatic regions in the United States. *(Based on A.I.A. Research Corporation, 1978.)*

wing walls; avoid valley sites where cold air flows at night or on hilltops where winds are greatest — the warmest microclimate is located on slopes; use long sloping roofs to deflect wind over the building and create "quiet" zones on the leeward side; use earth berms to deflect wind around and over the building.

To increase winter solar heat gain: site the building south to face the winter sun; locate living or important activity spaces near the south of the building; locate most window area on the south to increase solar heating; promote passive solar heating by using large area of south glass and internal thermal storage mass to dampen temperature swings; use a south-facing sunspace (greenhouse) to collect solar heat in the winter; use light-colored ground surface materials to reflect additional solar heat onto the south wall.

To reduce summer solar heat gain: use louvered overhangs and other horizontal shading devices over south-facing windows to block high-angle summer sun while allowing breezes to cool the building envelope; use operable exterior louvered shutters to shield east and west windows from low summer sun angles; use light-colored roofs and walls to reflect solar heat; shade east and west windows with vertical fins or louvers angled toward the north; use deciduous trees to shade east and

west windows; avoid skylights — they are directly exposed to high summer sun angles and are difficult to shade; use double roof with air space to reduce solar heat gain through the ceiling; provide shaded outdoor places, especially on the north side of the building, for comfortable outdoor activities.

To reduce daily temperature swings: use massive wall materials to delay heat transmission through the wall; add thermal mass to the roof by covering with sod to delay heat transmission; add thermal mass inside the thermal envelope to reduce temperature swings due to solar heat gain.

To reduce annual temperature swings: use deep underground construction; use open-loop underground ducts to cool summer and warm winter ventilation air; use closed-loop underground ducts to cool recirculated indoor air. When underground air ducts are used, insure that they are tightly sealed to prevent radon gas infiltration, and accessible for cleaning.

To increase summer ventilation cooling: landscape to direct summer breezes into the building; use roof belvederes and open interiors to exhaust indoor warm air by the "stack" effect; use leeward-facing high, clerestory windows to combine "stack" effect and wind ventilation; use attic vents to circulate air above the building envelope; use raised floors to circulate air below the building envelope; use narrow plans to increase cross-ventilation.

To increase summer evaporative cooling: locate fountains and sprayed patios where breezes can blow over them before entering the building; use hybrid evaporative coolers instead of mechanical air conditioners; spray roofs and walls to cool by indirect evaporation; add interior pools and greenhouses to add moisture sources. Use wetted loose-weave curtains to cool ventilation air by evaporation; flood roof ponds to use evaporation to augment radiative cooling.

To increase radiative cooling: expose roof surfaces to the night sky, while protecting them from solar gain with north-sloping louvers; provide a static roof pond exposed to night sky and covered during the day with movable insulation; install a thermocirculating "cool pool" exposed to the night sky at night and shielded from solar gain.

RECOMMENDED CONSERVATION LEVELS FOR SOLAR BUILDINGS

Conservation is the reduction of transmission and infiltration heat transfer through the building envelope. In designing any solar building, conservation measures are in direct competition with solar components for construction dollars. Both conservation and solar investments are governed by the law of diminishing returns: each additional dollar spent generates smaller annual saving than the previous dollar.

CONSERVATION FACTOR METHOD

Balcomb, et al. (1984) developed a method balancing the levels of insulation and solar in a building so that an additional construction dollar spent on either one will yield the same savings. Levels of insulation and building airtightness which are appropriate for a passive solar heated building can be calculated based on a *conservation factor* (*CF*). CFs for low and high fuel costs for selected locations are included in Appendix F; or CFs can be read from the map in Fig. 6.3. It is emphasized that the objective of this method is to provide a proportional balance between investments in conservation and in solar. The uncertainty of future energy costs makes it impossible to determine an optimum value for conservation; however, the conservation factor provides a useful starting point based on climate. In practice, building codes and local construction practices may ultimately determine the conservation measures actually selected.

$$R_{wall} = 14 \times CF$$

$$R_{ceiling} = 22 \times CF$$

where R_{wall} and $R_{ceiling}$ are the overall R-values (h•°F•ft²/Btu) of the opaque wall and ceiling insulation (taking into account all air layers and materials).

$$R_{perimeter} = (13 \times CF) - 5$$

$$R_{basement} = (16 \times CF) - 8$$

where $R_{perimeter}$ and $R_{basement}$ are the values of insulation *added to* the perimeter or basement walls. Perimeter refers to insulation that is added to the outside of foundation walls or under the slab perimeter in slab-on-grade construction. Normally this insulation is installed 2 ft down the foundation wall or 2 ft wide under the slab.

$$N_{E,W,N} = 1.7 \times CF$$

where $N_{E,W,N}$ refers to the number of window glazings to be used on east, west, and north windows. (Use the closest integer value; if this number exceeds 3, consider using either double glazing combined with movable insulation or using low-conduction "superglazing" with U-value less than 0.3 Btu/h•°F•ft².)

$$ACH = 0.42 \div CF$$

where ACH is the effective air changes per hour cause by natural infiltration and forced ventilation. (It is the sum of the natural infiltration and the non-heat-recovered portion of the forced ventilation.)

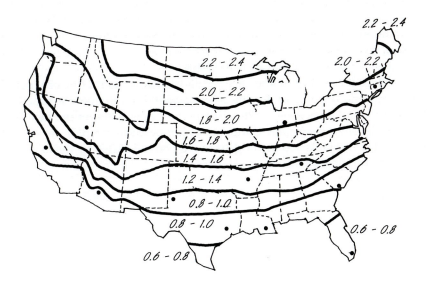

Figure 6.3: Conservation factors (CF) for low and high fuel costs for locations in the United States. *(Redrawn from Balcomb et al., 1984, by permission.)*

CONSERVATION EXAMPLE PROBLEM *(see worksheet, Fig. 6.4)*

Use the following formulas to calculate recommended values for insulation and airtightness levels:

Description

Determine the recommended conservation levels (of insulation and airtightness) for a one-story commercial office building located in Indianapolis.

The building dimensions are 120 ft (east-west) by 30 ft by 10 ft high. Triple-glazed areas (windows and glass doors) include: north 80 ft², west 60 ft² (completely shaded by adjustable awning), south 80 ft² (completely shaded during the summer by a fixed overhang), and east 24 ft² (unshaded); none of the glazing has inside shading. Construction is brick veneer over insulated studs, slab-on-grade floor, and 2x4 truss roof with insulated flat ceiling. Heating and cooling is provided by an air-to-air heat pump. The building is typically occupied 9 hours per day.

Project and site data

Enter the following data on the top of the building load worksheet (Fig. 6.4; blank worksheets included in Appendix F): annual heating degree-days (55°F base — because this is a commercial building) = 3440; annual cooling degree-days = 902; winter outdoor design temperature = +2°F; winter thermostat setpoint temperature = 68°F; summer outdoor design temperature = 92°F; summer thermostat setpoint temperature = 78°F; vertical solar radiation, VT (Jan) = 574 Btu/ft²•day; heating fuel cost = $0.14/kWh (an estimate based on probable demand and consumption rates for commercial buildings from the local utility); fuel cost = high (compared to natural gas, for example); heat value of fuel (from Table 5.1) = 3413 Btu/kW; shading coefficient (from Table 6.1) = 0.75; heating equipment efficiency factor = 2.5 (typical heating coefficient of performance — COP — for heat pump; available from manufacturer's literature); recommended conservation factor (from Fig. 6.3 or Appendix D; use higher value due to high fuel costs) = 1.76; cooling equipment coefficient of performance, COP = 2.0; and number of hours the building is occupied per day = 9.

Recommended conservation guidelines

Enter the following calculations on the worksheet (round off to nearest integer): total wall R-value = 14 x 1.76 = R-25; total ceiling R-value = 22 x 1.76 = R-39; R-value of insulation added to slab perimeter = (13 x 1.76) - 5 = 18; number of recommended glazing layers = 1.7 x 1.76 = 3; recommended airtightness level = 0.42 ÷ 1.76 = 0.24 air changes per hour (since this is below 0.5, an air-to-air heat exchanger is recommended).

HEATING LOADS

The heating loads (heat loss) of a building are expressed as *total load coefficients* (TLC). There are two components to the TLC: *transmission load* (which includes all heat transfer through the building envelope itself), and *infiltration load* (which includes heat lost by means of indoor/outdoor air exchange through cracks and normal door operation).

TRANSMISSION LOAD

Heat is transferred through building envelope elements (such as walls) by a combination of conduction, internal convection, and radiation across enclosed airspaces. The accepted practice for determining "conductive" heat transfer through the envelope is to use empirically determined R-values which are corrected to include the interrelated effects of conduction, convection, and internal radiation.

The total resistance through a building element (such as wall, ceiling, or floor over crawl space) is calculated as the sum of the R-values through all of the composite layers of the construction plus the insulating inside and outside air films. Depending on their configuration, these R-values may be per inch of thickness (typical for homogeneous materials such as insulating materials) or for a total prefabricated unit (typical for complex shapes such as a hollow concrete masonry unit). R-values for common building materials are given in Table 6.2.

The reflectivity and emittances of various surfaces is given in Table 6.3. R-values for indoor and outdoor air films and for airspaces are given in Table 6.4; the values for these vary depending on the emissivity of adjacent surfaces. If these surfaces have a low emissivity (that is, foil-like with a high IR reflectivity) then the heat transfer by radiation across the space is reduced. Note, however, that these R-value increases are only possible when an airspace is adjacent to the low-emissivity surface; if no airspace is present and the foil surface is in contact with another surface, heat is transferred by conduction and radiant transfer is negligible.

Envelope thermal resistance is typically expressed as *UA* (the product of the *U*-value and the area of the envelope element, even though the practical method of calculation varies). While the precise calculation of the heat lost through the various envelope components can be quite complex, for design purposes the transmission heating loads may be calculated by the following simplified formulas (Balcomb, et al., 1984):

Opaque walls:	$(UA)_{wall}$ =	Area of opaque walls ÷ total R-value of walls
Ceiling:	$(UA)_{ceiling}$ =	Area of insulated ceiling ÷ total R-value of ceiling.
Windows:	$(UA)_{glass}$ =	1.1 x Area of glass ÷ no. of glazings (conventional glass), or
	$(UA)_{glass}$ =	Area of glass x U-value of window assembly (for high-performance glazing materials).
Floor (crawl space):	$(UA)_{roof}$ =	Area of floor ÷ total R-value of floor.

Slab-on-grade: $(UA)_{perim}$ =   4.17 x slab *perimeter* in ft ÷ (*R*-value of insulation added + 5).

Basement: $(UA)_{base}$ =   10.7 x basement *perimeter* in ft ÷ (*R*-value of insulation added + 8).

INFILTRATION LOAD

Infiltration includes heat lost by means of indoor/outdoor air exchange through cracks and normal door operation. It depends on the airtightness of the construction and on the amount of door operations. Both variables are difficult to predict and vary further depending on wind conditions. The heat lost by infiltration is calculated by the *air change method* as follows:

Infiltration: $(UA)_{infiltration}$ =   0.018 x VOL x ACH x ADR

where   VOL   =   building volume (floor area x ceiling height), ft^3

ACH   =   ventilation rate in air changes per hour (1.5 is typical for conventional construction; 0.5 is a very well weatherstripped building; less than 0.5 requires an air-to-air heat exchanger).

ADR   =   Air density ratio (from Appendix E or Fig. 12.1).

The above air change method makes an overall estimate of the rate of infiltration as a function of building volume, the airtightness of the building, and whether an air-to-air heat exchanger is used. An alternative method is the crack method which considers the total linear feet of window and door crackage.

LOAD COEFFICIENTS

The *total load coefficient* (TLC) is the steady-state load (or heat loss) of a building per degree of inside/outside temperature difference per day. It is the sum of the transmission loads and the infiltration load over a 24-hour period and is calculated as:

TLC   = 24 x sum of *UA*

SIZING HEATING EQUIPMENT

In order to size the auxiliary heating system for the building, determine the inside design temperature (T_{set} thermostat setpoint) and the 97.5 percent winter design condition for the local site (T_{winter} from Appendix E or ASHRAE, 1989). Calculate the *design heat loss, q_H*:

q_H (Btu/h)   =   sum of *UA* x $\Delta t_{heating}$

where $\Delta t_{heating}$ = $T_{set} - T_{winter}$

HEAT LOSS EXAMPLE PROBLEM *(see worksheet, Fig. 6.4)*

Continuing the previous example on the Building Load Worksheet 1:

Heating load calculations

Select the actual materials and construction to be used in the proposed building (these selections are based on practical construction and design considerations as well as the recommended conservation levels calculated on the top part of the worksheet).

On part III of the worksheet:

• The net opaque wall area = gross wall area less window area = 300 ft perimeter x 10 ft height – 224 window = 2776 ft^2. (For simplicity, the glazed doors are treated as windows.) The total *R*-value for wall is equal to the sum of the components, including the effects of the outside and inside air films: 0.17 (outside air film) + 0.44 (4 in. brick x 0.11/in. from Table 6.2) + 1.84 (0.5 in. airspace facing aluminum foil facing on insulation, from Table 6.4) + 17.15 (5.5 in. fiberglass insulation and wood studs 16 in. o.c., from Table 6.2) + 0.45 (0.5 in. gypsum board, from Table 6.2) + 0.68 (inside air film, from Table 6.4) = *R*-20.7. (Using 8-in. studs instead of 6-in. would have increased the total to *R*-26, but would have required custom windows and would have reduced the net floor area by 37 ft^2.) UA_{wall} = 2776 ÷ 20.7 = 134 Btu/h•°F.

- The ceiling area = exterior length x width = 3600 ft^2. The total R-value for the ceiling is equal to the sum of the components: 0.17 (outside air film assumed for vented attic space, Table 6.4) + 25.12 (top 8-in. layer of fiberglass blanket insulation) + 17.15 (lower 5.5-in. fiberglass batts between 2x6 truss joists) + 1.25 (0.5-in. acoustical tile, from Table 6.2) + 0.61 (horizontal inside air film, from Table 6.4) = R-44.4. While the roof is gable-shaped, the insulation covers the horizontal ceiling. $UA_{ceiling}$ = 3600 ÷ 44.4 = 81 Btu/h•°F.

- Length of slab perimeter = 2 x length + 2 x width = 300 ft. Because of the difficulty of installing a greater thickness, add R-12.5 (2 in. urethane foam, from Table 6.2) to the perimeter of the slab. $UA_{perimeter}$ = 4.17 x 300 ÷ (12.5 + 5) = 71 Btu/h•°F.

- Total glazed area = 224 ft^2. Triple glaze all windows and doors. UA_{glass} = 1.1 x 224 ÷ 3 = 82 Btu/h•°F.

- Volume = length x width x height = 36,000 ft^3. Assume an airtightness of 0.25 air changes per hour (based on tight conventional construction practices and a medium-efficiency air-to-air heat exchanger). ADR = 0.97 (from Appendix E). $UA_{infiltration}$ = 0.018 x 36,000 x 0.25 x 0.97 = 157 Btu/h•°F.

- Sum of the $UA_{heating}$ = 134 + 81 + 82 + 71 + 157 = 525 Btu/h•°F.

- Total heating load coefficient = $TLC_{heating}$ = 24 x sum of $UA_{heating}$ = 24 x 525 = 12,600 Btu/degree days (DD) .

- Design temperature difference = Δt_{winter} = winter thermostat setpoint temperature — winter outdoor (OD) design temperature = 68 — (+2) = 66°F.

- Design heating load = q_H = sum UA x Δt_{winter} = 525 x 66 = 34,650 Btu/h.

COOLING LOADS

The building cooling load consists of sensible and latent heat gains. The sensible (temperature-related) component is the sum of:

- Heat transmission through opaque building envelope (due to the combined effects of temperature difference and absorbed solar radiation)

- Outside air (both infiltration and ventilation)

- Solar gains through glazing (windows and skylights)

- Internal sensible heat gain (due to people, lights, and equipment).

The latent (moisture-related) component of the cooling load is the sum of:

- People

- Appliances

- Outside air (both infiltration and ventilation).

While the building *heating* calculations above conservatively assume nighttime conditions and no internal heat gains, *cooling* calculations are much more complex. The air temperature difference between indoors and out (which greatly influences heat loss) is less important. Solar gain through windows, the effect of solar absorption by opaque building surfaces, and heat gain due to internal sources (lights, people, and equipment) all contribute substantially to heat gain and must be included. Because the time of day determines the solar heat gain contribution as well as the likelihood of gain from anticipated activities, the hour for which calculations are done must be chosen. ASHRAE (1989) currently recommends several calculation methods, including the CLTD/CLF (cooling load temperature differential/cooling load factor) method. By comparison with heat loss calculations, these heat gain calculation methods are tedious to do manually, are best suited for microcomputer analysis, and are beyond the scope of this book.

COOLING LOAD

Stein and Reynolds (1992) have described a simplified method for estimating the cooling load that is suitable for preliminary design analysis of light commercial and residential buildings. Because this method cannot respond to hourly changes and to thermally massive construction, it should only be used for an approximation. As a starting point for preliminary passive-cooling sizing (see Chapters 13 through 17) for typical buildings, however, it should be helpful. The total cooling load is the sum of sensible and latent loads.

Sensible loads

For "open" buildings which utilize cross-ventilation and stack-effect ventilation as the primary cooling strategies, sum the heat gains from parts A, C, and D of Table 6.6.

q_{sc} = sum of sensible heat gains (from parts A, C, and D of Table 6.6.) x A_{floor}

where q_{sc} = sensible cooling load, Btu/h

A_{floor} = total building floor area, ft²

For "closed" buildings which utilize roof ponds, evaporative cooling, night-only ventilation, or mechanical air-conditioning, sum the heat gains from parts A, B, C, and D of Table 6.6. (If mechanical air-conditioning is used, part D must be included on the assumption that daytime ventilation would be eliminated — that is, windows and doors would be closed prior to starting mechanical cooling.

Cooling load q = sum of sensible heat gains (from parts A, B, C, and D of Table 6.6) x A_{floor}

Latent loads

Latent loads are due to the moisture in the air that must be removed in order to achieve the desired relative humidity in the conditioned space. In the absence of detailed information about moisture sources, the latent load may be approximated as 30 percent of the sensible load calculated above. Notice that this is typical of an office or commercial building and does not account for food preparation or other activities that produce large amounts of moisture. With this limitation, the total cooling load can be calculated using the following formula:

$$q_c = 1.3\, q_{sc}$$

Cooling load coefficient

The *cooling load coefficient* (CLC) is the equivalent cooling required per cooling degree-day, and is calculated by the following equation:

$$CLC = q_c \times 24 \div \Delta t_{cooling}$$

where   CLC   = cooling load coefficient, Btu/DD

q_c = cooling load, Btu/ft²

$\Delta t_{cooling}$ = summer outdoor design temperature – summer thermostat setting, °F

Required cooling equipment capacity

The capacity of cooling equipment required is calculated by the following equation:

$$C_c = q_c \div 12{,}000$$

where C_c = capacity of cooling equipment, tons

q_c = design cooling load, Btu/h

12,000   = conversion factor, Btu/h•ton

COOLING LOAD EXAMPLE PROBLEM

Continuing the previous office building example on the Building Load Worksheet 2, part IV (see Fig. 6.5):

A. External gain through the envelope (per ft² of floor area)

• Opaque wall gain = UA_{wall} (from part III, worksheet 1) x factor (from Table 6.6 part A1 for 90° summer OD design temperature) ÷ total floor area = 134 x 15 ÷ 3600 = 0.56 Btu/h•ft².

• Opaque roof gain = UA_{roof} (from part III, worksheet 1) x factor (from Table 6.6 part A2) ÷ total floor area = 81 x 35 ÷ 3600 = 0.79 Btu/h•ft².

• Shaded window gain = shaded window area (on west and south only) x factor (from Table 6.6 part A3) ÷ total floor area = 120 x 16 ÷ 3600 = 0.53 Btu/h•ft².

• Unshaded east window gain = east window area x glass load factor (GLF; from Table 6.5 for east windows with no inside shading) ÷ total floor area = 24 x 70 ÷ 3600 = 0.47 Btu/h•ft².

- Unshaded north window gain = north window area x GLF (from Table 6.5 for north windows with no inside shading) ÷ total floor area = 80 x 27 ÷ 3600 = 0.60 Btu/h•ft^2.

B. External gain due to infiltration or ventilation (per ft^2 of floor area)

- Since this building is equipped with an air-to-air heat exchanger with a known *effective* ventilation rate of 0.25, the second factor for ventilation will be used. (The actual ventilation rate is higher, but because the unit exchanges heat between the exhaust and intake air, the 0.25 rate is used here for heat loss or gain purposes.) Using values determined previously for heat loss (part III, worksheet 1), the ventilation gain rate = VOL x ACH x ADR x factor (from Table 6.6 part B line 2) ÷ building floor area = 36,000 x 0.25 x 0.97 x 0.27 ÷ 3600 = 0.66 Btu/h•ft^2.

C. Internal gains due to people and equipment (per ft^2 of floor area)

- People factor (from Table 6.6 part C for office buildings) = 2.5 Btu/h•ft^2.

- Equipment factor (from Table 6.6 part C for office buildings) = 3.4 Btu/h•ft^2.

D. Internal gain due to lighting (per ft^2 of floor area)

- Since this building has most working areas within 15 ft of a window wall (although the window area is moderate), assume the intermediate value for daylighting and enter the lighting factor (from Table 6.6 part D for office buildings) = 2.0 Btu/h•ft^2.

Continuing Part IV:

- Total sensible heat gains = A + B + C + D = (0.56 + 0.79 + 0.53 + 0.47 + 0.6) + 0.66 + (2.5 + 3.4) + 2.0 = 11.3 Btu/h•ft^2.

- Design sensible cooling load = q_{sc} = total sensible heat gains x total floor area = 11.3 x 3600 = 40,680 Btu/h.

- Design total cooling load (including latent) = 1.3 x q_{sc} = 1.3 x 40,680 = 52,845 Btu/h.

- Design temperature difference = Δt_{summer} = summer OD design temperature – summer thermostat setpoint temperature = 92 – 78 = 14°F.

- Cooling load coefficient = CLC = q_C x 24 ÷ Δt_{summer} = 52,845 x 24 ÷ 14°F = 90,591 Btu/DD$_{cooling}$.

- Required cooling equipment capacity = C_C = q_c ÷ 12,000 Btu/h•ton = 52,845 ÷ 12,000 = 4.4 tons.

BALANCE POINT TEMPERATURE

The *balance point* of a building is defined as the outdoor temperature at which the heat generated inside the building balances the building's heat loss to maintain a desired inside temperature. If the balance point of a building is 50°F, then the building must be cooled when the outside temperature is above 50°F and heated when the temperature is below 50°F.

The balance point is a function of the rate of winter heat gain (from people, equipment, lights, and winter solar radiation) and the rate of heat loss (from conduction through the envelope and infiltration). Once the balance point is determined, it can be compared with the outside temperature at any time to assess the building's need for heating and cooling. This information is useful for determining when to use various passive heating and cooling strategies.

The balance point temperature is especially useful for illustrating the dramatic difference in the thermal behavior of residential versus commercial buildings. In conventional residential and other skin-load-dominated buildings, the internal heat gains are relatively small in comparison with heat losses and the balance point temperature is typically about 60 to 65°F. In energy-conserving residences (both passive solar heated and superinsulated) the solar and internal gains are larger in comparison with heat loss, and balance point temperatures are typically lower than 55°F. In larger nonresidential buildings, heat loss is comparatively small (due to the comparatively small surface area) while heat gains (due to people, lighting, solar radiation, and equipment) are high, and balance point temperatures are typically much lower (below 20°F is not uncommon). Therefore, in the latter building type, the principal thermal strategy is usually one of cooling in all but the coldest climates (Brown, 1985).

The fluidity of the balance point temperature

While the balance point temperature can be estimated for a building (using the procedure below), it is important to recognize that this estimate is based on specific heat gain conditions (number of people, electric lighting use, equipment use, solar radiation conditions, hours of occupancy), and that, in reality, the balance point changes constantly throughout a typical daily cycle as these conditions change. Thus, it would be a mistake to attach particular significance to the calculated balance point; it is better to consider it as representing a range of conditions that vary considerably throughout the day and year.

However, a very early estimation of the balance point temperature is useful to initially direct the designer toward either heating or cooling strategies; in fact, this is probably the single-most-important application of the balance point.

Calculating the balance point temperature

To determine the balance point of a building, first estimate the winter solar gain. This is an elusive quantity because solar gain varies depending on the month and on which window wall admits the most solar gain. Because of the low winter sun angle, it is likely that south-facing windows will be the dominant source of solar gain. January is usually selected as the month of interest because that is the time of lowest outdoor temperatures. Winter solar gain is calculated by the following formula:

$$Q_s = (VT)(A_{south})(SC) \div 24$$

where Q_s = average hourly winter solar gain

VT = average daily total radiation transmitted though a vertical, south-facing, single-glazed window

A_{south} = area of south-facing glass

SC = shading coefficient for south-facing glass

Next, calculate the internal winter heat gains using the following formula:

$$Q_i = (q_{people} + q_{equipment} + q_{light}) \times (T_{occupancy}) \times A_{floor} \div 24$$

where Q_i = internal gains in Btu/h

q_{people} = people gain (from Table 6.6, part C)

$q_{equipment}$ = equipment gain (from Table 6.6, part C)

q_{light} = lighting gain (from Table 6.6, part D)

$T_{occupancy}$ = number of hours building is occupied

A_{floor} = total floor area

Next, calculate balance point temperature using the following formula:

$$T_b = T_t - [(Q_s + Q_i) \div \text{sum } UA]$$

where T_b = balance point temperature, °F

T_t = thermostat winter setpoint temperature, °F

Q_s = average hourly winter solar gain, Btu/h

Q_i = internal winter heat gains, Btu/h

sum UA = total UA for building, Btu/h•°F

Continuing the present example:

Part V - balance point temperature

• Assuming the south window is unshaded in January, look up VT = 574 Btu/ft²•day. Since the glazing selected is regular triple glass, for the shading coefficient look up 0.75 from Table 5.1.

• Next, calculate the winter solar gain, Q_s = VT x (area of south glass) x SC ÷ 24 = 574 x 80 x 0.75 ÷ 24 = 1435 Btu/h.

• Assume that the building is occupied 9 hours per day in the winter. Calculate internal heat gain = Q_i = (q_{people} + $q_{equipment}$ + q_{light}) x ($T_{occupancy}$) x (A_{floor}) ÷ 24 = (2.5 + 3.4 + 2.0) x 9 x 3600 ÷ 24 = 10,665 Btu/h.

• Assuming a thermostat setpoint temperature of 68°F, then the balance point temperature, T_b = T_t - [(Q_s + Q_i) ÷ sum $UA_{heating}$] = (68) - [(1435 + 10,665) ÷ 525] = 45°F.

HEATING AND COOLING ENERGY ESTIMATES

DEGREE-DAYS

Base temperature, T_b (°F) is a fixed temperature against which the ambient temperature is compared for the purpose of degree-day calculations. Typically, it is the approximation of the lowest outdoor temperature at which a building would require no heating (solar or auxiliary) in order to maintain comfortable interior conditions, *assuming the "mean" of internal and solar heat gains throughout the heating season.*

The base temperature is equal to the average of all hourly balance point temperatures throughout the heating season. As such, the base temperature (which is based on *average* conditions) will always be higher than the balance point temperature (which is based on the "worst-case" assumptions of people occupancy, lighting and equipment usage, and incidental solar radiation gain).

Degree-day, DD (°F·day) is the difference between the base temperature and the mean ambient temperature for the day; if the mean ambient temperature is above the base temperature, no degree-days are counted. The number of degree-days in a month is the sum of the degree-days for each day of that month; similarly, annual degree-days are the same for all degree-days for all of the days of the year. Degree-days are used to calculate the monthly and annual heating energy used for buildings in a particular location. (*Note*: Unless otherwise noted, degree-days are heating degree-days; cooling degree-days are computed similarly for determining the cooling energy requirements based on indoor/outdoor temperature difference.)

ANNUAL HEATING ENERGY REQUIRED

The *degree-day* method for estimating heating energy requirements in nonsolar buildings is based on the assumption that, on a long-term average, internal and minor solar gains offset heat loss when the mean daily outdoor temperature is the base temperature or higher and that fuel consumption will be proportional to the degree-days in a particular period. It is a simplification of the variable-base degree-day (VBDD) method (ASHRAE, 1989), which is based on the balance point outdoor temperature.

It is important to recognize that this simplified method is primarily suited for conventionally-heated, non-solar residences. For this type building, assume a 65°F base temperature, and corresponding degree-day values from tables with this temperature base (for example, from Appendix D).

This simplified method may be used for small non-solar commercial buildings where internal gains are relatively small; use degree-day values from Tables with a 55°F base (for example, Appendix D).

This degree-day method is not applicable to solar-heated buildings; the LCR method presented in Chapter 12 should be used instead.

The total annual heating energy required (for conventionally heated buildings) may be calculated by the following equation:

$$Q_{heating} = TLC \times DD_{heating}$$

where $Q_{heating}$ = total annual heating energy required, Btu

TLC = total load coefficient (ASHRAE nomenclature: building load coefficient), Btu/DD

$DD_{heating}$ = annual heating degree-days (base temperature = 65°F for residences, 55°F for small commercial buildings)

ANNUAL HEATING ENERGY CONSUMED

The auxiliary heating energy *consumption* is typically more than the energy *required* due to the efficiency of the heating system used, and is calculated by the following equation:

$$E_H = Q_{heating} \div k$$

where E_H = Annual heating energy consumed, Btu

$Q_{heating}$ = Annual heating energy required, Btu

k = Average efficiency of the heating equipment (from Table 6.7)

HEATING FUEL CONSUMED

The heating fuel consumed annually is calculated by the following equation:

$$F_{heat} = E_H \div HV$$

where F_{heat} = Heating fuel consumed

E_H = Annual heating energy consumed, Btu

HV = Heat value of fuel (from Table 6.1)

Table 6.1: Approximate Heat Value of Fuels

Fuel	Heat value, HV		Typical seasonal efficiency (%)
Anthracite coal	14,600	Btu/lb	65 - 75
No. 2 oil	141,000	Btu/gal	70 - 80
Natural Gas	1,050	Btu/ft³	70 - 80
Propane	2,500	Btu/ft³	70 - 80
Electricity	3,413	Btu/kW	95 - 100
Wood (20% moisture)	7,000	Btu/lb	30 - 50

(Reprinted from Stein, et al., 1986, by permission.)

ANNUAL HEATING COST

The annual heating cost is calculated by the following equation:

$$Cost_{heat} = F_{heat} \times F_{cost}$$

where $Cost_{heat}$ = annual heating cost, $/yr

F_{heat} = heating fuel consumed

F_{cost} = average unit fuel cost (Note: for commercial buildings, this average unit fuel cost may be complex to determine for electric utility commercial rates which typically include a demand charge in addition to a consumption charge.)

ANNUAL COOLING ENERGY REQUIRED

The degree-day method may be used for estimating cooling energy requirements in a manner similar to that used for heating. However, because this method is based on the indoor/outdoor temperature difference (and does not take into account internal gains due to people, equipment, lighting, and solar), it is only applicable for buildings with envelope-dominated heat gains (such as residences and small commercial). Given this significant limitation, the cooling energy required is calculated by the following equation:

$$Q_{cooling} = CLC \times DD_{cooling}$$

where $Q_{cooling}$ = annual cooling energy required, Btu

CLC = cooling load coefficient, Btu/DD

$DD_{cooling}$ = annual cooling degree days (from Appendix D)

ANNUAL COOLING ENERGY CONSUMED

The cooling energy *consumption* is typically different than the energy required due to the efficiency of the cooling system used, and is calculated by the following equation:

$$E_c = 0.000293 \times Q_{aux\ cooling} \div COP$$

where E_c = annual auxiliary cooling energy consumed, kWh

0.000293 = conversion factor, kWh/Btu

$Q_{cooling}$ = annual cooling energy required, Btu

COP = coefficient of performance of the cooling system (ratio of the rate of cooling output to the rate of energy input)

Table 6.2: Thermal Properties of Typical Building Materials

Description	Density lb/ft³	Specific Heat	Emissivity	Resistance (R-value) per inch thickness	Resistance (R-value) thickness listed
BOARD MATERIALS					
Gypsum board, 0.5 in.	50	0.26	0.92	0.90	0.45
Plywood, 0.5 in.	34	0.29	0.90	1.24	0.62
Vegetable fiber sheathing, 0.5 in.	18	0.31	0.91	2.64	1.32
Sound deadening board, 0.5 in.	15	0.30	0.92	2.70	1.35
Acoustical tile, 0.5 in.	18	0.14	0.91	2.50	1.25
Particleboard, 0.5 in.	50	0.31	0.90	1.06	0.53
FLOORING MATERIALS					
Carpet and fiber pad	--	0.34		--	2.08
Carpet and rubber pad	--	0.33		--	1.23
Hardwood, 0.75 in.	--	--	0.90	0.90	0.68
INSULATING MATERIALS					
Fiberglass blanket and batt	0.6	--	0.94	3.14	--
3.5 in. with wood studs/joists	0.6	--	0.94	--	10.0
5.5 in. with wood studs/joists	0.6	--	0.94	--	17.15
Extruded polystyrene slab	2.0	--		5.00	--
Expanded polystyrene slab	1.5	--		4.7	--
Urethane foam slab	1.5	0.38		6.25	--
Isocyanurate foam slab	2.0	0.22		7.2	--
Cellulose (milled paper)	2.8	0.33	0.92	3.5	--
MASONRY MATERIALS					
Concrete, gravel aggregate	140	0.19	0.92	0.08	--
Concrete, lt-wt aggregate	60		0.92	0.59	--
Brick, face	130	0.19	0.93	0.11	--
Conc. block, sand aggregate					
three oval core, 4 in.	140	0.22	0.92	--	0.71
three oval core, 8 in.	140	0.22	0.92	--	1.11
three oval core, 12 in.	140	0.22	0.92	--	1.28
two rectangular core, 8 in.	140	0.22	0.92	--	1.04
same w/ insulation-filled core	140	0.22	0.92	--	1.93
Limestone or sandstone		0.19	0.90	0.08	--
PLASTER MATERIALS					
Cement plaster, stucco	116	0.20	0.91	0.20	--
Gypsum plaster	45	--	0.90	0.64	--
ROOFING MATERIALS					
Asphalt shingles	70	0.30		--	0.44
Built-up roofing, 0.375 in.	70	0.35		--	0.33
Wood shingles	32	0.31	0.90	--	0.94
SIDING & DECKING MATERIALS					
Shingles, wood	32	0.31	0.90	--	0.87
Siding, hardboard, 0.5 in.	40	0.28		0.67	0.33
Siding, wood, bevel	32	0.31	0.90	--	0.81
Solid Hardwoods	45	0.30	0.90	0.91	--
Solid Fir, Pine, etc.	32	0.33	0.90	1.25	--

(Data source — ASHRAE, 1985, reproduced by permission.)

Table 6.3: Reflectivity and Emittance Values of Various Surfaces and Effective Emittances of Airspaces

Surface	Far-IR reflectivity, %	Average emittance	Effective emittance of airspace: One surface emittance e; the other 0.90	Effective emittance of airspace: Both surfaces emittance e
Aluminum foil, bright	92 to 97	0.05	0.05	0.03
Aluminum sheet	80 to 95	0.12	0.12	0.06
Aluminum coated paper, polished	75 to 84	0.20	0.20	0.11
Steel, galvanized, bright	70 to 80	0.25	0.24	0.15
Aluminum paint	30 to 70	0.50	0.47	0.35
Non-metallic building materials:				
wood, paper, masonry	5 to 15	0.90	0.82	0.82
Regular glass	5 to 15	0.84	0.77	0.72

(Data source — ASHRAE, 1985, reproduced by permission.)

Table 6.4: R-values for Air Films and Airspaces
(Data source — ASHRAE, 1985, reproduced by permission.)

	Direction of Heat Flow	Effective Emittance Non-reflective e = 0.82 - 0.90	Effective Emittance Reflective e = 0.20	Effective Emittance Reflective e = 0.05
INDOOR STILL AIR FILM				
Horizontal	Upward	0.61	1.10	1.32
Sloping (45°)	Upward	0.62	1.14	1.37
Vertical	Horizontal	0.68	1.35	1.70
Sloping (45°)	Downward	0.76	1.67	2.22
Horizontal	Downward	0.92	2.70	4.55
0.5 in. AIRSPACE*				
Horizontal	Upward	0.75	1.29	1.57
Sloping (45°)	Upward	0.83	1.56	1.98
Vertical	Horizontal	0.90	1.84	2.46
Sloping (45°)	Downward	0.91	1.87	2.52
Horizontal	Downward	0.91	1.88	2.54
3.5 in. AIRSPACE*				
Horizontal	Upward	0.84	1.58	2.01
Sloping (45°)	Upward	0.86	1.67	2.17
Vertical	Horizontal	0.91	1.89	2.55
Sloping (45°)	Downward	1.00	2.28	3.30
Horizontal	Downward	1.22	3.86	8.17
OUTDOOR AIR FILM				
Winter (15-mph wind)	Any	0.17		
Summer (7.5-mph wind)	Any	0.25		

*mean airspace temperature = 50°F; 30°F temperature difference.

Table 6.5: Glass Load Factor (GLF)*
(Reproduced from ASHRAE, 1985, by permission.)

Design temperature, °F	Regular Single Glass 90	Regular Single Glass 100	Regular Double Glass 90	Regular Double Glass 100	Heat-Absorbing Double Glass 90	Heat-Absorbing Double Glass 100	Regular Triple Glass 90
No inside shading							
North	36	47	30	37	20	25	27
Northeast and Northwest	65	75	56	62	37	42	50
East and West	90	100	78	84	51	56	70
Southeast and Southwest**	81	91	70	76	46	51	63
South*	55	65	47	53	31	36	42
Horizontal Skylight	156	166	138	143	91	95	125
Draperies, Venetian Blinds, Translucent Roller Shades Fully Drawn							
North	19	27	16	22	14	18	16
Northeast and Northwest	38	42	30	35	24	29	28
East and West	46	54	41	46	33	38	39
Southeast and Southwest**	41	49	37	42	30	34	36
South**	28	37	25	31	21	25	24
Opaque Roller Shades, Fully Drawn							
North	15	23	14	19	12	17	13
Northeast and Northwest	26	34	24	30	22	26	23
East and West	36	44	33	38	30	34	32
Southeast and Southwest**	32	40	30	35	27	31	29
South**	22	30	20	26	19	23	20
Horizontal Skylight	60	68	57	62	52	57	57

*Glass Load Factors for single-family detached houses, duplexes, or multifamily with both east and west exposed walls or only north and south exposed walls, Btu/h•ft².
**Correct by +30% for latitude of 48° and by -30% for latitude of 32°. Use linear interpolation for latitudes from 40 to 48° and from 40 to 32°.

ANNUAL COOLING ENERGY COST

The annual cooling energy cost is calculated by the following equation:

$$Cost_{cool} = E_c \times F_{cost}$$

where $Cost_{cool}$ = annual cooling energy cost, $/yr

E_c = annual auxiliary cooling energy consumed, kWh/yr

F_{cost} = energy unit cost (average), $/kWh

Table 6.6: Approximate Heat Gains
(Adapted from Stein, et al., 1986, by permission.)

Part A. External Gain through Envelope [a] (Btu/h•ft² of Floor Area)

		Outdoor Design Temp. 90°F	Outdoor Design Temp. 100°F
1. Gains through opaque walls:			
Find: $(UA)_{wall}$ ÷ total floor area,	then multiply by	15	25
2. Gains through opaque roofs:			
Find: $(UA)_{ceiling}$ ÷ total floor area,	then multiply by	35	45
3. Gains through externally shaded windows:			
Find: total shaded window area ÷ total floor area,	then multiply by	16	21
4. Gains through unshaded windows and skylights:			
Find: total unshaded window area x GLF (from Table 6.4) ÷ total floor area [b]			

Part B. External Gain from Infiltration or Ventilation of "Closed" Building (Btu/h•ft² of floor area)

	Outdoor Design Temp. 90°F	Outdoor Design Temp. 100°F
1. Find: (total window + opaque wall area) ÷ total floor area, then multiply by	1.0	1.9
OR		
2. Find: known ventilation cfm of outdoor air ÷ total floor area, then multiply by	16	27.0

*Part C. **Internal Gains: People and Equipment** (Btu/h•ft² of Floor Area)*

Function	Area per Person (ft²)	Sensible Heat Gain (Btu/h ft² of Floor Area)[g] People[c]	Equipment[d]	Total
Office	100	2.5	3.4	5.9
School: elementary	100	2.5	3.4	5.9
School: secondary, college	150	1.7	3.4	5.1
Hospital	100	2.5	varies	2.5 plus
Clinic	50	5.0	varies	5.0 plus
Assembly: theater or arena[e]	15	15.3	--	15.3
Restaurant	25	11.0	varies	11.0 plus
Mercantile	50	5.0	varies	5.0 plus
Warehouse	1000	0.4	--	0.4
Hotels, nursing homes	300	0.8	3.4	4.2
Residences and Apartments[f]	300	0.8	(see note d)	(see note d)

Part D. Internal Heat Gain: Lighting — Daylighting and Electric (Btu/h•ft² of floor area)

Function	Sensible Heat Gain (Btu/h ft² of Floor Area)[g] Daylight Factor DF < 1	Daylight Factor 1 < DF < 4	Daylight Factor DF > 4
Office	5.1	2.0	0.5
School: elementary	6.3—6.8	2.5—2.7	0.6—0.7
School: secondary, college	6.3—6.8	2.5—2.7	0.6—0.7
Hospital	6.8	2.7	0.7
Clinic	6.8	2.7	0.7
Assembly: theater or arena[e]	3.8	1.5	0.4
Restaurant	6.3	2.5	0.6
Mercantile	5.1—6.8	2.0—2.7	0.5—0.7
Warehouse	2.4	1.0	0.2
Hotels, nursing homes	6.8	2.7	0.7
Residences and Apartments[f]	Up to 6.8	Up to 2.7	Up to 0.7

[a]Averaged from ASHRAE, 1989 data, *Design Cooling Load Factors Through Glass.* [b]Private correspondence with John. S. Reynolds. [c]Adapted from Buehrer (1978). [d]The usual load of 1.0 W/ft² is assumed. [e]Gains for these functions are only for the seating areas, not for lobbies, stage areas, kitchens, etc. [f]Residential internal gains are often assumed at 225 Btu/h per occupant plus 1200 Btu/h total from appliances. [g]Adapted from Northwest Power Planning Council, *Maximum Lighting Standards,* 1983.

BUILDING LOAD WORKSHEET 1

Project _EXAMPLE_   Date _____   Analyst _FM_   Location _INDIANAPOLIS_

Part I: PROJECT DATA (site data from Appendix D)

Annual heating DD 65 _____ ; Annual heating DD 55 _3440_; Annual cooling DD _902_ ; Winter OD design temp _±2_ °F

Winter thermostat setpoint _68_ °F;   Summer OD design temp (2.5%) _92_ °F;   Summer thermostat setting _78_ °F

Vertical solar radiation, VT _____ Btu/hft²; Heating fuel cost, F_{cost} _$0.14_ per _kWh_ ; Fuel cost : low / high

Heat value of fuel (Table 6.1), HV _3413 Btu_ per _kW_ ; Shading coefficient, SC for south-glass (from Table 5.1) _0.75_

Heating equipment efficiency factor (Table 6.7), k = _2.5_ ;   Recommended conservation factor, CF = _1.76_

Cooling equipment coefficient of performance, $COP_{cooling}$ = _2.0_ ; No. of hrs building is occupied per day = _9_ hrs.

Part II: RECOMMENDED CONSERVATION DESIGN GUIDELINES

Recommended wall total R-value: R_{wall} = 14 × CF   = _25_

Recommended ceiling total R-value: $R_{ceiling}$ = 22 × CF   = _39_

Recommended insulation R-value to be added to slab perimeter: $R_{perimeter}$ = (13 × CF) − 5   = _18_

Recommended floor (over vented space) total R-value: R_{floor} = 14 × CF   = _____

Recommended insulation R-value to be added to basement wall: $R_{basement}$ = (16 × CF) − 8   = _____

Recommended number of glazing layers on windows: N_{glass} = 1.7 × CF   = _3_

Recommended number of air changes per hour: ACH   = 0.42 ÷ CF   = _0.24_

Part III: HEATING LOAD CALCULATIONS (based on proposed design)

Building element: load formula (fill in blanks and calculate)   = Load, _UA_

Walls: $(UA)_{wall}$ = A_{wall} ÷ R_{wall} = _2776_ ÷ _20.7_   = _134_

Ceiling: $(UA)_{ceiling}$ = $A_{ceiling}$ ÷ $R_{ceiling}$ = _3600_ ÷ _44.4_   = _81_

Slab-on-grade: $(UA)_{perim}$ = 4.17 × P_{perim} ÷ (R_{perim} + 5) = 4.17 × _300_ ÷ (_12.5_ + 5)   = _71_

Floor: $(UA)_{floor}$ = A_{floor} ÷ R_{floor} = _____ ÷ _____   = _____

Basement: $(UA)_{base}$ = 10.7 × P_{base} ÷ (R_{base} + 8) = 10.7 × _____ ÷ (_____ + 8)   = _____

Glass: $(UA)_{glass}$ = 1.1 × A_{glass} ÷ number of glazings = 1.1 × _224_ ft² ÷ _3_   = _82_

Infiltration: $(UA)_{Infilt}$ = 0.018 × VOL × ACH × ADR = 0.018 × _36,000_ × 0.25 × 0.97 = _157_

                                                               Sum of UA = _525_

Heating total load coefficient: $TLC_{heating}$ = 24 × sum of UA = _12,600_ Btu/DD $_{heating}$

Design temperature difference: Δt_{winter} = winter thermostat setpoint − winter OD design temp = _66_ °F

Design heating load: q_H = sum of UA × $\Delta t_{heating}$ = _525_ × _66_ = _34,650_ Btu/h

Figure 6.4: Building load example worksheet 1 — heating load and energy estimate (blank worksheet in Appendix F).

BUILDING LOAD WORKSHEET 2

Part IV: COOLING LOAD CALCULATIONS   (based on proposed design)

A. External sensible gain through envelope:

1. Walls: $(UA)_{wall}$ x factor (from Table 6.6, part A1) ÷ total floor area:

   134 x 15 ÷ 3600 = 0.56 Btu/h•ft²

2. Roof: $(UA)_{ceiling}$ x factor (from Table 6.6, part A2) ÷ total floor area:

   81 x 35 ÷ 3600 = 0.79 Btu/h•ft²

3. Shaded window area x factor (from Table 6.6, part A3) ÷ total floor area:

   120 x 16 ÷ 3600 = 0.53 Btu/h•ft²

4. Unshaded window and skylight area x GLF (from Table 6.5) ÷ total floor area:

   Orientation E : 24 x 70 ÷ 3600 = 0.47 Btu/h•ft²

   Orientation N : 80 x 27 ÷ 3600 = 0.60 Btu/h•ft²

   Orientation ___ : ___ x ___ ÷ ___ = ___ Btu/h•ft²

B. External sensible gain from infiltration or ventilation:

EITHER Infiltration: (window area + opaque wall area) x (Table 6.6, part D1) ÷ total floor area:

   $q_{infiltration}$ = (___ + ___) x ___ ÷ ___ = ___ Btu/h•ft²

OR Ventilation: VOL x ACH x ADR x factor (from Table 6.6, part D 2) ÷ total floor area:

   $q_{ventilation}$ = $36,000$ x 0.25 x 0.97 x 0.27 ÷ 3600 = 0.66 Btu/h•ft²

C. Internal sensible gains — People and Equipment:

People factor (from Table 6.6, part C): q_{people} = 2.5 Btu/h•ft²

Equipment factor (from Table 6.6, part C): $q_{equipment}$ = 3.4 Btu/h•ft²

D. Internal sensible gains — Lighting:

Lighting (daylighting and electric) factor (from Table 6.6, part D) q_{light} = 2.0 Btu/h•ft²

Total sensible heat gains, q_t = sum sensible gains from above = (A + B + C + D) = 11.3 Btu/h•ft²

Design sensible cooling load: q_{sc} = total sensible gains x tot. flr. area = 11.3 x 3600 = $40,680$ Btu/h

Design total cooling load (including latent load): q_c = 1.3 x q_{sc} = 1.3 x $40,680$ = $52,845$ Btu/h

Design temperature difference: Δt_{summer} = summer OD design temp. – summer thermostat setpoint = 14 °F

Cooling load coefficient: CLC = q_c x 24 ÷ Δt_{summer} = $52,845$ x 24 ÷ 14 °F = $90,591$ Btu/DD cooling

Required cooling equipment capacity: C_c = q_c ÷ 12,000 Btu/ton = $52,845$ ÷ 12,000 = 4.4 tons

Part V: BALANCE POINT

Winter solar gain: Q_s = VT (from Part I) x (area of south glass) x SC (from Part I) ÷ 24 =

   574 x 80 x 0.75 ÷ 24 = 1435 Btu/h

Internal heat gain: Q_i = (q_{people} + $q_{equipment}$ + q_{light}) x (hrs occupied per day) x (floor area) ÷ 24 =

   (2.5 + 3.4 + 2.0) x 9 x 3600 ÷ 24 = $10,665$ Btu/h

Balance point: T_b = winter thermostat setpoint temperature – [(Q_s + Q_i) ÷ sum UA from Part III)] =

   68 – [(1435 + $10,665$) ÷ 525)] = 45 °F

Part VI: HEATING and COOLING ENERGY ESTIMATE (based on proposed design)

Annual heating energy required: $Q_{heating}$ = TLC x DD $_{heating}$ = $12,600$ x 3440 = 43.3 x 10⁶ Btu/yr

Annual heating energy consumed: E_H = $Q_{heating}$ ÷ k = 43.3 x 10⁶ ÷ 2.5 = 17.3 x 10⁶ Btu /yr

Annual heating fuel consumed: F_{heat} = E_H ÷ HV = 17.3 x 10⁶ ÷ 3413 = 5069 kWh /yr

Annual heating cost: Cost $_{heat}$ = F_{heat} x F_{cost} = 5069 x $\$0.14$ = $\$709$ /yr

Annual cooling energy required: $Q_{cooling}$ = CLC x DD $_{cooling}$ = $90,591$ x 902 = 81.7 x 10⁶ Btu /yr

Annual cool'g energy cons'd: E_c = 0.000293 x $Q_{cooling}$ ÷ COP = 0.000293 x 81.7 x 10⁶ ÷ 2.0 = $11,969$ kWh /yr

Annual cooling cost: Cost $_{cool}$ = E_c x F_{cost} = $11,969$ x 0.14 = $\$1676$ /yr

Figure 6.5: Building load example worksheet 2 — cooling load and energy estimate (blank worksheet in Appendix F).

Table 6.7: Heating Equipment Efficiency Factor, k
(Based on ASHRAE, 1985, data)

Heating Equipment	k
Electric Resistance Furnace	1.0
Electric Resistance Baseboards*	1.4
Air-to-Air Heat Pump	1.5 to 3.0
High-Efficiency Gas Furnace	0.8
Conventional Gas Furnace	0.6
Conventional Oil Furnace	0.6
Wood Stove or Furnace	0.4

*with individual room thermostats (this is an effective value based on the ability to reduce temperature in unused areas conveniently).

EXAMPLE HEATING AND COOLING ENERGY ESTIMATE

On part VI of the worksheet:

- Using heating degree days with a base of 55°F (from Appendix D), calculate annual heating energy required: $Q_{heating}$ = TLC x DD$_{heating \, (base \, 55°F)}$ = 12,600 x 3440 = 43.3 x 10⁶ Btu/yr.

- Calculate annual heating energy consumed: $E_H = Q_{heating} \div k = 43.3$ x 10⁶ ÷ 2.5 = 17.3 x 10⁶ Btu/yr.

- Calculate annual heating fuel consumed: $F_{heat} = E_H \div$ HV = 17.3 x 10⁶ ÷ 3413 = 5069 kWh/yr.

- Assuming a single electric rate that approximates the total of consumption and commercial demand costs, calculate annual heating cost: Cost$_{heat}$ = F_{heat} x F_{cost} = 5069 x $0.14 = $709/yr.

- Calculate annual cooling energy required: $Q_{cooling}$ = CLC x DD$_{cooling}$ = 90,591 x 902 = 81.7 x 10⁶ Btu/yr.

- Calculate annual energy consumed: E_C = 0.000293 x $Q_{cooling} \div$ COP = 0.000293 x 81.7 x 10⁶ ÷ 2.0 = 11,969 kWh/yr.

- Calculate annual cooling cost: Cost$_{cool}$ = E_C x F_{cost} = 11,969 x $0.14 = $1168/yr.

SUMMARY OF TERMS

Conservation factor, CF — a factor recommending levels of insulation and building airtightness for various locations in the United States and relative auxiliary fuel costs.

Mixed system — a combination of two or more passive solar heating system types in a single building. (This is differentiated from hybrid systems which utilize active components — such as a fan — in conjunction with passive systems.)

Total load coefficient, TLC (Btu/°F•day) — the steady-state load (or heat loss) of a building per degree of inside-outside temperature difference per day. (TLC is the same as building load coefficient, BLC, in ASHRAE terminology; TLC is used here to clearly distinguish from net load coefficient — see below.)

Transmission load — heat loss or gain through the building envelope itself; excludes any solar gain through glazings.

Infiltration load — heat lost by means of indoor/outdoor air exchange through cracks and normal door operation.

Net load coefficient, NLC (Btu/°F•day) — the total load coefficient minus the load coefficient of the solar wall.

UA — the product of the *U*-value and the area of the building envelope element.

Building cooling load — total sensible and latent heat gains through the building envelope.

Sensible heat gain — the temperature-related component is the building cooling load; the sum of: heat transmission through opaque building envelope (due to the combined effects of temperature difference and absorbed solar radiation), outside air (both infiltration and ventilation), solar gains through glazing (windows and skylights), and internal sensible heat gain (due to people, lights, and equipment).

Latent heat gain — the moisture-related component of the building cooling load; the sum of: people, appliances, and outside air (both infiltration and ventilation).

Cooling load coefficient, CLC — the equivalent cooling required per cooling degree-day.

Cooling equipment capacity — the capacity of cooling equipment required for a building.

VT (Btu/ft^2•day) — Average daily total radiation transmitted through a vertical, south-facing single-glazed window (0.3 ground reflectance assumed).

Balance point — the outdoor temperature at which the heat generated inside the building balances the building's heat loss, to maintain a desired inside temperature.

Base temperature, T_b (°F) — a fixed temperature (typically 65°F for conventionally heated houses; lower for solar-heated and commercial buildings) against which the ambient temperature is compared for the purpose of degree-day calculations. The base temperature is equal to the average of all hourly balance point temperatures throughout the heating season.

Degree-day, DD (°F day) — the difference between the base temperature and the mean ambient temperature for the day; if the mean ambient temperature is above the base temperature, no degree-days are counted.

Coefficient of performance, COP — ratio of the rate of heating or cooling output to the rate of energy input; a measure of the operating efficiency of auxiliary heating and cooling equipment.

STUDY QUESTIONS

1. What are some ways to reduce winter and summer transmission heat loss?

2. What are some ways to reduce winter and summer infiltration heat loss?

3. What are some ways to increase winter solar heat gain?

4. What are some ways to reduce summer solar heat gain?

5. What are some ways to reduce daily temperature swings?

6. What are some ways to reduce annual temperature swings?

7. What are some ways to increase summer ventilation cooling?

8. What are some ways to increase summer evaporative cooling?

9. What are some ways to increase radiative cooling?

10. Using the conservation factor method, for Knoxville, Tennessee, determine the recommended wall total *R*-value, ceiling total *R*-value, insulation *R*-value to be added to the concrete floor slab perimeter, floor (over vented space) total *R*-value, insulation *R*-value to be added to basement wall, the number of glazing layers on windows, and infiltration rate. Assume a high fuel cost.

PASSIVE SOLAR HEATING:

GENERAL PRINCIPLES

Table 7.1: Strategies of Winter Climate Control

Mode of transfer	Conduction	Convection	Radiation	Evaporation
Promote gain			Promote solar gain	
Resist loss	Minimize conduction	Minimize Infiltration		
Heat sources		Atmosphere	Sun	

(After Labs, 1990.)

A *passive solar heating system* is one in which the thermal energy flow is by radiation, conduction, or natural convection. This is distinguished from an active solar heating system which uses fans or pumps for forced distribution of heat (Balcomb et al., 1984). While this may at first seem a relatively minor distinction (i.e., whether or not mechanical means are used to distribute heat), in fact, it implies major architectural design implications. In the case of an active system, the design of the solar heating system itself need not be integrated with (or affected by) the design of the building. The various active components (storage, heat distribution system, controls, collectors) can be positioned in almost any remote location, connected by means of pipes or ducts with little or no direct effect on the building design or construction method, and operate satisfactorily.

On the other hand, the passive system is intimately integrated into the architecture of the building. This level of integration is essential if the proper flow of heat is to occur naturally without mechanical assistance. Often the building is the collector and the heat storage system. Often the elements of a passive solar building serve multiple purposes. For example, a window on a south-facing wall not only provides interior light and a view but also collects the sun's heat. A wall, in addition to providing structural support, can provide thermal mass for heat storage to stabilize interior temperatures.

"ZONING" BUILDINGS FOR SOLAR

Because the position and movement of the sun and interior heat transfer is predictable, it is possible to design buildings in such a way as to maximize the benefits of this movement as shown in Figs. 7.2 and 7.3.

COMFORT IN PASSIVE-SOLAR-HEATED BUILDINGS

Physical thermal comfort

In most contemporary buildings that utilize conventional heating systems, air is the dominant means of conditioning the space. In such buildings, the temperature of the surrounding building surfaces (that is, the mean radiant temperature or MRT) is relatively constant and is virtually the same as the air temperature. Since the other variables of thermal comfort (air motion and humidity) are maintained at relatively constant levels, air temperature (specifically, dry-bulb temperature) is a direct and primary indicator of thermal comfort.

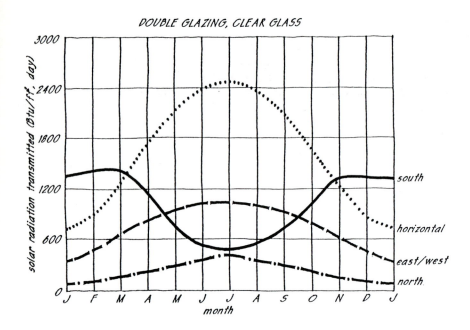

Figure 7.1: Clear day solar radiation transmitted through double-glazed windows throughout the year (40°N latitude). This graph illustrates the importance of orientation in passive solar buildings. In general, vertical south glazing is the most desirable in all United States climates. Notice how south-facing surfaces receive the maximum solar radiation during the heating season and very little during the summer. North-facing surfaces receive very little in the winter, and nearly as much as south facades during the summer. East and west facades are particularly bad, receiving the most during the summer and the least during the winter. Horizontal surfaces (skylights, for example) have the poorest balance with the greatest gain during the summer (nearly twice that of east and west facades) and the least during the winter.

However, in passive heated buildings, the MRT is often quite different from the air temperature. During the day, for example, the radiant warming effect of sunlight entering a room and directly striking its occupants is substantial (i.e., the MRT is comparatively high) and comfort is achieved at much lower dry-bulb air temperature. In fact, this higher MRT often necessitates the venting of collected solar heat if inadequate thermal storage mass is not available. This effect works in reverse at night if there are large expanses of cool glass exposed to the living space resulting in a low MRT and necessitating higher-than-normal air temperatures to compensate. Similarly, thermal storage walls provide large areas of mildly warm surfaces which raise the MRT and require lower dry-bulb temperatures to maintain comfort.

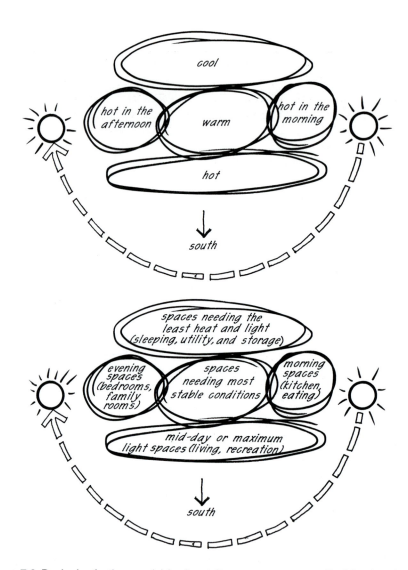

Figure 7.2: Designing for the sun: (a) horizontal temperature zones of building interiors, and (b) potential design response. *(After AIA, 1981.)*

The role of occupants in passive solar building operation

Many early passive solar buildings required the occupants to take an active role in maintaining their thermal comfort — for example, raising and lowering thermal shades, and operating vents to promote or reduce convection. One effect of these daily adjustments was that occupants became

WINTER   SUMMER

Figure 7.3: Potential design response to vertical zones of building interior. *(Redrawn from Stein et al., 1986, by permission.)*

intimately familiar with the thermal behavior of their dwelling and learned to operate it efficiently. More transient occupants, such as those in commercial and institutional buildings, often lack both the experience and economic motivation to operate these buildings efficiently (Kantrowitz, 1983). Recent developments in construction materials (particularly low-*E* glazings and selective surfaces) allow efficient passive heating operation without occupant intervention.

The U.S. Department of Energy has studied the effects of occupants on the performance of 23 buildings in the Passive Solar Commercial Buildings Program. The program concluded:

- Users will manipulate the building to achieve comfort, either by the means intended by the designer, or by any other means they can devise.

- Changes in occupancy patterns (number, timing, activity, and location) will have profound influence on energy use and operational characteristics of buildings.

- In buildings requiring occupant operation, only "educated" users and building operations staff are likely to achieve expected levels of energy performance, and the roles and responsibilities for building operation should be clear. (Where this level of awareness and participation by users is unlikely, the building should be designed to be as "self-regulating" as possible.)

- Some of the design features inherent in passive solar design (for example, exposed thermal mass, large areas of glass, and open space planning necessary for convection) contribute to acoustical and visual privacy problems.

The relatively large number of occupancy factors which influence building energy use point out the need for changes in architectural programming. The programming process for a passive solar commercial building must address issues of occupancy schedule, lighting, and acoustical requirements, and user functional requirements in ways that differ from the design of a simpler, residential building.

KEY DESIGN ELEMENTS

Balcomb et al. (1984) have concluded that the four most important elements affecting the thermal performance of a passive solar building are: (1) the size of the solar aperture (window, skylight, greenhouse, etc.), (2) the amount of energy conservation achieved (particularly as a result of envelope insulation and infiltration control), (3) the amount and placement of the thermal storage mass (to reduce excessive temperature swings and reduce overheating), and (4) the weather (principally, insolation and air temperature).

SOLAR APERTURE

Glazed openings (windows, for example) act as very efficient solar collectors. Glass is highly transparent to solar radiation (visible and near-IR wavelengths) but quite opaque to the far-IR spectrum. As a result, solar energy is readily transmitted through the glass, strikes interior surfaces, and warms them. These warmed surfaces reradiate longer far-IR wavelengths, some of which strike the glass and are absorbed (but *not reflected*), warming the glass. Ultimately, the warmed glass transfers this heat to both the exterior and the interior (by reradiation and convection). The quality that makes glass so effective for solar heating is its selective optical qualities (transparent to the solar spectrum and opaque to the longer far-IR). This is another example of the "greenhouse effect" introduced in the first chapter in the discussion of the ability of the earth's atmosphere to collect and store solar energy.

Generally speaking, the larger the solar aperture (if properly oriented) the greater the solar gain. Theoretically, the maximum solar heat can be collected using a south-facing aperture tilted at an angle normal to the winter sun. In practice, vertical south-facing glass is preferable in most circumstances. When the reflectance of the ground is taken into account (particularly the high reflectance of snow-covered winter months), the annual collection performance of vertical tilt is only slightly less than "optimally" tilted stationary surfaces. Vertically glazed apertures are easier to construct (easier to waterproof, glass strength), are safer (overhead glass should be tempered for safety reasons; some building codes even require wire glass), and are easier to shade.

But larger is not necessarily better; too large a solar aperture (in addition to being expensive to construct) can cause either overheating or a wasteful venting of collected solar heat. It can also increase the heat loss at night. If the useful solar gain is not efficiently used and the heat loss potential is increased, then the large aperture cannot be justified.

Projected collector area

The size of solar aperture is the projected collector area, A_p. For most types of passive solar heating systems (direct gain, Trombe wall, and water wall) the projected area is equal to the net glazing area. For sunspace designs, it is the glazing area projected onto a vertical surface.

CONSERVATION

Prevention of heat loss through the building envelope is essential to efficient passive solar heating. The most important means of energy conservation are the insulation (to reduce conductive heat loss) and sealing (to reduce infiltration) of the envelope. The more effective the envelope in reducing heat loss, the less energy required to properly heat the building. Very tightly sealed buildings can result in indoor air pollution resulting in health concerns; some amount of outside air ventilation is necessary. While conservation measures increase the construction cost (and, above a certain level, the extra costs cannot be justified by potential energy savings), in general, conservation costs less than increasing the size of the solar aperture and thermal storage. This is the basis for the adage, "Conservation first, then solar."

The law of diminishing return

While both the solar aperture and energy conservation contribute to the goal of reducing the cost of heating, both are also construction measures that cost money. Both of these respond to the law of diminishing return. The initial square feet of solar aperture (or *R*-value of insulation) installed can be most fully utilized, and is thus the most efficient in reducing auxiliary heating costs. As the size of the aperture increases to ever greater size, its additional solar input can only be utilized during the most extreme (and infrequent) weather conditions; for most of the heating season this input is excess and wasted. In the case of insulation, each time the *R*-value is doubled, the cost is approxi-

mately doubled, but the amount of heat lost is halved; each additional dollar spent on insulation results in less and less heat saved.

Building loads

The methods of determining the building heating loads were discussed in Chapter 6. For the purposes of passive solar heating performance calculations, there are two building load quantities of interest: The total load coefficient (TLC), which includes all of the building load, and the net load coefficient (NLC), which includes all of the building load with the exception of that of the solar wall. More precisely, TLC (Btu/°F•day) is defined as the steady-state load (or heat loss) of a building per degree of inside-outside temperature difference per day, while the NLC (Btu/°F•day) is defined as the total load coefficient minus the load coefficient of the solar wall.

THERMAL STORAGE

Heat is stored in passive solar buildings in those components (masonry walls, concrete floors, water containers, etc.) that absorb, store, and later release the heat in the interior. The principle function is to stabilize the interior temperature. During the day, when there is excess solar heat, the thermal mass absorbs the excess to prevent overheating (thus eliminating the need to exhaust this valuable heat to the exterior). At night, the thermal mass releases the heat to keep the building warm. The larger the thermal mass, the less the temperature swing during this daily cycle, the greater the level of thermal comfort, and the less auxiliary heat needed.

COMPONENT INTEGRATION

All three of these components (solar aperture, conservation, and thermal mass) reduce heating costs and all increase the cost of construction. The cost of each must be weighed against the energy cost savings that they produce. All three are, in essence, competing for the same limited construction dollar. The principle of *balancing solar and conservation* requires that the amount of construction funds spent on each of these three components (aperture, conservation, and storage) should be ideally balanced so that if one additional dollar is spent on each then all three improvements would result in the same added savings in auxiliary heating.

While this approach of balancing solar and conservation is useful in determining the *proportion* of funds that should be spent on each, determining the optimum *total amount* is more difficult. The latter requires a life-cycle cost analysis that attempts to resolve the trade-off of increased construction cost versus reduced long-term operating costs. It requires assumptions about the long-term future cost of auxiliary fuels, construction financing costs, maintenance costs, available tax incentives, and even the rate of return of alternative investments.

LOCAL CLIMATE

Ambient dry-bul*b air temperature and insolation (in*cident solar radiation) are the two climatic variables of interest in determining passive solar heating performance. Humidity has virtually no impact on building heating performance (cooling performance is, of course, a different matter). Wind speed affects the building heat loss (primarily by infiltration); however, the prediction of this for an annual heating season is virtually impossible. In practice, a conservative allowance is made for the effects of windspeed based on an assumed constant windspeed, and this effect is built in to most infiltration heat loss estimation procedures.

MEASURING SOLAR HEATING PERFORMANCE

For a given climate and passive solar system type, the two primary determinants for heating performance are the net heating load of the building and its collector area. These two factors may be expressed as a ratio — the *load-collector ratio* (LCR) — and it is this ratio that forms the basis for predicting heating performance. Recall from the previous chapter that the net load coefficient, NLC, is the total load coefficient minus the load coefficient of the solar wall. Then LCR is defined as the ratio of the net load coefficient to the projected collector area.

For a given location, LCR is the variable that most influences the net solar heating performance of a building. It largely determines the average increase in indoor building temperature over the average ambient temperature and is the most important parameter influencing the solar heating performance. It reveals the relationship between energy conservation (which is determined by NLC) and the amount of solar gain (determined by A_p). The relationship between LCR and the solar heating performance depends on the amount of incident sunshine and the degree-days and therefore varies with each locality.

SOLAR HEATING FRACTION VS. SOLAR SAVINGS FRACTION

Solar savings is the energy savings due to a passive solar heating system relative to the energy requirement of a comparable nonsolar building that has

an energy-neutral wall in place of the solar wall and a fixed indoor reference temperature.

Solar savings fraction (SSF) is the dimensionless ratio of the solar savings to the net reference load. In essence, SSF compares the auxiliary heat needed by a solar-heated building with that needed by a comparable "reference" building that is nonsolar but otherwise similar (for simplicity, in the reference building, the wall replacing the solar wall is "energy-neutral"). It is important to understand that this is not the same as the building's solar heating fraction (SHF), which is the percentage of the solar building's heating requirement that is supplied by solar.

This distinction is important to understand because most the total annual heat loss of a passive solar building is usually greater than for a comparable nonsolar reference building, even though the total auxiliary heat required is less (as a result of the contribution of solar heating). Because of this, it is possible to have one solar building with a higher SHF (but with a high total heat requirement) actually use more auxiliary heat than an alternative solar building with a lower SHF (and a lower total heat requirement) as shown in Fig. 7.4.

Because the SHF can be misleading, its use is discouraged in favor of the SSF (which has emerged as the most widely accepted basis for performance evaluation). In any case, the ultimate measure of heating performance is the auxiliary heat required.

Balcomb et al. (1984) have developed recommended starting points for LCR for various locations in the United States (see Fig. 7.5).

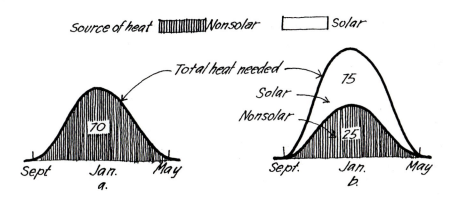

Figure 7.4: Performance comparison of: (a) "reference" non-solar building and (b) passive solar building. *(Redrawn from Stein et al., 1986, by permission.)*

TYPES OF PASSIVE SOLAR HEATING SYSTEMS

Passive solar heating systems are most commonly classified according to their physical configuration: direct gain, thermal storage wall, sunspace (or greenhouse), and convective air loop.

Direct gain is a passive solar heating system type consisting of south-facing windows that admit winter sunshine directly into the building's interior where it is absorbed by thermally massive materials (see Chapter 8).

Thermal storage wall is a passive solar heating system type consisting of a south-facing wall constructed of heavy masonry (Trombe wall) or water-filled containers (water wall). The outside south-facing surface is glazed to admit sunlight and reduce night heat losses (see Chapter 9).

Sunspace is a passive solar heating system type consisting of a glassed-in room (like a greenhouse, atrium, or conservatory) located on the south side of a building and separated from other building spaces by a common wall. Heat is transferred from the sunspace to the adjacent living areas either by conduction (through a masonry wall) or by convection (through vent or window openings in the wall). Thermal mass, in the form of water containers or masonry walls and floors, serves to stabilize the temperature in both the sunspace and the building (see Chapter 10).

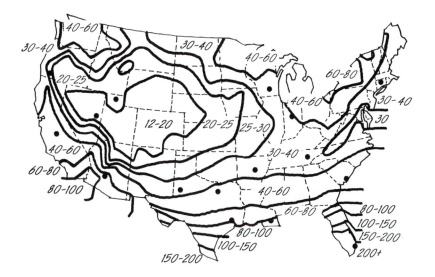

Figure 7.5: Recommended starting-point load collector ratios (LCR) for residential buildings for locations in the United States. These values have been determined to yield a life-cycle optimum for selected passive solar, conservation, auxiliary heat, and financing costs. *(Redrawn from Balcomb et al., 1984, by permission.)*

Convective air loop is a passive solar heating system that consists of a solar collector and a thermal storage mass (usually a rockbed) isolated from the living spaces. Air is used to transfer heat from the collector to the storage and the living spaces (see Chapter 11).

Roof pond is yet another passive system type that is most notable for its cooling performance and is therefore considered in Chapter 16, Passive Cooling: *Radiation.*

GENERAL DESIGN GUIDELINES

The following guidelines are suggested by Balcomb et al. (1984) and apply to all types of passive solar heating systems:

Rule 1. Conservation levels — Recommended levels of insulation and building airtightness are based on the conservation factor, CF (as calculated in Chapter 6).

Rule 2. Distribution of solar glazing — The solar glazing area should be distributed throughout the building proportional to the heat loss of each building area or zone.

Rule 3. Orientation — The optimum orientation of the solar glazing of all systems is within 5° of true south. If the orientation departs from true south, the penalty in solar heating performance increases slowly at first and more rapidly as the departure increases. In some climates, the performance penalty is less for deviations toward the west than toward the east; this is a result of higher afternoon air temperatures and the likelihood of clearer afternoon sky conditions.

Rule 4. Glazing tilt — For a given glazing area, an increase in performance can be achieved by tilting the solar glazing. The optimum winter heating angle is in the range of 50 to 60° for all locations in the United States. However, vertical glazing, while not optimum, is a very efficient collection angle for winter heating once the high ground reflectance characteristic of winter months is considered. Furthermore, vertical glazing reduces unwanted summer heat gain, is easier to construct, and facilitates the installation of night insulation. For these reasons, vertical glazing is recommended for most passive system types.

Rule 5. Number of glazing layers — the recommended number of glazing layers is given below:

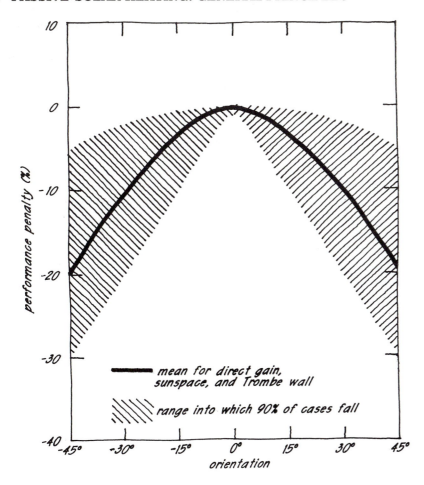

Figure 7.6: Performance penalty for orientations away from due south. *(Redrawn from Balcomb et al., 1984, by permission.)*

Rule 6. Night insulation and low-E glazings— Night insulation or low-emissivity glazing materials will greatly improve the performance of any passive solar system in any climate; however, the cost effectiveness (and indeed even the necessity) for these increases as the winter climate becomes colder. Direct gain is the most sensitive of all passive systems types to the use of such strategies for reducing glazing heat loss. Most earlier buildings which performed well utilized night insulation. However, recent component developments, such as low-*E* glazings, have largely replaced the use of night insulation due to their greater convenience, operational reliability, and durability.

Rule 7. Mixed systems — Mixing passive heating system types can improve both the comfort and character of passive solar buildings. By choosing systems that complement one another, the designer can provide solar heat when it is needed. An effective procedure is to size direct-gain window area based on nonsolar or daylighting considerations, typically in the range of 5 to 10 percent of the floor area. Locate the direct-gain windows on the south walls or in clerestories. Double- or triple-glazed east and west windows usually have no winter thermal penalty, but they should be located so that they will be shaded in the summer (to prevent overheating). Design east, west, and north windows to achieve proper lighting, visual access to the outside, ventilation, and emergency egress. Then, if more solar heating performance is desired, use indirect systems (Trombe or water walls, or sunspaces, for example) to achieve the total desired collection area.

SUMMARY OF TERMS

Passive solar heating system — one in which the thermal energy flow is by radiation, conduction, or natural convection.

Active solar heating system— one in which the thermal energy flow is effected by fans or pumps for the forced distribution of heat.

Solar aperture — the glazed opening in the building envelope for admitting sunlight (for example, window, skylight, greenhouse).

Solar aperture tilt — the vertical angle between the glazing and horizontal (vertical = 90° tilt).

Table 7.2: Recommended Number of Glazing Layers

Winter climate	No night insulation or selective surface**	Night insulation*, low-E glazing, or selective surface**
Mild (less than 2,500 DD)	1 or 2	1
Moderate (2,500 to 6,000 DD)	2 or 3	1 or 2
Severe	3 or 4	2
*Minimum *R*-4 to *R*-5	**on thermal storage walls	

(Reproduced from Balcomb et al., 1984, by permission.)

Solar aperture orientation — the horizontal angle between the direction the glazing is facing and south.

Phase-change material, PCM — one which has a melting point near the human comfort zone allowing it to absorb and store latent heat as it liquifies.

Insolation — incident solar radiation.

Night insulation — Operable thermal shades or shutters that are positioned to cover solar glazing at night to reduce heat loss, and removed during the day to admit solar radiation.

Mixed system — a combination of two or more passive solar heating system types into a single building.

Hybrid system — a predominantly passive solar heating system which utilizes an active component (such as an electric fan to force heated air from a sunspace into a building).

Direct gain — a passive solar heating system type consisting of south-facing windows that admit winter sunshine directly into the building's interior where it is absorbed by thermally massive materials.

Thermal storage wall — a passive solar heating system type consisting of a south-facing wall constructed of heavy masonry (Trombe wall) or water-filled containers (water wall). The outside south-facing surface is glazed to admit sunlight and reduce night heat losses.

Sunspace — a passive solar heating system type consisting of a glassed-in room (like a greenhouse, atrium, or conservatory) located on the south side of a building and separated from other building spaces by a common wall. Heat is transferred from the sunspace to the adjacent living areas either by conduction (through a masonry wall) or by convection (through vent or window openings in the wall). Thermal mass, in the form of water containers or masonry walls and floors serves to stabilize the temperature in both the sunspace and the building.

Convective air loop — a passive solar heating system that consists of a solar collector and a thermal storage mass (usually a rockbed) isolated from the living spaces. Air is used to transfer heat from the collector to the storage and the living spaces.

Net load coefficient, NLC (Btu/°F•day) — the total load coefficient minus the load coefficient of the solar wall.

Net reference load, NRL (Btu) — the product of the net load coefficient and the local annual heating degree-days.

Load-collector ratio, LCR (Btu/°F•day•ft²) — the ratio of the net load coefficient to the projected collector area.

Solar savings — the energy savings due to a passive solar heating system relative to the energy requirement of a comparable nonsolar building that has an energy-neutral wall in place of the solar wall and a fixed indoor reference temperature.

Solar savings fraction (SSF) — the dimensionless ratio of the solar savings to the net reference load; the most widely accepted measure of *relative* passive solar heating performance.

PASSIVE SOLAR HEATING:

DIRECT GAIN

The direct-gain passive solar building has south-facing windows that admit the winter sun directly into the occupied space. These solar gains serve to either meet part of the current heating needs of the building or are stored in the thermal mass to meet heating needs that arise later. Most direct-gain buildings include: (1) large, south-facing windows to admit winter sun; (2) thermal mass inside the insulation envelope to reduce temperature swings; (3) calculated overhang above the south glass (or other strategy) to shade the glass in the summer while admitting lower-angle winter insolation; and (4) a means of reducing heat loss at night (night insulation, for example).

In a direct-gain building, sunlight is admitted directly to the interior through south-facing glazing. It strikes massive interior surfaces (typically concrete floor and masonry wall surfaces), is absorbed, and is converted to heat. Some of the heat from the surface is immediately released back into the room interior (by convection and IR radiation). The remainder of the heat absorbed is conducted into the thermal mass which slowly warms up; later, at night, the stored heat is released back to the interior. Because glass is opaque to far-IR radiation, this reradiated heat is trapped by the familiar greenhouse effect.

The thermal mass is critical to effective operation. With the large amount of solar radiation admitted during the day, if only lightweight surfaces were available to absorb heat, the temperature of these would rise rapidly causing

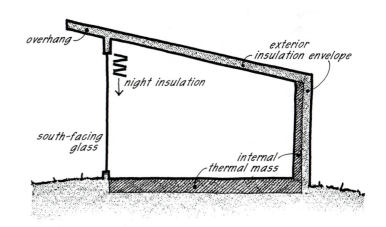

Figure 8.1: Diagrammatic section, direct-gain passive solar building. The overhang provides summer shading while admitting full winter sun. The floor and/or wall provide thermal mass to stabilize interior temperature and as such must be located inside of the insulation envelope, preferably with maximum exposure to direct sunlight.

the interior to overheat and necessitate venting excess heat to the outside to maintain comfort. This exhausted heat is wasted, and must be replaced later at night by auxiliary heat.

Because of the large glass area that is exposed directly to the interior, heat loss back out through that glazing is comparatively large at night. In addition, the cool glass surface lowers the MRT of the space and requires higher air temperatures to maintain comfort. For these reasons, some form of night insulation is usually employed in direct-gain buildings. Finally, the overhang is effective in shading the summer sun (to reduce overheating) while admitting lower winter sun angles for heating.

ADVANTAGES AND DISADVANTAGES

Direct-gain buildings are intuitively obvious in operation, provide daylight in the building, and provide views to the south. The incremental cost (relative to a comparable nonsolar building) is small, especially if the preferred building materials are inherently massive (such as adobe in the southwest, concrete floor slab-on-grade in the southeast, and in many commercial buildings).

Direct-gain buildings, because of their requirements for distributing thermal mass, place limitations on the choice of materials and construction methods. The use of decorative floor and wall coverings in this passive solar system type is limited; carpet and large rugs, for example, act as insulating covers and prevent heat from absorbed insolation from being stored in the floor slab resulting in overheating. Interior finishes (especially upholstery and carpeting) are subject to fading and degradation from exposure to sunlight (Guerin, 1979). See Chapter 20 for a discussion of interior finishes appropriate for direct-gain buildings.

The presence of large amounts of direct sunlight in a living space presents several visual problems. If the sun is in direct view of the observer, the resulting direct glare can cause discomfort. The intensity of sunlight illuminating a visual task (a book, for example) can be so great as to cause fatigue. Just the presence of sunlit and shadow areas presents such a contrast that shadow areas are perceived as dark (as the eye adapts to the intensity of the bright sunlight) even though the measurable illumination in these shadows might be more than adequate under less contrasty conditions. Privacy, particularly if a public access passes to the south, can be compromised by the large south windows which must be left undraped in order to be thermally effective.

Some occupants consider the required morning and evening operation of night insulation typically used in a direct-gain building to be an inconvenience. In practice, most people find the daily routine is similar to the operation of conventional drapes, a ritual of welcoming sunlight in the morning and making the house private at night. Perhaps the greatest disadvantage of night insulation surfaces occurs during prolonged absences by the occupants; it is usually left closed if thermostatically

controlled auxiliary heating is available (thermostat is set back to a lower temperature) and open if manual auxiliary heating, such as a woodstove, is used. With adequate thermal mass and insulation, interior temperatures in direct-gain buildings will not normally drop to freezing in continental U.S. locations. This is because the solar heat gained will offset the relatively small heat loss that accompanies low interior temperatures.

SUNTEMPERED BUILDINGS

These are direct-gain buildings with no intentional thermal mass (for example, a conventionally constructed wood frame with 1/2-in. gypsum board walls and ceiling and wood floor over crawlspace). In general, without adequate thermal mass, suntempered buildings experience overheating if the south-facing glazing areas exceed 15 percent of the heated floor area.

Overglazing with insufficient mass
These buildings are often built-for-sale by well-meaning builders in an effort to provide (and advertise) "passive solar" features without the added expense of thermal mass. Even with large areas of south-facing glazing, these buildings are poor performers in virtually every climate. In fact, without night insulation, large glazing areas actually lose more heat at night than they collect during the day resulting in negative heating performance; it is not possible to achieve more than 15 percent SSF in cold climates regardless of aperture size. The addition of R-9 night insulation helps considerably, but it is still difficult to achieve more than about 20 percent SSF in cold climates unless very large areas of glazing (or high levels of insulation) are used. It is this poor performance of low-mass, sun-tempered buildings that has slowed the acceptance of passive solar buildings.

DIRECT-GAIN CASE STUDIES

SUNSCOOP

David Wright's house, *Sunscoop*, is the most influential direct-gain example of the early passive solar designs developed in the southwest. Built in 1974 on the outskirts of Sante Fe, New Mexico (6100 degree-days), this small (612-ft^2) two-story house remains the purest example of the type, incorporating all of the important features of direct-gain buildings: south-facing glazing, internal mass (14-in. adobe walls, insulated on the exterior with 2 in. polyurethane rigid foam, and brick flooring), overhang (designed to provide summer shading while providing full winter solar

Figure 8.2: David Wright's direct-gain-passive-solar heated residence; note overhang, south-facing glass, and night insulating shutters (D. Wright, architect). *(Photo courtesy of J. D. Balcomb.)*

penetration), and a means of minimizing nighttime heat loss (double glazing and insulating foam shutters). There are a minimum number of windows on nonsouth facades, and an entry vestibule reduces infiltration. While by contemporary standards, this pioneering design is overglazed and underinsulated and, as a result, tends to overheat during the afternoon, its heating performance was impressive (the supplemental woodstove consumed less than one cord of firewood), pleased the owner-builder, and exerted considerable influence on the many passive houses that have been built in that region subsequently (Wright, 1976).

This is the first intentionally-designed solar adobe that I know of — though unintentional ones have happened. The adobe bench — the banco — that faces the collector windows will still register 100°F at 7 pm. It's really super to lie down there on a cold winter night. The bedroom on the loft level is great at bedtime, because during the day the temperature has been rising and the walls have been absorbing it. It's 4 to 5°F warmer upstairs at bedtime.

We haven't used the shutters to hold the heat in since February. The nighttime lows outside in April were around 16°F; inside it never dropped below 62°F. The only time we drop the shutters at night is

when we know the outside low will be below 10°F. Barbara and I have adapted to the temperature swing since we first started living in the house, and we've developed an intuitive ability to forecast the weather.

With the overhangs we sometimes get into trouble late in autumn during the so-called Indian Summer. Outside temperatures are not that cold yet, but the sun has dropped and we're getting quite a bit of solar gain. During those times I wish the overhang projected further. In later designs, I've started adding shades to give the system flexibility. The idea is not to lock yourself in with a set calculated overhang, because the weather is fickle and can vary up to 40% at any time of the year.

— David Wright (1976)

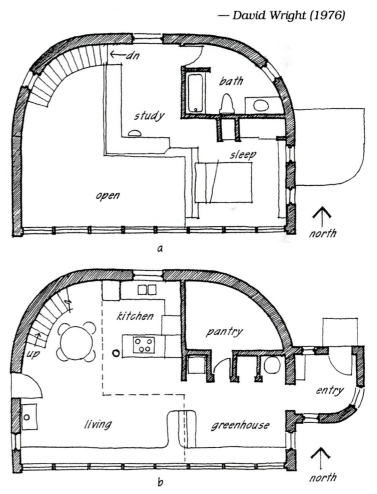

Figure 8.3: David Wright's residence: (a) upper plan, and (b) lower plan. *(After Wright, 1976.)*

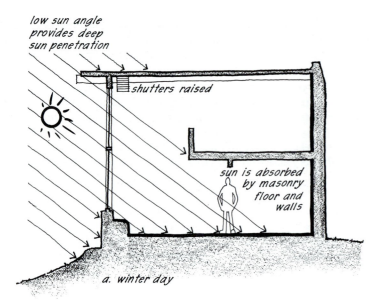

low sun angle
provides deep
sun penetration

shutters raised

sun is absorbed
by masonry
floor and
walls

a. winter day

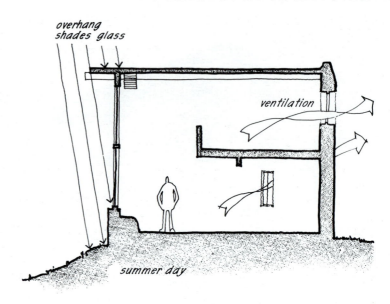

overhang
shades glass

ventilation

summer day

Figure 8.5: David Wright's residence — summer day passive cooling.

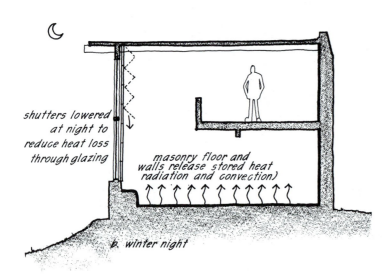

shutters lowered
at night to
reduce heat loss
through glazing

masonry floor and
walls release stored heat
radiation and convection)

b. winter night

Figure 8.4: David Wright's residence — passive solar heating operation: (a) winter day, and (b) winter night.

PATOKA INTERPRETATIVE NATURE CENTER

Located in Birdseye, Indiana, this direct-gain passive solar building was designed by the author to house nature exhibits at this Indiana state park. It has a floor area of 3200 ft^2 and functions as the point of departure of hiking trails and is used for lectures and slideshows (Moore, 1983). The building's design includes a glu-lam "A-frame" roof structure with the south-facing 1390 ft^2 60°-slope double-glazed solar roof aperture. A reflective ceiling on the north slope reflects insolation directly down to the thermal mass below (quarry tile floor on slab and two rows of fiberglass water storage tubes).

Two of the client's design requirements of the building were that it be a "visually exciting" demonstration of solar heating, and that daily operation of the solar components be automatic. Beadwall (see Harrison, 1976) night insulation was chosen to provide *R*-20 insulation over the large south-facing double glazing. The glazing has a 4-in. airspace between the two layers of tempered glass. In the winter, polystyrene beads are "blown" into the interglazing space at night from large storage tanks using vacuum motors; during the day, these beads are "vacuumed" out of the glazing assembly and returned to the storage tanks. In the summer, to prevent solar heat gain, the beads are left in the glazing during the day.

Figure 8.6: Patoka Interpretative Nature Center (F. Moore, architect): (a) from the southeast (sloped south glazing is insulated at night with polystyrene beads blown into 4-in. interglazing airspace; here the right portion is filled with beads and the left portion is empty), and (b) north facade, showing bead insulation storage tanks and clerestory.

Figure 8.7: Patoka Interpretative Nature Center interior, showing south-facing glazing, reflective north ceiling, top gable vent with shutter, and water tubes and quarry tile floor for thermal storage.

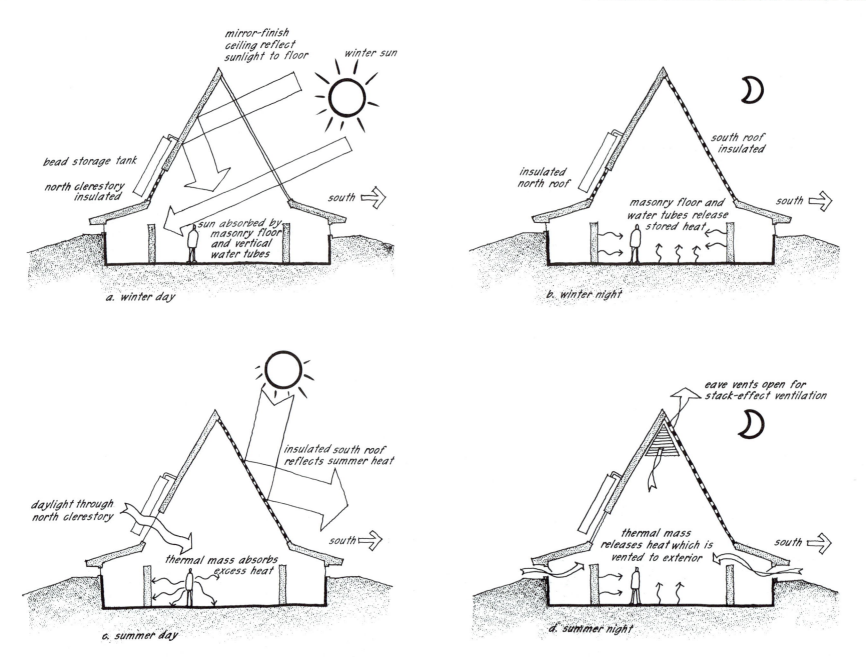

Figure 8.8: Patoka Nature Center modes of operation: (a) winter day, (b) winter night, (c) summer day, and (d) summer night. The building uses "night flushing" as a summer ventilation cooling strategy. Sixteen small awning windows over the exhibit booths admit air while large louvered exhaust eave vents are very effective in inducing stack effect night ventilation during the summer.

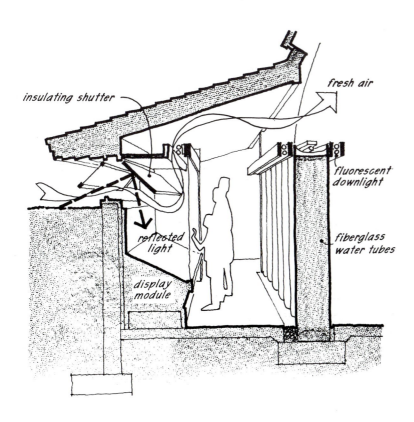

Figure 8.9: Detail section perspective showing thermal storage water tubes and daylighted display modules.

NEW HAMPSHIRE CONSERVATION CENTER

While this building is primarily direct gain, it is an excellent example of the sophistication that more recent passive solar buildings have achieved in combining multiple passive solar strategies to suit the various thermal and functional requirements of various parts of the building. In addition to its administrative function, this building was designed as a showcase for native forest products and energy conservation. As the design architect, C. Stuart White, Jr., said in an address to the International Solar Architecture Conference in Cannes in 1982, "You can't get much more elemental than sun and water and earth ... We have been removed from elementary considerations for architecture for the last 30 years or so, particularly in the U.S., and it seems time to get back to them."

Figure 8.10: New Hampshire Conservation Center. *(Banwell White & Arnold, architects; Robert O. Smith, energy consultant; photo courtesy of R. Smith.)*

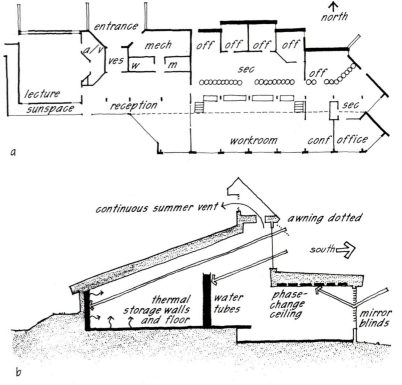

Figure 8.11: New Hampshire Conservation Center: (a) plan, and (b) section. *(Redrawn from Murphy, 1983, by permission.)*

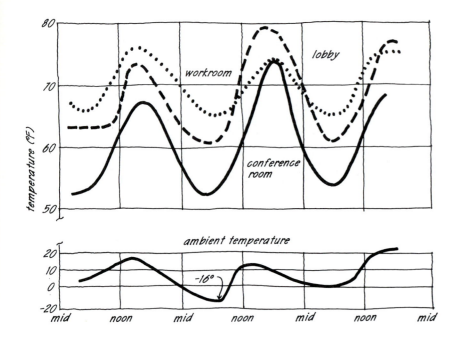

Figure 8.12: During a 72-hr. period in January 1982, the wood-fired boiler in the Conservation Center's headquarters did not come on. All three days were sunny. The ambient temperature ranged from 20 to –16°F. The temperatures recorded during the period are shown for the workroom, lobby, and conference room. (No data were recorded at night when the building was unoccupied so the temperature swings shown are interpolated.) *(Redrawn from Germer, 1983, by permission.)*

Sited on a high bluff overlooking Concord, New Hampshire, and the Merrimack River to the south, the plan of the building is long and narrow, with the main axis extending east-west providing ample exposure to the view and southern sun. The design program called for the facility to be about 7000 ft² with workspace for 20 employees, a lecture space, reception, book sales area, and lavatories. It was designed to be primarily (40 to 60 percent) passive solar-heated, to use waste-wood pellets for auxiliary heat, and demonstrate energy conservation in design.

Three distinct passive solar strategies were used in the design, not only to match the particular thermal requirements of each space, but to provide an educational showcase for the differences available in passive solar design (Murphy, 1983). Water-filled translucent fiberglass tubes (forming an interior partition) and the back (north) masonry wall receive the most direct sunshine; in addition to efficiently storing heat, the watertubes transmit diffused light to

the secretarial and office spaces beyond. In the workroom, mirror-finish "venetian" blinds (installed concave side up) reflect sunlight onto the ceiling (in addition to preventing the glare of direct sunlight onto desks). Some of this re-reflects (providing a soft, diffuse overhead illumination) and some is absorbed by the metal ceiling. This absorbed heat is stored in a phase-change material (eutectic salts) in bags laid onto metal ceiling panels. As warm air accumulates at the highest points in the building (near the clerestory), it is drawn (by means of a fan) through a continuous ceiling plenum, then through the voids in an insulated masonry wall on the bermed north side, and finally through a concrete floor plenum, by means of a fan. In the process, heat is stored in the masonry wall and the concrete floor.

DIRECT-GAIN DESIGN GUIDELINES

Continuing the general design guidelines presented in Chapter 7, the following guidelines specifically apply to direct-gain systems (Balcomb et al., 1984):

Rule 8. Mass distribution — For a given quantity of thermal mass, spread the mass over as large an area as practical consistent with locating mass within the direct-gain space. It is recommended that the area of exposed mass should be six times the glazing area (three times the glazing area should be the minimum; more than six times is desirable but usually difficult to achieve in practice). While mass in direct sunlight is most effective, mass out of direct sun but visible from sunlit areas is considered "radiatively coupled" and is also quite effective. "Convectively coupled" mass is not visible from sunlit areas and is only one-fourth as effective as radiatively coupled mass.

Rule 9. Mass thickness — Per pound, mass in thin sections is more effective than mass in thick sections. For masonry materials, added mass beyond about 4 in. in thickness is significantly less effective than that closer to the surface. For wood, because of its reduced conductivity, the corresponding thickness is only 1 in.

Rule 10. Color — Generally speaking, only floors in direct gain spaces should be dark in color. Light-colored walls and ceilings are desirable in order to reflect sunlight around the space and thus distribute the sunlight as much as possible before being absorbed.

Rule 11. Surface covering — Any insulating cover over thermal mass decreases heat storage effectiveness and building performance. Surface coverings should have good thermal contact with the mass (no air gaps) and an *R*-value of less than 0.1; a surface covering (such as a rug) with an *R*-value of 0.4 can decrease heat storage effectiveness by about 50 percent.

Rule 12. Concrete block masonry — When hollow-core concrete block is used for direct-gain heat storage, select a high-density block and grout the holes solid.

Rule 13. Floor materials — Concrete or brick flooring materials are recommended. If insulation is used under the flooring, it should be covered with at least 4 in. of mass; however, more than 6 in. of added thickness adds very little.

Rule 14. Limits on direct-gain glazing area — South-facing direct-gain glazing area should be limited to prevent large temperature swings, depending on the available heat storage. Recommended limits are 7 percent of floor area for low-mass buildings and 13 percent of floor area for high-mass buildings.

Rule 15. Glazing orientation — Vertical glazing facing directly south is the preferred orientation for direct-gain systems. The vertical geometry is easiest to build, easiest to shade during the summer with an overhang while admitting full winter sun (sloped glass requires bigger overhang to shade the lower areas of the glass), and does not require the special glass required for sloping overhead designs (for reasons of strength and safety). The heating performance penalty for departing from a due-south orientation by 15° is 10 percent or less, and by 30° is 20 percent or less; therefore it is recommended that direct-gain buildings be oriented within 15° of due south.

Rule 16. Night insulation — Annual solar heating performance of direct-gain systems is significantly better with the use of night insulation. However, both the initial and maintenance costs of these systems are high and must be carefully weighed against the resulting energy cost savings; the higher the cost of auxiliary heating fuel, the greater the justifiable night insulation cost. Night insulation should be used in all but the mildest climates. Recently developed "quad" glazing systems (two glass layers and two interior clear plastic glazing layers) and some low-emissivity (low-E) glazings have comparatively high transmittance and should be considered as an alternative to night insulation in severe climates or in buildings where night insulation operation is not practical (commercial buildings, for example).

Rule 17. Thermal insulation — Insulation should be located outside (the reverse of conventional brick veneer construction) of the thermal mass. This serves to reduce the loss of stored heat from the thermal mass to the exterior, while encouraging the free transfer of heat between the mass and interior. The amount of insulation should be determined using the conservation factor method (see Chapter 6).

SUMMARY OF TERMS

Direct gain — a passive solar heating system type consisting of south-facing windows that admit winter sunshine directly into the building's interior where it is absorbed by thermally massive materials. The glazing is protected from summer sun by an overhang. Some means of reducing night heat loss through the glazing (such as night insulation) is recommended in all but the mildest climates.

Sun-tempered buildings — direct-gain buildings with no intentional thermal mass (for example, a conventionally constructed wood frame with 1/2-in. gypsum board walls and ceiling and wood floor over crawl space). South-facing glazing area should be less than 7 percent of the floor area to prevent overheating.

STUDY QUESTIONS

1. Identify four components usually incorporated in a direct-gain passive solar heating system and briefly explain their function.

2. What is a suntempered building and why is its passive solar heating performance so poor in virtually every climate?

3. Explain how people can be comfortable in the winter in a passive solar building with a lower thermostat setting than in a conventional building.

4. Summarize the advantages and disadvantages in direct gain in comparison with other passive solar systems.

5. Thermal storage mass located in direct sunlight is the most effective type for reducing temperature swings in direct-gain buildings. However, thermal mass located out of direct sunlight can still be relatively effective. Explain why some non-sunlit thermal storage locations are more effective than others.

PASSIVE SOLAR HEATING:

THERMAL STORAGE WALL

Direct-gain buildings are configured so that sunlight is first admitted directly into the space, and then absorbed by thermally massive surfaces. In other words, the living space is adjacent to both the absorbing surface and the glazing, and is thus subject to the temperature variations experienced by each of these surfaces throughout the day and evening.

In a thermal storage wall system, the thermal mass is placed *between* the glazing and the living space. In the day, this arrangement requires the absorbed heat to transfer through the entire thermal mass, warming the entire mass in the process. At night, it buffers the living space from direct exposure to the cool glazing.

A thermal storage wall consists of the wall itself and the glazing over the outer surface. The large mass of the wall itself serves to store the solar energy, and is usually constructed either of solid masonry (Trombe wall) or water-filled containers (water wall).

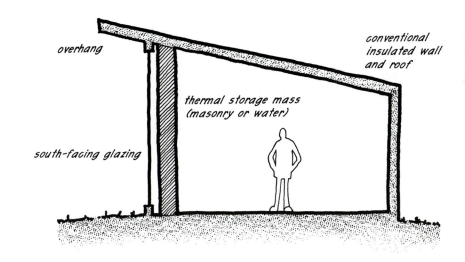

Figure 9.1: Schematic section showing principal components of a thermal storage wall passive solar building. Sunlight is transmitted through the glazing and absorbed by the storage wall surface. The resulting heat is transferred through the mass and into the interior space. While the wall itself is thermally massive (either masonry or water-filled containers), the remainder of the building envelope may be constructed of lightweight materials without affecting heating performance.

TROMBE WALL SYSTEMS

Edward Morse (1885) described the first use of solid masonry thermal storage walls for passive solar heating. These systems have been recently popularized as a result of the research of Felix Trombe and Jacques Michel in an experimental house in Odeillo, France (Trombe et al., 1976; also Trombe et al., 1977). They are usually dark on the glazing side to absorb insolation and, in turn, *conduct* heat slowly through the wall thickness. The thicker the masonry, the smaller the temperature swings in the living space and the longer the delay in conducting the heat through the wall. It is possible to optimize the thickness of the wall so that the maximum heating effect is predictably delayed to an evening time when the greatest heating is needed (for example, a 12-in.-thick masonry wall delays the maximum midday solar heat until just before bedtime).

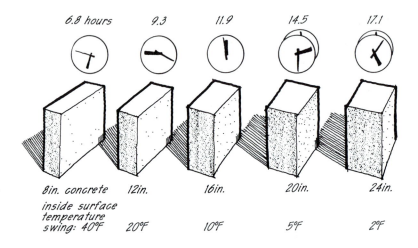

Figure 9.2: Effect of unvented concrete Trombe wall thickness on temperature swings and delay in conducting heat through the wall. *(Redrawn from Anderson and Wells, 1981, by permission.)*

The Trombe wall is an ideal complement to a direct-gain system because the time delay for heat transfer through the wall results in heat delivered to the space out of phase with direct-gain heat through windows. The result is an even flow of solar heat to the space.

THERMOCIRCULATION AIR VENTS

If one of the advantages of conventional (i.e., unvented) Trombe walls is their thermal stability, one of the related disadvantages is that they are "sluggish," requiring a long time to warm up in the morning after a night without sunlight. Midmorning interior temperatures as well as annual heating performance (SSF) of Trombe wall systems are increased with the addition of vent openings at the top and bottom of the masonry wall. This allows air warmed between the glazing and wall absorber surface to rise by natural

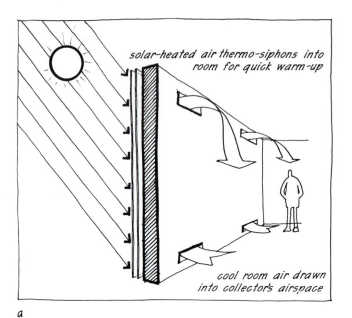

Figure 9.3: Trombe wall without thermocirculation vent controls: (a) vents allow faster warm-up in the morning due to convection warming, (b) but at night convective heat loss is excessive due to reverse thermocirculation resulting in performance that is worse than unvented wall. *(Redrawn from Mazria, 1979, by permission.)*

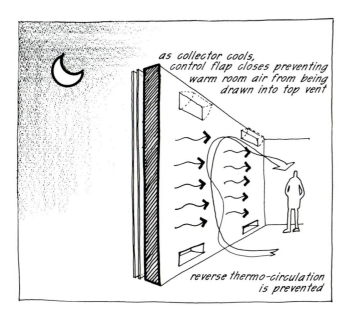

as collector cools,
control flap closes preventing
warm room air from being
drawn into top vent

reverse thermo-circulation
is prevented

Figure 9.4: Trombe wall with thermocirculation vent controls. The optimum solution for vents is the installation of an automatic control such as a lightweight flap valve that prevents reverse thermocirculation. *(Redrawn from Mazria, 1979, by permission.)*

convection, flowing into the room at the top, being replaced by the coolest air in the room drawn into the lower vent. The result is a quicker warmup in the morning (by convection through the vents) later being replaced by heat conducted through the wall (storing the heat for early evening use).

After dark the temperature of the wall absorber surface and the adjacent airspace drops below the room air temperature. This can cause the thermocirculation to reverse as the cool air in the glazing space becomes more dense, drops down the wall, and flows into the room through the lower vent. It is replaced by the warmest room air near the ceiling being drawn into the top vent. Unfortunately, this "reverse thermocirculation" becomes a very efficient "cooling" process, losing all of the early morning heating performance gains. In fact, the annual performance of a vented Trombe wall is worse than an unvented equivalent system unless some means are provided to block the reverse circulation at night.

Preventing reverse thermocirculation

Reverse thermocirculation can be controlled through the use of some method of blocking the airflow through either the top or bottom vents. Manually operated dampers (or "doors") are not recommended because they

are both inconvenient and unreliable. Not only are the occupants absent at the proper opening and closing time, but without a sensitive indicator such as smoke, it is virtually impossible to determine which direction the air is flowing and therefore what the appropriate door position is. The most practical and widely used vent control is a lightweight film which is top-hinged over the room side of the top vent. To prevent summer overheating, the vents should be closed permanently or care should be taken to adequately shade the wall with an overhang.

While vents (with appropriate control valves) provide a slight improvement in annual heating performance, they cost more to construct and can contribute to overheating in the summer. As an alternative to the vented Trombe wall, many designers combine unvented Trombe walls (for nighttime heating performance) with areas of direct gain (for daytime heating performance). The two systems are typically located in the building to reinforce the hours of greatest use: direct gain for daytime areas (living and dining areas) and Trombe wall for evening and nighttime areas (sleeping areas).

The direct-gain alternative to vents

The primary advantage of Trombe wall vents (quick morning warmup) can be achieved by mixing direct gain with unvented Trombe walls. As noted earlier, the unvented wall delays heat transfer to the space out of phase with direct gain through windows; this results in an even flow of heat to the space. This direct-gain/unvented Trombe combination eliminates some of the problems associated with the thermocirculation vents. The typically unattractive flap valves are eliminated, and dust accumulation of the absorber surface is minimized. And the addition of moderate direct-gain glazing provides daylighting and view, while providing aesthetic variety to an otherwise monotonous expanse of masonry. In general, this direct-gain/unvented Trombe combination is recommended over vented Trombe walls.

SELECTIVE SURFACES

In all Trombe walls (but especially in unvented ones) wall-to-glass radiant transfer is a substantial source of heat loss. A *selective surface* may be applied to reduce the wall-to-glass radiant transfer. Black foil is optically selective in that it absorbs solar radiation (because it is black and thus has a high absorptivity in the solar spectrum) while it reduces reradiation in the far-IR spectrum (because it is a metallic foil with low emissivity). Originally developed in Israel by Harry Tabor for use on solar water heaters, selective foil surfaces are now available commercially with a pressure-sensitive adhesive backing. The performance increase can be dramatic; a metal-foil selective surface is the equivalent of *R*-9 (2 in. of rigid foam) night insulation in its increase of SSF for an unvented Trombe wall. The performance increase for vented Trombe walls is less dramatic (due to the proportional greater losses due to convective circulation, and due to the increase in emissivity due to dust buildup).

TROMBE WALL ADVANTAGES AND DISADVANTAGES

Trombe walls perform well compared to other passive systems. They position the thermal mass between the living space and the sun and glazing, thus providing an intrinsic buffer between the occupants and the temperature variations of the solar absorber. They transfer the heat through the thermal storage mass slowly (by conduction). Because of this, temperatures are both delayed and moderated. This allows the delay of delivery of solar heat to the interior in a reliable and predictable manner (12 in. thickness delays the noon maximum gain until midevening but before bedtime).

Typically, the masonry wall also serves structural functions, and is typically used to support part of the roof. Masonry and concrete construction is familiar to the building trades; however, care must be taken to ensure that all masonry voids are filled with mortar to provide adequate conductive transfer. Because virtually all of the collection and storage functions are concentrated within the wall, there are few construction and room finish constraints on the rest of the building.

Generally, in Trombe wall systems, because room air is effectively isolated from the glazing by the masonry wall, night insulation is less important to annual heating performance and nighttime comfort than in direct-gain systems.

On the other hand, unvented Trombe walls are slow to provide heat in the morning. The addition of vents provides early morning warmup at the expense of evening delivery. Vented walls must be provided with flap valves to prevent undesirable reverse thermocirculation at night. Vented walls accelerate dust accumulation on the inner glazing surfaces and on the absorber surface. The space between the glazing and wall is too narrow to provide access for maintenance; therefore glazing must be removed for cleaning and repainting of the absorber surface (sliding doors provide one solution to this accessibility problem). The installation, operation, and maintenance of the night insulation is difficult (to increase performance, a selective surface is recommended instead). The entire assembly is expensive (due to the amount of floor area lost as well as the additional construction expense). Instead of vents, it is recommended that unvented Trombe walls be combined with direct-gain windows (for the reasons discussed previously).

TROMBE WALL CASE STUDIES

Kelbaugh house

Designed by owner/architect Douglas Kelbaugh, this well-publicized pioneering house (see Kelbaugh, 1976a, 1976b, 1976c, 1978, and 1983) was the first application of the Trombe wall in the United States and must be credited with popular and professional acceptance of this passive solar type (it has been published in over 50 books and magazines). The 2100-ft^2 residence is located in Princeton, New Jersey (40° north latitude, 5100 heating degree-days, in a relatively cloudy, temperate climate).

The two-story house is frame construction, with a linear plan arrangement to provide all rooms southern exposure. The dominant feature of the house is the 15-in.-thick concrete thermal storage wall that extends across the entire south facade. The wall is painted black to absorb insolation and is covered with a single layer of glass spaced 6 in. from the wall to provide a convective airspace. Vent openings in the concrete wall have an additional layer of fixed glazing to provide light, view, and direct solar gain to the interior spaces. The solar wall is unshaded in the summer; unwanted solar gain is reduced by venting the airspace to the outside using four small fans. Replacement air is

Figure 9.5: Kelbaugh house showing south facade with Trombe wall. *(Photo courtesy of D. Kelbaugh.)*

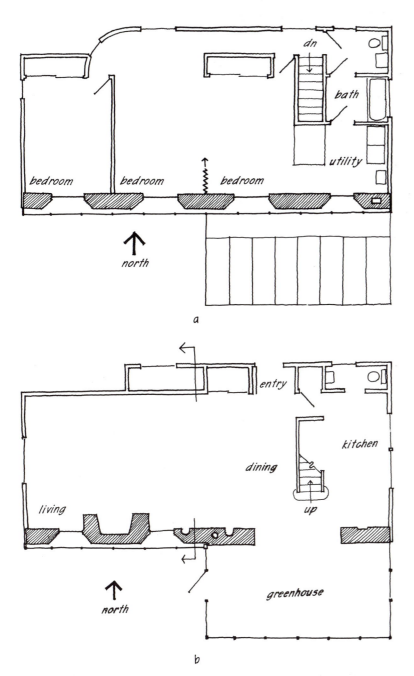

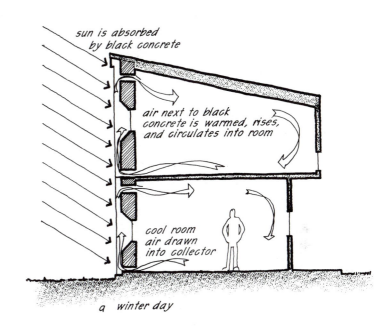

Figure 9.6: Kelbaugh house: (a) upper and (b) lower floor plans. *(After Kelbaugh, 1976.)*

Figure 9.7: Kelbaugh house winter operation: (a) day, and (b) night. *(After Skurka and Naar, 1976.)*

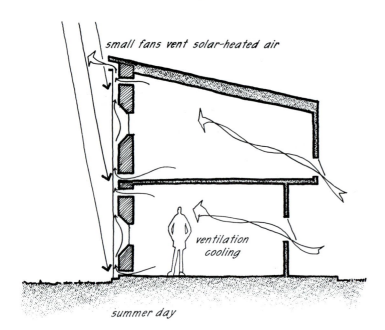

small fans vent solar-heated air

ventilation cooling

summer day

Figure 9.8: Kelbaugh house summer day operation. *(After Skurka and Naar, 1976.)*

drawn into the house from the north side providing forced ventilation cooling. A sunspace is attached to the south facade and is used primarily for plant growing. During the first year of operation, the single-glazed sunspace (with no night insulation) was open directly to the living spaces and lost an excessive amount of heat at night.

Since the first year of operation, Kelbaugh has made numerous changes and assessed their effect on the thermal performance and comfort of the house:

- 1976 — added second glazing layer to the sunspace (major improvement)

- 1976 — installed Trombe wall vent check valves to prevent reverse thermosiphoning at night (simple thin plastic film top-hinged over the upper screened vents; major improvement)

- 1976 — added movable insulation to two upstairs windows (very small improvement)

- 1976 — added water drums to provide additional thermal storage in the sunspace (small improvement)

- 1977 — added thermal curtain to provide separation between sunspace and living areas (curtain opening is varied to allow heat from the house to keep plants from freezing; major improvement)

- 1977 — added storm windows to existing double glazing on all nonsouth windows (small improvement)

- 1977 — added stairwell door in attempt to reduce the 5°F temperature stratification between the first and second story (no improvement; door removed later and never rehung)

- 1978 — added roof vents to improve ventilative cooling of second-story bedrooms (major improvement)

- 1980 — installed domestic hot-water solar collector in sunspace (major improvement)

- 1982 — added inside "storm" windows over south windows and skylight (small improvement)

Shelly Ridge Girl Scout Center

Designed by Bohlin Cywinski Jackson, architects (Burt Hill Kosar Rittlemann Associates, solar consultants), this building is the centerpiece of the Shelly Ridge Girl Scout Center and is the primary facility for year-round indoor and outdoor programs for Philadelphia. The 6000-ft² building is thermally dominated by the external energy forces of climate. This determined that solar strategies would be most helpful in offsetting the winter heating load. In the summer, the high humidity and small daily temperature swing suggested the primary cooling opportunity to be ventilation. Because summertime activities are largely out-of-doors, mechanical cooling was not required. Solar energy was used for heating domestic hot water and daylighting satisfies almost all of the building's lighting requirements (Cook, 1984).

Because of the compact plan, a single Trombe wall was selected for the main assembly hall because of its ability to function as a collector while still affording the lighting flexibility required for audiovisual presentations. The Trombe wall is 4-in.-thick brick and unvented, delivering the maximum heat during the day when the building is occupied. A more conventional 12-in. thickness would have delayed the pulse approximately 9 hr. to a time when the building was unoccupied.

The building has been widely published, and received a 1984 Honor Award from the American Institute of Architects.

a

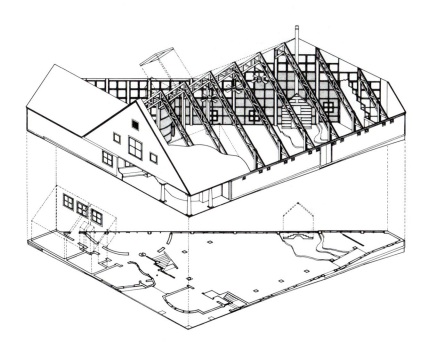

Figure 9.10: Shelly Ridge Girl Scout Center. *(Drawing courtesy of Bohlin Cywinski Jackson, architects.)*

b

Figure 9.9: Shelly Ridge Girl Scout Program Center: (a) exterior, and (b) interior (Bohlin Cywinski Jackson, architects). *(Otto Baitz, photographer, reproduced by permission.)*

WATER WALL SYSTEMS

Trombe and water walls collect and store heat in similar ways with one exception: water walls transfer heat through the walls as a result of convective circulation of the water while Trombe walls conduct heat through the thickness of the masonry. As a result of this convective circulation within the container, the water is constantly being mixed and the temperature is virtually the same from one side of the wall to the other (although there can be a gradient of temperature from the top to the bottom of the container). This causes the effect of heat absorbed on the solar side of the container to be felt almost immediately on the room side of the container (as a result of this circulation); in other words, in comparison with the Trombe wall, there is virtually no time lag. However, because the absorbed heat must raise the temperature of the entire container of water, the room-side temperature remains quite stable; like the Trombe wall, daily temperature swings are greatly reduced in comparison with direct-gain systems. Because of its high specific heat, water is a very efficient heat-storage medium. Although the heat transfer method is different, annual overall heat storage is similar for a water wall one-half the thickness of a comparable solid concrete Trombe wall.

Although water has the additional advantage of being virtually cost-free, its containerization is a substantial problem. Most metal containers (notably 55-gal. oil drums) will eventually rust through and leak. Even many "water-proof" liner materials (for example, polyethylene film) are subject to water penetration and deterioration after prolonged submersion and are thus unsuitable. Tall containers develop considerable hydrostatic pressure near the bottom, making even the structural containment of the water a problem. Because of the possible liability associated with consequential damage to the building and furnishings resulting from a large container rupture, many architects and contractors are reluctant to utilize large containers.

to Trombe wall systems). Water is an excellent thermal storage medium requiring approximately one-third of the volume and one-fifth the weight of masonry of comparable capacity. This efficiency reduces the weight of the required thermal storage mass and allows the use of water walls on upper floors of wood frame construction without major structural modifications. (In fact, of all of the passive system types, the water wall places the fewest restrictions on building construction and interior finishes; on the other hand, unlike Trombe walls, water walls provide no structural function.) The heat-storage material (water) is virtually free (although the containers can be expensive). Depending on configuration, water containers can be spaced so that access to operable windows and night insulation is possible, while admitting daylight and summer ventilation. The above mentioned containerization problem is the principle disadvantage.

WATER WALL CASE STUDIES

Baer Residence
Overlooking Albuquerque, New Mexico, and the Rio Grande Valley, the house was completed in 1972 and represents the most influential pioneering

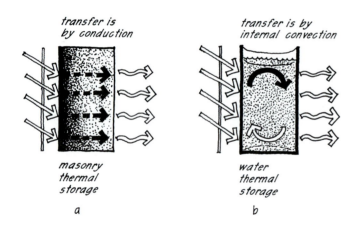

Figure 9.11: Comparison of heat transfer through thermal storage walls: (a) conduction through masonry, and (b) convection through water.

WATER WALL ADVANTAGES AND DISADVANTAGES

Water walls (like Trombe walls) position the thermal mass between the living space and the sun and glazing, thus providing an intrinsic buffer between the occupants and the variations of the solar wall. Unlike Trombe walls, they transfer the heat through the thermal storage mass promptly (because of internal convection). They perform comparatively well (comparable

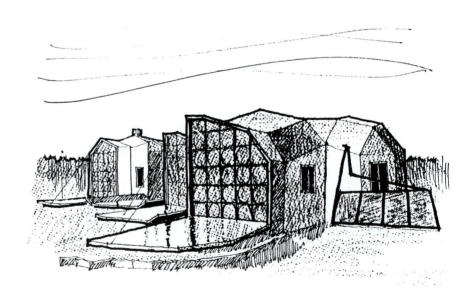

Figure 9.12: "Zomehouse" Baer Residence, Corralles, New Mexico, showing the solar collection walls with the bottom-hinged reflectors.

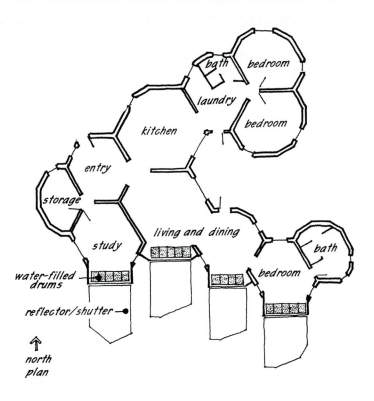

Figure 9.13: "Zomehouse" plan. *(After Cook, 1984.)*

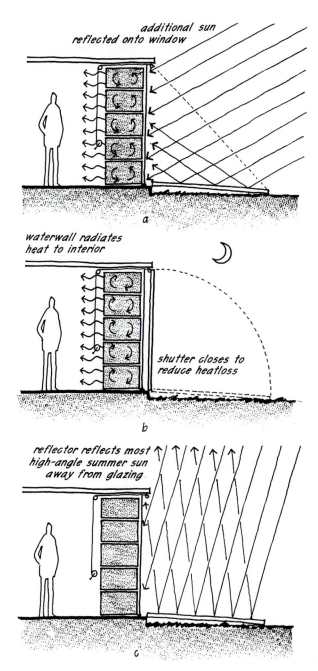

Figure 9.14: "Zomehouse," showing operation: (a) winter day, (b) winter night, and (c) summer day. Notice that the horizontal reflector significantly increases winter solar gain, while the higher solar angle in the summer results in little additional gain.

example of the use of water as the thermal storage wall material. Baer researched the geometry of crystalline structures to develop the zonohedron system that determined the form of the house. The resulting form incorporates numerous vertical south-facing walls for solar collection. Behind these double-glazed walls are recycled 55-gal. steel oil drums painted black on the solar side and supported horizontally (with the "bottoms" facing south) on steel racks. The water in the drums absorb the sun's heat during the day and reradiates it to the interior at night. The surfaces of the drums visible from the interior are painted white to lighten the rooms; the visual effect of the reflected light filtering around the drums during the day is visually pleasant (Cook, 1985; also Editors, 1974).

Each south-facing window wall is equipped with a bottom-hinged reflector/shutter that is lowered to horizontal during the day. The aluminum surface of this horizontal reflector provides an increase of approximately 50 percent solar radiation with no increase in glazing area (and without the increased heat loss that would accompany a simple enlargement of the collector area). At night, these shutters are raised to a closed position to provide insulation over the glazing to reduce nocturnal heat loss. The reflector/shutter is manually operated by an internal hand winch.

Kirley house

This compact two-story house is nearly cube-shaped, utilizes conventional post-and-beam construction, and was designed and constructed by the owner's company. The plan is efficiently compact and well suited for passive solar heating due to exposure of most living areas to the south solar wall. The thermal envelope is extremely well insulated with *R*-36 walls, *R*-46 roof, and 4-in. of extruded polystyrene "blue board" under the floor slab. The most distinctive visual elements of the house are the 8-ft-high, translucent fiberglass water tubes inside the south-facing windows. More than just an effect thermal storage system, these 12-in.-diameter cylinders refract light in constantly changing ways as the sun's position and sky conditions vary throughout the day. Gaps between the tubes allow some direct-gain sunlight to enter while providing access for operating the insulating shades installed between the glazing and tubes. The 8-ft water wall tubes (each holds 47 gal. of clear water and weighs 404 lbs) rest on the concrete floor slab which is thickened to 8 in., primarily for structural reasons. The water is treated with chlorine bleach to eliminate algae growth. Insolation of the south wall is increased by a white gravel reflector which extends twice the height of the south glazing (Cook, 1984).

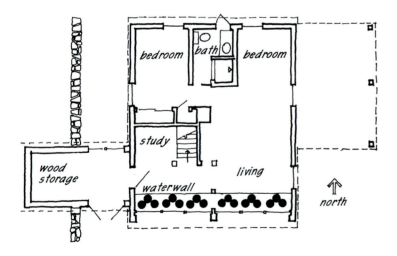

Figure 9.15: Kirley house lower plan: water tubes dominate the south wall. *(After Cook, 1984.)*

THERMAL STORAGE WALL DESIGN GUIDELINES

Continuing the general design guidelines presented first in Chapter 7, the following specifically apply to thermal storage wall systems (Balcomb, 1984):

Rule 18. Glazing azimuth — The optimum glazing azimuth (directional orientation) for thermal storage walls is due south: however, the effect of wall azimuth is relatively small for small deviations about due south. For azimuths within 30°F of due south, the performance penalty averages about 4 percent annually; for azimuths within 30° of due south, the performance decrease averages 10 percent annually. Beyond 30° the penalty increases rapidly up to nearly 50 percent for azimuths 90° off due south. Proportional performance penalty occurs with and without night insulation.

Rule 19. Vents — Vents are often omitted from Trombe walls, and this is generally recommended for residential applications. The increase in annual heating performance due to vents is small. Whether vents should be used depends on whether the building needs more daytime heat than is provided by direct gain. If so, then vents may be appropriate. Vents provide heated air to the building, which is useful primarily to offset immediate daytime heat loads. Vents combine with direct gain in driving building temperature swings. When used to excess, undesirable large swings will occur. For Trombe wall systems with SSF of 0 to 25 percent, make the total area of the top vents equal 3 percent of glazing area; SSF of 25 to 50 percent, 2 percent of glazing area; SSF of 50 to 75 percent, 1 percent of glazing area; more than 75 percent SSF unvented. The lower vent area should equal the upper vent area.

Rule 20. Glazing distance —In *unvented* Trombe systems, the space between the glass and masonry wall is not critical — one inch is adequate. In *vented* Trombe systems, the necessity for unrestricted airflow requires that the minimum clearance be at least 6 in.

Rule 21. Trombe wall thickness —Trombe wall optimum thickness varies between 16 and 10 in. depending on masonry material and whether vents are used. However, performance varies little within 20 percent of optimum values. Because of this, and for construction-cost reasons, 12-in. thickness is recommended for all materials. For buildings occupied only during the day (and where evening heating is not required), a thinner wall provides relatively quicker warmup, and should be used.

Rule 22. Water walls and phase-change-material (PCM) walls—The principal thermal advantage of using water or PCM in a thermal storage wall is the ability to achieve high values of thermal storage capacity within a smaller volume and with less weight than a masonry wall. Values of 60 to 120 Btu/°F•ft² of glazing are achievable and recommended.

Rule 23. Selective surfaces — A selective surface on the outside face of a thermal storage wall can be used to improve performance. The improvement is nearly as great as *R*-9 night insulation. It has the advantage of not requiring manual (or motorized) operation and is therefore particularly suited for buildings left unoccupied for extended periods. If a selective surface is used, vents should not be installed since dust accumulation may impair its selective optical qualities by increasing its emittance and decreasing its absorptance.

Rule 24. Absorber color—Thermal storage walls are very sensitive to the solar absorptance (color darkness) of the wall surface. As the absorptance decreases, performance of both Trombe walls and water walls falls off very rapidly; therefore use a black absorber surface. However, this characteristic applies only to opaque water storage containers; transparent fiberglass water cylinders transmit some *visible* solar radiation through the entire storage wall assembly as direct gain where it is absorbed by room surfaces beyond. The performance penalty is slight compared with painted black water containers, because virtually all IR (near- and far-) radiation is absorbed by the water. Transparent fiberglass tubes are attractive because of the manner in which they refract and diffuse light, and they can contribute to the daylight illumination of the rooms beyond.

SUMMARY OF TERMS

Thermal storage wall — a passive solar heating system type consisting of a south-facing wall constructed of heavy masonry (Trombe wall) or water-filled containers (water wall). The outside south-facing surface is glazed to admit sunlight and reduce night heat losses.

Trombe wall—a thermal storage wall system consisting of a dark, south-facing masonry wall covered with vertical glazing.

Water wall—a thermal storage wall system consisting of water-filled containers located behind a south-facing glazing.

STUDY QUESTIONS

1. Summarize the advantages and disadvantages of Trombe wall systems.

2. Summarize the advantages and disadvantages in Trombe wall vents.

3. Why is it advantageous to use a mixed system that is part direct gain and part unvented Trombe wall?

4. 12 in. is the most commonly selected Trombe wall thickness. Under what conditions would a substantially thinner masonry wall be advantageous?

5. Summarize the advantages and disadvantages of water wall systems.

10

PASSIVE SOLAR HEATING:

SUNSPACE

A *sunspace* is a solar collector that is also a useful space capable of serving other building functions. Other terms for this passive solar type are "solarium," "atrium," "conservatory," and "sunroom." The term "attached greenhouse" is also often used but can imply a plant-growing function as well as a solar heating function; for this reason, sunspace has evolved as the preferred descriptive term.

The sunspace is a direct-gain space in which heat is used directly to maintain a temperature for its intended secondary functions (such as occasional living space). But the primary purpose of the sunspace as a solar heating system is to deliver heat to the adjoining rooms. This may be by conduction through a masonry common wall and by natural convection through openings (doors, windows, or special vents) in the

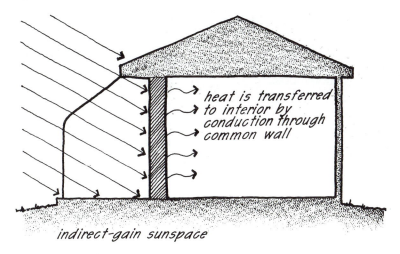

Figure 10.1: Indirect-gain sunspace building with common thermal storage wall. Conduction through the common wall is the primary means of heat transfer to living space.

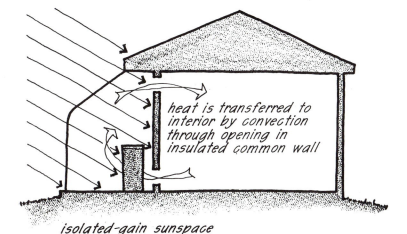

Figure 10.2: Isolated-gain sunspace building with free-standing thermal storage mass and insulated common wall. Convection (either fan-forced or natural) is the primary means of heat transfer to living space.

common wall. In this case, the sunspace system resembles a Trombe wall system. Or, if the heat-storage medium is freestanding water containers, the common wall is insulated and heat is transferred to the interior only by convection. In this configuration, a fan is sometimes used to assist convective heat transfer between the sunspace and surrounding rooms (Balcomb et al., 1984).

Sunspace Advantages and Disadvantages

The sunspace itself warms up quickly, while heat to the adjacent spaces may be transferred promptly (by convection through open windows and doors, for example) or delayed (by conduction through the masonry common wall). The heating performance can be impressive, often exceeding the performance of any other passive solar system type with the same solar aperture area. The separation of the glazing from the thermal storage wall permits convenient maintenance of the glazing (for cleaning and operation and maintenance of night insulation) and common wall (repainting, for example). Sunspaces are very popular building features, both for the attractive, sunlit living space that they offer as well as their ability to deliver heat to adjacent living spaces. As a result they are the most-often-retrofitted of all passive systems.

There are two schools of thought about sunspace glazing. Some designers strongly prefer to use only vertical glazing, accepting the slight winter heating performance penalty (15 to 25 percent, depending on climate). Others prefer to use some or all sloped glazing to get additional solar gain. But the geometry associated with sloped glazing introduces some unique construction problems. It is both difficult to shade and requires the use of tempered glazing (as a safety measure in the event of breakage overhead; tempered glass crumbles into relatively harmless small particles while conventional glass breaks into large and potentially dangerous shards).

Night insulating curtains or shutters are almost never used in sunspaces because they are awkward to install and operate, especially on sloped glazing. Although night insulation would theoretically help performance, the advantage is much less than for a direct-gain system, because the sunspace air temperature is usually allowed to "float" and frequently goes beyond the limits of the comfort zone.

The cost of sunspaces is comparatively high. Because sunspaces may contain useful living space, their cost effectiveness as a heating system often depends on whether the cost of the additional building floor area can be attributed to the integral cost of the house itself or whether its entire cost is assigned to the added cost of the solar heating system.

SUNSPACE CASE STUDIES

"Unit One," First Village

This pioneering sunspace mass wall house was designed and built by Wayne and Susan Nichols in 1976 under the U.S. Department of Housing and Urban Development (HUD) Cycle 1 program grants in Santa Fe, New Mexico (Nichols, 1976; Howard and Fraker, 1990). Its owner, J. Douglas Balcomb (a solar researcher at Los Alamos National Laboratory who led the development of the passive solar calculation procedures described in Chapter 12), was responsible for its instrumentation and monitoring, and, as a result, it is one of the better understood passive solar buildings. The house is two-story with all upstairs and downstairs rooms facing onto a large 20-ft-high sunspace.

The sunspace has approximately 400 ft² of double glazing facing south; two-thirds of this is sloped 50°. The floor area of the sunspace is triangle-shaped. The south wall of the sunspace is entirely glass (double glazed, no night insulation); the other two walls are adobe, 14-in. thick downstairs and 10-in. thick upstairs. This amount of adobe provides a large thermal storage

Figure 10.3: "Unit One" — First Village: exterior. *(Photo courtesy of J. D. Balcomb.)*

mass exposed to the sun and separates the living spaces from the sunspace. There are two distinct modes of passive heating operation.

First, the adobe wall acts as a Trombe wall, absorbing sunlight during the day, conducting heat through the wall, and transferring the heat from the back side of the wall to the living spaces by radiation and convection. As with a

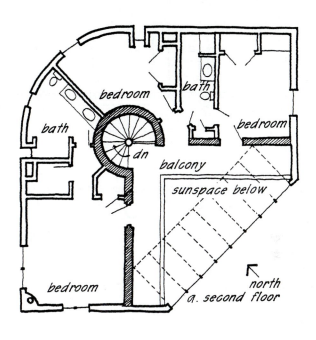

Figure 10.3 (continued): "Unit One" — First Village: (b) interior of sunspace. *(Photo courtesy of J. D. Balcomb.)*

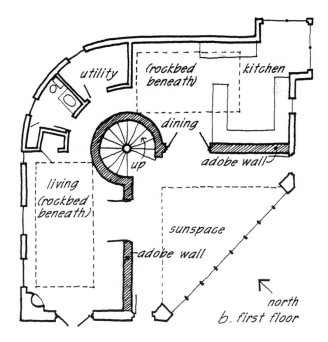

Figure 10.4: "Unit One" — First Village (a) upper, and (b) lower floor plans. *(Redrawn from Howard and Fraker, 1990, by permission.)*

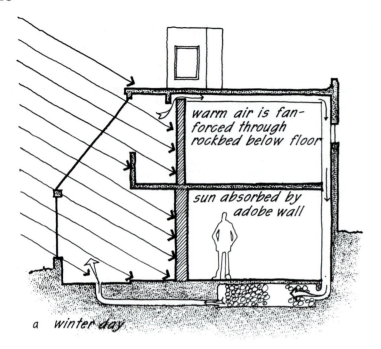

warm air is fan-
forced through
rockbed below floor

sun absorbed by
adobe wall

a *winter day*

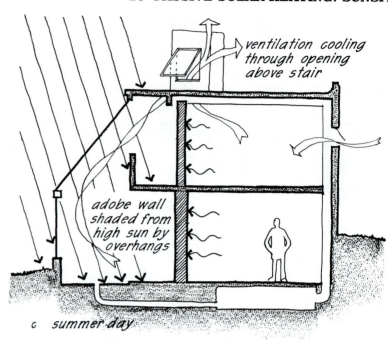

ventilation cooling
through opening
above stair

adobe wall
shaded from
high sun by
overhangs

c *summer day*

Figure 10.5 (continued): "Unit One" passive operation: (c) summer day. *(Redrawn from Howard and Fraker, 1990, by permission.)*

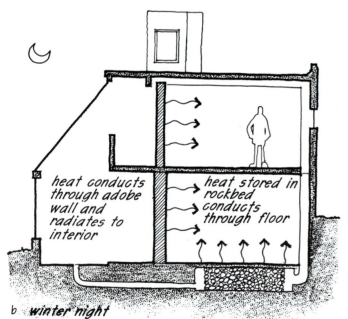

heat conducts
through adobe
wall and
radiates to
interior

heat stored in
rockbed
conducts
through floor

b **winter night**

Figure 10.5: "Unit One" passive operation: (a) winter day, and (b) winter night. *(Redrawn from Howard and Fraker, 1990, by permission.)*

vented Trombe wall, windows and doors can be opened in the morning to allow sunspace-heated air to circulate into the upper-level living spaces, which is replaced by cool air drawn from the lower-level living spaces. Of these two, convection is the most important heat transfer mechanism by far.

The second mode is an active-charge, radiant-discharge airloop system. Using two fans, warm air is drawn from the top of the sunspace and ducted down and through two underfloor rockbeds below the first-floor living areas, and finally returned to the bottom of the sunspace. The air transfers heat to the stones (4- to 6-in.-diameter) which store the heat, later releasing it gradually to the first-floor slab above. The combination of this radiant floor heating and the destratification of the greenhouse caused by the fan-forced air circulation helps to counterbalance the tendency for the lower story to be cooler than the upper story. The fans are controlled by a differential thermostat ("on" when upper sunspace air is warmer than the rockbed) and two back-draft dampers (to prevent reverse thermocirculation at night). Performance monitoring has revealed that this fan-forced mode is relatively unimportant to overall performance, with the primary advantage being a slight increase in thermal comfort. There is no night insulation.

Figure 10.6: Solargreen exterior showing south-facing sunspace.

Figure 10.7: Solargreen interior showing 12-in. masonry thermal storage wall on left, with sunspace beyond.

In the summer during the day, although there is no shading provided for any of the sunspace glazing, overheating is not a problem due to the shading of adobe thermal storage wall by the sunspace roof and by the balcony. In addition, a central circular staircase in the north corner has a clerestory vent window at the top and acts as a chimney to cool the sunspace by "stack effect" ventilation; outside air is drawn in through exterior sunspace doors to replace the air exhausted. During the hottest days, exterior and sunspace openings into the living spaces are closed; at night, to take advantage of the large temperature drop in this arid climate, the interior is cooled by "night-flushing" ventilation from the outside induced by the staircase stack effect. In the summer, the rockbed is dormant.

"Solargreen"

This sunspace design was the author's entry into the HUD Passive Solar Residential Design Competition (Moore, 1980a, 1980b; Franklin Research Center, 1979). The objective of the design was to develop a marketable dwelling that could be easily constructed using existing building practices. The basic design is a three-bedroom, two-story, 1600-ft^2 home with an attached greenhouse. The entry received a design award and five construction awards in the competition. Seventeen variations of the design have been built, including a vertically glazed, water wall version, and a wood-foundation, phase-change tube storage wall version.

The design utilizes a concept, "thermal layering," to establish an interrelated series of living zones which are ordered in response to time-of-day activities and the climatic loads of various seasons. In plan, this distributes the most frequently occupied areas next to the solar collection sunspace and the 12-in. solid masonry thermal storage wall, with circulation and utility zones along the north wall as a thermal buffer.

In section, the living area is at grade level, while sleeping areas are below grade. This positions daytime activities (living, dining, cooking, etc.) in the warmest area of the house, while sleeping areas (which require less light, cooler temperatures, and greater privacy) at the lowest level, with sunlight penetrating into the sleeping areas through the sunspace. This unconventional arrangement of activities (living above, sleeping below) is thus compatible with the natural air temperature stratification unlike the conventional arrangement which places living areas in the lowest (coldest) region and the sleeping areas in the highest (warmest).

The lower-level walls are constructed of reinforced concrete with 2-in. expanded polystyrene foam insulation on the outside. The upper level is conventional 2x4 wood stud construction with *R*-11 fiberglass batt insulation and prefabricated wood roof trusses with *R*-30 fiberglass batt insulation.

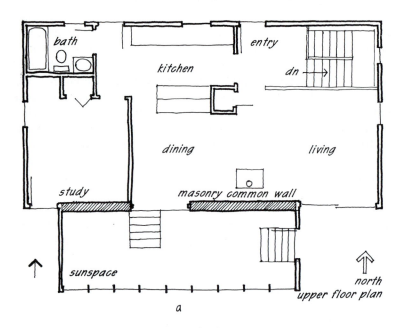

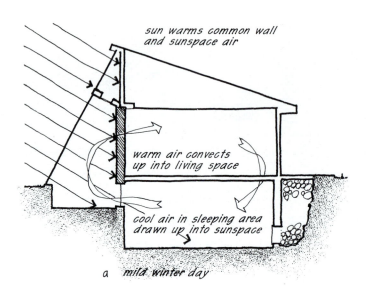

a   mild winter day

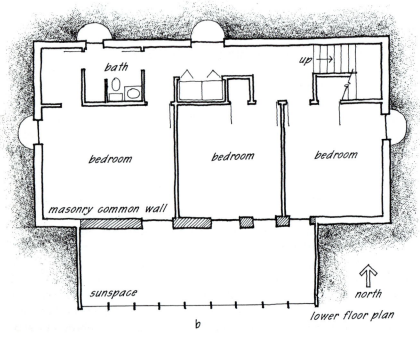

Figure 10.8: Solargreen floor plans: (a) upper level, and (b) lower level.

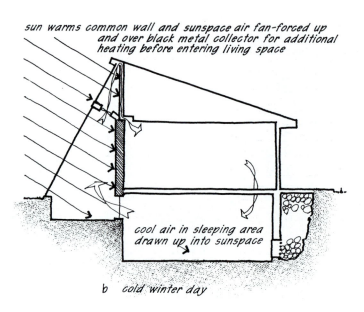

b   cold winter day

Figure 10.9: Solargreen passive operation: (a) winter day —passive heating only, and (b) winter day — with hybrid collector added.

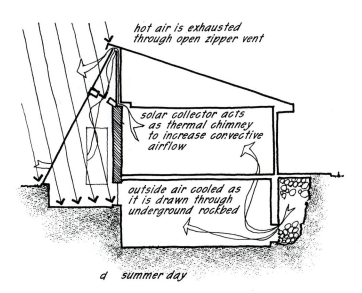

Figure 10.9 (continued): Solargreen passive operation: (c) winter night, and (d) summer day.

SUNSPACE DESIGN GUIDELINES

Continuing the general design guidelines presented first in Chapter 7, the following specifically apply to sunspace systems (Balcomb et al., 1984):

Rule 25. Effect of orientation— The performance of a sunspace depends on the orientation azimuth of its principle glazing relative to south. The optimum orientation is always due south, although (like other passive systems) there is little penalty for departures within a few degrees of south. For most cities, annual heating performance is reduced by about 5 percent for orientations 30° off due south; the penalties are greater for cold, sunny climates and least for cloudy climates. Summer overheating increases more rapidly for nonsouth orientations.

Rule 26. Use of mass— The use of mass increases the space's livability, its function as an entry, foyer, transit area, or greenhouse, and reduces any tendency to summer overheating. Effective locations for the thermal mass include a thermal storage wall separating the building, water containers along the common wall, or a masonry floor. The optimum thickness for a masonry wall is 12 in., although 8 in. performs nearly as well. As with the Trombe wall, all voids should be filled solid with grout. Insulated walls with water containers have no optimum amount of mass; performance continues to increase as thermal storage volume increases.

Rule 27. Area of mass— All the direct-gain rules for thermal mass apply to sunspaces except that a mass surface to projected glazing area ratio of at least 3:1 is recommended rather than the 6:1 ratio for direct gain. If water is used for the primary thermal mass, then the water mass should be approximately 0.5 ft³/ft² of projected glazing area, and the containers should be dark colored and located in the sun.

Rule 28. Water container shape— In the insulated-wall configuration, the shape of the water-storage containers has a small influence on the average annual performance. If a row of drums twice as high as the diameter is considered the base case, a small increase in performance can be achieved either by substituting very tall, thin containers (covering the common wall) or very short, deep containers (covering the floor), although the practicality of the latter is questionable. This improvement occurs because these extreme shapes have a higher surface-to-volume ratio, and therefore they absorb more solar radiation and release more heat by convection. However, because the volume of water has the dominant effect on performance (and because the cost of water is virtually free) the recommended shape is the one that allows the greatest volume of water to be placed in the sunspace.

Rule 29. Do not glaze the end walls— The use of glazed east and west end walls is not recommended on the basis of both winter and summer thermal criteria. Winter heating performance is reduced in every climate; however, the undesirable summer gain can be devastating. It is preferable to use insulated end walls, perforated with windows or doors adequate for summer cross-ventilation (Balcomb et al., 1984). Reflective foil wall covering on the end walls has been used to reflect sunlight back to the thermal storage mass to reduce sunspace overheating (Moore, 1980a); however, the effectiveness of this compared with light-colored endwalls is unknown.

Rule 30. Roof— The sunspace should be designed to shade internal sunspace mass in the summer while providing irradiation in the winter. If a portion of the roof is glazed, then provide for summer shading (using, for example, a curtain or awning).

Rule 31. Common wall— Sunspaces should be closable from the building living space (for example, by a door or operable window). The common wall is an effective and convenient location for thermal storage mass (masonry or water in containers), in which case it should not be insulated. Lightweight frame common walls should be insulated to at least *R*-10.

Rule 32. Common-wall vents — The primary thermal connection between sunspace and the adjacent building is normally by convection, and it is therefore necessary to give particular attention to this aspect of the design. The following are guidelines for sizing various opening types (all should be closable at night):

a. Doorways (assuming 6-ft 8-in. doors) = 15 percent of projected glazing area.

b. Window openings (assuming 3-ft-tall windows) = 20 percent of projected glazing area.

c. High and low vent pairs (assuming 8-ft vertical separation) = 10 percent of projected glazing area (combined for both vents).

Rule 33. Summer venting— Because most sunspace glazing is not shaded during the summer, vents (including windows and doors) to the outside are essential to prevent overheating. It is essential to provide both inlet (preferably low on the windward side of the building) and outlet vents (high on the leeward side) of generous size. Exhaust and ceiling fans can also be used.

Rule 34. Wall color — Generally, follow direct-gain rules with the following modifications:

a. If light-colored surfaces tend to reflect sunlight out of the sunspace, then they should be made darker (the color of lightweight objects does not affect performance).

b. If a sunspace is used as a greenhouse, then the surfaces in dark corners should be made light in color to improve plant photosynthesis.

Rule 35. Sunspace width — In the case of sunspaces with only one wall common, assuming that glazing area is kept constant, performance generally increases with sunspace width (although the improvement is small beyond widths of 15 to 20 ft). The effect is more significant for glazed end walls than for insulated end walls. The performance is different for semi-enclosed sunspaces (with three common walls); as width increases performance actually decreases. The reasons for this are: (1) the end-wall "losses" are to the adjoining rooms and not losses at all, (2) the thermal storage mass per unit of glazed area decreases as the sunspace increases because of the fixed amount of mass associated with the end walls, and (3) the effective absorptance of the sunspace increases as the cavity becomes deeper.

Rule 36. Color — Dark-colored sunspace surfaces tend to perform better than light-colored ones because less solar radiation is reflected back out through the glazing (before it can be absorbed). Dark thermal storage surfaces (masonry wall, floor, and water containers) are especially important because solar radiation absorbed by massive elements is partially retained as stored heat to be released later when it is needed. However, it is less critical that the thermal storage mass be dark in buildings achieving a low SSF ("weak" solar) because most of the solar heat collected goes immediately to satisfying daytime heating requirements and storage is less important. The color of lightweight ceilings and end walls has a negligible effect on performance.

Rule 37. Plants and other lightweight objects— Lightweight objects such as furniture and plants in the sunspace have the effect of rapidly transferring the solar energy into heated air. This is because the solar radiation absorbed by lightweight objects causes a rapid surface temperature increase and consequently a rapid transfer of heat by convection to the surrounding air. Because this heat is not being directly transferred to the thermal storage mass and thus contributes to overheating, the annual solar heating is reduced as the amount of lightweight material increases. This is most pronounced for "strong" solar designs which need to store heat to achieve high SSFs.

SUMMARY OF TERMS

Sunspace — a passive solar heating system type consisting of a glassed-in room (like a greenhouse, atrium, or conservatory) located on the south side of a building and separated from other building spaces by a common wall.

Common wall — the wall separating a sunspace from other living spaces.

Projected collector area — the projected area is the net glazing area projected onto a single vertical plane.

Greenhouse — a sunspace used primarily for growing plants.

Mixed system — a combination of two or more passive solar heating system types into a single building.

Hybrid system — a predominantly passive solar heating system which utilizes an active component (such as an electric fan to force heated air from a sunspace into a building).

STUDY QUESTIONS

1. Summarize the advantages and disadvantages of a sunspace passive solar heating system.

2. Explain the essential difference between an indirect-gain and an isolated-gain sunspace system.

3. Why is it less critical in sunspace buildings that glazing be shading during the summer than in other passive systems?

4. Explain why the east and west end walls of a sunspace should be opaque and insulated rather than glazed.

5. What are some of the considerations in determining the tilt of the sunspace glazing?

6. Many sunspaces are used as greenhouses for plant growing as well as for passive solar heating. Explain why plants can reduce sunspace heating performance.

11

PASSIVE SOLAR HEATING:

CONVECTIVE AIR LOOP

In convective air loop passive solar heating systems, air is typically heated by a sloped, glazed solar collector isolated from the living spaces. As the air is heated, it rises by natural convection and is replaced by cool air drawn in to the bottom of the collector. To provide thermal storage, the heated air may be circulated through a thermal storage bed of rocks (or hollow concrete floor slab). Heat is transferred to the rocks, and the air is cooled in the process. The cool air is returned to the collector for reheating.

To transfer the heat from storage to the house, cool air from the house is circulated through the rocks, where it is heated, rising by natural convection to enter the house. Because the airflow throughout the system is driven by

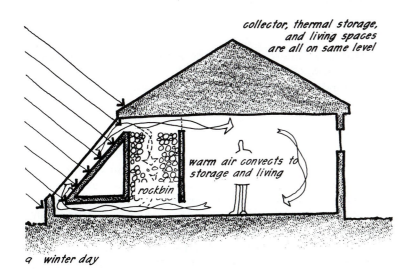

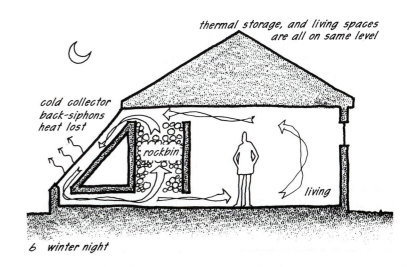

Figure 11.1: Positioning the collector, storage, and living areas at the same level in a convective air loop system: (a) winter day operation — level arrangement allows convective heating to occur during the day; (b) winter night operation — this "level" positioning of components permits unwanted back-siphoning, effectively cooling the system.

Figure 11.2: To prevent back-siphoning, the collector must be positioned below the rockbed, and the rockbed must be below the living space: (a) day operation, and (b) night operation.

natural convection, the vertical placement of the elements is critical to proper operation. The collector cannot be above the storage, and the storage cannot be above the living areas to be heated; air always flows up as it is heated (because it becomes more buoyant than adjacent cooler air).

CONVECTIVE AIR LOOP ADVANTAGES AND DISADVANTAGES

Most convective air loop systems are "isolated-gain" systems where the only heat transfer to the living space is by convection. As such, it has the advantage of being easily controllable (by closing the convective openings) and thus not prone to overheating. Because heat transfer is limited to convection, interior mean radiant temperatures (MRTs) closely follow air temperatures and thus have little effect on thermal comfort (in contrast with direct gain and thermal storage wall system where the MRT is often substantially different

from air temperature). Finally, the building envelope may be of any type (including lightweight wood frame).

On the other hand, the requisite locations of the components of convective air loop systems become a strong architectural design determinant. There is little spatial flexibility in this arrangement if the system is to work efficiently. While the component materials are relatively inexpensive, they occupy a large volume (in comparison with other passive systems); air channels must be quite large in comparison with fan-powered systems, for example, in order to get adequate volumetric flow rates at the very low velocities characteristic of natural convection. In addition, because most of the components are positioned outside of the building envelope, they are single-function. This differs from the components of direct-gain and Trombe wall systems, for example, which are best designed to fulfill structural and enclosure functions as well as heating. Depending on the location, the migration of groundwater or radon gas into the rock bed may be a problem. Finally, some researchers have expressed concern about the potential for growth of harmful organisms in rockbeds.

As a result, comparatively few convective air loop systems have been built (none recently). Compared with the other passive systems discussed in previous chapters, the convective air loop system is not an important catagory, and is included here primarily to recognize its historical significance within the passive solar movement.

CONVECTIVE AIR LOOP CASE STUDIES

Early work

As early as 1968, Steve Baer was successfully heating buildings using a thermosiphoning air passive solar collector and a thermal storage rockbed (Baer, 1975). In subsequent experiments, he demonstrated that it was possible to collect and store an average of 750 Btu/ft^2 in Albuquerque in December. This compared favorably with the active liquid collectors that were being touted by the engineering establishment at the time as the most efficient and cost-effective method of solar heating.

Using some simple experimental techniques to compare the performance of several convective systems in 1975, Baer concluded that multiple layers of expanded-metal lath worked well as the solar absorber. Until these experiments, most designers had assumed that the best design for an air collector was to pass air behind a black metal sheet, the front of which was exposed to the sun and covered with glazing. The multiple layers of black metal lath provided comparable absorption and greatly improved heat transfer (from the metal to the air) due to the greatly increased surface area.

Davis residence

This pioneering house, the most influential early example of a thermosiphoning air passive solar heating system, was designed and built by owner Paul Davis, an English professor at the University of New Mexico. The convective air loop system was designed by Steve Baer, Davis's next-door neighbor (Davis, 1976 and 1977; Skurka and Naar, 1976).

The two-level house is set into a south-facing hillside. The lower level has 600 ft^2 of living space, and a loft above provides another 300 ft^2 for bedrooms. The south-facing 400-ft^2 solar collector is located directly beneath a porch running across the building. It provides both space heating and hot water using the black expanded metal mesh absorber developed by Baer. The roof is covered by a movable overhang that is seasonally adjustable to provide shading or admit sunlight as required.

The rockbed is about 4 ft deep and holds about 43 ft^3 of "fist-size" washed river rock (2 to 4-in. diameter). Plenums above and below ensure uniform air distribution across the entire face of the rockbed. This combination was specified by Baer for optimum performance. Shallower depth or larger rocks would have resulted in incomplete heat transfer between the air and rocks; greater depth or smaller rocks would have increased the resistance of the system and reduced the flow velocity. All air channels were large (compared to ducts in fan-powered systems) to reduce resistance and assure adequate flow of low-velocity air. For example, registers for the warm air entering the living space are about 20 ft^2, and return grilles are of similar size. Flow is controlled by manually operated supply dampers between the storage and the living space.

In the following description of what happens when the dampers are opened, Davis (1977) also reveals the political and cultural values prevalent among most passive solar pioneers of that time:

The air rising convectively from the rock bin comes on "cat feet," waiting ten or fifteen seconds after the vents are opened before it begins to rise silently through the vents in the floor. This silence is a special property of air, a property removed by machines that push it against its will. The delay before rising is a natural pause like the moments between the appearance of the sunrise and the first feeling of morning warmth... The natural aesthetic of the thermosiphon house produces a sense of being in a warm place rather than a warmed place. Its simplicity, depending on the most obvious of scientific principles and having no parts to break, no plumbing to leak, make it an ideal system for the non-mechanic. Its simplicity also creates a sense of independence from the industrial complex, even if such psychological liberation is, in part, illusory.

Figure 11.3: Davis residence, Corrales, New Mexico — south facade showing the thermosiphoning air collector. The thermal storage rock bed is located below the porch.

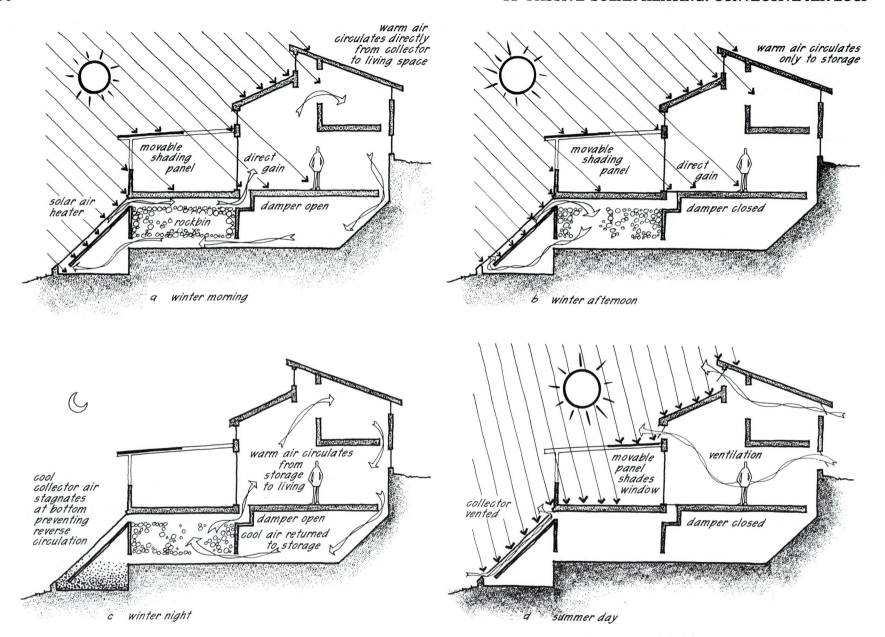

Figure 11.4: Davis residence operation: (a) winter morning — with dampers open, collector-heated air flows directly to house, bypassing the rock bed, while deck overhang is slid out to allow direct gain; (b) winter afternoon — dampers are closed to prevent overheating of the living spaces, and collector-heated air is diverted through the rock bed; (c) winter night — cool air stagnates at bottom of collector preventing back-siphoning, while open dampers provide air circulation from rock bed to living spaces and back; and (d) summer day — roof overhang moved back to provide shade, and open windows provide cross-ventilation (the offset position of the collector and storage minimize unwanted convective and radiative heating); recently, a vent in the top of the collector exhausts unwanted hot air to the exterior, keeping the storage cool.

A postscript: While the performance of his house has never been systematically monitored, in a recent interview Paul Davis said that earlier writings probably overemphasized the role of convective heating and underemphasized the contribution of direct gain and the thick, insulated adobe walls in maintaining comfort: "The house performs remarkably well with the dampers closed, even in cold weather."

Private residence, Santa Fe

Few recent examples of convective airloop buildings have been built. Most of these have been rockbeds under concrete floor slabs. One of the most famous and best documented is a house designed and built by Mark Jones (Scott Morris, solar consultant) for the speculative market located on a rural site near Santa Fe. The 1976 ft^2 house is single-story, 2x8 frame construction with R-27 walls and R-30 roof. It is primarily heated using a passive solar convective air loop system with a radiant-discharge underslab rockbed. The net collector area is 398 ft^2 and 55 tons of rocks provide thermal storage. The system provides an impressive 85 percent solar heating fraction (including the contribution of direct gain and a small greenhouse) and an overall system efficiency of 35 percent (Jones and Morris, 1980; Morris, 1981).

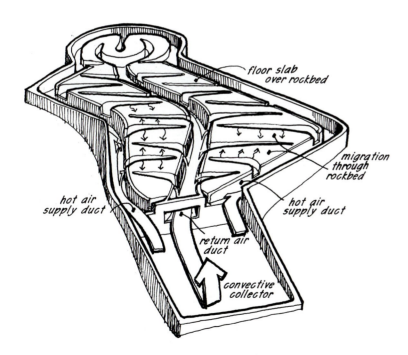

Figure 11.5: Santa Fe residence, overall arrangement of air-loop collector, ductwork, and radiant-release rock beds. *(Redrawn from Morris, 1980, by permission.)*

Large rectangular ducts feed hot air from the collector outlet around the perimeter of the building below the floor slab. A series of perforated ducts branch off into the 18-in.-deep rockbed area, which is in turn interspersed with perforated return air ducts feeding a central return air duct which flows back to the collector inlet. Night dampers prevent reverse thermosiphoning and isolate the rockbed from the collector during summer months.

CONVECTIVE AIR LOOP DESIGN GUIDELINES

Baer (1975) has proposed the following design guidelines for convective air loop systems:

1. Make D = at least 1/15 L.

2. Make rocks 2 ft deep if small gravel (1-in. diameter) and up to 4 ft deep if large rock (6 in. diameter).

3. Make the collector slant at least 45°.

4. Insulate storage box with at least 6 in. fiberglass insulation.

5. Make collector at least 6 ft long.

6. Keep all flow channels at least one-fifteenth of collector area.

7. Avoid corners in flow channels.

8. Make storage cross section at least one-third of collector area.

9. Insulate divider between downflow and upflow with at least 1-in. duct board.

10. Double glaze collectors if 7000 degree-day climate or more.

11. Hand place rock if possible to avoid layers of dirt in bin.

12. Place all of storage rocks above collector or use damper.

13. Build the house above storage bin.

14. Build vent flap at top of collector to open during summer to prevent overheating.

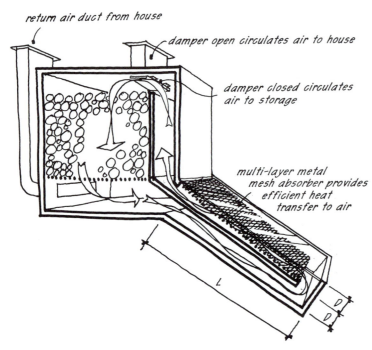

Figure 11.6: Section through convective air loop with rock bed thermal storage showing recommended dimensions. *(Redrawn from Baer, 1975, by permission.)*

HYBRID ROCKBEDS

A convective rockbed controlled by a fan is a reasonable choice for a design with large south windows (or greenhouse) that, for whatever reason, does not include mass in direct sunlight. It is also suitable in a solar retrofit where it may be easy to add more south-facing glass but difficult to add more mass. There are three types of fan-controlled rockbeds: *one-way, two-way,* and *radiant discharge* (Lewis et al., 1982).

DOUBLE-ENVELOPE CONVECTIVE AIR LOOP

First conceived by Lee Porter Butler, this variant of the convective air loop is the most controversial passive solar design to evolve in the late seventies. The design is characterized by a sunspace (usually two-story) on the south facade, a continuous enclosed airspace extended from the sunspace across the

Figure 11.7: One-way active discharge rockbed in a direct-gain passive home. Airflow is always in the same direction, with solar-heated air always circulated through the rockbed before being distributed to the house. Circulation continues at night, discharging the rocks to heat the house. A temperature wave moves through the bed in one direction; the length of the path through the rock bed determines the time lag introduced by the storage, while the total mass of the rock bed determines the temperature swings (more mass, less swing). *(Redrawn from Lewis et al., 1982, by permission.)*

Figure 11.8: Two-way active-discharge rock bed in a direct-gain passive house. Rockbed is "charged" in one direction, and "discharged" in the opposite direction. The rockbed is stratified, i.e., it has a hot and a cold side. Air being heated for return to the house always passes through the warmest rocks last. This configuration is most advantageous where high temperatures exist, and is thus the preferred type for active air-collector systems. In passive buildings, where lower temperatures are more typical, there is a smaller temperature difference across the rock bed and the advantage of stratification is less significant. *(Redrawn from Lewis et al., 1982, by permission.)*

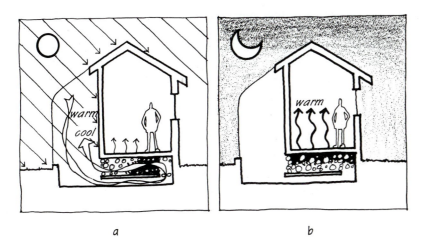

a   b

Figure 11.9: Radiant-release rockbed is actively charged by convection from collector during the day and passively discharged by conduction through the slab and finally by radiation and convection into the room at night. The slab tends to heated unevenly, being warmest above the intake of the rockbed; in practice, effect is minimal unless the path through the rockbed is long. *(Redrawn from Lewis et al., 1982, by permission.)*

upper-story ceiling, down the north wall, to a crawlspace below the lower floor (where heat is transferred to the soil, which acts as the system's thermal storage), and finally returning to the sunspace (Reno, 1980; Butler, 1978; Shurcliff, 1980; Editor, 1982; Huber, 1982).

Critics argue that this configuration violates good design practice for heat transfer by drastically increasing the area of heat transfer surface. Proponents respond that this configuration is effective because it results in heat being lost into the house; critics counter that even more heat is lost to the exterior because relatively high temperature air is circulated next to the cold outside environment.

Unlike rockbed passive systems, the storage (soil under the crawlspace) is positioned below the collector. Ideally, the warmest air in the system is used to charge the thermal storage; in the double-envelope design, the bottom location of the storage results in the coolest air coming in contact with soil after much of its useful heat has been lost (either to the interior or exterior). This is one of the paradoxes of the envelope concept: for the convective loop to work, air must lose heat and become more dense; yet, the objective is to preserve heat for charging the storage.

One of the problems in purely passive versions of this design is sluggish airflow which results in insufficient transfer of heat away from the sunspace and consequent overheating. Monitored results have revealed that air leaving the top

of the sunspace is typically 90°F (and often as high as 100°F), which results in excessive heat loss through the sunspace glazing.

Another problem is the ineffectiveness of the soil floor in the crawlspace for heat storage. Compared with rockbeds, the surface area of the soil exposed to air is small resulting in limited convective transfer. In addition, the ability of the soil to conduct heat away from (and back to) the surface (i.e., its *thermal diffusivity*) is poor compared with more dense conductive materials such as masonry or concrete. (Remember how hot the surface of the sand at the beach is on a sunny day...and how cool it is just below the surface. Soil is a comparatively poor heat conductor.) Construction of the double-envelope is complicated by the necessity of accommodating windows on the north side (which tend to interrupt the continuity of the convective space), and the necessity of providing fire-stops in the convection space to meet building code requirements.

Yet, in spite of these apparent thermodynamic shortcomings, the amount of auxiliary heat required to keep these designs comfortable is remarkably small. This has been confirmed by monitoring by independent researchers. Most conclude that the energy efficiency of double-envelope houses is attributable to their superinsulation construction and the sunspace, and that the contribution of the convective circulation around the envelope and crawlspace thermal storage is minimal (and, in some instances, even negative).

Double-envelope case study: Maston house

This house, designed by Lee Porter Butler, is representative of the double-envelope concept first proposed by this architect. It is located in Middletown, Rhode Island, and has three stories, including a finished basement, with approximately 2600 ft² of living area including the sunspace (Editor, 1982).

The house is framed with single 2x6 walls (R-19) on the east and west. The double north wall is framed with 2x4 studs (R-11) on the inside, and 2x6 studs (R-19) on the outside, with an 8-in. airspace between. The double wall is connected to a 12-in.-high subbasement crawlspace through the utility room on the north. The basement wood floor joists, supported by concrete blocks, are insulated with R-11 fiberglass batts. Air flows from the sunspace, across the attic, down the north wall, across the basement crawlspace, and back into the sunspace.

The house was monitored hour by hour for a seven-day period in January, 1980, by researchers from Brookhaven National Laboratory (BNL). During the test period, monitored auxiliary electric heaters were placed on each floor set to provide a nominal temperature of 65°F at all times. In addition to monitoring auxiliary heating energy, instrumentation recorded temperatures in several locations, relative humidity, and horizontal insolation. The auxiliary heating requirement varied from 3 Btu/°F•day•ft² (of floor area) under overcast conditions to about 2 Btu/°F•day•ft² for sunny days; this extrapolated to about 2 Btu/°F•day•ft² for the entire heating season (about one-quarter the level of a moderately insulated building).

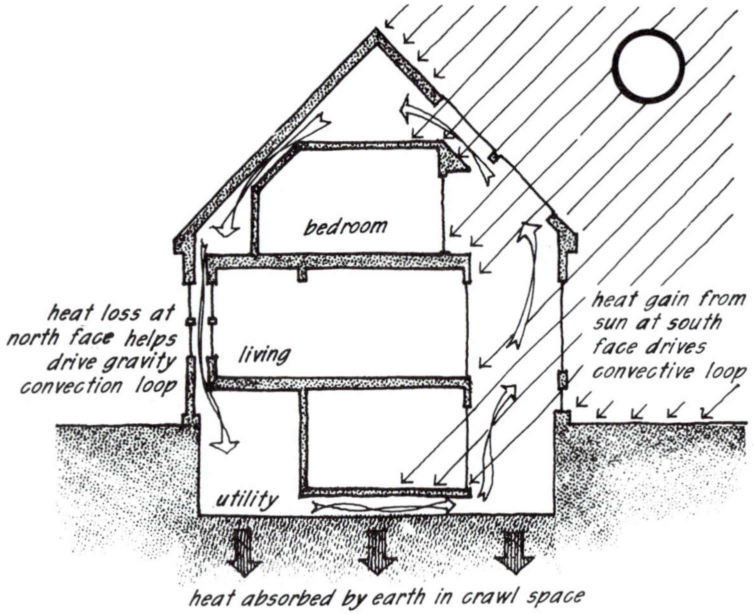

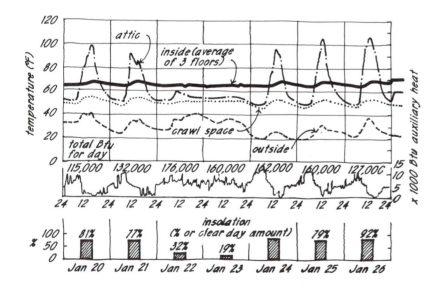

Figure 11.10: Maston double-envelope house: section showing airflow. *(Redrawn from Editor, 1982, by permission.)*

Figure 11.11: Maston double-envelope house: observed hourly performance, January 20 to 26, 1980. *(Redrawn from Editor, 1982, by permission.)*

The BNL researchers that monitored the house concluded, "The large temperature variations around the loop on clear days suggest that the airflow is not pronounced enough to transport much heat. The lack of forced circulation in the house results in stratification of air." When the convective loop was blocked, the blockage caused no increase in the auxiliary heat required. "If anything, the auxiliary heat needed was lower by about 5 to 20 percent with the convection loop blocked, depending on insolation. The merits of forced circulation with fans should be seriously considered in double-envelope houses. These can be coupled with more efficient thermal storage systems such as rockbeds and hollow-core concrete blocks . . . Another design alternative would be to insulate only the outer shell and use the radiative gain of the envelope to heat the interior space more directly."

MIXED SYSTEMS

Many recent solar houses mix two or more passive system types (i.e., a combination of direct gain in areas requiring quick warmup, and unvented Trombe wall in areas where delayed heating is desirable). This allows matching the differing passive performance characteristics of each type to the needs of the various spaces in the building, and thus improving the performance over any single system type alone.

MIXED SYSTEM CASE STUDY: THE SHREWSBURY HOUSE

One of the most ambitious passive solar houses was designed by solar inventor Norman Saunders (Shurcliff, 1982a). The house, located in Shrewsbury, Massachusetts (6500 degree-day climate), is 100 percent solar-heated and has no auxiliary heating system. The house is two-story frame construction with 2450-ft² floor area. The solar heating system is a combination of passive types including direct gain, sunspace, and fan-forced convective transfer to remote rockbed. It includes:

- A 480 ft² of south-facing solar aperture area sloped 34° and a high-temperature attic storage

- A rockbed below the lower floor for low-temperature storage

- Special thermosiphoning windows

- A solar greenhouse

- Domestic hot-water preheating in the attic.

Figure 11.12: Shrewsbury house (N. Saunders, solar consultant). *(Photo courtesy of R. Smith.)*

Figure 11.14: Shrewsbury house wintertime forced airflow: (1) outdoor cold air enters a slanting duct. (2) The duct leads to (3) a grille in a south room. The air diffuses through several rooms (4) and passes up through grilles leading to the attic. (5) The air diffuses to the upper end of the duct that carries air down to the north face of the rockbed beneath the lower-story floor. (6) A fan at the base of the duct drives the air south through the rocks. (7) The air enters the greenhouse and diffuses and (8) descends along the cold south glass of the greenhouse. (9) The air flows into a trough and (10) enters an exhaust duct that extends vertically up in the greenhouse and then extends along (11) to the peak of the roof where it (12) emerges through a vent to the outside. A single 1/4-hp fan powers all of these flows. The intake duct (2) surrounds the exhaust duct (11) to provide some heat recovery from the exhaust air. *(Redrawn from Shurcliff, 1982, by permission.)*

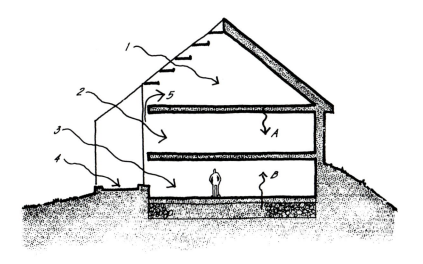

Figure 11.13: Shrewsbury house solar heating: (1) radiation enters the solar attic; (2) radiation enters upper south rooms; (3) radiation enters lower south rooms; (4) radiation is absorbed by the greenhouse earth; (5) radiation is absorbed within the triple-glazed south window, producing thermosiphon flow of warm air to the attic. The dotted arrows denote conductive and radiative energy flows: (a) downward from the attic to upper rooms (very small energy flow); and (b) up from the bin of stones and concrete slab to the lower rooms. *(Redrawn from Shurcliff, 1982, by permission.)*

The unique solar attic is the most remarkable feature of the house. It serves mainly as a large solar energy collection and high temperature storage system. The collector is the glazed south-facing roof (*R*-value is 6); the aperture is so large (and its thermal resistance so high) that a significant amount of solar energy is collected even when the sky is overcast. Yet in June, nearly all of the solar radiation striking the roof collector is reflected back to the sky. The effective noontime transmittance of direct radiation is only about 5 to 10 percent. This remarkable performance is the result of an ingenious configuration involving horizontal reflective louvers positioned below the sloped roof glazing which reflects high-angle summer insolation back out through the glazing, while reflecting lower-angle winter insolation into the sunspace and attic. This results in a seasonal selectivity that admits ten times the total insolation in the winter as in the summer.

SUMMARY OF TERMS

Convective air loop — a passive solar heating system that consists of a solar collector and a thermal storage mass (usually a rockbed) isolated from the living spaces. Air is used to transfer heat from the collector to the storage and the living spaces.

Hybrid system — A predominantly passive solar heating system which utilizes an active component (such as an electric fan to force heated air from one location to another).

Rockbed — a heat-storage component consisting of an enclosed volume of rocks (fist-size) with a plenum at each end. During the charging cycle, warm air (from a solar collector) is circulated through the rocks, warming them. During the discharge cycle, cool room air is circulated through the rocks where it is heated and returned to the room.

STUDY QUESTIONS

1. Summarize the advantages and disadvantages of a convective loop passive solar heating system.

2. What are some of the limitations on the locations of the collector and storage relative to the living areas?

3. Very few airloop convective systems with rockbed storage have been built. Identify reasons for this slow acceptance and some possible solutions.

4. Compare a one-way, a two-way, and a radiant release hybrid rockbed.

5. The "solar staircase" concept features sloped collector glazing with no overhang. Normally, this is avoided to prevent unwanted solar gain during the summer. Discuss how the "solar staircase" resolves this problem.

12

PASSIVE SOLAR HEATING:

LCR CALCULATIONS

As introduced in Chapter 7, the *solar savings* of a passive building is defined as the energy savings due to the solar system relative to the energy requirement of a comparable nonsolar building that has an energy-neutral wall in place of the solar wall and a fixed indoor reference temperature; it is expressed in Btus. The *solar savings fraction* (SSF) is the most widely accepted expression of the comparative performance of a passive solar building and is defined as the ratio of the solar savings of the solar building to the energy requirement of the comparable nonsolar building, expressed as a percentage.

The method for predicting the SSF of passive solar heated buildings is the load-collector ratio (LCR) method. It was developed at Los Alamos National Laboratory under funding by the U.S. Department of Energy by Passive Solar Group Q-11 from 1977 through 1984 (Balcomb et al., 1984). The Los Alamos group found that the primary factor that determines the performance of a solar building in a particular climate is the ratio of the building heat loss load to the area of the solar aperture — the load collector ratio (LCR). More precisely, LCR is defined as the ratio of the net load coefficient (NLC) to the projected collector area (A_p).

OVERVIEW OF THE *LCR* PASSIVE SOLAR DESIGN PROCESS

The process begins by looking up recommended passive solar design guidelines for a particular geographic location and relative fuel cost. These guidelines were developed after innumerable mainframe computer simulations intended to balance solar heating performance (and resulting auxiliary energy cost savings due to solar) against the probable extra construction cost of the solar heating components.

The guidelines recommend the level of conservation (insulation and airtightness), the recommended ratio of building heat loss to collector area (the load collector ratio LCR) and the resulting target solar heating performance (as measured by the SSF). From this recommended conservation factor (CF) and the designed building dimensions, the net load coefficient NLC (nonsolar heatloss) is determined.

To determine the optimum size of the passive solar heating system (glass area), the NLC is divided by the recommended LCR.

From this recommended "optimum" collector area, the designed collector area is chosen, the passive solar heating system type is selected, and the solar savings fraction SSF for this combination is calculated. This is compared with the original recommended SSF. This system is then redesigned if necessary, adjusting the collector area and system types as required.

Following this procedure will provide a cost-effective design that balances solar heating with conservation measures, while providing a comfortable thermal environment.

PROCEDURE

The annual LCR method is executed by following the steps listed below and entered on the Passive Solar Worksheet (Appendix F). In steps 1 through 3, determine the levels of insulation and airtightness as described in Chapter 6:

1. In Appendix D, look up the recommended CF, the recommended LCR, and the resulting target SSF for the site location and relative fuel cost. These recommendations are based on a combination of local weather conditions (solar and temperature) and balance typical construction costs against auxiliary fuel savings. Final designs which are close to these recommendations will be both cost effective and comfortable.

2. Based on the recommended CF, calculate the recommended insulation and airtightness levels using the procedure described in Chapter 6.

3. Based on these recommendations, select the actual insulation and airtightness levels for the construction planned (because of the availability of standard construction materials — especially insulation thicknesses — these values will probably vary somewhat from the above recommendations).

Next, calculate the passive solar heating performance of the proposed design as follows using Part II of the Passive Solar Worksheet:

4. Calculate the *UA* for each building element (except the solar wall) using the appropriate formula on the worksheet. The value of ADR is read from Fig. 12.1 (based on site elevation above sea level from LCR table in Appendix D).

5. Sum these *UA*'s.

6. Calculate the NLC = sum *UA* x 24 (to convert to degree-days).

7. Select an appropriate reference design from Appendix B [for additional reference designs see Balcomb et al., (1984); for mixtures of more than one system, see "Mixed Systems" below].

    Enter the name of the reference design (e.g., SSD2) and its $U_{collector}$ (from Appendix B) on the worksheet.

8. Determine A_p. As a preliminary guide for sizing a cost-effective passive solar heating system, the "recommended" A_p is approximately equal to the NLC (from step 6) divided by the recommended LCR (from step 1; this will yield a comfortable and cost-effective design based on local weather, probable construction costs, and auxiliary fuel cost savings). The designed A_p is based on this recommended A_p as adjusted for practical construction or design considerations (for example, make A_p a multiple of the net area of a standard-sized glazing component). By definition, the projected area

A_p of a direct-gain, Trombe wall, or water wall solar window is equal to the net glazing area. In the case of a sunspace, the projected area is the net glazing area projected onto a single vertical plane that has the same orientation as the "principle azimuth" or the sunspace. The principle azimuth is the area-weighted average azimuth — or orientation — of all glazings in the sunspace.

9. Calculate the LCR = NLC ÷ A_p.

10. Look up SSF in Appendix D and enter on worksheet as decimal fraction. Compare this to the *recommended SSF* from step 1. Within 15 percent is satisfactory; otherwise, change either the A_p or the system type as required.

11. Look up $U_{collector}$ from Appendix B. Calculate the $(UA)_{collector} = A_p$ x $U_{collector}$.

12. Calculate total load coefficient (for sizing auxiliary heating equipment) in Btu per degree-day:

    $$TLC = NLC + [24 \times (UA)_{collector}]$$

13. Look up annual heating degree-days DD (from Appendix D).

14. Calculate Q_{aux} = NLC x DD (1 – SSF). This is the amount of heat that will have to be supplied by the auxiliary heating system (e.g., furnace or stove).

EXAMPLE PROBLEM A (see worksheet, Fig. 12.2)

A preliminary design (with slab-on-floor) has been developed for Indianapolis, Indiana, as follows:

Exterior opaque wall area = 1050 ft²

Roof (insulated ceiling) area = 1550 ft²

E, W, N window area = 140 ft²

Slab-on-grade perimeter length = 170 linear ft

Volume (ceiling height x floor area) = 12,400 ft³

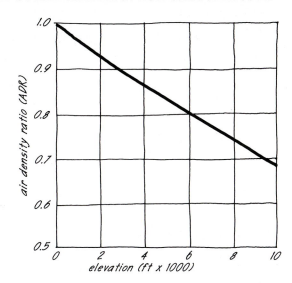

Figure 12.1: The air density ratio (ADR) for different elevations above sea level. *(Redrawn from Balcomb et al., 1984, by permission.)*

Begin by determining the levels of insulation and airtightness as described in Chapter 6 and entering the results in Part I of the Passive Solar Worksheet (from Appendix F):

1. In Appendix D, look up the recommended CF, the recommended LCR, and the resulting target SSF for the Indianapolis location and relative fuel cost (assumed high in this example): recommended CF = 1.76, recommended LCR = 40, and target SSF = 30.

2. Based on the recommended CF, calculate the recommended insulation and airtightness levels using the procedure described in Chapter 6:

R_{wall} = 14 x CF = 25

$R_{ceiling}$ = 22 x CF = 39

$R_{perimeter}$ = (13 x CF) – 5 = 18

$R_{basement}$ = (16 x CF) – 8 = 17

$N_{E,W,N}$ = 1.7 x CF = 3 glazing layers

ACH = 0.42 ÷ CF = 0.24

3. Based on these recommendations, select the actual insulation and air-tightness levels for the construction planned (see Chapter 5 for these calculation procedures):

R_{wall} = 22 (overall wall *R*-value: 2x6 studs, $5^1/_2$-in. fiberglass insulation, wood sheathing and siding, and drywall)

$R_{ceiling}$ = 40 (overall ceiling *R*-value: 12-in. blown cellulose insulation and drywall)

$N_{E,W,N}$ = 3 (number of glazing layers: triple glazing; alternatively, use double glazing with low-emissivity coating).

$R_{perimeter}$ = 20 (perimeter insulation *R*-value: 4-in. extruded polystyrene foam added).

Effective ACH = 0.25. (Since less than 0.5, a heat recovery unit is required: use a large unit with distribution and 70% efficiency: see Chapter 6.)

Next, calculate the passive solar heating performance of the proposed design as follows using Part II of the Passive Solar Worksheet.

4. Calculate the *UA* for each building element (except the solar wall) using the appropriate formula on the worksheet:

Walls: $(UA)_{wall} = A_{wall} \div R_{wall}$ = 1050 ÷ 22 = 48

Ceiling: $(UA)_{ceiling} = A_{ceiling} \div R_{ceiling}$ = 1550 ÷ 40 = 39

E, W, N glass: $(UA)_{glass} = 1.1 \times A_{E,W,N} \div$ number of glazings = 1.1 x 140 ft² ÷ 3 = 51

Slab-on-grade: $(UA)_{perim} = 4.17 \times P_{perim} \div (R_{perim} + 5) = 4.17 \times 170 \div (20 + 5) = 28$

Infiltration: $(UA)_{infil} = 0.018 \times VOL \times ACH \times ADR = 0.018 \times 12,400 \times 0.25 \times 0.97 = 54$ (the value of ADR is 0.97, based on Indianapolis elevation of 807 ft from LCR table in Appendix D).

5. Sum these *UA*'s to equal 220 Btu/h•°F.

6. Calculate the *NLC* = sum *UA* x 24 (to convert to DD) = 5280 Btu/DD.

7. Calculate the *recommended* A_p. As a preliminary guide for sizing a cost-effective passive solar heating system, the "recommended" A_p is approximately equal to the NLC (from step 6) divided by the recommended LCR (from step 1; this will yield a comfortable and cost-effective design based on local weather, probable construction costs, and auxiliary fuel cost savings).

Recommended A_p = NLC ÷ recommended LCR = 5280 ÷ 40 = 132 ft²

8. Select an appropriate reference design from Appendix B. Although the building may evolve with several passive system types, a preliminary calculation is made assuming only a single system — the major system.

In this case, a large sunspace is anticipated and system SSD2 (semienclosed, 50° sloped glazing, opaque end walls, double glazing, masonry common wall, night insulation) is selected. Enter the name of the reference design (SSD2 in this case) and its $U_{collector}$ (0.26 from Appendix B) on the worksheet.

9. The designed A_p is based on this recommended A_p as adjusted for practical construction or design considerations (for example, make A_p a multiple of the net area of a standard-sized glazing component).

Select a typical glazing unit (from manufacturer's literature for example) and determine the net glazed area in ft². For example, unframed insulated glass units 76 in. by 46 in. are used, then the net area is 75 x 45 ÷ 144 = 23.4 ft² (1 in. has been deducted from the glass dimensions for mounting in glazing stops; dividing by 144 converts in² to ft²).

Since the glazing slope β in this example is 50° (and cos β = 0.77), then the projected area per unit A_{unit} = 23.4 x 0.77 = 18 ft².

The required number of glazing units N_{unit} = recommended A_p ÷ A_{unit} = 132 ÷ 18 = 7.3. In this case, eight glazing units are selected for practical construction and design reasons. Therefore, the designed A_p = 8 x 18 = 144.

10. Calculate the design LCR = NCR ÷ A_p = 5280 ÷ 144 = 36.7 Btu/DD.

11. Look up SSF = 42 percent in Appendix D (for Indianapolis for system SSD2 and interpolate between LCR = 40 and 30) and enter on worksheet as decimal fraction 0.42.

Compare this to the *recommended SSF* from step 1 = 0.30. The system is appears moderately overdesigned, but is well within the recommended ±15 percent range.

12. Look up $U_{collector}$ from Appendix B (in Table B.5 for this SSD2 system) = 0.26. Calculate the $(UA)_{collector}$ = A_p x $U_{collector}$ = 144 x 0.26 = 37.4 Btu/h•°F.

13. Calculate total load coefficient (for sizing auxiliary heating equipment):

TLC = NLC + [24 x $(UA)_{collector}$] = 5280 + (24 x 37.4) = 6168 Btu/DD.

14. Look up heating DD_{55} = 3440 (from Appendix D for Indianapolis; use 55°F base temperature instead of 65°F because this building is passive-solar-heated and has a balance point temperature well below that of a conventional residential building).

15. Calculate Q_{aux} = NLC x DD x (1 – SSF) = 5280 x 3440 x (1 – 0.42) ÷ 10⁶ = 10.5 M Btu/yr.

MIXED SYSTEMS

For buildings that incorporate more than one passive system type, calculate a single LCR based on the NLC and the total projected area for all the apertures in the building. Then look up the SSF for each of the systems in Appendix B. The correct SSF for the building is the average of these SSF values weighted proportionally to the projected glazing area A_p.

EXAMPLE PROBLEM B (see worksheet Fig. 12.3)

This example follows the same building as the previous problem into a later stage of schematic design. Conservation levels are the same but the passive solar design has evolved into a mixture of three systems. As a result of the redesign, some of the building areas have changed:

Exterior opaque wall area = 1100 ft²

Roof area = 1520 ft²

E, W, N window area = 130 ft²

Perimeter length = 180 linear ft (slab on grade)

Volume (ceiling height x floor area) = 12,160 ft³

1 - 3. These steps remain unchanged (because the conservation factors have not changed).

4. Calculate the *UA* for each building element (except the solar wall) using the appropriate formula on the worksheet. As in the previous example, the value of ADR remains 0.97; selected *R*-values also are unchanged:

Walls: $(UA)_{wall} = A_{wall} \div R_{wall} = 1100 \div 22 = 48$

Ceiling: $(UA)_{ceiling} = A_{ceiling} \div R_{ceiling} = 1550 \div 40 = 39$

E, W, N glass: $(UA)_{glass} = 1.1 \times A_{E,W,N} \div$ number of glazings $= 1.1 \times 140$ ft² $\div 3 = 51$

Slab-on-grade: $(UA)_{perim} = 4.17 \times P_{perim} \div (R_{perim} + 5) = 4.17 \times 170 \div (20 + 5) = 28$

Infiltration: $(UA)_{infil} = 0.018 \times VOL \times ACH \times ADR = 0.018 \times 12,400 \times 0.25 \times 0.97 = 54$

5. Sum these *UA*'s to equal 219 Btu/h•°F.

6. Calculate the NLC = sum *UA* x 24 (to convert to *DD*) = 5256 Btu/DD.

7. Calculate the recommended projected area = NLC ÷ recommended LCR = 5256 ÷ 40 = 131.4 (in other words, between 120 and 140).

8. The reference designs are selected from Appendix B and include SSD2 (semienclosed sunspace with 50° sloped glazing, opaque end walls, double glazing, masonry common wall, night insulation), DGC3 (direct gain with double glazing, night insulation, with 4-in. thickness of brick thermal storage mass), and TWJ2 (unvented Trombe wall with 12-in. concrete wall, double glazing, selective surface, no night insulation).

Enter the name of the reference designs and their respective $U_{collector}$ (0.26, 0.26, 0.20) on the worksheet.

9. Determine the *design* projected area A_p (based on the above total recommended projected area and other design and construction considerations) for each reference design (sunspace SSD2 = 50 ft², direct gain DGC3 = 40 ft², and selective surface Trombe wall TWJ2 = 30 ft²) and sum for total A_p = 120 ft².

Enter the fraction of the total A_p for each system (0.417, 0.333, and 0.25, respectively).

Sum these to equal 120 ft² and enter under *design* A_p on the worksheet.

10. Calculate the LCR = NCR ÷ total A_p = 5256 ÷ 120 = 43.8 Btu/DD•ft² (note that the A_p used here is the design A_p).

11. For each design, look up SSF in Appendix D for LCR = 43.8: 37% (for SSD2), 27% (for DGC3), and 24% (for TWJ2), and enter these percent values of SSF as decimal values on the worksheet.

For each design, multiply the A_p fraction x the respective SSF = product of SSF and Fraction = 0.16 (for SSD1), 0.09 (for DGC1), and 0.06 (for TWJ2) for a sum total SSF = 0.31.

The *design* SSF almost matches the *recommended* SSF (0.31 vs 0.30), so the design is satisfactory.

12. Look up $U_{collector}$ from Appendix B for each system and calculate the $(UA)_{collector}$ for each:

$(UA)_{collector} = A_p \times U_{collector}$ (13.0, 10.4, and 6.0, respectively).

Sum the $(UA)_{collector}$ = total $(UA)_{collector}$ = 29.4 Btu/h•°F.

13. Calculate the total load coefficient (for sizing auxiliary heating equipment):

TLC = NLC + [24 x $(UA)_{collector}$] = 5256 + (24 x 29.4) = 5961 Btu/DD.

14. Look up Heating DD_{55} = 3440 (from Appendix D for Indianapolis).

15. Calculate Q_{aux} = NLC x DD x (1 − SSF) = 5256 x 3440 x (1 − 0.31) x 10^{-6} = 12.5 M Btu/yr.

PASSIVE SOLAR WORKSHEET

Project **Example A** Date — Analyst **FM** Location **Minneapolis** Fuel cost (circle one): low/**high**

Part I: RECOMMENDED DESIGN GUIDELINES (for this location and fuel cost)

Recommended CF (Appendix D) = **1.76**; recommended LCR (Appendix D) = **40**; target SSF (Appendix D) = **30** %.

Recommended wall total *R*-value: R_{wall} = 14 × CF = **25**

Recommended ceiling total *R*-value: $R_{ceiling}$ = 22 × CF = **39**

Recommended *R*-value to be added to slab perimeter: $R_{perimeter}$ = (13 × CF) − 5 = **18**

Recommended floor (over vented space) total *R*-value: R_{floor} = 14 × CF = **25**

Recommended *R*-value to be added to basement wall: $R_{basement}$ = (16 × CF) − 8 = **17**

Recommended number of glazing layers on E, W, N walls: $N_{E,W,N}$ = 1.7 × CF = **3**

Recommended number of air changes per hour: ACH = 0.42 ÷ CF = **0.24**

Part II: PERFORMANCE CALCULATIONS BASED ON PROPOSED DESIGN

Building element: **load formula** (fill in blanks and calculate)   = **Load, *UA***

Walls: $(UA)_{wall}$ = A_{wall} ÷ R_{wall} = 1050 ÷ 22 = **48**

Ceiling: $(UA)_{ceiling}$ = $A_{ceiling}$ ÷ $R_{ceiling}$ = 1550 ÷ 40 = **39**

E, W, N glass: $(UA)_{glass}$ = 1.1 × $A_{E,W,N}$ ÷ number of glazings = 1.1 × **140** ft² ÷ **3** = **51**

Floor: $(UA)_{floor}$ = A_{floor} × R_{floor} × ___ ÷ ___ = **NA**

Slab-on-grade: $(UA)_{perim}$ = 4.17 × P_{perim} ÷ (R_{perim} + 5) = 4.17 × **170** ÷ (**20** + 5) = **28**

Basement: $(UA)_{base}$ = 10.7 × P_{base} ÷ (R_{base} + 8) = 10.7 × ___ ÷ (___ + 8) = **NA**

Infiltration: $(UA)_{Infil}$ = 0.018 × VOL × ACH × ADR = 0.018 × **12,400** × 0.25 × 0.97 = **54**

Sum of *UA* = **220** Btu/h•°F

Net load coefficient NLC = 24 × Sum of *UA* = **5280** Btu/DD

Recommended projected area: A_p = NLC ÷ recommended LCR = 5280 ÷ 40 = **132** ft²

Design A_p (based on recommended A_p and construction considerations) = **144** ft²

Load collector ratio: LCR = NLC ÷ Design A_p = 5280 ÷ 40 = **36.7** Btu/DD•ft²

Name of reference design	Design Projected Area, A_p	Fraction of Projected Area		SSF for each ref. design		Product of SSF × Fraction	
SSD2	**144** ft²	x	**1.0**	x	**0.42**	=	**0.42**
	___ ft²	x	___	x	___	=	___
	___ ft²	x	___	x	___	=	___

total design A_p = **144** ft²   combined (sum) SSF = **0.42**

	A_p × U_{col} (Appx. B)		= $(UA)_{collector}$
	A_p × 0.26		= **37.4**
	A_p × ___		= ___
	A_p × ___		= ___

Total $(UA)_{col}$ = **37.4** Btu/h•°F

Total load coefficient (for sizing auxiliary heating equipment), TLC = NLC + [24 × $(UA)_{collector}$] = **6168** Btu/DD

Auxiliary heat, Q_{aux} = NLC × DD (1 − SSF) = **5280** × **3440** × (1 − **0.42**) ÷ 10^6 = **10.5** M Btu/year

Figure 12.3: Completed worksheet for Example Problem B (blank worksheet from Appendix F).

PASSIVE SOLAR WORKSHEET

Project _Example B_ Date _–_ Analyst _FM_ Location _Indianapolis_ Fuel cost (circle one): low / (high)

Part I: RECOMMENDED DESIGN GUIDELINES (for this location and fuel cost)

Recommended CF (Appendix D) = _1.76_; recommended LCR (Appendix D) = _40_ ; target SSF (Appendix D) = _30_ %.

Recommended wall total R-value:	R_{wall} = 14 × CF	= _25_
Recommended ceiling total R-value:	$R_{ceiling}$ = 22 × CF	= _39_
Recommended R-value to be added to slab perimeter:	$R_{perimeter}$ = (13 × CF) − 5	= _18_
Recommended floor (over vented space) total R-value:	R_{floor} = 14 × CF	= _25_
Recommended R-value to be added to basement wall:	$R_{basement}$ = (16 × CF) − 8	= _17_
Recommended number of glazing layers on E, W, N walls:	$N_{E,W,N}$ = 1.7 × CF	= _3_
Recommended number of air changes per hour:	ACH = 0.42 ÷ CF	= _0.24_

Part II: PERFORMANCE CALCULATIONS BASED ON PROPOSED DESIGN

Building element: load formula (fill in blanks and calculate)

					= Load, UA
Walls:	$(UA)_{wall}$	= A_{wall} ÷ R_{wall} = 1100 ÷ 22			= _50_
Ceiling:	$(UA)_{ceiling}$	= $A_{ceiling}$ ÷ $R_{ceiling}$ = 1520 ÷ 40			= _39_
E, W, N glass:	$(UA)_{glass}$	= 1.1 × $A_{E,W,N}$ ÷ number of glazings = 1.1 × 130 ft² ÷ 3			= _48_
Floor :	$(UA)_{floor}$	= A_{floor} × R_{floor} × ____ ÷ ____			= _NA_
Slab-on-grade:	$(UA)_{perim}$	= 4.17 × P_{perim} ÷ (R_{perim} + 5) = 4.17 × 180 ÷ (20 + 5)			= _30_
Basement:	$(UA)_{base}$	= 10.7 × P_{base} ÷ (R_{base} + 8) = 10.7 × ____ ÷ (____ + 8)			= _NA_
Infiltration:	$(UA)_{Infil}$	= 0.018 × VOL × ACH × ADR = 0.018 × 12,160 × 0.25 × 0.97			= _53_

Sum of UA = _219_ Btu/h·°F

Net load coefficient NLC = 24 × Sum of UA = _5256_ Btu/DD

Recommended projected area: A_p = NLC ÷ recommended LCR = 5256 ÷ 40 = _131.4_ ft²

Design A_p (based on recommended A_p and construction considerations) = _120_ ft²

Load collector ratio: LCR = NLC ÷ Design A_p = 5256 ÷ 120 = _43.8_ Btu/DD·ft²

Name of reference design	Design Projected Area, A_p		Fraction of Projected Area		SSF for each ref. design		Product of SSF × Fraction			$A_p \times U_{col}$ (Appx. B)	= $(UA)_{collector}$
SSD2	50	ft²	0.417	×	0.37	=	0.16		A_p × 0.26 =	13.0	
DGC3	40	ft²	0.333	×	0.27	=	0.09		A_p × 0.26 =	10.4	
TWJ2	30	ft²	0.250	×	0.24	=	0.06		A_p × 0.20 =	6.0	
total design A_p = 120 ft²			**combined (sum) SSF**			=	0.31		**Total $(UA)_{col}$** =	29.4	

Total load coefficient (for sizing auxiliary heating equipment), TLC = NLC + [24 × $(UA)_{collector}$] = 5256 + [24 × (UA) collector] = _5961_ Btu/DD

Auxiliary heat, Q_{aux} = NLC × DD (1 − SSF) = NLC × DD × (1 − SSF) = 5256 × 3440 × (1 − 0.31) ÷ 10⁶ = _12.5_ M Btu/year

Figure 12.2: Completed worksheet for Example Problem A (blank worksheet from Appendix F).

BEYOND THE LCR METHOD

The Los Alamos group has also developed a more detailed method for predicting the thermal performance of a building on a month-by-month basis: the monthly *SLR* method (Balcomb et al., 1984). This method is recommended for nonresidential buildings that have unusual occupancy and internal heat load patterns, and wherever a more detailed picture of solar heating performance is needed. The SLR calculations are considerably more extensive than the annual LCR method and are beyond the scope of this book. Because of their complexity, a number of computer programs and spreadsheet templates have been developed to facilitate analysis of various design options.

SUMMARY OF TERMS

Mixed system — a combination of two or more passive solar heating system types into a single building.

Total load coefficient, TLC (Btu/°F•day) — the steady-state load (or heat loss) of a building per degree of inside-outside temperature difference per day.

Net load coefficient, NLC (Btu/°F•day) — the total load coefficient minus the load coefficient of the solar wall.

Projected collector area (ft²) — the projected area A_p of a direct-gain, Trombe wall, or water wall solar window is equal to the net glazing area. In the case of a sunspace, the projected area is the net glazing area projected onto a single vertical plane.

Load-collector ratio, LCR (Btu/°F•day•ft²) — the ratio of the net load coefficient to the projected collector area.

Base temperature, T_b (°F) — a fixed temperature against which the ambient temperature is compared for the purpose of degree-day calculations.

Degree-day, DD (°F•day) — the difference between the base temperature and the mean ambient temperature for the day; if the mean ambient temperature is above the base temperature, no degree-days are counted.

Solar savings fraction, SSF (dimensionless) — the ratio of the solar savings (Q_{sav}; heat savings due to solar) to the net reference load (Q_{net}).

Solar savings, Q_{sav} (Btu) — the energy savings due to a passive solar heating system relative to the energy requirement of a comparable nonsolar building that has an energy-neutral wall in place of the solar wall and a fixed indoor reference temperature.

Net reference load, Q_{net} (Btu) — the building heat loss, excluding heat loss through the solar wall, over a period of time.

Auxiliary heat, Q_{aux} (Btu) — the amount of heat furnished by an auxiliary heating system (e.g., a furnace) to keep a building warm.

Internal heat, Q_{aux} (Btu) — the amount of heat generated within a building by incidental sources such as people, lights, appliances, etc. Internal heat does not include heat furnished by the auxiliary heating system.

Net glazing area, A_n (ft²) — the actual area of the solar wall glazing; the "solar aperture."

Tilt angle, TILT — the angle (measured in degrees) between the plane of the solar glazing and the horizontal plane; the angle of the glazing slope relative to the horizontal.

Azimuth angle, AZ — the orientation angle (measured in degrees) between true south and the orientation of the glazing angle. The azimuth angle of a south-facing glazing is zero; of an east-facing glazing is 90°E; of a west-facing glazing is 90°W.

Orientation — the compass direction that the glazing is facing.

STUDY QUESTION

1. Explain how it is possible for a direct-gain building to offset more than half of its total annual heat loss with solar gain and still use more auxiliary heating energy than a comparable non-solar building.

$$13$$

FORMAL SPECULATIONS ON THERMAL DIAGRAMS*

by Harrison Fraker, Jr.

In the history of modern architecture, approaches to the technology of environmental control have had a significant impact on the formal expression of many important buildings. As Reyner Banham has explained, the elegant abstraction and detailing of the Seagram Building would not have been possible without advances in HVAC technology, which provide comfort through the use of inexpensive "concealed power." Documenting a change in the attitude of designers about the importance of mechanical equipment, Banham cites Kahn's Richards Medical Building as a seminal expression of "exposed power."

Passive design is an obvious reaction to positions of both concealed and exposed power. Rather than relying on HVAC equipment and the consumption of hidden energy to provide comfort, passive design seeks to use the form and envelope of a building to act as mediator between climate and people, providing comfort by natural energy flows. Although there are many successful technical examples of this approach, the integration of passive design concepts into the formal language and aesthetics of architecture has been limited at best. The causes are complex and reveal in part the extent to which our reliance on HVAC systems and artificial lighting have cut us off from experiencing thermal and luminous phenomena.

In the early stages of the passive design movement, some designers took the approach of showing off the special features of passive design, such as Trombe walls or sunspaces. Because the mere presence of a passive element symbolized a conservation ethic, many designers were lulled into a sense of moral superiority and developed the architecture no further; or they became absorbed in solving the many detail problems of an emerging technology. In the best examples, the thermal diagrams became the architecture, and in the worst, passive elements were attached to buildings in a superficial or awkward fashion.

Most of the serious research going on concurrently focuses on understanding and validating the technical performance of design concepts, classifying systems into direct gain, mass wall (indirect gain), and sunspaces (isolated gain) and carefully defining such components as the collector, absorber, storage, and distribution subsystems. All of this activity is essential in any emerging technology. The principles and components of passive design, however, have physical consequences that go beyond technical performance. They can profoundly influence our perception of architectural space and our understanding of formal concepts. As we refine the technical performance of passive design prototypes, it is important that the designers begin to explore their latent formal content.

A complete understanding of the relevance of passive concepts on architectural form goes beyond the formal analysis of visual qualities alone. It requires the perception and understanding of thermal and luminous phenomena which are not visible in the same sense as architectural space. Boundaries in the thermal or luminous environment are subtle and not sharply defined, although a Trombe wall can create a radiant thermal space or a clerestory window can provide gradations of luminous space just as real as the boundaries of the architectural space. Before architects can make passive design concepts a part of their architectural language, they must understand the spatial implications of the thermal and luminous environment.

SPATIAL VS. SOLAR LAYERING

David Wright's simple direct-gain house in Santa Fe (Fig. 13.1a) has a strong differentiation between the back (north) and the front (south). The south side is entirely glass; the north side is almost entirely solid except for a

---

*Text and illustrations reprinted by permission from Fraker, H., 1984, "Formal speculations on thermal diagrams," *Progressive Architecture,* April, pp. 104-108.

few ventilation windows. This contrast can be described as an opposition between solid/void or open/closed. In this building, the thermal diagram and the formal object are almost synchronous; the progression from light to dark (luminous space) and the mass walls that create a radiant enclosure (thermal space) match the visible qualities of the object. With such a strong image or gestalt, it is easy to orient oneself both inside and outside the building. Yet, where does one enter? In Wright's plan, the little air-lock entry on one side is a modest response to an opportunity rich in potential. If the building were entered along a central axis (Fig. 13.1b), the composition would force a response to its frontality — to the experience of the building as a sequence of layers progressing from closed to open, from dark to light, from a heavy, warm radiant adobe to brittle cold glass. This axial sequence raises its own set of questions: What is to the right or left of the axis? Is the sequence made up of a chain of events with some structured rhythm or references to what might be at the end of the sequence? All of these questions are generic to a formal parti where the axial sequence and spatial layering are coincident with the solar orientation and thermal zones of the object. Having recognized this latent formal potential, it is interesting to examine how other solar buildings have explored this parti.

COINCIDENT SPATIAL AND SOLAR LAYERING

The New Hampshire Conservation Center by Banwell, White & Arnold (Fig. 13.2) has a similar kind of differentiation between open and closed as in David Wright's house. The entry axis is also from the north, but rather than approaching small air lock at the end of the building, one approaches a bermed, closed facade frontally with its entry slightly off center. This makes it similar in composition to the frontal, axial version of the Wright house.

On the simplest functional level, the entry axis divides the building into a public meeting room (right) and private offices and work area (left). The entry sequence approaches frontally the primary passive solar element, a two story direct-gain window, which, in turn, frames the major site view as the axial terminus beyond. The planar position of the window acts as a formal reference in plan and is transformed in section as one moves along its edge in either direction from the entry. On the left, it becomes a clerestory window providing heating and daylighting, with rows of thermal water tubes and structural columns creating a circulation spine for the work spaces. On the right, it becomes an attached sunspace, which provides heating for the meeting room and a link to an adjacent building. The solar collector thus organizes the building, providing a physical datum that creates different zones of thermal and luminous space appropriate to each function. The building's spatial organization is layered in response to these thermal and luminous zones

similar to Wright's plan. Unlike Wright's direct-gain window, however, this passive collector differs along its length, creating a rich spatial experience.

Donald Watson's little "Belvedere" house on Block Island (Fig. 13.3) explores similar formal ideas: a progression of spatial layers, from closed to open, which here is organized into a service zone, living zone, and solar zone. These layers are clearly delineated in both plan and section. However, Watson

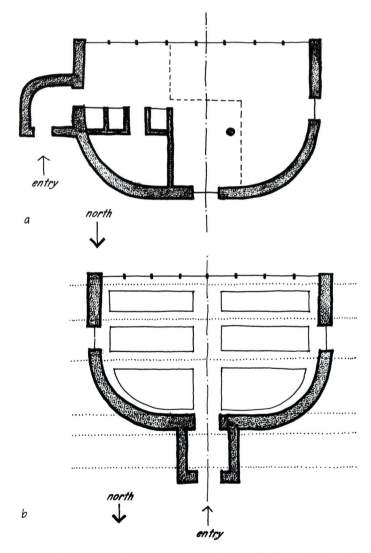

Figure 13.1: Residence, Albuquerque, New Mexico (D. Wright, architect): (a) plan as built, and (b) alternative plan, symmetrical with centered north entry axis.

has added an additional formal theme: The entry axis, fireplace, and belvedere create a strong centrality, reinforced by the lines of the hipped roof. The open deck with bowed seat, flanked by the symmetrical sunspaces, forms a protected niche and an appropriate end to the progression. In addition, the entry sequence has a clever move in plan and section that introduces the experience of centrality. The fireplace is positioned on axis, blocking passage,

forcing movement off axis. At this juncture, the section is opened to the belvedere, revealing it as a kind of baldacchino around which one must move. It is only after reoccupying the seating area around the hearth and underneath the belvedere that one is back on axis with relationship to the open deck and view. Thus, the thermal concepts of centralized natural ventilation and solar layering have been developed into primary and secondary architectural themes within a composition that has the integrity and directness of vernacular prototypes.

Both of the layered schemes discussed above have their entry sequence from north to south. The experience has an element of contradiction in approaching the closed back of the building and moving toward the open front. What are some of the formal potentials when the sequence is reversed, when the sun is at one's back and the approach is toward the solar front?

The prototype for the Mercer County Libraries by Harrison Fraker Architects (Fig. 13.4) explores some of these potentials. Again, the building is approached frontally, but the major passive solar element, a clerestory window that runs the entire length of the library, is in the middle of the building over the reading rooms. This massing creates a large-scale frame of reference against which the lower front section is perceived as preparatory to arrival in the main space.

The plan is organized into functional layers, which correspond to gradations in luminous space created by the clerestory and in thermal space created by the Trombe wall. The solar elements articulate important transitions between layers. The Trombe wall establishes the front plane of the building, while the clerestory marks the separation between staff and reading space and creates a sense of being outside. On the other side of the reading space, a colonnade of thermal water tubes forms a transition between the reading area and stacks. The spatial layers are "pinned" together by the entry axis, developed with a series of related architectural events: a semicircular sundial entry, a lobby with a pyramidal skylight, a kiosk for the card catalogs, and a periodical reading area carved out of the stacks.

Not only have the spatial layers been developed out of the thermal and luminous diagrams, but the solar elements, which make reference to historical forms, reveal intentions about each of the spatial layers they occupy. In this sense, formal qualities of the thermal diagram have been developed into an architectural language for the whole building.

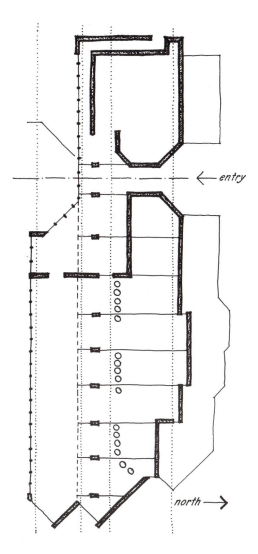

Figure 13.2: New Hampshire Conservation Center plan (Banwell, White, and Arnold, architects).

OPPOSED SOLAR AND SPATIAL LAYERING

Returning to the Wright house (Fig. 13.5), what if the object was approached on axis with its end rather than its center? The differentiation of open and closed would be experienced as a progression from side to side, with the axis of movement 90° to the spatial layering created by the thermal and luminous gradations. Architecturally, this is one of the more difficult partis to resolve because the building has two fronts, solar and entry. Furthermore, it is difficult to know both where and how to enter the end of a section that has such a strong contrast from side to side.

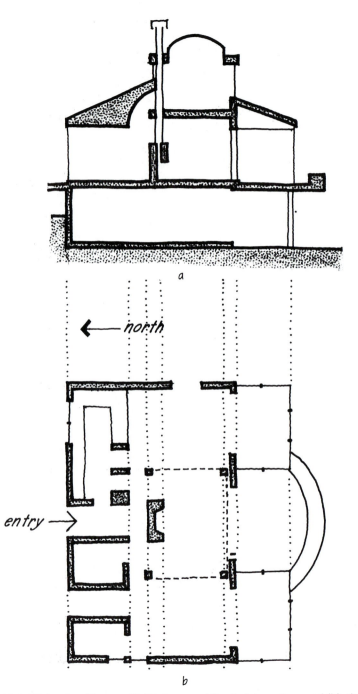

Figure 13.3: "Belvedere" house (D. Watson, architect): (a) section, and (b) plan.

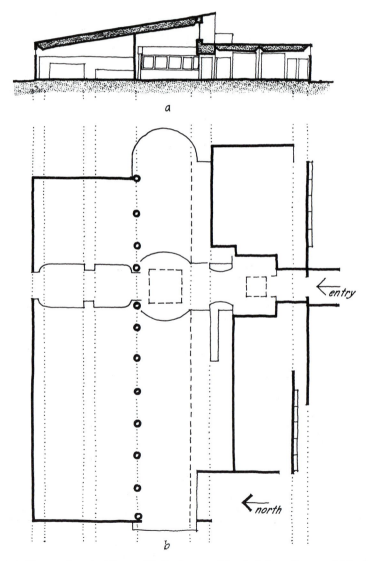

Figure 13.4: Mercer County Library (H. Fraker, architect): (a) section, and (b) plan.

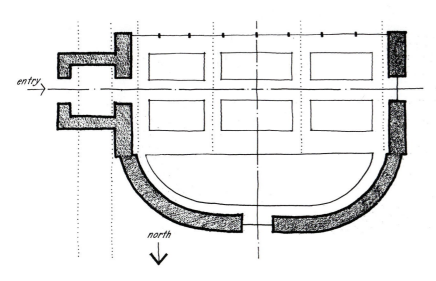

Figure 13.5: Residence, Albuquerque, New Mexico (D. Wright, architect): alternative plan, symmetrical about end entry axis.

One approach to that dilemma is taken by Kelbaugh & Lee in their Milford Reservation Environmental Center (Fig. 13.6). In this case the major circulation street is located along the edge of the solar glazing, that is, on the open side of the section. Thermal and luminous gradations occur at 90° to the direction of movement and correspond to a series of minor cross axes, in plan and section, which move from the public street to private sleeping quarters. Spatial definition along the axis of movement is provided by a modulation in the column grid at the cross axes and a corresponding widening of the street on one side to accommodate the front doors, windows, and stairs of the sleeping quarters. The movement along the line of glass and the frontality of the wall facing the solar orientation and the street create a tension generic to the parti. The architecture explores this tension well beyond the initial thermal diagram.

Entering such a building is extremely difficult. Kelbaugh's solution is one of the most direct. The building section and corresponding end elevation are sharply sloped toward the south, but rather than trying to find an intermediate entry point in the slope, he has pulled a small-scale portico forward at the low end, with its local symmetry centering on the circulation axis beyond. Thus the architecture of the entry is developed directly out of the formal interpretation of the thermal diagram.

By comparison, Buchanan and Watson have placed the entry to the New Canaan Horticultural Education Center (Fig. 13.7) on the center axis of its end elevation. Here again the south side is open (glazed) and the north is closed. Unlike the single-sloped roof in one direction at Milford, however, the two sides

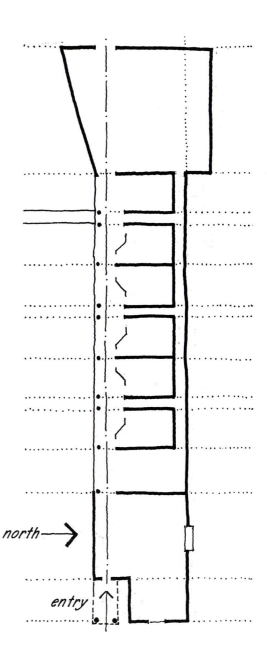

Figure 13.6: Milford Reservation Environmental Center plan (Kelbaugh and Lee, architects).

in New Canaan slope in opposite directions, creating a gabled shape. Relying on the unifying strength of this form, Watson plays up the distinction between north and south as a stark contrast between greenhouse and roof rather than

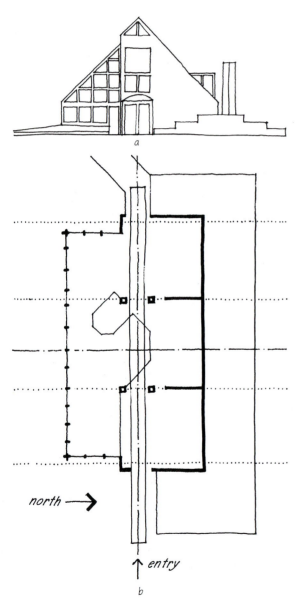

Figure 13.7: New Canaan Horticulture Education Center (Buchanan and Watson, architects): (a) elevation, and (b) plan.

as a progression from solid to void. The intersection of these similar yet contrasting halves creates a logical position for entry and the central circulation axis; a slight shift in the ridge of the greenhouse glazing further articulates the central spine and its continuous gabled skylight. The spine's strong linear sequence is divided into three bays. The central bay has a rotated stair and double-height space creating a minor center and frontality to the solar cross axis. The successful architectural development of these solutions demonstrates the formal potential inherent in the dilemma posed by an entry sequence at right angles to the solar orientation.

Both Milford and New Canaan respond to the differences between north and south created by the solar diagram through asymmetry—even at New Canaan, which is entered in the middle. By comparison, Princeton Professional Park (Fig. 13.8), designed by Harrison Fraker, Architects, has a symmetrical facade on its approach axis. Can a solar building ignore the differentiation between north and south? At Princeton, the facade's symmetry is countered by the asymmetrical operation of the glazed atrium's movable insulation and by the more or less even distribution of daylighting through the atrium clerestory windows in both directions. The luminous diagram thus enables a symmetrical entry when its axis is at right angles to the solar orientation.

SOLAR DATUM

Doug Kelbaugh's house (Fig. 13.9), as a formal object, has many of the same qualities of orientation, definition, and spatial layering as the Wright house, with one obvious difference. A concrete Trombe wall is placed just behind the all-glass south facade, introducing a contradiction: What is normally perceived as open or void is now closed. The Trombe wall dominates the plan, elevation, and section. Its orientation to the sun and its differentiation from the other walls create a powerful sense of place, both outside and inside, while its sheer size provides a datum or organizing element whose location, dimension, and treatment are of great architectural interest. As with the Wright house, the Kelbaugh house's thermal and formal diagrams are synchronous, producing a powerful gestalt with a number of possible architectural permutations.

Kelbaugh & Lee and Don Prowler have further developed the idea of using a solar element as a datum or formal reference for their winning submission to the Monroeville Civic Center competition (Fig. 13.10). The major datum or formal reference is not a solid Trombe wall, but a linear sunspace. Not only is it a multifunctioning solar device, but its size and linearity organize a series of disparate spaces which are plugged into one side. The sunspace also creates a powerful facade, which acts as a backdrop for a civic open space and isolates

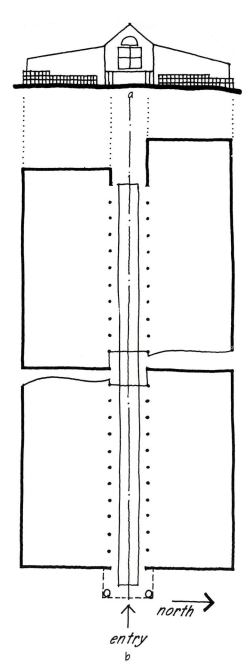

Figure 13.8: Princeton Professional Park (H. Fraker, architect): (a) elevation, and (b) plan.

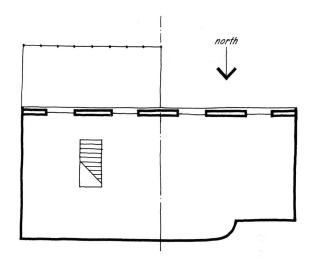

Figure 13.9: Residence, Princeton, New Jersey (D. Kelbaugh, architect), upper plan.

the town hall as a ceremonial object. The strong frontality of the entry sequence (coincident with the solar orientation) and the axial rotation of the town hall show how a single formal reference can help articulate subtle differences between the natural and man-made context.

AXIAL ROTATION

In Santa Fe, Unit One at First Village (Fig. 13.11), designed by Bill Lumpkins and Susan Nichols, illustrates another kind of latent formal potential. The spatial organization of the building wraps two wings of living space around a sunspace, with a spiral stair at the pivot, for both vertical circulation and natural ventilation. The orientation of the sunspace is due south, while the two wings are oriented at a 45° angle, producing a triangular plan. One of the thermal consequences of this organization is that the least amount of exterior wall area faces north. A more interesting formal consequence, however, is that the living space and facade are rotated 45° off the solar orientation. The thermal diagram is no longer synchronous with the formal orientation.

Unit One divides the two orientations by thermal storage walls, thus delineating the split. A further development, where some spaces are put on the solar orientation and others are oriented to the context, produces what Colin Rowe and Robert Slutzky have described as "phenomenal transparency," where the two orientations become overlaid. That raises several questions: How should one approach such an object? What elements should be placed on

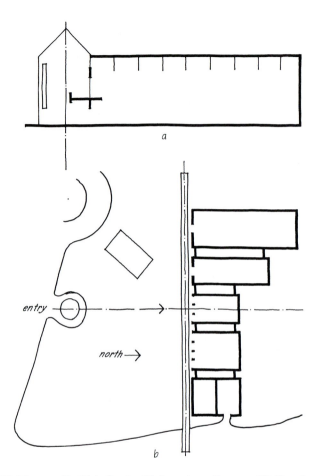

Figure 13.10: Monroeville Civic Center (Kelbaugh and Lee, and D. Prowler, architects): (a) section, and (b) plan.

which axis to articulate their difference? How should the rotation be experienced? And so on. All of these formal issues grow out of the potential opposition between the thermal and contextual orientations. The differentiations refer to real qualities of the site (context) and nature (sun) and not just to the building's own form.

DEFORMED OBJECT

One architectural approach to a building that has two diagonally opposed orientations is to deform it in response to one of the orientations. In the Shelly

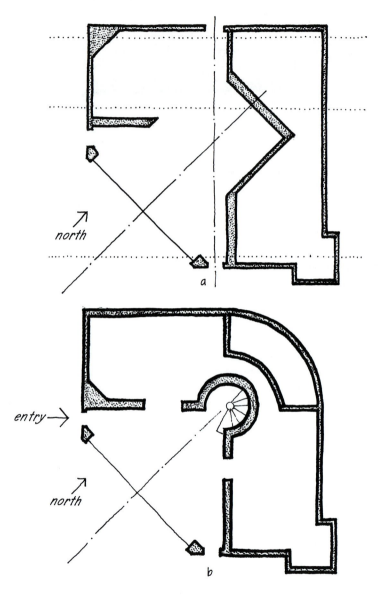

Figure 13.11: Unit One, First Village (W. Lumpkins and S. Nichols, architect and designer): (a) plan as built, and (b) alternative plan, with some spaces oriented to solar and others to context.

Ridge Girl Scout Center (Fig. 13.12) by Bohlin Cywinski Jackson, the main building has a large, gabled shape. While the entry axis corresponds to the long axis of the gable and to the symmetrical treatment of the windows in the upper

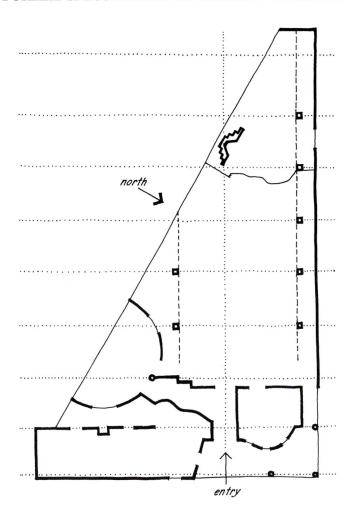

Figure 13.12: Shelly Ridge Girl Scout Center (Bohlin Cywinski Jackson, architects), plan.

face of the gable, the local asymmetry of the front porch responds to the deformation of the other end and side of the gabled form by an angled glass facade, oriented south (Cook, 1984).

The architects use the intersection between the primary axis of the gable and the angled facade to locate the fireplace, with the glazing that steps up around the fireplace creating a local center along the south facade. Procession from the entry to the fireplace is blocked by a central column, forcing a choice between moving around the column or turning to the side and proceeding

along a curvilinear path to an apsidal sundial space that fronts on the solar orientation. Thus, the architectural language has grown out of the "collision" of the two orientations.

SOLAR ORIENTATION FIXED, CONTEXT ROTATED

Another architectural response to diagonally opposed orientations occurs in a small house at the Girl Scout Center (Fig. 13.13). In contrast with the previous example, the primary axes of this centroidal house coincide with the solar orientation, rather than with the connected buildings. The two orientations, apparent in the house's angled entrance, come together at the hearth in the center of the plan, where the hearth and woodstove are rotated onto the geometry of the context and the four columns are rotated onto the geometry of the enclosing walls. The center not only has a kind of "phenomenal transparency," with one orientation overlaid on the other; it responds to the centroidal thermal space created by the wood stove. Thus, the architectural expressions of "transparency" and "centrality" have acquired meaning from a thermal concept and from the tension between a primary solar orientation and an angled context.

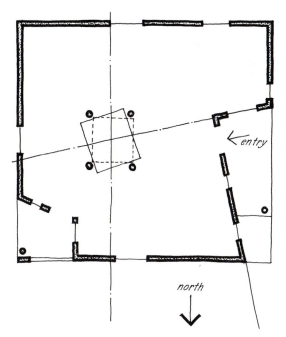

Figure 13.13: "Small house," Shelly Ridge Girl Scout Center (Bohlin Cywinski Jackson, architects), plan.

CONTEXT FIXED, SOLAR ORIENTATION ROTATED

Richard Levine's house (Fig. 13.14) reverses the primacy of the solar orientation over the context. The square plan sets up the primary orientation, with the solar orientation expressed as a diagonal transformation. The resulting "transparency" is best experienced on the central stair, which has the same orientation as the primary square envelope, but which also occupies the middle of a rotated center space that is oriented to the sloped solar glazing. The dialogue between the two orientations creates a rich architectural experience, compensating for the almost incidental entry. In all three of the examples above, the formal potential of "transparency" has been given a new meaning because of its generation out of solar and thermal necessity.

CONCLUSION

This only begins to articulate the architectural possibilities of passive design prototypes; many more remain to be explored. However, this beginning is intended to challenge designers to investigate these latent formal potentials—not only to diagram technical energy flows but also to appreciate the significance that they can have on architectural experience. The value and importance of diagramming the formal essence of energy-conserving prototypes cannot be overestimated. As models of an idea, they act as intermediaries which allow the designer to see thermal and luminous intentions, to interpret their potential formal experience, and to ask how the building can serve both.

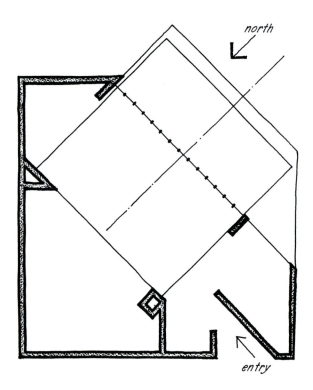

Figure 13.14: Residence (R. Levine, architect), plan.

14

PASSIVE COOLING:

GENERAL PRINCIPLES

The hills across the valley of the Ebro were long and white. On this side there was no shade and no trees and the station was between two lines of rails in the sun. Close against the side of the station there was the warm shadow of the building. And a curtain, made of strings of bamboo beads, hung across the open door into the bar, to keep out flies. The American and the girl with him sat at a table in the shade, outside the building. It was very hot and the express from Barcelona would come in forty minutes. It stopped at this junction for two minutes and went on to Madrid.

— from Hills Like White Elephants, *by Ernest Hemingway*

Passive cooling is the counterpart of passive space heating. While passive solar heating is driven only by the sun, passive cooling can utilize several heat sinks and a variety of climatic influences to create thermal comfort in warm regions. While passive heating has been widely adopted only recently, passive cooling has a much longer history of theory and application in indigenous buildings. However, few of these principles are widely found in contemporary building design. Because a general goal of passive cooling is to avoid overheating that is primarily generated by the sun, passive cooling is not "solar" at all but is, instead, nonsolar. . . even anti-solar (Cook, 1990). However, because passive heating and cooling both depend heavily on heat flow by natural means (convection, conduction, radiation, and phase change) they share many similar principles.

The primary comfort strategies in overheated climates are defensive; they avoid gains due to solar radiation (by shading and reflective barriers) and heat transfer through the envelope (by insulation and infiltration sealing), and were considered in Chapter 6.

Beyond these defensive strategies, passive cooling requires the evacuation of heat from the building to those natural heat sinks of the planet which normally offset the heat gained form the sun: the atmosphere, the sky, and the earth.

The *atmosphere* serves as a medium of heat exchange in two ways: *ventilation* and *evaporation*. Ventilative cooling intentionally flushes warm air from the building interior with cooler outside air; in addition, the air movement enhances perspiration skin cooling. Evaporative cooling, where building components are intentionally wetted and exposed to airflow, represents one of the most effective cooling strategies in all but the most humid regions.

The *sky* (or more precisely, limitless outer space beyond the atmosphere) has very little molecular substance, and is its temperature effectively absolute zero. As such, it is an absolute radiation absorber and, in the absence of any moderating effect due to atmosphere, causes rapid radiative heat loss by any comparatively warm surface exposed to it. At the earth's surface, the atmosphere's greenhouse effect tends to moderate this radiative cooling source, depending on the amount of moisture present in the air. If the humidity is low (as in desert regions), then the atmosphere has a comparatively small effect on retarding outgoing radiation, and exposed horizontal surfaces cool off quickly after sunset. Conversely, this effect is reduced considerably in humid regions. This effect is often termed *nocturnal radiation* (because the effect is most noticeable at night in the absence of the offsetting effect of solar radiation); however, the effect continues day and night and might be more precisely termed *outgoing radiation* to distinguish it from insolation (Cook, 1990).

The *earth* is a virtually infinite heat sink providing nearly stable temperatures (near the annual average surface temperature) at soil depths of 20 ft and greater.

PASSIVE COOLING CATEGORIES

Passive solar heating is divided into categories according to application configuration. On the other hand, passive cooling is better understood as a series of research fields that focus on the basic heat sinks. While this organization is helpful to scientists and inventors, it is a source of frustration for designers and policy makers (and authors trying to identify case studies) because so many workable systems involve multiple heat sinks (Cook, 1990). Nonetheless, this characterization of passive cooling will be used in the following chapters:

Ventilative cooling (see Chapter 15) — (1) exhausting warm building air and replacing it with cooler outside air; (2) directing moving air across occupants' skin to cool by a combination of convection and evaporation. In passive applications, the required air movement is provided either by the wind or by the "stack effect." In hybrid applications, movement may be assisted by fans.

Radiative cooling (see Chapter 16) — the transfer of heat from warmer surface to a cooler surrounding surface (or outer space). It may be used to cool the building (where warm building surfaces radiate heat to the sky) or to cool people (where the warm skin radiates heat to cooler surrounding room surfaces, to the cool walls of an underground building, for example).

Evaporative cooling (see Chapter 17) — the exchange of sensible heat in air for the latent heat of water droplets of wetted surfaces. It may be used to cool

the building (where wetted surfaces are cooled by evaporation), building air (cooled either directly by evaporation, or indirectly by contact with a surface previously cooled by evaporation), or the occupants (where evaporation of perspiration cools the skin surface).

Dehumidification (see Chapter 17) — the removal of water vapor from room air by dilution with drier air, condensation, or desiccation. In the case of condensation and desiccation, dehumidification is the exchange of latent heat in air for the sensible heat of water droplets on surfaces; both are the reverse of evaporative cooling and, as such, are adiabatic heating processes.

Mass-effect cooling (see Chapter 18) — the use of thermal storage to absorb heat during the warmest part of a periodic temperature cycle and release it later during a cooler part. "Night flushing" (where cool night air is drawn through a building to exhaust heat stored during the day in massive floors and walls) is an example of daily-cycle mass-effect cooling.

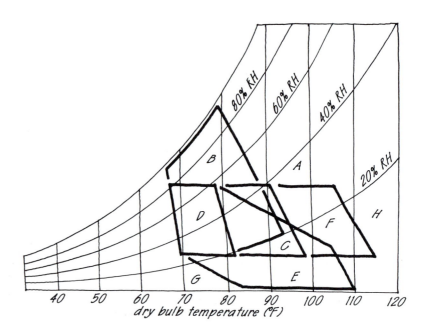

Figure 14.1: Psychrometric chart showing extensions of comfort zone with various passive cooling strategies: (a) conventional dehumidification, (b) ventilation, (c) high thermal mass, (d) comfort zone, (e) evaporative cooling, (f) high mass with nighttime ventilation, (g) humidification, and (h) conventional air conditioning. *(Based on Milne and Givoni, 1979; modified for the ASHRAE, 1989, comfort zone.)*

15

PASSIVE COOLING:

VENTILATION

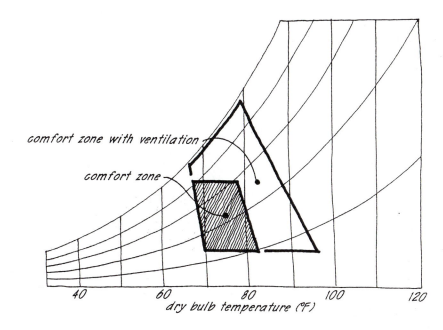

Figure 15.1: "People cooling"; extending the comfort zone by increasing air movement. *(After Milne and Givoni, 1979.)*

comfort zone with ventilation

comfort zone

dry bulb temperature (°F)

Ventilation is one of the most ancient of cooling strategies. In arid climates where there is a wide variation in daily temperatures and massive construction (particularly stone and adobe masonry), night-only ventilation ("night flushing") has been generally used. This takes advantage of the cool night air temperatures while isolating the interior from the extremely hot daytime conditions. However, hot-arid climates also have abundant other strategies (especially evaporation and nocturnal radiation).

BUILDING COOLING VERSUS PEOPLE COOLING

Ventilating a building results in an air exchange between the inside and outside at various rates (5 to 500 air changes per hour). This overall ventilative replacement of warmer inside air with cooler outside air is the source of building cooling. This cooler air also increases the cooling of the body by convection (which increases with the temperature difference between room air and the skin). In addition, the *air motion* generated by the ventilation process further increases bodily heat loss in two ways: by evaporation, and again by convection (here convection is increased because the warm layer of air next to the skin is exchanged more frequently). This distinction is important because building cooling depends on the introduction of outside air, while people cooling can be accomplished solely by the circulation of inside air (by a ceiling fan, for example . . . a remarkably energy-efficient mechanical strategy).

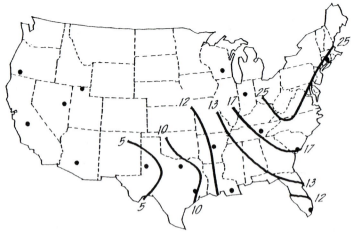

Figure 15.2: Percent savings in cooling energy possible from good natural ventilation in a low-mass residence. *(Redrawn from Chandra, et al., 1984, by permission.)*

UNDERSTANDING AIRFLOW

In order to anticipate how ventilation will occur in a proposed design, it is helpful to understand a few basic principles that govern airflow at the building scale as illustrated in Figs. 15.3 to 15.10:

high pressure   *low pressure*

Figure 15.3: Ventilation principle #1 — Air will always flow from a region of high pressure to a region of lower pressure.

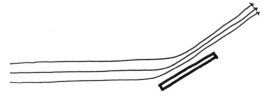

Figure 15.4: Ventilation principle #2 — Air has mass (and thus momentum) and it will tend to continue in its direction until altered by an obstruction or adjacent airflow.

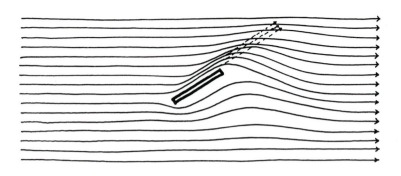

Figure 15.5: Ventilation principle #3 — The overall effect of wind at a site is so large that locally deflected airflow (by trees or buildings, for example) will tend to return to the direction and speed of the site wind.

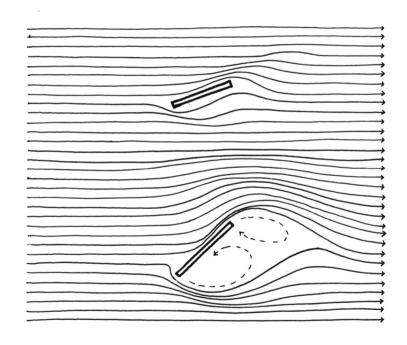

Figure 15.6: Ventilation principle #4 — "Laminar" airflow is smooth with adjacent air moving in similar direction and speed. Slow, gentle alterations of flow direction will preserve laminar flow, while abrupt alterations results in "turbulent flow" whereby adjacent air currents separate abruptly into swirling, unpredictable directions. When two currents of air are traveling in opposite directions, they will always be separated by eddies because adjacent particles of air always move in the same direction.

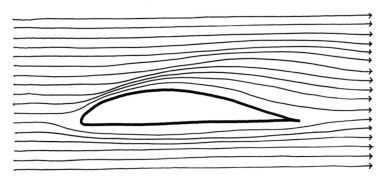

Figure 15.7: Ventilation principle #5 — The "Bernoulli effect" causes a decrease in pressure when air is accelerated in order to cover a greater distance than adjacent airflow. The classic example is the airplane wing which is shaped so that air passing over the top must travel further than that passing below; the Bernoulli effect reduces pressure on the top of the wing as the air is accelerated, creating "lift."

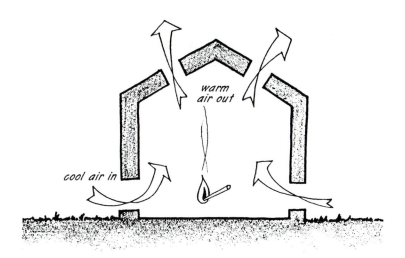

Figure 15.9: Ventilation principle #7 — The "stack effect" results when air in the building warms, becomes more buoyant than outside air, and rises to escape out of openings high in the building.

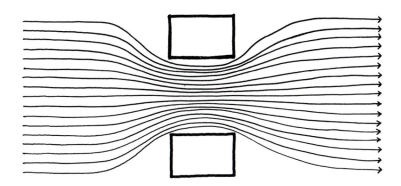

Figure 15.8: Ventilation principle #6 — The "Venturi effect" causes an acceleration when laminar airflow is constricted in order to pass through an opening (because the same volume of air must now pass through a smaller area). If the constriction is so abrupt as to create turbulence, Venturi acceleration is minimized.

WIND-DRIVEN VENTILATION

The configuration of buildings, rooms, and especially the locations of inlet and outlet openings within rooms have a major effect on the ventilation rates in buildings. These have been studied by various researchers using wind tunnels and scale models to develop design guidelines for effective ventilation. One seminal research project conducted at the Texas Engineering Experiment Station in the early 1950s sought to develop guidelines for ventilation that

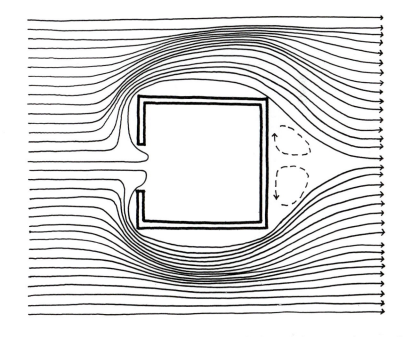

Figure 15.10: Ventilation principle #8 — Cross-ventilation requires an outlet as well as an inlet. (Analogy: water cannot be put into a bottle that is already full unless some old water is removed first — through a hole in the opposite end of the bottle, for example.)

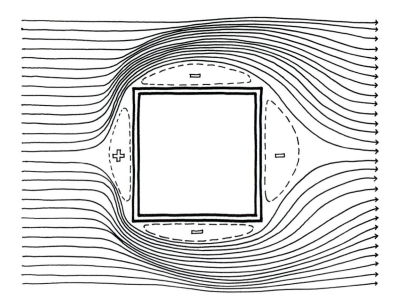

Figure 15.11: Low-pressure zones occur along the sides parallel to the wind and on the leeward side of the building. *(After Bowen, 1981.)*

would be applicable to the design of un-air-conditioned school buildings (Evans, 1957, 1979, and 1989; Holleman, 1951; and Reed, 1953). Bowen (1981) has summarized the results of this and other ventilation research in a comprehensive set of diagrams describing principles of ventilative airflow around and through buildings that are helpful to the designer in understanding specific common airflow patterns as illustrated in Figs. 15.13 to 15.16.

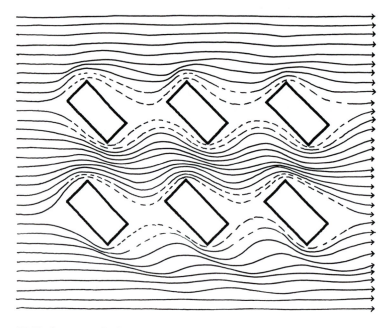

Figure 15.13: Staggered building arrangements result in reduced wind shadows. *(After Bowen, 1981.)*

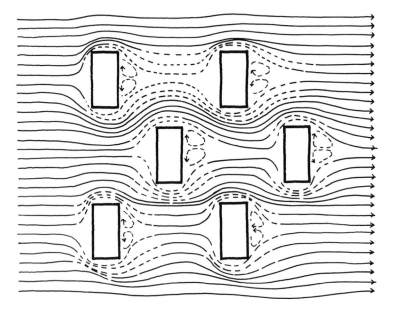

Figure 15.12: Multiple low-pressure zones are caused by linear arrangement of buildings resulting in wind shadow with a minimum ventilation potential. *(After Bowen, 1981.)*

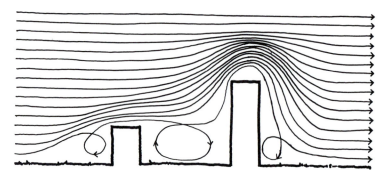

Figure 15.14: A low building placed in the windward path of a tall building produces a large amount of turbulence between the two. *(After Bowen, 1981.)*

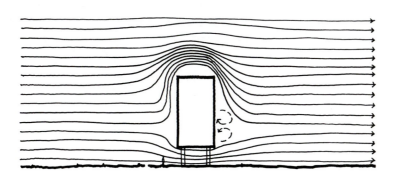

Figure 15.15: Raising a tall building on *piloti* reduces the high pressure on the windward side by allowing airflow under the building. *(After Bowen, 1981.)*

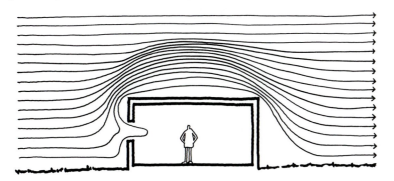

Figure 15.16: An opening on windward side only results in poor ventilation; an additional leeward opening — completing the connection between high and low pressure regions — is essential to promote airflow through the structure. *(After Bowen, 1981.)*

Window placement

Cross-ventilation in rooms where openings are on opposite walls creates the best airflow. Where windows are on adjacent walls, cross-ventilation can be improved by positioning of wing walls adjacent to the window openings. When cross-ventilation is not possible, wing walls adjacent to window have been found to be particularly effective at increasing ventilation in rooms with only one exterior wall. Full-scale tests were conducted at Florida Solar Energy Center comparing ventilation with and without wing walls.

Interior partitions

The location and orientation of interior partitions can affect the velocity and direction of airflow within a building. In general, partitions placed parallel to the direction that the airflow would otherwise take in their absence have the least effect.

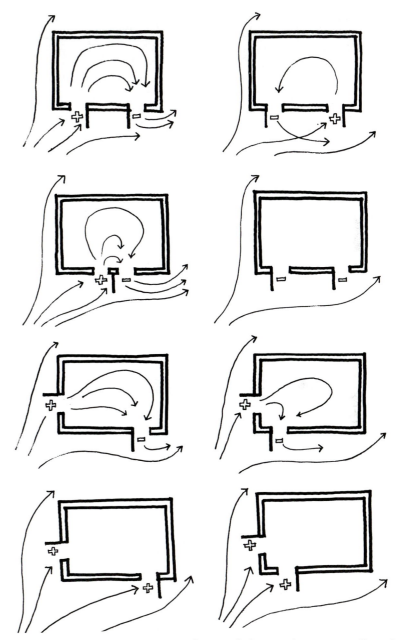

Figure 15.17: Wing wall design patterns for two windows on the same or adjacent walls showing probable airflow patterns and wind directions for improved ventilation performance due to wing walls: (a) excellent, (b) poor, (c) good, (d) poor, (e) excellent, (f) good, (g) poor, and (h) poor. *(After Chandra et al., 1983.)*

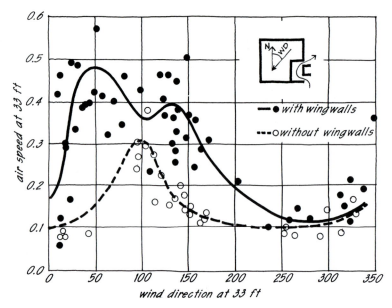

Figure 15.18: Airflow with and without wing walls obtained in full-scale experiments. Solid and dashed lines indicate researchers' opinion of data trends. _(Redrawn from Chandra et al., 1983, by permission.)_

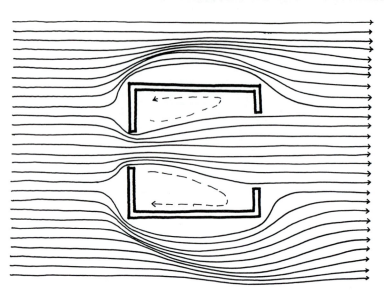

Figure 15.20: Maximum _interior airspeed_ is created when the inlet is smaller than the outlet, making this the optimum configuration when _people_ cooling is the goal. _(After Bowen, 1981.)_

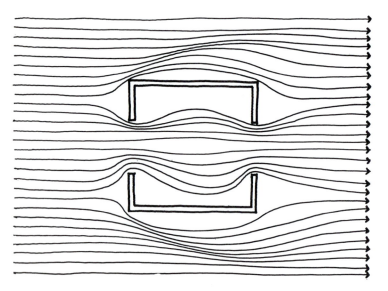

Figure 15.19: Openings of opposite walls relieve high pressure on the windward side, creating good cross-ventilation through the interior. Maximum _air exchange_ is created when the inlet and outlet areas are equal, making this the optimum configuration when _building_ cooling is the goals. _(After Bowen, 1981.)_

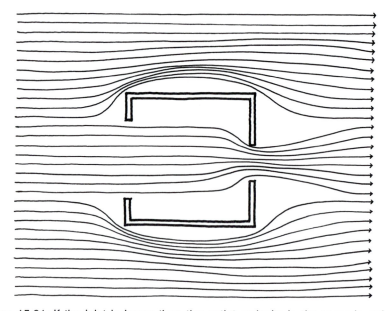

Figure 15.21: If the inlet is larger than the outlet, velocity in the room is reduced (although velocity outside just to leeward of the outlet is increased). This has potential for cooling a localized exterior area such as a patio. _(After Bowen, 1981.)_

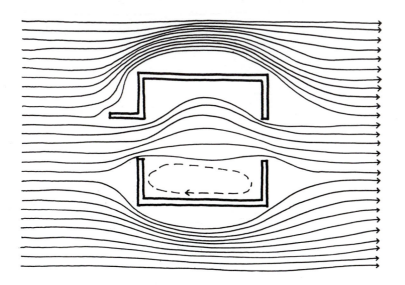

Figure 15.22: A baffle (wing wall, door, or casement window) placed perpendicular to the opening changes the direction of airflow through the space with only a small reduction in velocity. *(After Bowen, 1981.)*

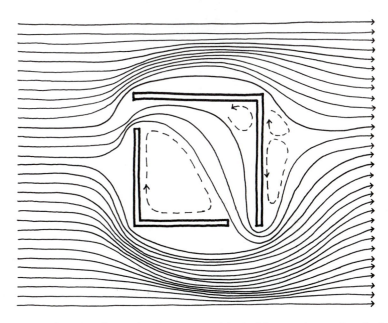

Figure 15.24: Openings located at the corners of the building as shown allow the inertia to continue the motion in the same direction in a smooth curve until the outlet is reached. *(After Bowen, 1981.)*

STACK-EFFECT VENTILATION

The stack effect is the result of air density decreasing as temperature increases. As discussed in Chapter 1, the greater the temperature difference between two connected bodies of air, the greater the difference in buoyancy of the two bodies. This buoyancy difference is the driving force behind stack-effect circulation, and is dependant on the temperature difference and the height difference. As the comparatively warm air in a building rises to escape through upper openings, it is replaced by cooler outside air admitted through low openings around the building perimeter. It is possible to enhance this stack effect by using the sun to create a solar thermal chimney to increase the convective flow by increasing the temperature differences within the system. This is accomplished by using a thermosiphoning air collector to heat the air after it is drawn from the occupied area of the building. The solar-heated air rises to a high outlet to be exhausted. Using this effect, airflow in the building increases as insolation on the collector increases. In principle, this generates the greatest airflow (and cooling effect) at times when it is most needed (that is, when the sun is strongest). In practice, two additional factors reduce the effectiveness of solar chimneys, and thus their cooling potential.

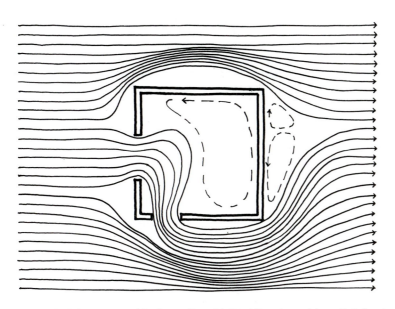

Figure 15.23: An inlet centered in the wall restricts airflow to a side outlet due to an abrupt change in direction; flow is increased by repositioning the inlet to a more diagonal location and adding a baffle directs entering air diagonally in the direction of the outlet. *(After Bowen, 1981.)*

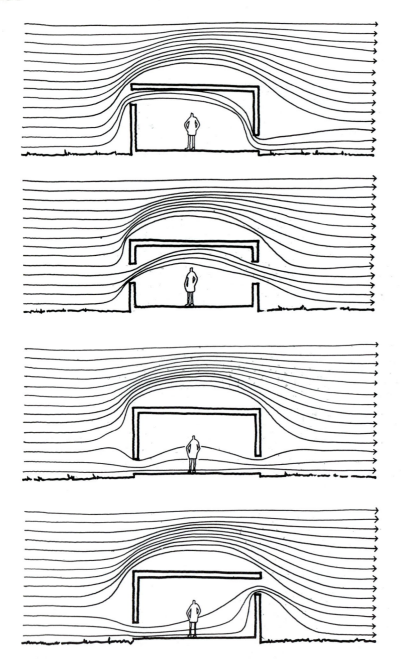

Figure 15.25: The vertical position of the *inlet* window is important in maximizing the airflow through the lower, occupied portion of the room; the low inlet is best for cooling. The *outlet* location has little effect on flow within the room. *(After Bowen, 1981.)*

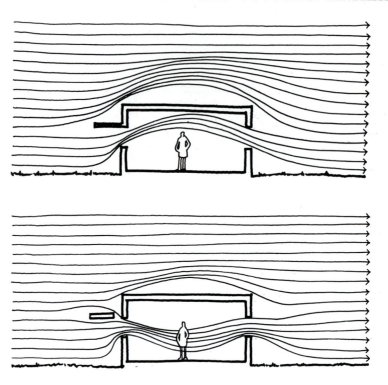

Figure 15.26: An overhang above the inlet window directs the interior airflow along the ceiling out of the occupied zone; the addition of a slot separating the overhang from the building redirects the flow down into the room, increasing the useful cooling effect. *(After Bowen, 1981.)*

First, while a vertical orientation of the solar collector is near optimum for winter heating and also for promoting stack-effect airflow, a much more horizontal attitude is better for summer solar collection (due to the much higher summer sun angles). This lower angle diminishes the vertical height of the airflow path and thus reduces both the convective driving force and the resultant air velocity.

Second, the driving force behind the solar chimney stack effect is small under the best of circumstances. If the high chimney outlet faces leeward, then any wind will enhance the stack effect. However, if the wind shifts, the air circulation may reverse, causing the solar-heated air to be blown down into the living space, effectively heating the building rather than cooling it. For this reason, any solar chimney should have a wind-activated ventilator cap to ensure that airflow is always positive.

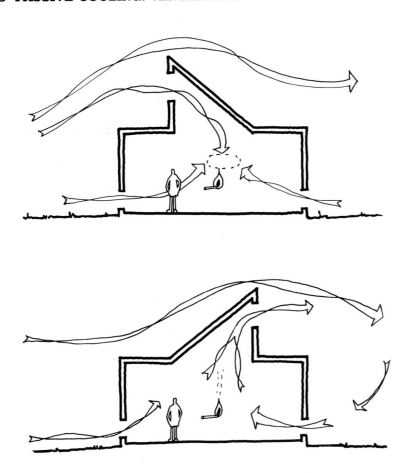

Figure 15.27: A high window acting as a windscoop inlet together with a low outlet must overcome the stack-effect tendency of the warm inside air to rise; reorienting the windscoop to leeward reinforces the stack effect and increases airflow.

Wind ventilator caps

Wind ventilators can be used to enhance ventilative airflow in buildings either in conjunction with the types of solar chimneys described above, or alone, depending solely on the force of the wind to induce a suction. In general, any object placed in the path of wind flow causes pressure differentials (positive on the windward side, negative on the leeward side). When the object is placed on the top of a ventilation chimney, these pressure differentials can be used to create a suction, increasing the airflow exiting the chimney. See Chapter 20 for a discussion of various wind ventilator caps.

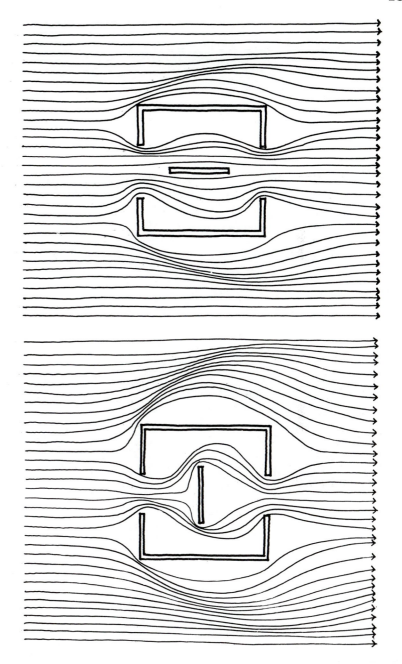

Figure 15.28: An interior partition added parallel to windflow has a minimum effect on velocity and direction, while a similar partition positioned perpendicular redirects the pattern and reduces the velocity. *(After Bowen, 1981.)*

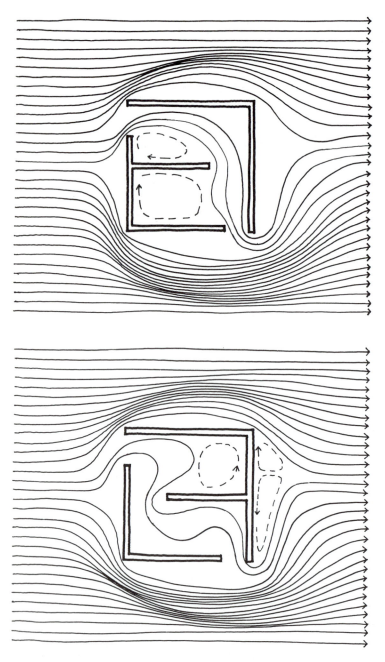

Figure 15.29: Similarly, partitions placed outside of the main airflow path have little effect while those blocking the path create a "dam" effect, creating stagnant areas. *(After Bowen, 1981.)*

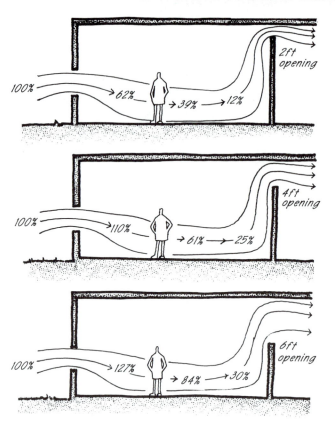

Figure 15.30: Depending on the size of interior partition openings, the velocity of incoming airflow near the inlet window can exceed that of the outside (expressed as percentages). *(Redrawn from Evans, 1989, by permission.)*

Double roof strategies

A major source of unwanted heat gain in buildings is the roof. As the roof surface is heated to high temperatures due to insolation in the summer, this heat conducts through the roof/ceiling assembly and ultimately radiates heat to the room below. A historically effective strategy is to introduce a ventilated airspace between the roof and the insulated ceiling below. One method common to current construction practices is to utilize the attic volume occupied by roof trusses as a ventilated space. Typically, the inlet is a continuous vent strip formed along the entire length of the soffit (with a screen or equivalent insect barrier). In older construction, triangular louvered eave vents provided the outlet; in more recent construction, continuous ridge vents are used. See Chapter 20 for further discussion of ventilation components and construction details.

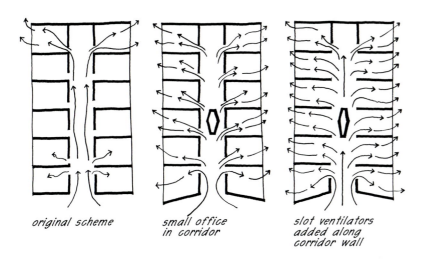

original scheme   *small office in corridor*   *slot ventilators added along corridor wall*

Figure 15.31: Site restrictions necessitated orienting the long dimension of the Elk City, Oklahoma, school parallel to prevailing winds (rather than the preferred perpendicular direction). Based on wind tunnel tests conducted during the schematic design phase, it was determined that a conventional corridor plan configuration resulted in most airflow occurring through the end classrooms. Introducing an "island" office in the corridor about 40 percent down from the inlet caused incoming air to build up pressure earlier and flow more uniformly through all classrooms (CRS, architects). *(After Evans, 1989.)*

VENTILATION CASE STUDIES

LEARNING FROM THE PAST

Traditional housing types indigenous to the Mississippi region utilize a variety of effective humid climate ventilation cooling strategies (Ford, 1982). The *dog trot* house derives its name from the "dog trot" that separated the two large main rooms. Whether the form came from Africa or from Celtic crofters' huts is unclear, but it owes much to the need to make log buildings stable by connecting them on four sides. Roofs extended over porches on front and back to shade the walls. Breezes accelerated to 150 percent of outside speeds (Aho, 1981) as they were constricted to pass through the open central hall. Furthermore, each room had potential open locations on all four sides. Porches were raised to resist insect damage and decay, while allowing more ventilation from below the floor.

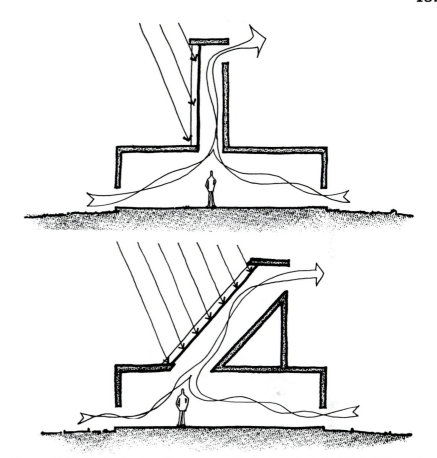

Figure 15.32: Vertical solar chimneys provide the greatest stack height for a given collector size but this tilt is not effective for summer collection. Sloped chimneys provide a better summer collection angle but must be taller to provide sufficient vertical "stack" height.

Another type is the white frame "raised" cottage represented by *Beauvoir*. Designed and built by James Brown in 1852, it was the last home of Jefferson Davis, president of the Confederacy. Located on the Mississippi gulf coast, it is oriented to the south with a superb view of the gulf from broad sheltered porches. It was really an enhanced dog trot elevated to the status of mansion. Rooms, shaded by large overhanging porches on all sides, open to each other via sliding doors, and to the outdoors via 12-ft-tall triple-hung windows. Breezes from the nearby gulf course through them and through the latticework that separates the ground from the floor, 9 ft above grade. The objectionable heat and fire hazard of the kitchen was located in a separate structure to the rear of the house (Ford, 1982).

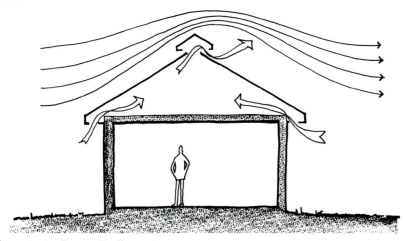

Figure 15.33: Bernoulli-effect attic ventilation utilizing continuous soffit and ridge vents.

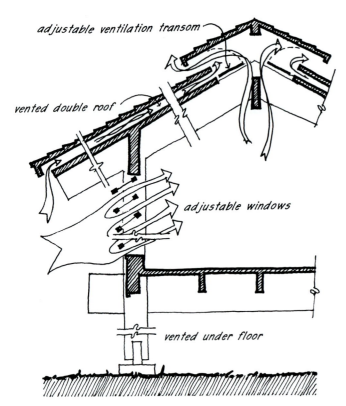

Figure 15.34: A roof-venting strategy for a contemporary house in south Florida that incorporates both adouble roof and cupola for ventilation cooling; note adjustable transom detail for controlling ventilation at ridge. *(Redrawn from Malt and Ripoll, 1981, by permission.)*

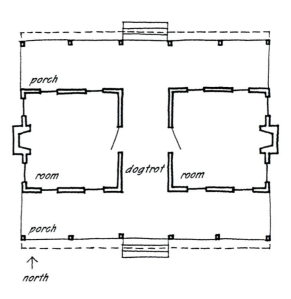

Figure 15.35: "Dog trot" house, c. 1840. *(Plan redrawn from Ford, 1982, by permission.)*

The *belvedere* (center section of the roof raised and surrounded by clerestory windows) evolved as a popular and effective ventilation strategy using the stack effect and Bernoulli effect to evacuate air from the large open center stair hall. *Waverly* is an excellent example designed by Charles Pond for Col. George Young. It is a large two-story house dominated by a large belvedere rising above the roof. Like the tog trot and Beauvoir, it has a formal, symmetrical plan. The windows were not protected by surrounding porches (as in the first two examples) but by operable wood louvered shutters that, when left closed allow natural ventilation and a soft diffuse daylight inside. All rooms except the central hall have openings on three sides for ventilation. The hall has doors on the north and south sides that allow air to enter and escape through the rooms or up through the belvedere (Ford, 1982).

DEJA-VU HOUSE

Robert Ford deliberately adopted the strategies of these three historical prototypes in the design of his own house in Starkville, Mississippi. Named the "deja-vu" house because of its traditional climatic design roots, it is heavily shaded by deciduous trees. The entrance is a procession that begins between a split garage, framing the house like the detached carriage houses of some traditional homes of the southeast, and proceeding across a 66-ft-long bridge

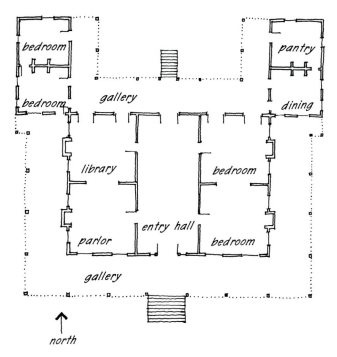

Figure 15.36: Beauvoir, near Biloxi, Mississippi, c. 1852. *(Plan redrawn from Ford, 1982, by permission.)*

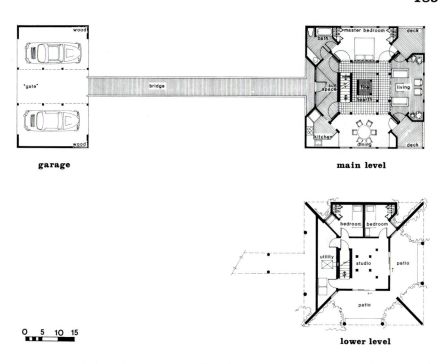

Figure 15.38: Deja-vu house, plans. *(Drawings courtesy of Robert Ford, architect.)*

Figure 15.37: Deja-vu house, Starkville, Mississippi, 1981, entrance showing flanking carports and bridge. *(Photo and drawings courtesy of Robert Ford, architect.)*

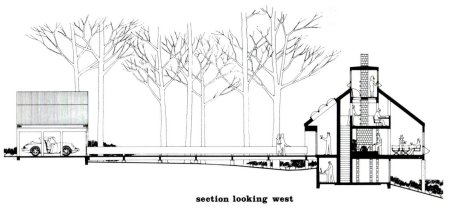

Figure 15.39: Deja-vu house, section. *(Drawings courtesy of Robert Ford, architect.)*

to the centered entrance. The projecting belvedere dominates the roof, dramatizing its role in ventilation and natural lighting. The deja-vu's plan is square and open with a raised floor.

From the bridge the house is entered through a sunspace that serves as a thermal buffer zone and passive solar collector. Doors isolate the sunspace from the interior main living areas. The first-floor rooms open to each other and to the outside. The second level is a study open on three sides to the rooms below and separated from the upper sunspace that can be opened for winter solar heat. The highest level is the belvedere which pierces the roof housing the masonry chimney and is surrounded by a free ventilation area and window on all sides. The unusual height of the house (36 ft from basement to belvedere) provides the necessary height to drive the strong stack-effect ventilation, drawing air in through awning windows on three sides.

The house's cooling performance is impressive. While most conventional houses in the northern Mississippi climate require mechanical cooling from early May through October, this house's passive strategies are adequate for a 6-week period at the beginning and at the end of the summer, requiring supplemental mechanical cooling for a much shorter period — mid-June to mid-September.

Figure 15.40: Florida A&M School of Architecture (Clements, Rumpel Associates, architects). *(Photo courtesy of the architect.)*

FLORIDA A&M SCHOOL OF ARCHITECTURE

The School of Architecture building at Florida A&M University, designed by Clements, Rumpel Associates, Architects, was the first institutional application of the use of thermal chimneys for ventilative cooling and heating in the warm-humid southeastern United States. Conceptually the building is a collection of five "buildings" differentiated by thermal requirements. They are linked with exterior circulation and arranged to create exterior courtyards while optimizing the orientation and exposure requirements of each building. The modes of operation and control were designed to differ from "building" to "building" as appropriate to the thermal and humidity requirements of the activities housed (Fisher, 1985).

The basic massing of the building provides each wing with a large south-facing wall and sloped roof. These were designed with a "chimney" space backed by painted metal and glazed with translucent fiberglass. These south-facing collector spaces were designed to heat the air and generate an updraft. In the passive-heating mode, this hot air is collected by a duct near the peak and returned to the building's air-handling system for circulation throughout the building. In the ventilating mode, motorized dampers open the ridge ventilator and the hot air in the chimney is exhausted by the stack effect, pulling cool air from the north courtyard into the room through operable windows.

Unfortunately, many of the innovative passive thermal strategies included in the original design were lost during post-design budget cuts. Twenty-one HVAC-related items were deleted or modified prior to construction. The

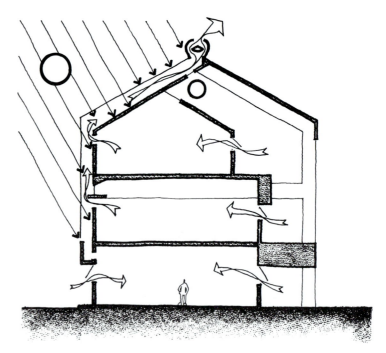

Figure 15.41: Florida A&M School of Architecture: ventilating mode showing thermal chimney zone with exhaust through the ridge ventilator. *(Redrawn from Fisher, 1985, by permission.)*

ability to passively solar heat was removed from wings 1 and 3 entirely, although the thermal chimneys remained to operate in natural ventilation mode. Only wing 2, the studio wing, remained with the "passive ductwork" system which allows the heated air to be collected and used. "This single move, after the design process was completed, calls into question the entire design strategy for climate response . . ." (Ubbehlohde, 1986).

PREDICTING VENTILATION IN BUILDINGS

VENTILATION RULES-OF-THUMB

Experiments have demonstrated that a constant airflow of 15 air changes per hour (ACH) in a residence of typical construction (frame, slab-on-grade) will maintain the average interior air temperature within 3°F of ambient, with a peak of 5°F above ambient in late afternoon. Raising the ventilation rate to 30 ACH brings the average house temperature within 1.25°F of ambient (Chandra et al., 1986). Reynolds (1984) has developed some simplified rules-of-thumb for estimating the performance of both cross-ventilation and stack-effect ventilation.

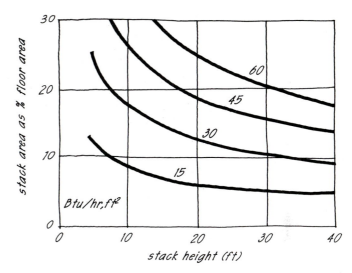

Figure 15.43: Stack-effect ventilation rule of thumb, for heat removed per unit floor area. The total stack area is the minimum of: inlet free area, cross section through the vertical stack, and outlet free area. Internal air temperatures are assumed to be at least 3°F higher than the exterior. *(Redrawn from Reynolds, 1984, by permission.)*

WINDOW VENTILATION CALCULATIONS

The Florida Solar Energy Center (Chandra et al., 1983) has also developed a simplified worksheet procedure to determine the window size required to produce the desired ventilation rate. The following worksheet (Fig. 15.44) shows the window area calculations for an example house in suburban Orlando, Florida, having a floor area of 1334 ft^2 and oriented with the principal window walls facing SSE and NNW. Since it is a residence in a humid area, 24-hour ventilation is assumed. For security reasons, assume that doors will not be depended on for ventilation. A blank worksheet is included in Appendix F.

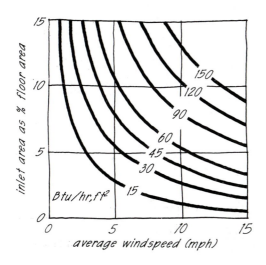

Figure 15.42: Cross-ventilation rule of thumb, for heat removed per unit of floor area, and the relationship of inlet opening area and wind speed. Total inlet opening area is expressed as a percent of total floor area. Note that the method assumes the outlet areas at least equal to inlet area and internal air temperatures are at least 3°F higher than the exterior. *(Redrawn from Reynolds, 1984, by permission.)*

VENTILATION SCALE MODELS

Scale models may provide a more accurate method of studying ventilation in small buildings than computer simulations. A low-cost outdoor scale-model test procedure has been developed and validated against full-scale buildings at the Florida Solar Energy Center Passive Cooling Laboratory. The agreement on airspeed at various points within the interior between that simulated in the model and that measured in the full-scale building was found to be excellent (Chandra et al., 1983).

Worksheet for Calculating Window Areas of Naturally Ventilated Houses

Project **ORLANDO EXAMPLE**   Analyst **FM**

1. Building conditioned floor area = **1334** (1) ft²

2. Average ceiling height = **8** (2) ft

3. House volume = (step 1) x (step 2) = **10,672** (3) ft³

4. Design air change rate / hour (recommended value is 30) = **30** (4) ACH

5. Required airflow rate, cfm = (step 3) x (step 4) ÷ 60 = **5336** (5) cfm

6. Design month (recommended: May for Florida and Gulf Coast; June elsewhere) = **MAY** (6)

7. Name of nearest city = **ORLANDO** (7)

8. From maps in Appendix C, determine windspeed (WS) and direction (WD) for the design month: WS = **9** (8a) ; WD = **SE** (8b) mph

9. From prevailing direction, determine the incidence angle on the *windward* wall having the *largest area* of window (0° = perpendicular to wall) = **20°** (9) deg.

10. From Table 15.1, determine inlet-to-site 10-meter windspeed ratio = **0.35** (10)

11. Determine windspeed correction factors:

11a. For house location and ventilation strategy, determine terrain correction factor from Table 15.2 = **0.67** (11a)

11b. For neighboring buildings, assume neighborhood convection factor = 0.77; no surrounding buildings = 1.0 = **0.77** (11b)

11c. For windows for the second floor (or for house on stilts), use a correction factor of 1.15 (otherwise, use 1.0). Correction factor = **1.0** (11c)

12. Calculate windspeed correction factor = (step 11a) x (step 11b) x (step 11c) = **0.52** (12)

13. Calculate site windspeed in ft/min = (step 8a) x (step 12) x 88 = **412** (13) ft/min

14. Calculate window inlet airspeed = (step 13) x (step 10) = **144** (14) ft/min

15. Calculate net aperture inlet area = (step 5) ÷ (step 14) = **37** (15) ft²

16. Determine total effective inlet + outlet area (screened) = 3.33 x (step 15) = **123** (16) ft²

17. Determine total effective area as % of floor area = (step 16) ÷ (step 1) x 100 = **9.2** (17) %

18. This total effective area requirement can be met by the same area of net opening. If windows or doors are used, then this area must be increased to allow for their effective opening area by applying the following effective opening factor: single- or double-hung window = 0.45; single- or double-sliding window = 0.45; hopper = 0.45; awning window = 0.75; casement window = 0.9; jalousie windows = 0.75; sliding door = 0.45; hinged door = 0.95.

19. Select openings and calculate their total effective area:

Opening type: frame opening area (ft²) x effective opening factor (step 18) x no. of this opening type:

Opening type	frame opening area (ft²)		effective opening factor (step 18)		no. of this opening type			
casement	**8**	x	**0.9**	x	**14**	=	**101**	ft²
awning	**4**	x	**0.75**	x	**12**	=	**36**	ft²
		x		x		=		ft²
		x		x		=		ft²

20. Total effective area as designed and installed (should equal or exceed step 16) = **137** ft²

Figure 15.44: Window sizing example worksheet. *(After Chandra et al, 1983, by permission of Florida Solar Energy Center.)*

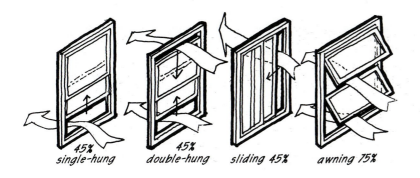

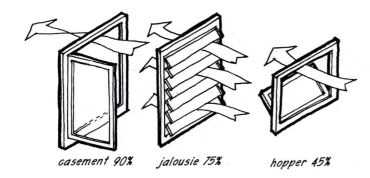

Figure 15.45: Effective open area of various window types. *(Redrawn from Vieira and Sheinkopf, 1988, by permission.)*

Table 15.1: Inlet-to-Site 10-Meter Windspeed Ratios, WSR

(Reproduced from Chandra et al., 1983, courtesy of Florida Solar Energy Center.)

Wind Incidence Angle (deg)	WSR
0 - 40	0.35
50	0.30
60	0.25
70	0.20
80	0.14
90	0.08

Note: Incidence angle = 0 when wind is directly entering the window.

Table 15.2: Terrain Correction Factor, TCF

Terrain Type	24 h. ventilation (humid)	Night-only ventilation (arid)
Oceanfront	1.3	0.98
Airports or flatland	1.00	0.75
Rural	0.85	0.64
Suburban or Industrial	0.67	0.50
Center of large city	0.47	0.35

(Reproduced from Chandra et al., 1983, courtesy of Florida Solar Energy Center.)

SUMMARY OF TERMS

Wind-driven ventilation—ventilation where the driving force is the air pressure differences that result from wind flow around the building.

Stack-effect ventilation — ventilation where the driving force is the relative buoyancy of warmer inside air.

Fan-forced ventilation — ventilation where the driving force is a mechanical fan.

"Building cooling" — using outside air to replace warm inside air and to cool building interior surfaces by convection.

"People cooling" — using air movement to cool skin surfaces by increasing evaporation of perspiration; air may be outside air or inside, recirculated air.

Laminar airflow— changes in direction caused by obstructing surfaces is gradual, resulting in smooth, continuous, predictable airflow direction with little change in speed.

Turbulent airflow — changes in direction caused by obstructing surfaces is abrupt resulting in discontinuous, unpredictable airflow direction with greatly reduced airspeed.

Bernoulli effect — a decrease in pressure when air is accelerated in order to cover a greater distance than adjacent airflow.

Venturi effect — an acceleration when laminar airflow is constricted in order to pass through an opening (because the same volume of air must now pass through a smaller area).

Piloti — columns used to raise a building up above the ground.

Awning window — a top-hinged window that projects out at the bottom.

Hopper window — a bottom-hinged window that projects in at the top.

Casement window — a side-hinged window that projects out when opened.

Double-hung window — a window divided into two parts that slide vertically.

Triple-hung window — similar in operation to a double-hung; a very large traditional window extending to the floor and doubling as a door. Common in traditional tropical architecture.

Ridge vent — a continuous vent along the ridge of a roof; utilizes a combination of the stack and Bernoulli effects to exhaust attic air.

Soffit vent — a continuous vent along the soffit of a roof overhang.

Eave vent — a screened, louvered vent installed in the eave for the purpose of ventilating an attic.

Ceiling fan — a large fan suspended from a ceiling used to circulate interior air.

Whole-house fan — a fan which draws warm room air through the ceiling into the attic and exhausts hot attic air to the outside.

Wind ventilator cap — a device located on the top of a ventilating stack to enhance ventilation rate while excluding rain.

Double roof — one exterior roof (for shading and rain protection) and a second lower roof separated by an airspace vented at the top and bottom to create stack-effect airflow.

"Dog trot" house — a traditional housing type indigenous to the Mississippi region, the house derives its name from the "dog trot" that separated the two large main rooms.

Belvedere — the center section of the roof raised and surrounded by clerestory windows.

Solar chimney — a ventilation strategy that uses solar heat to increase stack-effect ventilation.

STUDY QUESTIONS

1. Compare the use of ventilation for "cooling buildings" versus "cooling people."

2. Explain the difference between the Bernoulli effect and the Venturi effect. Draw a diagram showing the application of each in building ventilation.

3. It is desirable to place the windward ventilation opening low and the leeward opening high. Why is this the best combination?

4. What window type is best for ventilation and why?

5. Explain the purpose and operation of a "double roof."

6. Explain how ventilation works in a dog-trot house.

16

PASSIVE COOLING:

RADIATION

Radiative cooling is the transfer of heat from a warmer surface to a cooler surrounding surface (or outer space). It may be used to cool the building (where warm building surfaces radiate heat to the sky) or to cool people (where the warm skin radiates heat to cooler surrounding room surfaces — to the cool walls of an underground building, for example). It is a common method of rejecting heat from the earth's surface. Indeed, it is the only heat transfer means by which the earth can lose heat, and an amount equal to the total solar radiation absorbed by the earth must be reradiated to outer space to maintain the thermal balance required for temperature stability (Martin, 1990).

SKY TEMPERATURE

In general, the drier the atmosphere, the more readily terrestrial surfaces can radiate heat to outer space. If there were no atmosphere at all, then radiative loss to outer space would be extremely rapid; it would be just as though an impossibly cold shell (absolute zero, or –460°F or –273.15°C) surrounded the earth. Because the atmosphere is somewhat less transparent than a vacuum, terrestrial radiation to the sky is reduced — in effect, the sky "seems" warmer. Water vapor is particularly opaque to terrestrial infrared radiation (far-IR), and so the higher the humidity (or the greater the cloud cover), the "warmer" the sky seems to radiating surfaces (such as buildings). *Sky temperature* is the equivalent radiant temperature above the horizon that would create the same radiative heat loss from terrestrial surfaces; it is independent of outdoor air temperature around the building and directly related to the amount of moisture in the atmosphere above the site. It is this reduced moisture (and consequent reduced sky temperature) that is responsible for the large drop in nighttime temperatures in desert regions.

This "nocturnal radiation" effect can be costly to agriculture, causing frost at above-freezing air temperatures. Some fruit crops are sensitive to freezing and are protected from early morning frosts by the use of smudge pots and wind generators. The smudge pots burn a fuel which induces smog, producing a radiative "blanket" which inhibits the radiation of ground heat to the sky (raising the sky temperature); contrary to popular belief, the direct heating effect of the smudge pots is insignificant by comparison. Furthermore, because sky temperature is typically lower than the air temperature, any air movement tends to counterbalance nocturnal radiation. The frost danger is greatest on still, clear nights, and large electric fans (reverse windmills) are used in orchards to stir up the stagnant cool air layer that forms near the ground as a result of nocturnal radiation (Martin, 1990).

long on the east-west axis, were created. An adobe wall was built on the south side of each pond, high enough to shade the entire width of the pond during the ice-making season and shield it from the convective warming effect of the wind. Lower endwalls shielded the ponds from early morning and afternoon sun. On cloudless winter nights, the ponds were filled with water. Although there is some conductive warming effect from the ground, the radiative cooling to the clear night sky is sufficient to freeze the ice several inches in thickness. This was cut the following day and stored in covered, insulated pits for storage until the summer. While this method has been discontinued for health reasons (due to bacterial contamination of the ice), it demonstrates the effectiveness of radiative cooling (Bahadori, 1978).

Figure 16.2: An ancient Iranian ice pond. These were several hundred meters in length, and produced ice by radiative cooling to clear night sky; high adobe walls provided shading and deflected convective warming winds. *(After Bahadori, 1978.)*

COURTYARDS

Enclosed patios and courtyards benefit from radiative cooling. Chapter 3 described the daily cooling cycles of traditional courtyards, including the radiative cooling of courtyard surfaces (walls and ground) if these are exposed to the night sky. (If the view of the sky from the courtyard is obstructed by trees, nocturnal radiation is reduced; however, this loss of night radiative cooling is typically more than counterbalanced by protective daytime shading and the increased evaporation and transpiration.)

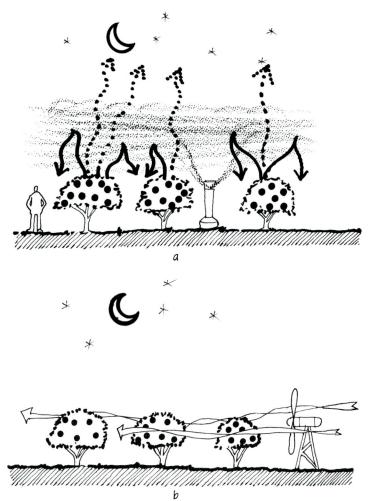

Figure 16.1: Frost-suppression strategies in agriculture: (a) using smog-producing smudge pots to create a radiation blanket and (b) wind generators to induce convective warming. Because the wind dissipates the smoke, the two strategies are not compatible.

RADIATIVE ICE PONDS

Radiative cooling was used to produce ice in hot-arid regions of ancient Iran. While the process was not used for summer comfort conditioning, it clearly demonstrates the potential of radiative cooling. The winter nighttime temperature often dropped within a few degrees of freezing. Shallow rectangular ponds, 30 to 60 feet wide on a north-south axis and several hundred feet

The roof can be designed to enhance this courtyard cooling cycle. If the roof surrounding the courtyard is sloped toward the courtyard, as the roof cools by radiation at night, the layer of air above the roof is also cooled and (being relatively more dense than surrounding air), "drains" into the courtyard, displacing the warmer air. In practice, this configuration is common in order to drain rainwater into the court, collecting valuable moisture for evaporation.

In addition to the radiative, convective, and evaporative cooling processes that make the courtyard an effective design strategy in hot-arid climates, the additional aesthetic and psychological effect of this contained "oasis" should not be underestimated. Reynolds et al. (1983) analyzed traditional courtyards in Colima, Mexico, and concluded that the subjective perception of coolness in these enclosures exceeded the measurable effects:

> *This study has reinforced my impression that comfort is a state of mind first and only secondarily a measurable set of factors. These courtyards invariably seemed much cooler at midday than either side of the street, more so than the measurements suggest. I believe that this approach to passive cooling succeeds largely because it visibly integrates so many things that are indicators of coolness. Taken separately, the more common shallow courtyard's measurements often seem but slight improvements upon those of the street. When all such courtyards' impressions are taken together, however, they provide an environment that is distinctly more comfortable than the street beyond.*

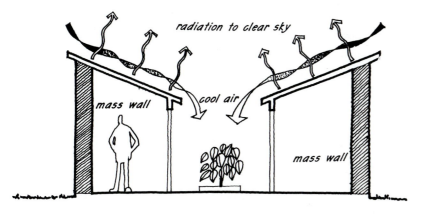

Figure 16.3: Courtyard which combines radiantly cooled convective air "drainage" together with massive exterior walls to delay conductive heat transfer. *(After Trombe, 1967.)*

ROOF PONDS

SKYTHERM SYSTEM

Harold Hay invented a roof-pond system that provided both passive summer cooling (radiative) as well as winter passive solar heating (Hay and Yellott, 1970). His invention was demonstrated by some early proof-of-concept experiments whereby a foam box was filled with water and the lid removed to receive insolation during the day and replaced at night to reduce heat loss. The measured increase in the water temperature demonstrated the passive solar heating potential of the system. Then by simply reversing the positions of the insulating lid (*on* during the day to prevent solar heat gain, *off* at night to allow cooling by radiation and evaporation), radiative cooling was effected.

The patented Skytherm system has subsequently been tested in a full-scale test room and an occupied house (Hay and Yellott, 1970). It consists of a single-story building with a level, uninsulated, metal-pan structural roof. The roof supports a plastic "bag" filled with water (similar to a simple water bed) 6 to 8 in. deep. The upper layer of the bag was transparent while the bottom layer was black to increase absorption. Finally, the roof is equipped with horizontally sliding insulating panels which slide into place to cover the roof and off to one side (over an unconditioned area, such as a garage or porch).

In operation, during a summer day, the water absorbs heat through the metal roof/ceiling from the room below and is protected from solar heat gain by the insulating panels. At night, the panels are removed, allowing the water bags to radiate heat to the night sky. During a winter day, the water bags are uncovered and absorb solar heat; this heat is conducted through the metal ceiling/roof and radiated to the room below. At night, the bags are covered by the insulating panels to reduce heat loss. Operation is enhanced by the use of a second covering plastic layer slightly inflated to provide an insulating air space. During the summer, the top surface may be flooded or sprayed to promote evaporative cooling. In addition, ceiling fans can be used to increase the convective transfer between the room air and the metal ceiling. With the use of these two enhancements (evaporative flooding/spraying and ceiling fans), research based on computer simulations (validated by test building experiments) have demonstrated that roof-pond cooling can provide comfort in every location in the United States. A comprehensive single-source document that addresses schematic and detailed design, construction, heating, and cooling performance and economics for this system is available from the National Technical Information Center (Marlatt et al., 1984). A number of enhancements of the basic roof-pond systems have been proposed; for example, researchers at the University of Nebraska have suggested pumping water above the insulation rather than moving the insulation.

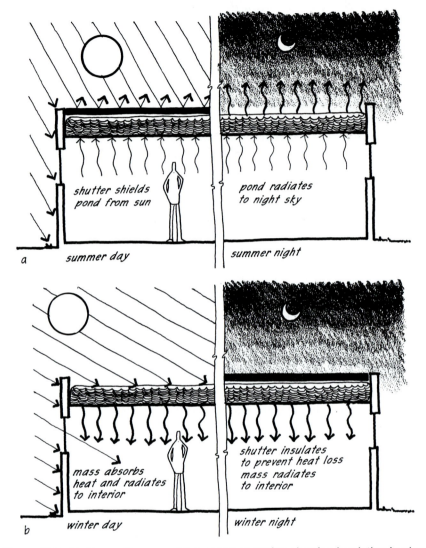

Figure 16.4: Skytherm diagrams: (a) summer operation showing insulation in place over water mass during the daytime and retracted at night, and (b) winter operation showing insulation retracted during the daytime and in place at night.

The system is most effective in mild climates which have both heating and cooling requirements. The system installed in the Atascadero, California house provided 100 percent of the heating and cooling (Hay, 1976). In colder climates, the horizontal slope is a very inefficient collector orientation (because of the low winter altitude of the sun at northern latitudes). In addition, the

presence of snow and ice may interfere with the operation of the insulating shutters that are essential to the system's performance. Several alternatives have been proposed for colder climates which provide a sloped roof cover.

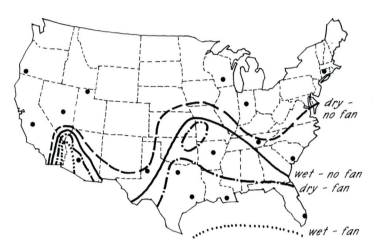

Figure 16.5: Southern limiting comfort contours achieved by wet and dry roof pond residences with and without ceiling fans (6 p.m. on a July $2^1/_2$ percent ASHRAE design day). *(After Fleischhacker et al., 1983.)*

Figure 16.6: Roofpond residence, Atascadero, CA. The horizontal sliding insulation panels are stored above the carport when not covering the waterbag. *(Photo courtesy J. D. Balcomb.)*

COOL POOL

The *cool pool* is an innovative passive roof-cooling system (Crowther and Melzer, 1979; Crowther, 1979). It consists of an open roof pond shaded from summer sun by sloping louvers which still allow exposure of the pond to the north sky. In addition to evaporation, the pool is cooled by radiation to the sky. The cooled water is piped to a large water storage tube inside the building below so that thermocirculation occurs any time the roof pool is cooler than the storage tube. The cooling performance of this system is impressive. A test demonstrated that a small, well-insulated room could be kept between 68°F and 77°F even after three days of 100-plus weather (peak 106°F with a wet-bulb temperature of 78°F).

Cool pool tubes could be designed to function as a water wall for winter passive heating by locating them behind south glazing and blocking circulation to the roof pond.

ENHANCING RADIATIVE COOLING

Horizontal surfaces are the most efficient radiative cooling surfaces because they are most directly exposed to the sky; tilted cooling surfaces are exposed to warmer terrestrial surfaces below the horizon, and thus experience a higher effective sky temperature.

There should be a maximum thermal coupling between the conditioned space and the radiating surface (usually the roof); the area should be as large as practical and the thermal resistance should be minimized, allowing the heat to be readily transferred from the room to the roof—in effect, warming the roof. The warmer the roof, the greater the difference between the roof and sky temperatures and the greater the cooling effect. Even small differences in roof temperature can make a large difference in the daily cooling rate; for example, a difference of only 4°F warmer roof surface will approximately double the cooling rate.

Because sky temperatures are typically below ambient air temperatures surrounding the building, any airflow across the radiative cooling surface heats it by convection. Therefore, any strategy that reduces airflow across the collector will enhance the cooling process. The measured air velocity immediately above a flat roof with a surrounding parapet has been found surprisingly low in comparison with that further away from the building, suggesting that conventional building elements such as parapet walls may be effective in suppressing convection (Clark et al., 1983).

Considerable research has been done on the development of windscreen coverings for cooling radiators that suppress convection warming while being

Figure 16.7: Cool pool building: (a) day, and (b) night cooling operation.

transparent to IR radiation. Such materials are unusual; the minimum optical requirement is that they be highly transparent in the spectral region between 8 and 13 microns. Glass and most common building materials are virtually opaque in this far-IR region. Most materials used for infrared lenses are too expensive for rooftop glazing systems. To date, the only practical material yet identified for IR-transparent windscreens are thin sheets of polyolefin plastics, and high-density polyethylene in particular. An inherent problem with these materials is that they rapidly degrade when exposed to air and sunlight, reducing their IR transparency and mechanical strength (Martin, 1990).

SUMMARY OF TERMS

Radiative cooling — the transfer of heat from a warmer surface to a cooler surrounding surface (or outer space) by electromagnetic wave radiation.

Sky temperature — the apparent temperature of the sky, for radiative cooling purposes; more specifically, it is the equivalent radiant temperature above the horizon that would create the same radiative heat loss from terrestrial surfaces. Sky temperature is independent of outdoor air temperature around the building and is directly related to the amount of moisture in the atmosphere above the site. It is this reduced humidity (and consequent reduced sky temperature) that is responsible for the large drop in nighttime temperatures in desert regions.

Nocturnal radiation — radiation to a clear, low-humidity night sky. (Radiation to the clear sky occurs at all times but is counterbalanced during the day by direct and diffuse solar radiation.)

Roof pond — a passive cooling system using water as the primary heat-storage medium and exhausting building heat to the sky by radiation. Examples of roof-pond cooling systems include Skytherm and Cool Pool.

Skytherm — a patented passive cooling and solar heating system invented by Harold Hay. It typically consists of a single-story building with a level, uninsulated, metal-pan structural roof. The roof supports a plastic "bag" filled with water. The roof is equipped with horizontally sliding insulating panels which slide into place to cover the roof and off to one side (over an unconditioned area, such as a garage or porch). See text for discussion of operation.

Cool pool — a passive cooling system consisting of an open roof pond shaded from summer sun by sloping louvers which still allow exposure of the pond to the north sky. In addition to radiation to the sky, the pool is cooled by evaporation. The cooled water is piped to a large water storage tube inside the building below so that thermocirculation occurs anytime the roof pool is cooler than the storage tube.

STUDY QUESTIONS

1. Explain the difference between "sky temperature" and "air temperature."

2. What were the functions of the high adobe walls that were typically located on three sides of ancient Iranian ice ponds?

3. Describe the design and operation of a Skytherm roof pond building.

4. Discuss the suitability of a roof pond for multistory buildings.

5. Discuss the suitability of a roof pond for cold climates.

6. Why is it inappropriate to insulate the ceiling of a roof-pond building?

7. Why does a ceiling fan increase heating performance in roof pond buildings?

8. If ventilation is generally such an effective cooling strategy, why is wind detrimental to the performance of a radiative cooling panel?

17

PASSIVE COOLING:

EVAPORATION AND DEHUMIDIFICATION

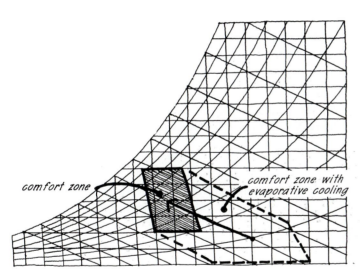

Figure 17.1: Evaporation is a constant-enthalpy process (the latent heat gained equals the sensible heat lost) and occurs along the wet-bulb/enthalpy lines on the psych chart. The comfort zone is shaded and the dotted line defines conditions that can be made comfortable using direct evaporative cooling.

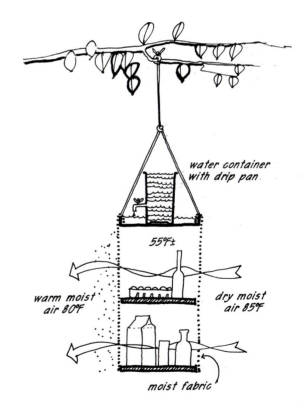

Figure 17.2: Evaporative food cooler; dripping water keeps open-weave, absorbent fabric "walls" wet, cooling dry breezes. *(Redrawn from Wright, 1978, by permission.)*

EVAPORATION

Evaporative cooling is the exchange of sensible heat in air for the latent heat of water droplets on wetted surfaces. It may be used to cool the building (where wetted surfaces are cooled by evaporation), building air (cooled either

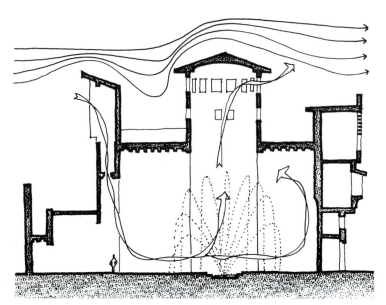

Figure 17.3: *Malkaf* or wind-catch used in old houses in Cairene, Egypt. Air is drawn down and through an interior fountain which cools the air by evaporation. *(After Fathy, 1973.)*

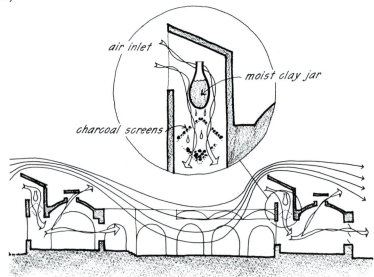

Figure 17.4: Ventilation/evaporation system in girls' primary school in New Gourna, Egypt (H. Fathy, architect). Air is drawn in through wind catches past damp, porous water jars and down through wetted charcoal screens where it is cooled 18°F below ambient temperatures. *(After Fathy, 1973.)*

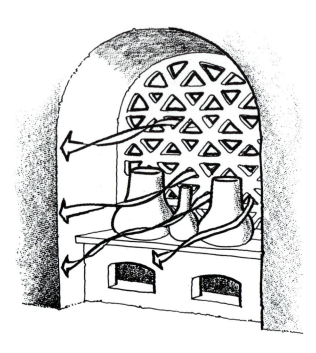

Figure 17.5: Screened wall opening in New Gourna, Egypt (H. Fathy, architect), cools by ventilation and evaporation as air flows around damp, porous water jars. *(After Fathy, 1973.)*

directly by evaporation or indirectly by contact with a surface previously cooled by evaporation), or the occupants (where evaporation of perspiration cools the skin surface). While this would include the physiological process of perspiration cooling, the present discussion will focus on building design strategies that utilize evaporation.

Ideally, evaporative cooling is an *adiabatic* (or constant-enthalpy) process; that is, *sensible* heat is extracted from the air (dry-bulb temperature is reduced), while an equal amount of *latent* heat (in the form of water vapor) is added. The enthalpy (or total heat) remains the same.

DIRECT EVAPORATION

Direct evaporative cooling occurs when relatively dry air is blown over a wetted surface. For example, a breeze blowing through a fountain or over a pond or irrigated field is cooled by direct evaporation. In fact, such landscaping features are among the best ways to implement this cooling strategy because

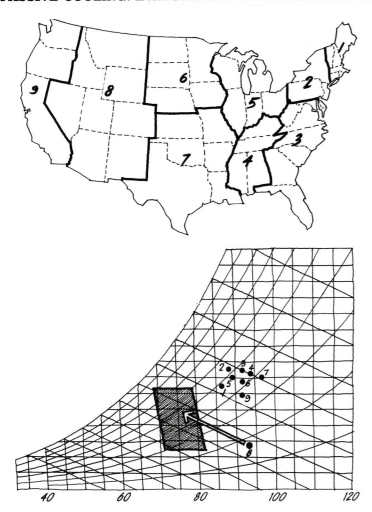

Figure 17.6: Psychrometric chart showing direct evaporative cooling potential for each of the nine DOE climatic zones. The dots represent the outdoor summer conditions that are the basis for sizing cooling equipment. Notice that only region 8 can achieve comfort solely by direct evaporative cooling. *(Redrawn from Yellott, 1990, by permission.)*

of their aesthetic benefits in addition to a relatively automatic control of the process. The disadvantage is that the moisture and cooling effect of such outdoor strategies is often dissipated (and thus wasted) outside of the building. The courtyard has traditionally been used to minimize the evaporative loss from the minioasis of vegetation and fountains that is surrounded by building living spaces.

"Swamp coolers"

Between World War I and II, commercially manufactured direct evaporative cooling units became popular throughout the southwest, where the low wet-bulb temperature of outside air allowed substantial sensible cooling. These units were commercialized in the form of a mass-produced perforated metal box with three sides packed with pads of shredded aspen wood ("excelsior") that could be saturated with water from slotted pipes that ran along their upper edges. The belt-drive centrifugal blower within the box could draw outside air through the wet pads and discharge it into the house through the bottom (because of the motor, they are considered "hybrid" rather than strictly passive). These simple coolers could reduce the dry-bulb temperature of the incoming air to within 5 to 10°F of the outdoor wet-bulb temperature. During the spring and fall, they could produce very acceptable indoor conditions. They were reliable, inexpensive, and required only a small amount of electricity to operate. A major weakness was their inability to cope with the higher wet-bulb temperatures that prevail in the southwest during the most uncomfortable period of the summer (Yellott, 1990).

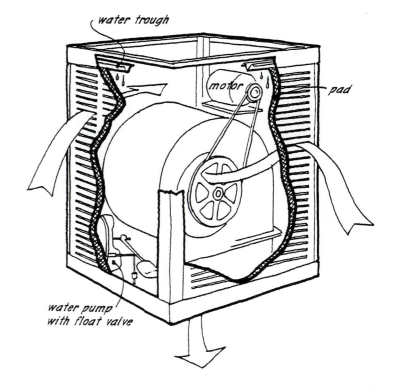

Figure 17.7: Direct evaporative air cooler. *(Redrawn from Yellott, 1990, by permission.)*

INDIRECT EVAPORATION

Indirect evaporative coolers separate the evaporatively cooled air from the conditioned room air. This technique allows reducing the dry-bulb temperature without adding humidity to the room air, and is particularly well-suited where humidity is too high for direct evaporative cooling but where the dew-point temperature is sufficiently low to achieve comfort using only the sensible component of the evaporative process.

This is usually done by a conductive divider which serves as a heat exchanger. Because a motor is usually employed, it is typically a hybrid process rather than a purely passive one. One method is an open-loop process which sprays exhaust air from the room, cooling it by evaporation; this cooled exhaust air is used to indirectly cool incoming hot, dry air from the outside.

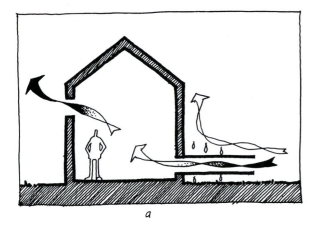

a

b

Figure 17.8: Indirect evaporative air coolers: (a) open-loop, and (b) closed-loop systems.

The alternative indirect process is closed-loop, spraying the outside air to cool it by evaporation; before being exhausted back to the exterior, this cool moist air in turn cools recirculating room air by means of a heat exchanger. While indirect evaporation has the advantage of not increasing the humidity, there is some loss of effectiveness due to the inherent inefficiency of the heat exchange process. In most cases, commercial indirect evaporative coolers have cooling efficiencies of around 65 percent. Virtually all evaporative strategies involving spraying or flooding building surfaces are indirect because the humidity added during the evaporation process remains outside, isolated from the interior air.

Dual-rock-bed coolers

Researchers (Morse, 1968; Dunkle, 1966) have developed a low-cost, hybrid, indirect open-loop evaporative cooling system that utilizes two parallel rock beds as heat exchangers. Room air is cooled by spraying, and is blown through a bed of rocks (cooling the rocks — "charging") before being exhausted to the exterior. Outside hot-dry air is drawn through a separate, identical cool rock bed ("discharging"), cooling the air before entering the building. After a short period of operation (10 to 20 minutes), an air diverter damper changes the circulation pattern, reversing the roles of the rock beds. It is important that the rocks be impervious to water to minimize the residual moisture carried over to the next cycle.

Evaporative cooling of building surfaces

Exterior building wall and roof surfaces heated by radiation (insolation) or convection (air temperature) may be cooled by spraying them with water. As the water evaporates (and its temperature lowered), it cools the surface. The surfaces do not have to be sprayed continuously; it is sufficient to keep the surfaces moist. Thus effective cooling can be achieved by intermittent spraying. Sprays can reduce heat transmission through roofs by 80 percent compared with comparable dry roofs (Reaves and Reaves, 1981). This general strategy can be categorized as a form of indirect evaporation (because the humidified outside air is usually kept separated from the interior); however, because heat transfer through the building envelope is so inefficient, it is usually considered to be a gain-reduction defensive strategy rather than an overt cooling strategy.

Evaporative cooling case study: Princeton Professional Park

A contemporary example of the use of evaporative roof spraying is the Princeton Professional Park (1983, Short and Ford, and Harrison Fraker, architects; Princeton Energy Group, consultants) located in Princeton, New Jersey (a relatively humid, temperate climate). This 64,900 ft² complex is divided into three separate buildings, each with a linear central atrium. At 15-

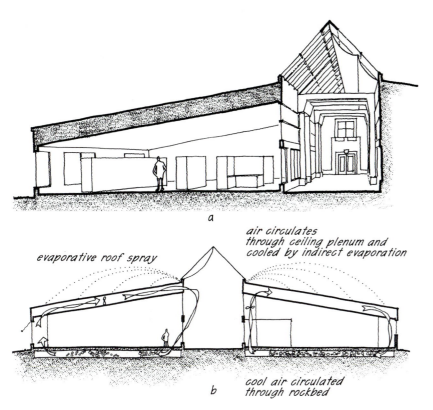

Figure 17.9: Princeton Professional Park: (a) section perspective, and (b) cooling section showing daytime gain-suppression by spray evaporation (left) and night spray evaporation and night sky radiation cooling with cooled air circulation through rock bed under floor (right). *(After Ternoey et al., 1985.)*

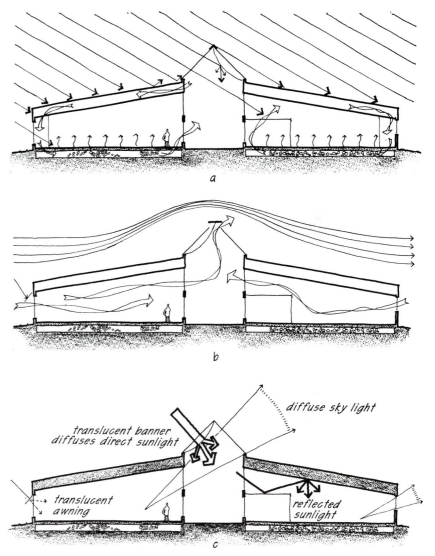

Figure 17.10: Princeton Professional Park: (a) passive solar heating section, (b) ventilative cooling section, and (c) daylighting section. *(After Ternoey et al., 1985.)*

min. intervals, water is sprayed over the metal roof. Peak exterior roof surface temperatures are lowered below 100°F with this system. This component nearly paid for itself by reducing the peak cooling capacity required for the mechanical air conditioning system; because of this the "payback" time was nearly zero, and net savings in operating cost began to occur immediately. The metal roof and spray system also provide a means to purge heat from the rock beds during summer nights. Spray evaporation and night sky radiative cooling can reduce the temperature of the metal roof to about 60°F. A plenum created between the metal roof and the insulated lower panels attached to the bottom chord of the wood trusses permits circulating air past this cool surface, cooling the rock bed to about 65°F, making the office floors a daytime heat sink. The only added expense in this system is the cost of sealing the plenum bound-

aries. This heat-rejection technique and natural ventilation are estimated to reduce the cooling energy needed by the complex by 90 percent. In addition to these cooling strategies, the buildings utilize passive solar heating and daylighting to reduce energy consumption and demand (Ternoey et al., 1985; Cook, 1984).

DEHUMIDIFICATION

While the summer temperature extremes of the humid southeast are not as great as the arid southwest, the high humidity (that is, after all, responsible for the more moderate temperature swings because of the greenhouse effect) is the primary source of discomfort. *Dehumidification* is the removal of water vapor from room air by three means: dilution with drier air, condensation, or desiccation.

VENTILATIVE DILUTION USING DRY AMBIENT AIR

The humidity ratio in un-air-conditioned buildings (particularly residences) is typically higher than outside air due to perspiration, cooking, bathing, and plants. Because of this, ventilative dilution is the simplest and cheapest source of dehumidification. This occurs naturally in the process of ventilative cooling, and is desirable whenever the outdoor dew point is low enough and the ambient dry-bulb temperature is high enough. The design strategies are the same as for ventilation cooling.

CONDENSATION ON PASSIVELY COOLED SURFACES

Ideally, condensation dehumidification is an *adiabatic* (or constant-enthalpy) process; that is, *latent* heat (in the form of water vapor) is extracted from the air, while an equal amount of *sensible* heat (in the form of raised temperature) is added. The enthalpy (or total heat) remains the same.

In warm-humid climates, passive systems rarely can achieve surface temperatures sufficiently low to effect sufficient condensation to control humidity (although wall condensation is a common problem in uninsulated underground structures in humid climates). Control of relative humidity below 70 percent during the night typically requires dew points below 60°F. Even idealized roof radiation systems are unable to provide temperatures this low.

However, passive strategies that utilize seasonal storage of winter cold (for example, deep underground) can provide a condensation surface cold enough to produce dew points near or even below 60°F. Air flowing through earth tubes located deep below ground surrounded by conductive soil can be significantly dehumidified, particularly if the air is recirculated through the tubes in a

closed loop. Underground dehumidification using air tubes poses a number of problems, including disposal of condensate water that collects in the tube, and the presence of underground animals and organisms which may be difficult to clean or remove. Water pumped through underground aquifers in Alabama can yield water cold enough to provide 62°F dew point control by conventional air coils throughout the year (Brett and Schaetzle, 1982).

DESICCANT DEHUMIDIFICATION

Desiccant dehumidification (like condensation) is the psychrometric reverse of evaporative cooling and is thus a constant-enthalpy process. As moisture is absorbed out of the air into the desiccant material, latent heat (water vapor) is removed, sensible heat is added, and the dry-bulb temperature of the air is raised. In other words, the air leaves the desiccant dry and warm. This usually means that if desiccants are used to absorb water vapor in warm-humid climates, additional sensible cooling is necessary to counterbalance the sensible gain that is inherent in the desiccation process. While a number of passive desiccant dehumidification systems for buildings have been proposed, none have proven practical in operation. Absorption refrigeration is a hybrid application of desiccant dehumidification and is discussed in Chapter 19.

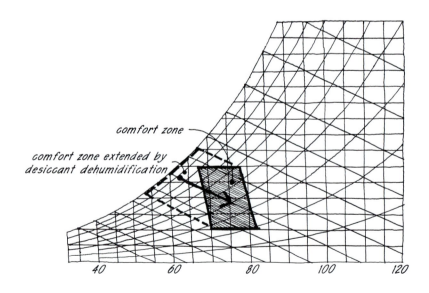

Figure 17.11: Psychrometric chart showing desiccant dehumidification as a constant-enthalpy process.

SUMMARY OF TERMS

Evaporative cooling — the exchange of sensible heat in air for the latent heat of water droplets of wetted surfaces.

Direct evaporative cooling — a cooling process where relatively dry air is blown over a wetted surface and the sensible temperature is lowered and the humidity is increased.

"Swamp cooler" — a fan-powered (hybrid) direct evaporative cooling unit.

Indirect evaporative cooling — a cooling process that separates evaporatively cooled air from the conditioned room air, allowing the reduction of the dry-bulb temperature without adding humidity to the room air.

Open-loop cooling — supply air is drawn in from the outside and cooled before being introduced in the building; return air is exhausted to the outside.

Closed-loop cooling — room air is cooled and recirculated.

Dehumidification — the removal of water vapor from room air by three means: dilution with drier air, condensation, or desiccation.

Ventilative dilution — dehumidification by diluting moist interior air with drier outside air. (Interior air is typically more moist than outside air as a result of cooking, bathing, perspiration, etc.)

Condensation dehumidification — an adiabatic (or constant-enthalpy) dehumidification process.

Desiccant — a chemical drying material that removes moisture (latent heat) from air while raising the temperature (adding sensible heat); the enthalpy (total heat) remains unchanged.

STUDY QUESTIONS

1. What is evaporative cooling and what are the different ways that it can contribute to thermal comfort in buildings?

2. What is dehumidification?

3. Evaporation and desiccant dehumidification are both adiabatic processes. Distinguish between the two.

4. Distinguish between direct and indirect evaporative cooling.

5. Explain the role of solar heating in the desiccant dehumidification process.

6. Why doesn't convective solar-heated desiccant regeneration work well?

18

PASSIVE COOLING:

MASS EFFECT

Buildings with substantial mass utilize their thermal storage capabilities to achieve cooling in three ways: (1) by dampening out interior daily temperature swings, (2) by delaying daily temperature extremes, (3) by ventilating ("flushing") the building at night, and (4) by earth contact to achieve seasonal storage.

DAMPENING DAILY TEMPERATURE SWINGS

If *interior* building materials used for walls and floors are of conductive, massive construction (for example, concrete, masonry, or even water storage containers), they provide a thermal "flywheel" effect, gradually absorbing and releasing heat. The average temperature remains unchanged; only the variation on either side of this average changes. If the building is well-insulated, the thermal mass is entirely within the insulation envelope, and internal heat enters and exits the mass from the *same side,* this moderation occurs with no appreciable time delay. Even without any time delay, this moderation is a substantial advantage in hot-arid climates that experience a substantial daily change in outdoor air temperature.

Even noncoastal humid locations experience sufficient daily temperature variation to make internal mass advantageous. (The stable daily temperatures of Miami, Florida, is often cited as evidence that thermal mass in warm-humid climates is unnecessary; in fact, Miami, located at the end of the Florida peninsula and surrounded by water of stable temperature, is not typical of most inland humid locations which experience considerably greater daily and seasonal temperature ranges.) Internal thermal mass is also effective in diluting the peak effects of intermittent internal heat sources such as people,

equipment, lighting, and absorbed solar heat. Even in the most stable temperature environments (typically coastal), thermal mass is not a disadvantage, although it may be difficult to justify its additional cost on the basis of thermal performance alone. However, conductive massive materials (such as terrazzo, marble, and tile flooring) are cool to the touch (because they rapidly conduct heat away from the surface) and are popular in southeastern coastal regions.

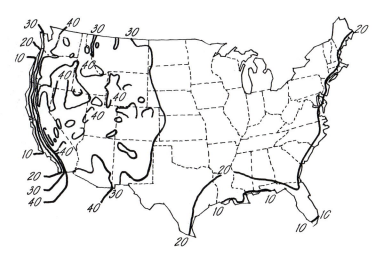

Figure 18.1: Normal daily range of temperature (°F) in July. Notice how close those contours having the lowest values are spaced near the coast, indicating the effect of proximity to a large mass of water on reducing daily temperature swings. *(After U.S. Department of Commerce, 1978.)*

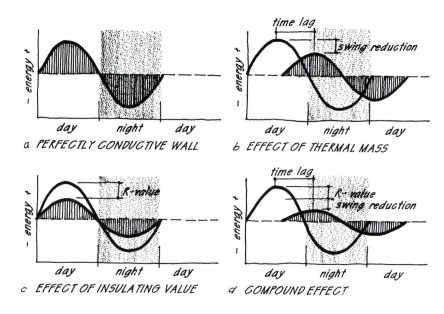

Figure 18.2: Effect of thermal mass and insulation on interior temperature: (a) conductive, low-mass envelope (high swings, no lag), (b) high-mass envelope (e.g., uninsulated masonry; time lag plus reduced swings), (c) insulated, low-mass envelope (reduced swings, no lag), (d) insulated, high-mass envelope (e.g., masonry with exterior insulation; time lag with greatly reduced temperature swings). Notice that in every case, the average temperature remains unchanged. *(After Howard and Fraker, 1990.)*

DELAYING DAILY TEMPERATURE EXTREMES

The exterior envelope of the building behaves somewhat differently because heat enters one side of the material and must conduct through the entire thickness of that material before it finally exits the other side into the interior. If building materials used for walls and roofs are of conductive massive construction (for example, concrete, masonry, or even water storage containers), there is a significant time delay, or *lag*, in addition to the reduction of temperature swing. These two distinct (but related) effects are most obvious in traditional massive construction such as adobe (and contemporary Trombe walls), where there is a minimum of insulating materials. Massive envelope materials are especially appropriate where delaying the effect of the peak daily air and building surface temperatures to a later, cooler period is advantageous.

In hot climates where substantial daily air temperature swings exist (typically in arid areas), the daytime temperature is often so high that ventilative cooling is not only ineffective but may add to discomfort, increasing the cooling load. However, night often brings outdoor air temperatures low enough to contribute to building cooling. If the building interior is massive, this night ventilative cooling can be used to "flush" the building of heat absorbed during the day. For this strategy to be effective, it is important that the ventilating airflow come in direct and intimate contact with the thermal mass. While this can be accomplished to a limited degree depending solely on naturally induced ventilation (wind and stack-effect), the additional cooling effect possible from higher ventilation rates may make the hybrid strategy of utilizing fans cost effective. Night flushing is especially effective in buildings occupied only during the day, allowing the mass to be more effectively cooled (discharged) at night using air temperatures below the comfort zone.

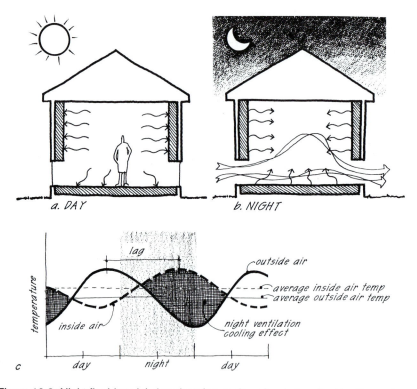

Figure 18.3: Night flushing: (a) day charging cycle — heat absorbed by thermal mass no ventilation to prevent daytime gain, (b) night discharging cycle — heat removed by, thermal mass and exhausted by ventilation of cool night air, and (c) effect on daily temperatures.

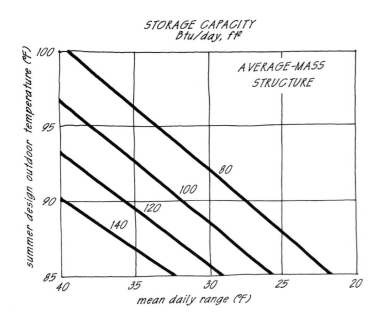

Figure 18.4: Rule of thumb for heat storage capacity in "average-mass" structure using night ventilation, in Btu/day•ft². Assumes a mass structure having 1 ft² of surface exposed per 1 ft² of floor area, of a 4-in. odinary-density concrete slab, with no other significant thermal mass. *(Redrawn from Reynolds, 1984, by permission.)*

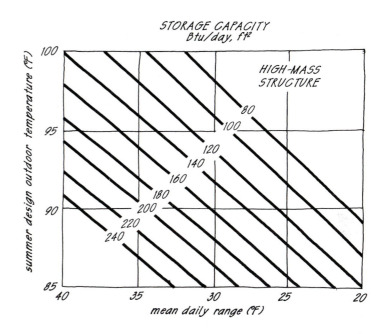

Figure 18.5: Rule of thumb for heat storage (cooling) capacity in "high-mass" structure using night ventilation, in Btu/day•ft². Assumes a mass structure having 2 ft² of surface exposed per ft² of floor area, of a 3-in. ordinary-density concrete (this could also be both sides of a 6-in. concrete wall or slab exposed), with no other significant thermal mass. *(Redrawn from Reynolds, 1984, by permission.)*

One problem with the night flushing ventilation strategy is that, in many climates, wind speed is lowest at night due to the absence of solar radiation as the driving force. For that reason, it may be necessary to use fans to insure the required airflow.

Estimating performance of night ventilation cooling

Reynolds (1984) has suggested rules of thumb for estimating the heat storage capacity of medium- and high-mass buildings using night ventilative cooling (flushing), the maximum hourly cooling rate, and the temperature difference between the outside air and inside mass that exists during the time of maximum cooling. These can be used in conjunction with the charts shown in Figs. 18.4 to 18.7 to determine the required ventilation rates.

EARTH CONTACT

The earth is a virtually infinite heat sink. The magnitude of its heat storage capacity makes it possible to use it for seasonal storage purposes. At depths below 20 ft, the soil temperature is virtually stable and equal to the average annual surface temperature (which is typically two or three degrees warmer than the average annual air temperature, as a result of insolation and the higher temperature of the deep core of the earth). At shallower depths, the soil temperature annual swings are reduced as depth increases. In addition, there is a time lag that increases with depth (e.g., the annual peak soil temperature at a depth of 12 ft typically occurs about three months after that of the surface). The thermal characteristics of soils vary with soil type (constant), compaction (nearly constant), and moisture (varies with rain and groundwater conditions).

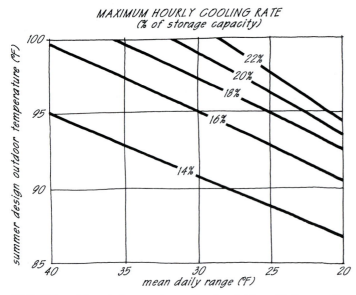

Figure 18.6: Rule of thumb for maximum hourly night ventilation cooling rate (expressed as an approximate percent of the total daily heat stored that is removed during the hour of maximum cooling. *(Redrawn from Reynolds, 1984, by permission.)*

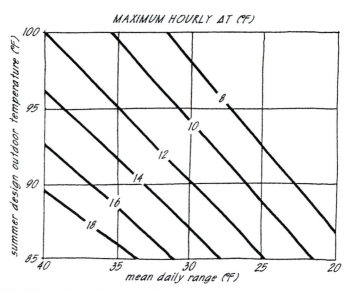

Figure 18.7: Rule of thumb for determining the temperature difference (Δt) between outside air and inside thermal mass that exists during the hour of maximum cooling. *(Redrawn from Reynolds, 1984, by permission.)*

In addition, surface conditions (shade, insulating ground cover, sky temperature) affect soil temperatures.

There are two basic strategies for utilizing earth contact for building cooling: *direct contact* (where the building envelope is partially or completely buried underground), and *indirect contact* (where the building is cooled by buried heat-exchangers such as pipes or air tubes).

DIRECT CONTACT

Earth sheltering is the strategy of covering the walls and/or the roof with soil. In some instances, this may involve constructing the building underground with openings only for entrances and windows. At the other extreme, it may be limited to "berming" (mounding) earth against one or more walls. The primary purpose of establishing direct contact between the building surfaces and the ground is to utilize the mass of the soil for thermal storage. In cases where the soil thickness is relatively thin (for example, a 2-ft thickness of soil on the roof), then the thermal storage is sufficient only for moderating daily (at the most weekly) temperature variations. In cases of completely underground construction, the increased thermal mass of soil provides nearly stable annual temperatures resulting in seasonal storage (i.e., heat gained by the surface in

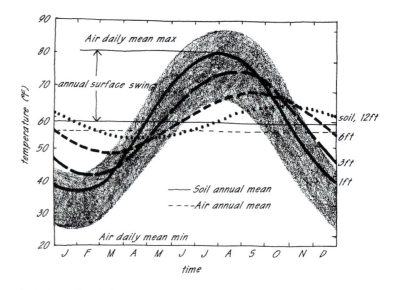

Figure 18.8: Annual variation in air and soil temperatures for a location near Lexington, Kentucky. Notice that as the depth increases, temperatures become more stable (i.e., variation decreases), time lag increases, while the mean temperature remains unchanged. *(After Labs, 1990.)*

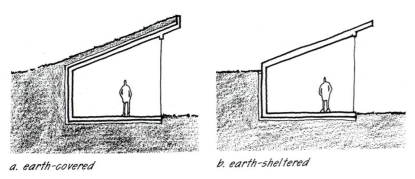

a. earth-covered

b. earth-sheltered

Figure 18.9: Degrees of earth sheltering: (a) *underground* construction (large structural roof loads; extensive, inaccessible waterproofing), vs. (b) *bermed* construction (walls are basement-type construction; roof is wood frame construction with conventional insulation and roofing). Conclusion: given the special structural, waterproofing, and insulation requirements for earth-covered roofs, it is unlikely that the added construction cost can be justified solely on the basis of energy savings (in comparison with, for example, well-insulated, conventional frame roof construction above bermed wall construction).

struction, greater acoustical privacy, reduced exterior surface area for maintaining, and reduced exterior visibility. Disadvantages include increased structural costs, expensive roof waterproofing systems that are inaccessible for repair, expensive moisture- and vermin-resistant rigid foam insulation, humidity control necessary to prevent condensation in cool, humid climates, and the necessity for installing thermal breaks to prevent conductive heat losses through structural walls and roof.

A common misconception holds that underground structures need be dark, cool, and damp; on the contrary, numerous strategies have evolved to utilize direct-gain passive solar heating and daylighting extensively, making them cheerful as well as energy-efficient dwellings. Elevational (primary rooms arranged in a row along one elevation) and atrium plans are two alternatives that provide generous access to the sun for lighting and heating.

One thermal problem inherent in earth-sheltered designs is "thermal nosebleed" — the conductive heat loss that occurs when the building structure is continuous from interior to exterior. This is a particular problem because the large structural loads are typically supported by concrete members (walls, roof, floor) that need to be continuous structurally as they penetrate the building envelope. To prevent excessive heat loss, it is necessary to install

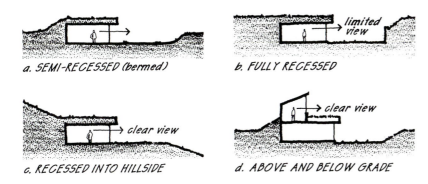

a. SEMI-RECESSED (bermed)

b. FULLY RECESSED → limited view

c. RECESSED INTO HILLSIDE → clear view

d. ABOVE AND BELOW GRADE → clear view

Figure 18.10: Relationship to surface of earth-sheltered design alternatives: (a) fully recessed, (b) semirecessed (bermed), (c) recessed into hillside, and (d) above- and below-grade rooms combined. *(After Underground Space Center, 1979.)*

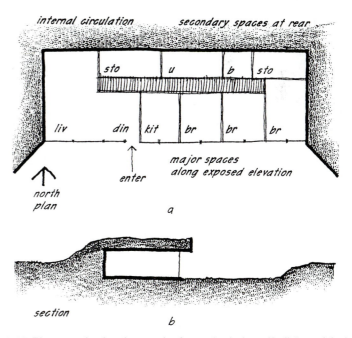

Figure 18.11: Plan organizational strategies for earth-sheltered buildings: (a) elevational plan (all major rooms face toward south elevation). *(After Underground Space Center, 1979.)*

the summer is stored several months to offset heat loss, and in the summer the relatively cool soil provides a large heatsink that is an asset for cooling.

The advantages of earth-sheltered construction include reduced heating and cooling loads (due to reduced conductive and infiltrative transfer, and the potential for seasonal storage), the possibility of increasing the area of vegetation on the site (in the case of earth-covered roof), fire-resistive con-

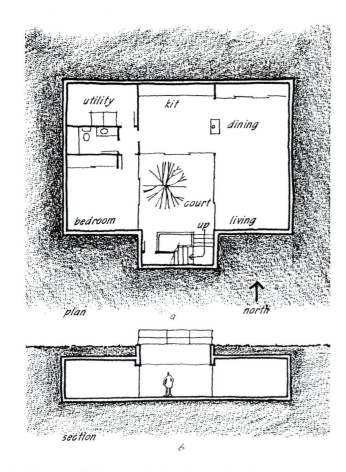

Figure 18.11 (continued): Plan organizational strategies for earth-sheltered buildings: (b) courtyard (open atrium) plan. *(After Underground Space Center, 1979.)*

thermal breaks to effectively isolate the exterior part of the structure from the interior.

Condensation control

A second problem with earth-sheltered designs is the occurrence of condensation on perimeter walls in contact with the earth mass. This problem is most common immediately after construction of cast-in-place concrete. Water vapor is continuously released into the interior environment as the concrete cures, resulting in abnormally high humidity (which, in turn, causes condensation on the walls). This temporary problem often persists for several

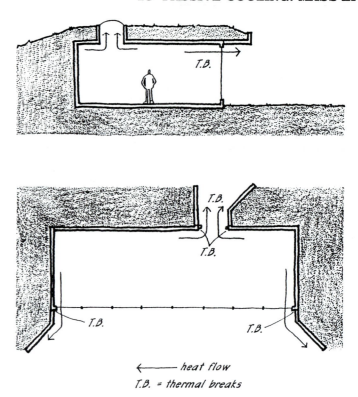

Figure 18.12: Thermal breaks are required (at locations like those labeled "T. B.") to prevent "thermal nosebleed" conductive losses in underground structures. *(After Underground Space Center, 1979.)*

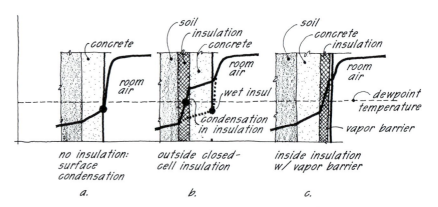

Figure 18.13: Temperature profiles showing the generation of condensation on cool, earth-contact surfaces: (a) no insulation, (b) insulation outside wall, and (c) insulation inside wall.

months (years in some cases), and is exacerbated by the presence of the waterproofing membrane which limits the moisture release to the interior wall surface only.

Wall condensation can be a continuing problem in cool, humid regions (northeastern United States, for example), where it is common for the soil temperature to drop below the dew point. While direct wall contact with this cool soil is an effective cooling strategy, in this case it is too much of a good thing. Insulation between the wall and the soil becomes important not only to reduce winter conductive heat loss but also to buffer the wall from the cooling effect of the soil in the summer (allowing the wall surface temperature to follow more closely to the interior air temperature) and therefore remain above the critical dew-point temperature. If insulation is to be installed inside of the concrete wall (for example, by installing wood furring strips and insulation and covering with finish surface) it is important to install a vapor barrier to prevent hidden condensation from occurring behind the insulation on the concrete surface; this can result in deterioration of materials in contact with the concrete.

In either case, condensation is undesirable, resulting in moisture damage to interior finish surfaces (paint, plaster, wallpaper, carpet) as well as the formation of mildew. Increased ventilation of affected rooms tends to warm the wall by convection nearer to the room air temperature and may be sufficient to eliminate the problem. The alternatives are a portable dehumidifier or mechanical air conditioning, both of which offset the energy-saving advantages of earth sheltering.

Further reading

Earth sheltering is an energy-conservation strategy that has been widely publicized by the popular and professional press, but about which few comprehensive and authoritative handbooks exist. Labs (1990) has identified two books published by the University of Minnesota's Underground Space Center (Underground Space Center, 1979 and 1983) and a Naval Facilities Engineering Command manual (Naval Facilities Engineering Command, 1983) as the three most important books available on the subject for architects designing an underground building.

INDIRECT CONTACT

In this strategy, a fluid (air or liquid) is cooled as it is circulated through an underground conduit (tunnels, ducts, pipes, etc.). The fluid, in turn, cools the structure. The circulation pattern can be *open-loop* (air drawn from outside through tubes and into the building) or *closed-loop* (air is circulated from building out through the underground conduit and back to the building).

A historic example of an open-loop, indirect contact system is the Villa Aeolia, built in 1550 by Count Francesco Trento, which was cooled by air drawn through large underground caverns (Fanchiotti and Scudo, 1981). The caverns had been excavated previously in the process of digging out slabs of marble as far back as the empire of Augustus (27 B.C. — 14 A.D.). Air is introduced in a hillside opening above the cavern which is connected by a tunnel to the villa below. Because of this vertical arrangement, convective airflow occurs as the air is cooled and becomes more dense than outside air. The performance of this ancient system has been measured; the temperature in the caverns is practically constant 52°F (11.5°C) throughout the year, while typical summer day temperatures reach 90°F (32°C). The system provides a supply of air at 55 to 57°F to the villa where the interior air temperature is maintained at a near-constant 68 to 71°F.

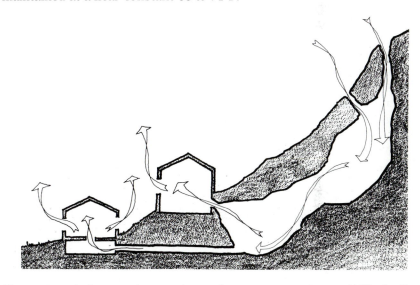

Figure 18.14: Indirect-earth-contact, open-loop system used to cool Villa Aeolia, c. 1550; A. Palladio, architect. Flow is by natural convection as air enters high, is cooled in underground caverns, and flows down through tunnels into the villa below, maintaining air temperature around 70°F while outdoor air temperature reaches 90°F. *(Redrawn from Fanchiotti and Scudo, 1981, by permission.)*

Recently, open-loop earth tube systems have been installed in several buildings, drawing in outside air through buried tubes where the air is cooled sensibly (often below the dew point, resulting in condensation) before entering the building. Virtually all of these systems are hybrid, using fans to generate the required airflow. Akridge (1982) has suggested the following design guidelines for earth tubes:

- Small-diameter tubes are more effective per unit surface area than are larger tubes.

- Air reaches the adjacent ground temperature relatively quickly, so long tubes are unnecessary.

- A large-diameter tube of a given length will transfer more energy than a small-diameter tube of the same length; therefore multiple small tubes should be used.

- Tubes should be placed as deeply as possible so that the surrounding soil temperature is the lowest and relatively constant.

- Exit temperature is highly dependent on inlet temperature; thus, using outside air drawn through open-loop earth-cooling tubes results in higher exit temperatures, higher soil temperatures, and a higher relative humidity (than a comparable closed-loop configuration which recycles interior air).

- Ground thermal resistance is so high that tube thermal resistance is immaterial (i.e., plastic or concrete tubes perform as well as copper tubes).

- While higher airflow rates result in greater cooling, this results from more air being cooled than from more efficient conductive heat transfer between the tube and air.

Stein and Reynolds (1992) suggest the following rule-of-thumb procedure for approximating earth tube performance:

- Air velocity within each tube should be 500 ft/min (fan should be sized accordingly).

- air volume, ft^3/min = (500 ft/min) x (tube cross section, ft^2)

- Sensible cooling will be about 1.3 Btu/h•°F per ft of length (maximum length 300 ft) times the difference between the earth temperature and the outside air temperature.

Abrams (1986) provides additional information on earth tube design and construction. Boyer and Johnston (1981) suggested a "plan design index" methodology which evaluates the floor plan of earth-sheltered residences on the basis of thermal comfort, energy efficiency, and occupant utilization on an overall rating scale (from 0.0 poor to 1.0 excellent).

Figure 18.15: Regional earth-tube condensation index. July 21 values equal 2 to 12-ft-depth soil temperature average *minus* maximum daily dew-point temperature (°F). Large positive values (i.e., dew point much less than soil temperature) such as those found in the arid southwest indicate condensation is unlikely; large negative values are found in the northeast where condensation is most likely and can be used for dehumidification. *(Redrawn from Labs, 1981, by permission.)*

EARTH-CONTACT ENHANCEMENT

One of the most overlooked aspects of earth-contact cooling are the opportunities for intentional alteration of the natural temperature of the ground (Labs, 1990), including:

- Reduction of deep ground temperature by intentionally "supercooling" the soil (e.g., using a curtain of vertical air drains filled with pebbles surrounding the structure, so that cool winter air "drains" into the open shafts) as proposed by Givoni (1980).

- Summer surface temperatures (and, consequently, subsoil temperatures) can be depressed by restricting the amount of solar radiation absorbed by the surface (by providing shading, using light-colored surfaces, and dissipating heat by evaporative spraying).

- Manipulation of soil thermal properties (by localized irrigation to keep soil moist, and consequently more conductive).

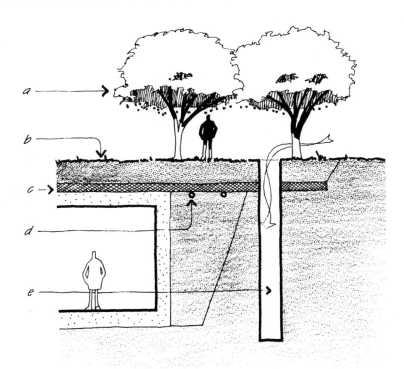

Figure 18.16: Composite showing several strategies for intentional alteration of subsurface soil temperatures: (a) surface shading to retard phase of ground, (b) surface treatments to increase albedo (reflection) and irrigation for latent heat dissipation, (c) horizontal insulation underground to resist conducted heat gain from surface, (d) subirrigation to enhance conductivity of backfill in summer, and (e) air drain curtain. *(Redrawn from Labs, 1981, by permission.)*

An example of earth-contact enhancement is a house using a closed-loop earth-tube hybrid cooling system designed by the author for the U.S. Department of Housing and Urban Development Cycle Five Demonstration Program. Built in Cincinnati, the house utilizes four 6-in.-diameter PVC tubes 70 ft long buried 8 ft below ground. During the winter, cold outside air is circulated through the underground tubes using a 1/10-hp fan and exhausted back to the outside; this "discharge" winter cycle "supercools" the earth mass well below the normal underground temperature in preparation for the following summer cooling season. During the summer, with the manual repositioning of two dampers, the same fan circulates room air down through the tubes (where it is cooled), and back into the residence. While the system has operated without problem for several years, its performance has never been monitored.

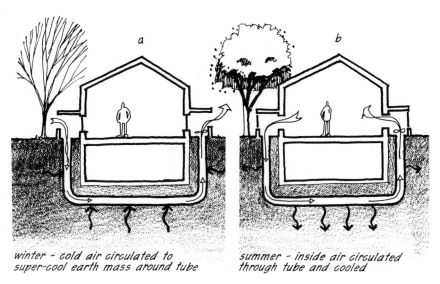

winter - cold air circulated to super-cool earth mass around tube

summer - inside air circulated through tube and cooled

Figure 18.17: Closed-loop earth-tube-cooled residence, Cincinnati, Ohio (F. Moore, architect); (a) winter "discharging" cycle supercools earth mass, and (b) summer cycle is "closed-loop" circulating indoor air through the tubes and back to the interior again.

SUMMARY OF TERMS

Mass-effect cooling — a passive strategy that utilizes thermal storage for cooling: (1) by dampening out interior daily temperature swings, (2) by delaying daily temperature extremes, (3) by ventilating ("flushing") the building at night, and (4) by earth contact to achieve seasonal storage.

Night flushing — ventilating a building interior at night in order to cool internal thermal mass.

Earth-contact cooling — using the cool temperature of subsurface soil temperatures to cool building interiors.

Thermal break — insulating building component installed to conductively isolate the interior part of an earth-sheltered structure from the exterior.

Earth-cooling tubes — underground ducts which draw air through them in order to be cooled before being supplied to a building interior.

STUDY QUESTIONS

1. How can buildings with substantial mass utilize their thermal storage capabilities to achieve cooling?

2. Why should building thermal storage materials be both massive and conductive?

3. What are the two thermal effects of an adobe wall in a pueblo structure?

4. What is "night flushing"? Explain why it is such an attractive cooling strategy in commercial buildings.

5. For a high-mass building in a climate with a summer outdoor design temperature of 90°F and a 30°F average daily temperture range, what is the rate of cooling due to night ventilation?

6. Compare direct-contact and indirect-contact earth-contact cooling.

7. What are the advantages and disadvantages of earth-sheltered construction?

8. What are the two primary means of controlling wall condensation in earth-sheltered buildings?

9. Briefly compare open-loop and closed-loop earth cooling tubes.

19

MECHANICAL HEATING AND COOLING[*]

While passive solar heating and cooling systems are effective in conserving energy, it is usually not cost-effective (or, in most cases, possible) to achieve 100 percent of the annual heating or cooling by these means alone. Like conservation measures, the design of passive solar heating and cooling systems is determined by the principle of diminishing return. Small systems can be effectively utilized throughout most of the season. As the systems are made larger (and more expensive) in an attempt to achieve higher percentages of passive conditioning, they are fully utilized fewer and fewer times during the year. In the extreme case, the final system enlargement necessary to achieve passive conditioning through the worst-case condition (may occur only once every several years) is completely idle the remainder of the time. It is not possible to justify the cost of these very large systems on the basis of the small savings achieved under the worst-case periods. In virtually every building, there is a need to supplement passive strategies with mechanical heating and air conditioning systems. Chapter 12 described the method for determining a cost-effective balance of passive and mechanical heating systems.

MECHANICAL HEATING

Mechanical heating sources may be catagorized as *boilers* (which heat water or steam for distribution to the building in pipes), *furnaces* (which heat air for distribution in ducts), *heat pumps* (which heat air or water by extracting heat from the surounding outdoor environment using a refrigeration cycle),

and *electric resistance* (which most typically heat air locally for circulation within the room, or heat ceiling or wall surfaces for direct radiation within the room; because of high operating cost, electric resistance is seldom used as the heat source for a furnace or boiler). Boilers and furnaces are most commonly used in large buildings. Heat pumps are more commonly used in small- and medium-sized buildings. Electric-resistance radiant heating is used primarily in small buildings, although electric resistance may be used in air ducts in larger buildings to reheat air immediately before being supplied to rooms.

Both boilers and furnaces burn fossil fuels to generate heat. Usually these are natural gas or fuel oil; because of the difficulty of controlling combustion emissions, coal is rarely used directly for building heating but may be used in a central generating plant which supplies steam to several buildings. These combustion processes require a source of combustion air and a chimney for exhausting combustion emissions. Heat pumps require electrical power for the mechanical refrigeration cycle, and a source of heat (typically outdoor air or ground water).

Electric resistance requires only wiring for heat distribution and production, converts all of the electrical energy into heat, and produces no on-site pollution. However, significant pollution is concentrated at the electric generating plant, power transmission is relatively inefficient, and the cost of heat delivered to the building is the highest of most available alternatives. Because of that, electric resistance is considered only where low construction cost is the principal consideration or where pipe and duct distribution systems are impractical.

---

[*]With the exception to the portions noted, this chapter was substantially reproduced from "HVAC Systems," monograph in the *Architects Handbook of Energy Practice* by permission of the American Institute of Architects.

MECHANICAL COOLING

The refrigeration machine (that component that "pumps" heat) is the essential element of any mechanical cooling system. There are two methods suitable for building applications: vapor compression and absorption. The vapor compression cycle is less expensive and more commonly used. They have the added capability of functioning as a source of heat (heat pump) by reversing the cycle. The absorption cycle is suitable when there is a low-cost source of heat available and is the system typically used in conjunction with active solar collectors to create "solar air conditioning."

VAPOR-COMPRESSION REFRIGERATION

The compressive refrigeration cycle is based on the following two phenomena:

1. A large amount of heat (heat of vaporization) must be added to change a liquid into a gas; the same amount of heat (heat of condensation) is released when the gas condenses back into a liquid.

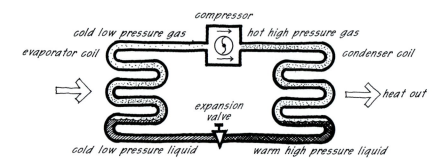

Figure 19.1: The vapor-compression refrigeration cycle. The compressor maintains the left side of the diagram at low pressure and the right side at high pressure. As warm refrigerant liquid passes from the high-pressure side through a small opening in the expansion valve to the low-pressure side (evaporator coil), it vaporizes due to the low pressure. As this vaporization occurs, it absorbs heat from the evaporator coil (this creates the cooling process that is the goal of the process). The compressor pumps the refrigerant cold gas over to the high-pressure side (condenser coil). Because any gas heats up when put under higher pressure, this gas (and the condenser coil containing it) becomes hot and releases heat. As heat is released, the temperature drops below the high-pressure condensation temperature and warm liquid refrigerant collects at the bottom of the condenser coil. This warm, high-pressure liquid is drawn through the expansion valve to complete the cycle. *(Redrawn from Lechner, 1991, by permission.)*

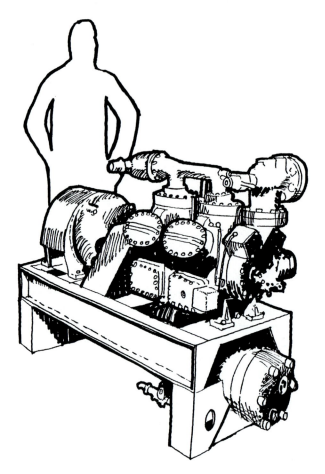

Figure 19.2: Reciprocating compressor (used in compressive refrigeration cycle).

2. The boiling/condensation temperature of any material varies with pressure. When pressure is reduced the boiling/vaporization point temperature is also reduced.

ABSORPTION REFRIGERATION

The absorption refrigeration cycle depends on the same two phenomena plus the following:

Figure 19.3: Air-cooled condensing unit.

3. Some liquids (for example, lithium bromide or ammonia) have a strong tendency to absorb water vapor. Once saturated with water, these absorbers can be regenerated by heating to evaporate the water.

Unlike the compressive cycle, absorption refrigeration machines require no compressor pumps or other moving parts. However, they do require a source of heat such as a gas flame or the waste heat from an industrial process.

HVAC SYSTEM TYPES

Centralized mechanical heating, ventilating, and air-conditioning (HVAC) systems are generally classified according to the heat-transfer fluid delivered to the occupied space: air, air and water, water, or refrigerant. In addition, decentralized systems may be installed at the point of use.

ALL-AIR SYSTEMS

In all-air systems, the air treating and refrigeration units may be located some distance from the conditioned space in a central mechanical room. The central treating station not only cleans the air but also heats or cools, humidifies or dehumidifies. Only the final cooling-heating medium (air) is brought into the conditioned space through ducts and distributed within the space through outlets or mixing terminals. The available all-air systems can be classified as single-path or dual-path:

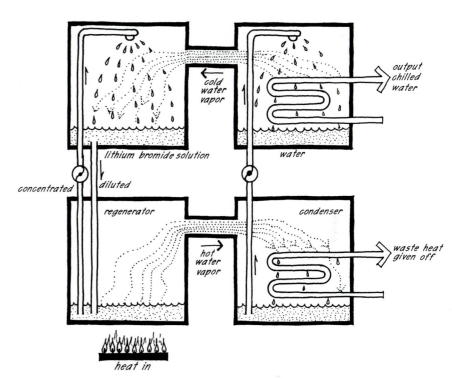

Figure 19.4: The absorption refrigeration cycle. In chamber "A" water evaporates and in the process draws heat from the chilled water coil (cooling output). The water vapor migrates to chamber "B" where it is absorbed by the lithium bromide (or ammonia) solution. Consequently, the vapor pressure is reduced and more water can evaporate to continue the cooling process. When the lithium bromide begins to dilute to further absorb water, it is piped into chamber "C" (the regenerator) where it is heated (by solar heat, waste industrial process heat, or some other low-cost heat source) to boil the water off. The regenerated lithium bromide is returned to chamber "B" while the hot water vapor is condensed back into water in chamber "D." The water is returned to chamber "A" completing the cycle while waste heat is released to outside. *(Redrawn from Lechner, 1991, by permission.)*

- Single-duct, constant-volume

- Single-duct, variable-volume

- Single-duct, reheat (constant- or variable-volume)

- Dual-duct (including dual-duct variable-volume)

- Multizone

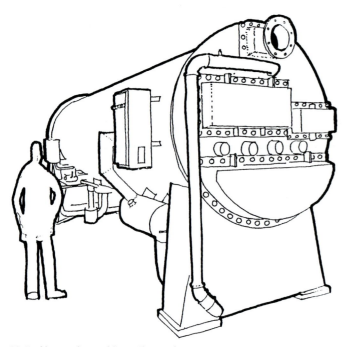

Figure 19.5: Absorption refrigeration unit.

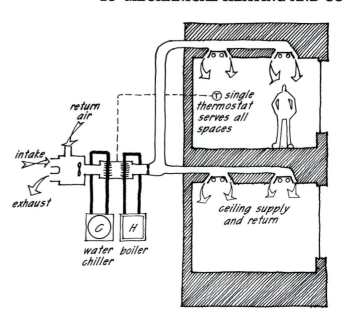

Figure 19.6: Single-duct, single-zone system. *(Redrawn from American Institute of Architects, 1982, by permission.)*

The *single-duct, constant-volume* is a single-zone system that can be quite effective but its range of application is somewhat limited. The *single-duct, variable-volume* system is a multizone system that is clearly superior to the remaining all-air systems designed to deliver constant-temperature air. This system satisfies the severest zone load and gives smaller volumes of the same constant-temperature air to other zones with lesser loads. This system is especially effective for groups of interior zones where loads do vary but generally not rapidly nor frequently. The most serious problems would occur in zones with lesser heat loads but which produce larger quantities of moisture, dirt or odor that are too large to be eliminated by low volumes of air. Spaces with no cooling loads but a minimum air supply volume can become too cool.

Constant-volume, multizone systems can satisfy different loads by varying air temperature only. Unfortunately, the normal control strategy is to cool all of the air to the level required by the severest load and to reheat the air delivered to all zones with lesser loads as necessary. This technique offers finely tuned control but can waste energy.

The *variable-volume* (VAV) systems, in addition to eliminating wasteful reheating, have other energy conservation benefits. Controls can be designed

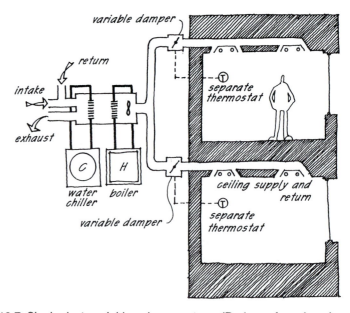

Figure 19.7: Single-duct, variable-volume system. *(Redrawn from American Institute of Architects, 1982, by permission.)*

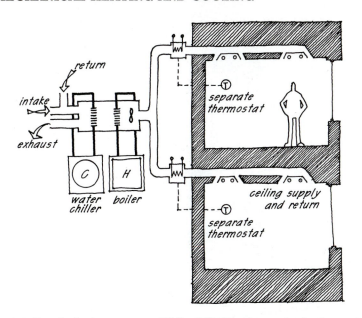

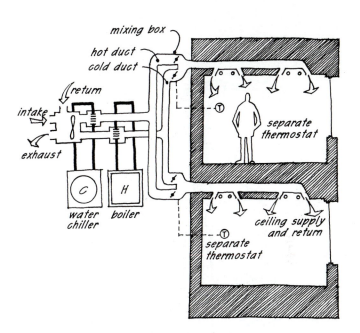

Figure 19.8: Terminal reheat system. While air is the primary distribution system, the use of hot water reheat coils make this a mixed system: all-air and air-water. The reheat source may also be electric resistance which is less expensive to install but more expensive to operate. *(Redrawn from American Institute of Architects, 1982, by permission.)*

Figure 19.9: Dual-duct system. *(Redrawn from American Institute of Architects, 1982, by permission.)*

so that as the total of all the various zone loads decreases and as more VAV dampers reduce the volume, the delivery air temperature can be increased and/or the system air volume reduced. This significantly reduces fan power consumption.

All-air systems characteristics include:

Advantages:

- Adaptable to humidification, heat-recovery systems, and automatic seasonal changeover.

- Adaptable to complex zoning schemes, with ability to provide year-round heating and cooling.

- Adaptable to close control of temperature and humidity, e.g., in computer rooms.

- Can use untreated outside air instead of mechanically cooled air more often in summer.

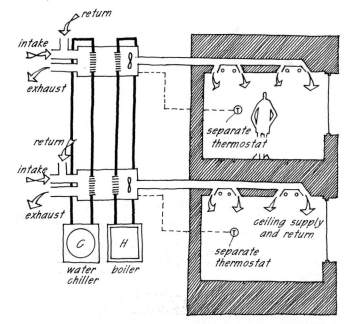

Figure 19.10: Constant-volume, multizone system. *(Redrawn from American Institute of Architects, 1982, by permission.)*

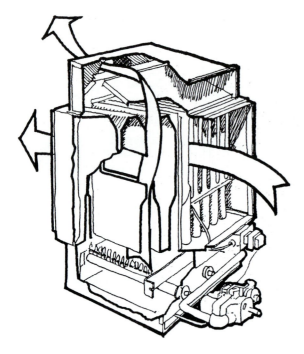

Figure 19.11: Horizontal-flow, gas-fired duct furnace. *(Redrawn from American Institute of Architects, 1982, by permission.)*

Disadvantages:

• Special care required with terminal device placement and surrounding structural elements to ensure accessibility to terminal units for maintenance and repair.

• In cold climates, radiation heating needed at perimeter during unoccupied hours to avoid having to heat entire building.

• Higher structural costs and increased HVAC loads, due to large duct spaces that increase building volume.

Other general characteristics of all-air systems include:

• Suitability for laboratories or other applications requiring abnormal exhaust makeup.

• Provides least infringement on rentable floor space.

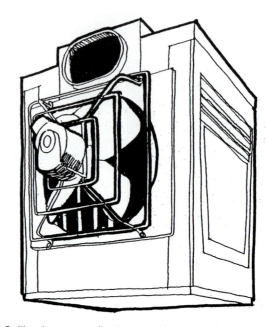

Figure 19.12: Ceiling-hung, gas-fired convection space heater.

Figure 19.13: Vane axial fan.

- Provides flexible control of air motion.

- Does not interfere with window drapes; minimum damage risk to furnishings.

- Perimeter systems not available for use as rapidly as radiation systems during building construction.

- Absence of built-in automatic zone devices for rapid easy balancing when a single air system serves areas which are not rented simultaneously.

- Sometimes difficult to prevent unwanted air noise and motion.

- Often difficult to provide for proper fire safety separations.

AIR-WATER SYSTEMS

Air-water systems combine the cost and energy efficiency of water systems with the flexibility of air systems, to provide forced-air ventilation, central control humidity, and rapid response to load fluctuations in a variety of zones.

In these systems both air and water are delivered to each space, and heating and cooling functions are carried out by changing the temperature of one or both media to control space temperatures year-round.

Water's high specific heat allows it to deliver a given amount of heating and cooling capacity in a much smaller volume than air requires. This results in distribution pipes much smaller than comparable air ducts, a feature that makes water attractive in highrise and other buildings where space is at a premium.

Further, the pumping necessary to circulate the water throughout the building is usually about one-sixth the fan power that would be required for an all-air system. The savings on operating cost can be quite substantial when compared with medium- or high-pressure, all-air, constant-volume systems.

When water is the primary conditioning medium, the system can be designed so that the air supply is equal to ventilation or exhaust requirements, eliminating the need for return air ducts and fans.

Air-water systems are primarily applicable to multiple perimeter spaces where a wide range of sensible loads exists and where close control of humidity is not required. Where significant fluctuations in air-conditioning requirements can occur at the same time on a given exposure, individual room control is available.

For all systems using outdoor air, there is an outdoor temperature, the changeover temperature, at which mechanical cooling is no longer required. At this point, the system can accomplish cooling through the use of outdoor air; at lower temperatures, heating rather than cooling is needed. With all-air systems capable of operating with up to 100 percent outdoor air, mechanical cooling is often not required at outdoor temperatures below 50 to 55°F. An important characteristic of air-water systems, however, is that refrigeration for secondary water cooling may continue to be needed even when the outdoor temperature is considerably less than 50°F.

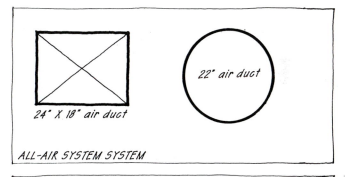

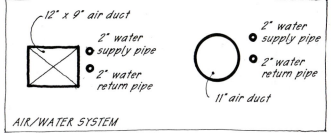

Figure 19.14: Comparison of space requirements for air-air and air-water distribution systems. *(Redrawn from American Institute of Architects, 1982, by permission.)*

Air-water systems generally have the following characteristics:

Advantages:
- Ability to handle a variety of loads by separate sources of heating and cooling in each space.

- Capacity for centralized humidification, dehumidification, and filtration.

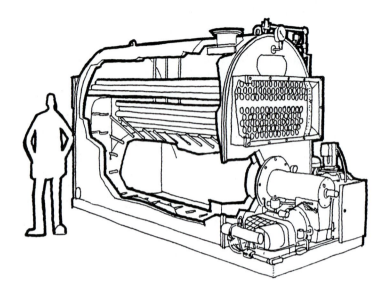

Figure 19.15: Oil-fired, high firebox boiler.

• Smaller central air handler needed because of reduced air volume.

• Capacity for space heating by water system alone, without fans, at night or during power emergencies if wall units are located under window.

Disadvantages:

• Air at low dew-point temperature is necessary when primary system accomplishes all dehumidification.

• Inability to prevent condensation caused by open windows or other sources of humidity.

• Humidity control requires water chilled to low temperatures or even chemical dehumidification.

• Reliance on mechanical cooling even when the outdoor temperature is considerably less than 50°F.

As shown in the following illustrations, the in-space equipment will generally be either induction units or fan-coil.

Air-water induction systems

In an air-water induction unit, centrally conditioned air is supplied to the unit plenum at high pressure. It then flows through induction nozzles and induces air from the room to flow over the water coil and become heated or cooled. The primary and secondary air are mixed and discharged to the room.

A wide variety of induction unit configurations is available, including units with low overall heights or with extremely large coil face areas, to suit the particular needs of space or load.

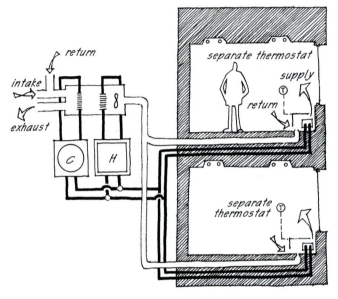

Figure 19.16: Air-water induction system. *(Redrawn from American Institute of Architects, 1982, by permission.)*

Fan-coil conditioner systems with primary air

Fan-coil conditioner units are versatile room terminals that can be used with both air-water and water-only systems. Despite the shortcomings in the quality of air-conditioning achieved with water-only systems, the fan-coil units have been more commonly associated with that type of system than with air-water systems. Many of the standard features of the units are accordingly used for the water-only applications.

The basic elements of fan-coil units are a finned-tube coil and a fan. The fan recirculates air continuously from within the perimeter space through the coil, which is supplied with either hot or chilled water. In addition, the unit can contain an auxiliary heating coil, which usually functions by electric resistance, steam, or hot water. The primary air system for areas using fan-coil units need not be integrated with the fan-coil system.

Air-water systems are characterized as two-, three-, and four-pipe systems. Incorporating both cooling and heating capabilities for year round air conditioning, they all function in the same way, although the details of system design differ significantly.

Two-pipe system

The water-coil output of each terminal is controlled by a local space thermostat, and can vary from 0 percent to 100 percent of capacity as required to maintain space temperature. Two-pipe systems are generally satisfactory during the winter and summer seasons. The intermediate seasons, however, can create problems because of the system's inability to provide simultaneous heating and cooling to different parts of the building. Primary air temperatures must be reset as outside air temperature changes and thus both a temperature reset schedule and calculation of primary air quantities become critical to the design.

Three-pipe systems are not widely used. They can be wasteful of energy, especially when there are wide variations between zone loads, because as with all-air systems the mixing is actually heating and cooling the same space at the same time. Also, there are only minor savings from deleting one pipe, but major control problems.

Four-pipe systems

Four-pipe systems have four pipes to each terminal unit: one each for chilled water supply and return, and two more for warm water supply and return. As four-pipe systems do not mix the hot and chilled water in a common return pipe, they are superior to three-pipe systems in reducing the energy needed to reheat and rechill the water after it returns to the central unit.

The controls for four-pipe systems are generally simpler than for two- or three-pipe systems, and the first costs often work out to be quite close. Energy and operating costs for four-pipe systems are generally comparable as well.

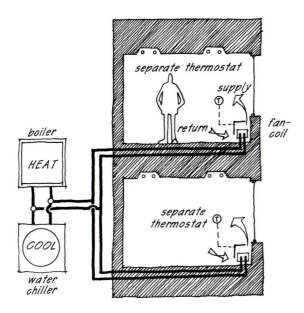

Figure 19.17: Two-pipe system. *(Redrawn from American Institute of Architects, 1982, by permission.)*

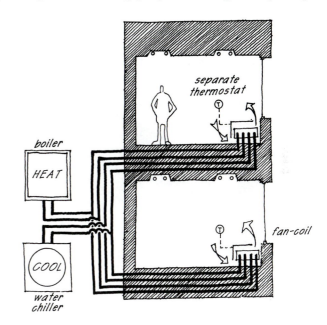

Figure 19.18: Four-pipe system. *(Redrawn from American Institute of Architects, 1982, by permission.)*

Three-pipe systems

Three-pipe systems have three pipes to each terminal unit: a cold water supply, a hot water supply, and a common return. Hot and cold water are usually used in the unit selectively, depending on temperature requirements.

Air-water systems have other advantages and disadvantages.

Advantages:
• Pipework and ducting that lasts as long as 20 to 25 years.

- Positive-ventilation air supply.

- Recirculation that occurs only within each room when all primary air is outdoor air, and thus reduced cross-contamination.

- High-quality air filtration.

- Reduced cooling capacity, with the building load rather than the sum of room peaks determining capacity requirements.

Disadvantages:
- Applicable only to the perimeter of most buildings.

- Frequent cleaning of room units is required.

- Usually not possible to shut off primary air supply in individual rooms.

- Supplementary ventilation air is needed for spaces with high exhaust requirements.

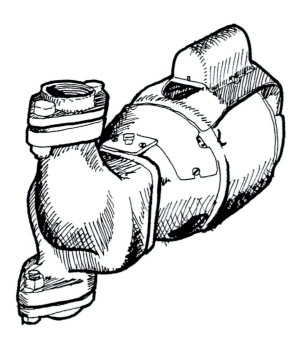

Figure 19.19: In-line circulating pump used for air-water and all-water systems.

ALL-WATER SYSTEMS

All-water (or hydronic) systems use fan-coils or unit ventilators with unconditioned ventilation air supplied by an opening through the wall or by infiltration. Cooling and dehumidification are provided by circulating chilled water or brine through a finned coil in the unit. Heating is provided by supplying hot water through the same or a separate coil, using two-, three-, or four-pipe water distribution from central equipment. Electric heating at the terminal can be used to enhance system flexibility. In residences, all-water baseboard hydronic convectors are used with no provision for outside air (see "Decentralized Systems" section below).

All-water systems can be especially economical and compact, but their effectiveness as space conditioners is limited to buildings with small interior spaces, such as motels, apartments, and small office buildings.

UNITARY SYSTEMS

All of the mechanical distribution systems discussed thus far are designed to take advantage of the performance efficiencies of large central plant equipment. Most refrigerant systems, on the other hand, are designed for decentralization. Inefficiencies in performance are offset by the following advantages:

- Individual room control, air distribution, and ventilation system for each room, usually with simple adjustment by the occupant.

- Heating and cooling capability always available independently of operation of other spaces in the building.

- Only one terminal zone or conditioner affected in the event of equipment malfunction.

- Usually low initial cost.

- Reliable, manufacturer-matched components (usually with certified ratings and published performance data), assembled by manufacturer.

- Ability to shut down equipment in unoccupied rooms for extended periods.

Unitary systems rarely have the variations of coil configurations, evaporator temperatures, air-handling arrangements, and refrigerating capacities available in central systems. Thus, unitary equipment often requires a higher level of design ingenuity and performance to develop superior system performance. Yet, because of factory control in component matching and of quality control in interconnection, application of unitary equipment seldom leads to serious breakdowns.

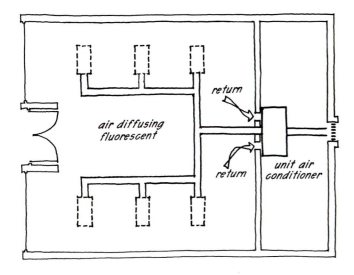

Figure 19.20: Single packaged unit with variable air volume and bypass. *(Redrawn from American Institute of Architects, 1982, by permission.)*

Multiple units come either as window air conditioners or through-the-wall units, also called packaged terminal air conditioners (PTACs). PTACs generally include a heating section, while window air conditioners do not.

Unitary systems are generally located on the roof; at least the fan and evaporator of a rooftop system is mounted on the roof. The air distribution ductwork penetrates the roof. The compressor and condensing section can be mounted remotely, but they are more often packaged with the fan and evaporator. The complete system consists of the unitary equipment, air distribution and air delivery system(s), interlocking controls, structural supports, and vibration-isolation system.

Unitary systems can also be equipped with variable-volume terminals, either the bypass or squeeze-off type. Unitary systems are designed for constant-air-volume control units and do not have the capacity for adjusting fan speeds. For small outside air percentages, bypass terminals avoid increases in duct static pressure and do not allow the cooled air to mix with warm room air before circulating it again.

As indicated earlier, unitary systems are well suited to logical zoning, with one unit per zone. A variation on this theme is the use of a single unitary system to supply preconditioned air to other unitary systems in the building. Under mild weather conditions, such a unit continues in operation even if the zone thermostats have one or more other units off. This prevents the introduction of hot, humid air into the conditioned spaces under periods of light loading. This strategy can also be adapted to highrise buildings.

Direct-expansion water-loop heat pumps deserve special attention because heat recovery and redistribution are among their inherent energy-conserving characteristics. They are used as terminal equipment to heat and cool a zone when connected to a closed-loop piping circuit with means for adding heat to, or rejecting heat from, the water circuit. With supply-loop water temperature maintained between 60 and 90°F, and with a water flow rate of 2 to 3 gal/min•ton, the terminal equipment can operate on either heating or cooling to maintain temperature in its zone.

Water circulated within the closed loop becomes either a sink or a source of heat. Units on the heating mode extract heat from the water. Units on the cooling mode reject heat to the water. Heat rejected from the central core units is carried in the loop water to perimeter units for use in the heating season. Unlike air-source heat pumps, heat available for units of this system does not

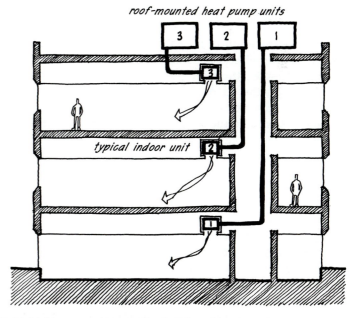

Figure 19.21: Multiroom, multistory office building with unitary air conditioners. *(Redrawn from American Institute of Architects, 1982, by permission.)*

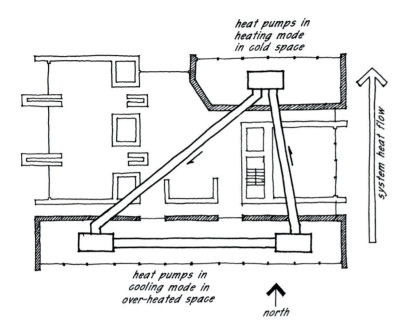

heat pumps in
heating mode
in cold space

system heat flow

heat pumps in
cooling mode in
over-heated space

north

Figure 19.22: Closed-loop, water-loop heat pump system. *(Redrawn from American Institute of Architects, 1982, by permission.)*

depend on outdoor temperature, since the water loop is the primary source, and a secondary source of heat is usually provided.

In the cooling mode, the heat pump operates as a water-cooled air conditioner. In the heating mode, the functions of the evaporator and the condenser are reversed so that the equipment operates as a water chiller. Heat is removed from the water in the water-to-refrigerant heat exchanger, which acts as the evaporator. That heat, plus the heat from the compressor, is rejected through the refrigerant-to-air heat exchanger (acting as the condensor) and heats the room.

The multiple-water-loop heat pump system offers zoning capability, since terminal equipment can be selected with cooling capacity as low as 7,000 Btu/h. Since equipment can be placed in interior areas, the system can accommodate future relocation of partitions with a minimum of modifications.

This system is twice as efficient in heating than in cooling, because waste heat entering spaces from the terminal compressors enhances the system's heating capacity, but detracts from its cooling capacity.

Many applications of this system lend themselves well to heat storage. Installations that operate in winter on the cooling cycle most of the day and the heating cycle at night (such as a school) are excellent candidates for heat storage. This can be accomplished by installing a large storage tank in the

closed-loop circuit ahead of the boiler and adjusting the controls of the heat rejector to allow the loop temperature to build up to 95°F during the day. The volume of water at 95°F can be used during unoccupied hours to maintain heat in the building, allowing the loop temperature to drop from 95 to 65°F (instead of 70°F minimum without storage). The boiler would not be called on until the loop had dropped the entire 30°F. The storage tank operates as a flywheel to prolong the period of operation between the limits where neither heat makeup nor heat rejection is required.

Terminal units are available in a variety of sizes and types, including the following:

- Finished console cabinets for window or wall flush mounting

- Floor-mounted vertical units for concealed installation

- Ceiling-concealed models hung from floors above and connected to ductwork

Selection of terminal equipment will require close coordination of architectural, engineering, and lighting details. Access for service and maintenance must be provided for ceiling units.

A secondary heat source (boilers—gas, oil or electric) and heat rejection equipment (usually closed-circuit evaporative cooling) are required when the water-loop temperature goes out of the 10 to 95°F range.

DECENTRALIZED HEATING SYSTEMS

Electric and gas space heating are simple to distribute and control and are used in residences, schools, as well as certain commercial and industrial applications. A decentralized electric system provides heating units to individual rooms or spaces. In terms of heat output, electric in-space heating system types include natural convection, radiant, or forced air (Sun and Park, 1981).

Natural convection units

Electric heating units for wall mounting, recessed placement, or surface placement ("baseboard" units, for example) are made with elements of incandescent bare wire or lower temperature bare wire or sheathed elements. An inner liner or reflector is usually placed between elements so that part of the heat is distributed by convection and part by radiation. Electric convectors should be located so that air movement across the resistance elements is not impeded (by furniture or drapes, for example).

Electric baseboard units are particularly low in initial cost and are frequently installed in residences which do not require mechanical cooling. Each room may be controlled by a separate thermostat. While the unit cost of electric resistance heating is comparatively high, the ability to control the temperature of each room separately makes it possible for a conscientious occupant to operate this system economically.

Radiant heating units

Radiant heating warms objects directly (not the air) and is suited only for locations where the occupants are in direct view of the warmed surface. Manufactured electric resistant radiant panels may be wall- or ceiling-mounted. Radiant ceilings may be field-fabricated by imbedding resistance wiring in ceiling plaster.

Suspended unit radiant heaters (either electric resistance or gas-fired) are often utilized to heat people directly where it is impractical to warm the air. Factories, automotive service bays, warehouses, baths, and outdoor waiting areas are examples of suitable applications for radiant heaters.

Forced-air units

Unit ventilators and heaters combine common convective heating with controlled fan-forced ventilation. The electric units are most often mounted on an outside wall for air intake and below windows to prevent the down-draft of cold air; they may be surface-mounted or recessed.

ZONING

Heating, lighting, dehumidifying, and cooling are interrelated activities that not only affect each other but vary considerably in different spaces and at different times of the day and year. They challenge the designer to create an energy-efficient, cost-effective system that satisfies all these interrelated and changing needs.

OCCUPANCY

Space conditioning and the lighting, hot water, and circulation needs of a building are determined by the varying schedules of its occupants. Schedules can be developed in the preliminary phase of design. Depicted graphically, occupancy schedules describe the dynamic nature of occupancy-related loads over a period of time. Internal heat gains due to lights, machines, and people are proportional to occupancy. During periods of low or zero occupancy, space conditioning and building service requirements are at a minimum. Therefore,

occupancy becomes a major determinant of loads. Occupancy schedules are necessary before accurate load schedules can be derived.

In developing occupancy schedules, it can be useful to group together individual spaces with similar occupancy characteristics, since different spaces or zones often have widely diverse occupancy schedules. Zoning strategies based on occupancy can have beneficial impacts on energy use.

Variations in the system loads of these spaces can then be handled more economically. Occupancy characteristics are the primary determinants of whether central system or decentralized (unitary) HVAC systems are more efficient.

Individual control of zones with similar occupancy characteristics can also be applied to lighting, hot water, elevators, and other services. An energy management system can be used to control equipment on a predetermined schedule or on the basis of sensors in individual zones. Controls can also be located in the zone or space.

CLIMATE

Variations in climate can also affect load schedules. Climate varies over 24-hour and annual cycles. Climate schedules indicate how temperature, humidity, solar insolation, and wind vary over time. The effect of climate on system loads will change according to:

- The degree to which the building envelope insulates against and controls the external climate. A well-insulated building tends to reduce the impact of climate variation on system loads. Buildings with minimum exposed areas, such as buildings in urban sites, tend to be affected less by climate than freestanding buildings. Climate will play a larger role in poorly insulated buildings or buildings with operable windows and vents. It should be emphasized, however, that good design can often use the external climate to reduce system loads.

- The quantity of ventilation air required of the HVAC system. If outdoor ventilation air needs to be heated/cooled or humidified/dehumidified, it represents a load on the HVAC system. Often, however, outdoor air is more economical to use than recycled return air. Free cooling, in buildings with large internal loads, can be accomplished using outdoor air up to 75°F within an acceptable humidity range. An air economizer control on an HVAC system considers the temperature and humidity of both return and outdoor air to determine which is more energy-conserving. Operable windows and vents do not offer this type of sensitive control and are often misused.

HVAC systems are often zoned by orientation where external climate causes variations in thermal loading. HVAC systems have trouble meeting widely varying thermal loads within a zone efficiently. The type of HVAC system selected will depend on the "thermal flexibility" that can be tolerated while maintaining efficiency. If it is not possible for a centralized HVAC system to provide for thermal load variation efficiently, decentralized HVAC systems should be considered.

HVAC systems should be zoned to account for climate and occupancy wherever possible. HVAC systems are zoned according to orientation in perimeter spaces (spaces with exterior wall or roof), where thermal-load variation between these orientations exceeds the efficient "flexibility" of the system. Internal spaces (spaces with no outdoor exposure) are very often zoned separately from peripheral zones. Internal zones usually require only cooling. For this reason, buildings that require interior cooling and ventilation usually divide HVAC systems into "internal" and "perimeter" zones.

Tall buildings must often be separated into vertical zones as well, because of the "stack effect" phenomenon, in which hot air rises through elevator shafts and stairwells, increasing exfiltration at the top and infiltration at the bottom of the building.

LOAD CONTROL

In large buildings, a main objective of energy-conscious design is to reduce annual system load. Care should be taken that such strategies do not raise the peak loads on a system or cause wide fluctuations in system loading. Large areas of south-facing glazing, for example, can significantly reduce heating loads in winter. Shadows from neighboring buildings, however, can cause large variations in the heating loads in specific spaces. A centralized HVAC system would have difficulty maintaining comfort and economy where this large load variation exists. Summer heat gains through glazing can also increase peak cooling loads unless adequate sunshading is provided.

REDUCING PEAK LOADS

Residential buildings are subject to a simple electric utility *consumption* rate structure that is solely based on the total energy consumed during a rate

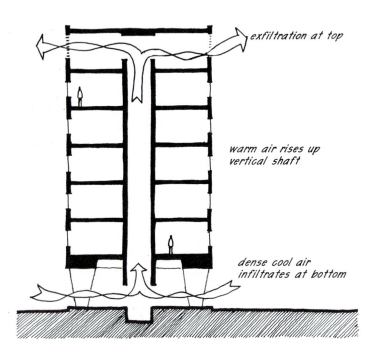

Figure 19.23: Stack effect in multistory building. *(Redrawn from American Institute of Architects, 1982, by permission.)*

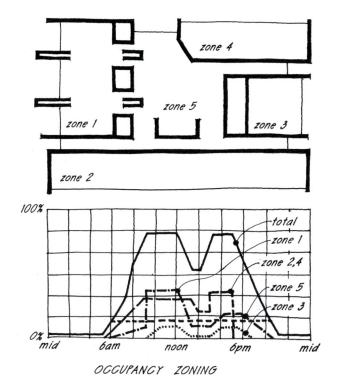

Figure 19.24: Effect of occupancy zoning on energy use in large buildings. *(Redrawn from American Institute of Architects, 1982, by permission.)*

period. By contrast, nonresidential customers pay not only a charge for consumption, but also an additional *demand* charge based on the peak rate of use (because it is this peak usage that determines the required utility generating capacity). In commercial buildings such as office buildings where the peak cooling, equipment, and lighting loads frequently coincide in early afternoon, this demand charge may be the largest component of the building's energy cost. For this reason, strategies that reduce peak demand may actually be more cost-effective than those that simply address reducing consumption.

In addition to reducing demand utility charges, reducing peak loads on systems permits a reduction in the size and quantity of system elements. A double economy of energy and material is achieved. The best opportunities for peak load reduction are found with HVAC and lighting systems. The two basic strategies for reducing peak loads are:

- *Basic system load reduction* — including most energy design strategies; examples are conservation (Chapter 6) to reduce heating and cooling loads and daylighting to reduce illumination loads (Chapters 22 to 24).

- *Peak load shedding* — by deferring loads from peak load periods to periods of low loads it is possible to flatten the system load schedule. Maintaining a constant occupancy schedule for a space or building is one strategy for shedding cooling peak loads. The peak heating and cooling loads may also be reduced by avoiding reheat and recool periods associated with varying occupancy.

Storage systems

Occupancy scheduling and heat- and cold-storage systems can be used to supplement HVAC heating and cooling loads during peak periods. During off-peak periods, central HVAC systems can divert some of their heating and cooling capacity to mass storage systems. As the heating or cooling load rises above the capacity of the system, the heated or cooled storage system is used to supply extra capacity.

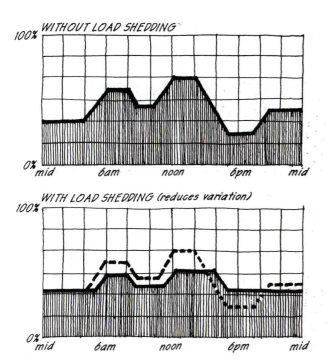

Figure 19.25: Effect of peak load shedding on energy use in large buildings. *(Redrawn from American Institute of Architects, 1982, by permission.)*

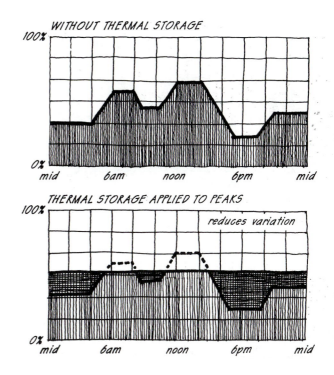

Figure 19.26: Effect of thermal storage on energy use in large buildings. *(Redrawn from American Institute of Architects, 1982, by permission.)*

Thermal storage systems have the following advantages:

- More efficient system because heating and cooling plants operate closer to maximum capacity and, therefore, maximum efficiency, for longer periods of time.

- Potential integration of solar heating and cooling by using a common storage system.

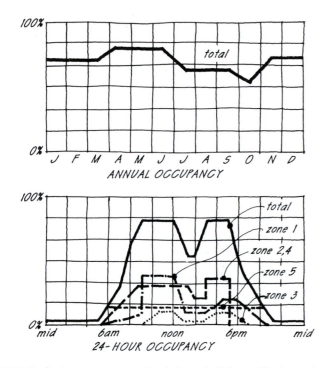

Figure 19.27: Typical occupancy profiles in large buildings. *(Redrawn from American Institute of Architects, 1982, by permission.)*

Load variation over time

Many of the concepts that apply to peak load shedding also apply to load variation over time. Energy-conserving buildings tend to reduce system load variation. Large variations in system load due to occupancy and climate can adversely affect the effectiveness and efficiency of energy-consuming systems.

The rate and cycle period over which these loads change is just as important as the size (scale) of load variation. HVAC and lighting systems can be especially sensitive to system load variations.

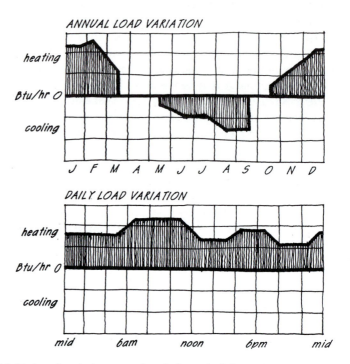

Figure 19.28: Load variation over time in large buildings. *(Redrawn from American Institute of Architects, 1982, by permission.)*

In HVAC systems, fluctuating thermal loads in spaces mean that HVAC systems will run at significantly less than 100 percent capacity for long periods. HVAC systems, however, are usually less efficient when operating at these reduced loads. The rate at which thermal loads change can also tax the ability of the system to adjust efficiently and effectively to demands.

Seasonal variations in thermal load are characterized by a low rate of change over a yearly cycle. The magnitude of the load variation can be large, however. Since thermal loads in the intermediate seasons (spring and fall) can be far less than the peak loads of winter and summer, inefficiencies might be expected during these intermediate seasons. Some central HVAC systems have modular or incremental heating and cooling plants to overcome these load variations. These systems are made up of a number of smaller modular units connected in series. Modular units always operate at or near 100 percent capacity; as heating or cooling loads fluctuate, units are turned on or off to meet the demand. Decentralized HVAC systems and electrically driven systems tend to maintain efficiency during off-peak thermal load conditions.

Rapid thermal load variations in a building are characteristic of the hourly and daily cycles of occupancy and climate. A passive strategy for retarding and reducing thermal fluctuations is the addition of thermal mass to the envelope and interior. If wide thermal load variations remain (usually due to occupancy), HVAC systems should be selected so as to minimize the time lag between the actual load change and the system's ability to sense and provide for this change. All-water systems usually have long time lags, whereas all-air HVAC systems have shorter time lags. Decentralized (unitary) HVAC equipment located in the space it serves can often react very quickly to load variation.

Load variation between spaces

At a given time, system loads can vary widely between different spaces and zones. Both the occupancy schedules of specific spaces and climate-related factors contribute to this load variation. It is often possible to arrange spaces and zones so that both occupancy and climate-related system loads are accommodated.

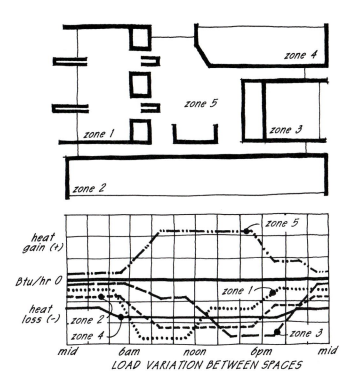

Figure 19.29: Load variation between spaces in large buildings. (Redrawn from American Institute of Architects, 1982, by permission.)

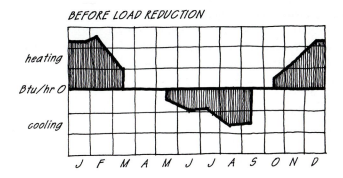

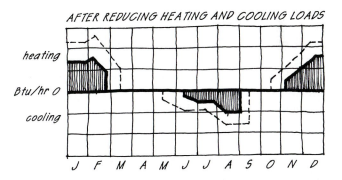

Figure 19.30: Reducing heating and cooling loads in large buildings. (Redrawn from American Institute of Architects, 1982, by permission.)

AIR FILTRATION AND ODOR REMOVAL

Air filter selection is determined by the degree of cleanliness required. Variables involved in the selection of the filtration system include initial cost, ease of maintenance, improvement of housekeeping, health benefits, product quality, and size and quantity of dust and contaminants (Patel, 1981).

Filters are usually located at the air-return inlet of the HVAC equipment to provide protection to the equipment as well as the space served. In special cases, filters are located at the equipment discharge and at entry into the room in critical air-quality conditions (for example, in critical health care rooms, operating rooms, and industrial "clean" rooms).

Filter types include (in order of increasing cost and effectiveness): throwaway dry media (fine mesh screens), throwaway viscous (sticky) media, renewable media (washable media, roll mats, and panels), and electrostatic (to remove smoke and pollen).

Odors are best controlled by limiting the source. Dilution of odors by direct exhaust ventilation is the most common control method. Air washer and carbon filters are most often used to clean recirculated air; in some circumstances, ozone treatment and aerosol masking of odors may be used.

HEAT RECOVERY IN LARGE BUILDINGS

In contrast to the residential-scale air-to-air heat exchangers described in Chapter 20, the following types are best suited for larger buildings.

THERMAL WHEELS

Thermal wheels, also called heat wheels, are packed with a heat-absorbing material such as aluminum or stainless steel wool. The wheels transfer energy from one airstream to another or, for large boiler plants, from flue gas to combustion air. The thermal wheel can only be installed when the hot and cold airstreams are immediately adjacent and parallel. Two types of thermal wheel are available: one transfers sensible heat only, the other transfers both sensible and latent heat.

Thermal wheels are driven by electric motors, which use energy and decrease summer efficiency because of motor-generated heat. Efficiencies are generally 60 to 80 percent for sensible heat transfer and 20 to 60 percent for latent heat transfer.

HEAT PIPES

Heat pipes running through the adjacent walls of inlet and outlet ducts can be an efficient means of transferring heat from the warmer duct to the

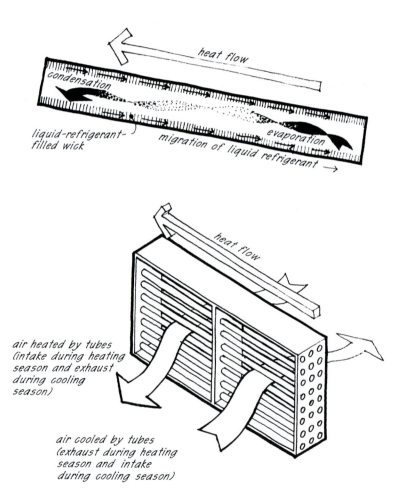

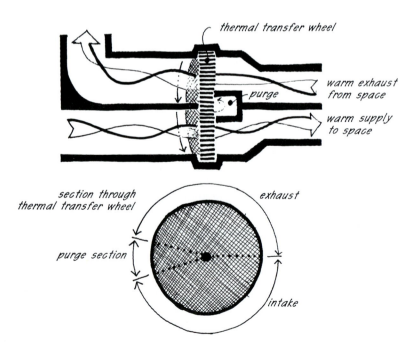

Figure 19.31: Thermal wheel heat exchanger. *(Redrawn from American Institute of Architects, 1982, by permission.)*

Figure 19.32: Heat pipe. *(Redrawn from American Institute of Architects, 1982, by permission.)*

cooler one. The heat pipes are short lengths of copper tubing, sealed tightly at the ends with wicks or capillaries and containing a charge of refrigerant. For single-direction heat flow, the refrigerant moves by capillary action to the warmer end of the tube and evaporates, absorbing heat in the process. The warmer end of the pipe is slightly lower than the cooler end, where it condenses, releases its heat to the cooler duct, and remigrates to the lower end. For dual-direction heat flow (summertime cooling recovery) heat pipes must be installed level. All liquid flow is then by capillary action only.

RUN-AROUND COILS

A run-around coil system is composed of two or more extended surface fin coils installed in air ducts and interconnected by piping. A heat-exchange fluid of ethylene glycol and water is circulated through the system by a pump; the fluid absorbs heat from the hot airstream and releases it into the cold airstream (or vice versa). A run-around coil system can be used in winter to preheat cold outdoor air and in summer to cool hot outdoor air. Where there is no possibility of freezing, water can also be used as the heat transfer medium. Run-around coils are most often used when it is physically difficult to locate the exhaust air duct in close proximity to the makeup air duct. They are substantially less efficient than heat wheels and heat pipe heat exchangers.

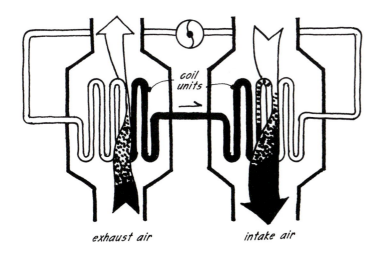

Figure 19.33: Run-around coil heat exchanger. *(Redrawn from American Institute of Architects, 1982, by permission.)*

When double bundle condensers are used for heat recovery, a cooling coil can be placed in the exhaust air duct to remove the heat before dumping to the outside. This heat is transferred via the chiller to the condenser side. This is one of the most efficient forms of exhaust air heat recovery possible. It should be considered if other system requirements support it.

HEAT RECOVERY FROM EQUIPMENT

Some systems are specifically designed to cool machinery and lighting fixtures before their heat is released into the space. Water-cooled equipment reduces the cooling load in this way and provides a high-level source of waste heat. The hot water generated can be applied to space heating, absorptive refrigerant space cooling, and domestic hot water systems.

The major method for recovering lighting heat is plenum-return systems. Ducted-air systems can provide a direct means of controlling and redistributing heat dissipated by lighting fixtures. A lighting fixture provided with slots, through which return air is drawn into the ceiling plenum, is one approach. As air passes over the lamps, ballasts, and sheet metal of the luminaire, it picks up as much as 80 percent of the electrical energy used by the light as dissipated heat and carries it into the plenum.

Plenum heat can be used in space conditioning systems in many ways. In some systems the plenum can be the source of heat for air supply, with supplementary heat supplied by duct heaters or water coils piped to the water side of a double-bundle condenser.

Heat from air-return lighting fixtures can be drawn off and discharged outdoors rather than being used to heat occupied space. This approach reduces the cooling load for the building and can result in economies in distribution ductwork and refrigerator equipment. Another advantage is that removing heat from the lighting fixtures can increase their efficiency 10 to 20 percent.

HEAT RECOVERY CONTROL

The integration of heat recovery strategies, localized and variable air-conditioning, and lighting needs, and potentially rapid fluctuations in outdoor conditions can create the need for automated control of energy-related systems. Energy management systems currently available range from relatively simple devices that offer peak-demand control, load cycling and time-of-day scheduling to highly sophisticated computerized systems that monitor indoor and outdoor temperature, humidity, and light levels, and respond accordingly. The latter systems have already demonstrated their effectiveness

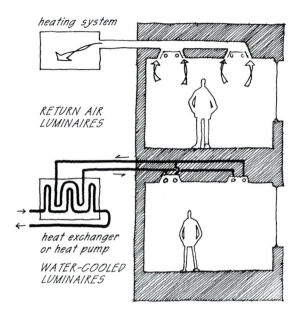

heating system

RETURN AIR
LUMINAIRES

heat exchanger
or heat pump
WATER-COOLED
LUMINAIRES

Figure 19.34: Heat recovery from lighting systems. *(Redrawn from American Institute of Architects, 1982, by permission.)*

in providing comfort control, energy conservation and facilities maintenance functions in larger buildings. Doubtless reductions in the cost of microcircuitry will soon make these systems useful and cost-effective for smaller, less complex buildings as well.

"FREE" COOLING

The hourly and daily changes in humidity and temperature of outdoor air can also be put to advantage in the design of HVAC systems. Unlike strategies for recovering waste heat from energy already expended, these designs avoid expending it in the first place.

An enthalpy optimizer control is used in hot weather to sense both dry- and wet-bulb temperatures of the outside air and the return air. The optimizer uses this information to determine the enthalpy or total heat content (sensible plus latent heat) of the two airstreams. In this way, the optimizer can select whichever requires the least heat removal. This control is the basis of the economizer cycle.

The economizer cycle is often used in HVAC systems to avoid unnecessary cooling of air in cool weather. It is particularly applicable to night flushing of high-mass commercial buildings. A sensor registers the dry-bulb and wet-bulb temperatures of outside and return air. If outside air is appropriately cool, it regulates how much outside air should be taken in. For example, the outside air may have a higher dry-bulb temperature than return air, but may also contain much less moisture, i.e., have lower overall heat content. It will require less energy to cool the outside air than to dehumidify the return air.

Balance and changeover temperatures also can help the designer integrate HVAC systems with the local elements. The balance temperature is the outside air temperature at which mechanical heating is no longer required because the internal gains from people, lights, equipment, and solar heat gains are exactly equal to the losses from infiltration, ventilation, and conductance through the envelope. The changeover temperature is the outside air temperature at which mechanical cooling is no longer required because the combination of infiltration, transmission losses, and ventilation using 100 percent cold outside air is just equal to the internal gains.

Usually no heat is required above the balance temperature and no cooling is required below the changeover temperature. However, some buildings with high internal gains, such as hospitals, have balance points as low as 10°F. While a summation of total gains and total losses may be zero, substantial perimeter zone heating and makeup air heating will exist.

The composite room load profiles shown for typical interior and perimeter areas have been based on occupied conditions. Composite room load profiles can also be drawn for unoccupied daytime periods, night periods, or other combinations of operational periods and load factor combinations to determine room heat flow characteristics under different sets of operating conditions. The actual loads used for constructing room load profiles may be expressed in terms of total Btu/h or Btu/h•ft^2 or floor area of the space being analyzed, for quantifying heat flow at partial load operation.

The *thermocycle economizer* avoids use of the mechanical compressor — the single largest energy consumer in a refrigeration machine when the outdoor wet-bulb temperature is suitable. If the design temperature for the chilled water is 55°F, for example, whenever outdoor wet-bulb temperature is around 45°F, it is possible to turn off the compressor but still use the evaporative cooling cycle. This is done by using the cooling tower to cool the condenser water down close to the outside wet-bulb temperature, in effect reversing the temperature differential of the refrigerant cycle.

The condenser water causes the refrigerant to condense. By installing a pipeline for the refrigerant to bypass the compressor, and a small pump sufficient to move the refrigerant to spray nozzles above the evaporator coils, the relatively warmer chilled water will cause the refrigerant to evaporate just as it would if the compressor with its much larger motor were in operation.

The basic requirement of the thermocycle economizer, that the outside wet-bulb temperature be 5 to 10°F cooler than the design temperature for the chilled water, occurs frequently in many parts of the country.

These concepts can give insights into such decisions as the type of distribution system, feasibility of thermal storage, cost/benefit of various heat-recovery strategies, and, perhaps most important, the relative weight on an annual basis of the heating and cooling loads. For example, a design with a balance temperature of 38°F would need an investigation of weather data to see how much of the time the temperature falls between 51 and 42°F. The larger this period of time, the more beneficial the system with the higher changeover becomes. If the period is relatively short, then the choice of system can be made on other grounds.

The worst-weather conditions (the coldest day in winter and hottest, most humid day in summer) can be dealt with in a relatively straightforward manner by simply sizing the system to meet these loads. The real challenge and potential for energy conservation lies in the varied 363 days between the extremes.

COGENERATION

Cogeneration is the term used for systems that use fossil fuels to generate electricity on site and use the heat of generation for space conditioning, domestic hot water, or other purposes. The appeal of cogeneration systems is that they avoid the considerable conversion and transmission losses which occur when fossil fuels are used to produce electricity at a central utility, and are able to beneficially use the thermal by product of electrical generation. In contrast, the thermal by-product of electrical generation at central power plants can become a thermal pollutant as it is discharged into the atmosphere or streams.

As with district heating and cooling, cogeneration systems have found most use in large installations with consistently high loads like shopping centers, universities, and hospitals. Consideration of cogeneration systems for any application should follow careful analysis of the loads to be met, the local fuel situation, the added investment required by a cogeneration plant, and service and maintenance costs, as well as federal regulations concerning power generation.

District systems, which provide steam or chilled water produced outside the building, have long existed in cities and on campuses and military installations. Today, however, when we seek opportunities to integrate our energy usage patterns, the economies of scale possible with district systems merit consideration for a greater variety of applications.

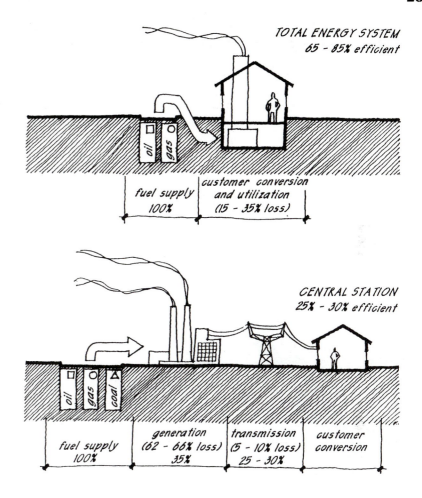

Figure 19.35: Cogeneration and central-station efficiencies. *(Redrawn from American Institute of Architects, 1982, by permission.)*

MECHANICAL EQUIPMENT SPACE REQUIREMENTS

In general, the mechanical and electrical equipment requires a total of between 6 and 9 percent of the gross floor area of most buildings (ASHRAE, 1989). In terms of building size, smaller buildings (and those with heavy cooling loads) require the largest percentage of floor area for HVAC purposes (3 to 9 percent), while large buildings enjoy the economies of scale and require less area (1 to 3 percent). In terms of system type, all-air systems require the most area (3 to 8 percent), air-water systems slightly less (3 to 6 percent), all-water systems less (1.5 to 5 percent), and smaller package units throughout the building or roof-mounted the least (1 to 3 percent; Stein et al., 1986).

Air-handling equipment room

   In larger buildings employing all-air systems, the air-handling equipment room should be centrally located to minimize the distance the air has to travel from the room to the furthest air-conditioned space. The fan noise transmission to adjacent rooms should be considered, and if the equipment room is to be located near sound-sensitive areas (such as a conference room, auditorium,

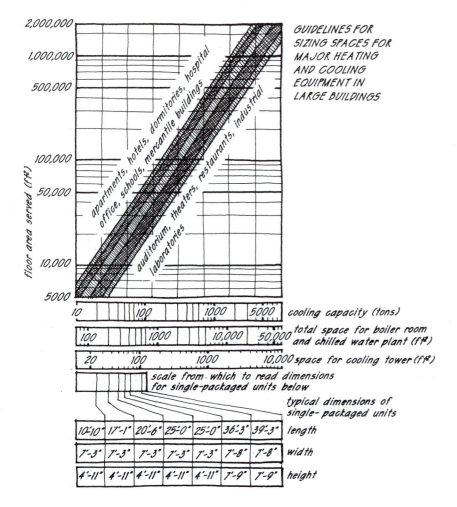

Figure 19.36: Guidelines for sizing spaces for major heating and cooling equipment in large buildings. *(Redrawn from Allen and Iano, 1989, by permission.)*

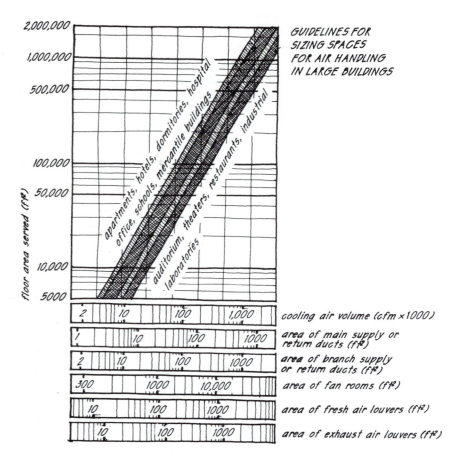

Figure 19.37: Guidelines for sizing spaces for air handling in large buildings. *(Redrawn from Allen and Iano, 1989, by permission.)*

sleeping area, or sound studios) then special attention should be given to isolating air and structure noise and vibration from surrounding areas (Patel, 1981).

SYSTEM SELECTION

   The selection of a particular HVAC system is influenced by many factors, including economics, design temperatures, physical space availability, the need for maintaining separate thermal temperature zones, the availability of

design objective	Variable Air Volume	VAV Reheat	VAV Induction	Dual-Duct VAV	Single-Duct Const. Vol.	CAV Reheat	Multizone	Air-Water Induction	Fan-Coil Terminals	Closed-Loop Heat Pump	Hydronic Convectors	Packaged Term. Units
Minimize first cost					●							●
Minimize operating cost	●				●				●			
Maximize control of air velocity+quality	●	●		○	●	○	○					
Maximize individual temp control	●	●	○	○		○	○	●	●	○		●
Minimize system noise	●	●		○	●	○	○				●	
Minimize visual obtrusiveness	●	●	○	○	●	○	●				●	
Maximize flexibility of rental space	●	●	○	○	●	○	○	●	●		●	
Minimize floor space for mech'cal			○				○	●	●	●	●	●
Minimize floor-to-floor height			○				○	●	●	●	●	●
Minimize system maintenance	●				●						●	
Avoid having a chimney												●
Minimize construction time												●

● frequently used
○ infrequently used

Figure 19.38: Heating and cooling system selection for large buildings. *(Redrawn from Allen and Iano, 1989, by permission.)*

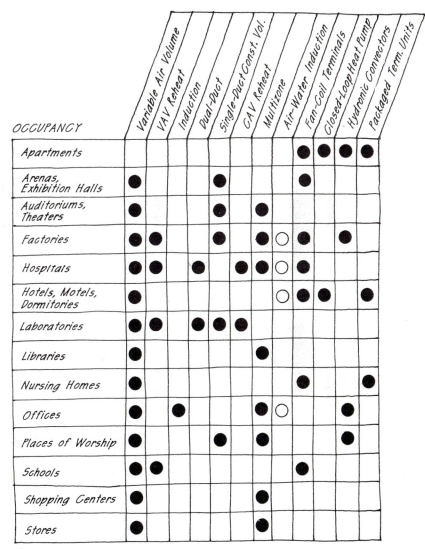

● frequently used
○ infrequently used

Figure 19.39: Some typical choices of heating and cooling systems for large buildings. *(Redrawn from Allen and Iano, 1989, by permission.)*

energy (particularly of the source of energy), aesthetics, hours of operation, and the type of occupancy. Certain air-conditioning systems are appropriate for certain structures. Hospitals, factories, and office buildings each use their own type of air-conditioning system.

Office buildings

Office buildings should be designed for a shifting tenant occupancy. They should have many independent zones of control and great flexibility to permit rearrangement of these zones as the population shifts. Small one- or two-story offices can be served by rooftop, packaged, air-cooled units. These lack some flexibility, but the capital cost is low and other types of zoning systems become quite expensive in small increments.

The use of double-duct or multizone systems is decreasing. Double-duct systems provide great flexibility, however, both in zoning and in revising the system, and have been widely applied to office buildings in the past.

Highrise buildings are frequently served by induction-type systems for perimeter zones and either variable-volume or double-duct for the core zone. Normally, the core of such a structure requires no heat. Induction systems call for a minimum of shaft space and relatively small ducts and pipes. The system can be very flexible and has a great potential for zoning.

Fan-coil units are also suitable for large office buildings. These types may not have the flexibility of the induction system or the double-duct system; however, some of the capital cost can be deferred until tenant space is leased.

Theaters

Although they need not be zoned for temperature, theaters must be quiet, well-ventilated, and low in humidity. They are frequently air-conditioned with single-zoned fan-coil units using chilled water or direct expansion refrigeration. This system is not noisy and uses outside air for ventilation. It also has a high dehumidifying capacity essential where many people assemble in a small space and would create high latent heat loads with air-conditioning.

Factories

Factories are most often single-story structures with a large, clearspan height. Most factories are heated and ventilated only, although there is a growing trend toward more comfort cooling. Temperature and humidity in textile and color printing factories must be controlled to maintain production quality. Assuming that workers produce more and make fewer errors in comfort-controlled atmospheres, air-conditioning may be economically feasible in factories. Separate thermal zones, if they exist at all, are usually large and can be handled by independent units. Both large self-contained air conditioners and central chilled-water plants with fan coils are effective in factories.

Hospitals

Comfort systems for hospitals are under severe regulatory code restrictions. Normally outside air must be used in surgical suites to flush out odors and hazardous vapors. Exhaust openings are usually located near the floor of surgical suits to capture heavy gases, and humidity control is essential because of the presence of explosive vapors that might be ignited by static electric discharges.

Nurseries, delivery rooms, intensive care areas, and cardiac areas are all subject to special temperature and humidity control requirements.

To keep hazardous organisms from spreading, pressure differentials between different parts of the hospital must be maintained. This is especially important for isolation wards, which are often air-conditioned using induction units or individual fan coil units for patient areas, provided adequate air filtration is included. Fiberglass ductwork is usually not specified for hospital air conditioning, since ducts provide a good breeding ground for microorganisms.

Schools

As classrooms require separate zoning, they are usually served by fan coil units or heat pumps located in the room under the windows or operated by remote control. Rooms must be adequately ventilated and free of noise.

Stores and shopping centers

Some large shopping malls use central water-chilling and water-heating systems. Individual stores are air-conditioned using separate fan coil units served by chilled and/or hot water for each store. Smaller shopping centers and individual stores that are not a part of a shopping center usually are air-conditioned with self-contained rooftop packages. Air distribution is less critical in commercial establishments than in office buildings and hospitals, because shoppers are moving about and are not as sensitive to drafts.

Multiresidential buildings

Low-rise apartments, from one- to three-stories, can be served from forced-air furnaces located in each apartment, with cooling coming from a remote air-cooled condensor, usually mounted on the roof. Central chilled water plants have been applied to such buildings with individual fan coils for each apartment. Water-to-air heat pumps with a circulating heat sink from which the individual heat pumps can either accept or reject heat have also been successfully applied to apartments.

High-rise structures for housing are most likely to use central water chilling and water-heating plants with individual fan coil units for each apartment. Water-to-air heat pumps are also a suitable choice.

Every tenant expects to control the heating and air-conditioning in his or her own apartment — not only the temperature, but the hours of operation.

Houses

Most houses are heated with forced-air furnaces that force air through a direct-expansion cooling coil. This coil is connected by refrigerant piping to a remote air-cooled condensing unit to furnish the cooling. Larger residences are often divided into separate zones, usually into sleeping and living areas.

SUMMARY OF TERMS

HVAC — heating, ventilating, and air-conditioning.

Compressive refrigeration cycle — a refrigeration cycle that utilizes a mechanical compressor to compress a refrigerant fluid.

Absorption refrigeration cycle — a refrigeration cycle that utilizes a liquid desiccant and a heat source for regenerating ("drying") the desiccant.

All-air — an HVAC system which utilizes air as the heat-distribution medium exclusively.

Air-water — an HVAC system in which air and water are delivered to each space, and heating and cooling functions are carried out by changing the temperature of one or both media to control space temperatures.

Single-duct, constant-volume — an all-air, single-zone HVAC system that regulates air temperature by on-off operation.

Single-duct, variable-volume — an all-air, multizone HVAC system that regulates air temperature in each zone by varying the volume of conditioned air delivered to that zone by means of a variable damper.

Single-duct, reheat — an all-air, multizone HVAC system that conditions to supply air to the lowest temperature required by any zone and then locally reheats air to the temperature required by each other zone.

Dual-duct — an all-air, multizone HVAC system that mixes hot and cold air locally to meet the temperature requirements of that zone.

Fan-coil unit — a finned-tube coil and a fan.

Air-water induction unit — centrally conditioned air is supplied to the remote unit plenum at high pressure where it flows through induction nozzles and induces air from the room to flow over the water coil and become heated or cooled. The primary and secondary air are mixed and discharged to the room.

Balance point — the outside air temperature at which mechanical heating is no longer required because the internal gains from people, lights, equipment, and solar heat gains are exactly equal to the losses from infiltration, ventilation, and conductance through the envelope.

Changeover temperature — the outside air temperature at which mechanical cooling is no longer required because the combination of infiltration, transmission losses, and ventilation using 100 percent cold outside air is just equal to the internal gains.

Unitary system — a pre-assembled HVAC system.

Packaged terminal air conditioner (PTAC) — a small self-contained HVAC unit mounted through-the-wall designed to serve a single room or small zone.

Window air-conditioning unit — a small self-contained, cooling-only unit mounted through-the-wall designed to serve a single room or small zone.

Heat pump — a compressive-refrigeration-cycle heating system which extracts heat from the surrounding environment and supplies it to the interior of the building.

Baseboard convector — a heating unit that uses either hot water or electric resistance to heat air which circulates by natural convection.

Economizer cycle — the use of cool outside air in HVAC systems to avoid unnecessary refrigeration cooling in cool weather.

Cogeneration — the use of fossil fuels to generate electricity on site and use the heat of generation for space conditioning, domestic hot water, or other purposes.

Thermostat — a control device that measures the temperature in a representative location in a building zone to determine the need for heating or cooling.

Zone — an area of the building having relatively uniform heating and cooling requirements and thus able to be satisfied by a single HVAC supply controlled by a single thermostat.

Refrigerant — the heat-transport fluid in a compressive refrigeration cycle that changes from liquid to vapor, and vice versa.

Filter — a device for removing undesirable particles from air before it is supplied to the conditioned space.

Coefficient of performance (COP) — the ratio of the net heat removal by the evaporator to the total energy input to the compressor.

Thermal (or heat) wheel — an air-to-air heat exchanger used to transfer energy from one airstream to another.

Heat pipe — short length of copper tubing, sealed tightly at the ends, with wicks or capillaries and containing a charge of refrigerant.

Run-around coil — an air-to-air heat exchanger composed of two or more fin coils installed in air ducts and interconnected by piping.

STUDY QUESTIONS

1. Describe the compressive refrigeration cycle.

2. Describe the absorption refrigeration cycle.

3. What are the advantages and disadvantages of all-air HVAC systems?

4. Identify and briefly describe some all-air systems typically used for larger buildings.

5. What are the advantages and disadvantages of air-water HVAC systems?

6. Identify and briefly describe some air-water systems typically used for larger buildings.

7. Describe an economizer cycle.

8. Distinguish between balance point and changeover temperatures.

9. Identify and briefly describe some heat exchangers typically employed in large-building HVAC systems.

10. Explain cogeneration.

20

MATERIALS, COMPONENTS, AND DETAILS

In general, energy-efficient construction materials and methods follow standard construction practices with special attention to insulation and air-tightness details. This chapter introduces construction techniques and components that are applicable to energy-efficient construction in general, and passively heated and cooled buildings in particular.

INSULATION

Insulating materials are intended to reduce conductive heat transfer through the building envelope. Sometimes referred to as resistive insulation (to distinguish them from reflective insulation or radiant barriers), these materials typically have a very low density due to the large amount of dead air contained within. As noted in Chapter 1, air is a poor conductor and is thus a good insulator (provided it is confined in small compartments to prevent convection circulation). All commercially available resistive insulation materials are characterized by a large amount of air isolated in small compartments within the material.

The three general categories of insulation commonly used in buildings are blanket, loose-fill materials, and foam.

BLANKET INSULATION

Blanket insulation is most commonly used in wood frame construction to fill wall cavities and above ceilings. It usually consists of loosely matted fiberglass held together by binding material. Batt is one form of blanket insulation; common dimensions are thicknesses of 1 in., 2 in., $3^1/_2$ in., $5^1/_2$

in., and 8 in., widths of $14^1/_2$ and $22^1/_2$ in. (to fit between conventional 16-in. and 24-in. framing spacing), and 4- and 8-ft lengths. Roll insulation is similar to batt with longer length and a paper or foil backing to facilitate handling and installation.

LOOSE-FILL INSULATION

Loose insulation materials include cellulose and other mineral fiber materials which are "blown" into place in attics and in existing wall cavities. Cellulose is an inexpensive product typically manufactured from recycled newspaper and rendered flame-retardant by chemical additives. Masonry-fill insulation materials include perlite and vermiculite.

One problem with loose-fill insulation is itstendency to settle over time resulting in a reduced R-value. This is a particular problem for retrofit insulation of existing stud wall cavities. One alternative for retrofits is the blown-in-batt system (BIBS), which utilizes a resin binder, completely fills the cavity, does not settle or shrink, and achieves about R-4 per in.

FOAM INSULATION

Foam insulation is usually installed in the form of rigid foam boards and sheets. Expanded polystyrene (white "beadboard") is an inexpensive foam material well-suited for dry locations; because of its open-cell structure, moisture will migrate throughout the material, greatly reducing its insulating qualities. Extruded polystyrene ("blue board") is a more expensive foam material well-suited for both dry and moist environments (particularly where in contact with soil); because of its closed-cell structure, moisture migration is minimized and its insulating qualities are maintained.

Urethane and isocyanurate rigid foam sheets are particularly good insulators but are comparatively expensive and typically used only where the highest *R*-value for a given thickness is important; they are often faced with aluminum foil and used as nonstructural wall sheathing.

In addition to rigid foam materials, urethane can be foamed-in-place to fill cavities. In new construction, spray foam is typically used to seal cracks to reduce insulation. For retrofitting existing uninsulated walls, urethane foam is injected through drilled holes to fill wall voids.

NIGHT INSULATION

As noted in Chapter 7, movable window insulation reduces the large heat loss inherent with large areas of glazing at night, while admitting useful solar radiation when opened during the day. The performance of direct-gain systems is particularly sensitive to the presence of night insulation — in northern climates, it is difficult to achieve more than about 20 percent SSF without it. While the calculation procedure in Chapter 12 is based on *R*-9 night insulation (approximately equal to a tight-fitting shutter constructed of 2-in. thick polystyrene foam), approximately 80 percent of this performance gain (over no night insulation) is achieved with *R*-4.

Night insulation also contributes to comfort in direct-gain systems. Exposure of occupants directly to cool glass in the winter reduces the mean radiant temperature (MRT) of the room and results in discomfort in air temperatures that would yield a comfortable environment under normal conditions. It is necessary to raise the air temperature to compensate the radiant cooling effect of the large glass surfaces. Night insulation, by providing an insulating thermal buffer between the occupants and the glass, results in a warmer interior surface and thus a higher MRT.

Movable window insulation may be categorized by its location relative to the glazing: interior (on the room side), intraglazing (between the glazing layers), and exterior.

INTERIOR MOVABLE INSULATION

The principal advantages of locating the night insulation on the interior include convenient operation, comparative cost, and protection from weather conditions.

The principal disadvantage of the interior location is condensation. Because night insulation is effective in thermally isolating the glazing from the

heat from the interior, glass temperatures become much cooler than would occur without night insulation. Because the humidity ratio (and the dew-point temperature) of interior air is typically higher than that of outside air (due to moisture sources such as breathing, cooking, bathing, laundry, and plants), as this moist air comes in contact with the cool glass surface, condensation occurs. In extremely cold climates where high *R*-value night insulation is used, the temperature of the glazing may drop below freezing and frost will occur. While this is especially true with single glazing, it is common even with double glazing. When the insulation is removed in the morning and the warm air melts the night's accumulation of frost, as much as a half-cup of condensate may drain onto surfaces below a 3 ft by 6 ft double-glazed greenhouse panel.

There are a number of strategies to minimize the condensation problem. Reduce interior humidity by venting kitchen hoods, clothes dryers, and bathroom exhausts directly to the outside (use a timer switch and automatic dampers to minimize heat loss). Prevent the interior moisture from reaching the glass by using an impermeable insulation material with a nearly airtight perimeter seal and a small vapor vent hole through the window frame to the outside. Capture condensate along the bottom of the window in a small trough preventing it from damaging the sill and wall and floor finishes below, and allowing it to evaporate back into the room air.

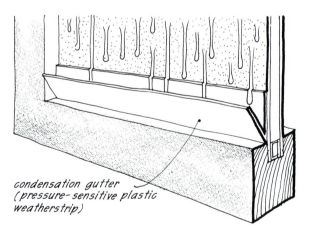

condensation gutter (pressure-sensitive plastic weatherstrip)

Figure 20.1: Use of plastic weatherstrip material (with pressure-sensitive backing) to trap condensate and allow it to reevaporate into the room air. *(Reproduced from Langdon, 1980, by permission.)*

Movable panels

A very simple, inexpensive, and thermally effective type of night insulation are solid shutters. They are installed over the glass at night and manually removed to another location during the day. They are suitable for small

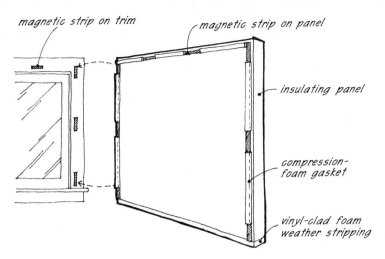

Figure 20.2: Edge-sealed, pop-in shutter. *(Reproduced from Langdon, 1980, by permission.)*

windows with adjacent wall space onto which the shutters can be hung when not in use. As the window area increases, these panels become awkward to handle and store.

They are typically constructed of either rigid insulating foam or multiple layers of corrugated cardboard. If foam is used, it should be sealed on all surfaces with foil to minimize the dangers of toxic fumes in the event of fire. Most fire codes restrict the use of flammable materials in nonresidential interiors. The shutters may be held in place using either a friction fit around the perimeter or magnetic tape.

Hinged and sliding shutters

For larger windows, shutters may be side-hinged to facilitate operation by swinging flat against the wall when not in use. Where standard-sized units can be used, flush hollow-core doors are a cost-effective insulating shutter. The principle disadvantage is the large sweep into the room that this configuration makes, reducing furniture location options. Bifold doors may be used to reduce the sweep and adjacent wall storage area required. Top-hinged shutters controlled by remote control lines are often used for inaccessible clerestory installations.

Pocket shutters may be constructed in a manner similar to pocket sliding doors. However, care needs to be taken to provide adequate fixed insulation in the pocket area. This provides an attractive and convenient installation that is virtually hidden when the shutters are open. However, special construction

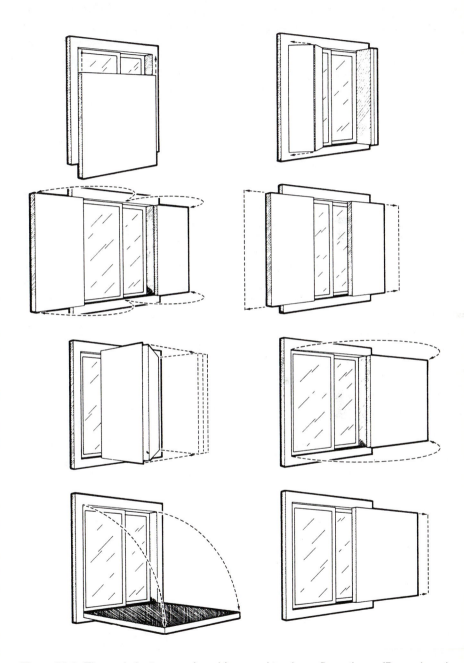

Figure 20.3: Thermal shutters: various hinge and track configurations. *(Reproduced from Langdon, 1980, by permission.)*

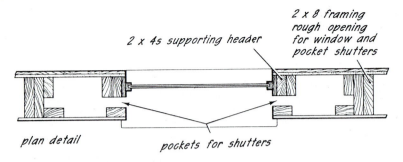

Figure 20.4: Thermal shutters: 8-in.-thick wall is required for pocket shutters. *(Reproduced from Langdon, 1980, by permission.)*

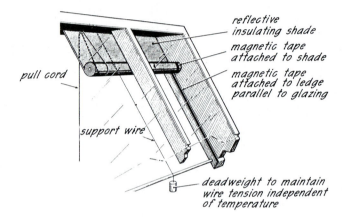

Figure 20.5: Reflective roll-down shade in large greenhouse installations, with magnetic edge seals. *(Reproduced from Langdon, 1980, by permission.)*

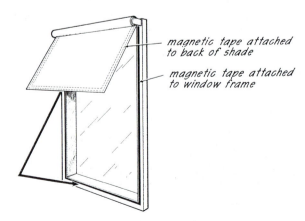

Figure 20.6: Pull-down shade with magnetic edge seals. *(Reproduced from Langdon, 1980, by permission.)*

is required and this configuration is seldom cost-effective on the basis of energy savings alone.

Roll shades

A relatively inexpensive alternative to rigid interior shutters is roll-down shades (similar in operation to the familiar bamboo shade). These may be constructed of quilt-like fabric materials (resistance insulation), far-IR reflective materials (reflective insulation) such as "space blanket" fabric, or a combination of both. Reflective materials have the advantage of being thin for compact storage while having a high R-value (relative to conventional thin sheet materials).

In order for any insulating shade or shutter to be effective, a tight perimeter seal to maintain a dead-air space must be made between the component and the glazing. Without a perimeter seal, the difference in buoyancy between warmer room air and the cooler air in the space next to the glazing will cause a strong thermosiphoning effect. Because the edges of these shades do not slide up or down the jamb, magnetic tape may be installed on both surfaces to create a tight edge seal.

A series of thin layers of material insulates against heat flow due to the airspaces and air films formed by each layer. Reflective foil layers further reduce heat flow by reducing radiant transfer between layers. Multiple-foil layers have been used for years in the walls of commercial refrigerators. More recently, thin reflective layers of plastic film have been worn by astronauts for

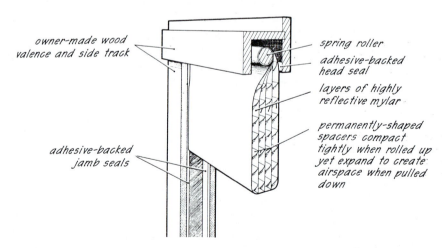

Figure 20.7: High-R insulating Shade (no longer manufactured) had five layers of reflective plastic film resulting in an impressive R-10. The layers were separated with curved plastic strips which flattened when drawn onto a roller. These strips also helped localize and reduce convection currents between shade layers. *(Reproduced from Langdon, 1980, by permission.)*

protections from extremes in temperatures in outer space. The modern space suit has as many as 14 layers of thin, metalized fabric with thin nylon scrims to trap air between each layer.

Using multiple foil layers is a way to provide high R-values in window shades. Several layers of reflective materials can be drawn onto a roller with a minimum of bulk. The problem with foil layers is getting them to separate when the shade is down. If the layers remain in tight contact, then heat conducts through them as though they were one layer. Figures 20.7 and 20.8 show how two commercial multiple-layer insulating shades that were manufactured for a short period during the early eighties achieved this layer separation. Figure 20.9 shows an ingenious skylight louver system that operates automatically without electrical power.

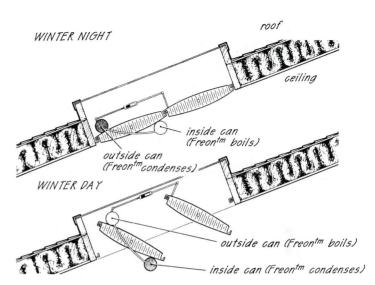

Figure 20.9: Skylid (manufactured by Zomeworks, Albuquerque, New Mexico) is a unique skylight shutter consisting of insulating louvers that open and close automatically from the shifting weight of Freon between two canisters (one located on the sun-facing side and the other on the shaded room side). When the sun comes out, the Freon in the sunny canister boils and moves to the shady side where it condenses and collects until the increased weight of the inboard canister tips louvers open. At night, Freon reenters the outside canister, which tips the louvers closed. A manual override prevents opening on hot summer days. *(Reproduced from Langdon, 1980, by permission.)*

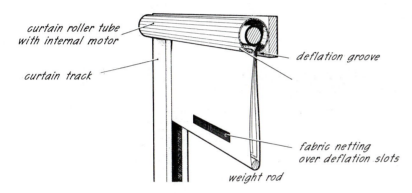

Figure 20.8: Self-inflating curtain wall shade (no longer manufactured) had four layers of highly reflective fabric. When this shade was lowered, the air temperature differences on the two opposite sides of the shade generated air currents inside the shade that caused it to "inflate" and yielded an R-value of about 10. Raised and lowered by an electric motor, this system was suited only for large glass areas. *(Reproduced from Langdon, 1980, by permission.)*

INTRAGLAZING MOVABLE INSULATION

Locating the insulating material between glazing layers reduced the components' exposure to physical damage and dust accumulation. If the glazing void is vented to the outside, condensation is minimized. However, operation is necessarily remote and requires more sophisticated control mechanisms than simple manual interior systems. And maintenance and cleaning (when required) are more difficult (Langdon, 1980).

In addition to the components shown above, venetian blinds can be enclosed in the void between glazing layers. Commercially available units

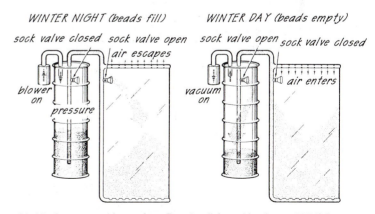

Figure 20.10: A patented invention, Beadwall (see Harrison, 1976) is a system that consists of polystyrene beads used to fill the void between two glazing layers at night. In the morning the beads are "vacuumed" out of the glazing and stored in large tanks. In the evening, a second motor operating in the opposite direction "vacuums" the beads out of the storage tanks and fills the glazing void. *(Reproduced from Langdon, 1980, by permission.)*

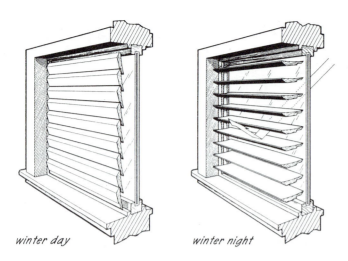

winter day   *winter night*

Figure 20.11: The RIB (Reflective Insulating Blind) is a prototype developed by Hanna Shapiro and Paul Barns of Oak Ridge National Laboratory. The louvers are about 4 in. wide with an interlocking edge seal. The top of each louver is curved so that all of the incoming sunlight is reflected onto the ceiling where it is diffusely re-reflected down onto desktops. While the prototype louvers were constructed of wood, they could be manufactured using high-density foam for greater R-value. *(Reproduced from Langdon, 1980, by permission.)*

(such as the Pella Slimshade) are quite effective at controlling the amount of solar radiation entering a space (reducing heat gain by up to 50 percent), but the thin, metal strips offer little thermal resistance (reduces heat loss through double glazing by about 20 percent). The addition of a metallic, mirror-finish surface increases the insulating value by reducing radiant transfer.

EXTERIOR MOVABLE INSULATION

Exterior insulating shutters are more popular in Europe and eliminate the condensation problem associated with interior systems. Properly designed, they can be used as reflectors (to enhance solar collection in the winter), as overhangs (to provide shading during the summer), and can provide increased security.

The disadvantages of exterior shutters include exposure to weather (sun, water, great temperature extremes), greater structural requirements due to wind loading and vandalism, the difficulty in achieving a tight perimeter seal, and the need for remote operation (especially in multistory buildings).

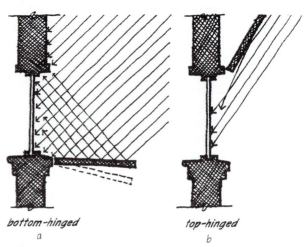

bottom-hinged   *top-hinged*
     a   *b*

Figure 20.12: (a) Bottom-hinged shutter is coated with mirror-like specular top surface reflects sunlight to increase the solar heating effectiveness during the day while reducing heat loss at night. (b) Top-hinged shutter can provide summer shading and a very small winter increase. *(Redrawn from Langdon, 1980, by permission.)*

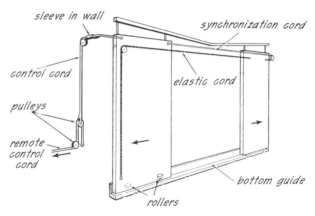

Figure 20.13: Sliding shutters are best suited over large areas of glazing where opaque adjacent wall areas are available. They are difficult to edge seal and are thus thermally inefficient. This configuration shows a control system designed by Clinton Sheerr. *(Reproduced from Langdon, 1980, by permission.)*

NIGHT INSULATION OPERATION

For residential applications, manual operation of night insulation is quite satisfactory. In general, the times of appropriate operation coincide with the natural inclination to open window coverings (drapes, for example) in the morning to admit light, and close them at night for privacy. While concern is often expressed about the inconvenience of operating manual shutters, in practice most passive solar homeowners find the routine of directly participating in saving energy and maintaining comfort to be a pleasant one. Obviously, the controls need to be convenient and few in number if this enthusiastic participation is to be maintained.

For nonresidential applications, particularly where the building may be unoccupied for extended periods (over weekends and holidays, for example), manual operation may not be suitable. Under these conditions, motorized operation may be preferable. However, motorized systems are less reliable mechanically and require skilled maintenance. Non-operating alternatives

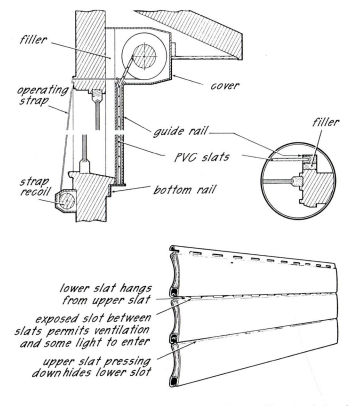

Figure 20.14: Rolladen-type shutters are popular in Europe. The slats have slots along one edge that recess into the adjoining section when the shutter is completely lowered. They open when the upper part of the shutter is raised slightly so that each slat hangs from the one above. This allows a small amount of light and ventilation to occur even when the shade is in the down position, making it ideal for controlling heat gain in hot climates. However, even versions with foam-filled slats achieve only a relatively low *R*-2 in spite of their relatively high cost. *(Reproduced from Langdon, 1980, by permission.)*

(such as low-*E* glazing, high-transmittance quad-glazing, and selective surface thermal storage walls) should be considered where manual operation is undependable (for example, in commercial buildings or rented apartments) and motorized operation unsuitable.

NIGHT INSULATION COST-EFFECTIVENESS

While significant performance increase is possible with night insulation, this must be balanced against the installed and maintained costs of the system. While life-cycle cost analysis of night insulation is relatively complex and involves many factors (fuel cost, fuel inflation rate, tax status and rate of heating costs, night insulation installation and maintenance costs, nonthermal value of the system, etc.), for the *R*-values recommended in Chapter 6, the maximum justifiable cost of installation and maintenance for eight years is between $5 and $8 per square foot of glazing area (1992 prices). In general, night insulation is most cost-effective when installed over a small number of large, vertical glazing areas for manual operation. The cost of small, motorized shades can seldom be justified on the basis of energy savings alone. Irregular-shaped glazing (such as the ends of greenhouses) is usually impractical to equip with night insulation.

OPTICAL MATERIALS

Because the optical properties of building materials affect radiant energy transfer, they are especially important in passive solar and other energy-efficient buildings.

SELECTIVE SURFACES

As presented in Chapter 1, *emissivity* is the ability of a surface to emit radiation at a given temperature. Within a certain portion of the radiation spectrum, a surface's emissivity is exactly equal to its absorptivity (Kirchhoff's Law). Thus, most conventional (i.e., nonmetallic) building materials, which are good IR absorbers, are equally good IR emitters. When they are warmed (by any means), they readily radiate energy to surrounding surfaces. Conversely, polished metallic surfaces, once warmed, are poor IR emitters and tend to retain heat longer than comparable nonmetallic surfaces.

The "ideal" solar collector surface is both black (for maximum solar absorption) and has a low thermal emissivity (to minimize heat loss by reradiation). Materials with this unique combination of selective optical properties are commonly referred to as "selective surfaces." Both water wall and Trombe wall systems with a selective foil absorber perform comparable to identical nonselective absorbers equipped with *R*-7 night insulation. This level of performance enhancement is surprising until one considers that the selective surface is reducing heat loss 24 hours a day while night insulation is, by definition, only operational at night. Selective surfaces have the additional advantages of not requiring manual operation (making them particularly suited for nonresidential buildings which may be unoccupied for extended periods) and requiring minimum maintenance.

Selective foils

Metallic selective surfaces were first developed by Harry Tabor in Israel in 1948 for use as absorbers on solar water heaters. This type of surface is now available commercially as a pressure-sensitive foil that can be applied on flat-plate collectors in active solar systems and on thermal storage walls (water tubes and Trombe masonry walls).

In order to be effective in transmitting absorbed heat into the thermal storage wall, it is essential that the adhesive bond between the foil and wall be good, providing continuous intimate contact. Even small air gaps interrupt the essential conductive transfer; the resulting radiative and convective transfer across the gap is much less efficient and results in wasteful overheating of the selective surface. Achieving this level of tight adhesion is easy on smooth surfaces (such as metal or fiberglass water containers); it is problematic on masonry, concrete, or stucco surfaces which tend to be "friable" or dusty, preventing good adhesion. A good masonry surface preparation is a coating of a cementacious waterproofing compound (such as Thoroseal) which dries to a smooth semigloss finish. Gypsum plaster finishes can achieve a similar smooth, dust-free surface but are less thermally conductive and thus less suited for this application.

Selective paints

Recently, special paints have been developed which have limited selective optical qualities. While the performance increase due to these paints is less than selective foils, it is still substantial; their lower costs and ease of application make them an attractive alternative to select foil surfaces.

REFLECTORS

For all commonly available building materials (including paints and metal surfaces), reflectance in the near-IR region is similar to reflectance in the visible region, and can be evaluated on the basis of lightness or darkness of color. Therefore, sunlight maintains the same proportion of visible and near-IR

radiation after being reflected by a white surface. There is thus little thermal advantage in reflecting sunlight from a white roof surface before entering compared with transmitting a comparable amount of direct sunlight. (This is not literally true because the outside white surface does absorb some radiation in both regions, and this is dissipated by convection outside of the building envelope. However, this advantage is not due to any selective reflectance.)

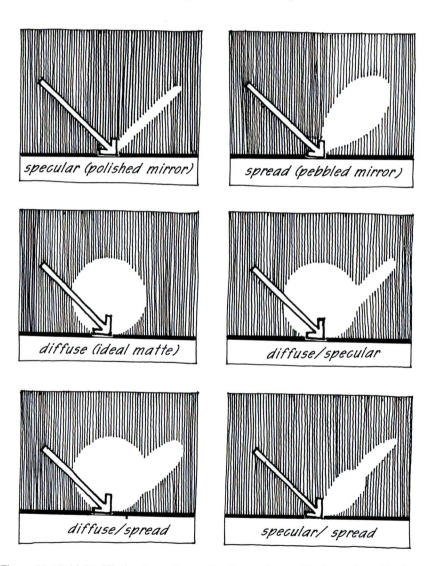

Figure 20.15: Light diffusion by various reflective surfaces. (*Redrawn from Kaufman, 1981, by permission.*)

In the far-IR region, high reflectance is primarily associated with metallic surfaces; virtually all other non-metallic opaque materials are highly absorptive in the far-IR region.

Reflected diffusion

Flat, polished metallic surfaces reflect specularly (like a mirror). Conversely, ideal matte surfaces reflect diffusely, with an even distribution in all directions. In practice, most building materials exhibit some combination of specular and diffuse reflection.

Solar modulator

Reflective blinds may be used to reflect sunlight onto ceilings deep within a room for passive solar heating (concrete ceilings provide thermal storage mass) and daylighting (sunlight is diffusely rereflected from a matte white ceiling). Adjustable mirror-finish louvers have the capability of reflecting all direct sunlight onto the ceiling for all sun angles throughout the year. Lebens (1979) has described the adaptation of commercially produced venetian blinds — "solar modulators" — for that purpose. The slats are inverted (concave up)

with the top mirror finished. The curved profile provides a controlled diffusion of reflected sunlight onto the ceiling. The slat curvature and spacing determine the number of seasonal adjustments. It was found that a single curvature (2.9 in. radius for a 1.0 in. slat) with two spacings (0.62 in. for Boston and wider at lower latitudes) is suitable for control with a minimum number of adjustments per year. The above optimum radius is slightly larger than most commercially available blinds which are approximately 2 in. in radius. However, this radius is satisfactory, requiring slightly more frequent adjustment. In practice, adjustment every two weeks is sufficient for most working hours.

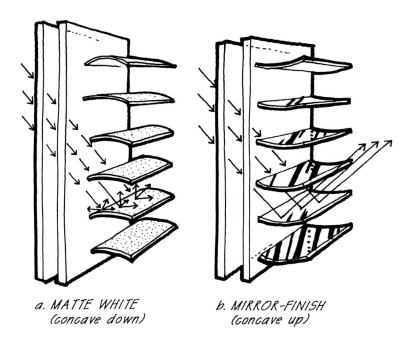

a. MATTE WHITE
(concave down)

b. MIRROR-FINISH
(concave up)

Figure 20.16: Adjustable louver reflection of sunlight: (a) white venetian blinds, concave down, and (b) mirror-finish ("solar modulator") venetian blinds, concave up. *(Redrawn from Lebens, 1979, by permission.)*

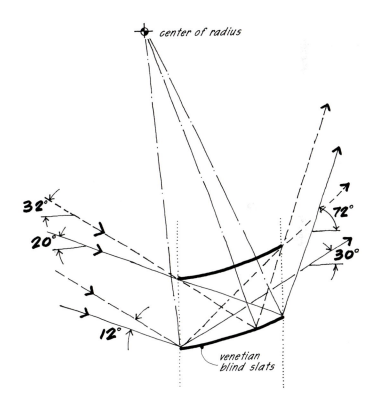

Figure 20.17: Ray diagram analysis of inverted venetian blinds with top surface mirror finish ("solar modulator"). In this configuration, 12° is the accepted profile-angle range for this adjustment. *(Redrawn from Lebens, 1979, by permission.)*

Lebens's studies were directed at passive solar heating applications of the "solar modulator." In a later study, Rosen (1981) investigated its daylighting potential for commercial office buildings. He concluded:

1. Under overcast skies, reflective blinds outperform conventional white blinds. The reflective blinds are clearly able to reflect diffuse skylight. They result in improved daylight distribution and increased light levels at the rear of the room. With the sun greater than 25°, daylight levels at the room's rear were increased by more than 20 footcandles.

2. Under clear skies, the reflective blinds greatly increase interior light levels when direct sun is on the windows. However, when there is no direct sun on the windows, the reflective blinds have little effect on interior light levels.

3. The combination of reflective blinds and white blinds wasn't notably better than using all white blinds.

Horizontal reflectors

Any solar window receives sunlight reflected from the ground as well as directly from the sun. The reflectance of the ground plane has a significant effect on the radiation received, increasing as reflectance increases. In colder climates, the higher reflectance of winter snow provides for significantly enhanced solar collection on south walls. This makes vertical glazing an attractive alternative to sloped glazing (which would perform significantly better if ground reflectance is not taken into account).

Specular (mirror-finish) reflectors can enhance solar collection of vertical walls even more than matte surfaces (such as snow or white gravel). At 40° latitude, a horizontal specular reflector located in front of a south-facing window (width of reflector equals width of window and depth of reflector equals the height of the window) will increase the incident solar radiation 30 percent during the heating season. Unlike the alternative of simply enlarging the window, the addition of a horizontal reflector avoids the increased heat loss associated with the larger glazing area. Thus the addition of a reflector may increase heating performance the equivalent of increasing the window size to 150 percent of the base case.

While horizontal reflectors are ideal for reflecting low-angle winter sunlight onto south-facing windows, higher-angle summer sunlight is reflected back to the sky and contributes little to summer overheating. This is only true of specular reflectors; diffuse reflectors are much less sensitive to the incidence angle and thus increase incident solar radiation through the year. Because of this, specular reflectors are preferred for enhancing winter heat gain (without the penalty of increasing summer overheating), while white reflectors are better suited for enhancing daylighting throughout the year.

This strategy is best suited for use on flat-roofed buildings with clerestories that project above. Position the reflector (specular for solar heating, white for year-round daylighting) in front of any south-facing clerestory windows. In this case, the base for the reflector is already constructed and hidden, and only the reflective surface need be added.

Ground-mounted reflectors are best suited for thermal storage wall systems (they cause glare problems in direct-gain buildings). One alternative is to integrate the reflector with an exterior, bottom-hinged insulating shutter (see the Baer residence in Chapter 9). Another is to install the reflective surface on a concrete slab. In the summer, the reflector can be covered with a durable, low-reflectance covering (such as indoor-outdoor carpet) to provide a useful patio area.

RADIANT BARRIERS

In warm climates, most of the heat transferred through the roof construction — from the roof deck through a vented attic space and through the insulated ceiling — is radiant. (Convection transfer occurs only when the warmer surface is below the cooler surface — in the winter.) A radiant barrier is a layer of aluminum foil placed in an airspace to block radiant heat transfer between a heat-radiating surface (such as a hot roof) and a heat-absorbing surface (such as conventional attic insulation; Fairey, 1986).

Radiant barriers can reduce heat gain through R-19 insulated ceilings by over 40 percent. If the ceiling portion of the total cooling load is 20 percent, this is a reduction of 40 percent of 20 percent — about 8 percent of the total cooling load.

Melody (1987) has identified the five most common radiant barrier materials:

- Single-sided foil (foil one side) with another material backing such as kraft paper or polypropylene. Some products are further strengthened by fiber webbing sandwiched between foil and backing. The strength of the backing material is important since unreinforced foil tears easily.

- Double-sided foil with reinforcement between the foil layers. Reinforcement may be cardboard, kraft paper, Mylar, or fiber webbing.

- Foil-faced insulation. The insulating material may be polyisocyanurate, polyethylene "air bubble" packing, or other materials that impede heat conduction.

- Multilayered foil systems. When fully extended and installed so that the foil layers do not touch, these products also form insulating airspaces.

- Although not by definition a "radiant barrier," low-emissivity paints are available that can be applied directly to the underside of the roof deck.

In selecting a radiant barrier material, consider emissivity (the lower the better — preferably 0.1 or less), and fire rating (as required by building codes); in general, foil-faced blanket fiberglass insulation cannot be left exposed (for example, in an attic) because of the flammability of the adhesive used to attach the foil.

Single-sided radiant barrier materials should be installed with the foil side facing down (utilizing the low emissivity rather than the reflective quality of the foil). At first, a single-sided barrier will work equally well with the foil facing either up or down. But over time dust will accumulate on the surface of the foil facing up and reduce its effective emissivity, causing it to absorb radiation rather that reflect it.

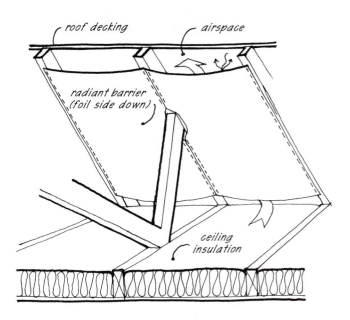

Figure 20.19: Retrofitting radiant barrier materials in existing attic spaces. *(Redrawn from Melody, 1987, courtesy of Florida Solar Energy Center.)*

GLAZING MATERIALS

Glazings are used in buildings for a variety of radiation control purposes including admitting light, admitting solar heat, allowing view in and out, and blocking or allowing radiant losses from the interior. In addition to radiation control, glazings are used as a barrier to convection. (Glazing materials have a relatively high conductance, and do not contribute directly to reducing conductive losses.) While other materials are equally effective in controlling convection, glazings are unique in their capability to control radiation (Moore, 1985).

Three regions of the radiation spectrum

As noted previously, when radiation strikes a surface it is either transmitted, reflected, or absorbed. It is obvious that different glazings vary in transmittance, reflectance, and absorptance. It is not as obvious (but very important in energy-efficient design) that for a given glazing material, transmittance, reflectance, and absorptance vary considerably depending on the radiation wavelength.

As discussed in Chapter 1, there are three regions of the radiation spectrum that are of particular interest in building design. These are the

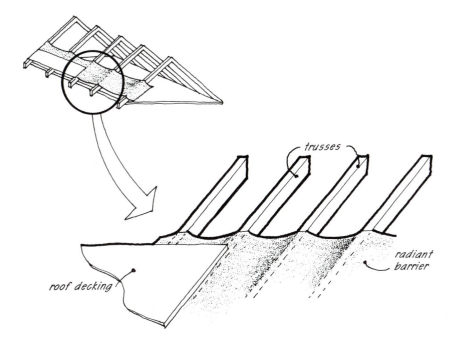

Figure 20.18: Installing a radiant barrier. In new residential construction, staple large sheets of the radiant barrier material to the top of the trusses before installing the roof decking. Install single-sided barriers foil side down. Install double-sided barriers loosely, allowing it to "sag" between trusses, creating an air space between the barrier and roof deck. Leave openings in the barrier at the ridge and eave, and install continuous ridge and soffit vents to prevent hot-air buildup and keep roof temperatures low. *(Redrawn from Melody, 1987, courtesy of Florida Solar Energy Center.)*

visible, *near-IR* (near infrared), and *far-IR* (far infrared) regions of the electromagnetic spectrum. The visible region is that part of the total solar spectrum that is visible to the eye and thus useful for lighting (0.4 to 0.7 microns). The near-IR region is the invisible portion of the solar spectrum (0.7 to 0.4 microns). The small *ultraviolet* solar region (0.3 to 0.4 microns) is also invisible but architecturally significant only for its effect on the fading of interior finishes and plant growth. The far-IR region is the invisible portion of the spectrum emitted from warm room surfaces (greater than 8.0 microns). The distinction between the near-IR and far-IR regions is particularly important architecturally because of the different behavior of glazing materials in these regions.

Radiation (in either of these regions) that is transmitted or reflected retains similar wavelength characteristics. However, absorbed radiation is converted to heat which is then conducted, convected, or reradiated. This reradiation occurs only in the far-IR region and should thus not be confused with transmitted or reflected radiation. In glazings, this absorbed energy is transferred (by radiation and convection) to both the room side and the exterior depending on their temperature relative to the glass. Thus, in the summer, absorbed heat tends to flow to the cooler room interior, while in the winter more heat is radiated to the exterior.

Glazing spectral response

There are seven basic types of glazings that are important to daylighting and solar heating/cooling applications because of their distinctly different behavior in the three regions of the radiation spectrum. These are: (1) clear glass, (2) gray/bronze glass, (3) "heat-absorbing" green glass, (4) light-reflecting film, (5) far-IR-reflecting film, (6) near-IR-reflecting film, and (7) IR-transparent plastic. The following discussion is a conceptualization of these types in terms of their more important different spectral responses; commercially-available examples differ from these simplified categories. For clarity, these types will first be considered as single layers (even though some, such as mirror finishes, are usually applied to a different layer). The combined effects of multiple layers will be considered subsequently.

Clear glass

Clear glass is highly transparent in both the visible and near-IR regions, highly absorptive in the far-IR region, and reflective in none of the regions. It is most suited for solar heat collection, for viewing from light to dark areas (such as through display windows), and for best color rendition. Even standard "clear" glazing typically contains iron oxide, which imparts a greenish color to the edge. "Water white" glass contains less iron oxide and thus has slightly greater visible and near-IR transmittance.

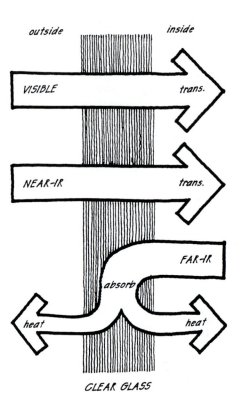

Figure 20.20: Ideal clear glass: section showing spectral transmission, absorption, and reflection. *(Reproduced from Moore, 1985, by permission.)*

Gray glass

Gray (and "bronze") glass is pigmented to increase visible and near-IR absorption (and thus decrease transmittance). Like clear glass, it is also highly absorptive in the far-IR, and reflective in none of the regions. It is best suited for viewing from dark to light areas (such as view windows to the exterior) because it reduces the brightness contrast between the view and surrounding interior surfaces. It is also used for reducing solar heat gain, but is less effective than "mirror" glasses because energy not transmitted is absorbed as heat, much of which is ultimately transmitted to the interior in the summer. Because of its neutral tint, gray glass is preferred to bronze where color rendition is important.

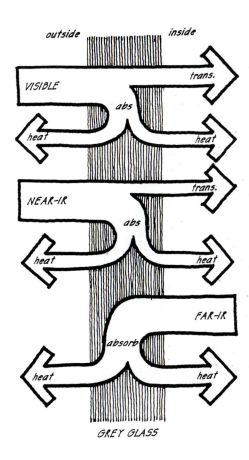

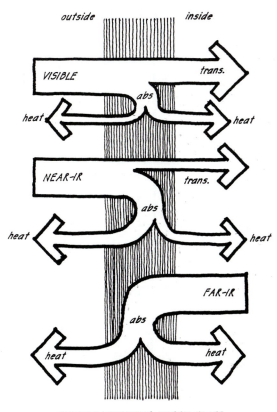

Figure 20.21: Ideal gray glass: section showing spectral transmission, absorption, and reflection. *(Reproduced from Moore, 1985, by permission.)*

Figure 20.22: Ideal "heat-absorbing" green glass: section showing spectral transmission, absorption, and reflection. *(Reproduced from Moore, 1985, by permission.*

"Heat-absorbing" green glass

Green-tinted glass is lightly pigmented to increase near-IR absorption with only a small increase in visible absorption. For this reason, it is preferred for many daylighting applications where the maximum light (compared with total solar energy admitted) is admitted while minimizing heat gain. This selectivity advantage occurs at the expense of slightly reduced color rendition. Like clear glass, it absorbs most far-IR.

Light-reflective film

A light-reflective film is created by depositing a metallic coating on a transparent substrate, producing a mirrorlike appearance. This type of film is usually reflective in the IR regions as well as the visible. The spectral qualities of the substrate (usually glass) combine with those of the coating. The combined characteristics differ depending on the interior or exterior location of the film.

Far-IR-reflective film

Selkowitz (1979) has described commercially available reflective films that, like clear glass, have a high visible and near-IR transmittance. Unlike glass, which absorbs far-IR, these coatings reflect in this region, further reducing heat loss. Theoretically, this would be the ideal glazing for passive solar heating applications. In practice, available commercial products have

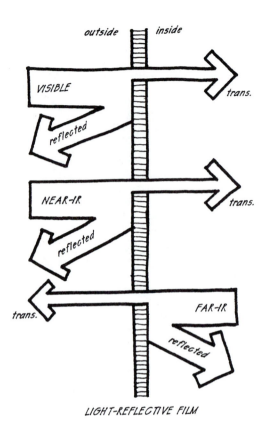

Figure 20.23: Ideal light-reflective film: section showing spectral transmission, absorption, and reflection. *(Reproduced from Moore, 1985, by permission.)*

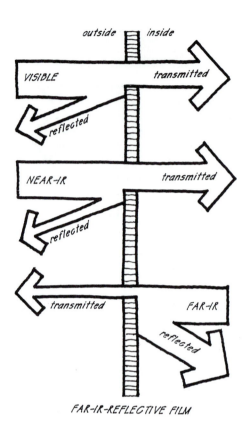

Figure 20.24: Ideal far-IR-reflective film ("residential heat mirror"): section showing spectral transmission, absorption, and reflection. *(Reproduced from Moore, 1985, by permission.)*

significantly reduced visible and near-IR transmittance compared with clear glazing, making it less suited for passive heating than for non-south residential window applications.

Near-IR-reflective film

Rosen (1982) has described a more recent development: a film which, like glass, has a high visible transmittance, but, unlike glass, has a high reflectance in both near-IR and far-IR regions. This combination is particularly attractive for daylighting in internal-load dominated buildings because of the rejection of the nonvisible solar region (which contributes only to the structure's heat gain).

IR-transparent plastic

Certain plastic materials (i.e., polyethylene and Nylon 6) are highly transparent in the far-IR spectrum. This reduces the "greenhouse" effect common to glass, greatly increasing heat loss to the exterior. This transparency is important, however, for certain radiative cooling applications. Clark and Blanpied (1979) have described the use of IR-transparent plastics for windscreen coverings to reduce convective warming of night-sky roof radiation cooling panels. Other plastics, more commonly used for building glazing (acrylic, polycarbonate, etc.) are typically also more transparent to far-IR than glass, but less so than polyethylene. Since spectral qualities vary considerably with thickness as well as material, manufacturer's specifications should be consulted.

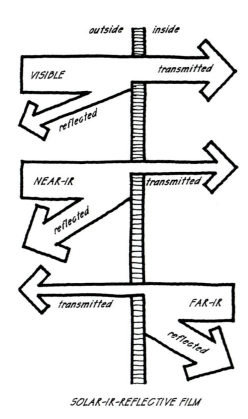

SOLAR-IR-REFLECTIVE FILM

Figure 20.25: Ideal near-IR-reflective film ("commercial building heat mirror"): section showing spectral transmission, absorption, and reflection. *(Reproduced from Moore, 1985, by permission.)*

Multiple glazing

The spectral response of multiple layers of the same material differs little from that of an individual layer. However, combining two or more types into a "sandwich" may produce a totally different response. This is particularly true in the common case where one layer is glass and one layer is a reflective film. Placing the reflective layer on the outside causes the far-IR to be absorbed and the heat dissipated to each side by convection and by reradiation to the interior. Conversely, placing the reflective layer on the room side reflects far-IR before it can be absorbed by the glass.

While the possible combinations of multilayer glazings are very large, the response for any combination can be derived from the individual layers discussed above. It should be noted that commercially available products

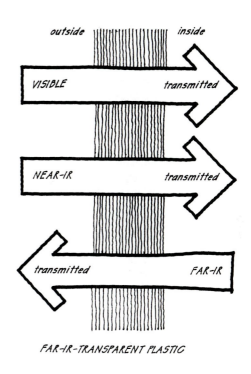

FAR-IR-TRANSPARENT PLASTIC

Figure 20.26: Ideal *far-IR* transparent plastic: section showing spectral transmission, absorption, and reflection. *(Reproduced from Moore, 1985, by permission.)*

(especially IR-reflective types) will differ from these ideal examples. In some cases, the performance difference is so great as to make it unsuitable for the application recommended for the ideal sample. For example, some low-E glazings (which have a high far-IR reflectivity) may not be suitable for passive solar heating applications because the reduced heat loss (due to the low emissivity) is more than offset by the reduced solar transmittance of the low-E film. Manufacturer's test results for spectral response in each of the three regions should be studied. Unfortunately, many manufacturers do not differentiate between transmission in visible and near-IR regions in standard literature.

Glazing diffusion

In general, the transmittance and reflectance discussed above is primarily a function of the material used to form the glazing. If the surfaces are flat and polished, then transmission and reflection are specular (i.e., transmitted light

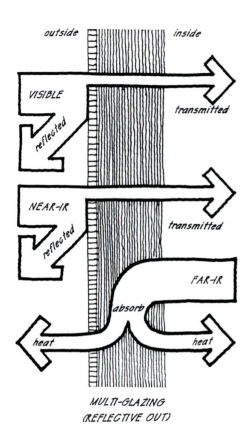

Figure 20.27: Multiple glazing: reflective out: section showing spectral transmission, absorption, and reflection. *(Reproduced from Moore, 1985, by permission.)*

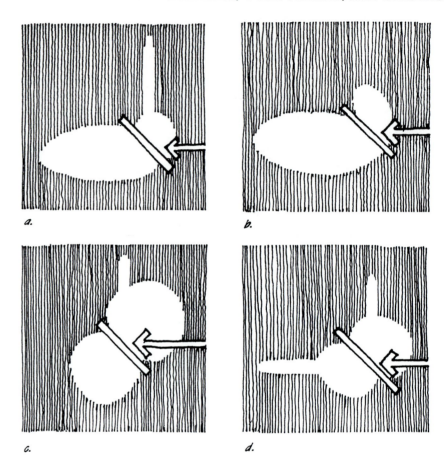

Figure 20.28: Transmitted light diffusion. *(Redrawn from Kaufman, 1981, by permission.)*

continues in the same direction and reflections are mirrorlike). If one or both surfaces are rough, then reflection and transmission are diffused. In most cases this diffusion is only dependent on surface texture; in some materials (such as translucent white glass or plastic), white pigment suspended in the material diffuses the light internally. Transmission can be characterized as clear, diffuse (where diffusion is complete and uniform in all directions), and spread (where diffusion is complete but not uniform, with the largest component in the incident direction).

While the exact amount of transmission, reflection, and spread of diffusion can only be determined by laboratory measurement, useful design information can be gained by visual inspection of glazing samples. As a general rule, for commercially available glazing materials, increased diffusion results in decreased transmission.

INTERIOR FINISHES IN DIRECT GAIN BUILDINGS

A major disadvantage of direct gain systems is the necessary prolonged exposure of interior finishes to sunlight. Fabrics are especially sensitive to deterioration. In addition to fading, fabrics used for drapes and thermal shades are subject to moisture exposure from condensation. Resistance to shrinkage from moisture absorption is an important consideration in selecting fabrics for this application. In general, fabrics which most readily absorb moisture are most prone to shrinkage. Even a preshrunk cotton fabric guaranteed to shrink less than 3 percent can cause serious problems in an 80-in.-long thermal

Table 20.1: Stability of Fibers to Environmental Conditions

Fiber (trade name)	Effect of Sunlight	Effect of Heat	Effect of Moisture
Cotton	Gradual loss of strength; gradual yellowing.	Excellent resistance to degradation by heat.	Medium absorbency; subject to mildew and rot if stored wet.
Linen	Gradual loss of strength.	Discolors at high temperatures.	High absorbency.
Silk	Moderate loss of strength (more than cotton); depends on dye and additives.	Less affected than wool.	Medium absorbency.
Wool	Loss of strength; gradual fading.	Loses softness from prolonged exposure.	High absorbency.
Acetate (Acele, Celanese, Estron)	Slight loss of strength; little color loss.	Little degradation.	Low absorbency.
Acrylic (Acrilan, Creslan, Orlon, Sefkrome, Zefran)	Very little loss of strength; no discoloration.	Little degradation	Low absorbency.
Glass (Fiberglas)	None.	None.	None.
Leather	No loss of strength; slight discoloration.	Embrittlement; stabilized by care.	Low absorbency.
Modacrylic (Dynel, Elura, Kanakalon, Levil)	Very little loss of strength.	Little degradation.	Low absorbency.
Nylon (Antron, Cardon, Caprolan, Cumuloft, Nomex, Perlon, Qiana)	Gradual loss of strength; little color loss.	Little degradation.	Low absorbency.
Olefin (Durel, Herculon, Marvess, Meraklon, Polycrest, Polypropylene).	Moderate loss of strength; gradual embrittlement; can be stabilized.	Embrittlement; moderate decomposition.	None.
Polyester (Dacron, Fortrel, Kodel, Textura)	Very gradual loss of strength; no discoloration.	Little degradation.	Low absorbency.
Rayon (Avril, Coloray, Jetspon, Zantrel, Bemberg)	Gradual loss of strength; affected more than cotton.	Little degradation.	High absorbency.
Vinyl (Nagahyde)	No loss of strength; slight discoloration.	Gradual embrittlement.	None.

(After Guerin, from Langdon, 1980, by permission.)

shade, which, cut to fit when installed, may shrink 2 in. within a year. In general, synthetic fabrics (including acrylic, polyester, nylon, and modacrylic) are best suited to prolonged exposure to direct gain conditions; of the common natural fibers, wool is superior. Synthetic dyes are relatively stable, while vegetable dyes fade rapidly.

Wood (in paneling, furniture, and flooring) is also subject to degradation in passive solar buildings. Like fabrics, wood tends to fade with exposure to interior sunlight. If exposure is not uniform (under small rugs, for example), permanent changes in coloring may occur that are particularly noticeable. This fading tendency may be retarded or, in some cases, accelerated by the application of stain coatings. Most interior coatings (varnishes and paints) are not formulated to either resist deterioration of the coating by ultraviolet radiation or protect the underlying wood from discoloration; coatings (particularly varnishes) formulated for exterior applications (especially marine environments which have UV-inhibitive additives) may be more suitable for direct-gain interiors. In general, opaque coatings (paint) are more durable than transparent ones (varnishes) because UV penetration is limited to the top layer of the coating.

Another consideration in direct-gain interiors is the degradation of wood materials due to too much moisture (rot) and too little moisture (excessive drying, shrinkage, checking, and glue-joint failure). Most coatings transmit moisture, and at best, simply retard the drying or saturation process.

Epoxy coatings and adhesives

Epoxy is an exception to this characteristic of coating moisture permeability; properly applied, it produces a vapor-proof coating. Virtually unused in the building construction industry, epoxy coatings are widely used in the marine industry and have revived wood as a boat-building material. The "wet epoxy saturation technique" (WEST) system (Gougeon and Gougeon, 1988) involves coating wood components with three coats of low-viscosity two-part epoxy. Conventional paint and varnish coatings are permeable to water vapor and thus allow wood to become saturated in a marine environment, losing approximately half of its structural strength and creating conditions conducive to rot. Because epoxy is virtually impermeable to water vapor, wood so coated maintains its original moisture content and structural characteristics and is virtually impervious to rot. While the epoxy is water clear, it is subject to UV degradation and must be coated with a UV-inhibitive varnish. However, its impermeability to water vapor transmission makes it superior to conventional coating in direct-gain interiors which are subject to rapid changes in humidity and resultant shrinkage and cracking. It is also a superior coating for wood components exposed to rot environments (such as condensation on windowsills, or leakage under water wall containers).

In addition to its coating superiority, epoxy may be mixed with a cotton-fiber thickening additive to make it suitable for use as an adhesive. Depending on the amount of thickener added, the viscosity of the epoxy can be increased from motor oil consistency to that of peanut butter. Because of the superior strength and "bridging" capacity of the adhesive, tightly fitted joints are unnecessary; standard boat-building practice requires only rough-shaping of wood components, applying a liberal amount of thick epoxy, and joining the pieces under light pressure to squeeze out the excess adhesive. Curing time is 8 to 12 hours.

The same epoxy can be mixed with various powdered phenolic additives to create either a structural filler (for creating fillets to eliminate the need for wood strips at perpendicular plywood joints) or an extremely lightweight filler that is easily sanded.

INFILTRATION CONTROL

In well-insulated buildings, infiltration becomes a major source of heat loss and gain. There are two sources of infiltration: opening and closing exterior doors and air leakage through cracks in the building.

Infiltration due to door openings can be reduced by airlock entry vestibules and revolving doors. If the cost of construction of the additional floorspace for such a vestibule is taken into account, the energy savings alone can seldom justify such a feature in a residence where the number of openings is relatively small. However, in commercial and institutional buildings the frequency of door openings make such strategies essential, especially in cold climates.

Air leakage can be minimized by the use of weatherstripped windows and doors that have demonstrated their airtightness through independent laboratory testing. While fixed glazing has the inherent advantage of minimizing infiltration in comparison with operable windows, the latter has the advantage of allowing ventilation cooling during mild seasons and should be included for that reason. During construction, after the windows and doors are set, the gaps between the rough opening and the frame should be filled either with expanding foam spray or with pieces of fiberglass insulation forced into the crack.

Gaps between the sill plate and the foundation wall should be filled with expanding foam spray or by prior installation of a thin layer of fiberglass "sill-sealer" batt insulation. In frame construction, caulk between the perimeter band joist and the subfloor and again between the wall base plate and the subfloor.

In general, caulking should be installed for both water-resistance and air-tightness in joints where dissimilar materials meet on the exterior (especially where one is concrete). Where expansion is likely to occur, select a caulking material that has good elongation (stretching) characteristics as well as good adhesion and resistance to UV. For gaps larger than 1/4 in. install a backing strip to ensure that the proper thickness and shape of the caulk joint is maintained. Seal around electrical outlets that penetrate the exterior envelope with special gaskets for that purpose.

Table 20.2: Caulking Material Characteristics

Product	Rel. Cost	Adhesion	Elongation (%)	Life (yrs.)	Service Temp, °F	Resist. to UV
Urethane (1 pt)	$2 — 3	Excellent	300 — 450	20+	-58 to 135	Good
Silicone	$3 — 4	Good (Excell. with Primer)	100 — 200	20+	-76 to 400	Excell.
Acrylic Terpolymer	$3 — 4	Excellent		20+	185 max.	Very Good
Hypalon	$2	Very Good	15 — 50	15 — 20	-4 to 230	Good
Polysulfide	$2 — 4	Excell.	200 — 250	20+	-58 to 248	Very Good
Butyl Rubber	$1 — 2	Very Good	75 — 125	7 — 10	-40 to 275	Fair
Acrylic Latex	$1 — 2	Excell. (exc. w/metal)	25 — 60	2 — 14	-22 to 212	Fair
Oil	$1	Fair to Good	5	1 — 7	-13 to 185	Poor

(Source: Northeast Solar Energy Center, 1980, by permission.)

Install an infiltration barrier sheet around the entire exterior walls over the sheathing but prior to the installation of windows and doors or siding. Cut the required door and window openings by cutting an "X" diagonally from corner to corner and folding the excess around the frame and stapling on the inside of the framing before final trimming. This material should be especially manufactured for this purpose of infiltration control and *must be vapor-permeable* while being a barrier to airflow. The vapor permeability is essential to prevent inadvertently creating a vapor barrier on the cold side of the wall which could result in condensation within the wall insulation.

INDOOR AIR POLLUTION

Traditionally, the amount of infiltration that inadvertently occurred in buildings was enough to dilute any common indoor contaminants. Air leakage was considerable due to poorly sealed windows and doors and little if any caulking of construction joints. Furthermore, the construction materials used resulted in little contamination of indoor air (Shurcliff, 1981 and 1982).

Today, the increased concern for energy conservation has minimized infiltration, which has prevented the previous dilution of contaminants from occurring. In addition, the increased use of plastics and other building materials which give off far greater hazardous gaseous products into the interior air than did more traditional materials has contributed to indoor air pollution. A common pollutant is formaldehyde, a chemical found in many building materials (including most glues used for plywood), which continues to release toxic gases for several years.

Table 20.3: Indoor Pollutant Characteristics, Impacts, and Controls

Pollutant	Major sources	Form	Exposure Levels Indoors	Health Impacts	Control Strategies
Sulfur Dioxide	Ambient air indoor: fossil fuel combustion	Gas	Ambient source: significantly lower than outdoors	Risk of acute and long-term respiratory effects in conjunction with particulates, heart disease, neoplams	Absortive surfaces, source ventilation, ventilation
Nitrogen Oxides	Ambient air, vehicle emission; indoor combustion: carbonaceous fuels (gas stoves and heating, wood and tobacco combustion)	Gas	Ambient source: lower or approx. same as ambient levels. Indoor source: significant levels with unvented combustion.	Risk of acute respiratory effects, possible increased mortality from cardiovascular disease and cancer.	Source removal, source ventilation; absorption by activated carbon, ventilation.
Carbon Oxides	Ambient air, vehicle emission. Indoor combustion, infiltration from garage	Gas	Ambient source: approximates patterns of outdoor levels. Indoor source: significant levels with unvented combustion.	Lower concentrations: headache, dizziness. Higher concentrations: Nausea, vomiting, asphyxiation, death.	Source removal, source ventilation, catalytic oxidation, complete combustion.
Photochemical oxidents	Ambient air		Ambient source: significantly lower than outdoors	Eye irritation, respiratory discomfort, chronic exposure not understood.	Absorptive surfaces, ventilation.
Particulates	Ambient air; indoor combustion resuspension from physical activity.	Particulate	Ambient sources: lower than outdoors. Indoor source: significant levels from indoor combustion.	Varied: range from respiratory to cardiovascular disease and cancer.	Source removal, material substitution or sealing.
Asbestos	Insulation or decorative sprays	Particulate fiber	Indoor source: variable significance of levels unknown.	Asbestosis to bronchogenic carcinoma to neoplasms. Risk of acute exposure: pleural or peritoneal mesothelioma 15 years later.	Source removal, material substitution or sealing.
Hydrocarbons	Ambient air; indoor combustion; pesticides; spray propellants; cleaning solvents	Gas	Ambient source: approximates outdoor levels; Indoor generation: acute exposure can be extremely high.	Risk of a variety of severe, acute and long-term effects including depression of the central nervous system	Source removal, source ventilation, absorption by activated charcoal, ventilation
Formaldehyde	Building materials, wallboard, insulation, tobacco smoke	Gas	Indoor source: can be significant depending on building materials	Low levels: eye, nose, and upper respiratory tract irritation. Chronic exposure: unknown	Source removal, material substitution, activated carbon absorption, ventilation, absorption by special surfaces, oxidation
Radon	Surrounding soil and fill; building materials (bricks, concrete, stone); natural gas, groundwater.	Gas and particulate	Significantly higher than outdoor levels dependent on ventilation levels.	Enhanced risk of lung and other cancers.	Radon Gas: activated charcoal absorption, ventilation. Radon daughters: electrostatic precipitators, filters, ventilation, barriers.

(Reproduced from Scott and Scott, 1980, by permission.)

Radon is a naturally occurring radioactive gas that is found in the soil in varying concentrations depending on location. It leaks into the building through cracks in the foundation and basement slab, and in newer, relatively airtight construction can be a source of serious health concern. Most local health departments can provide information on low-cost testing for the concentrations of radon in buildings.

The remedy for indoor air pollution is not simply to reduce the airtightness of the buildings. A building with sufficient infiltration on days that have mild temperatures and no wind may receive ten times that amount of infiltration on cold and windy days; the energy wasted by such an uncontrolled process is simply too great.

AIR-TO-AIR HEAT EXCHANGERS

The solution is to achieve a constant fan-forced ventilation rate, with a heat exchanger that allows the heat from the polluted exhaust air to be transferred to fresh, outdoor makeup air. There are two basic configurations of air-to-air heat exchangers.

Flat-plate exchangers use a continuous transfer of heat through fixed sheets (usually plastic films) that keep the two airstreams separate. These have the virtue of no moving parts other than the blower.

Rotary exchangers achieve sequential transfer with a slowly turning (7-rpm) honeycomb rotor wheel. Each passage of the wheel remains in the stream of outgoing air for a few seconds, absorbing heat from it; it then moves into the incoming stream and releases heat to it. Rotary exchangers have a greater heat-transfer area per unit of volume. In addition, they can recover water vapor with high efficiency provided the air-passage surfaces are coated with a hygroscopic material which extracts water vapor from the outgoing air and then releases it a few seconds later to the incoming air.

The efficiency of these exchangers ranges from 60 to 80 percent (in other words, 60 to 80 percent of the temperature *difference* between indoor and outdoor air is added to the outdoor temperature of the intake air).

VENTILATION

WINDOWS

While windows were formerly made at the construction site, virtually all are now produced in factories for efficiency, lower cost, and higher quality. The traditional material for window frames was wood, and it continues to be an excellent choice for residential applications. Other materials used in contemporary construction include aluminum, steel, and plastics used singly or in combination. Wood has moderate insulating qualities and is easily worked; however, it shrinks and swells with changing moisture content and requires periodic repainting. Plastic or aluminum is often used to add a permanent outer finish to a wood structural core, providing most of the advantages of each material. Aluminum is comparatively inexpensive and easy to work (its extrudability is a special advantage over wood and steel) and requires no repainting; however, it conducts heat so well that condensation and frost will form on interior sash surfaces unless interrupted by a thermal break of rubber or plastic. The primary advantage of steel is its strength, allowing relatively thin mullion sections; it is difficult to work and achieve even a moderate level of airtightness; as a result, steel is seldom used in energy-efficient construction (Allen and Iano, 1985).

Fixed windows are the least expensive and least likely to leak air or water because of the lack of movable components. *Single-hung* and *double-hung* windows have one or two movable sashes (the frames in which the glazing is mounted). The sashes slide up and down in recesses in the frame of the window. In older windows the sashes were held in position by cords and counterweights; newer versions use springs to counterbalance the weight of the sashes. A *sliding* window is essentially a single-hung unit on its side; it shares with single- and double-hung windows the advantage that the sashes are secured in the tracks at all times allowing their construction to be more

lightly built than those in *projected* windows where the sashes pivot in their frames and therefore must have sufficient stiffness to resist wind loads. Hung and sliding windows can only be opened to half their total area.

All projected windows can be opened to their full area. *Casement* windows are helpful in catching passing breezes and inducing ventilation in the building (especially in rooms with a window on only one wall; see Chapter 15). They are typically tall and narrow but several can be arranged together to cover a large area. *Awning* windows can be broad and relatively short and are often used below fixed glazing; they are hinged to project out at the bottom when open and thus shed rain. *Hopper* windows are similar to awning windows except that they project in at the top when open; because they project into the room and can be an obstruction, hoppers are used most often in nonresidential construction above an HVAC room unit (in a school room for example). See Fig. 15.47 for the effective open area of various window types.

WIND VENTILATOR CAPS

As noted in Chapter 15, wind ventilators can be used to enhance ventilative airflow in buildings either in conjunction with the types of solar chimneys described above, or alone depending solely on the force of the wind to induce a suction. In general, any object placed in the path of wind flow causes pressure differentials (positive on the windward side, negative on the leeward side). When the object is placed on the top of a ventilation chimney, these pressure differentials can be used to create a suction, increasing the airflow exiting the chimney. Rotating wind "turbine" ventilation caps are a popular, low-cost device for accomplishing this while providing protection from rain. Long used for industrial applications, these "chef's hats" provide a visually dynamic symbol of energy conservation that made them popular among designers of passively cooled houses during the 1970s. While these rotating ventilators may be impressive visually, experimental testing has revealed that their ventilation performance is modest in comparison with several alternatives.

MOISTURE CONTROL

The effort to create tighter buildings by reducing heat loss and air infiltration must include some serious consideration of the presence and movement of moisture (in the form of water vapor) within the building. Water vapor is introduced into the interior by occupants (breathing and perspiration) and their activities (bathing, cooking, dishwashing and laundering). These contribute as much as one gallon per person per day. In addition, interior plants and dirt floors in basements and crawlspaces contribute additional moisture. Although water vapor movement can be influenced by air movement, the primary driving force is diffusion from an area of high concentration (high vapor pressure) to areas of low pressure. In winter, moisture tends to move from inside through the building shell to the outside. Water vapor is carried out either by air leaking through gaps in the envelope, or directly through materials as it diffuses from the moisture-laden interior (Schwolsky, 1980a and 1980b).

Moisture as a vapor will not harm the building. However, as vapor moves through the building shell, it may encounter cool surfaces that cause it to condense into water. This can damage the building's structure (due to rust and

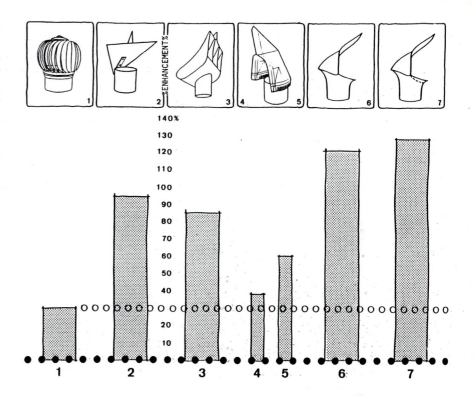

Figure 20.30: Comparison of ventilation rates generated by six different ventilator caps showing enhancement (%) over base case rotating turbine cap. *(Reproduced from Schubert and Hahn, 1983, by permission.)*

rot) and thermal performance (*R*-value is sharply reduced as insulation materials become saturated). Mildew and wood-staining fungi will grow well on a wetted surface at 60°F and 60 percent RH. For wood-eating fungi to grow, wood fibers must be saturated (about 30 percent moisture content) and warm. The decay-causing fungi grow fastest at 50 to 60°F but may occur as low as freezing. Consistently high humidities and cool temperatures in combination with an inadequate vapor barrier combine to produce this level of concealed condensation (Bliss, 1984).

VAPOR BARRIERS

Vapor barriers (technically, these are vapor retarders) are those materials that effectively resist the passage of water vapor. In addition to the materials listed in Table 6.2, foil-backed wall boards, closed-cell insulative sheathings,

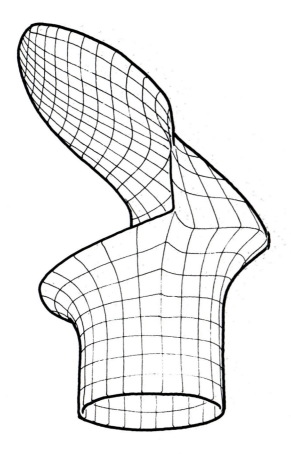

Figure 20.29: Experimental fiberglass ventilator cowl. *(Redrawn from Schubert and Hahn, 1983, by permission.)*

and vapor-retardant paints retard vapor permeation. Generally, the separate sheet barriers are much more effective than other barriers (including those supplied on insulation). The actual performance is very dependent on the quality of its insulation.

Polyethylene is the most commonly used vapor barrier. The continuity of the barrier is critical to its effectiveness. After monitoring a number of test walls for two years, researcher Gerald Sherwood of the Forest Products Laboratory (FPL) in Madison, Wisconsin, concluded: "Puncturing the vapor retarder, as with an electrical outlet, can completely change the moisture patterns in the wall," and that, once punctured, 6-mil polyethylene film performed no better than kraft paper (Bliss, 1984).

Vapor barriers are necessary on perimeter walls and ceiling framing to resist the movement of moisture into the insulated cavities, where it can cause serious problems where the insulation temperature drops below the dew point and condensation occurs. The condition is particularly bad because it is hidden from view and only becomes apparent after serious damage has occurred. Install the vapor barriers on the "warm" side of the wall insulation: inside in predominantly cool climates, outside in predominantly hot climates. Install over insulation by stapling to studs before applying the finish material. Minimize joints and any tears and openings with duct tape. Carefully seal around openings cut for electrical outlets and fixtures. Sheet barriers should be extended across windows and door openings and later carefully trimmed to the inside of the jambs.

Install vapor barriers under interior concrete slabs to resist the movement of ground moisture into the building. Install after all plumbing, electrical, and drainage lines are in place and the gravel bed leveled. Minimize the number of joints, and tape all joints and openings. Extend the barrier up the foundation wall and hold in place with tape; trim after the slab is cured.

Dirt floors in crawlspaces should be evened and raked prior to laying the polyethylene, removing any rocks and construction scraps that could tear the sheets. Lap joints 4 in. minimum and seal splices with duct tape. Weight the perimeter of the barrier at the foundation wall with soil.

Retrofitting vapor barriers

Older buildings, even without any installed vapor barriers, seldom experience intra-wall condensation. This is because the large number of cracks (lack of weatherstripping and insulation) dilute the interior humidity below the level where condensation problems would occur. When older buildings (particularly houses with many interior moisture sources) are renovated, wall insulation is typically added (by blowing in fill or foamed-in-place insulation to the wall cavity), and weatherstripping installed. The result is a much higher winter humidity ratio and, without the provision of a vapor barrier, the occurrence of intra-wall condensation. In many cases, this results in invisible

structural damage to the wall studs due to rot. The recommended solution, assuming that adding a sheet vapor barrier is impractical, is to coat the walls and ceiling with a vapor-retardant paint. Paints formulated especially for this purpose are available from major manufacturers. Alternatively, an aluminum paint with a high aluminum-powder-solids content is satisfactory.

MOISTURE DILUTION BY VENTILATION

Moisture buildup can also be controlled through the use of controlled ventilation. Areas of concentrated moisture (such as baths, laundries, and kitchens) should be vented directly to the outside during periods of moisture generation by means of exhaust fans or hoods. Such devices should only be operated when necessary to prevent excessive heat loss; a timer switch is recommended.

Moisture that enters roof cavities and attic spaces must be carried out to the building by air moving through vented openings. In the winter, if the moisture is not removed, it may condense on the underside of the cool roof sheathing and then drip back onto the ceiling insulation. In addition, adequate ventilation keeps the attic air temperature near that of the outdoor temperature and thus reduces cooling loads in the summer. In general, sloped roofs are adequately ventilated by continuous soffit vents and a continuous ridge vent (as shown in the following section on construction details).

Venting also reduces damaging moisture buildup in crawlspaces. In addition to the polyethylene ground cover recommended above, screened operable vents should be installed in the foundation walls near each corner of the foundation. Most local building codes specify the number and areas of vents required. If the crawlspace is insulated around the perimeter, the vents may be closed in the winter to reduce heat loss; if the floor itself is insulated, the vents should be left open throughout the year to reduce moisture migration to the interior.

THERMAL STORAGE COMPONENTS

MASONRY

Masonry (concrete block and brick) and concrete (floor slabs and walls) are efficient thermal storage components. In general, the more dense and conductive the material, the better for thermal storage; light-weight concrete and masonry units should be specifically avoided as the air-entrainment necessary to make these materials light acts as insulation and inhibits the conduction in and out of the material. With this exception, virtually all common masonry materials are suitable for thermal storage. Ensure that where hollow units and multiple wythes are used, all voids are filled solid with cement grout so that no thermal breaks inhibit thermal conduction through the material.

WATER CONTAINERS

As noted in Chapter 1, water can store five times the amount of heat per unit of weight (three times per unit volume) as concrete for a comparable temperature rise. This advantage (and the availability of water at virtually no cost) is offset by the problem of containerization and its inherent lack of structural support capability.

A variety of container types and designs are available. Some containers are manufactured with an attractive interior finish and may be left uncovered. Others are not intended for exposure, and may be enclosed in walls or incorporated components such as planters or window seats. In general, the less expensive the container, the more likely that it must be concealed. Unfortunately, covering the containers will degrade the system's performance (because direct radiation and convection transfer between the container and the adjacent living space is interrupted by the enclosure; Levy, 1983).

Regardless of the container type selected, the water should be treated (with 1:400 parts chlorine bleach) to inhibit algae growth. In the case of metal containers, they should incorporate a plastic liner or inner coating to prevent corrosion.

Fiberglass tubes are manufactured for the specific purpose of water thermal storage. They are often left exposed for functional and aesthetic reasons. They are made of thin, UV-stabilized fiberglass sheets rolled into a cylinder. Prior to filling, the tubes are lightweight and easy to install but are relatively fragile and special care must be taken to prevent crackage and punctures during the construction process. Earlier installations painted these tubes dark (or dyed the water) to maximize solar absorption; however, comparative testing determined that clear tubes performed nearly as well thermally as opaque ones with the additional advantage of admitting daylight and being more attractive visually. The tubes are available in standard diameters 12 and 18 in. and in heights from 4 to 10 ft. The tubes need to be braced at the top to prevent overturning. A cap is recommended to keep out dust and minimize evaporation.

Metal culvert pipe can be used for water storage. Culverts can be cut to any height, providing more design flexibility than with fiberglass tubes. Furthermore, culverts are sturdier than fiberglass and less subject to construction damage. Their heavier weight should be considered in the structural design of supporting construction. A plate is welded to the bottom. In galvanized steel culverts, because the welding process damages the galvanized coating, a plastic liner is recommended to prevent corrosion-related leaks. To protect the liner from puncture at the bottom (from sharp edges resulting from the welding process), build up the bottom to the culvert 3 or 4 in. by pouring in a thin cement grout. For the liner use polyethylene film in tube form (used for packaging or for inflatable ducting in commercial greenhouses) sized to match the diameter of the culvert. To eliminate the need for creating a seal, the polyethylene should be cut slightly longer than twice the height of the culvert, folded in half and the folded end inserted to the bottom with both ends projecting from the top. Fill either end of the tube, and seal to top with a "twist-tie" to exclude dust from the water and cover the polyethylene to prevent UV degradation. Again, structural bracing is required to prevent overturning. The exterior of the culvert is usually painted (dark on the solar side); two coats of zinc chromate primer followed by two coats of the finish paint are recommended.

Metal drums can be used as water storage containers. The cost is quite low for used drums; drums previously containing oil or grease actually provide an inherent corrosion resistance. Thirty-gallon drums are preferred to the larger, more common fifty-five-gallon size. The smaller diameter is sufficient for solar applications and the smaller size is more easily moved or supported.

Five-gallon high-density polyethylene drums are available for use as water storage containers. These are self-supporting and will stack safely with proper lateral support to prevent overturning. The small size makes them easy to handle, but a large number is required to provide sufficient storage area.

In the late 1970s and early 1980s several companies began manufacturing modular water wall containers designed to fit into conventional wood framing construction systems. While several of these were innovative and resolved the problems of containerization, few of these are still commercially available. While many do-it-yourselfers have recognized the performance and construction advantages of water for thermal storage, the potential liability for consequential damages resulting from water spillage has discouraged manufacturers from developing and marketing water containers for this purpose. One company discontinued production upon determining that product liability insurance for the water containers for one residence was $2000 — more than the cost of the components. And in an era of escalating construction litigation, designers are similarly discouraged from specifying water thermal storage components.

ROCK BED CONSTRUCTION

As discussed in Chapter 11, rock beds are an effective means of thermal storage in convective air-loop systems. The two types of rock beds are *convective discharge* (where air is used to transfer heat from the rock bed to the living space) and *radiant-release* rock beds (where the rock bed discharges by conduction through a floor slab — or wall component — and transfers heat from the floor slab to the space by radiation). Both types are charged by hot air heated by a remote collector and circulated through the rock bed either by natural convection or (in the case of hybrid systems) by a fan (Lewis et al., 1982).

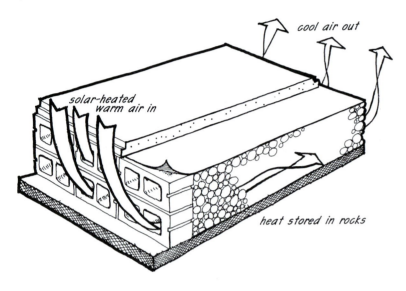

Figure 20.31: Radiant-release rock beds are typically located under the conditioned space and are covered with an uninsulated concrete slab. *(Redrawn from Lewis et al., 1982, by permission.)*

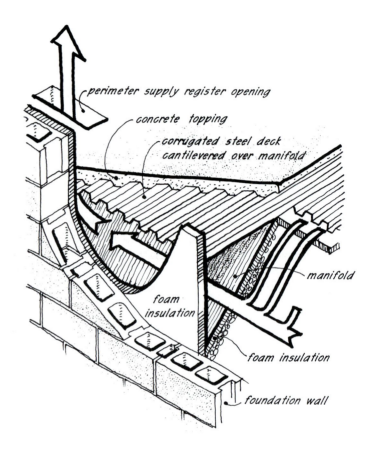

Figure 20.32: Use of steel decking to form air channels under floor slab. At the perimeter, the decking is cantilevered to form a manifold plenum which collects air from the channels and supplies it to the room through register openings (developed by William Chaleff, architect). *(Redrawn from Lewis et al., 1982, by permission.)*

The most desirable rock is about fist-sized (2 to 4 in. diameter) washed river gravel. Crushed gravel is also satisfactory provided it is thoroughly washed to remove small particles and dust. Slag is not satisfactory due to cleanliness and odor problems.

Most rock beds operate without odors or other evidence of bacterial problems. When occasional problems occur, they are almost always associated with the presence of moisture within the system, usually resulting from the installation of rocks that were not adequately dried after the recommended washing to remove dust. This moisture will evaporate as rock-bed temperatures rise; once stabilized the problem is not likely to reoccur.

On the other hand, moisture is almost always a problem when a rock bed is used for cooling hot, humid air in the summer. Most reports of odor problems deal with rock beds used for cooling, and because of this, this application is not recommended.

RADIANT FLOOR CONSTRUCTION

Radiant floors operate similarly to radiant-release rock beds in that they are charged by hot air from a remote solar collector. They differ in that heat is stored in the floor slab itself instead of underlaying rocks. Various strategies have evolved for creating voids under the slab for the required air passage (Lewis, 1982).

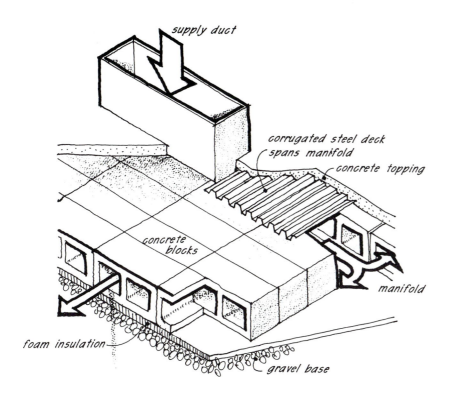

Figure 20.33: Use of concrete blocks to create air channels under slab; corrugated steel deck spans manifold (developed by Robert Mitchell, architect). *(Redrawn from Lewis et al., 1982, by permission.)*

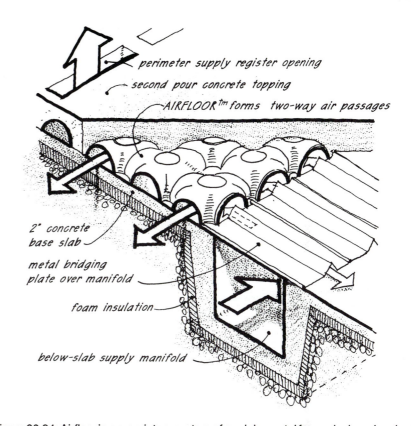

Figure 20.34: Airfloor is a proprietary system of modular metal forms designed and sold since the 1950s specifically for the construction of radiant floor slabs (developed by William Chaleff, architect). *(Redrawn from Lewis et al., 1982, by permission.)*

PHASE-CHANGE MATERIALS

The thermal storage materials discussed above (masonry and water) are "sensible" in that they gain and release heat by changing temperature. Phase-change materials (PCMs) store and release most of their collected heat by changing state or "phase," usually from a solid to liquid and back. In effect, when heated by sunlight, the solid PCM melts without significantly changing temperature. Later when heat is required in the living spaces, the now-liquid PCM begins to solidify, giving off heat to the space (Levy, 1983).

Various PCM products require different amounts of heat to cause this change of state and (depending on the precise chemical composition) will change phase at different temperatures. Ideally, a PCM will store a great deal of heat as it changes phase and the phase change temperature will be slightly higher than that of the comfort zone of the room, resulting in a thermal storage component that is more compact and lighter than "sensible heat" alternatives while stabilizing the room temperature near the comfort zone. This size and weight advantage allows PCMs to be used in frame construction in locations not otherwise suitable for thermal storage (in ceilings in conjunction with blinds that reflect sunlight onto the ceiling, for example).

A major concern in selecting a PCM is the possibility of degradation over time. Some materials perform well initially, but after repeated "freeze-thaw" cycles become reluctant to change phase as intended. Another concern is that some materials are reliable only if completely and absolutely isolated from moisture; even humidity in the air seriously degrades performance.

Containerization is also a problem. The containers of most PCMs must be completely vapor-tight to absolutely prevent moisture migration over long periods. In addition, because many PCMs are corrosive, most metal containers are unsatisfactory (stainless steel is satisfactory but expensive). Flexible foil-lined plastic pouches are low-cost containers used by several PCM manufacturers. Because there are no recognized testing or performance standards, most design professionals remain cautious about specifying PCMs until more information is available about long-term reliability.

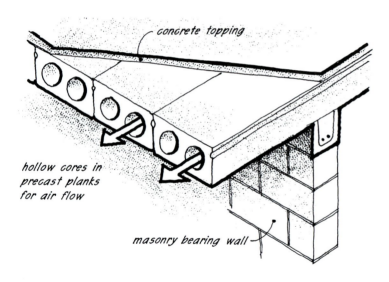

Figure 20.35: Use of cored precast concrete planks to create radiant slabs on second level. *(Redrawn from Lewis et al., 1982, by permission.)*

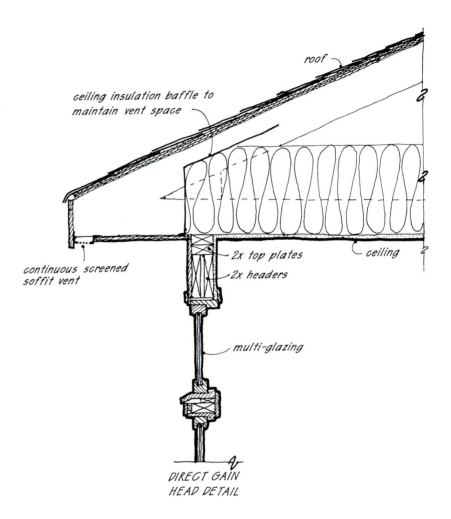

Figure 20.36: Direct gain: eave detail, wood frame construction. Use overwidth truss with no top chord extension (instead of conventional width with extended top chord for overhang); install vertical spacer between upper and lower truss chords above the bearing point. This configuration allows full roof insulation thickness above the wall and raises the bottom of the overhang to allow full exposure of the glazing to the sun in the winter. Note the use of baffle to ensure 1.5-in. vent space above insulation. Install continuous soffit vent. Provide insulation at the header above window and door openings.

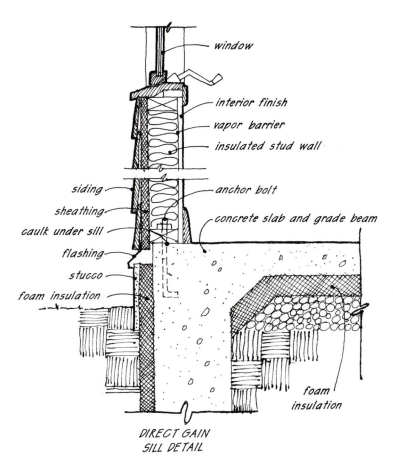

DIRECT GAIN
SILL DETAIL

Labels: window; interior finish; vapor barrier; insulated stud wall; siding; sheathing; caulk under sill; flashing; stucco; foam insulation; anchor bolt; concrete slab and grade beam; foam insulation

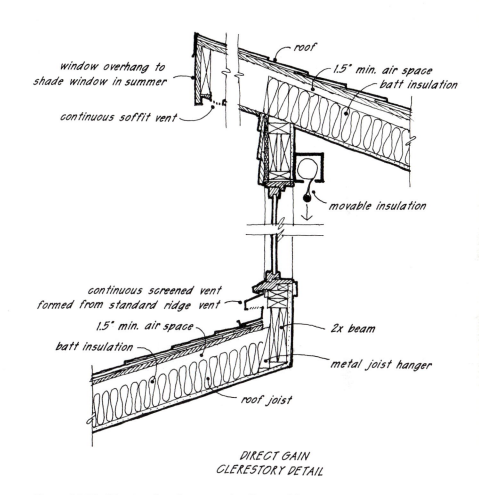

DIRECT GAIN
CLERESTORY DETAIL

Labels: window overhang to shade window in summer; continuous soffit vent; roof; 1.5" min. air space; batt insulation; movable insulation; continuous screened vent formed from standard ridge vent; 1.5" min. air space; batt insulation; 2x beam; metal joist hanger; roof joist

Figure 20.37: Direct gain: foundation detail, wood frame and slab-on-grade construction. Install extruded polystyrene ("blueboard" — white beadboard is porous and not satisfactory) perimeter foundation insulation in thickness recommended in Chapter 6. Extend insulation to the bottom of foundation wall. Insulation must be protected where exposed above grade; cement plaster over wire lath or other methods may be employed (as recommended by insulation manufacturer). In cold climates, underslab insulation is optional if slab is installed over gravel fill; recommended if installed over sand or other dense fill. Install continuous "sill sealer" thin layer of fiberglass insulation (or expanding foam caulk) to seal against infiltration. Concrete slab should be either 3000 psi (or higher) or reinforced with 6-in. welded wire mesh.

Figure 20.38: Direct gain: clerestory detail, wood frame construction. Fabricate a screened vent with integral flashing using half of a section of standard ridge vent. Where sloped ceilings are used in cold climate, joist depth may limit the thickness of fiberglass blanket insulation; add one or more layers of urethane foam insulation to achieve the insulation levels recommended in Chapter 6. Top-hinged insulating shutter may be used instead of roll shade. (Redrawn from Winter, 1983, by permission.)

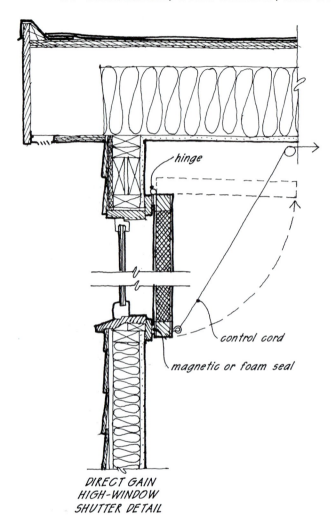

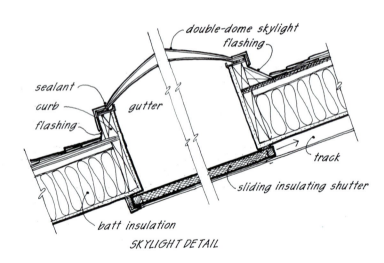

SKYLIGHT DETAIL

DIRECT GAIN
HIGH-WINDOW
SHUTTER DETAIL

Figure 20.39: Direct gain: skylight detail, wood frame construction. *(Redrawn from Winter, 1983, by permission.)*

Figure 20.40: Top-hinged interior shutter detail. Notice that the pivot point of the shutter is behind the center-of-gravity of the shutter panel. This is essential in order for the shutter to close completely due to gravity.

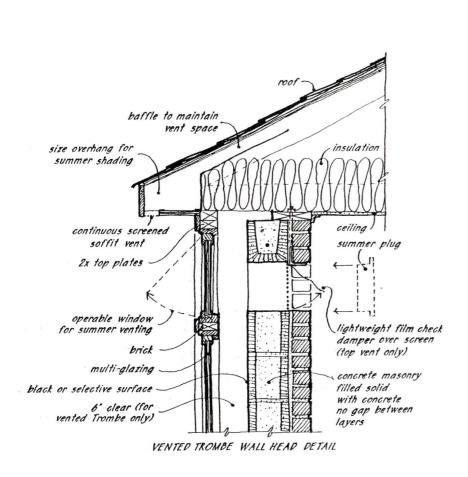

VENTED TROMBE WALL HEAD DETAIL

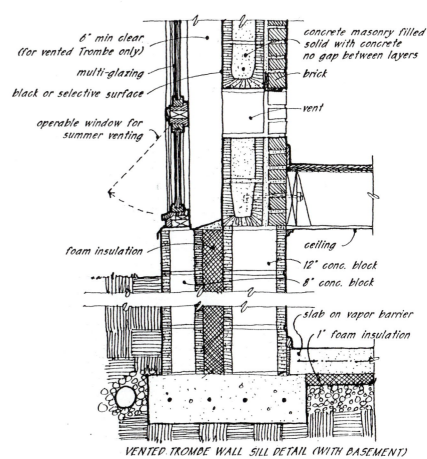

VENTED TROMBE WALL SILL DETAIL (WITH BASEMENT)

Figure 20.41: Trombe wall (vented) head: window wall is constructed independently of masonry in order to provide 6-in. minimum unobstructed air circulation space. Masonry must be solid to ensure maximum conduction through the wall. Ensure that all voids (especially between separate wythes of masonry) are filled completely with grout. Provide continuous screened soffit vent and baffles to maintain vent space above ceiling insulation. Movable insulation is not recommended unless the space behind glazing is a minimum 24-in.-wide to permit maintenance or glazing assembly is easily removable. Instead of night insulation, use pressure-sensitive selective surface foil. To ensure adequate adhesion between selective surface foil and masonry, prepare dust-free subsurface by coating masonry with smooth cementacious waterproofing (such as Thoroseal). If an overhang is used to provide summer shading, outside venting is not necessary to prevent overheating. *(Redrawn from Winter, 1983, by permission.)*

Figure 20.42: Trombe wall (vented) at the foundation wall. *(Redrawn from Winter, 1983, by permission.)*

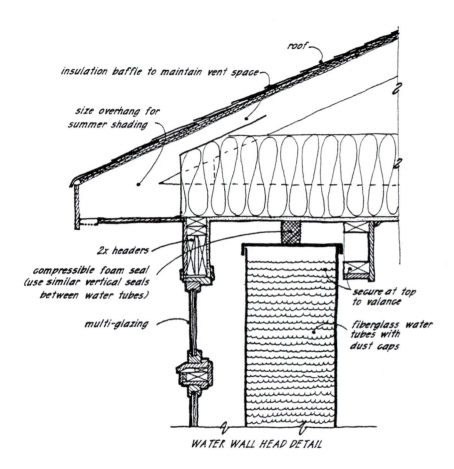

WATER WALL HEAD DETAIL

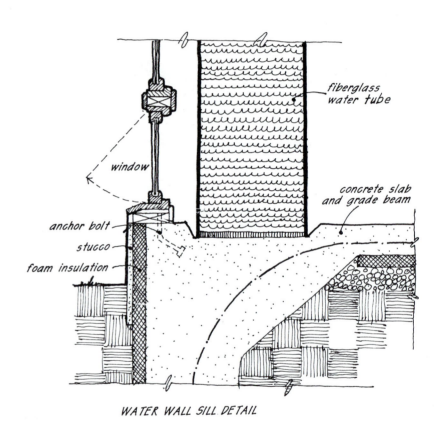

WATER WALL SILL DETAIL

Figure 20.43: Water wall: head detail, wood frame construction. Use overwidth truss with no top chord extension (instead of conventional width with extended top chord for overhang); install vertical spacer between upper and lower truss chords above the structural bearing point. This configuration allows full roof insulation thickness above the wall and raises the bottom of the overhang to allow full exposure of the glazing to the sun in the winter. Note the use of baffle to ensure 1.5-in. vent space above insulation. Install continuous soffit vent. Provide insulation at the header above window and door openings. Securely anchor water containers at top to prevent overturning. Use top cap to minimize dust and prevent overturning. Add chlorine bleach to eliminate algae growth. Use night insulation only if water tubes can be easily emptied and moved for maintenance of night insulation. Otherwise use extra glazing layers, low-E glazing, or selective surface on water containers to reduce heat loss. (Redrawn from Winter, 1983, by permission.)

Figure 20.44: Water wall: foundation detail, wood frame construction. Form 1-in. deep trough with drainholes through slab to exterior to contain any leakage. Install extruded polystyrene ("blueboard" — white beadboard is porous and not satisfactory) perimeter foundation insulation in thickness recommended in Chapter 6. Extend insulation to the bottom of foundation wall. Insulation must be protected where exposed above grade; cement plaster over wire lath or other methods may be employed (as recommended by insulation manufacturer). In cold climates, underslab insulation is optional if slab is installed over gravel fill; recommended if installed over sand or other dense fill. Install continuous "sill sealer" thin layer of fiberglass insulation (or expanding foam caulk) to seal against infiltration. Concrete slab should be either 3000 psi (or higher) or reinforced with 6-in. welded wire mesh. (Redrawn from Winter, 1983, by permission.)

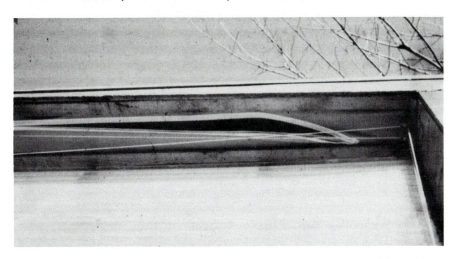

Figure 20.45: Zipper vent closure suitable for long convection vents (viewed from below). This one is 40-ft long and installed on the underside of a soffit above a greenhouse. It provides a reliable near-airtight closure that can be remote-controlled using a pull-cord and pulleys. The curved ends and off-center zipper location allow the flap to fall open by gravity when the zipper is opened. Have a sailmaker construct this out of dacron sailcloth and use a "hot knife" to seal the edges to eliminate loose threads which can jamb the zipper. A backing layer of fiberglass insect screen can be sewn in at the time of fabrication.

SUMMARY OF TERMS

Insulation — materials with high *R*-values that are intended to reduce conductive heat transfer through the building envelope.

Blanket insulation — loosely matted fiberglass held together by binding material.

Foam insulation — an expanded, low-density plastic usually installed in the form of rigid foam boards and sheets.

Loose insulation — materials include cellulose and other mineral fiber materials which are "blown" into place in attics and in existing wall cavities.

Night insulation — movable insulation positioned to increase the thermal resistance of glazing at night, and removed during the day to admit light and solar heat.

Selective surface — a surface having high solar absorptivity and low thermal emissivity.

Solar modulator — mirror-finish venetian blinds (slats concave up) intended to reflect sunlight onto the ceiling for indirect daylight illumination (and passive solar heating) while retaining view.

Horizontal reflector — a mirror-finish surface positioned below a south-facing window for the purpose of increasing passive solar heat or daylight collection.

Radiant barrier — a layer of aluminum foil placed in an airspace to block radiant heat transfer between a heat-radiating surface (such as a hot roof) and a heat-absorbing surface (such as conventional attic insulation).

Gray glass — glass glazing material pigmented to increase visible and near-IR absorption (and thus decrease transmittance).

Heat-absorbing green glass — glass that is lightly pigmented to increase near-IR absorption with only a small increase in visible absorption.

Light-reflective film — created by depositing a metallic coating on a transparent substrate, producing a mirrorlike appearance, this type of film is usually reflective in the IR as well as the visible regions.

Far-IR-reflective film — a reflective film that, like clear glass, has a high visible and near-IR transmittance. Unlike glass, which absorbs far-IR, this coating reflects in this region, further reducing heat loss.

Near-IR-reflective film — a film which, like glass, has a high visible transmittance, but, unlike glass, has a high reflectance in both near-IR and far-IR regions; suitable for daylighting in internal-load-dominated buildings.

IR-transparent plastics — highly transparent in the far-IR spectrum, these materials are useful for windscreen coverings to reduce convective warming of night-sky roof radiation cooling panels.

Shading coefficient, SC — the ratio of the solar heat gain through a fenestration system to the solar gain through a single layer of double-strength glass.

Fenestration — a glazed opening (such as a window or skylight) including any devices in the immediate proximity of the opening that affect light distribution (such as baffles, louvers, draperies, overhangs, light shelves, jambs, sills, and other light-diffusing components).

Caulking — a sealant installed for both water-resistance and airtightness in joints where dissimilar materials meet on the exterior of a building.

Window — a vertical, operable glazing unit including the frame, hinge, screen, and operating hardware.

Wind ventilator cap — a device located at the top of a ventilation chimney for the purposes of increasing the ventilation rate while excluding precipitation.

Vapor barrier — a relatively impermeable building material that effectively resists the passage of water vapor and thus controls condensation.

Phase-change material, PCM — a material that stores and releases heat by changing state or "phase," usually from a solid to liquid and back.

STUDY QUESTIONS

1. Compare and give examples of inside, intra-glazing, and outside night insulation.

2. Describe selective surfaces, and discuss their application in passive solar construction.

3. Draw two section diagrams illustrating how a horizontal reflector increases winter solar collection while minimizing additional summer gain.

4. Describe a *solar modulator* and its operation.

5. What is a "radiant barrier" and how is it effective in reducing cooling loads in buildings?

6. Why is "heat absorbing" green glass better than gray glass for daylighting applications?

7. Compare the two types of "heat mirror" films available.

8. Why are air-to-air heat exchangers recommended in many passive solar-heated buildings?

9. What are phase-change materials and why are they desirable for passive solar-heating applications?

21

THE LUMINOUS ENVIRONMENT

. . . And as each unalike star shine
Each ray of light is forever gone
To leave way for a new ray
And a new ray, as from a fountain
Complete unto itself, full, flowing.
So are some souls like stars
And their words, works and songs
Like strong, quick flashes of light
From a brilliant, erupting cone.

— *Johnny Cash*
from line notes of Bob Dylan's
album "Nashville Skyline"

It is difficult to completely separate the thermal environment of a building from its luminous enviroment. Introducing sunlight for passive solar heating brings light into a building. One cannot design a direct-gain building properly without considering lighting issues such as daylight illumination, glare, visual contrast and comfort, privacy, and view. The use of various shading devices and glazing materials to control heat gain inevitably affect the quantity and quality of daylight admitted to the interior. Conversely, lighting (especially in commercial buildings) is one of the principal sources of heat gain and directly affects the selection of HVAC equipment. In some cases, the lighting and HVAC systems are integral. HVAC systems are often intentionally configured to recirculate the passive-solar-heated air resulting from daylighting. In some cases, such as heat-recovery lighting fixtures, the individual components involve simultaneous lighting and thermal considerations.

PHOTOMETRY*

While a complete knowledge of photometry (the science of the measurement of light) is not essential as a basis for good lighting design, certain principles and definitions provide an important foundation upon which creative and appropriate design decisions can be based.

LUMINOUS FLUX

The photometric term for the time rate of light flow is *luminous flux*. It is analogous to the rate of flow of water from a sprinkler head (measured in gallons per minute). The unit of measurement of luminous flux is the *lumen*.

* Portions of this section were excerpted from Moore, F., 1985, *Concepts and Practice of Architectural Daylighting.* New York: Van Nostrand Reinhold, by permission.

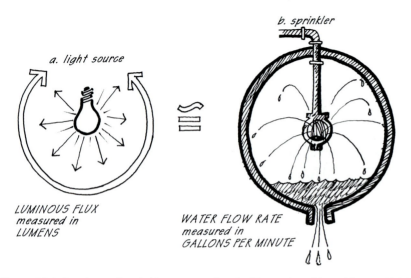

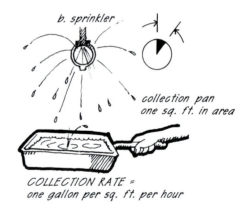

Figure 21.1: Luminous flux (with water analogy). *(Reproduced from Moore, 1985, by permission.)*

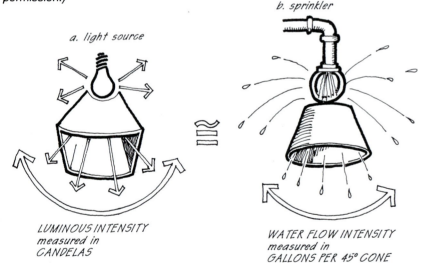

Figure 21.2: Luminous intensity (with water analogy). *(Reproduced from Moore, 1985, by permission.)*

LUMINOUS INTENSITY (CANDLEPOWER)

A light source emits luminous flux in various directions away from its surface. The amount emitted in each direction may vary. *Luminous intensity*

is the amount of *luminous flux* in a given direction measured in lumens per solid angle. It is analogous to the gallons of water per minute sprayed with a 15° cone. The unit of measurement is *candelas* (or lumens per steradian).

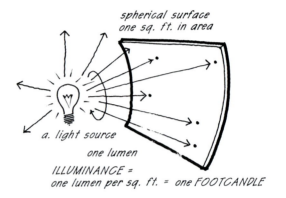

Figure 21.3: Illuminance (with water analogy). *(Reproduced from Moore, 1985, by permission.)*

ILLUMINANCE

When luminous flux strikes a surface, that surface is said to be illuminated. *Illuminance* is the density (concentration) of luminous flux incident on a surface. It is analogous to the gallons of water per minute sprayed onto a 1-ft^2 surface area. The unit of measurement of illuminance is the *footcandle* (lumens per square foot) or *lux* (lumens per square meter).

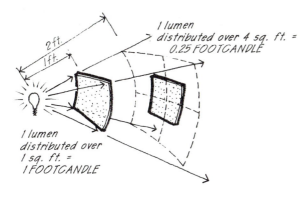

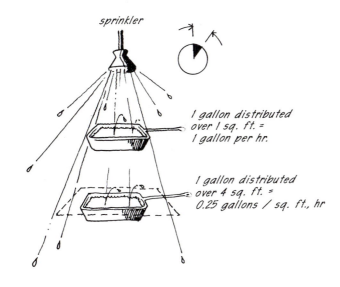

Figure 21.4: The inverse square effect: illuminance as a function of distance (with water analogy). *(Reproduced from Moore, 1985, by permission.)*

Effect of distance on illuminance

Like all radiation, the direction of luminous flux is always divergent away from the light source. Because the direction is not parallel, luminous flux is spread over an ever-larger area as it travels further from the source (that is, the flux within a solid angle remains constant at all distances). Because of this, illuminance is an inverse square function of the distance from the source. For example, when the distance from a source is doubled, the same amount of light

flux is spread over an area four times as large (because the dimension of the receiving surface is doubled in each of two directions), and the illuminance (footcandles = lumens per square foot) is reduced to 25 percent. Similarly, when the distance is tripled, the illuminance is reduced to one-ninth.

Effect of incidence angle on illuminance

If a surface is oriented perpendicular to the direction of the light, it receives (intercepts) the greatest amount of light flux possible for its area. However, if the surface is tilted relative to the direction of light, the area projected to the source is less, fewer lumens are intercepted, and illuminance is reduced. If the surface is further tilted until it is parallel to the light direction, no light flux is intercepted and illuminance is zero. For surfaces that are not normal to the source (i.e., angle of incidence is greater than 0), illuminance is reduced by the cosine of the angle of incidence. This *cosine effect* is analogous to a glass used to collect rainwater; the greatest amount of water is collected when the opening is perpendicular to the path of the raindrops.

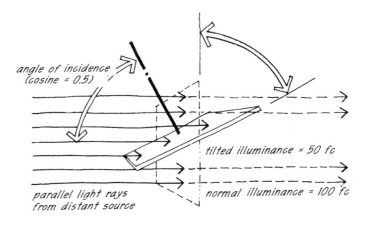

Figure 21.5: The cosine effect: illuminance as a function of angle of incidence. *(Reproduced from Moore, 1985, by permission.)*

Measurement of illuminance

Illuminance is typically measured using a photocell housed behind a flat translucent diffusing disk. The device measures the illuminance in the plane of the diffusing disk in footcandles. Two characteristics of an illuminance meter are of particular interest for daylighting applications. First, it must be "color-corrected" in order to duplicate the sensitivity of the eye in the radiation spectrum. Second, it must be "cosine-corrected" so that it measures the illuminance in a flat plane and accurately responds to the cosine reduction at

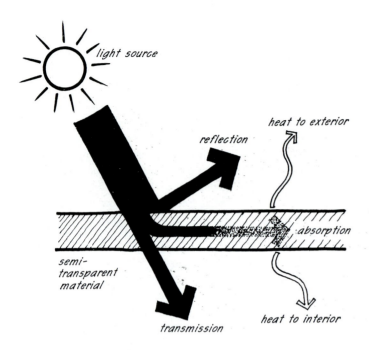

Figure 21.6: Light reflectance, absorptance, and transmittance. *(Reproduced from Moore, 1985, by permission.)*

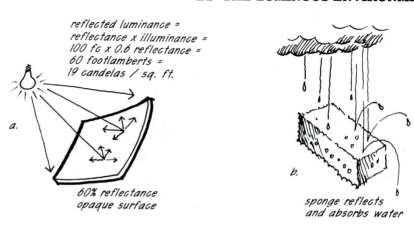

Figure 21.7: Reflected luminance as a function of illumination and reflectance (with water analogy). *(Reproduced from Moore, 1985, by permission.)*

high incidence angles. Incident-type photographic light meters, which typically have a hemispheric diffuser, are not cosine-corrected, and are thus unsuitable for illuminance measurement.

REFLECTANCE, LUMINANCE, AND SUBJECTIVE BRIGHTNESS

When luminous flux strikes an opaque surface, it is either reflected or absorbed. *Reflectance* is the ratio of reflected flux to incident flux. *Absorptance*, conversely, is the ratio of absorbed flux to incident flux.

Reflected brightness is the photometric measure of "brightness" of an illuminated opaque surface, and is the product of illuminance and reflectance. It is analogous to water bounced off of a sponge. *Subjective brightness* is the visual sensation equivalent of *luminance* and is influenced by such factors as the state of adaptation of the eye as well as *luminance*. (While the term *brightness* is often used when referring informally to measurable luminance, the preferable term for photometric quantity is *luminance*, thus reserving

brightness for the subjective visual sensation.) The unit of luminance is either *candela per square foot* (or candela per square meter) or *footlambert* (one footlambert equals 0.318 cd/ft^2).

Real surfaces are not perfect diffusers and reflect light unequally in different directions. The reflectance (and thus the luminance) of such a surface is dependent on the angles of incidence and reflectance, and the surface's diffusion characteristics. Glossy surfaces reflect light specularly (i.e., like a mirror), and thus exhibit qualities similar to the original source.

Transmittance

Nonopaque surfaces can transmit light either specularly (e.g., clear, transparent glass) or diffusely (e.g., frosted, transparent glass). Light transmittance is the ratio or transmitted light to incident light (less than 1.0). Transmitted luminance is a function of illumination on the reverse side (in footcandles) and transmittance. As with reflecting surfaces, the units of transmitted luminance are either candelas per square foot or footlamberts. For real translucent surfaces (which are not perfect diffusers), luminance is dependent on the angle of transmittance and the surface's diffusing qualities.

Measurement of luminance

Luminance is typically measured using a color-corrected photocell that is shielded to receive light only within a very narrow angle of acceptance (typically one degree or less). The device is aimed at the subject surface from the appropriate direction and is calibrated to measure surface luminance in either candelas per square foot (or meter) or footlamberts.

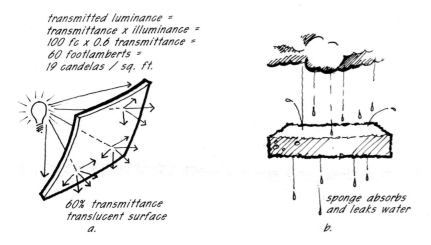

transmitted luminance =
transmittance x illumination =
100 fc x 0.6 transmittance =
60 footlamberts =
19 candelas / sq. ft.

60% transmittance
translucent surface
a.

sponge absorbs
and leaks water
b.

Figure 21.8: Transmitted luminance as a function of illumination and transmittance (with water analogy). *(Reproduced from Moore, 1985, by permission.)*

daylight and sunlight as the primary sources of terrestrial radiation, it is not surprising that the limits of eye sensitivity closely approximate the solar spectrum. Vision is particularly vital because of its use for most functions requiring perception of both spatial relationships and detail.

Initially, this includes a process of orientation and the formation of spatial impressions. This is followed by the scanning of various information cues, making comparisons, and ordering mental priorities. There is also the process of communication — involving both the identification of meaningful information sources and the subsequent gaining of detailed quantitative and qualitative information. Lastly, vision interprets movement and rates of change in the surrounding environment.

VISION AND THE EYE

Light enters the eye through the pupil, which is an opening in the iris, which is variable in diameter to control the amount of light admitted. The cornea and the lens focus the light by refraction onto the retina, which is the light-sensitive surface on the rear of the eye. The fovea is the small portion of the retina (opposite the iris) that constitutes our center of vision. This fovea region contains a high proportion of "cone" retinal cells, and is most sensitive to detail and color, but less sensitive to movement and low levels of light. As such, the fovea region of the retina is analogous to a slow-speed, fine grain, color photographic film.

VISUAL PERCEPTION

Architecture (and the activities within) are experienced primarily through vision. Vision is the eye's ability to sense that portion of the radiation spectrum that is defined as light. Because most of human evolution has occurred with

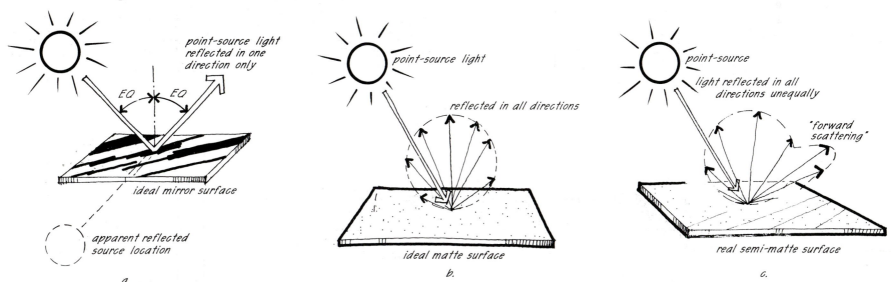

point-source light
reflected in one
direction only

EQ EQ

ideal mirror surface

apparent reflected
source location

a.

point-source light

reflected in all directions

ideal matte surface

b.

point-source

light reflected in all
directions unequally

"forward
scattering"

real semi-matte surface

c.

Figure 21.9: Comparison of: (a) specular, (b) diffuse, and (c) semidiffuse reflectance. *(Reproduced from Moore, 1985, by permission.)*

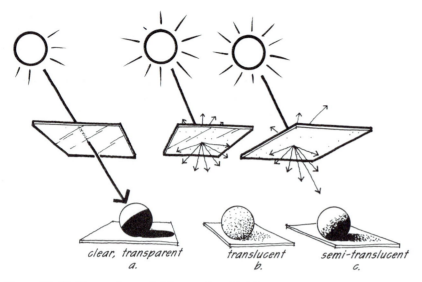

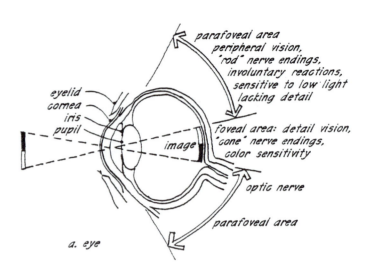

Figure 21.10: Comparison of: (a) specular, (b) diffuse, and (c) semidiffuse transmittance. *(Reproduced from Moore, 1985, by permission.)*

The larger para-fovea surrounding portion constitutes our peripheral vision. This para-fovea region contains an increasingly large proportion of "rod" retinal cells, which are extremely light-sensitive (sense light 1/10,000 as bright as required for cone cells) and motion-sensitive, but lack color and detail sensitivity. This accounts for poor color perception at low light levels, when "rod" vision predominates. The para-fovea region of the retina is analogous to a high-speed, course grain, black-and-white film.

Humans have binocular vision with both eyes focusing on the same center of vision. The slight difference in image that each eye receives provides three-dimensional depth cues. The total visual field of both eyes is about 180° wide. However, facial features (eyebrows, cheeks, and the nose) obstruct portions of the field of each eye.

ADAPTATION

The human eye is remarkable in its adaptability to various lighting conditions. All visual experience (of brightness, color, distance, perspective, etc.) is measured relatively against some reference experience. This experience may be present (in the form of the surrounding luminous environment), or past (in the form of expectations based on prior experience — an effect known as constancy). There are two visual effects of present environment that are particularly related to daylight illumination: *general adaptation* and *local brightness contrast*.

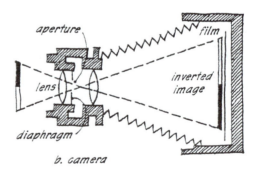

Figure 21.11: Comparison of the human eye with a camera. In the eye, depth focusing is accomplished by changing the shape of the lens; in a camera, the lens-to-film distance is changed. *(After Stein et al., 1986.)*

General adaptation

At night, electric lighting is totally under the control of the designer. The quantity and quality of illumination is completely controllable and usually constant. The resulting illumination is predictable in terms of absolute quantity (that is, footcandles). During the day, because of changing sky and sun conditions, absolute illumination levels are not predictable. The designer, by determining the size and position of windows, can determine the *proportion* of the available daylight that will be admitted, but cannot determine the absolute amount.

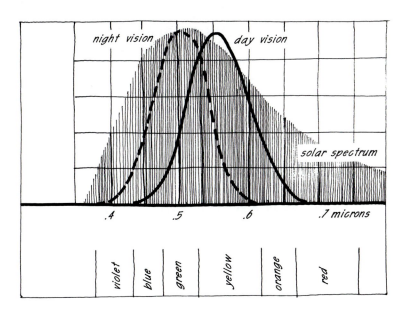

Figure 21.12: Spectral sensitivity of the human eye compared with the spectral distribution of solar energy. *(Reproduced from Moore, 1985, by permission.)*

This inability to predict absolute amounts is a source of concern for some illumination engineers accustomed to the predictability of electric sources, and for this reason, unfortunately, the utilization of daylight for illumination is sometimes discouraged. The eye does not perceive light in the absolute terms of the photometer. The large variations inherent in daylight do not result in correspondingly great perceived changes on the interior. This is because of the wide range of adaptation of the eye to changing overall levels of illumination. On an overcast day, it is virtually impossible to estimate illumination level visually (for example, even experienced photographers necessarily rely on light meters under these conditions).

The physiological process of adaptation is a combination of rapid changing of the pupil diameter (controlling the amount of light admitted) and a slower change in retinal sensitivity. Generally, changes in sky brightness conditions occur slowly enough to allow comfortable adaptation of the eye. However, visual discomfort occurs when the eye is required to adapt to repeated and abrupt changes in overall brightness. A typical example occurs when the visual field must be shifted back and forth between a large area of high brightness (such as the sky or wall areas) and an interior object (such as a book or machine).

Local brightness contrast

The eye generally adapts to the average of the various brightnesses within the field of view, being affected most by brightnesses nearest the center of vision. If an area of high brightness is seen next to an area of much lower brightness, the eye tends to adapt to the average, making it difficult to discern detail in either area, especially the low brightness area. While the eye could adapt to either of these brightness levels alone, it is the adjacency of these within the field of view at the same time that is the source of discomfort and reduced visual acuity.

Local brightness contrast can be reduced by the use of similar surface reflectances, and (in the case of windows and other daylighting apertures) ensuring that surfaces surrounding the opening have a relatively high luminance (that is, receive light and are high reflectance).

To achieve a comfortable brightness balance, it is desirable and practical to limit brightness ratios between areas of appreciable size from normal viewpoints as follows:

1 to 1/3	Between task and adjacent surroundings.
1 to 1/10	Between task and more remote darker surfaces.
1 to 10	Between task and more remote lighter surfaces.
20 to 1	Between fenestration (or luminaires) and adjacent surfaces.
40 to 1	Anywhere in the field of view.

Brightness constancy

Constancy is the visual tendency to perceive the environment as the way it is known to be, rather than on the basis of appearance alone. There are many types of constancy. An example of "size constancy" is that of seeing drawings of three persons on a grid of converging lines (which is interpreted in western cultures as a perspective grid leading to a point at infinity). The three figures, drawn the same size on the paper, appear to be of greatly different sizes depending on their location in the drawing as a result of size constancy.

Although rarely noticed, brightness constancy is always present in a lighted interior. For example, the light reaching a white ceiling from side windows may be, at the back of the room, only one twentieth of the light on the ceiling at the front of the room. Yet the eye sees the ceiling as white all over (rather than white near the window and dark gray near the back). It is possible to demonstrate that the measured luminance of a dark gray card placed on the ceiling near the window may be as great as the white ceiling at the back, but it is not perceived as such by the eye. The observer knows from experience that the ceiling is uniformly white, and thus discounts the fact that all areas of the ceiling do not receive the same illumination. This is reinforced by the awareness of the location of the window light source. From experience, the observer knows that objects near a light source appear brighter than those further away. Thus, the observer unconsciously concludes that, because the location of the source is consistent with the appearance of brightness gradation, the ceiling is uniformly white.

If the ceiling were viewed only through a small hole in a box, it would be impossible for the observer to determine whether the ceiling were brightly illuminated gray or dimly lit white. Brightness constancy is only effective if the observer is able to survey the entire surrounding environment, including the source and the surface receiving light. This information is necessary to separate the illumination component perceptually from the reflectance component of a bright surface.

VISUAL PERFORMANCE AND COMFORT

Visual acuity is the ability of the observer to distinguish fine detail (such as that measured by familiar optician's chart of letters of decreasing size). Up to a point, visual acuity increases with increased illuminance of the task surface.

Contrast sensitivity is a measure of the eye to distinguish differences in luminance, and is also a function of task illumination. Under poor illumination, it may not be possible to distinguish between a black card and an adjacent dark gray card; under better illumination, the difference is obvious.

While the high brightness that accompanies high levels of illumination usually improves seeing, unwanted high brightness (glare) can reduce both visual acuity and contrast sensitivity. Glare can be categorized on the basis of its effect on the observer as disability glare and discomfort glare.

Disability glare results from areas in the field of view of such brilliance that they cause a scattering of light within optical matter of the eye, causing a "veiling effect" which reduces visual contrast to such a degree that seeing is reduced. A familiar example of disability glare occurs when driving at night. In the absence of other vehicles, the road ahead is visible under headlight illumination as a result of the lighter surfaces reflecting more light (and appearing brighter) than darker surfaces. When oncoming headlights are encountered, the light scattered within the eye exceeds the light reflected from both light and dark road surfaces, resulting in a temporary loss of useful vision. With some extreme exceptions (sky seen through a window at the end of a dark corridor, reflections from a glossy work surface, etc.), disability glare is seldom a major building design consideration.

Discomfort glare is defined as glare which produces discomfort, but does not necessarily interfere with visibility or visual performance. It may result from bright sources within the field of view that are not inherently distressing, but are seen in much darker surroundings.

Glare can also be categorized on the basis of the path of the light. *Direct glare* is caused by sources directly visible within the field of view. *Reflected glare* is glare from a glossy surface which reflects an image of the light source. (Discomfort and disability glare can be caused by either direct or reflected light.)

Veiling reflections are reflected glare that occurs on the task surface. A familiar example is the image of an overhead skylight or electric lighting fixture reflected on the surface of a glossy magazine. Veiling reflections reduce visibility because the brightness of the reflected image causes an increase in the brightness of both the light and dark features of the task (for example, the brightness of both the black lettering and the white surrounding page are increased to very high levels and the contrast between the two is eliminated). Because veiling reflections are specular (mirrorlike), they can be anticipated whenever concentrated light sources occur within the reflected field of view of the work surface. In other words, if the work surface were a mirror, any source within the area seen in the reflection is a potential source of veiling reflections.

Veiling reflections can be controlled by:

- Locating all relatively concentrated light sources outside of the reflected field of view.

- Reducing source luminance by distributing the light source over a larger area (for comparable illumination at the workplane, a luminous ceiling minimizes the effect of veiling reflections compared with a concentrated source in the reflected field of view).

SELECTING ILLUMINANCE LEVELS

Lighting guidelines for the illuminance needed to perform a visual task have changed considerably since they were first recommended in 1899. In the early 1900s, electric lighting was relatively new, and recommended levels were low. As the use of electric lighting has increased and become an integral part of daily life, there has been a corresponding increase in the illuminance levels recommended by various guidelines. In 1910, 1 fc was recommended as

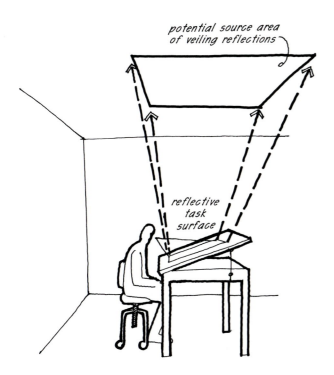

Figure 21.13: Areas subject to cause veiling reflections on a horizontal work surface. *(Reproduced from Moore, 1985, by permission.)*

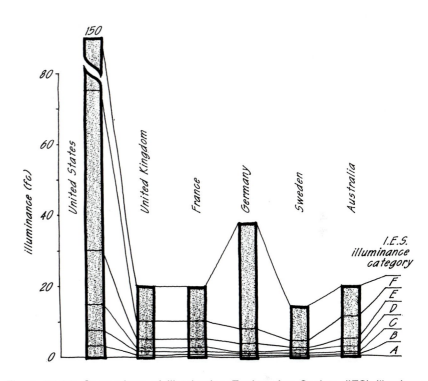

Figure 21.14: Comparison of Illuminating Engineering Society (IES) illuminance guidelines in various countries, as of 1981. Illuminance categories are represented as follows: (A) public spaces with dark surroundings, (B) simple orientation for short temporary visits, (C) visual tasks are only occasionally performed, (D) visual tasks of high contrast or large size, (E) visual tasks of medium contrast or small size, (F) Visual tasks of low contrast or very small size. *(Redrawn from Robbins, 1986, by permission.)*

satisfactory for reading 8-point black type on white paper. In 1917, and again in 1921, 3 to 6 fc were recommended in libraries. Since then, there has been a steady increase in the levels recommended, especially in the United States. For example, by 1930 the guidelines of the Illuminating Engineering Society/ United States (IES/US) for libraries had increased to 18 fc, to 30 fc by 1950, to 150 fc by 1972, and 50 to 200 fc in 1981. Recommendations have also increased in European countries, but at a much more moderate rate. The current IES/US lighting standard recommends illuminance ranges rather than a single value. This allows the lighting designer more flexibility in designing lighting systems for various tasks (Robbins, 1986).

ILLUMINANCE CATEGORY DIFFERENCES

Because of the characteristics of the functions in Categories A through C (Table 21.1), illuminances are required over the entire area of the interior space

considered. For example, in a lobby area, one visual task is walking to the elevator. This visual task remains constant throughout time and space; therefore, a general level of illuminance should be provided throughout the lobby.

Categories D through F, however, are for tasks that remain relatively fixed at one location for meaningful visual performance, although tasks may change considerably from one location to another within a particular space. For example, an accounting office may have a secretarial pool where reading felt-tip pen handwritten notes and proofreading typed originals are prominent tasks, while at the same time accountants may be reading computer printouts. Each task calls for a particular illuminance for satisfactory visual performance, and so each task should be lighted accordingly. For this reason, categories D through F should be applied to the appropriate task areas only.

Categories G through I are for extremely difficult visual tasks that may be difficult to illuminate. For practical and economic reasons, lighting systems for these tasks may require a combination of general overall illumination and task illumination (Kaufman, 1984).

SELECTING THE DESIGN (TARGET) ILLUMINANCE VALUES

Select the illuminance value from the three values recommended, depending on: occupant age (higher values for older occupants), room or task background surface reflectances (higher values for low reflectances), and task speed and accuracy requirements (higher values for more critical requirements).

The final selection of the target illuminances is left to the designer. *In general, current IES illuminance guidelines remain quite generous; one-half or even one-fourth of these recommended levels will produce quite satisfactory lighting while resulting in considerable energy savings due to reduced lighting and cooling requirements, particularly in nonresidential buildings.*

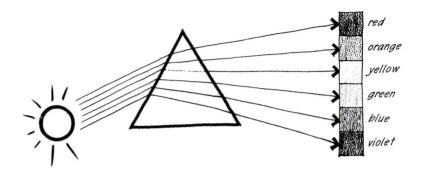

Figure 21.15: White light is a mixture of different wavelengths of light. As white light passes through a prism, each wavelength (light color) is refracted at a different angle, creating a "rainbow" spectrum of light colors.

COLOR

COLOR SPECTRUM

A light source emitting radiant energy relatively balanced in all visible wavelengths will appear white to the eye. However, a beam of "white" light passing through a glass prism will refract each wavelength at a slightly different angle so that a rainbowlike spectrum is produced. This refraction separates each of the different colors of light that originally combined to make the white mixture. The normal eye will see three wide bands of blended color (violet, green, and red) with several narrower bands (blue, yellow, and orange) blended between the wider bands. Persons with deficient color perception ("color blind") see only gradations of gray, or perhaps only some of the colors (IES Education Committee, 1985).

The three dimensions of surface colors (pigments) are hue, chroma, and value.

Hue is that attribute that defines a color as red, yellow, blue, etc.; variations of hue are distributed *around* the perimeter of the color wheel.

Chroma is that attribute of a pigment that determines its saturation and ranges from pure (high chroma) to gray (low chroma). For example, "brick" red has a low chroma; "bright" red has a high chroma. The chroma of a pigment is reduced by adding a small amount to the *complementary* hue (exactly opposite on the color wheel). Mixing a balanced amount of any two complementary colors will create gray (because some pigments are "stronger" than others,

Table 21.1: Illuminance Categories and Illuminance Values Recommended for Generic Types of Activities in Interiors

Illuminance Category	Type of Activity	Footcandles	Reference Workplane
A	Public spaces with dark surroundings	2-3-5	General lighting throughout spaces
B	Simple orientation for short temporary visits	5-7.5-10	General lighting throughout spaces
C	Working spaces where visual tasks are only occasionally performed	10-15-20	General lighting throughout spaces
D	Performance of visual tasks of high contrast or large size	20-30-50	Local lighting on task
E	Performance of visual tasks of medium contrast or small size	50-75-100	Local lighting on task
F	Performance of visual tasks of low contrast or very small size	100-150-200	Local lighting on task
G	Performance of visual tasks of low contrast or very small size over a prolonged period	200-300-500	Combination of general and local lighting on task
H	Performance of very prolonged and exacting visual tasks	500-750-1,000	Combination of general and local lighting on task
I	Performance of very special visual tasks of extremely low contrast and small size	1,000-1,500-2,000	Combination of general and local lighting on task

(Reproduced from Kaufman, 1984, by permission.)

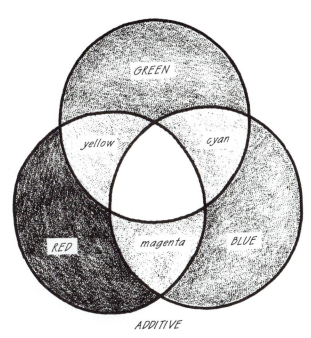

ADDITIVE

Figure 21.16: *Additive* color mixing is achieved by superimposing beams of colored light. The primary additive colors are red, blue, and green; pairs of these primary colors combine to make the secondary additive colors: (a) red light and blue light combine to make magenta, (b) blue light and green light combine to make cyan (blue-green), and (c) red light and green light combine to make yellow. (d) Combining all three primary colored lights in the proper balance creates white. In each case, the primary light colors combine in an additive manner to create secondary colored lights that are *lighter* than the originals. Some of the additive mixes (for example, red + green = yellow) seem strange because of our experiences with subtractive color mixing of paints (where red + green = dark gray).

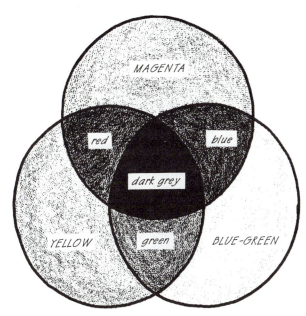

SUBTRACTIVE

Figure 21.17: *Subtractive* color mixing is achieved by combining pigments (or transparent colored filters). The primary subtractive colors are cyan, magenta, and yellow (the same as the secondary *additive* colors); pairs of these primary colors combine to make the secondary subtractive colors: (a) cyan and yellow make green, (b) yellow and magenta make red, and (c) magenta and cyan make blue. (d) Combining all three subtractive colors (pigments or sandwiching colored filters) in the proper balance combine to make gray (pigments) or black (sandwiching colored filters). In each case, the primary colors combine in a subtractive manner to create secondary colors that are usually *darker* than the originals.

different quantities of the complements may have to be mixed to achieve a neutral gray).

Value is that attribute of a pigment that determines its lightness or darkness. When white is added to a pigment, it produces a *tint*; it becomes lighter and its value is increased. Conversely, when black is added to a pigment, it produces a *shade*; it becomes darker and its value is decreased.

Munsell system

Munsell (1941) developed a system of color notation based on these three dimensions; it is the most widely used system for classifying surface colors. Although the normal human eye can differentiate several million different colors, for the sake of practicality, the basic Munsell system uses only about

1500 different color samples. A particular color sample is first classified by its hue, and all color samples of that hue are arranged on the same page. Next, the sample is classified according to its value from 1 (darkest) to 9 (lightest). Finally, the sample is classified according to its chroma from 0 (grayest) to 14 (most saturated; purest).

COLOR IN LIGHT SOURCES

In order for colored surfaces to appear natural, they must be illuminated by a full-spectrum mixture of "white" light. A red surface illuminated by a "white" light source will make the surface appear red because most of the red

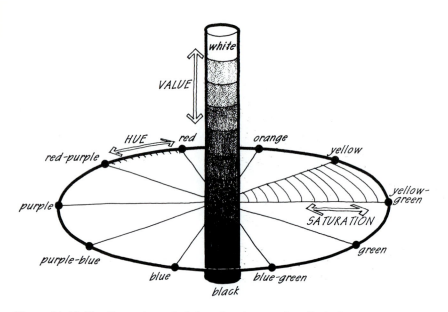

Figure 21.18: The three characteristics of a pigment: *hue* ("color" — e.g., "redness"), *chroma* (saturation or "grayness"), and *value* (darkness). *(After Stein et al., 1986.)*

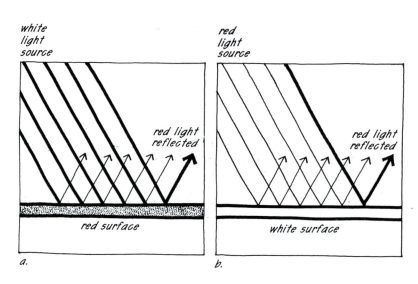

Figure 21.20: Absorption and reflection. Red-appearing surfaces can be created in two ways: (a) illuminating a red surface with white light (the surface absorbs all wavelengths of the white light except those perceived as red), and (b) illuminating a white surface with red light (the surface reflects all wavelengths, but in this case the only wavelengths striking the surface are red).

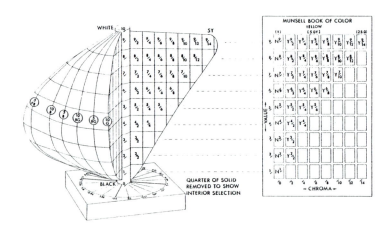

Figure 21.19: A conceptual model of the Munsell system of color classifications. Each radial segment of the solid corresponds to a hue and is depicted on a page of color samples. *(Reproduced from IES Education Committee, 1985, by permission.)*

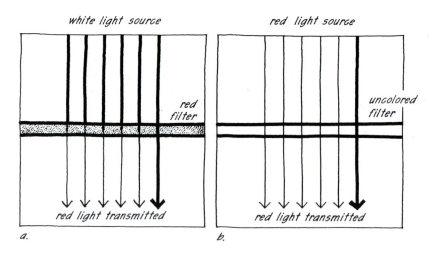

Figure 21.21: Absorption and transmission. Similarly, a piece of translucent paper may appear red in two ways: (a) backlighting a red paper with white light (the paper absorbs all wavelengths of the white light except those perceived as red), and (b) backlighting a white paper with red light (the paper transmits all wavelengths equally but, in this case, the only wavelengths striking the paper are red).

wavelengths are reflected toward the eye while all of the other (nonred) wavelengths are greatly absorbed. However, if the same surface is lighted with a green light, it will appear much darker and more colorless (brownish gray) because there is very little red energy in the green light to be reflected. The important principle is that, regardless of the characteristics of a surface finish, the eye cannot see colors from the surface that are not contained in the light source.

Color temperature

Even "white" light can vary in color — from the "warm" light of an incandescent lamp to noon sunlight to "cool" light from a clear blue sky. Light sources are often designated with a color temperature to indicate their relative "warmness" (orangish) or "coolness" (bluish). Based on the Kelvin scale, color temperature is based on the temperature to which a black body must be heated to radiate a light approximating the color of the source in question. *Color temperature* is literally applicable to a light source that produces light by heating (such as an incandescent lamp); other sources that produce light by different processes (such as fluorescent lamps), are assigned *correlated* color temperatures that most nearly match their chromaticity. It is ironic that bluish light sources that have a higher color temperature (greater than 6000°K) are intuitively referred to as "cool," while orangish sources with a lower color temperature (less than 4000°K) are termed "warm."

While the human eye is remarkable in its ability to adapt to light sources of different color temperatures and still perceive colored surfaces illuminated by these sources correctly (a phenomenon known as color constancy), there is still a noticeable difference is the way that various colors appear under different color temperature sources. In general, "warm" colors (reds, oranges, yellows, flesh tones) appear lighter and more saturated when illuminated by "warm" light sources (incandescent lamps, candlelight) than do "cool" colors, which appear darker and more "gray." Conversely, bluish "cool" light sources tend to enhance surfaces of similar color (blue and green) and depress reds and oranges.

This ability to selectively enhance certain colors is a well-known marketing tool. In supermarkets, lamps used in the meat displays are typically richer in the red spectrum ("warmer", lower color temperature) than used for other merchandise. Furniture stores specializing in residential furnishings can avoid unpleasant customer surprises by installing lamps that approximate the color temperature (and thus color rendition of the furniture) of the incandescent lamps that can be expected in most homes. For the same reason, office furnishings are best marketed under fluorescent lamps that are typical of the commercial environment. Similarly, clothing intended for daylight, office, or evening wear is most appropriately displayed under lamps that most closely approximate the color temperature typical of those environments.

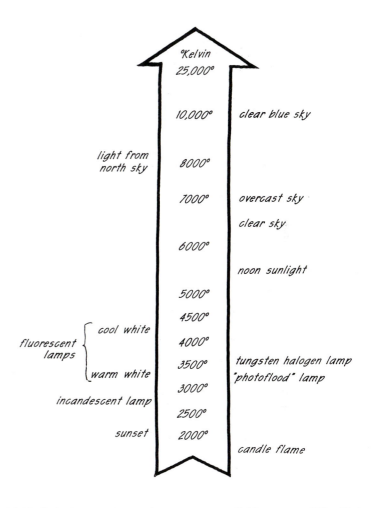

Figure 21.22: Color temperatures of some common light sources. *(After Stein et al., 1986.)*

Effect of light level on color perception

At relatively low light levels, colors appear most natural under warm, reddish light (low color temperature). Conversely, at higher levels, colors appear more natural under cool, bluish light (high color temperature). This may be a result of the fact that human vision evolved at a time when daylight was the only primary source of light. At sunrise and sunset, when the sun is at the horizon and light levels are low, daylight is quite "orangish" and color temperature is low, and colors appear natural under this combination. As the

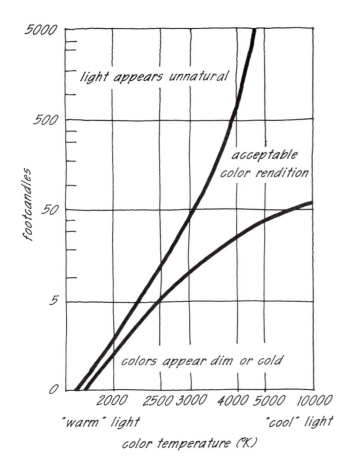

Figure 21.23: Human preference for color temperature. *(Redrawn from IES Education Committee, 1985, by permission.)*

LIGHTING DESIGN

Richard Peters (a noted lighting designer and professor of architecture at Berkeley) has often expressed his disdain for the distinction made between daylighting and electric lighting: "daylight . . . electric light . . . it's all light!" His point is that the eye perceives both, and that the same approach to distribution and control may be used regardless of the original source, and that both can and should be consciously manipulated in order to achieve design goals.

Thus, while the following two design approaches were originally proposed by the Illuminating Engineering Society (Kaufman, 1987) for electric lighting, they apply equally well to daylighting and have been so adapted here. They are the *luminous environment* design approach, and the *visual task* design approach.

LUMINOUS ENVIRONMENT DESIGN APPROACH

This approach is based on the concept of considering all of the visual surfaces in a room as potential reflectors whose importance is consciously emphasized (or deemphasized) by their respective brightness (or perceived luminance). This is controlled by a combination of the illumination of these surfaces and their respective reflectances or colors. As such, this method is best suited for general lighting design: for occupant orientation, for organizing the visual priorities within the space, and for revelation of the architecture itself. The method may be considered as the following steps: (1) the determination of the desired visual composition in the space, (2) the determination of the desired appearance of visual tasks and objects in the space, and (3) the selection of luminaires that fit the concept of visual composition and implement the desired appearance of objects.

Step I: Determining the visual composition of the space
The designer can specify the combination of room surfaces to be lighted or left dark through the design and placement of lighting elements. The patterns of brightness can be used to merge or reinforce the physical pattern of the space and enclosing elements. Or the patterns of brightness can be used in response to the activities within the space — to identify centers of interest and attention and otherwise complement the activities of the space.

Focal Centers — The lighting system should properly identify centers of primary and secondary attention (for example, a display, a picture, or a featured wall). Depending on the relative dominance desired, the luminance of these focal areas should range from 5 to 10 times that of surrounding surfaces.

sun is higher and light levels are higher, daylight is more "bluish" and color temperature is high, and colors also appear natural under this combination.

However, when lamps that give off "daylight-corrected" (color temperature similar to daylight — 6000°K) are used to produce low levels of illumination (lighting an outdoor area at night), colors will appear unnaturally cold and dim. Conversely, if low-temperature lamps (incandescent, for example) are used to achieve high light levels (in a merchandising display, for example), colors will appear unnaturally warm. It is important, therefore to match the color temperature with design lighting levels in a manner that is consistent with the natural daily cycle of daylight (low color temperatures for low light levels and vice versa).

The Overhead Zone — The ceiling is usually of secondary interest (relative to the activity) in a space, yet it is a preferred location for luminaires, skylights, and monitors. The relatively higher luminance of these potentially make them strong elements in the visual composition of the room. A ceiling pattern unrelated to the rest of the interior design is spatially confusing despite the fact that workplane illumination and visual comfort might be both relatively good. Conversely, a well-designed luminaire pattern can reinforce the design emphasis of the space (activity zones, circulation patterns, spatial hierarchy, structural elements, etc.).

The Perimeter Zone — Where task lighting is subordinate to the objective of creating a restful atmosphere, the perimeter brightness should be greater than the brightness of the overhead zone. In this situation, visual simplicity is desirable in the perimeter zone. Visual clutter here may cause confusion in spatial comprehension and orientation. It may also complicate identification of meaningful focal centers (for example in merchandising areas and in travel centers).

The Occupied Zone — The functional or activity emphasis is usually in this zone. For this reason, illumination objectives are usually task-related and determined from Table 21.1. In general, the overall effectiveness of the lighting design is determined by the balance of this occupied zone and the perimeter and overhead zones.

Transition between Zones — When the luminance ratio between adjoining spaces and activities approximates 2 or 3 to 1 or less, the sense of visual change is minimal and almost unnoticeable. Where a sense of change is desirable (rather than continuity), luminance differences should substantially exceed this ratio. For a clearly noticeable transition, use a 10-to-1 luminance ratio; for a dominant or abrupt change, use 100 to 1 or greater. Another variable for controlling continuity or change is the light color ("whiteness" or color temperature).

Level of Stimulation — General luminance levels below about 3 cd/ft^2 (or 10 fL) tend to be associated with twilight conditions and may appear "dingy" unless bright accents are included. Warm colors tend to stimulate occupants, while cool colors tend to sooth. Saturated colors are more stimulating than tints. Areas of darkness tend to be subduing or relaxing, but may be dramatic if focal accents are provided.

Step II: Determining the desired appearance of objects in the space

In addition to the spatial factors considered above, the desired appearance of the objects within the space must be considered.

Diffusion — Diffuse light (from a large source area) tends to reduce variations that relate to object form, pattern, and texture. Conversely, point-source lighting emphasizes these characteristics. In particular, oblique lighting emphasizes surface texture; for example, a luminaire or strip skylight in the ceiling adjacent to a masonry wall acts as a "wall washer" emphasizing (even exaggerating) the inherent surface variations. Sculpture should generally be developed with some directionality in lighting but with significant diffusion to relieve harshness. Portrait photographers usually favor large diffuse light sources (large translucent screens or reflective "umbrellas") with some directionality in order to subdue facial wrinkles while providing sufficient modeling to define the larger facial features.

Sparkle — Use of point-light sources to create small areas of high brightness — sparkle and highlight — to enhance the sense of vitality in a space and of particular polished objects.

Color Rendition — Color schemes for the interior (paint, fabrics, carpeting) should always be chosen under light sources identical to those to be used in the space. While the eye will adapt to color temperature of the lighting source, different colors will be brightened while others will be subdued. For example, under a relatively cool daylight source, cool surface colors such as blues and greens will be enhanced and brightened, while warmer surface colors (reds, browns, oranges) will be subdued or made grayer.

Step III: Selection of lighting oomponents

This section implements the objectives defined in the first two steps by selecting components (luminaires, windows, skylights, and monitors) to fit the concept of visual composition and to implement the desired appearance of objects. In selecting the most suitable components, a number of engineering and architectural aspects should be considered.

Visual Dominance of the Lighting System — A primary decision in the design of the lighting system is the decision where the system itself should be visually subordinate or dominate. In general, components that are recessed and thus hidden from view (such as recessed and cove mounted luminaires, "hidden" windows and skylights, and indirect components where reflective room surfaces are the "source") are visually subordinate to other architectural features of the space. Conversely, large, decorative luminaires (such as chandeliers and other sculptural designs) as well as daylighting components are used to dramatize an architectural concept (such as an atrium, or a large skylight defining a primary circulation spine in the building).

Brightness, Color, Scale, and Form — Is the visual appearance of the components compatible with the architectural composition?

Space Requirements and Architectural Detailing — Are the physical space allowances sufficient? Is the spatial volume and design of the room sufficient to provide for necessary lighting cavities and recesses?

Coordination with other Environmental Control Systems — Is the lighting system functionally and physically compatible with other systems (HVAC, sound, plumbing, sprinkler)? In particular, consider coordination with other ceiling elements and wall systems.

Distribution Characteristics and Color of Light —Can the selected components achieve the desired visual result (both spatial and task illumination) as determined in the first two steps?

Dimensional Characteristics and Form —Are the physical characteristics (shape and size) generally appropriate to the illumination concept? Reflector size and finish, lamp-to-enclosure distance, shielding and cutoff angles, and lamp ventilation must be considered as well as the dimensional intrusion of the component into the space when pendant or bracket is involved.

Lighted and Unlighted Appearance of the Component —Is the appearance and quality of detail consistent with the other parts of the building?

Initial and Operating Costs — Are the costs of the components (initial, maintenance, and operating) consistent with the general design objectives of the building? Is the system energy efficient? Can electric components be dimmed for effective supplementation of daylighting?

Maintenance —Are the components accessible for lamp replacement and cleaning? Are the characteristics regarding dirt collection and consequent lumen loss compatible with the use of the space? What is the recommended maintenance interval?

VISUAL TASK DESIGN APPROACH

In areas where the primary function of the lighting system is to provide illumination for the quick, accurate performance of visual tasks, the task itself is the starting point in the lighting design.

Step I: Identifying the visual task

Identify the most commonly found visual tasks. Determine how the task should be portrayed by the lighting. Decide whether the lighting is to be diffuse or directional. Determine if the task will be subject to veiling reflections. Determine if color rendition is important. Determine what illuminances should be provided.

Step II: Defining the task environment

Determine the dimensions of the area and the reflectances of the surfaces. Determine if the surface luminances should minimize transient adaptation effects and whether this can be accomplished without creating a bland visual environment. Determine if the surrounding surfaces will create reflected glare. Determine if illumination uniformity is desirable.

Step III: Luminaire selection

Identify the type of distribution, control medium, and spectral quality needed to properly portray the task (for diffusion, shadows or avoiding veiling reflections) and provide a comfortable environment (visually, thermally, and sonically). Identify the type needed to illuminate the area surfaces (for transient adaptation, for avoiding reflected glare). Conceptualize what the luminaire looks like and how it should be mounted (see previous design approach). Determine the condition of the area atmosphere and, therefore, the type of maintenance characteristics needed. Assess the economics of the lighting system.

Step IV: Calculation, layout, and evaluation

Determine the layout of luminaires that will portray the task best (illuminance, direction of illumination, veiling reflections, disability glare). Determine what layout will be most comfortable (visually — direct and reflected glare —and thermally). Determine which layout will be most pleasing aesthetically. Determine what energy management considerations apply.

SUMMARY OF TERMS

Light — radiant energy that is capable of exciting the retina and producing a visual sensation. The visible portion of the electromagnetic spectrum extends from about 0.38 to 0.77 microns.

Sky light — daylight from the sky dome only (excluding direct sunlight).

Skylight — a relatively horizontal glazed roof aperture for the admission of daylight.

Sunlight —light directly from the sun excluding light from other portions of the sky.

Infrared radiation — invisible radiation with wavelengths longer than 0.77 microns and less than 100 microns.

Near-infrared — infrared radiation in the 7.7- to 8.0-micron region and typical of that radiated from surfaces near room temperature.

Far-infrared — infrared radiation in the 8- to 100-micron region and typical of that radiated from surfaces near room temperature.

Ultraviolet radiation (UV) — invisible radiant energy within the wavelength range of 0.001 to 0.38 microns.

Luminous flux, lm — the time rate of flow of light.

Lumen (lm) — unit of luminous flux; the luminous flux emitted within a unit solid angle (one steradian) by a point source having a uniform luminous intensity of one candela.

Luminous intensity — the luminous flux per unit solid angle in the direction in question; units are candelas or lumens per steradian.

Candela, cd — the unit of luminous intensity; one candela is one lumen per steradian.

Candlepower — luminous intensity expressed in candelas.

Steradian, sr — (unit solid angle) — a solid angle subtending an area on the surface of a sphere equal to the square of the sphere radius.

Illuminance — the density of the luminous flux incident on a surface, expressed in units of footcandles (or lux).

Footcandle, fc — the illuminance on a surface one square foot in area on which there is a uniformly distributed flux of one lumen.

Lux, lx — the SI unit of illuminance; equal to one lumen per square meter.

Inverse square effect — the reduction of illuminance as the inverse square function of the distance from the source.

Cosine effect — the reduction of illuminance as a function of the cosine of the angle of incidence. The angle of incidence is the angle between the normal to the surface and the direction of the incident light.

Illuminance meter — a photometer for measuring illuminance from visible flux on a plane; as such, it must be color-corrected and cosine-corrected .

Reflectance — the ratio of the reflected flux to the incident flux.

Absorptance — the ratio of radiant flux absorbed by a medium to the incident radiant flux (see absorption).

Luminance — the luminous intensity of a surface in a given direction; the units of luminance are candelas per square foot and footlamberts.

Brightness — the subjective perception of luminance.

Footlambert, fL — a unit of luminance equal to 0.318 cd/ft^2; an unobstructed sky of one-footlambert uniform luminance contributes one footcandle of illuminance on a horizontal plane.

Transmission — the process by which incident flux leaves a surface or medium on a side other than on the incident side, without change in frequency.

Transmittance — the ratio of the transmitted flux to the incident flux.

Diffuse reflection — the process by which incident flux is redirected over a range of angles.

Diffuse transmission — the process by which the incident flux passing through a surface or medium is scattered.

Specular reflection — the process by which incident light is re-directed at the specular (mirror) angle.

Matte surface — one from which the reflection is predominantly diffuse, with or without a negligible specular component; see *diffuse reflection.*

Visual acuity — a measure of the ability to distinguish fine details.

Visual perception — the qualitative assessment of impressions transmitted from the retina to the brain in terms of information about a physical world displayed before the eye.

Retina — the light-sensitive membrane lining the posterior part of the inside of the eye.

Fovea — the small portion of the retina (opposite the iris) that constitutes the center of vision where acuity and color discrimination are greatest.

Para-fovea — the portion of vision surrounding the fovea that constitutes the peripheral vision where motion and low-level light sensitivity are greatest.

Accommodation — the process by which the eye changes focus from one distance to another.

Adaptation — the process by which the visual system becomes accustomed to more or less light resulting from a change in the sensitivity of the eye to light.

Dark adaptation — the process by which the retina becomes adapted to a luminance of less than 0.003 cd/ft^2 (0.01 fL).

Contrast — luminance differences.

Visual surround — all portions of the visual field except the task.

Visual task — those details and objects that must be seen for the performance of a given activity, including the immediate background of the details or objects.

Workplane — the plane at which work usually is done, and on which the illuminance is specified and measured. Unless otherwise indicated, this is assumed to be a horizontal plane 30 in. above the floor.

Glare — the sensation produced by luminance within the visual field that is sufficiently greater than the luminance to which the eye is adapted to cause annoyance, discomfort, or loss in visual performance and visibility.

Blinding glare — glare which is so intense that, for an appreciable length of time after it has been removed, no object can be seen.

Direct glare — glare resulting from high luminances or insufficiently shielded light sources in the field of view.

Disability glare — glare resulting in reduced visual performance and visibility.

Veiling reflection — specular reflections superimposed upon diffuse reflections from an object, which partially or totally obscure the details to be seen by reducing the contrast.

Reflected glare — glare resulting from specular reflection of high luminances in polished or glossy surfaces in the field of view; see *veiling reflection.*

Hue — that attribute of a color that determines whether it is red, blue, etc.

Chroma — that attribute of a color that determines its saturation (purity).

Value — that attribute of a color that determines its lightness or darkness.

Tint — the process of adding white to a color pigment in order to lighten it, increasing its value.

Shade (color) — the process of adding black to a color pigment in order to darken it, decreasing its value.

Shade (light control) — a screen made of opaque or translucent material to prevent a light source from being directly visible at normal angles of view.

Color temperature (of a source) — a measurement used to evaluate the color of "white" light sources; equal to the absolute temperature of a black-body radiator having a chromaticity equal to that of the light source.

STUDY QUESTIONS

1. Distinguish between luminous flux and luminous intensity, and give their units.

2. Distinguish between illuminance, luminance, and brightness, and give their units.

3. Describe brightness constancy and give an architectural example.

4. What are veiling reflections, what is their effect, and how can they be controlled?

5. Compare additive and subtractive color mixing.

6. Identify and describe the three dimensions of color.

7. What is "color temperature," and how is it quantified?

8. What is the "luminous enviroment" lighting design approach, and what are its principal steps?

9. What is the "visual task" lighting design approach, and what are its principal steps?

22

DAYLIGHTING:

*SOURCES AND CONCEPTS**

Inside the temple there was a cool, cavernous darkness, tempered only by the faint daylight filtering in through a pair of small lattice windows and by the seven lamps that hung, like a halo of yellow, quivering stars, above the head of the image on the altar. The light . . . of the last hour before dusk. It's just stopped raining and the sun has come out again, brighter than ever. Bright with the preternatural brightness of slanting light under a ceiling of cloud, the last, doomed afternoon brightness that stifles every surface it touches and deepens every shadow.

—*Aldous Huxley, 1962*

DAYLIGHT SOURCES

For design purposes, daylight sources may be categorized as direct (direct sunlight and diffuse skylight) and indirect (light from reflective or translucent diffusers that were originally illuminated by primary or other secondary sources).

DIRECT SUNLIGHT

Direct sunlight illuminates normal (perpendicular) surfaces with 6,000 to 10,000 fc. As such, it is too intense to be used directly for task illumination. Because of this, many illumination engineers typically prefer to exclude direct sunlight completely from interiors. This is unfortunate, because the movement and sparkle associated with controlled shafts of sunlight add consider-

ably to the visual variety and excitement of a space. Even where visual tasks are fixed in location and subject to direct glare, occupant controls (such as shades and blinds) are preferable to permanent exclusion. In addition, when the glazing is south-facing and vertical, it contributes favorably in the winter to psychological as well as thermal comfort.

Efficacy

Efficacy is a measure of the luminous efficiency of a light source. Any light source introduces heat into a building in the process of introducing light. More specifically, efficacy is the ratio of lumens emitted to watts (a watt is equal to 3.4 Btu) of heat introduced into a building by daylighting (or watts consumed by an electric lamp) since virtually all building illumination is ultimately absorbed as heat inside of the building.

Because of its importance to passive solar heating, direct solar radiation is often considered undesirable for illumination purposes because of its

* Portions of this chapter were excerpted from Moore, F., 1985, *Concepts and Practice of Architectural Daylighting.* New York: Van Nostrand Reinhold, by permission.

associated thermal content. This is a popular misconception. As can be seen from Table 22.1, the efficacy of direct sunlight (while less than clear sky light) is still considerably greater than commonly used electric alternatives. Virtually all of the energy from each source is ultimately converted to heat within the building (at the rate of 3.4 Btu/W). Thus, direct sunlight introduces less heat per lumen into a building than do most electric alternatives. This makes even direct sunlight an attractive strategy for reducing cooling loads in buildings due to lighting, *assuming that it can be effectively distributed and fully utilized for illumination.*

Since most sunlight entering a building is ultimately absorbed and converted to heat, it also contributes favorably to winter heating performance if the glazing is oriented in a direction where solar gain exceeds glazing heat loss (i.e., vertical, south-facing). This is particularly true for buildings where the thermal load is dominated by convective envelope losses.

Table 22.1: Efficacy of Various Light Sources

Light Source	Efficacy
Sun (altitude = 7.5 deg)	90 lm/W
Sun (altitude > 25 deg)	117 lm/W
Sun (suggested mean)	100 lm/W
Sky (clear)	150 lm/W
Sky (average)	125 lm/W
Global (average)	115 lm/W
Incandescent (150 W)	16 - 40 lm/W
Fluorescent (40 W, CWX)	50 - 80 lm/W
HP Sodium	40 - 140 lm/W

(Reproduced from Moore, 1985, by permission.)

Sunpath diagrams . . . again

Because of the importance of the contribution of direct sunlight to illumination and solar heating, a method for visualizing its position in the sky is valuable to the designer. The movement of the sun across the sky at a given site latitude can be visualized using a sunpath diagram (introduced in Chapter 5). Similar diagrams for other U.S. latitudes in 4° increments are provided in Appendix A.

DIRECT SKY LIGHT

Sky light is diffuse light from the sky dome resulting from the refraction and reflection of sunlight as it passes through the atmosphere. Under clear skies, the very small size of the particles causes only the wavelengths of light in the blue portion of the spectrum to be refracted, imparting this color to the sky. Under such clear conditions, the sky is darkest 90° from the sun and brightest near the sun.

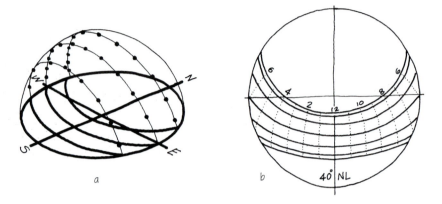

Figure 22.1: (a) Typical sky dome with sun paths and (b) corresponding plan diagram for 40° north latitude. *(Reproduced from Moore, 1985, by permission.)*

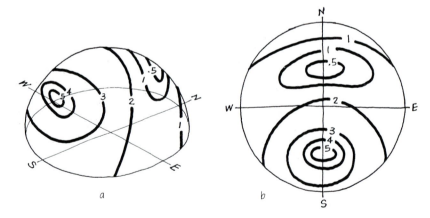

Figure 22.2: (a) Typical "clear" sky dome and (b) plan with isoluminance contours showing 10 to 1 distribution ratio (greatest near sun, least 90 degrees from sun). *(Reproduced from Moore, 1985, by permission.)*

Under overcast skies, the relatively larger water particles diffusely refract/ reflect all wavelengths equally in all directions. This results in a white-colored sky, about three times brighter at the zenith (directly overhead) than at the horizon.

While sunlight is a point source of illumination, sky light (from either a clear or overcast sky) is a distributed (area) light source. This produces a soft, nondirectional, relatively shadow-free illumination. The resulting illuminance levels are considerably less; typically 500 to 2,000 fc overcast or clear conditions (excluding direct sunlight) compared to 6,000 to 10,000 fc direct sunlight.

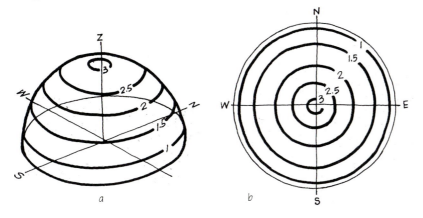

Figure 22.3: (a) Typical "overcast" sky dome and (b) plan with isoluminance contours showing 3 to 1 ratio (greatest at zenith, least at horizon). *(Reproduced from Moore, 1985, by permission.)*

Traditionally, daylighting has been achieved by employing large north window areas to receive diffuse north sky light while excluding direct sunlight. With the recent interest in passive solar heating, this north-oriented approach has been criticized because of the large associated net winter heat losses. This criticism is valid for buildings with skin-dominant thermal loads. These typically include residences and small commercial buildings with large surface-to-volume ratios and little internal gains from equipment, etc., in colder climates. All of these tend to favor south orientations with the associated increased winter solar heat gain.

For larger buildings, with smaller surface-to-volume ratios, daytime occupancy, and large internal gains, the choice between dominant south and north orientation is less obvious. In such buildings, where winter heating requirements are minimal and cooling loads dominate, north sky light may be preferred. Furthermore, such buildings are subject to utility charges for peak power demand as well as total power consumption. Under such rate structures, reduced power consumption does not necessarily translate to lower energy costs. It is thus important to recognize that optimizing energy costs in such buildings becomes much more complex than the south-dominated passive solar heating strategies that have proven so successful for residences.

INDIRECT SOURCES

When a matte reflective (i.e., flat white) surface is illuminated by a primary source (i.e., sunlight or sky light), its resulting luminance makes it an indirect source of illumination. Because it is a distributed source, the quality and distribution of its light is virtually identical to direct sky light admitted through a similar-sized opening. If directly sunlit, white reflector luminance can be as high as 1600 to 3200 cd/ft^2 (about 5000 to 10,000 fL), substantially more than the luminance of the sky dome (160 to 640 cd/ft^2, or about 500 to 2,000 fL). In a similar manner, translucent glazing materials can be used as indirect sources.

VISUALIZING DAYLIGHT ILLUMINATION

In order to understand daylighting, it is helpful for the designer to have a conceptual model to help visualize the effects of the various factors which affect the distribution of daylight in the building.

SOURCE-PATH-TARGET

One such conceptual model is to consider light in the sequential terms of *source-path-target*. The location of the light source and the target are determined and a direct or reflected path between the two is arranged. As arrows are used to represent light direction, this is an obvious, simple, and convenient visualization for designers.

This *source-path-target* model provides a valid basis for intuitive understanding only when the light emanates from a *point source* (sun, incandescent lamps) and the *path* is specular (clear glazing or mirror reflectors). These conditions are typical of those associated with solar heating and shading design. However, it is difficult to extend this convention to include *distributed sources* (such as the diffuse sky vault or a luminous surface) or *diffusing path* elements (such as translucent glazing or matte, white reflectors). This diffusion results in such a confusion of "arrows" (either mental or graphic) that the method becomes ineffective as a conceptual model for design.

Luminance x apparent size

In order to develop a workable alternative, first consider illumination as a function of areas of brightness that can be "seen" by the *target*. The basis for this approach is that the amount of light at the target is the result of exposure to all of the bright and dim surfaces within the view of that target. More precisely, the light contributed to (illuminance of) the target is the product of

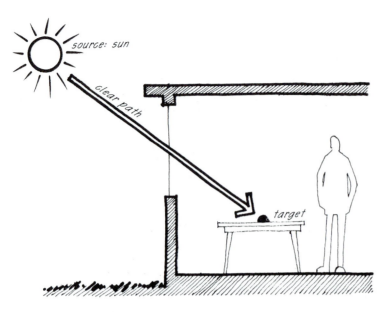

Figure 22.4: Source-path-target conceptual model (point source, clear path) provides a simple, valid method of visualizing daylight from a point source. *(Reproduced from Moore, 1985, by permission.)*

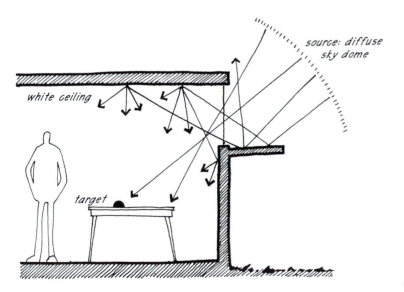

Figure 22.5: Source-path-target conceptual model (diffuse path) becomes ineffective because of the profusion of arrows in all directions. *(Reproduced from Moore, 1985, by permission.)*

the *luminance* of a particular source times its *apparent size* as viewed from the receiver. (For simplicity, the effect of "cosine reduction" is ignored here, but will be considered later.)

This concept does not differentiate between various sources; i.e., a cloudy sky "viewed" through a clerestory window contributes the same quality and quantity of light to a receiver as an illuminated white wall surface (assuming equal luminance, color, and apparent size).

The apparent size of the source as seen from the receiving point is a function of source size, object-to-reflector distance, and source tilt relative to the point.

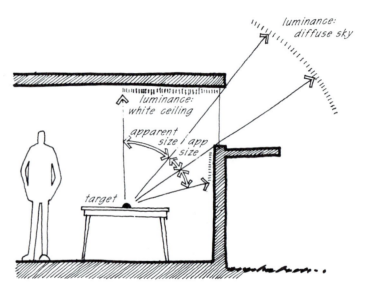

Figure 22.6: Luminance x apparent size conceptual model. *(Reproduced from Moore, 1985, by permission.)*

Reflecting diffusers

If the distributed source is a white reflector, the tilt of the reflector relative to the receiver does not affect reflector luminance (assuming an ideal matte finish). This reflector-receiver tilt does however affect the apparent size (exposure decreases as tilt increases). Thus for a given reflector location, this apparent size is maximized when the reflector is tilted normal toward the receiver. This tilt is invariably different from the tilt that maximizes reflector luminance. The optimum tilt becomes a compromise between these two tilts, just as if the reflector were a mirror. Note that this optimum tilt is not a function of specular focusing (as a mirror would be) but is instead the result of compromising the reflector area projected to both the source and receiver.

Because of this (and unlike a specular reflector), considerable design deviation from this optimum is possible with little effect on the illumination of the receiver.

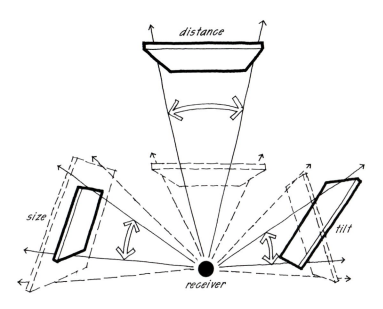

Figure 22.7: Apparent size of distributed source as a function of size, tilt, and distance. *(Reproduced from Moore, 1985, by permission.)*

Translucent diffusers

Translucent diffusers, such as patterned glass or white fabric, become indirect sources when illuminated from behind. While the resulting luminous surface is distributed (similar to white reflectors), translucent diffusers are of particular value in lighting building areas away from the direct source (i.e., when located between the target and the direct source). Perfectly diffuse glazing has many qualities analogous to white reflectors. It has the greatest luminance when oriented normal to the direct source, and contributes the greatest apparent size when the opposite side is oriented normal to the target point. The optimum tilt for maximum illumination of the target is between these two.

Like white reflectors, translucent diffusers permit considerable design freedom in deviating from this optimum, with little effect on illuminating performance. However, if the translucent diffuser is also used as exterior glazing, thermal performance becomes an important consideration. The need for reducing transmitted solar gain in the summer usually makes a vertical south-facing orientation most desirable.

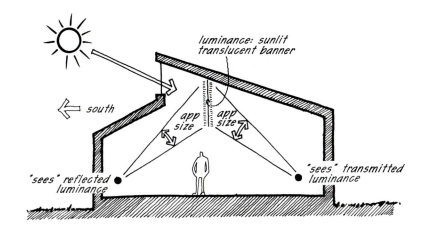

Figure 22.8: Illumination by a transmitting/reflecting diffuser. *(Reproduced from Moore, 1985, by permission.)*

The high reflectance of high-diffusion opal material can be used advantageously on the interior to diffuse light in both directions. Suspended white fabric banners behind south-facing clerestories reflect light back to south building areas, while diffusely transmitting to north areas.

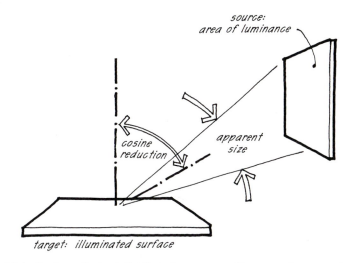

Figure 22.9: Cosine effect of distributed source position on reference plane illuminance. *(Reproduced from Moore, 1985, by permission.)*

Source position (cosine effect)

This luminance x apparent size concept, as stated so far, is an oversimplification. If the target is a two-dimensional surface (i.e., working plane) then the position of the light source relative to the receiving surface becomes a consideration (because of the cosine effect). As discussed previously, light normal to the reference plane contributes more illumination than if oblique. If the reference plane is horizontal (i.e., a table surface), then an overhead light source location would maximize illumination. If the reference plane is vertical (i.e., an artist's easel or bookshelves, vertical exhibits), then a source level with the reference would provide maximum illumination. However, other considerations, such as veiling reflections and the user's shadow tend to favor oblique lighting over normal incidence. A 45° angle of incidence from above only reduces illumination by 30 percent (due to the cosine effect) for either vertical

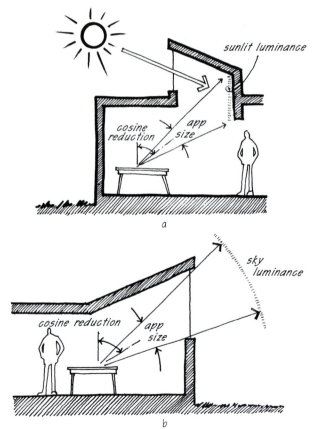

Figure 22.10: Reference plane illuminance by distributed sources: (a) sunlit white reflector and (b) diffuse sky dome. *(Reproduced from Moore, 1985, by permission.)*

or horizontal reference planes, while minimizing ceiling reflections and source glare in the occupant's field of view.

Therefore, the conceptual model for reference plane illuminance becomes luminance x apparent size x source position (cosine reduction).

SUMMARY OF TERMS

Zenith — directly overhead; 90° altitude angle.

Direct sunlight — beam illumination directly from the sun; typically 6,000 to 12,000 fc normal incidence, depending on atmospheric conditions, elevational altitude, and solar altitude angle.

Efficacy, lm/W — the ratio of lumens emitted to watts of heat introduced into a building by daylighting (or watts consumed by an electric lamp).

Sky light — diffuse light from the sky dome (either clear or overcast) resulting from the refraction and reflection of sunlight as it passes through the atmosphere.

STUDY QUESTIONS

1. The greatest amount of exterior horizontal daylight illuminance is likely to occur on a partly cloudy day. Explain why this is true.

2. Why are clear skies blue?

3. Describe the source-path-target visualization model and explain why it is valid for direct sunlight but not for diffuse daylight.

4. Describe the "luminance x apparent size" visualization model and explain why it is more suitable for diffuse light sources.

5. What is meant by the "apparent size" of a daylight source and what factors affect it?

6. Direct sunlight is an effective source of solar heating. Explain how a building can utilize direct sunlight for daylighting and still have a lower cooling load than a comparable building illuminated with electric lights only.

23

DAYLIGHTING:

DESIGN STRATEGIES

Strict invisible wedge untaken, immortal interval whose slow in-crease moves with millenial patience; dark core in light, shadow of noon which defeating us light us now: north light: my windows that have now sunrise or set save by reflection; snow-light; leaf-light; outward, earnest . . .

— *W. T. Scott (1962)*

SITE DESIGN STRATEGIES

Access to daylight in cities has long been a concern of lawmakers. The ancient Greeks and Romans mandated minimum lighting standards for their cities. The British Law of Ancient Lights (which dates to 1189) and its later embodiment into statute law, "The Prescription Act of 1832," provided that if a window enjoyed uninterrupted access to daylight for a twenty-year period, right to that access became permanent. In 1912, William Atkinson proposed a geometry for limiting building heights in urban areas. Based on similar geometry, the New York 1916 zoning ordinance was the first comprehensive municipal attempt to ensure minimum street-level standards for daylight. The city was divided into five "height districts" which attempted to recognize the perceived utility, neighborhood character, and the need for pedestrian ame-nity. A 1980 New York zoning revision provides for graphic evaluation of the amount of the sky obstructed by a proposed building (Bryan et al., 1981).

If daylighting is to be utilized in a proposed building, it is necessary to determine its availability on the site. Surrounding objects such as other buildings, trees, and landforms all act as daylight obstructions by blocking either direct sunlight or portions of the sky dome as visible from the building location. Because of its potentially large contribution to illumination, and because of its directionality, the position of the sun is of particular interest to the designer. In addition to its effect on illumination, solar position is important because of its effect on winter sun penetration for passive heating, and on the design of summer shading devices.

PLANNING FOR DAYLIGHTING

Robbins (1986) has suggested goals that should be established in the early site-planning stage to ensure access to daylight. These goals fall into two categories: daylight planning goals (which ensure that daylight is available around and within buildings as needed), and daylight safeguard goals (which protect the site for future development or protect surrounding sites).

Daylight planning goals (with applications):
1. Ensure that daylight is present on and between the facades of buildings in order to provide good interior and exterior illumination (new buildings and land development or zoning).

2. Ensure that daylight is available where it is wanted, either in particular rooms or at particular exterior locations (new buildings, land development or zoning, building renovation, and site rehabilitation).

Daylight safeguard goals (with applications):
3. Ensure that daylight is safeguarded within all new projects (new buildings and site rehabilitation).

4. Ensure that daylight is safeguarded on all land likely to be developed (land development or zoning).

5. Ensure that daylight is as fully safeguarded in rehabilitated or renovated buildings as possible, given the existing conditions (land development or zoning and building renovation).

6. Ensure that daylight is safeguarded in buildings and land developments adjacent to the proposed project (new buildings, land development or zoning, building renovation, and site rehabilitation).

DAYLIGHT OBSTRUCTION SURVEY

A daylight obstruction survey is helpful for evaluating the potential for a proposed design or existing building to meet both the *design planning and safeguard goals* above. The survey (based on the *angle of acceptance* method described by Robbins, 1986) identifies obstructions to both sunlight or daylight. It is based on determining whether there are any site features (buildings, landforms, trees) which project above the *sky exposure angle*. The

sky exposure angle (Table 23.1) is defined as the vertical angle above the horizon above which unobstructed exposure of a point 6 ft above the ground (or floor) to the sky is necessary to ensure 15- or 20-ft daylight penetration. For clear sky without the sun, the sky exposure angle varies with latitude (greater sky exposure is required at higher latitudes due to the comparatively lower sky luminance). While clear sky brightness varies with the location of the sun with respect to the aperture, for simplicity, the same sky exposure angle is used for all orientations. The sky exposure angle for overcast sky conditions is assumed to remain constant for all latitudes (although sky brightness at lower latitudes is greater due to higher sky luminance).

The sky exposure angle can be applied in two ways: to ensure access of the project site to daylight (design planning goals), and to safeguard the daylighting of the surrounding areas from obstruction by the project building (design safeguard goals):

Table 23.1: Sky Exposure Angles

Latitude	Required Sky Exposure Angle, Φ	Vertical-to-Horizontal Scale Ratio (SR)
< 24°	50°	1.18
28°	52°	1.27
32°	53°	1.35
36°	55°	1.45
40°	57°	1.55
44°	59°	1.69
48°	62°	1.86
52°	64°	2.08
56°	66°	2.42
All latitudes, overcast	50°	1.20

(Based on data from Robbins, 1986.)

Ensuring site access to daylight
The first consists of ensuring that outside obstructions (limited in height and proximity to the building by the sky exposure line) do not shield the sky visible from the critical 6-ft height on the facade of the building.

Safeguarding the daylighting of surrounding areas
The second consists of using the same sky exposure angle to limit the volume of the project building (that is, its height and setback) in order to assure that it does not obstruct surrounding buildings or sites at their 6-ft height above the ground.

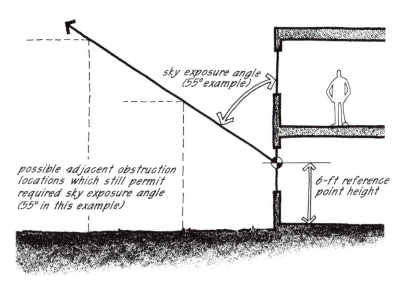

Figure 23.1: Ensuring site access to daylight. Using the relationship of the required sky exposure angle (clear day, 36° latitude, from Table 23.1) and the vertical-to-horizontal scale ratio: (a) section shows sky exposure angle which limits the height of surrounding objects without reducing daylighting effectiveness.

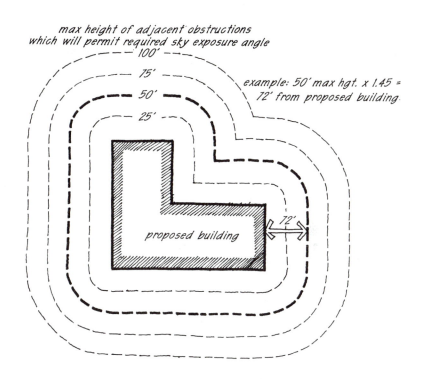

Figure 23.1 (continued): Ensuring site access to daylight: (b) site plan showing the use of the vertical-to-horizontal scale ratio to create a graphic scale that defines the minimum horizontal distance that surrounding objects of various heights can be without becoming an obstruction. For example, at 36° latitude, an object 50 ft higher than the 6-ft-high reference point can be no closer than 72 ft to the perimeter of the building (height x vertical-to-horizontal scale ratio or 50 x 1.45 = 72).

BUILDING DESIGN STRATEGIES

FORM

In early design stages, building shape has a primary effect on daylighting performance. As a general rule, daylighting is a function of the exposure of interior spaces to the sky vault.

Single-story structures (and the top story of multistory buildings) are particularly suited for daylighting because of the accessibility of virtually all interior areas to the sky dome. Furthermore, overhead light sources are more efficient for illuminating horizontal task surfaces (such as tables and desks) than are side sources because the cosine reduction is less. Because overhead sources tend to occur above the normal field of view of the occupants, the potential for direct glare is reduced. On the other hand, the potential for veiling reflections on horizontal surfaces is greater with overhead skylights; for applications such as reading and desk activities, side lighting may be preferable.

If, as a result of nondaylight considerations, multiple stories are to be used, exposure to the sky dome becomes a function of the narrowness of the plan. With careful fenestration design, a 15-ft perimeter zone can be task-lighted primarily by daylight, the next 15 ft, partially daylighted with supplemental electric lighting, with the remainder requiring entirely electric illumination. Prior to the widespread use of air conditioning, office building plans tended to be narrow (about 65 to 70 ft wide), to provide adequate ventilation as well as daylight illumination. With a center circulation zone, all of the work areas were within about 30 ft of the exterior. With the increased availability of air conditioning, plans became deeper, leading to the present dependence on fluorescent lighting due to the average increased distances to the exterior wall (Moore, 1985).

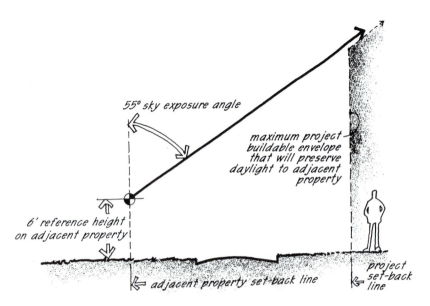

Figure 23.2: Safeguarding the daylighting of the surrounding areas from obstruction by the project building using the required sky exposure angle (clear day, 36° latitude, from Table 23.1) and the vertical-to-horizontal scale ratio: (a) section shows sky exposure angle (used to limit the project building volume) extending from the 6-ft height at the closest point on adjacent property on which a building can be built.

Building form design guidelines for daylighting

To utilize daylighting effectively in multistory buildings

* Use narrow plans to keep work areas within 30 ft of the exterior.

* "Finger" plans can be used where other conditions make a straight plan undesirable.

* However, if the structure is tall and the space between wings is narrow, each wing becomes a sky dome obstruction to those adjacent.

* This effect can be minimized by the use of light-colored exterior surfaces.

ORIENTATION

Small buildings (where daylighting is less of a design priority and where energy performance is dominated by the envelope) must balance the desirability of southern exposure for passive solar heat gain against minimizing

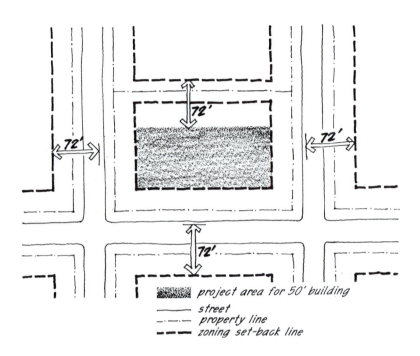

Figure 23.2 (continued): Safeguarding the daylighting of the surrounding areas: (b) site plan showing contours that limit the maximum volume of the proposed building in order to comply with setbacks while preserving the sky exposure angle to all adjacent property locations.

perimeter area to reduce heat loss. In larger, daylit buildings, heat loss is less of a concern (because of greater internal loads) and the need for exposure to relatively uniform lighting levels predominates. In general, southern and northern exposures are the most desirable while east and west exposures are to be minimized.

Because light (and sun) on the south facade is abundant, relatively uniform, and because excess solar gain in the summer can be controlled with overhangs, this is the most desirable facade for daylighting access, and its dimension should be maximized.

Daylight exposure is less abundant on the north facade, but the near-constant availability of diffuse sky light and the absence of summer sunlight make it the second most desirable orientation. The large net heat loss through north glazing is still a disadvantage but not to the degree associated with smaller buildings (with minimum internal gains and large envelope losses).

Both east and west orientations afford only half-day exposure to sunlight, making optimum fenestration design more difficult. Both (especially the west)

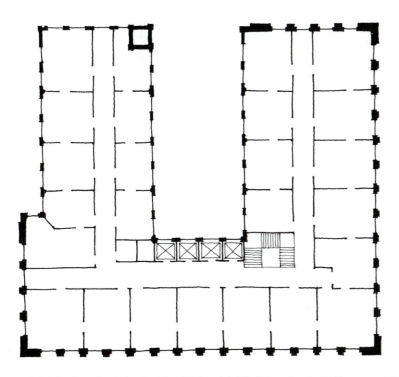

Figure 23.3: The "notched plan" of the Wainwright Building (Louis Sullivan, architect) allows side light and ventilation penetration. *(After Ternoey et al., 1985.)*

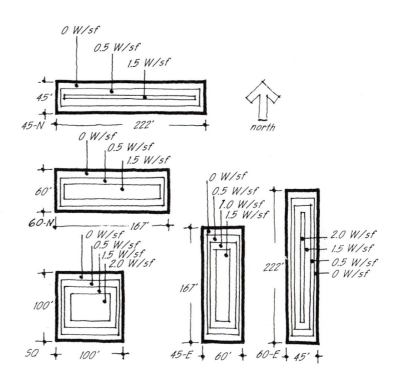

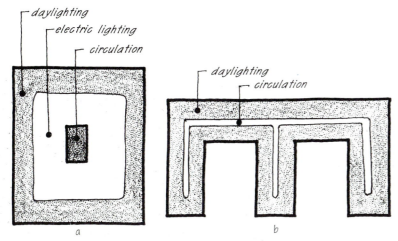

Figure 23.4: Access to daylighting increases as the surface-to-volume ratio increases: (a) typical 1970s office building and (b) its 1940s predecessor. *(Reproduced from Moore, 1985, by permission.)*

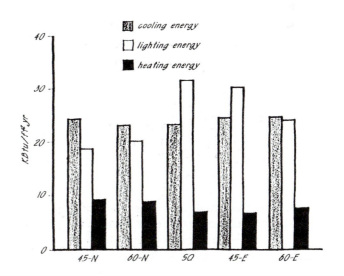

Figure 23.5: Effect of building orientation on building energy consumption for a prototypical commercial office building. *(After Ternoey et al., 1985.)*

experience large summer heat gain at unwanted times, while providing little winter passive solar contribution. For these reasons the east and west facade dimensions should be minimized.

Building orientation design guidelines for daylighting

*   To the extent permitted by siting and other constraints, the multistory building plan should be elongated with the maximum length facades on the north and south. In addition to proportioning facade exposures properly, this results in a narrow building, allowing maximum interior exposure to daylight.

*   In single-story and low-rise buildings, the availability of the roof for admitting daylight makes this plan elongation less important (Moore, 1985).

SIDELIGHTING

Sidelighting systems are so named because light sweeps across tasks from either side. The oblique incidence angle on the workplane causes a significant reduction of illuminance due to the cosine effect, but it also results in virtually no veiling reflections and as a result is a valuable source of illumination. Sidelighting apertures can also provide view glazing to maintain a visual connection with the surrounding environment. Daylight *penetration* is defined as the distance into the room that daylight reaches along the task plane at a predetermined illuminance level. In general, for a given window area, higher windows provide better penetration and more uniform distribution. This desirable height is often in conflict with view requirements. Consider separating the two functions: a high strip of windows for daylighting and relatively narrow vertical slits to frame selected views. In order to reduce the brightness contrast around the windows, locate them adjacent to perpendicular partition walls to utilize the reflectance of the wall to bounce light back on the wall surrounding the window (Robbins, 1986).

Sidelighting components: overhangs

Overhangs (particularly on the south) are desirable to limit unwanted solar gain. Unfortunately, they also reduce the view of the sky from within the room and thus reduce interior daylight illumination. From a daylighting standpoint, the room begins at the edge of the overhang and the location of the window wall merely defines the usable portion of the space below the roof. The workplane illuminance near the window decreases substantially; illuminances at the center and the rear of the room are less affected. While illuminances are reduced, uniformity of distribution is improved (Villecco et al., 1979).

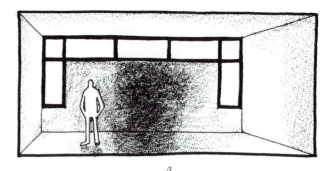

Figure 23.6: Window shapes that combine high glazing (for daylighting) and vertical glazing (for views): (a) better distribution, poorer view, and (b) better view location but high surround contrast, dark corners.

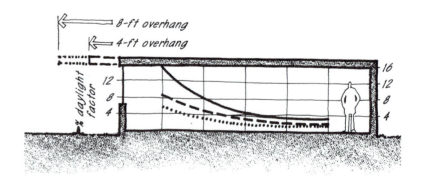

Figure 23.7: Effect of overhangs on daylight distribution in a room. In terms of daylighting, the room begins effectively at the edge of the overhang and the window wall merely defines the usable portion of the space. *(Data based on daylighting model studies tested under an "overcast" artificial sky at Rice University. Redrawn from Villecco et al., 1979, by permission.)*

Sidelighting components: horizontal reflectors

Illumination through windows (on all orientations) is increased with the addition of a horizontal reflector below the glazing. It has the effect of increasing the ground-reflected component. For clear glazing, with no other fenestration (as is typical of north facades) this component is beneficially directed to the ceiling only, where it is then diffusely reflected down onto the working plane. If the reflector is used with diffusing fenestration (translucent glazing or white louvers), then its reflected component will increase transmitted luminance (still desirable but with the tendency to increase glare because the increased brightness occurs lower in the field of view).

The contribution of under-window reflectors to interior illuminance is directly affected by ceiling reflectance. Back wall reflectance also affects interior illuminance, but its contribution is primarily limited by its exposure to direct sky light, and to a lesser degree to light reflected from the ceiling; the exposure of the back wall to the horizontal reflector directly is negligible.

Similarly, clerestory windows (which, by definition, rise above an adjacent roof surface) provide a cost-effective way to increase daylight entering the window. Simply use a light-reflecting roofing surface adjacent to the window. While a specular horizontal reflector is best suited for passive solar heating applications (low winter sun is reflected onto the glazing while most high-angle summer sun is reflected back to the sky), for daylighting purposes (where maximum enhancement throughout the year is the goal) a diffuse white surface is preferable. White marble gravel provides a suitable surface that requires little maintenance (Moore, 1985).

Sidelighting components: lightshelves

Lightshelves are often used to divide upper and lower glazing. They reflect additional light through the upper glazing, while acting as an overhang for the lower window, shading it from direct sun and obstructing the sky vault.

Contrary to popular belief, a lightshelf does not increase the amount of light in a space far from the window, but instead lowers the level near the window without decreasing it further back in the room. This results in more uniform distribution, and (once the eye adapts to the overall lower illumination level) a *perception* of greater illuminance deep in the interior.

The contribution of lightshelves to interior illuminance is directly affected by ceiling reflectance. Back wall reflectance also affects interior illuminance, but its contribution is primarily limited by its exposure to direct sky light, and to a lesser degree to light reflected from the ceiling; the exposure of the back wall to the horizontal reflector directly is negligible.

The location of the lightshelf reflector relative to the exterior building plane affects its exposure to the sky (and thus its reflection of light onto the ceiling). As a general rule, the less effective overhang above the shelf, the greater the lightshelf's contribution to interior illuminance.

Interior obstructions

Sidelighting, because of its inherently low angle of direction, is particularly subject to interior obstructions. These include furnishing (such as filing cabinets, etc.) as well as interior partitions. As a general rule, work surfaces that cannot "see" the window directly will receive reduced illuminance. This poses a particular problem for the designer due to the lack of control of the placement of movable obstructions during the life of the building. When the architect does not control the interior design directly, considerable collaboration with interior designers and occupants is required to avoid decisions that reduce daylight penetration.

- Orient ceiling beams and interior partitions perpendicular to the principal window wall to minimize the obstruction to light penetration.

Sidelighting case study: Farm Credit Bank Building

The Farm Credit Bank Building of Spokane, Washington (Walker McGough Foltz Lyra, architects), is an 18-story office building completed in 1982. A major contributor to the energy conservation was the plan configuration of the building. Elongated east-west to provide a maximum southern exposure, the plan is relatively narrow (65-ft interior dimensions). This minimizes the interior zones that cannot be daylighted. Orientation of the north and south window walls and open office plans reduce the need for electric lighting during daytime hours.

The building is protected from excessive heat gain during spring, summer, and fall periods by deeply recessing the clear glazing on the south facade and providing an intermediate lightshelf to shade the lower part of the glazing while reflecting light to the deep interior. In addition, the wide exterior sill below the

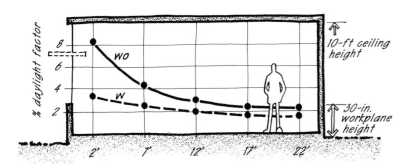

Figure 23.8: Daylight illuminances with and without an intermediate light shelf (overcast sky). *(Reproduced from Moore, 1985, by permission.)*

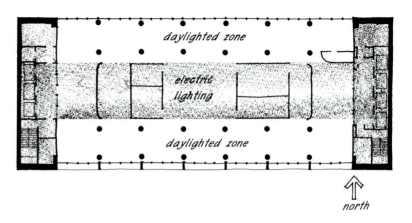

Figure 23.10: Farm Credit Bank Building: typical floor plan. Notice the elongation of the plan east/west to maximize desirable south and north facades. Service cores (which require no daylight) are located on the east and west facades which are devoid of any glazing to minimize undesirable morning and afternoon solar gain in the summer.

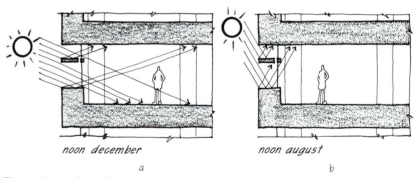

Figure 23.11: Farm Credit Bank Building sections showing the effect of the south-facade light shelf: (a) winter, and (b) summer. *(After Owings-Corning, 1981.)*

lower south window is white and also acts as a reflector. This surface is in direct view of the occupant and is a potential source of direct brightness glare (similar to looking out onto a patch of sunlit snow). However, the visual size of this bright area is relatively small (unless the occupant is seated close to the window) and, in reality, is not a source of discomfort. The north window wall is flush with no intermediate lightshelf or wide sill. Both facades are equipped with a roller-mounted vinyl solar shade that is manually operated by the occupants to control direct sunlight and direct sky glare while maintaining view.

Figure 23.9: Farm Credit Bank Building (Walker McGough Foltz and Lyerla, architects) exterior showing south-facing light shelves and "blind" east facade. *(Photo courtesy of J. Reynolds.)*

Utility areas (stairs, storage, mechanical, elevators, toilets) which do not require daylighting are located on the short east and west facades which have no windows. Supplemental general electric lighting is recessed fluorescent with mirror-finish parabolic wedge louvers to minimize direct glare in the field of view; these are equipped with dimming ballasts with photocell controls.

In addition to the above passive features, the building's mechanical system includes an electric heat recover chiller, 150,000-gal thermal storage water tanks (mechanically heated, cooled, and circulated), and natural gas boiler. Fan-motor energy for circulating conditioned air throughout the buildings reduced with variable-air-volume (VAV) supply systems augmented by fan-powered induction boxes. The thermostatically controlled boxes recover heat from lighting fixtures, using only the minimum amount of air necessary to provide comfort in various spaces After hours, dampers in the supply connection at each floor will admit air only as required. Heat recovery (heat pump) refrigeration machines, with water storage, transfer internal heat to the perimeter of the building when needed.

Sidelighting case study: Emerald People's Utility District Headquarters

The Emerald People's Utility District (EPUD) headquarters (Eugene, Oregon; designed by Equinox Design, and WE Group Architects and Planners, architects; Virginia Cartwright, daylighting consultant) is a remarkable example of a successful integration of daylighting with passive heating and cooling. EPUD is a young progressive public utility that aggressively promotes conservation and the use of renewable energy resources. EPUD was determined that its new office building reflect these values. The 24,000-ft^2 office building was too small for an atrium, so its designers selected an elongated form. They used the rule of thumb that the distance from any point in the building should be no more than 2.5 times the window's height. The building's window heights were set early in the design process at 12 ft, due to the building's total allowable width of 60 ft and the correspondingly narrow plan. The building was oriented with this long direction east-west in order to maximize southern exposure. Passive solar heat is stored in large amounts of thermal mass provided by concrete floors and masonry walls oriented perpendicular to the south-facing windows. This provided for solar absorption and storage while not obstructing daylight penetration. Acoustical baffles were suspended from the ceiling (again perpendicular to the south-facing windows to avoid obstructing daylight) to absorb sound in an otherwise very reverberant "hard" space. Passive cooling strategies include daytime ventilation and "night-flushing" ventilation of thermal mass (Novitski, 1989).

To ensure distribution of daylight into the core of the building, the designers utilized exposed concrete structure (to allow maximum window height without increasing building height) and T-shaped windows. The upper part of the windows run the full width to the structural bay (24 ft) to ensure

a

b

Figure 23.12: Emerald People's Utility District (EPUD) headquarters south facade: (a) at spring equinox, and (b) winter solstice showing effectiveness of louvered shading devices. *(Photo courtesy of J. Reynolds, from Stein and Reynolds, 1992, by permission.)*

deep penetration of daylight to the interior. The narrower lower leg of the T provides illumination to nearby desks while providing view. The top and bottom parts are divided by a lightshelf. Venetian blinds control light through the lower view windows; employees are encouraged to adjust the blinds to reflect the sunlight upward, thus bouncing light back into the office while preserving the view for other workers. No blinds are used on the upper windows above the lightshelves.

The size and louver spacing of the window overhangs were carefully designed to shade only in the summer and not in the winter. Deciduous vines planted near the south-facing windows grow on the louvered overhangs, which double as trellises. The vines block direct sun from May to October, and let it in from November to April. Virginia creeper was selected because it grows and drops its leaves at the best times for radiation control in the building, and because it is not destructive to building materials as some ivies are.

Figure 23.13: EPUD building cross section. *(Drawing courtesy of V. Cartwright.)*

Figure 23.14: EPUD "T-shaped" window as built results in dark areas on each side of the view window. Redesign suggested by designers included a recessed fluorescent lamp or space between the shelf and wall to lighten this area. *(After Cartwright and Reynolds, 1991.)*

TOPLIGHTING

In addition to the sidelighting strategies described above, single-story buildings and the top story of multistory buildings can employ skylights (horizontal and shallow-sloped glazing) and monitors (vertical and steeply sloped glazing) to introduce daylight. This is particularly advantageous for large-area floor plans with interior areas remote from perimeter windows.

Components: skylights

Because of the large amount of sunlight on horizontal surfaces during the summer, skylights introduce considerable heat gain and are often avoided in order to reduce cooling loads. However, if the aperture area is carefully controlled so that all admitted sunlight can be effectively used for lighting, the increase in cooling load will actually be less than would result from comparable electric lighting. This is because of the high efficacy of the sunlight (about 95 lm/W) compared with the supplemental fluorescent lighting (about 60 lm/W) together with the modest aperture areas which prevented "overlighting." In other words, even though daylighting results in heat gain, it introduces less heat than a comparable amount of electric lighting. The key to preventing unnecessary cooling loads is the use of moderate aperture area to ensure that all admitted daylight can be necessary to achieve the design lighting level.

For simple domed skylight configurations, clear glazing transmits more light than translucent glazing; however, if the sunlight beam through clear glazing penetrates to the floor, its high intensity is wasted for lighting purposes. Clear domed skylights are most effective when used with deep light wells which receive and diffusely reflect sunlight. Clear domes are also preferred in predominantly overcast climates (such as the Pacific Northwest).

Translucent skylight domes are preferred where the ceilings are relatively thin and no well is available to diffuse sunlight by reflection. Even though the visible transmittance is lower than for clear glazing, the transmitted diffusion results in more useful illumination per unit of heat admitted to the building.

Components: skylight reflectors

Baer (1986) has described the "sunbender," a commercially manufactured reflector/shade. The component is installed above a conventional skylight. In the winter position, the two-position reflector reflects additional sunlight through the skylight aperture. The reflector is curved in one direction to focus the sun's rays through the skylight aperture; after crossing, the rays diverge to distribute the sunlight over a large area. In the summer position, the reflector is lowered manually to provide shade on the skylight to reduce heat gain. In this lowered position, the reflector still directs light reflected from the roof back down into the skylight.

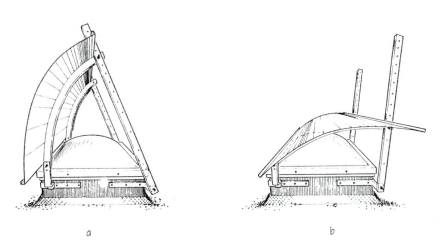

Figure 23.15: Sunbender south-facing reflector/shade installed on a conventional domed skylight: (a) winter position reflects sunlight down into skylight, and (b) summer postion provides shade, reducing solar heat gain. *(Drawings courtesy of Zomeworks Corporation, Albuquerque, New Mexico.)*

Skylight case study: *Window Rock School*

This building, designed by Don Felts and Associates, Architects and Engineers, is located on the Navajo Indian Reservation in Window Rock, Arizona. It consists of an addition of 16,000 ft^2 of instructional and administrative space to an existing building. A central atrium garden provides a pleasant circulation area and acoustic buffer between the perimeter classrooms and offices.

Daylight is admitted into the spaces by a unique system of skylights, reflectors, and translucent diffusers. A Sunbender reflector increases the amount of light admitted through the horizontal skylights considerably (this same reflector is lowered manually during the summer to shade the skylight from excessive heat gain). An interior diffuser/reflector distributes the light throughout the classroom spaces and shields the occupants from direct sunlight and excessive brightness while providing more uniform distribution. The system is economical compared with a roof monitor school (Ganado High School) designed by the same architect for a nearby location; providing comparable daylighting performance, the incremental cost per classroom was approximately $5,150 for the skylight/reflector system compared with $10,500 for the roof monitor scheme (Felts, 1985).

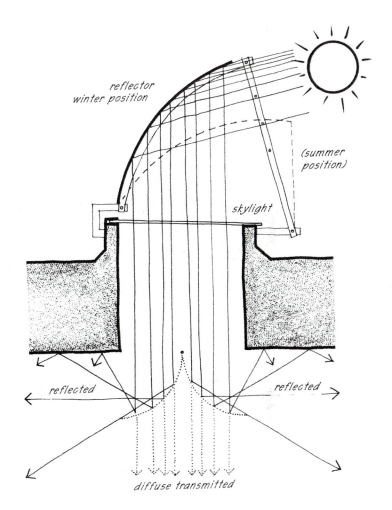

Figure 23.16: Window Rock School (Don Felts, architect), detail of skylight/reflector. *(Redrawn from Felts, 1985, by permission.)*

Components: *roof monitors*

Monitors are roof structures that utilize vertical or steeply sloped glazing. This allows contribution of roof reflected light, and (in the case of south-oriented glazing) more direct exposure to winter sunlight. Typically, north-facing monitors employ clear glazing for maximum transmission since diffusion is inherent in the sky light and roof-reflected sunlight. South-facing monitors must employ translucent glass or white baffles to diffuse direct sunlight. The combination of direct north sky light and twice reflected sunlight (roof + monitor interior) provides about half the illumination (with similar distribution) as does a horizontal translucent skylight. A comparable south-facing monitor with translucent glazing transmits illuminance comparable to the flat skylight, but the greatest illuminance occurs slightly north of the opening (Moore, 1985).

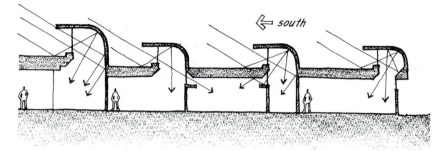

Figure 23.17: Ganado High School (Don Felts, architect), section through classrooms. Cost of this monitor daylight system was approximately twice that of the Window Rock system shown in Fig. 23.16. *(Redrawn from Felts, 1985, by permission.)*

Figure 23.18: Mount Airy Library, south and west facades.

Figure 23.19: Mount Airy Library interior (with monitor detail) showing ceiling level diffusing baffles under south-facing daylighting monitors.

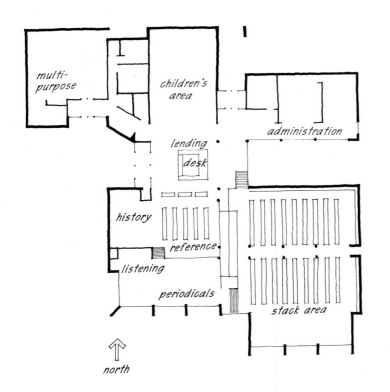

Figure 23.20: Mount Airy Library floor plan. *(Redrawn from Fisher, 1983, by permission.)*

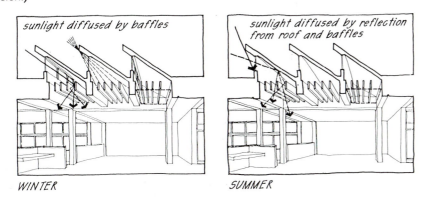

Figure 23.21: Mount Airy Library roof monitor section showing: (a) winter, and (b) summer operation. Notice that the diffusing baffles are precisely spaced so that no direct sunlight can ever quite penetrate to the interior. Conversely, no sky can be seen through these monitors from anywhere in the interior. *(Drawing courtesy of Edward Mazria.)*

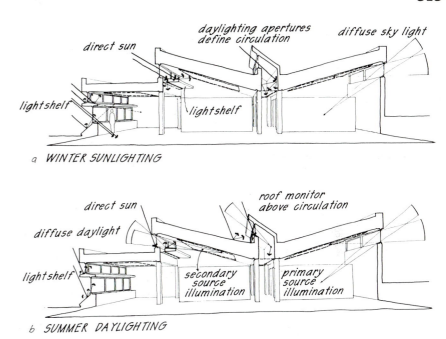

Figure 23.22: Mount Airy Library section through stack area showing typical recessed south window, clerestory and central monitor above stack circulation aisle: (a) sunlighting, and (b) diffuse daylighting. *(Drawing courtesy of Edward Mazria.)*

Roof monitor case study: Mount Airy Library

Sited on 3 acres near the center of Mount Airy, North Carolina (noted for its locally quarried white granite), this 14,000-ft^2 municipal library was designed by architects J. N. Pease Associates, and Mazria/Schiff and Associates (Fisher, 1983; Editors, 1983). In keeping with the nature of the site and the surrounding buildings in the town, the library is low-lying and spread into several wings. The resulting large perimeter makes the whole building easier to daylight and no part of the building is devoid of daylight. The total area equals 12 percent of the total floor area—a moderate ratio. Most of the daylight enters through south-facing monitors and windows allowing passive solar heating during winter months.

The dominant daylighting strategy is a series of south-facing sawtooth monitors on the roof that bring daylight to parts of the interior distant from the perimeter. The vertical glazing of each monitor is shaded from direct summer sun by a small overhang, while admitting lower-angle winter sun. At ceiling level under each monitor, a group of louvers are precisely spaces so that no sunlight enters directly, but is instead diffused by reflection off of their white surfaces. Along the south facade, light shelves above the recessed view windows reflect sunlight deep into the interior, aided by a light-colored ceiling.

The most important of the cooling strategies in the building isn't a cooling strategy per se — it is the high daylighting level achieved throughout the building which introduces less heat per lumen than comparable fluorescent lighting. Other cooling strategies include the extensive use of plants for shading, recessed windows, and very massive construction (which moderates the effects of afternoon high temperatures by "night-flushing" ventilation).

COURTYARDS AND ATRIA

Courtyards and atria (covered courtyards) are a traditional response to climate. In a Mediterranean house, the atrium walls shade the space in summer while the night air cools the masonry courtyard surfaces. The courtyard plan is the most compact variation of the "finger" plan, and thus creates the most "self-obstruction" of the sky dome. It does, however, provide some daylight access to the center of an otherwise deep plan. Because interior locations typically are unable to "see" the sky in a courtyard configuration, illuminance is particularly sensitive to exterior wall illuminance. A horizontal lightshelf or scoop is particularly effective. There is one advantage inherent in the geometry of courtyards. While the opposite wall obstructs the sky dome, it also obstructs low-angle direct sunlight, reducing glare problems and the need for wide overhangs.

The enclosed atrium is a buffer space providing a transition zone between inside and out. In the process, this central buffer space has assumed such large proportion as to become the focal space in the building. The lighting performance of an atrium is very similar to that of a courtyard of similar dimensions because the same sky dome obstructions are present. A clear atrium roof glazing simply replaces courtyard window glazing. There are, however, major thermal differences. In cold climates, the atrium remains habitable in the winter, at the expense of considerable summer heat gain. If an opaque roof, with clerestories, is used to cover the atrium, sky dome obstruction is increased, and illuminance is reduced accordingly. Based on the monitored performance of a small number of atrium office buildings it is not clear that life cycle costs are lower for buildings with an atrium than for comparable courtyard buildings.

The proportions of the atrium are critical to its daylighting performance. The proportions of the atrium section (its height-to-width aspect ratio) determines the amount of solar radiation reaching the floor of the atrium and lower surrounding rooms. The proportions of the atrium plan (its width-to-depth aspect ratio) should be elongated east and west to best utilize winter solar exposure while minimizing the summer impacts of east and west low-

angle sunlight. The taller the atrium, the greater the potential for stack-effect ventilation. While both courtyard and atrium configurations increase the *effective* perimeter area available for daylighting, the atrium minimizes the actual exterior surfaces that must be weather-resistant, thereby reducing construction costs.

Atrium case study: Bradbury Building

The Bradbury Building (Los Angeles, 1893; George Wyman, architect) is the model for many contemporary atrium office plan buildings. The 47-ft by 119-ft atrium serves as a grand interior lobby surrounded by galleries on each of the five floors onto which each office opens. The Italian Renaissance-style exterior is finished in brown brick and terra cotta. The atrium has the character of a Victorian street lined by brick facades. The clear-glass skylight provides abundant daylight, approaching outdoor levels. Large open marble stairs with wrought-iron rails are located at opposite ends of the atrium, while dramatic open-cage wrought-iron elevators dominate each of the long sides of

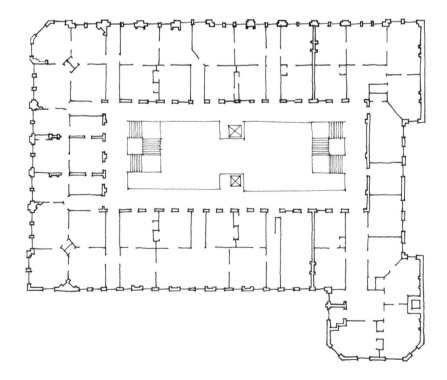

Figure 23.23: Typical floor plan, Bradbury Building. *(After Bednar, 1986.)*

the atrium. Built before the invention of the electric light, daylight was the predominant light source, supplemented by gas lamps (replaced later by electric). Ventilation entered through exterior windows, through the offices and the interior door transoms into the atrium. Warm air was exhausted out the pivoted windows around the top of the atrium perimeter by the stack effect (Bednar, 1986).

Atrium case study: Lockheed Building 159

The primary design objective for Lockheed Building 159 (Sunnyvale, California, 1983; Leo A. Daly, architect), a high-security office building, was to create a high-quality environment with minimal energy use. The building form itself was conceived to collect and distribute daylight effectively. The elongated plan maximizes north and south exposures while locating the core elements at each end to block low-angle morning and afternoon summer sun (see typical plan).

The 60-ft-wide atrium is located in the center in order to balance the daylighting for the 90-ft deep office bays while providing a visual focus. The building section controls and distributes daylight throughout the office areas. The general strategy for side lighting is to provide low-transmittance glazing in lower view windows and clear glazing above a reflective lightshelf. This approach reduces the illuminance variation across the deep bay while minimizing the sky brightness glare for perimeter locations.

Figure 23.24: Atrium of Bradbury Building, (Los Angeles, 1893; George Wyman, architect). Note clear glazing and perimeter ventilation windows below the skylight.

Figure 23.25: Lockheed Building 159, Sunnyvale, California (Leo A. Daly, architect), south and west facades. *(Photo courtesy of the architect.)*

Figure 23.26: Lockheed Building 159 atrium with sawtooth glazed roof. *(Photo courtesy of Leo A. Daly, architect.)*

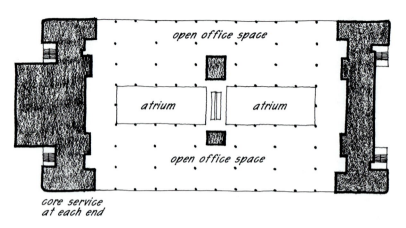

Figure 23.27: Lockheed Building 159 typical floor plan showing atrium with service cores at each end. *(Redrawn from Gardner, 1984, by permission.)*

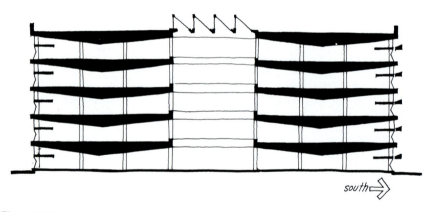

Figure 23.28: Lockheed Building 159 transverse section showing atrium with sawtooth top glazing. *(Redrawn from Gardner, 1984, by permission.)*

A ceiling which slopes from a 15-ft height at the perimeters to 10 ft at the center of the bay provides low-brightness ambient illumination. On the north and south facades, daylight enters through clear glass and is reflected against the ceiling from 13-ft-deep reflective lightshelves. On the south facade, a 5-ft projection reflects additional sunlight through the upper clear window while shading the reflectively coated (17 percent transmittance) view window below. Model studies have demonstrated that 85 percent of the daylight reaching the interior from the north and south perimeter comes from above the light shelves.

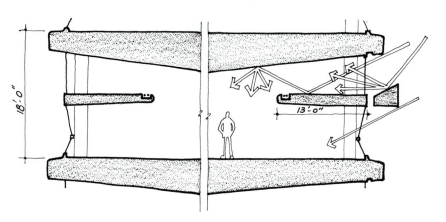

Figure 23.29: Lockheed Building 159 detail sections showing north and south window designs. *(Redrawn from Gardner, 1984, by permission.)*

Continuous sawtooth skylights span the atrium with their slopes facing south. Translucent glazing on the glazing slopes diffuse the direct sunlight. The general fluorescent lighting has a very low power density — 0.9 W/ft^2 — and is dimmable, controlled by photocells located in the ceiling. Addition local electric lighting provides task illumination. The HVAC system utilizes the stack effect created in the atrium and above the lightshelves to exhaust hot air. Variable-air-volume fan systems supply air through linear diffusers located in the ceilings (Bednar, 1986; Gardner, 1984).

LESSONS FROM AALTO'S LIBRARIES

Daylighting was a primary design determinant for most of the buildings designed by the Finnish architect, Alvar Aalto. In particular, Aalto's libraries are rich in examples of the application of indirect (reflected) daylighting (Moore, 1985; Moore and May, 1983).

Seinajoki Library

There are four visual task areas in the main reading room: the reading counter (between the columns), the sunken reading area, the stacks, and the charging desk.

The large, high south window has clear glazing, with horizontal diagonal-slope exterior louvers. The louvers are white on both sides with a cutoff angle of 45°; in other words, at angles higher than 45°, no sunlight or sky light penetrates directly, but is instead reflected twice by the parallel louvers. As a result, the high window performs like a translucent diffuser to high light

Figure 23.30: Seinajoki Library, (a) north and (b) south exterior. *(Reproduced from Moore and May, 1983, by permission.)*

sources. Its large area adequately illuminates the reading areas from above the field of view of the reader. The result is generous illumination evenly distributed, little cosine reduction, and minimal glare because of the high source location.

At angles below the 45° cut-off angle, direct sky light (and in the winter, direct sunlight) enters directly. Most of the direct sunlight strikes the lower part of the large, curved reflective "light scoop." The lower portion of this scoop has a high luminance level (due to its orientation relative to the window). This bright surface becomes the principle source for the vertical bookstacks along the exterior wall. Note the large apparent size of the scoop as "seen" from the stack. It is not as obvious from the section that the stacks perpendicular to the

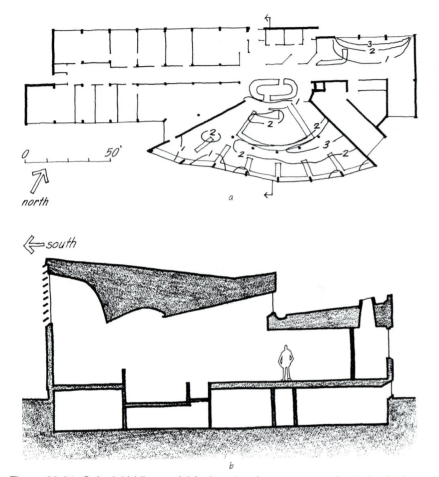

Figure 23.31: Seinajoki Library, (a) isolux pian (as a percent of exterior horizontal illumination, excluding direct sun), and (b) section. *(Reproduced from Moore and May, 1983, by permission.)*

wall receive diagonal illumination from the scoop as well as directly from the window (due to the fan-shaped wall curvature in plan).

The top of the scoop receives light reflected from both the lower part of the scoop as well as the top of the louvers and exterior ground. The exterior wall (below the window and above the stacks) receives light from the lower part of the scoop. While both the upper scoop and this wall portion in turn contribute to the general illumination of the room, their luminance is important in reducing the brightness contrast around the window.

Figure 23.32: Seinajoki Library, (a) interior showing light scoop, (b) with explanation. *(Reproduced from Moore and May, 1983, by permission.)*

The opposite side of the scoop serves as an eyebrow to screen the circulation desk librarian from most of the low-angle glare from the high south window. The charging desk has poor daylight illumination because most of the south window is obstructed by this eyebrow and the north clerestory is directly overhead. This results in a small apparent size of each source from this location. It appears that the structural requirements of the building prevented placing the north clerestory even further to the north (which would have increased its apparent size, and thus the illumination, in this area). However, the sloped ceiling receives light reflected from the snow on the adjacent roof, and to a lesser extent, directly from the sky.

The sunken reading area "sees" two large, bright secondary sources: the high south window and the north clerestory. The sunken location places both sources high, reducing the cosine reduction from both sources onto a horizontal reading plane, while keeping them above the reader's field of view to reduce glare.

Figure 23.33: Mount Angel Library, (a) south, and (b) north exteriors. *(Reproduced from Moore and May, 1983, by permission.)*

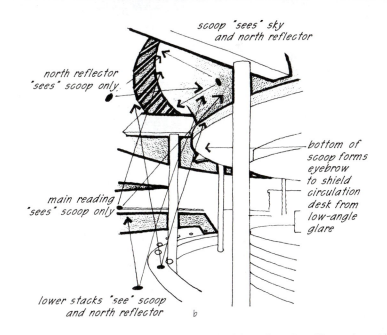

Figure 23.34: Mount Angel Library, (a) interior, with (b) explanation. *(Reproduced from Moore and May, 1983, by permission.)*

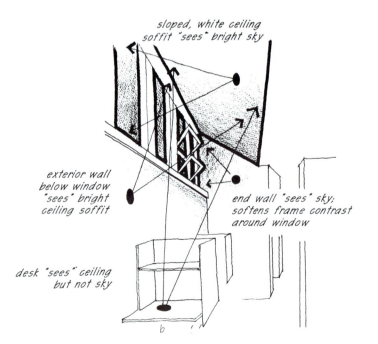

In addition to a fan-shaped plan (such as that at Seinajoki), most Aalto libraries employ a sunken study area located in the center of the main library space. This creates a strong spatial focus. It also allows stacks to be located in the center without blocking visual control from the circulation desk. In those libraries where light is admitted only from the perimeter, the sunken floor configuration keeps the high side light above the field of view of the reader while reducing the cosine reduction of illumination on reading tables.

Mount Angel Library

Aalto designed several other libraries that demonstrated a large and sophisticated vocabulary of daylighting strategies (including those at Wolfsburg, Rovaniemi, Otaniemi, and Vipuri). The last library to be designed by Aalto is located at Mount Angel Abbey, a Benedictine monastery near Portland, Oregon. Using the familiar fan-shaped plan, light is introduced over the center reading area by a north-facing, crescent-shaped roof monitor, with a white "scoop" behind clear glazing sloped about 60°. The sectional profile is shallow, allowing direct sky illumination in one direction and reflection from the scoop in the opposite. This provides generous illumination to the reading stations surrounding the sunken mezzanine crescent and the mezzanine level itself. In addition, adequate light penetrates down past the mezzanine into the basement open stack area to allow selection of books.

sloped, white ceiling
soffit "sees" bright sky

exterior wall
below window
"sees" bright
ceiling soffit

end wall "sees" sky;
softens frame contrast
around window

desk "sees" ceiling
but not sky

b

Figure 23.35: Mount Angel Library, (a) high north window, with (b) explanation. *(Reproduced from Moore and May, 1983, by permission.)*

Figure 23.36: Mount Angel Library, roof monitor.

On the main level, stacks radiate out from this center light chamber, allowing visual control from the circulation desk. At the perimeter of the main level, open carrels are illuminated from above by high window light which is reflected from the sloped ceiling. This straight "scoop" also washes the wall below the window to reduce the brightness contrast of the sky seen through the windows. A similar sloped ceiling is positioned above corner windows in the small lecture room. In addition to light reflected by the sloped ceiling, each lower wall is washed from the adjacent perpendicular window.

SUMMARY OF TERMS

Daylight design planning goals — those which ensure access of the project site to daylight.

Daylight design safeguard goals — those which safeguard the access to daylight of the surrounding areas from obstruction by the project building.

Sky exposure angle — the vertical angle above the horizon above which unobstructed exposure of a point 6 ft above the ground (or floor) to the sky is necessary to ensure 15- or 20-ft daylight penetration.

Fenestration — the entire aperture assembly, including glazing, overhang, mullions, screens, louvers, blinds, draperies, reflectors, etc.

Orientation — the compass direction which exterior wall surfaces face.

Sidelighting — daylighting which uses windows as the primary apertures (i.e., light sweeps across tasks from either side).

Daylight penetration — the distance into the room that daylight reaches along the task plane at a predetermined illuminance level.

Overhang — a fenestration component consisting of a horizontal slab or trellis located above a window for the purpose of providing shade or other climatic protection.

Horizontal reflector — a high-reflectance (white or mirrorfinish) horizontal surface located outside under a window for the purpose of increasing daylight through a window by means of daylight.

Intermediate light shelf — a horizontal reflector that divides upper and lower glazing.

Interior daylight obstruction — a partition, furnishing, or structural element above the workplane which obstructs daylight penetration.

T-shaped windows — windows which are very wide near the ceiling for maximum daylight penetration and are narrower below for viewing.

Roof monitor — a raised section of a roof that includes a vertically (or near-vertically) glazed aperture for the purpose of daylight illumination.

Courtyard — an enclosed or semienclosed outdoor area completely surrounded by a building.

Atrium — usually a dominant, daylighted, roofed, multistory architectural space.

Core daylighting — daylight illumination of the deep interior of a multistory building.

Beam daylighting — the use of tracking reflectors or refractors to focus narrow beams of direct sunlight to deep interior locations.

STUDY QUESTIONS

1. Differentiate between daylight planning goals and daylight safeguard goals and give examples of each.

2. Using the site plan in Fig. 23.1b, assume the latitude to be 48° and the site to be level. Draw the boundary of the closest locations allowable for adjacent 46-ft tall structures.

3. What are the daylighting advantages and disadvantages in "finger" floor plans?

4. Why is it desirable to elongate a daylighted building on the east-west axis?

5. What are the advantages of a T-shaped window?

6. In daylighted buildings, what is the most advantageous direction (or orientation) for exposed beams, ducts, and interior partitions? Why?

7. Describe the daylighting rationale behind the floor plan of the Farm Credit Bank Building.

8. Describe the unique shading devices used on the Emerald Public Utility District headquarters building.

9. What is the primary energy-related function of an atrium in a multistory office building? Why is it preferable to separate the atrium from surrounding areas with a glazed partition?

24

DAYLIGHTING:

ANALYSIS

There are two principle types of daylighting calculations: illuminance (which estimates the interior illuminance level at a particular instant in time), and energy use (which estimates the energy and cost savings due to the use of daylighting during a typical period of time).

ILLUMINANCE CALCULATIONS

DAYLIGHT FACTOR

Because interior illuminance due to daylight changes as a function of sky conditions, absolute measurements of illuminance are not directly indicative of actual building performance. The *daylight factor* is a ratio of interior horizontal to exterior horizontal illuminance under an overcast, unobstructed sky (expressed as a percentage) and remains constant regardless of changes in sky luminance. Daylight factors are usually expressed as a percentage; a factor of 15 percent at a given interior location means that location receives 15 percent of the illuminance that would be received under an unobstructed sky.

In addition to eliminating the effect of changing sky conditions, daylight factors are a more realistic measure of perceived illuminance. This is due to the adaptive abilities of the eye, which make relative differences more significant perceptually than absolute measurements.

Graphic representation of illuminance

Illuminance data from measurements in buildings, daylighting model studies, or calculations, can be presented graphically in the form of contours of either equal footcandle or daylight factors plotted over a building floor plan. Known as *isolux contours*, this graphical method facilitates visual assessment of illuminance distribution throughout a room (closely spaced contours represent a strong illuminance gradient, while widely spaced contours indicate a relatively even distribution). While illuminances or daylight factors can be interpolated for specific locations, the primary value of isolux contours is their indication of distribution, which is the quantitative factor most representative of visually perceived illumination quality in an architectural environment.

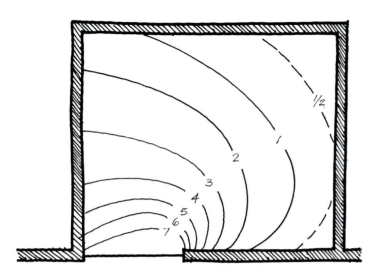

Figure 24.1: Floor plan with daylight factor isolux contours. *(Reproduced from Moore, 1985, by permission.)*

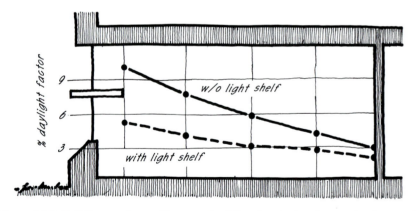

Figure 24.2: Building sections with a graph of illuminance levels are also frequently used to show distribution. This is particularly useful to compare illuminance data (such as measurements from daylight model studies of alternative window configurations). *(Reproduced from Moore, 1985, by permission.)*

Illuminance calculations estimate the illuminance at an interior reference point (or an average throughout the room) given certain outside sky conditions. Methods range from simple rules of thumb to detailed computer simulations which are able to account for unusual room and aperture geometries as well as particular sky conditions. Generally, the more complex the method the more reliable and accurate the results.

RULES OF THUMB

The 2.5 rule

This traditional rule (Illuminating Engineering Society, 1924) assumes that sufficient daylight for office tasks penetrates 2.5 times the height of the window head above the workplane. It is most applicable where clear glazing is used, the window width is half of the exterior perimeter length, sky conditions are either overcast (or the room is north-facing or controllable blinds are provided), interior ceiling and wall reflectance are relatively high, and there are no major obstructions. For a 9-ft head height above the floor, this would provide daylight to a depth of about 16 ft from the window on a 30 in.-high workplane.

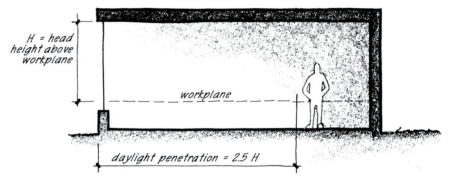

Figure 24.3: Section showing the 2.5 rule of thumb which assumes that adequate daylight for office tasks will penetrate to a depth of 2.5 x the height of the window head above the workplane. *(After Robbins, 1986.)*

The 15/30 rule

Another rule of thumb assumes that it is possible to provide sufficient daylight for office tasks in the outer 15-ft perimeter and that partial daylighting can be achieved to a 30-ft depth (sufficient for general background lighting but requires supplemental electric task lighting).

Spatial proportions

Robbins (1986) has described two basic spatial relationships that can be used to assess the potential of a building for daylighting. They are: the ratio of envelope surface area to floor area (E/F) and the ratio of volume to floor area (V/F). Daylighting tends to increase the surface area of the envelope, so the E/F ratio is often larger for daylighted buildings than for comparable nondaylighted ones (because more of the interior areas are near a perimeter

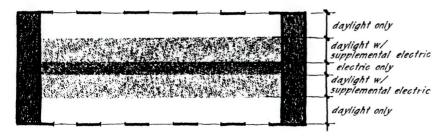

Figure 24.4: Plan showing daylighted areas using the 15/30 rule of thumb. For preliminary design purposes, assume that the 15-ft-wide zone can be illuminated entirely by daylighting, while the next 15 ft can be partially daylighted with supplementary electric; areas further than 30 ft from the window wall receive daylight that is sufficient only for circulation.

wall or roof). Similarly, the V/F ratio is typically larger in daylighted buildings (a result of higher ceilings and windows, allowing greater daylighting penetration from sidelighting).

Table 24.1: Spatial Proportions Typical of Daylighted and Nondaylighted Buildings

Floor Area	Nondaylighted		Daylighted	
(sq. ft.)	E/F	V/F	E/F	V/F
5,000	1.89	11.9	2.24	13.0
10,000	1.77	13.0	2.17	16.7
25,000	1.34	9.0	2.09	17.9
50,000	1.06	12.0	1.53	15.2
100,000	0.64	12.3	0.89	16.2
1,000,000	0.38	9.6	0.45	12.0

(Reproduced from Robbins, 1986, by permission.)

SIMPLE FORMULAS

One of the simplest formulas is that the minimum *daylight factor* (DF) in the room is equal to one-tenth of the window area (expressed as a percentage of the floor area). In other words, multiply the required daylight factor by 10 to get the percentage of floor area required for window area. For example, a classroom with 700 ft^2 floor area has a design illuminance level of 30 fc. Assuming typical outdoor illuminance equal to 1000 fc throughout the winter, a daylight factor of 3 percent is required. Thus 30 percent (ten times 3 percent) of the 700 ft^2 — or 210 ft^2 — of window area is required (about 6 ft by 35 ft).

Hopkinson and Kay (1969) have suggested the following simplified formulas:

For side lighting,

$$DF \text{ (at a reference point)} = \frac{10(W)(H)^2}{(D)(D^2 + H^2)} + \frac{4(G)(R)}{F(1-R)}$$

where: DF = daylight factor, %

W = width of window, ft

H = height of window above the workplane, ft

D = distance from window wall to reference point, ft

G = glass area, ft^2

R = wall reflectance, %

For top lighting,

$$DF \text{ (at a reference point} = \frac{(S)(U)(G)}{(F)}$$

where: DF = daylight factor, %

S = sky obstruction factor (unobstructed sky = 1.0)

U = coefficient of utilization (0.4 for typical horizontal skylights with average interior reflectance)

G = glass area, ft^2

F = floor area, ft^2

GRAPHIC METHODS

Chapter 22 described a conceptual model that recognizes interior daylight illuminance as a function of three variables: (1) luminance of the light source (the sky dome, for example), (2) apparent (angular) size of the light source (the part of the sky visible through the window), and (3) the position of the source relative to the reference plane (cosine effect). Virtually all graphic methods are based on this conceptual model; that is, they involve measuring the angular field of view of the primary daylight source (the sky) from a selected interior reference point, assume a sky luminance, and provide a correction for the cosine effect.

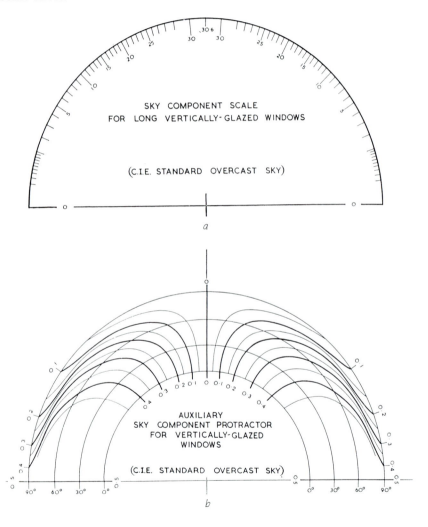

Figure 24.5: BRS daylight factor protractor: (a) top half is "primary" protractor for use over section, (b) bottom half is "auxiliary" protractor for use over floor plan to determine the width correction factor. A complete set for various glazing slopes for both overcast and uniform sky conditions are available. *(Reproduced from Hopkinson, 1963, by permission of Her Majesty's Stationery Office.)*

DAYLIGHT FACTOR PROTRACTOR

The Building Research Station (BRS) has developed a series of daylighting design tools. The most widely used of these are the BRS protractors (Dufton, 1946), first developed for uniform sky conditions to simplify the calculation of daylight and to enable daylight measurements to be made directly from architectural drawings. These were revised (Longmore, 1967) to include the CIE (Commission Internationale de l'Eclairge) standard overcast sky and more recent information on glazing transmission. The BRS protractors are based on the daylight factor method (also known as the CIE method) for calculating the interior illuminance under *overcast sky* conditions.

As discussed previously, the daylight factor is the ratio of interior horizontal illuminance to exterior horizontal illuminance under an unobstructed sky, and is expressed as a percentage. It is the sum of three components (each of which is a percentage of exterior unobstructed illuminance):

- *Sky component* — the illuminance received at the interior reference point directly from the sky through the window or skylight.

- *External reflected component* — the illuminance received at the interior reference point from reflecting exterior surfaces above the horizon (surfaces below the horizon cannot be "seen" directly from the horizontal reference plane).

- *Internal reflected component* — the illuminance received at the interior reference point from all light reflected from interior room surfaces.

Each BRS protractor is actually two semicircular protractors. The "primary" protractor is overlaid on a building section for measuring the sky component for an infinitely long window. The "auxiliary" protractor is overlayed on a corresponding floor plan to determine a correction factor for the given window length. The same protractor is used to measure the external reflected component and a reduction factor (typically 0.1) is applied to correct for the reduced luminance of the external obstructions (compared with sky luminance). Table 24.2 is used to estimate the internal reflected component. The *initial daylight factor* is the sum of the sky component, the external reflected component, and the internal reflected component. This is further reduced by multiplying light-reduction factors for mullions, glazing transmittance (if other than single clear glass), and dirt. The final product is the *maintained daylight factor* (%).

To determine the footcandle illuminance, multiply the daylight factor by the horizontal exterior illuminance (overcast sky). Typical midday exterior illuminances under an overcast sky are: 1000 fc (December), 1500 fc (March

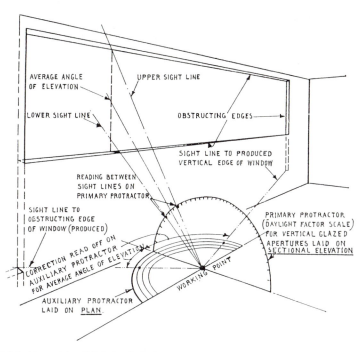

Figure 24.6: Use of the BRS daylight factor protractor. *(Reproduced from Hopkinson, 1963, by permission of Her Majesty's Stationery Office.)*

and September), and 2000 fc (June). Thus a reference point in a room with a maintained daylight factor of 3.0 percent would receive about 30 fc in December and 60 fc in June under overcast skies.

CLEAR SKY DAYLIGHT FACTOR PROTRACTORS

The BRS protractors described above are limited to uniform sky and CIE overcast sky conditions. While these conditions are representative of northern Europe, they are less suited for the greater occurrence of clear sky conditions characteristic of many parts of North America. As discussed previously, under clear sky conditions, sky brightness is greatest near the sun and least perpendicular to the sun (approximately 10 to 1 ratio). Thus, not only does the average sky luminance change through the day (as with an overcast sky) but

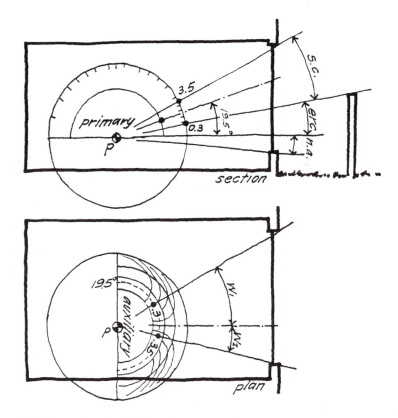

Figure 24.7: Example using BRS protractor to estimate sky component and external reflected component (see example worksheet in Fig. 24.8). *(Reproduced from Moore, 1985, by permission.)*

Table 24.2: Internal Reflected Component of Daylight Factor

Glass area (as a % of floor area)	Floor Reflectance (%)											
	10				20				40			
	Wall Reflectance (%)											
	20	40	60	80	20	40	60	80	20	40	60	80
	(%)	(%)	(%)	(%)	(%)	(%)	(%)	(%)	(%)	(%)	(%)	(%)
2	—	—	0.1	0.2	—	0.1	0.1	0.2	—	0.1	0.2	0.2
5	0.1	0.1	0.2	0.4	0.1	0.2	0.3	0.5	0.1	0.2	0.4	0.6
7	0.1	0.2	0.3	0.5	0.1	0.2	0.4	0.6	0.2	0.3	0.6	0.8
10	0.1	0.2	0.4	0.7	0.2	0.3	0.6	0.9	0.3	0.5	0.8	1.2
15	0.2	0.4	0.6	1.0	0.2	0.5	0.8	1.3	0.4	0.7	1.1	1.7
20	0.2	0.5	0.8	1.4	0.3	0.6	1.1	1.7	0.5	0.9	1.5	2.3
25	0.3	0.6	1.0	1.7	0.4	0.8	1.3	2.0	0.6	1.1	1.8	2.8
30	0.3	0.7	1.2	2.0	0.5	0.9	1.5	2.4	0.8	1.3	2.1	3.3
35	0.4	0.8	1.4	2.3	0.5	1.0	1.8	2.8	0.9	1.5	2.4	3.8
40	0.5	0.9	1.6	2.6	0.6	1.2	2.0	3.1	1.0	1.7	2.7	4.2
45	0.5	1.0	1.8	2.9	0.7	1.3	2.2	3.4	1.2	1.9	3.0	4.6
50	0.6	1.1	1.9	3.1	0.8	1.4	2.3	3.7	1.3	2.1	3.2	4.9

(Reproduced from Hopkinson, 1963, by permission.)

BRS DAYLIGHTING PROTRACTOR WORKSHEET

Project __Example__　　　Analyst __FM__　　　Conditions __Overcast__

PART I: SKY COMPONENT

Reading on primary sky component scale	upper reading =	**3.5**	1
	lower reading =	**0.3**	2
Primary sky component for window of infinite length (step 1 – step 2)		**3.2**	3
Angles of elevation of visible sky	upper reading =	**29** °	4
	lower reading =	**10** °	5
Average angle of elevation: (step 4 – step 5) x 2		**19.5** °	6
Readings from auxiliary scale:	left reading =	**0.3**	7
	right reading =	**0.35**	8
Correction factor for window width: (step 7 ± step 8)	=	**0.65**	9
Sky component for window of finite length (step 3 × step 9)　*double glazed, clear*	=	**2.08**	10
Factor for glazing material (1.0 for single glazing)	=	**0.9**	11
Factor for window mullions and frames (0.75 is typical)	=	**0.8**	12
Factor for dirt on glazing (0.9 for clean, 0.6 for very dirty)	=	**0.8**	13
Combined factors (step 11 x step 12 x step 13)	=	**0.576**	14
Corrected sky component (step 10 x step 14)	=	**1.20**	15

PART II: EXTERNALLY REFLECTED COMPONENT

Readings on primary sky component scale:	upper reading =	**0.3**	16
	lower reading =	**0.0**	17
Primary sky component for window of infinite length (step 16 – step 17)	=	**0.3**	18
Angles of elevation of visible sky	upper reading =	**10** °	19
	lower reading =	**5** °	20
Average angle of elevation: (step 19 – step 20) x 2			21
Readings from auxiliary scale:	left reading =	**0.30**	22
	right reading =	**0.35**	23
Correction factor for window width: (step 22 ± step 23)	=	**0.65**	24
External reflected component for window of finite length (step 18 x step 24)	=	**0.195**	25
Correction factor for relative luminance of external obstruction (0.2 typically)	=	**0.2**	26
Corrected externally reflected component (step 25 x step 26 x step 14)	=	**0.04**	27

PART III: INTERNAL REFLECTED COMPONENT

Internal reflected component (from Table 24.2)　*glass area = 35% floor area*	=	**1.8**	28
floor reflectance = 20% ; walls, 60%			

PART IV: DAYLIGHT FACTOR

Daylight factor (step 15 + step 28)	=	**3.04**	29

comments:

Figure 24.8: BRS protractor example problem worksheet (see Fig. 24.7; blank worksheet in Appendix F). (*After Longmore, 1967.*)

the location of greatest luminance changes with the sun's location. The luminance range throughout the clear sky is much greater than the overcast sky. As a result of these variables, a much more complex set of protractors and procedures is required for clear sky conditions. Bryan and Carlsberg (1982) have such a set of protractors that are based on the CIE clear sky function, and is similar in format to the BRS protractors.

DOT CHARTS

Several authors (Pleijel, 1954; Turner, 1971) have described daylight factor dot charts for graphically estimating the sky component for overcast skies; similar charts have been developed for clear skies (Moore, 1984). The charts are a pattern of dots distributed as a function of the sky luminance distribution, and the cosine correction for the angle of incidence. In use, the chart is overlayed with an obstruction mask showing the angular size and location of window/skylight openings visible from a given interior reference location. (In the case of clear sky conditions, the dot chart is rotated relative to the obstruction mask to account for the relative solar azimuth.) The number of dots visible in the opening area determines the sky component of the daylight factor at that location.

IES LUMEN METHOD

The "lumen method" recommended by the Illuminating Engineering Society of North America (Kaufman, 1984) for predicting daylight illumination is empirically based on a process of interpolating actual test data. As such, its accuracy is limited to the general type of room, fenestration, and conditions actually tested (that is, the top of the window is at the ceiling level, the sill is at the desk height, the window width is equal to the room length, etc.).

Interior illumination is determined by calculating the contributions of various components (various windows, skylights, sky and ground contributions, etc.) and then adding them together.

The method can be extended to bilateral daylighting where the windows are on opposite walls (calculate separately and add together); the method is not applicable where there are windows on adjacent walls (because the three locations where illuminance is calculated would not coincide).

Lumen method — sidelighting

The IES lumen method for sidelighting is outlined in the worksheet example in Fig. 24.9 (see Appendix F for blank worksheet; for a more detailed explanation, especially regarding other methods for considering the effects of

overhangs and draperies, see Kaufman, 1984). The side window calculations yield illuminances at three locations in the room in the horizontal workplane 30 in. above the floor: "maximum" (5 ft from the window), "middle," and "minimum" (5 ft from the wall opposite the window).

Lumen method — toplighting

The IES lumen method for toplighting determines the average illuminance on the workplane due to horizontal (or near-horizontal) roof openings. The procedure is outlined in the worksheet example in Fig. 24.10 (see Appendix F for blank worksheet).

Table 24.3: Room Coefficients of Utilization for Toplighting
(Based on 20 percent floor reflectance)

Ceiling Reflectance (percent)	RCR	Wall Reflectance		
		50 percent	30 percent	10 percent
80	0	1.19	1.19	1.19
	1	1.05	1.00	0.97
	2	0.93	0.86	0.81
	3	0.83	0.76	0.70
	4	0.75	0.67	0.60
	5	0.67	0.59	0.53
	6	0.62	0.53	0.47
	7	0.57	0.49	0.43
	8	0.54	0.47	0.41
	9	0.53	0.46	0.41
	10	0.52	0.45	0.40
50	0	1.11	1.11	1.11
	1	0.98	0.95	0.92
	2	0.87	0.83	0.78
	3	0.79	0.73	0.68
	4	0.71	0.64	0.59
	5	0.64	0.57	0.52
	6	0.59	0.52	0.47
	7	0.55	0.48	0.43
	8	0.52	0.46	0.41
	9	0.51	0.45	0.40
	10	0.50	0.44	0.40
20	0	1.04	1.04	1.04
	1	0.92	0.90	0.88
	2	0.83	0.79	0.76
	3	0.75	0.70	0.66
	4	0.68	0.62	0.58
	5	0.61	0.56	0.51
	6	0.57	0.51	0.46
	7	0.53	0.47	0.43
	8	0.51	0.45	0.41
	9	0.50	0.44	0.40
	10	0.49	0.44	0.40

(Reproduced from Kaufman, 1984, by permission.)

SIDELIGHTING DAYLIGHT ILLUMINANCE WORKSHEET (Lumen Method)

Project __Example__   Analyst __FM__   Location __Oxford, OH__ .

Date to be analyzed (circle one): Jun 21; (Mar/Sep 21) Dec 21; Time (circle one): 8 a.m. 10 a.m. (noon) 2 p.m. 4 p.m.

Room Length (parallel to window) = __30__ ; Room Width = __20__ ; Ceiling Height = __10__ ; Wall Reflectance = __70__ %

Latitude = __38__ ; Predominant sky condition (circle one): clear / (overcast) Window facing direction (N, E, S, W) __E__ .

1. Enter the vertical illuminance from the sky on the glazing surface for the predominant sky condition for the above date and time (either clear diffuse from Table 24.5, or overcast from Table 24.4; do not include direct sun) __7__ kilolux × 100 fc/kilolux = E_s = __700__ fc

2. Determine the ground reflectance, (typically 0.2; 0.6 for snow) = ρ_g = __0.2__

3. Determine the total horizontal illuminance on the ground for the predominant sky condition (due to both sun and sky; from Table 24.6) __32__ kilolux × 100 fc/kilolux = E_h = __3200__ fc

4. Calculate vertical illuminance due to ground = $E_h \times \rho_g \times 0.5$ = (__3200__)(__0.2__)(__0.5__) = E_g = __320__ fc

5. Enter the gross window area A_w above the 30 in. workplane height = E_h = __150__ ft²

6. Estimate the mullion factor, MF = reduction factor applied to gross window area to allow for mullions and other obstructions in the window plane (0.75 is typical; that is 25% of the window is obstructed by mullions, 75% is glass area). MF = __0.8__

7. Calculate net glazing area = (A_w)(MF) = (__150__)(__0.8__) = A_g = __120__ ft²

8. Determine the net transmittance, T_{net} (less than 1.0, it is the product of such light loss factors as glazing transmittance, dirt factor, drapery transmittance, etc.; for example, double-glazed clear glass in an office building with no draperies has a net transmittance of about 0.65; single-glazed clear glass in a factory with no draperies has a net transmittance of about 0.55). T_{net} = __0.65__ .

9. From Table 24.7 a or b, look-up C_{max}, C_{mid}, C_{min}, K_{max}, K_{mid}, and K_{min} sky-contributed coefficients of utilization:

   Sky-contributed: C_{max} = __.0143__ ; C_{mid} = __.010__ ; C_{min} = __.0079__ ; K_{max} = __.129__ ; K_{mid} = __.116__ ; and K_{min} = __.112__

10. From Table 24.7 c or d, look-up C_{max}, C_{mid}, C_{min}, K_{max}, K_{mid}, and K_{min} ground-contributed coefficients of utilization.

    Ground-contributed: C_{max} = __.0102__; C_{mid} = __.0094__; C_{min} = __.0082__; K_{max} = __.140__; K_{mid} = __.122__; and K_{min} = __.110__

11. Sky-contributed $E_{int, sky}$ at Max = $(E_s)(A_g)(T_{net})(C)(K)$ = (__700__)(__120__)(__.65__)(__.014__)(__.13__) = __99__ fc

    Ground-contributed $E_{int, gnd}$ at Max = $(E_g)(A_g)(T_{net})(C)(K)$ = (__320__)(__120__)(__.65__)(__.01__)(__.14__) = __100__ fc

    Total interior illuminance E_{int} at Max = $(E_{int, sky})$ + $(E_{int, gnd})$ = __199__ fc

12. Sky-contributed $E_{int, sky}$ at Mid = $(E_s)(A_g)(T_{net})(C)(K)$ = (__700__)(__120__)(__.65__)(__.01__)(__.12__) = __65__ fc

    Ground-contributed $E_{int, gnd}$ at Mid = $(E_g)(A_g)(T_{net})(C)(K)$ = (__320__)(__120__)(__.65__)(__.01__)(__.12__) = __86__ fc

    Total interior illuminance E_{int} at Mid = $(E_{int, sky})$ + $(E_{int, gnd})$ = __151__ fc

13. Sky-contributed $E_{int, sky}$ at Min = $(E_s)(A_g)(T_{net})(C)(K)$ = (__700__)(__120__)(__.65__)(__.008__)(__.11__) = __48__ fc

    Ground-contributed $E_{int, gnd}$ at Min = $(E_g)(A_g)(T_{net})(C)(K)$ = (__320__)(__120__)(__.65__)(__.0082__)(__.11__) = __65__ fc

    Total interior illuminance E_{int} at Min = $(E_{int, sky})$ + $(E_{int, gnd})$ = __113__ fc

Figure 24.9: Sidelighting daylight illuminance calculation worksheet example (lumen method; blank worksheet in Appendix F).

TOPLIGHTING DAYLIGHT ILLUMINANCE WORKSHEET (Lumen Method)

Project __Example__ Analyst __FM__ Latitude = __38__ ; Sky condition (circle one): clear / (Overcast)

Date to be analyzed (circle one): Jun 21, (Mar/Sep 21) Dec 21; Time (circle one): 8 a.m. (10 a.m.) noon 2 p.m. 4 p.m.

Room length = __30__ ft; Room width = __20__ ft; Ceiling height = __10__ ft; Wall reflectance = __50__ %

Ceiling reflectance = __80__ % ; Number of skylights __6__ ; Skylight gross area (each) __4__ ft²; Skylight well height __1.5__ ft

Skylight well width, __2__ ft; Skylight well length __2__ ft; Skylight well reflectance __80__ %

1. Determine the exterior horizontal illuminance, E_h (use total of direct sun plus sky for
   clear conditions; from Table 24.6) __15__ kilolux × 100 fc/kilolux = E_h = __1500__ fc

2. Calculate total gross area of skylights, A_t = (gross area of one skylight)(# of skylights) = A_t = __24__ ft²

3. Determine the T_g = transmittance of the glazing medium (from manufacturer's literature,
   or assume 0.85 for clear double domes and 0.44 for translucent double domes) = T_g = __0.85__

4. Calculate the skylight well index, WI = $\dfrac{\text{(height)(width + height)}}{2\text{(width)(length)}} = \dfrac{(1.5)(2+2)}{2(2)(2)}$ = WI = __0.75__

5. Determine the well efficiency, N_w (from Fig. 24.11) N_w = __0.65__

6. Estimate the mullion factor, MF = reduction factor applied to gross window area to
   allow for mullions and other obstructions in the skylight (0.75 is typical; that is 25% of
   the window is obstructed by mullions, 75% is glass area). MF = __0.8__

7. Determine the transmittance of any controls, T_c (louvers, for example; 1.0 if none) = T_c = __1.0__

8. Determine the net transmittance, T_{net} = (T_g) (N_w) (MF) (T_c) = (__.85__) (__.65__) (__0.8__) (__1.0__) = T_{net} = __0.442__

9. Calculate RCR = $\dfrac{5\text{(room height} - \text{workplane height)(room width + room length)}}{\text{(room length)(room width)}}$ =
   $\dfrac{5(10 - 2.5)(20 + 30)}{(30)(20)}$ = RCR = __3.125__

10. Look-up the room coefficient of utilization, RCU (Table 24.3) = RCU = __0.82__

11. Calculate the utilization coefficient, K_u = (RCU) (T_{net}) = (__3.125__)(__0.442__) = K_u = __1.38__

12. Calculate the light loss factor: K_m = skylight and room wall dirt depreciation factors
    (typically between 0.4 for factories and 0.8 for offices) = K_m = __0.8__

13. Workplane average illuminance:
    $E_{wp} = \dfrac{(E_h)(A_t)(K_u)(K_m)}{\text{(room length)(room width)}} = \dfrac{(1500)(24)(1.38)(0.8)}{(30)(20)}$ = E_{wp} = __66.2__ fc

comments:

Figure 24.10: Toplighting daylight illuminance calculation worksheet example (lumen method; blank worksheet in Appendix F).

Table 24.4: Exterior Vertical Illuminance on a Clear Day, in Kilolux
(Multiply by 100 for Footcandles.) *(Reproduced from Kaufman, 1984, by permission.)*

Latitude (degrees north)	Component	December 21					March and September 21					June 21				
		8 AM	10 AM	Noon	2 PM	4 PM	8 AM	10 AM	Noon	2 PM	4 PM	8 AM	10 AM	Noon	2 PM	4 PM
Facing North																
30	Direct	0	0	0	0	0	0	0	0	0	0	10	0	0	0	10
	Diffuse	3	4	4	4	3	6	6	5	6	6	8	7	7	7	8
	Total	3	4	4	4	3	6	6	5	6	6	18	7	7	7	18
34	Direct	0	0	0	0	0	0	0	0	0	0	6	0	0	0	6
	Diffuse	3	4	4	4	3	5	5	5	5	5	8	7	6	7	8
	Total	3	4	4	4	3	5	5	5	5	5	14	7	6	7	14
38	Direct	0	0	0	0	0	0	0	0	0	0	0	0	0	0	0
	Diffuse	3	4	4	4	3	5	5	5	5	5	8	7	6	7	8
	Total	3	4	4	4	3	5	5	5	5	5	8	7	6	7	8
42	Direct	0	0	0	0	0	0	0	0	0	0	0	0	0	0	0
	Diffuse	2	3	3	3	2	5	5	5	5	5	7	6	6	6	7
	Total	2	3	3	3	2	5	5	5	5	5	7	6	6	6	7
46	Direct	0	0	0	0	0	0	0	0	0	0	0	0	0	0	0
	Diffuse	2	3	3	3	2	5	5	5	5	5	7	6	6	6	7
	Total	2	3	3	3	2	5	5	5	5	5	7	6	6	6	7
50	Direct	0	0	0	0	0	0	0	0	0	0	0	0	0	0	0
	Diffuse	0	3	3	3	0	5	5	4	5	5	7	6	6	6	7
	Total	0	3	3	3	0	5	5	4	5	5	7	6	6	6	7
Facing South																
30	Direct	26	64	74	64	26	20	42	50	42	20	0	5	11	5	0
	Diffuse	8	12	14	12	8	8	11	11	11	8	7	8	8	8	7
	Total	34	76	88	76	34	28	53	61	53	28	7	13	19	13	7
34	Direct	20	63	75	63	20	21	46	55	46	21	0	11	19	11	0
	Diffuse	8	12	14	12	8	8	11	12	11	8	7	8	8	8	7
	Total	28	75	89	75	28	29	57	67	57	29	7	19	27	19	7
38	Direct	13	61	75	61	13	23	50	60	50	23	0	17	26	17	0
	Diffuse	7	12	14	12	7	8	11	12	11	8	7	8	8	8	7
	Total	20	73	89	73	20	31	61	72	61	31	7	25	34	25	7
42	Direct	5	57	72	57	5	24	53	64	53	24	1	23	33	23	1
	Diffuse	6	12	14	12	6	8	11	13	11	8	7	9	8	9	7
	Total	11	69	86	69	11	32	64	77	64	32	8	32	41	32	8
46	Direct	0	51	68	51	0	25	56	68	56	25	5	28	40	28	5
	Diffuse	5	11	13	11	5	8	12	13	12	8	8	9	8	9	8
	Total	5	62	81	62	5	33	68	81	68	33	13	37	48	37	13
50	Direct	0	41	60	41	0	25	58	70	58	25	9	34	48	34	9
	Diffuse	5	10	12	10	5	8	12	14	12	8	7	10	7	10	7
	Total	5	51	72	51	5	33	70	84	70	33	16	44	55	44	16
Facing East																
30	Direct	36	39	0	0	0	68	48	0	0	0	69	45	0	0	0
	Diffuse	10	10	7	5	3	13	11	7	5	4	14	11	7	6	4
	Total	46	49	7	5	3	81	59	7	5	4	83	56	7	6	4
34	Direct	28	37	0	0	0	67	48	0	0	0	69	45	0	0	0
	Diffuse	9	10	7	5	2	13	11	7	5	3	14	11	7	6	4
	Total	37	47	7	5	2	80	59	7	5	3	83	56	7	6	4
38	Direct	17	35	0	0	0	65	47	0	0	0	69	44	0	0	0
	Diffuse	8	9	7	5	2	13	11	7	5	3	14	11	7	6	4
	Total	25	44	7	5	2	78	58	7	5	3	83	55	7	6	4
42	Direct	6	32	0	0	0	63	46	0	0	0	69	44	0	0	0
	Diffuse	7	9	8	5	2	13	11	8	5	3	14	11	7	6	4
	Total	13	41	8	5	2	76	57	8	5	3	83	55	7	6	4
46	Direct	0	27	0	0	0	60	45	0	0	0	69	44	0	0	0
	Diffuse	8	8	8	5	1	13	11	8	5	3	14	11	7	6	4
	Total	8	35	8	5	1	73	56	8	5	3	83	55	7	6	4
50	Direct	0	22	0	0	0	56	44	0	0	0	67	44	0	0	0
	Diffuse	8	8	7	4	0	13	11	7	5	3	16	11	7	6	4
	Total	8	30	7	4	0	69	55	7	5	3	83	55	7	6	4

Continued on next page.

Table 24.4 (continued): Exterior Vertical Illuminance on a Clear Day, in Kilolux
(Multiply by 100 for Footcandles.) *(Reproduced from Kaufman, 1984, by permission.)*

Facing West

Latitude (degrees north)	Component	December 21					March and September 21					June 21				
		8 AM	10 AM	Noon	2 PM	4 PM	8 AM	10 AM	Noon	2 PM	4 PM	8 AM	10 AM	Noon	2 PM	4 PM
30	Direct	0	0	0	39	36	0	0	0	48	68	0	0	0	45	69
	Diffuse	3	5	7	10	10	4	5	7	11	13	4	6	7	11	14
	Total	3	5	7	49	46	4	5	7	59	81	4	6	7	56	83
34	Direct	0	0	0	37	28	0	0	0	48	67	0	0	0	45	69
	Diffuse	2	5	7	10	9	3	5	7	11	13	4	6	7	11	14
	Total	2	5	7	47	37	3	5	7	59	80	4	6	7	56	83
38	Direct	0	0	0	35	17	0	0	0	47	65	0	0	0	44	69
	Diffuse	2	5	7	9	8	3	5	7	11	13	4	6	7	11	14
	Total	2	5	7	44	25	3	5	7	58	78	4	6	7	55	83
42	Direct	0	0	0	32	6	0	0	0	46	63	0	0	0	44	69
	Diffuse	2	4	7	9	7	3	5	8	11	13	4	6	7	11	14
	Total	2	4	7	41	13	3	5	8	57	76	4	6	7	55	83
46	Direct	0	0	0	27	0	0	0	0	45	60	0	0	0	44	69
	Diffuse	1	4	6	8	5	3	5	8	11	12	4	6	7	11	14
	Total	1	4	6	35	5	3	5	8	56	72	4	6	7	55	83
50	Direct	0	0	0	22	0	0	0	0	44	57	0	0	0	44	69
	Diffuse	0	4	6	8	0	3	5	7	11	12	4	6	7	11	14
	Total	0	4	6	30	0	3	5	7	55	69	4	6	7	55	83

* Atmospheric extinction coefficient = 0.21.
† More exact multiplier is 92.9.

Table 24.5: Exterior Vertical Illuminance Facing Any Direction an Overcast Day, in Kilolux
(Multiply by 100 for Footcandles.) *(Reproduced from Kaufman, 1984, by permission.)*

Latitude (degrees north)	Component	December 21					March and September 21					June 21				
		8 AM	10 AM	Noon	2 PM	4 PM	8 AM	10 AM	Noon	2 PM	4 PM	8 AM	10 AM	Noon	2 PM	4 PM
30	Direct	0	0	0	0	0	0	0	0	0	0	0	0	0	0	0
	Diffuse	2	4	5	4	2	4	6	7	6	4	5	8	8	8	5
	Total	2	4	5	4	2	4	6	7	6	4	5	8	8	8	5
34	Direct	0	0	0	0	0	0	0	0	0	0	0	0	0	0	0
	Diffuse	1	4	5	4	1	4	6	7	6	4	5	7	8	7	5
	Total	1	4	5	4	1	4	6	7	6	4	5	7	8	7	5
38	Direct	0	0	0	0	0	0	0	0	0	0	0	0	0	0	0
	Diffuse	1	3	4	3	1	3	6	7	6	3	5	7	8	7	5
	Total	1	3	4	3	1	3	6	7	6	3	5	7	8	7	5
42	Direct	0	0	0	0	0	0	0	0	0	0	0	0	0	0	0
	Diffuse	1	3	4	3	1	3	5	6	5	3	5	7	8	7	5
	Total	1	3	4	3	1	3	5	6	5	3	5	7	8	7	5
46	Direct	0	0	0	0	0	0	0	0	0	0	0	0	0	0	0
	Diffuse	0	2	3	2	0	3	5	6	5	3	5	7	8	7	5
	Total	0	2	3	2	0	3	5	6	5	3	5	7	8	7	5
50	Direct	0	0	0	0	0	0	0	0	0	0	0	0	0	0	0
	Diffuse	0	2	2	2	0	3	5	5	5	3	5	7	8	7	5
	Total	0	2	2	2	0	3	5	5	5	3	5	7	8	7	5

* Typical nonprecipitative minimum.
† More exact multiplier is 92.9.

Table 24.6: Exterior Horizontal Illuminance, in Kilolux
(Multiply by 100* for Footcandles.) *(Reproduced from Kaufman, 1984, by permission.)*

Latitude (degrees north)	Component	December 21			March and September 21			June 21		
		8 AM 4 PM	10 AM 2 PM	Noon	8 AM 4 PM	10 AM 2 PM	Noon	8 AM 4 PM	10 AM 2 PM	Noon
Clear Day†										
30	Direct	9	42	55	34	72	87	52	86	99
	Diffuse	8	12	13	11	14	15	13	15	16
	Total	17	54	68	45	86	102	65	101	115
34	Direct	5	35	48	32	68	82	52	86	98
	Diffuse	7	11	12	11	14	15	13	15	16
	Total	12	46	60	43	82	97	65	101	114
38	Direct	3	29	41	29	64	77	53	84	96
	Diffuse	6	10	12	11	14	15	13	15	16
	Total	9	39	53	40	78	92	66	99	112
42	Direct	1	22	33	27	59	71	53	83	94
	Diffuse	5	10	11	10	13	14	13	15	16
	Total	6	32	44	37	72	85	66	98	110
46	Direct	0	16	25	24	54	65	53	80	91
	Diffuse	4	9	10	10	13	14	13	15	16
	Total	4	25	35	34	67	79	66	95	107
50	Direct	0	10	18	21	49	59	52	78	87
	Diffuse	0	8	9	10	12	13	13	15	15
	Total	0	18	27	31	61	72	65	93	102
Partly Cloudy Day‡										
30	Direct	0	13	20	9	33	44	19	44	55
	Diffuse	9	22	27	20	34	39	27	40	45
	Total	9	35	47	29	67	83	46	84	100
34	Direct	0	9	16	8	30	40	20	44	54
	Diffuse	7	20	25	19	33	38	27	40	45
	Total	7	29	41	27	63	78	47	84	99
38	Direct	0	6	12	7	27	36	20	43	52
	Diffuse	6	17	22	18	31	36	28	39	44
	Total	6	23	34	25	58	72	48	82	96
42	Direct	0	4	8	6	24	32	20	42	50
	Diffuse	4	15	19	17	29	34	28	39	43
	Total	4	19	27	23	53	66	48	81	93
46	Direct	0	2	5	4	20	28	20	40	48
	Diffuse	2	12	16	16	27	32	28	38	42
	Total	2	14	21	20	47	60	48	78	90
50	Direct	0	1	2	3	17	24	19	38	45
	Diffuse	0	10	13	15	25	29	27	37	41
	Total	0	11	15	18	42	53	46	75	86
Overcast Day§										
30	Direct	0	0	0	0	0	0	0	0	0
	Diffuse	4	11	13	9	16	18	13	19	21
	Total	4	11	13	9	16	18	13	19	21
34	Direct	0	0	0	0	0	0	0	0	0
	Diffuse	4	9	12	9	15	18	13	19	21
	Total	4	9	12	9	15	18	13	19	21
38	Direct	0	0	0	0	0	0	0	0	0
	Diffuse	3	8	10	8	15	17	13	19	21
	Total	3	8	10	8	15	17	13	19	21
42	Direct	0	0	0	0	0	0	0	0	0
	Diffuse	2	7	9	8	14	16	13	18	20
	Total	2	7	9	8	14	16	13	18	20
46	Direct	0	0	0	0	0	0	0	0	0
	Diffuse	1	6	8	8	13	15	13	18	20
	Total	1	6	8	8	13	15	13	18	20
50	Direct	0	0	0	0	0	0	0	0	0
	Diffuse	0	5	6	7	12	14	13	17	19
	Total	0	5	6	7	12	14	13	17	19

Table 24.7: Coefficients of Utilization: "C" and "K" Factors
(Ceiling Reflectance = 80%; Floor Reflectance = 30%.) *(Reproduced from Kaufman, 1984, by permission.)*

A. Illuminance from an overcast sky, without window controls

C — Room Length / Wall Reflectance (per cent) / Room Width

Pos	Room Width (M)	(FT)	6.1 M (20 FT) 70	30	9.1 M (30 FT) 70	30	12.2 M (40 FT) 70	30
MAX	6.1	20	.0276	.0251	.0191	.0173	.0143	.0137
	9.1	30	.0272	.0248	.0188	.0172	.0137	.0131
	12.2	40	.0269	.0246	.0182	.0171	.0133	.0130
MID	6.1	20	.0159	.0117	.0101	.0087	.0081	.0071
	9.1	30	.0058	.0050	.0054	.0040	.0034	.0033
	12.2	40	.0039	.0027	.0030	.0023	.0022	.0019
MIN	6.1	20	.0087	.0053	.0063	.0043	.0050	.0037
	9.1	30	.0032	.0019	.0029	.0017	.0020	.0014
	12.2	40	.0019	.0009	.0016	.0009	.0012	.0008

K — Ceiling Height / Wall Reflectance (per cent) / Room Width

Pos	Room Width (M)	(FT)	2.4 M (8 FT) 70	30	3 M (10 FT) 70	30	3.7 M (12 FT) 70	30	4.3 M (14 FT) 70	30
MAX	6.1	20	.125	.129	.121	.123	.111	.111	.0991	.0973
	9.1	30	.122	.131	.122	.121	.111	.111	.0945	.0973
	12.2	40	.145	.133	.131	.126	.111	.111	.0973	.0982
MID	6.1	20	.0908	.0982	.107	.115	.111	.111	.105	.122
	9.1	30	.156	.102	.0939	.113	.111	.111	.121	.134
	12.2	40	.106	.0948	.123	.107	.111	.111	.135	.127
MIN	6.1	20	.0908	.102	.0951	.114	.111	.111	.118	.134
	9.1	30	.0924	.119	.101	.114	.111	.111	.125	.126
	12.2	40	.111	.0926	.125	.109	.111	.111	.133	.130

B. Illuminance from a clear sky, without window controls

C

Pos	Room Width (M)	(FT)	6.1 M (20 FT) 70	30	9.1 M (30 FT) 70	30	12.2 M (40 FT) 70	30
MAX	6.1	20	.0206	.0173	.0143	.0123	.0110	.0098
	9.1	30	.0203	.0173	.0137	.0120	.0098	.0092
	12.2	40	.0200	.0168	.0131	.0119	.0096	.0091
MID	6.1	20	.0153	.0104	.0100	.0079	.0083	.0067
	9.1	30	.0082	.0054	.0062	.0043	.0046	.0037
	12.2	40	.0052	.0032	.0040	.0028	.0029	.0023
MIN	6.1	20	.0106	.0060	.0079	.0049	.0067	.0043
	9.1	30	.0054	.0028	.0047	.0023	.0032	.0021
	12.2	40	.0031	.0014	.0027	.0013	.0012	.0012

K

Pos	Room Width (M)	(FT)	2.4 M (8 FT) 70	30	3 M (10 FT) 70	30	3.7 M (12 FT) 70	30	4.3 M (14 FT) 70	30
MAX	6.1	20	.145	.155	.129	.132	.111	.111	.101	.0982
	9.1	30	.141	.149	.125	.130	.111	.111	.0954	.101
	12.2	40	.157	.157	.135	.134	.111	.111	.0964	.0991
MID	6.1	20	.110	.128	.116	.126	.111	.111	.103	.108
	9.1	30	.106	.125	.110	.129	.111	.111	.112	.120
	12.2	40	.117	.118	.122	.118	.111	.111	.123	.122
MIN	6.1	20	.105	.129	.112	.130	.111	.111	.111	.116
	9.1	30	.0994	.144	.107	.126	.111	.111	.107	.116
	12.2	40	.111	.116	.130	.118	.111	.111	.120	.118

C. Illuminance from a uniform ground, without window controls

C

Pos	Room Width (M)	(FT)	6.1 M (20 FT) 70	30	9.1 M (30 FT) 70	30	12.2 M (40 FT) 70	30
MAX	6.1	20	.0147	.0112	.0102	.0088	.0081	.0071
	9.1	30	.0141	.0112	.0098	.0088	.0077	.0070
	12.2	40	.0137	.0112	.0093	.0086	.0072	.0069
MID	6.1	20	.0128	.0090	.0094	.0071	.0073	.0060
	9.1	30	.0083	.0057	.0062	.0048	.0050	.0041
	12.2	40	.0055	.0037	.0044	.0033	.0042	.0026
MIN	6.1	20	.0106	.0071	.0082	.0054	.0067	.0044
	9.1	30	.0051	.0026	.0041	.0023	.0033	.0021
	12.2	40	.0029	.0018	.0026	.0012	.0012	.0011

K

Pos	Room Width (M)	(FT)	2.4 M (8 FT) 70	30	3 M (10 FT) 70	30	3.7 M (12 FT) 70	30	4.3 M (14 FT) 70	30
MAX	6.1	20	.124	.206	.140	.135	.111	.111	.0909	.0859
	9.1	30	.182	.188	.140	.143	.111	.111	.0918	.0878
	12.2	40	.124	.182	.140	.142	.111	.111	.0936	.0879
MID	6.1	20	.123	.145	.122	.129	.111	.111	.100	.0945
	9.1	30	.0966	.104	.107	.112	.111	.111	.110	.105
	12.2	40	.0790	.0786	.0999	.106	.111	.111	.118	.118
MIN	6.1	20	.0994	.108	.110	.114	.111	.111	.107	.104
	9.1	30	.0816	.0822	.0984	.105	.111	.111	.121	.116
	12.2	40	.0700	.0656	.0946	.0986	.111	.111	.125	.132

D. Illuminance from the "uniform sky", without diffuse window shades

C

Pos	Room Width (M)	(FT)	6.1 M (20 FT) 70	30	9.1 M (30 FT) 70	30	12.2 M (40 FT) 70	30
MAX	6.1	20	.0247	.0217	.0174	.0152	.0128	.0120
	9.1	30	.0241	.0214	.0166	.0151	.0120	.0116
	12.2	40	.0237	.0212	.0161	.0150	.0118	.0113
MID	6.1	20	.0169	.0122	.0110	.0092	.0089	.0077
	9.1	30	.0078	.0060	.0067	.0044	.0044	.0041
	12.2	40	.0053	.0033	.0039	.0028	.0028	.0024
MIN	6.1	20	.0108	.0066	.0080	.0052	.0063	.0047
	9.1	30	.0047	.0026	.0042	.0023	.0029	.0020
	12.2	40	.0027	.0013	.0022	.0012	.0018	.0011

K

Pos	Room Width (M)	(FT)	2.4 M (8 FT) 70	30	3 M (10 FT) 70	30	3.7 M (12 FT) 70	30	4.3 M (14 FT) 70	30
MAX	6.1	20	.145	.154	.123	.128	.111	.111	.0991	.0964
	9.1	30	.141	.151	.126	.128	.111	.111	.0945	.0964
	12.2	40	.159	.157	.137	.127	.111	.111	.0973	.0964
MID	6.1	20	.116	.116	.115	.125	.111	.111	.101	.110
	9.1	30	.0952	.113	.105	.122	.111	.111	.110	.122
	12.2	40	.111	.105	.124	.107	.111	.111	.130	.124
MIN	6.1	20	.0974	.111	.107	.121	.111	.111	.112	.119
	9.1	30	.0956	.125	.103	.117	.111	.111	.115	.125
	12.2	40	.111	.105	.125	.111	.111	.111	.133	.124

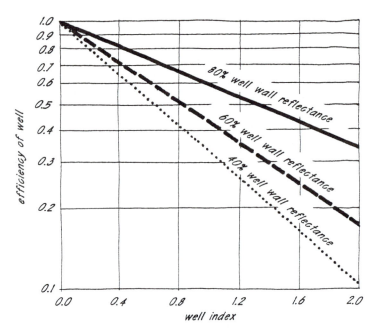

Figure 24.11: Skylight well efficiency factors for various depths of skylight wells. *(Reproduced from Kaufman, 1984, by permission.)*

PHYSICAL MODELS

Models provide a means of accurately predicting interior daylight illumination in buildings. Unlike most other physical models where the behavior of the phenomenon does not scale down properly (for example, thermal conduction, structural bending, acoustics, and airflow), light model studies require no scaling correction. A daylighting model that exactly duplicates a full-scale building space, if tested under identical sky conditions, will yield identical results. Although it is not always practical to exactly duplicate a full-scale space, the advantages of using physical scale models can significantly outweigh the disadvantages.

These advantages include:

• Accurate, quantitative results, even when crude models are used.

• Ease of making comparisons by changing a single design component.

• Familiarity of most designers with constructing and using scale models.

• Opportunity for qualitative evaluation (such as identification of potential glare problems and client demonstration) through visual observation or photography.

Disadvantages include:

• Cost of model (in labor and material).

• Time required to construct and test.

• Accurate instrumentation required.

• Either waiting for suitable weather for outdoor testing or artificial sky simulator required.

It is essential that sky exposure and obstruction geometry be accurate if models are to be used for daylighting analysis. Sectional models (where one wall or the ceiling is removed) that are often used for other architectural studies obviously admit extraneous light and are thus useless for illumination analysis. Similarly, by observing a model interior through window openings, the observer's head (or camera) becomes a significant obstruction. It is thus essential that observation intrusion be considered and minimized throughout the design, construction, and use of daylight models.

CONSTRUCTION

Because most models will be used for design purposes to compare various alternatives, the construction should be modular to accommodate inserts representing the competing configurations. For example, in comparisons of sidewall configurations, the entire sidewall may be replaceable. To vary room heights, either the floor or ceiling should be adjustable.

Special care should be taken to detail accurately all fenestration. The three-dimensional aspects of openings and mullions should be reproduced. Care should be taken to eliminate extraneous light from entering (or leaving) the interior. Model surface reflectances should match those of the building. For quantitative studies, shades of gray can be used; for qualitative studies colors should be used.

Clear glazing materials can be omitted from the model (and a correction factor applied to the interior measurements at a later time); for translucent materials, glazing can be represented by the actual material (full thickness) or by an acrylic plastic of similar transmittance.

TESTING

Daylight model testing can be conducted under a real or artificial sky.

Testing under a real sky is the cheapest and easiest to perform. However, unpredictable weather and sky conditions change absolute interior illuminances considerably. Even on two "identical" days, sky luminance measurements will typically vary more than 15 percent. For that reason, it is recommended that relative illuminance (i.e., daylight factor) measurements be used as a basis for comparing alternative designs. Sun angles throughout the year can be simulated by tilting the model relative to the sun to achieve the desired solar altitude and azimuth angle.

To control the problems associated with varying and unpredictable sky conditions, many daylight researchers prefer to work with an artificial sky that approximates the luminance distribution of an "ideal" overcast sky (that is, the 1 to 3 CIE standard overcast sky luminance distribution).

One type of artificial sky in general use is the hemispherical dome. Domes are usually opaque white and illuminated by interior perimeter lights. The model is located in the center and receives reflected light from the surrounding dome in a manner similar to a building receiving light from an overcast sky.

A less expensive alternative to the artificial sky dome is a mirror box. It combines a luminous "ceiling" and mirror walls to create a sky with an "infinite" horizon as a result of multiple interreflections. Because some light is absorbed with each mirror reflection, this configuration tends to approximate naturally the luminance distribution of an overcast sky (brighter at the zenith than at the horizon). The height-to-width ratio of the box controls the actual luminance distribution.

While a large (room-sized) box can be used, allowing the insertion of a freestanding model, most are smaller with the model window exposed to the box interior through an opening in one mirror wall. Such boxes can be modified to allow a portion of the model to penetrate into the box (thus allowing skylights to be tested).

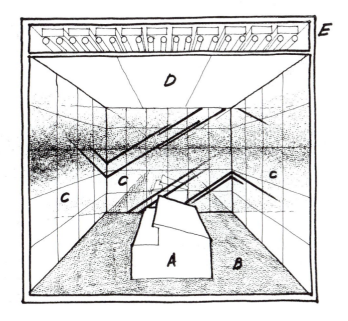

Figure 24.13: Section perspective, mirror box artificial sky: (a) model, (b) gray ground plane, (c) mirror walls, (d) translucent diffuser, and (e) fluorescent lamps. *(After Moore, 1985.)*

MEASUREMENT

An important (and expensive) aspect of physical modeling is the need for accurate and convenient measurement of interior and exterior model illuminances. These measurements are taken with a cosine-corrected, color-

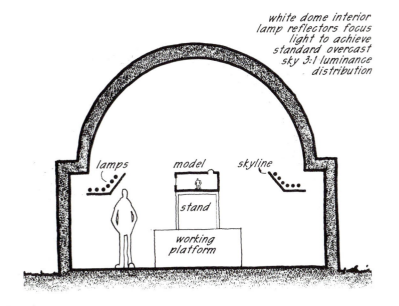

white dome interior lamp reflectors focus light to achieve standard overcast sky 3:1 luminance distribution

lamps *model* *skyline*

stand

working platform

Figure 24.12: A typical dome artificial sky used to simulate CIE standard overcast sky.

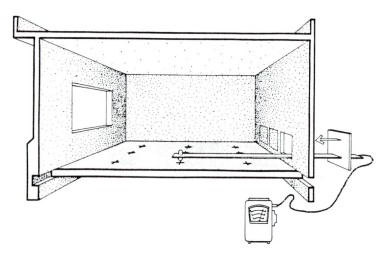

Figure 24.14: Remote photosensor mounted on a stick to facilitate placement at model reference locations (care should be taken to exclude extraneous light through these wall openings. *(Reproduced from Moore, 1985, by permission.)*

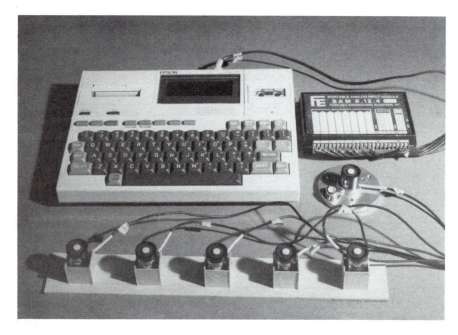

Figure 24.15: Multisensor photometer for model measurements. *(Photo courtesy of Fowlkes Engineering, Bozeman, Montana.)*

corrected photometer. Cosine correction is necessary to measure illuminance in a plane. (Incident-reading photographic meters incorporate a hemispherical diffuser, are intentionally not cosine-corrected, and are not suitable for lighting measurements.) Color-correction requires that sensitivity match that of the human eye. (Ordinary photocells and solar pyranometers are sensitive to ultraviolet and infrared as well as visible radiation, and are thus unsuited for lighting measurements.)

Most hand-held meters (which incorporate the sensor and the display in the same enclosure) are poorly suited for model studies because of their large size, and because of the difficulty in observing the readings without obstructing the windows. If such a meter must be used, it should be inserted through an opening in the floor of the model, allowing the display to project below for observation. Ensure that extraneous light through the opening is minimized by use of a shielding "skirt" fitted around the neck of the meter.

Sensors which are remote (on a wire) from the display are a desirable alternative to the self-contained meter. Multisensor photometers allow near-simultaneous measurements to be made at several locations inside and outside the model, saving time and minimizing the effect of changing sky conditions. Multisensor photometers can be combined with a data acquisition microcomputer to facilitate calibration in the field, storing data on cassette or paper tape, and simultaneous data analysis to compute and plot daylight factors, etc.

SELECTING THE BEST METHOD

Rules of thumb are best used for the very earliest design studies to determine room depths, buildings widths, and the approximate window areas needed.

Protractor methods described above have one major advantage over other methods (such as the lumen method described earlier in this chapter): they provide the designer with a direct visual representation of the various factors affecting interior illumination. For example, it is obvious in these methods how different locations in the room "see" a different angular size of the window opening. The geometric effect of overhangs and external obstructions is self-evident. The results of this graphic analysis are so immediate that the protractor can actually be used as a design tool to suggest aperture size and location necessary to provide a required daylight factor. Protractors for overcast conditions are simple to use, but are better suited for the climate of Great Britain (where they were developed) than for much of the United States. The necessarily complex clear sky protractors lose the very simplicity that makes the overcast protractors so useful in the early design stages.

The lumen method has the advantage of applicability in either clear or overcast conditions and is most useful for determining the maximum and minimum range of illumination within a space. It lacks the ability of protractors to take into account the geometric effects of unusual inside or outside obstructions. It also lacks the visual representation of the design factors involved. It is best suited for simple room shapes which closely approximate the standard conditions upon which the method is based.

Physical models provide the best method for predicting illumination in unusual room shapes or when complex fenestration is used. They provide the only method for assessing the qualitative aspects of the design (visual comfort, view). They require that design alternatives be identified prior to constructing the model. Models are expensive (in terms of construction and instrumentation), but this cost is small in comparison with the cost of constructing an actual building with a daylighting systems that does not work as anticipated.

ANNUAL SAVINGS DUE TO DAYLIGHTING

The preceding portions of this chapter address estimating the quantity of daylight illumination at one specific instant in time. They have attempted to define the illumination performance of a building design under a set of prescribed sky conditions (overcast or clear). This results in "if....then" type conclusions. "*If* a 1000-fL equivalent overcast sky condition exists, *then* daylight illuminance at a point will be 27 fc, and 13 fc additional electric illumination is required to reach the design illuminance." While these if...then conclusions are useful for comparing design alternatives, they tell nothing about the annual energy and cost savings that can be expected due to local climatic conditions.

To predict annual lighting energy savings, it is necessary to know the relative frequency of various sky conditions during the hours of operation of the building. The traditional method has been to base projections on the relative frequency of clear and overcast conditions as recorded by weather bureau observers. This method may be further refined if this information is available for various work-day time periods; estimates of these data have been recently developed and considerably improve the potential accuracy of such annual estimates.

Robbins and Hunter (1982) have developed a method for estimating the annual energy savings attributed to daylight based on predicting the percentage of the year that the electric lighting system is not in use. This percentage is a function of the electric lighting control strategy used (dimming or various types of switching), standard working hours, local weather data, and the amount of daylight as a daylight factor reaching a given reference point in the building. The weather data used are based on recent daylight and sunlight

availability research for selected cities in the United States. However, the method is tedious to apply manually and is best suited for microcomputer analysis.

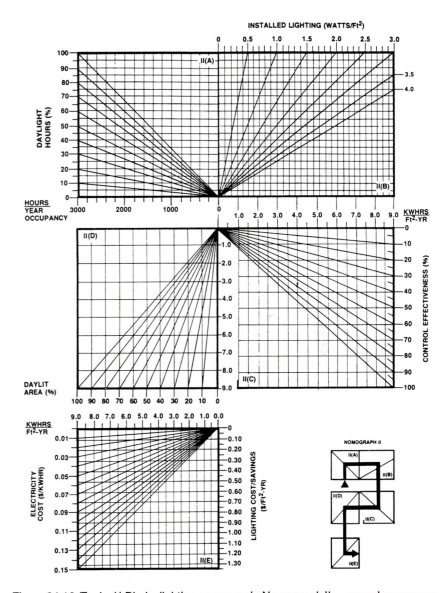

Figure 24.16: Typical LBL daylighting nomograph: Nomograph II — annual energy use and cost for daylighted vs. nondaylighted buildings. *(Reproduced courtesy of Lawrence Berkeley Laboratory, University of California.)*

LBL DAYLIGHTING NOMOGRAPHS

The daylighting nomographs developed by the Windows and Lighting Program, Lawrence Berkeley Laboratory (LBL) are an attractive alternative to the Robbins-Hunter method described above (Selkowitz and Gabel, 1983). They are intended to assist designers in making initial decisions concerning daylighting's potential as a strategy for energy conservation and load management in commercial buildings.

A nomograph is a graphic representation of the relationships that exist between several variables of a mathematical equation. It allows the user to determine quickly the numerical values in formulas having three or more variables. They have the advantage (compared with mathematical formulas) of representing relationships in a graphic format that visually reveals the relative importance of various parameters to the overall solution.

The LBL nomographs provide the designer with an all-important "feel" for energy considerations because the relative impact of the various parameters is visible graphically. Because of this, for the schematic design phase (when most of the important decisions affecting building energy usage are made), they are superior to other methods that require more detailed information and are more time-consuming to use. Moore (1985) includes the complete set of LBL nomographs with instructions for use.

SUMMARY OF TERMS

Daylight factor — the ratio of interior horizontal illuminance to exterior horizontal illuminance under an unobstructed sky, expressed as a percentage.

Sky component — the illuminance received at the interior reference point directly from the sky through the window or skylight.

External reflected component — the illuminance received at the interior reference point from reflecting exterior surfaces above the horizon (surfaces below the horizon cannot be "seen" directly from the horizontal reference plane).

Internal reflected component — the illuminance received at the interior reference point from all light reflected from interior room surfaces.

Isolux line — a line plotted on any appropriate set of coordinates to show all the points on a surface where the illuminance is the same.

BRS protractor — a protractor for computing the sky component and the external reflected component of the daylight factor directly from building plans and sections.

Dot charts — a graphic method of calculating the sky component and external reflected component of the daylight factor.

Lumen method — an empirically based method of predicting interior illuminance due to daylighting.

Artificial sky — a device for simulating the effect of daylight on a building model.

Hemispherical dome — a type of artificial sky used for simulating daylight; consists of a large dome (usually opaque white) illuminated by interior perimeter lights.

Mirror box — A type of artificial sky used for simulating daylight; combines a luminous "ceiling" and mirror walls to create a sky with an "infinite" horizon as a result of multiple interreflections.

Photometer — an instrument for measuring either illuminance (footcandle or lux meter) or luminance (luminance meter).

Cosine-corrected — a special configuration of the diffusing disk on a footcandle (lux) meter that accurately reproduces the cosine effect when measuring illuminance.

Color-corrected — the use of filters in the construction of a photometer in order for its spectral sensitivity to match that of the human eye.

Nomograph — a graphic representation of the relationships that exist between several variables of a mathematical equation.

STUDY QUESTIONS

1. What is a daylight factor and explain why it is a better measure of daylight illumination in buildings than an absolute measurement (such as footcandle)?

2. Explain the 15/30 daylighting rule.

3. Identify and explain the three components of daylight illumination that are typically summed to total the daylight factor in most calculation procedures.

4. Describe the function of "primary" and "auxiliary" BRS daylight protractors.

5. Why is it more difficult to predict the daylight factor under clear sky conditions than under overcast conditions?

6. Explain how the BRS daylight protractors and the IES daylighting lumen method are fundamentally different in the way that they were developed.

7. Describe the advantages and disadvantages of using models for daylighting analysis.

8. What are the daylighting model test environment alternatives?

9. What are the two most important features for any illuminance meter? What additional features are desirable for instruments used to test daylight models?

10. Contrast methods which predict daylight factors with those that predict annual savings due to daylighting.

25

ELECTRIC LIGHTING:

COMPONENTS

ELECTRIC LIGHT SOURCES*

"Lamp" is a man-made (usually electric) source of light. In professional use, the word "bulb" is reserved for the glass enclosure portion of the lamp, whereas "lamp" includes the base, filament, etc., as well as the bulb.

The electric lighting industry produces over 14,000 different types of lamps with applications ranging from building interiors and exteriors to roadways to parking lots to sports events. These can be divided into three categories: *incandescent filament, fluorescent,* and *high-intensity discharge (HID)*.

INCANDESCENT FILAMENT LAMPS

Incandescent filament lamps are basically a "hot wire in a bottle" and consist of the following principal components:

Bulb — an airtight transparent or translucent enclosure made of soft glass (hard glass in lamps with higher temperatures; quartz in tungsten-halogen lamps).

Filament — a coil of tungsten wire heated to incandescence by an electric current.

Filling gas — an inert gas, usually a mixture of nitrogen and argon that reduces tungsten evaporation.

Support wires — hold the filament in place.

Base — connects the lamp to an electric circuit and permits easy lamp replacement.

Selection

In most applications, incandescent lamps with a rated lamp life of 750 to 1,000 hours are the most economical. Longer-life lamps are available but are typically used only for those applications where the labor cost for lamp replacement is unusually high.

One of the best ways to compare light sources is to look at their efficacy (the lumens produced divided by input wattage). For example, a 100-W lamp that produces 1,740 lm has an efficacy of 17.4 lm/W, while a 300-W lamp that produces 6,360 lm has an efficacy of 21.2 lm/W. (As a comparison, high-pressure sodium lamps are currently one of the most efficient white light sources available, with efficacies up to 140 lm/W.)

Incandescent lamp identification

A code is used to identify each lamp type; for example: *25T10/IF 120V*. The first part of the code is the wattage. In this example, the wattage is 25 W. The

---

* Portions of this section were excerpted from IES Education Committee (1985) by permission.

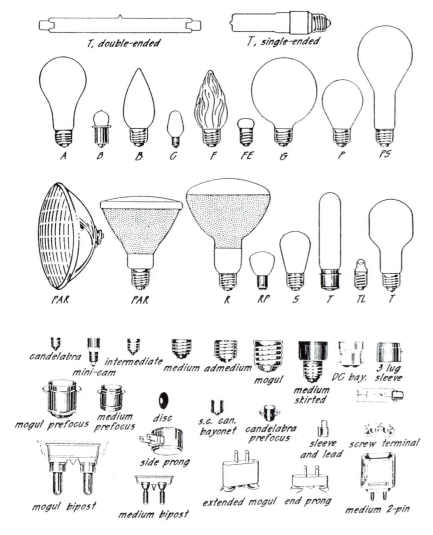

Figure 25.1: Incandescent lamp shapes and bases. *(Reproduced from IES Education Committee, 1985, by permission.)*

second part is a letter (or letters) indicating the shape of the bulb ("T" in this example). The third part is the diameter of the lamp expressed in eighths of an inch (in this example, the "10" means 10 eighths of an inch, or $1^1/_4$-inch in diameter). The next part of the code is the finish of the lamp (IF is inside frost; others include W = white, CL = clear). The last part of the code is the rated voltage (120 V in this example). The overall length is measured in inches from the top of the lamp to the bottom of the base. The lamp base is the other component of lamp identification.

Incandescent lamp types

General service lamps are the most familiar and are characterized by their A-shape bulbs; bulb finishes include *clear*, *inside frost*, and *white* (similar to inside frost but with greater diffusion).

Reflector lamps have a special shape and reflective coating to direct the light in a particular pattern. The *R-type* reflector pattern may be *flood* (a broad pattern produced by a combination of reflector shape and heavy frosting) or *spot* (a concentrated pattern produced by a deeper shape and little or no frosting). *PAR* (parabolic specular reflector) lamps are a heavier, cast-glass construction and used where more precise pattern distribution is required and for outdoor applications; PAR lamps are also available in spot and flood patterns. *ER* (elliptical reflector) is a specialized reflector lamp which reflects the light through a focus point about 2 in. in front of the lamp face, permitting less light loss in stacked baffle downlights commonly used in commercial applications. In addition, other reflector types include low-voltage PAR and R, heat-reducing PAR, and colored PAR and R.

Tungsten-halogen lamps are brighter than other incandescent lamps. In these lamps, a selected gas of the halogen family (bromine or iodine especially) is used to fill the bulb. As the lamp operates, the gas combines with the tungsten molecules that evaporate off the filament and deposits the tungsten back on the filament rather than on the bulb wall. This keeps the inside of the bulb clean and minimizes the falloff of light output throughout the service life. Because of the high temperature (over 500°F) necessary for the halogen cycle to occur, quartz is used as the preferred bulb material. Most tungsten-halogen lamps are either tubular (type T) or reflector (PAR and R types). Advantages of tungsten-halogen lamps include excellent color rendition and compact size of both filament and bulb to allow precise light focusing.

FLUORESCENT LAMPS

The first practical fluorescent lamp was introduced in 1938. Today, fluorescent lamps provide about 70 percent of the light generated in North America. While the efficacy of incandescent lamps is in the 10 to 25 lm/W, fluorescent efficacies range from 50 to 80 lm/W. Not only does this result in energy savings due to lighting, in most commercial applications this also results in energy savings due to reduced cooling loads.

Most fluorescent lamps are tubular. The inside surface of the tube is coated with fluorescent phosphors. At each end of the tube is a cathode (a type of electrode that is a coil of tungsten wire similar to the filament in an incandescent lamp). The tube also contains a small quantity of mercury and inert gas (argon, krypton, neon) at near vacuum. With the application of electric current, electrons flow from one electrode to the other. These electrons collide with the mercury atoms causing an excitation that results in the emission of invisible ultraviolet (UV) radiation. When this UV radiation strikes the phosphorus coating, the coating "fluoresces" and reradiates wavelengths in the visible spectrum. The color of the light emitted by the phosphor varies depending on the composition of the phosphor. Color and efficacy are directly related. Standard cool white is one of the most efficient (79 lm/W) but has only moderate color-rendering qualities. Warm white deluxe has superior color rendering capability at the expense of higher cost and lower efficacy (62 lm/W). Approximately 80 percent of the fluorescent lamps sold are cool white; about 10 percent are warm white, with the other colors comprising the remaining 10 percent.

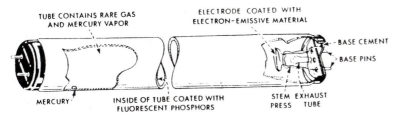

Figure 25.2: Construction of a rapid-start fluorescent lamp. *(Reproduced from IES Education Committee, 1985, by permission.)*

In addition to the conventional tubular shape, compact fluorescent lamps are available in the form of small U-tubes and double U-tubes. Some are mounted with an integral ballast and screw base and can directly replace an incandescent lamp while providing considerably higher efficacy and resulting energy savings.

Ballasts

Once the arc between the cathodes is established, resistance decreases as current increases. This creates a condition similar to a "short circuit" which if uncontrolled could destroy the lamp quickly. *Ballasts* are electrical components which limit the current while providing the proper starting and operating voltage. All ballasts produce a humming sound; the volume varies with the quality of construction and cost, and ballasts are rated from A (most quiet) to F (most noisy). While most ballasts are mounted within the luminaire (lighting fixture), they can be mounted in a remote location to reduce noise.

Ballasts are available in both high and low (normal) power factors. The wattage of each is the same, but the low-power-factor type draws nearly twice as much line current (amperes) as the high. While the initial cost of low-power-factor ballasts is lower, wiring cost could be higher, and in commercial applications, some utilities have penalties in the rate schedules for low-power-factor ballasts. Recently, dimmable ballasts have become commercially available, allowing energy costs to be reduced by the automatic dimming of fluorescent lamps as required to supplement daylight illumination.

Circuit types

Today, most fluorescent lamps are the "rapid-start" circuit type; the ballast quickly heats the cathodes and, when sufficient ionization of the lamp has occurred, the open circuit voltage strikes the arc and starts the lamp in one or two seconds. Older configurations, including "preheat" (where the cathode is preheated for several seconds by a separate circuit) and "slimline" (which apply a high voltage to initiate the arc), are still manufactured but seldom installed in new construction. While there are some exceptions, generally the lamp type and ballast type must be matched for successful operation (for example, rapid-start lamps must be used with rapid-start ballasts).

Lamp life

Fluorescent lamp life is many times that of the longest incandescent lamp and is directly related to the burning interval (hours per start) because emission material leaves the cathode with each start. While longer burning intervals lengthen lamp life, this savings is offset by the resulting increased energy cost. Traditional practice has been to leave fluorescent lamps on continuously unless they could be left off for more than 45 minutes. However, recent higher energy costs have shortened this "break-even" point; today,

Table 25.1: Common Applications of Fluorescent Lamp Types

Application	Typical Lamp Selection	Watts	Lumens	Efficacy
Office	F40CW, or	40	3150	79
	F40CW/RS/Energy Saving	34	2770	81
Super Market	F96T12/CW	75	6300	84
Discount	F96T12/CW/Energy Saving, or	60	5500	92
Department Store	F96T12/CW/HO, or	110	9150	83
	F96T12/CW/HO/ Energy Saving	95	8300	87
Warehouse	F96T12/CW/1500 mA	215	15,250	71
Light Industry	F96T12/CW/1500 mA/Energy Saving	195	13,000	67

(Reproduced from IES Education Committee, 1985, by permission.)

lamps should be turned off if the space is unoccupied for more than five minutes.

HIGH-INTENSITY DISCHARGE (HID) LAMPS

The HID lamp is similar to the fluorescent lamp in that both produce light by discharging an electrical arc through a mixture of gases and gaseous metals, both require ballasts to provide proper starting and operating voltages, and both have much higher efficacies than incandescent filament lamps. The HID lamp differs from the fluorescent in that the discharge is confined to a small arc tube and operates at greater pressure and higher brightness.

Mercury lamps

In the mercury lamp, voltage is applied to initiate an arc between a starting electrode and a nearby operating electrode within an arc tube containing argon and mercury. This arc vaporizes the mercury. After 5 to 7 min, the lamp develops full light output. Restrike (startup after a power interruption) requires a cool-down period of about 10 min to reestablish the arc. A significant portion of the energy radiated by the mercury arc is in the UV region. Phosphor coating on the inside surface of the outer bulb envelope converts some of the UV into visible light by the same process as in fluorescent lamps.

In general, the color rendition of mercury lamps is poor due to the absence of red radiation; blue, green, and yellow colors are emphasized while red and orange appear brownish. This is especially true for low- and medium-pressure lamps; the color rendition of high-pressure mercury lamps is slightly better but still poor in comparison with other lamp types.

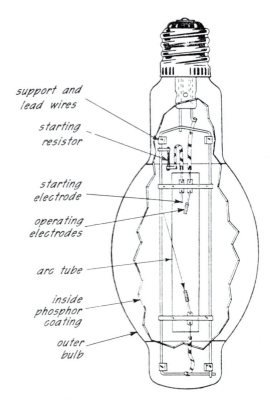

Figure 25.3: Construction of a mercury vapor lamp. (*Reproduced from Kaufman, 1984, by permission.*)

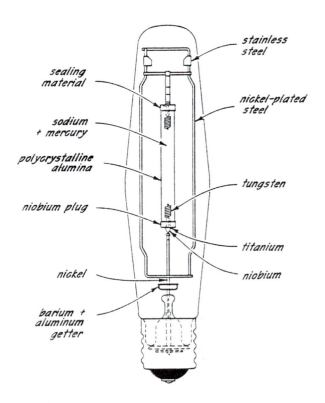

Figure 25.4: Construction of a high-pressure sodium lamp. (*Reproduced from Kaufman, 1984, by permission.*)

The three basic types of HID lamps are *mercury* (introduced about 1930), *metal halide* (about 1960), and *high-pressure sodium* (about 1965). Each has special characteristics that make it suitable for certain applications.

Mercury lamps are most commonly used for interior industrial applications and many outdoor uses such as street, general security, and floodlighting. The characteristic blue-green color is especially suited to lighting landscapes.

Metal halide lamps

Metal halide lamps are similar to mercury with the primary difference being that metal halides are added to the arc tube. These improve both the efficacy and color rendition of the lamp in comparison with mercury or high-pressure sodium, at the expense of reduced lamp life. Because metal halide lamps have several spectral components (which is responsible for the improved color rendering), color is less consistent than other HID lamps and lamp-to-lamp variations can be severe.

High-pressure sodium (HPS) lamps

In the HPS lamp, light is produced by electric current passing through sodium vapor. HPS lamps (in contrast to low-pressure sodium) have a higher percentage of red radiation and thus improved color rendition. Because of the small diameter of a HPS lamp arc tube, no starting electrode is necessary in the arc tube (as is the case with the mercury lamp). Most HPS lamps can operate in any position. HPS lamps may be "frosted" for diffusion, but phosphors (like those used in mercury and metal halide lamps) are not used because high-pressure sodium does not produce the ultraviolet radiation that is necessary to excite them. The purpose of the diffusing coating is to reduce glare when the lamps are mounted at low heights.

Dimming

Like fluorescent lamps, HID lamps are suitable for dimming as a result of recent developments in solid-state controls. This makes them suitable for integration with daylighting and can result in significant energy savings. Lamp light of dimmed HID lamps is generally as good as with undimmed lamps. The slow warmup and hot restrike delay characteristic of HID lamps also apply to dimming applications. They respond to dimming much more slowly than fluorescent or incandescent sources; the typical times required to go from maximum to minimum light output (and vice versa) are 3 to 10 min. However, as much as 50 percent variation is possible depending on HID source and lamp wattage. While not as good as fluorescent and incandescent, HID color and efficacy are reasonably good down to 50 percent lumen output, making them quite satisfactory for energy savings and daylight supplementation applications; in fact, the slow response time provides additional system stability and minimizes occupant distraction (Kaufman, 1984).

LUMINAIRES

Commonly called a "lighting fixture," a *luminaire* is the preferred professional term and is defined as a complete lighting unit consisting of a lamp or lamps together with the parts designed to distribute the light, to position and protect the lamps, and to connect the lamps to the power supply.

REFLECTION AND TRANSMISSION

As discussed in previous chapters, when light (or any radiant energy) strikes a surface, it is absorbed, reflected, and (if the material is not opaque) transmitted. In general, this transmission and reflection are primarily functions of the material. If the surfaces are flat and polished, then transmission and reflection are specular (i.e., transmitted light continues in the same direction and reflections are mirrorlike). If one or both surface surfaces are rough, then reflection and transmission are diffused. In most cases, this diffusion is only dependent on surface texture; in some materials (such as translucent white glass or plastic) white pigment suspended in the material diffuses the light internally.

Flat, polished metallic surfaces reflect specularly (like a mirror). Conversely, ideal matte surfaces reflect diffusely, with an even distribution in all directions. In practice, most building materials exhibit some combination of specular and diffuse reflection.

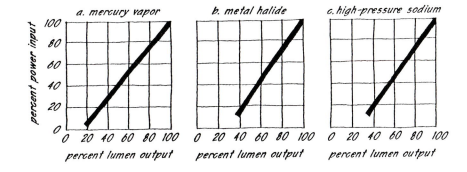

Figure 25.5: Percent lumen output vs. percent ballast input for 400-watt clear high-intensity discharge lamps: (a) mercury vapor, (b) metal halide, and (c) high-pressure sodium. *(Redrawn from Kaufman, 1984, by permission.)*

Transmission can be characterized as specular (clear), diffuse (where diffusion is complete and uniform in all directions), and spread (where diffusion is complete but not uniform, with the largest component in the incident direction).

While the exact amount of transmission, reflection, and spread of diffusion can only be determined by laboratory measurement, useful design information can be gained by visual inspection of glazing samples. As a general rule for most materials, increased diffusion results in decreased transmission.

REFLECTORS

The different types of reflection described above are used for different applications. Diffuse reflection is used when a widely spread source of light is needed. If some light directionality and control are needed, a spread-type reflector is used; and when precise light control is needed, a specular reflector is typically used. By shaping a specular reflector, light can be directed to the precise point at which it is needed. If a specular surface is shaped into a semicircle and the source is placed at the focal point of the circle (center), then all of the light striking the reflector will be directed back through the source. If the reflector is elliptical and the source is placed at one of the two focal points, the rays will converge at the other focal point. If the reflector is parabolic with the source at the focal point, the rays leaving the reflector will be parallel (if the source is moved to a point between the parabolic reflector and focal point, the rays will diverge).

REFRACTORS

When light passes from one transparent medium into another (as from air into glass) at an oblique angle, the direction changes. The amount of the change depends on the difference in the optical densities of the two materials (1.0 for air; approximately 1.5 for glass). This refraction may be calculated by Snell's law (the law of refraction):

$$n_1 \sin i = n_2 \sin r$$

where n_1 = index of refraction of first medium

   i = angle of incidence

   n_2 = index of refraction of second medium

   r = angle the refracted light ray forms with the surface

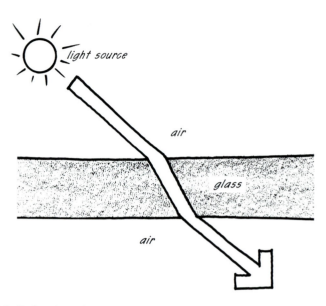

Figure 25.6: Refraction of light at a plane surface. *(Redrawn from IES Education Committee, 1985, by permission.)*

This optical phenomenon has important implications in the design of lenses for luminaires for the purpose of controlling light distribution. Lenses may be used to concentrate light or scatter it in a diffuse pattern. The most common materials used in luminaire refractors are glass and plastic.

LIGHT DISTRIBUTION

The combination of a specific lamp in a specific luminaire produces a unique distribution pattern of light. This can be quantified in candlepower (or luminous intensity) distribution in various directions. It is typically measured using an illuminance (footcandle or lux) meter measuring perpendicular to the source at a constant distance (five to ten times the largest dimension of the luminaire) in a plane. The luminous intensity (in candelas) is then calculated:

Luminous intensity = footcandles x distance (ft)^2

While accurate measurements cannot be taken close to the luminaire (because it is not a point light source), it is helpful to remember that at 1-ft distance, the number of candelas equals the number of footcandles (and at 1-m distance equals the lux).

These measurements are made by rotating the illuminance meter around the luminaire and are plotted typically on polar coordinates to generate a candlepower distribution curve (CDC). Each is unique for each lamp/luminaire

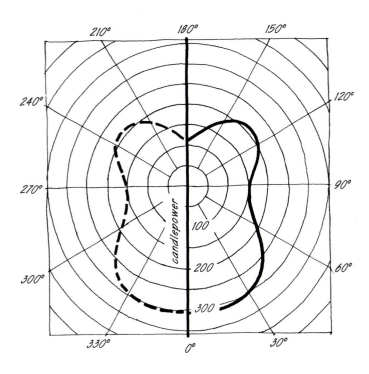

Figure 25.7: Typical candlepower distribution curve for a general diffuse-type luminaire. Since the unit is symmetrical about its vertical axis in all directions, only the right side of this single curve is shown due to symmetry. *(After Stein et al., 1986.)*

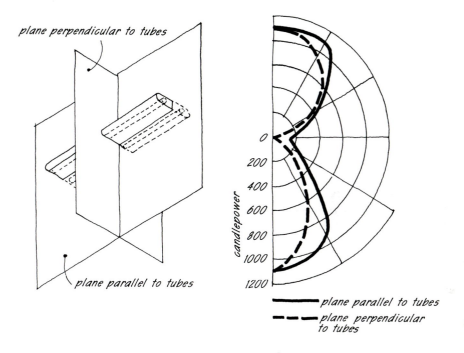

Figure 25.8: Typical candlepower distribution curve for a fluorescent luminaire typically shows distribution in vertical planes parallel and perpendicular to the lamp orientation.

combination and is typically published as part of the luminaire manufacturer's data sheet. For luminaires that are symmetrical in all directions (such as most incandescent lamps, downlights, and open circular reflectors) only one CDC is required. For nonsymmetrical luminaires (such as fluorescents), CDCs in additional vertical planes (parallel, perpendicular, and in some cases diagonal, to the lamp) are required.

The shapes of these distribution curves visually represent the distribution of light from the fixture. From these curves, the designer can determine how widely the light is spread, as well as assess potential direct glare problems. A circular distribution pattern centered about the luminaire reveals a uniform distribution in all directions (from a point source or a diffusing globe, for example). A long, teardrop pattern below the luminaire is characteristic of a concentrating downlight. A triangular pattern below the luminaire reveals a widespread pattern which would allow wider spacing of units. For general illumination, beware of patterns that show strong distribution between 45° below the horizontal and horizontal; these suggest a likelihood of direct glare in the view of the occupant.

A useful characteristic of the polar format is that they can be easily interpreted to assess the relative illuminance across a horizontal work plane. A triangular CDC for a luminaire suggests a wide distribution pattern with more of the light directed out to the sides than straight down. However, once the cosine effect is taken into effect, the flat bottom of the CDC means uniform illuminance across the workplane. In other words, the greater concentration of light out to the sides exactly compensates for the natural falloff due to the cosine effect.

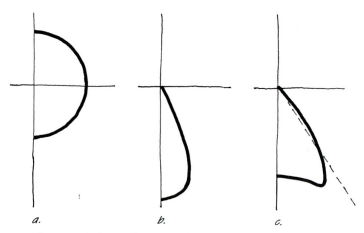

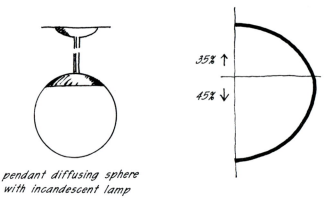

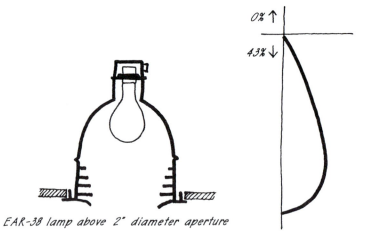

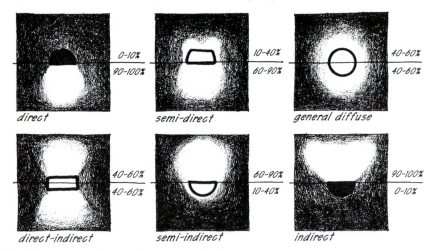

Figure 25.9: Characteristic candlepower distribution curves for (a) point source — or ideal diffuse globe, (b) concentrating downlight, (c) moderate-spread downlight to provide uniform distribution. In the triangular pattern, the bottom of the curve is flat, revealing the greatest concentration out toward the sides; this compensates for the cosine effect (reduced illuminance as the angle of incidence increases). Thus, the flat bottom of the curve translates to a uniform illuminance out to about 35°. If the flat bottom extended beyond about 45° then direct glare gets to be a problem due to the high brightness visible to the occupant at low viewing angles.

Figure 25.11: *Diffusing Sphere*—a *general diffuse* luminaire that is nondirectional and decorative. Often used in public and residential applications (for example, in an outdoor mall or an entry). The diffuser is made of transparent or translucent glass or plastic. Since light is emitted equally in all directions, either low-wattage lamps or a large translucent diffuser should be used to minimize direct glare. *(Redrawn from Kaufman, 1984, by permission.)*

Figure 25.10: Luminaires for general lighting are classified by the percentage of total luminaire output emitted above and below horizontal: direct, semi-direct, general diffuse, direct-indirect, semi-indirect, and indirect. The candlepower distribution curves may take many forms within the limits of upward and downward distribution, depending on the lamp and luminaire type. *(Redrawn from IES Education Committee, 1985, by permission.)*

Figure 25.12: *Downlights* — a direct luminaire used when decorative highlighting is needed, or for general illumination. Incandescent downlights are often used to highlight merchandising displays. For larger areas, and where increased energy efficiency and reduced maintenance costs are primary considerations, HID downlights should be used, especially in areas with high ceilings. *(Redrawn from Kaufman, 1984, by permission.)*

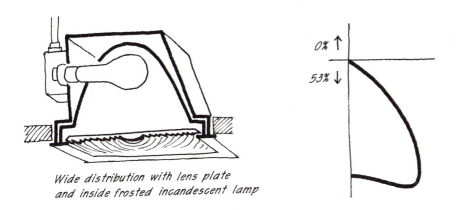

*Wide distribution with lens plate
and inside frosted incandescent lamp*

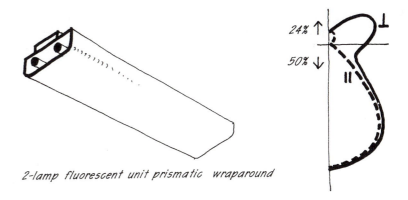

2-lamp fluorescent unit prismatic wraparound

Figure 25.13: *Recessed Enclosed Incandescent* — these direct luminaires are used when a lens or diffuse-bottom closure for a recessed incandescent downlight is required. These are typically used in low ceiling areas where moisture or dirt accumulation may be a problem. The internal reflector is usually made of specular aluminum. *(Redrawn from Kaufman, 1984, by permission.)*

Figure 25.15: *Wraparound Fluorescent* — these general diffuse luminaires are suitable for locations where some indirect lighting is required; they may be surface- or pendant- (suspended) mounted. The enclosure is either translucent or prismatic plastic. *(Redrawn from Kaufman, 1984, by permission.)*

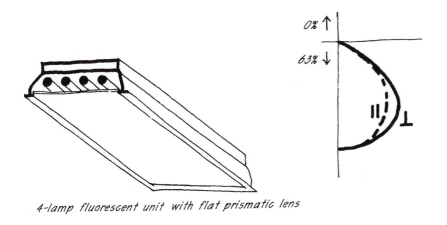

4-lamp fluorescent unit with flat prismatic lens

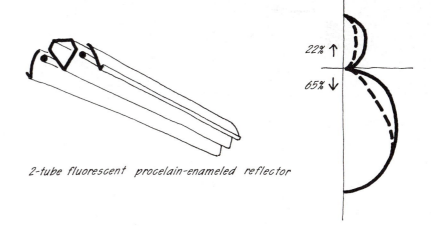

2-tube fluorescent procelain-enameled reflector

Figure 25.14: *Recessed Enclosed Fluorescent* — these direct luminaires are used when lower luminances in the glare zone (below 45°) are needed. The reflector is usually a white paint with a diffuse-specular finish; the refractor is usually plastic. *(Redrawn from Kaufman, 1984, by permission.)*

Figure 25.16: *Open Reflector Fluorescent* — these semidirect luminaires are used primarily in industrial spaces such as a warehouse. The reflector is usually diffuse/specular white paint or porcelain. The deep center-V reflector provides shielding from low viewing angles. The narrow slots in the top allow a small amount of light to be directed upward, relieving dark contrasts above the luminaire plane. *(Redrawn from Kaufman, 1984, by permission.)*

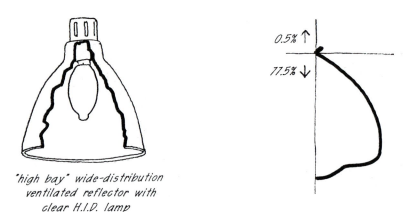

*"high bay" wide-distribution
ventilated reflector with
clear H.I.D. lamp*

Figure 25.17: *High bay HID* — this direct luminaire is used primarily in industrial interiors with high mounting heights. The reflector is available in a variety of finishes, depending on the required distribution pattern (including semispecular flat aluminum, with specular, semispecular, or diffuse finishes). It is designed to project the maximum light to the workplane and to minimize the direct glare from the high-luminance HID lamp. *(Redrawn from Kaufman, 1984, by permission.)*

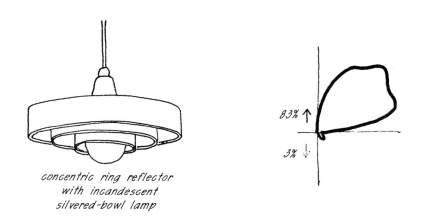

*concentric ring reflector
with incandescent
silvered-bowl lamp*

Figure 25.18: *Concentric Ring* — this indirect luminaire depends on ceiling reflection for final diffusion. It is used with a silvered-bowl lamp which directs all of the light upward. Used in schools prior to the widespread adoption of fluorescent systems. *(Redrawn from Kaufman, 1984, by permission.)*

LUMINAIRE CLASSIFICATION

Interior luminaires are often classified on the basis of the percentage of total light output (lumens) above and below the horizontal.

ELECTRIC LIGHTING CONTROL FOR DAYLIGHTED BUILDINGS

Perhaps the most successful overall approach to integrating electric lighting and daylighting is the British method of *permanent supplementary artificial lighting in interiors* (PSALI), which is widely used throughout Europe (Lynes et al., 1966; Ne'eman and Longmore, 1973; Stein et al., 1986). The method is a design approach which views electric lighting a supplementary to daylighting and not vice versa. PSALI recognizes that a nonresidential building is principally occupied during the day, and that sufficient daylight is available during most of these hours to provide much of the building's illumination needs. It is based on three assumptions:

- The large variation of interior daylight illuminance that occurs during the course of a typical day will not affect visual performance, even when the actual illuminance levels fall below accepted recommendation, because of the adaptive ability of human vision.

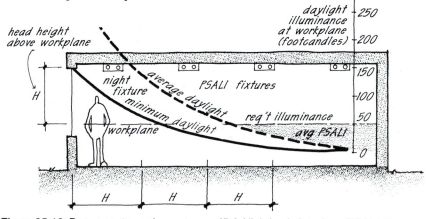

Figure 25.19: Permanent supplementary artificial lighting in interiors, PSALI. Because even with minimum daylighting conditions there is sufficient daylight to meet requirements to a depth equal to the window height, the first luminaire is used only for nighttime lighting. The second and third would be either automatically switched or dimmed (depending on the level of daylighting available), and the last would be lighted during all hours of building use. *(After Stein et al., 1986.)*

- The *task* illuminances are those recommended by the Illuminating Engineering Society of North America (Kaufman, 1984; see Table 21.1), and the *general* illuminances are one-third of the recommended task illuminance.

- Electric light can be used to successfully supplement daylight when the latter is insufficient.

Daylighting can save energy only if it can reliably displace electric lighting usage.

Manual switching can be effective where users perceive that they have a large measure of control over the interior lighting environment. Under these circumstances manual light control can be more energy conserving than automated dimming or switching controls. In the U.S. Department of Energy (DOE) commercial buildings program (Burt Hill Kosar Rittelmann Associates and Min Kantrowitz Associates, 1987; see Chapter 27), occupants were found to be often willing to work at lower lighting levels than those recommended by industry standards. This voluntary action was apparently connected to the high degree of personal control that users perceived in those buildings.

However, in large nonresidential buildings where this control is not available to the end user, no amount of provision for convenient manual switching (even for 50 percent reduction) will result in useful energy savings. For significant savings to be achieved in these buildings (in lighting and cooling energy and in peak-demand utility costs), electric lighting control must be automatic. Automatic controls are made up of a combination of a sensing device (to measure daylight) and a controller which either switches or dims the electric lighting (Sain, 1983).

The recent increase in daylight utilization (particularly in larger commercial buildings) has been facilitated by the commercial availability of standard electric lighting controls. These controls can be generally categorized as (1) switching, and (2) dimming. Each has certain characteristics that may be desirable or undesirable depending on the application.

SWITCHING CONTROLS

Switching controls turn off electric lights when there is ample daylight. The control may be two-step (off / on), three-step (off, 1/2 on, and all on), four-step (off, 1/3 on, 2/3 on, and all on), and five-step (off, 1/4 on, 1/2 on, 3/4 on, and all on).

DIMMING CONTROLS

Dimming controls reduce electric light proportionally as the daylight increases. An ideal dimming control sequence is shown graphically in Fig. 25.20e. Unfortunately, "ideal" dimming devices (which consume no power themselves) are not available at this time although some approach this ideal.

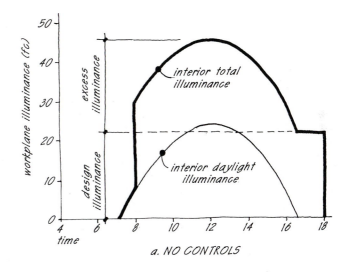

a. NO CONTROLS

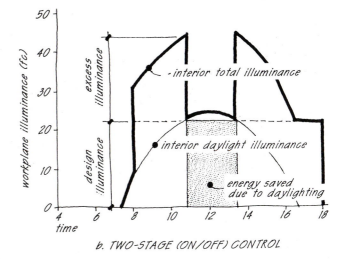

b. TWO-STAGE (ON/OFF) CONTROL

Figure 25.20: Response of various control strategies to a selected interior design illuminance for various daylight conditions: (a) no controls, and (b) two-stage (on/off) switching control. *(After Robbins and Hunter, 1982.)*

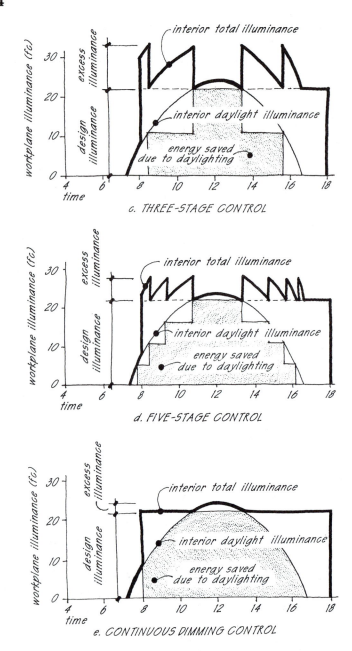

Figure 25.20 (continued): Response of various control strategies to a selected interior design illuminance for various daylight conditions: (c) three-stage switching control, (d) five-stage switching control, and (e) continuous dimming. *(After Robbins and Hunter, 1982.)*

Dimming controls for incandescent lamps are the closest to the ideal. These dimmers reduce the power consumption proportionally to the light output; however, the dimming control consumes a small amount of power itself. An incandescent dimmer has a slight increase in power consumption over an ideal dimmer, particularly at lower levels. Incandescent dimming systems for daylighting purposes are not commercially available as an integrated unit, but can be readily assembled from available components.

Fluorescent with standard lamps and ballasts

Dimming controls for fluorescent lights with standard lamps and ballasts are available in a variety of forms and with many special features. They can be divided into two generic types: multiple- and single-fixture dimmers.

Multiple-fixture dimmers are useful when simultaneous dimming is required for a large number of fixtures. One sensor is used to read the daylight level, converting this to an electronic signal to operate a controller and dim the lights. In this type of system, one sensor and one controller dim several hundred watts of lighting. Overall costs are decreased when the maximum number of watts possible is dimmed by each controller. However, care should be taken to ensure that all areas dimmed are receiving equal daylight.

Single-fixture dimmers normally control one or two ballasts only. Typically, this type of system uses a fiber-optics tube to sense the light level on the work surface below the fixture, transferring this light signal to the control box on top of (or in) the ballast housing. The control box contains all electrical and/ or mechanical devices, thus reducing the cost of the sensing device. Each fixture in a daylit area is equipped with a sensor and controller to make maximum use of the daylight available. However, care should be taken to select a controller which is adjustable from below the ceiling.

One manufacturer of daylighting controls has added an on-off switch to its dimming system for standard lamps. The control dims the lights down to the minimum level of 25 percent light output, then waits until daylight can provide all of the required light before turning the electric lights off. When the daylight decreases, the lights are turned back on. Designers should recognize, however, that standard fluorescent lamps and ballasts must be turned first to 100 percent power and then dimmed. Note that not all lamps can be dimmed by the fluorescent controls. Some energy-saving lamps cannot be dimmed; manufacturer's literature should be consulted before combining dimmers and energy saving lamps.

Fluorescent with dimming ballasts

Dimming controls for fluorescent lights with dimming ballasts are very similar to dimmers for standard lamps except that they can dim the full 100-percent range. This type of system can also be used for those electronic ballasts that are designed to be dimmed. At present, this type of system is only available in the multiple-fixture form described above.

High intensity discharge (HID)

The power consumption characteristics for dimming controls for HID lights are similar to those of fluorescent controls. However, dimming HID lamps has a severe effect on the color rendition of the lamps and may reduce the life of both lamps and ballasts. Manufacturer's literature should be consulted for recent developments in these products.

CONTROL SENSOR LOCATION

Controls can be categorized by their placement — at the *task* or at the *source*. Both can be used directly to control one fixture, an entire circuit, or relays can be added to switch several circuits (depending on the relative location of those fixtures to the sensor).

Source-sensing devices sense the quantity of daylight by installing the sensor on the exterior of the building (at the "source" of the daylight). The operating mechanism must be adjustable for high levels of light (100 to 2,000 fc) so that the required inside light level (that is, 50 fc) can be matched with the appropriate source level (that is, 1,000 fc). The primary disadvantage of source-sensing is that it does not actively take into account any interior circumstances (the position of blinds or drapes used to shield direct sunlight, for example); however, it has the advantage of simplicity and of encouraging maximum occupant utilization of daylight.

Task-sensing devices control luminaires by sensing the light level at the task. Photocells used must be (1) adjustable and (2) capable of sensing at least two levels of light. An adjustment control makes the same device appropriate for various spaces with different lighting requirements. The device should sense when there is twice as much daylight as required (to compensate for electric light) and turn off (or dim) the lights, and sense when the quantity of lights drops below the required level and turn the lights back on. If switching control is used, either a time-delay feature or a "dead band" will prevent annoying on-off switching during partly cloudy days. Task-sensing devices vary in their ability to provide constant illumination levels using a dimming system depending on location. In the simplest case, the photosensor is located on the work surface and the system operates by maintaining a constant light level on the sensor itself. However, this location is impractical since the sensor is then sensitive to the effects of body shadows, loose papers, and other light-obstructing objects.

SELECTION OF ELECTRIC LIGHTING CONTROLS

Proper selection of electric lighting controls is an important step in the design of a daylighted building and should involve the following considerations (Sain, 1983):

Quality of space — Daylighting controls can affect the quality of the interior space. They can cause annoying changes in the light level, poor color rendition, appearance of burned-out lamps, and other items that may reduce the quality and/or rentability of building space. If illuminance level changes are sudden (as in the case of two-stage switching), occupants may be annoyed. This is critical in task areas such as office spaces, where light switching may reduce productivity resulting in economic losses that far exceed the energy savings. Some recent installations have utilized various occupant sensors which prevent lowering electric lighting when anyone is present in the room. Color and perceived burnout must also be addressed for each application and control system.

Lamp and ballast type — The type of lamp and ballasts used in the space will affect the selection of electric light controls. Several controls are made specifically for certain lamp types, but some controls, such as switching, can be used on any lamp type. The designer should be aware of this compatibility of controls and lamp types. For example, switching HID or fluorescent lamps can reduce their life, but if they are switched off half of the normal working hours and their life is reduced 25 percent they will still last 25 percent longer than standard lamps with no controls.

Fixture layout and room size — The selection of controls can be affected by the fixture layout or room size. Multifixture dimming and switching systems rely on layouts where many fixtures are receiving similar quantities of daylight. In large buildings where this occurs, the multifixture systems are typically cheaper and easier to maintain. However, in small buildings or individual rooms, the single-fixture controls are more appropriate.

Quality of light — The daylighting strategy and its resultant daylight level in the space can affect the control device selection. Since most dimming devices have a minimum power consumption of approximately 30 percent, they may not be appropriate for areas where large amounts of daylight are available, or where low illuminance levels are required. On the other hand, in areas where the required light level is high and the daylight source is small, a switching device may never operate.

Cost — The cost of daylighting controls will have a major effect on final system selection. When a designer bases a decision on economic feasibility, it is in an attempt to save the most energy for the lowest initial cost. Prices for each control system will vary slightly between manufacturers, but the actual cost of the total system will vary much more depending on the application. (This is especially true for retrofit projects.) Using a multifixture device on a few fixtures will cost more than, say, two single-fixture units. One system which is much higher in first cost is a fluorescent dimming system with dimming ballasts which would be extremely hard to justify on the basis of energy savings alone.

Other considerations — Other miscellaneous items can also affect the control selection. Control systems will require some maintenance and some devices are easier to maintain than others. They may also cause radio interference with other equipment in the space. Another concern with dimming or switching fluorescent lights is the adverse effect this may have on the power factor. If the space contains a large inductive motor load, the fluorescent lights will help alleviate the problem. However, if the fluorescent lights are not there, a capacitor bank may be required to control the power factor.

SUMMARY OF TERMS

Lamp — a man-made light source consisting of a bulb, base, and other components necessary for the generation of light.

Bulb — an airtight transparent or translucent enclosure made of glass.

Base — connects the lamp to an electric circuit and permits easy lamp replacement.

Incandescent filament lamp — a lamp in which light is produced by a filament heated to incandescence by an electric current.

Filament — a coil of tungsten wire heated to incandescence by an electric current; the source of light in an incandescent lamp.

Filling gas — an inert gas, usually a mixture of nitrogen and argon, that reduces tungsten evaporation in incandescent filament lamps.

Tungsten — the preferred material for incandescent filaments because of its high melting point.

Tungsten-halogen lamp — a gas-filled tungsten-filament lamp containing a certain proportion of halogens; quartz-iodine lamps are included in this category.

Fluorescent lamp — a low-pressure mercury electric-discharge lamp in which a phosphorus coating transforms some of the ultraviolet energy generated by the discharge into light.

Efficacy, lm/W — the ratio of lumens emitted to watts consumed by an electric lamp (or watts of heat introduced into a building by daylighting).

Ballast — a device used with an electric-discharge lamp to obtain the necessary circuit conditions (voltage, current, waveform) for starting and operating.

Rapid-start — a type of fluorescent lamp circuit where the ballast quickly heats the cathodes and, when sufficient ionization of the lamp has occurred, the open circuit voltage strikes the arc and starts the lamp in one or two seconds; used in virtually all new installations.

Preheat — an obsolete type of fluorescent lamp circuit where the cathode is preheated for several seconds by a separate circuit.

Slimline — an obsolete type of fluorescent lamp circuit which applies a high voltage to initiate the arc.

High-intensity discharge (HID) lamp — an electric discharge lamp in which the light-producing arc is stabilized by wall temperature, and the arc tube has a bulb wall loading in excess of 3 W/cm²; includes mercury, metal halide, and high pressure sodium lamps.

Mercury lamp — a high-intensity discharge (HID) lamp in which voltage is applied to initiate an arc between a starting electrode and a nearby operating electrode within an arc tube containing argon and mercury, vaporizing the mercury.

High-pressure sodium (HPS) lamp — a high intensity discharge (HID) lamp in which light is produced by radiation from sodium vapor.

Color rendering — general expression of the effect of a light source on the color appearance of objects in conscious or subconscious comparison with their color appearance under a reference light source.

Luminaire — a complete lighting unit consisting of a lamp or lamps together with the parts designed to distribute the light, to position and protect the lamps, and to connect them to the electrical supply.

Fixture — a commonly used term meaning luminaire.

Refraction — the process by which the direction of a ray of light changes as it passes obliquely from one medium into another.

Candlepower (intensity) distribution curve — a curve, generally polar, representing the variation of luminous intensity of a lamp or luminaire through the light center.

Specular surface — one from which the reflection is predominantly mirrorlike.

Direct — a luminaire type having a light distribution pattern of 0—10 percent upward and 90—100 percent downward.

Semi-direct — a luminaire type having a light distribution pattern of 10—40 percent upward and 60—90 percent downward.

General diffuse — a luminaire type having a light distribution pattern of 40—60 percent upward and 40—60 percent downward, and relatively evenly distributed horizontally as well as vertically.

Direct/indirect — a luminaire type having a light distribution pattern of 40—60 percent upward and 40—60 percent downward, with most of the light directed vertically and relatively little horizontally.

Semi-indirect — a luminaire type having a light distribution pattern of 60—90 percent upward and 10—40 percent downward.

Indirect — a luminaire type having a light distribution pattern of 90—100 percent upward and 0—10 percent downward.

Ambient lighting — lighting throughout an area that produces general illumination.

General lighting — lighting designed to provide a substantially uniform level of illumination throughout an area, exclusive of any provision for special local requirements.

Local lighting — lighting designed to provide illumination over a relatively small area without providing any significant general surrounding lighting.

Directional lighting — lighting provided on the workplane or on an object predominantly from a preferred direction.

Direct glare — glare resulting from high luminances or insufficiently shielded light sources in the field of view; usually associated with bright areas, such as luminaires, ceilings, and windows, which are outside the visual task or region being viewed.

Task lighting — lighting directed to a specific surface or area that provides illumination for visual tasks.

Indirect component — the portion of the luminous flux from a luminaire arriving at the workplane after being reflected by room surfaces.

Pendant — a device (tube or cord) for suspending a luminaire.

Troffer — a recessed lighting unit, usually long and installed in the opening flush with the ceiling; derived from "trough" and "coffer."

Workplane — the plane at which work is usually done and on which the illuminance is specified and measured; 30 in. above the floor unless otherwise indicated.

Permanent supplementary artificial lighting in interiors, PSALI — a lighting design approach which considers electric lighting as supplementary to daylighting; widely used throughout Europe.

Contrast ratio — the ratio of task luminance to surround luminance.

Switching control — a device to turn off electric lights when there is ample daylight.

Dimming control — a device to reduce electric lights proportionally as the daylight increases.

STUDY QUESTIONS

1. Distinguish between a lamp and a bulb.

2. Describe an incandescent lamp and explain its operation.

3. Describe a fluorescent lamp and explain its operation.

4. Describe the function of a ballast in conjunction with fluorescent lamps.

5. What are the major fluorescent lamp circuit types that are commercially available?

6. Contrast a typical high-intensity discharge (HID) lamp with a fluorescent lamp.

7. What is a "luminaire"?

8. Luminaires are generally classified according to their light distribution patterns. Explain what this means and describe the six commonly used classifications.

9. What is a candlepower distribution curve and how is it useful to a designer?

10. What is *permanent supplementary artificial lighting in interiors* (PSALI) and what are the assumptions that underlie it?

26

ELECTRIC LIGHTING:

ANALYSIS

We were born of light. The seasons are felt through light.
We only know the world and it is evoked by light.
— Louis Kahn

There are two fundamental approaches that are commonly used for calculating illuminance due to electric lighting. The first approach (average illuminance determined by the *lumen method*) is derived from the lumen definition and the fact that one footcandle is equal to one lumen incident on one square foot of area. This method is best suited for calculating the average illuminance over an area where luminaires are evenly spaced. The second approach (the *point method*) uses the candlepower distribution curve in conjunction with the cosine effect and inverse-square effect to calculate the illuminance at a single point due to one or two luminaires (indirect light reflected from the walls or ceiling are not included).

$$\text{Illuminance} = \frac{\text{luminous flux}}{\text{area}}$$

$$\text{Footcandles} = \frac{\text{lumens}}{\text{square feet}}$$

$$\text{Lux} = \frac{\text{lumens}}{\text{per square meter}}$$

For example, if 6000 lm are striking an area 10 ft by 10 ft then:

$$\text{Illuminance} = 6000 \text{ lm} \div 100 \text{ ft}^2 = 60 \text{ lm/ft}^2 = 60 \text{ fc}$$

COEFFICIENT OF UTILIZATION, CU

The above definition and example assumes that the quantity of lumens which strikes the given area (workplane) is known. In practice, this is seldom

AVERAGE ILLUMINANCE — *LUMEN METHOD*

By definition, if the total lumens striking an area are known and the area is known, then the illuminance can be determined (IES Education Committee, 1985):

the case; while the lumens emitted from a lamp are known (from manufacturer's data), the amount of usable lumens actually reaching the workplane is less. A more useful approach considers that only a portion of the lumens produced by a lamp in a luminaire will actually reach the workplane, and that portion depends on the particular lamp and luminaire selected as well as the installation environment. *Coefficient of utilization* (CU) is the term used to describe this portion (expressed as a percentage), and is a function of three factors:

- Room surface (ceiling, wall, and floor) reflectances

- Room size and proportions

- Luminaire characteristics (efficiency and intensity distribution)

For example, if a particular luminaire/room combination had a CU of 0.75, then 75 percent of the lumens produced by the lamp would reach the workplane. The other 25 percent of the lumens would be lost (absorbed and converted to heat). Some would be absorbed inside of the luminaire, and some would be absorbed by rooms surfaces (such as walls, ceilings, and floors). Each of these will be discussed individually.

Room surface reflectances

All surfaces in the room (walls, ceilings, floors, furniture, machines, and people) absorb and reflect light. If these surfaces are highly reflective, less light

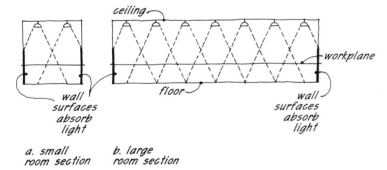

a. small room section   b. large room section

Figure 26.1: In small rooms, a larger percentage of the total light produced by luminaires strikes the walls than in large rooms. Note that in the small room (a) a large part of the light from the luminaire strikes the walls, while in the large room (b) some of the light from the end luminaires hits the wall, but the luminaires in the center send all of their light directly to the workplane. As a result, the same luminaires will have a higher CU in large rooms. *(Redrawn from IES Education Committee, 1985, by permission.)*

is absorbed and more light is reflected back into the space. Since some of this light will eventually reach the workplane, luminaires will perform more efficiently in rooms with high-reflectance surfaces.

Room size and proportions

Except in a totally indirect lighting system, light travels directly from the luminaire to the workplane while other light travels to the walls where some is absorbed and some reflected toward the workplane. In small rooms, a larger percentage of the total light produced by luminaires strikes the walls than in large rooms. As a result, the same luminaires will have a higher CU in large rooms. Similarly, luminaires will have a higher CU in rooms with a relatively low fixture mounting (or ceiling) height.

Type of luminaire

The design and light distribution characteristics and efficiency of the luminaire also affect the CU. Some luminaires (such as recessed deep-baffle downlights) have interior surfaces or cavities that trap or absorb light; others have low or medium transmittance lenses or translucent closures that absorb light to varying degrees. Still others are designed to direct all of the light to the ceiling from which it is reflected back to the workplane. All of these types will typically be less efficient (and have a lower CU) than open-bottom luminaires with high-reflectance interior surfaces that reflect and direct light to the workplane.

INITIAL AVERAGE WORKPLANE ILLUMINANCE

The workplane is the height at which the task is performed; for office work, it is considered to be 30 in. above the floor (normal desk/table height). The room cavity height is the distance from the luminaire to the workplane.

Consider an office 15 ft long by 10 ft wide by 8.5 ft high, ceiling reflectance $\rho_c = 80$ percent, wall reflectance $\rho_w = 50$ percent, and floor reflectance $\rho_f = 20$ percent, and a workplane height of 30 in. From Table 21.1, select 50 fc for this office environment from illuminance category E.

Calculate the room cavity ratio, RCR:

$$RCR = \frac{5(\text{room cavity height})(\text{room length} + \text{room width})}{(\text{room lenght})(\text{room width})}$$

For the example room, $RCR = \dfrac{5(6)(15 + 10)}{(15)(10)} = 5$

	Typical Luminaire	Typical Intensity Distribution and Per Cent Lamp Lumens	
		Maint. Cat.	SC
35		V	1.5 / 1.2
	2 lamp prismatic wraparound	$11\frac{1}{2}\%$ ↑ $58\frac{1}{2}\%$ ↓	

ρ_{CC} →	80			70			50			30			10			0	
ρ_W →	50	30	10	50	30	10	50	30	10	50	30	10	50	30	10	0	WDRC
RCR ↓	Coefficients of Utilization for 20 Per Cent Effective Floor Cavity Reflectance ($\rho_{FC} = 20$)																
0	.81	.81	.81	.78	.78	.78	.72	.72	.72	.66	.66	.66	.61	.61	.61	.59	—
1	.71	.69	.66	.69	.66	.64	.64	.62	.60	.59	.58	.56	.55	.54	.53	.50	.204
2	.64	.59	.56	.61	.58	.54	.57	.54	.51	.53	.51	.49	.49	.48	.46	.44	.184
3	.57	.52	.48	.55	.50	.47	.51	.48	.45	.48	.45	.42	.45	.42	.40	.38	.168
4	.51	.46	.41	.49	.44	.41	.46	.42	.39	.43	.40	.37	.41	.38	.35	.34	.156
5	.46	.40	.36	.44	.39	.35	.41	.37	.34	.39	.35	.32	.37	.33	.31	.29	.147
6	.41	.35	.31	.40	.35	.31	.38	.33	.30	.35	.31	.28	.33	.30	.27	.26	.137
7	.37	.31	.27	.36	.31	.27	.34	.29	.26	.32	.28	.25	.30	.27	.24	.23	.129
8	.33	.28	.24	.32	.27	.23	.30	.26	.22	.29	.25	.22	.27	.24	.21	.19	.122
9	.30	.24	.20	.29	.24	.20	.27	.23	.19	.26	.22	.19	.24	.21	.18	.17	.116
10	.27	.22	.18	.26	.21	.18	.25	.20	.17	.23	.19	.16	.22	.18	.16	.15	.110

Figure 26.2: Typical coefficient of utilization (CU) table for a fluorescent luminaire. CU tables for specific luminaires are available from manufacturer's literature. CU tables for various generic luminaires are provided in Appendix E. *(Reproduced from Kaufman, 1984, by permission.)*

Table 26.1: Data for Selected Lamps

Description	Watts	Base	Initial Lumens	Initial Lumens/ Watt	Lamp Lumen Depreciation, %	Rated Average Life (hours)
Incandescent A-19 frosted	100	Medium	1,740	17.4	90.5	750
Incandescent PS-30 frosted	200	Medium	3,700	18.5	85	750
Tungsten Halogen T-3 clear	500	RSC	10,500	20.8	96	1,500
Incandescent R-40 flood	300	Medium	3,600	12.0	90	2,000
Fluorescent 48" T-12 RS CW	41	Med. Bi.	3,150	76.8	84	20,000
Fluorescent 48" T-12 RS CWX	41	Med. Bi.	2,200	53.6	84	20,000
Fluorescent 96" T-12 RS CW	113	Rec DC	9,150	76.8	82	12,000
Fluorescent 96" T-12 RS CWX	113	Rec DC	6,533	53.6	82	12,000
Mercury HID H37KC-250/C	250	Mog.	18,850	75.4	89	24,000
Metal Halide HID M58PH-250	250	Mog.	20,500	82.0	78	10,000
HP Sodium HID S50VC-250	250	Mog.	26,000	104.0	90	24,000

(Data from Kaufman, 1984, by permission; for other lamps, see manufacturer's literature.)

Reading from the table in Fig. 26.2 for RCR = 5, ρ_c = 80 percent and ρ_w = 50 percent, CU = 0.46. (In more typical cases, the value of the RCR will not be a simple integer and interpolation will be necessary.)

Modifying the formula:

$$\text{Footcandles} = \frac{\text{lumens}}{\text{square feet}}$$

$$\text{Footcandles} = \frac{(\text{lumens per lamp})(\text{no. lamps per luminaire})(\text{CU})}{\text{floor area}}$$

From Table 26.1 (or the lamp manufacturer's literature), for a fluorescent 48" T-12 RS CWX lamp, the initial lumen output per lamp is 2,200 lm. There are two lamps in this luminaire. Thus the average initial illuminance can be calculated:

$$\text{Initial average illuminance per luminaire} = \frac{(200)(2)(0.46)}{150} = 13.5 \text{ fc}$$

LIGHT LOSS FACTORS

The initial illuminance must be reduced by the *light loss factor, LLF,* to determine the maintained illuminance. The LLF is the product of a number of subfactors (each of which is 1.0 or less):

Luminaire ambient temperature factor, LATF — if the ambient temperature of fluorescent lamps is significantly higher or lower than normal room temperature, then the lamp lumen output is reduced by the LATF (available from lamp manufacturer's literature or see Fig. 26.3). No adjustment is necessary for either incandescent or HID lamps because their output is not normally affected by temperature.

Voltage to luminaire factor, VLF — if the service voltage will be predictably high or low, an adjustment factor should be applied (see Fig. 26.4).

Ballast factor, BF — typically use a 0.95 BF for fluorescent and HID lamps, and 1.0 for incandescent lamps.

Luminaire surface depreciation factor, LSDF — luminaire surfaces depreciate over time (due to corrosion of reflectors, lens discoloration, etc.). Unless specific data is available, assume 1.0.

Lamp burnout factor, LBF — in the past, it was common practice of allow a certain percentage of lamps to burn out before relamping. Presently, with higher energy costs, lamps are typically replaced immediately and this factor can be omitted (equal to 1.0).

Lamp lumen depreciation factor, LLDF — lumen output gradually and predictably decreases throughout the life of the lamp. This factor is typically in the 0.8 to 0.9 range and is available for selected lamps from Table 26.1 or from manufacturer's literature.

Luminaire dirt depreciation factor, LDDF — lumen output is reduced due to an accumulation of dirt on the lamp and luminaire. This factor depends on the construction of the luminaire (varies with category of luminaire, I—VI; see CU table in Appendix E or manufacturer's literature), the dirt conditions within the space, and the frequency of luminaire washing (see Fig. 26.5).

Room surface depreciation factor, RSDF — the accumulation of dirt on room surfaces reduces the amount of light reflected to the workplane (see Fig. 26.6).

In the present example, these factors are:

Luminaire ambient temperature factor, LATF = 1.0 (operating at normal room temperature).

Voltage to luminaire factor, VLF = 1.0 (operates at rated voltage).

Ballast factor, BF = 0.95 (ballast factor for fluorescent lamps).

Luminaire surface depreciation factor, LSDF = 1.0 (anticipate no deterioration due to age).

Lamp burnout factor, LBF = 1.0 (burnouts will be replaced immediately).

Lamp lumen depreciation factor, LLDF = 0.84 (from Table 26.1).

Luminaire dirt depreciation factor, LDDF = 0.86 (from Fig. 26.5; assumes "very clean" conditions for office environment; category V luminaire maintenance

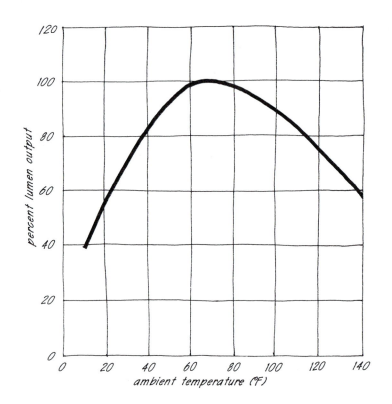

Figure 26.3: Luminaire ambient temperature factors, LATF, for F-40 fluorescent lamps (incandescent and HID lamps have an inherent LATF of 1.0). *(Redrawn from Kaufman, 1984, by permission.)*

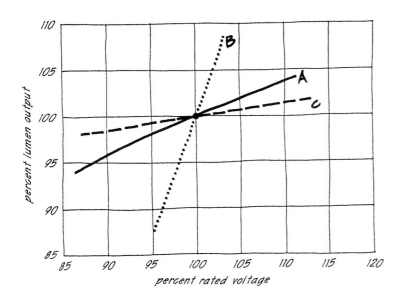

Figure 26.4: Voltage to luminaire factor, VLF: (a) fluorescent, (b) incandescent and mercury with non-regulated ballast, and (c) mercury with constant-wattage ballast. *(Redrawn from Kaufman, 1984, by permission.)*

classification from CU table in Fig. 26.2 or Appendix E or manufacturer's literature; and 36-month luminaire cleaning interval).

Room surface depreciation factor, RSDF = 0.94 (see Fig. 26.6; based on RCR = 5, 10 percent expected dirt depreciation with this "semidirect" luminaire — some light is up, most is down).

Thus the light loss factor,

$$LLF = (LATF)(VLF)(BF)(LSDF)(LBF)(LLDF)(LDDF)(RSDF)$$

$$= (1.0)(1.0)(0.95)(1.0)(1.0)(0.84)(0.86)(0.94) = 0.69$$

MAINTAINED ILLUMINANCE PER LUMINAIRE

Average maintained illuminance per luminaire = (initial illuminance per luminaire)(LLF) = (13.5)(0.69) = 9.3 fc

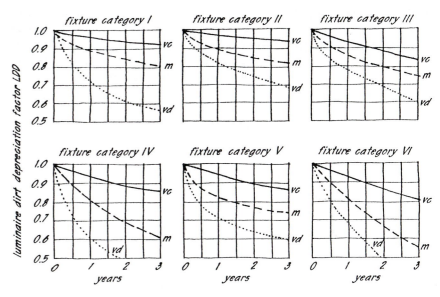

Figure 26.5: Luminaire dirt depreciation factor, LDDF, is a measure of the effect of air cleanliness and luminaire design on reducing lumen output over a period of time. The curves are for very clean (solid line), average (dashed line), and very dirty (dotted line) for six maintenance categories of luminaires. See the coefficient of utilization table from manufacturer's literature to determine the maintenance category (for example, the fluorescent luminaire in Fig. 26.2 is category "V"). *(Redrawn from Kaufman, 1984, by permission.)*

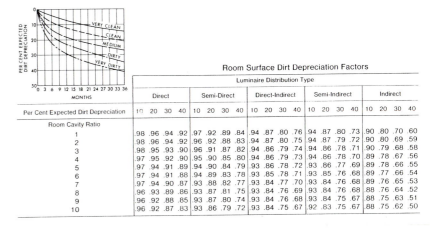

Room Surface Dirt Depreciation Factors

	Direct				Semi-Direct				Direct-Indirect				Semi-Indirect				Indirect			
Per Cent Expected Dirt Depreciation	10	20	30	40	10	20	30	40	10	20	30	40	10	20	30	40	10	20	30	40
Room Cavity Ratio																				
1	.98	.96	.94	.92	.97	.92	.89	.84	.94	.87	.80	.76	.94	.87	.80	.73	.90	.80	.70	.60
2	.98	.96	.94	.92	.96	.92	.88	.83	.94	.87	.80	.75	.94	.87	.79	.72	.90	.80	.69	.59
3	.98	.95	.93	.90	.96	.91	.87	.82	.94	.86	.79	.74	.94	.86	.78	.70	.89	.78	.67	.56
4	.97	.95	.92	.90	.95	.90	.85	.80	.94	.86	.79	.73	.94	.86	.78	.70	.89	.78	.66	.55
5	.97	.94	.91	.89	.94	.90	.84	.79	.93	.86	.78	.72	.93	.86	.77	.69	.89	.77	.66	.54
6	.97	.94	.91	.88	.94	.89	.83	.78	.93	.85	.78	.71	.93	.85	.76	.68	.89	.77	.66	.54
7	.97	.94	.90	.87	.93	.88	.82	.77	.93	.84	.77	.70	.93	.84	.76	.68	.89	.76	.65	.53
8	.96	.93	.89	.86	.93	.87	.81	.75	.93	.84	.76	.69	.93	.84	.76	.68	.88	.76	.64	.52
9	.96	.92	.88	.85	.93	.87	.80	.74	.93	.84	.76	.68	.93	.84	.75	.67	.88	.75	.63	.51
10	.96	.92	.87	.83	.93	.86	.79	.72	.93	.84	.75	.67	.92	.83	.75	.67	.88	.75	.62	.50

Figure 26.6: Room surface dirt depreciation factor, RSDF, is a measure of the effect of dirt accumulation on room surfaces reducing reflection to the workplane over a period of time. *(Redrawn from Kaufman, 1984, by permission.)*

NUMBER OF LUMINAIRES

Establish the *design illuminance level* for the room (for example, from recommendations in Table 21.1). In this example, the design illuminance level is established as 50 fc. Calculate the number of luminaires required:

$$\text{Number of luminaires} = \frac{\text{design illuminance level}}{\text{net illuminance per luminaire}}$$

Thus, the number of luminaires required $= \dfrac{50}{9.3} = 5.4$ or 6

A worksheet is provided for these calculations in Appendix F; Fig. 26.8 shows the completed worksheet for the example.

LIMITATIONS OF METHOD

The lumen method as presented here is a simplification of the zonal cavity method. It assumes that luminaires are surface-mounted; however, it may be applied where the luminaire-to-ceiling distance is comparatively small and wall reflectance above the luminaire plane equals the ceiling reflectance. For large ceiling cavities the more complex general zonal cavity procedure (Kaufman, 1984) is recommended.

ILLUMINANCE AT A POINT — *POINT METHOD*

The lumen method discussed above calculates the illuminance in a workplane averaged over the entire floor area. However, the illuminance at any point may vary considerably at a specific location. For critical locations, it is desirable to calculate the illuminance at one specific point. This point method includes only the direct component of the illuminance from a luminaire; one of its principal disadvantages is that it does not include any indirect light reflected from ceilings or walls.

INVERSE-SQUARE EFFECT

The most widely used method of point illuminance calculation is based on the inverse-square effect which can be expressed:

$$E = \frac{I}{d^2}$$

where E = illuminance in footcandles

I = luminous intensity of the source in candelas

d = distance from the source in feet

In other words, if the source has a luminous intensity of one candela, then the illuminance on a surface at a distance of one foot from the source is one lumen per square foot or one footcandle. When the distance is doubled, the area over which the same lumen is spread is proportionally doubled in width and doubled in height (or 4 ft^2) so that the illuminance is 0.25 fc (lumens per foot). Similarly, moving to three feet from the source distributes the same one lumen over an area of 9 ft^2 resulting in an illuminance of 1/9 fc. In other words, there is an inverse relationship between the illuminance and the square of the distance from the source.

COSINE EFFECT

While the above inverse-square formula gives the illuminance at a point on a plane normal (perpendicular) to the direction of light, in practice this perpendicular relationship is rarely encountered. In most instances, a correction must be applied that reduces the illuminance as the angle of incidence (tilt; the angle between light rays and the perpendicular of the plane) increases. This correction is equal to the cosine of the angle of incidence, and modifies the above formula to become:

$$E = \frac{I}{d^2} = \cos \beta$$

where β = angle of incidence (the angle between light rays and the perpendicular of the plane)

AVERAGE ILLUMINANCE WORKSHEET - ELECTRIC LIGHTING

1. Project name *Example* Room *office* Designer *FM*
2. Illuminance category (from Table 21.1 recommendations or other) _____ *E* Design illumination **50** fc
3. Luminaire manufacturer *Fig 26.2*
4. Luminaire mfg'rs. catalog no. *Fig 26.2* **2280**
5. Lamps: type and color *48" T-12 RS CWX*
6. Initial lumen output (per lamp) **2280**
7. Number of lamps per luminaire **2**
8. Total lumens per luminaire **4400**
9. Fill in sketch:

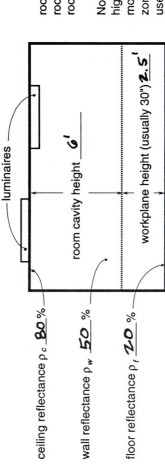

room length **15'**
room width **10'**
room area **150**

luminaires

room cavity height **6'**

workplane height (usually 30") **2.5'**

Note: If ceiling is substantially higher than the luminaire mounting height, the general zonal cavity method must be used (see Kaufman, 1987).

ceiling reflectance ρ$_c$ **80** %

wall reflectance ρ$_w$ **50** %

floor reflectance ρ$_f$ **20** %

10. Calculate the room cavity ratio, RCR:

$$RCR = \frac{5(\text{room cavity height})(\text{room length} + \text{room width})}{(\text{room length})(\text{room width})} = \frac{5(\ 6\ )(\ 15\ + 10\ )}{(\ 15\ )(\ 10\ )} = 5$$

11. Coefficient of utilization, CU (from manufacturer's literature or Kaufman, 1984) = **0.46 (from fig 26.2)**

12. Initial av. illuminance per luminaire = $\dfrac{(\text{lumens per lamp})(\#\ \text{lamps per luminaire})(CU)}{\text{floor area}} = \dfrac{(2280)(2\ )(0.46)}{(\ 150\ )} = $ **13.5**

13. Determine light loss subfactors:

Luminaire ambient temperature factor, LATF **1.0**
Ballast factor, BF **0.95**
Lamp burnout factor, LBF **1.0**
Luminaire dirt depreciation factor, LDDF **0.86**

Voltage to luminaire factor, VLF **1.0**
Luminaire surface depreciation factor, LSDF **1.0**
Lamp lumen depreciation factor, LLDF **0.84**
Room surface depreciation factor, RSDF **0.94**

Light loss factor, LLF = (LATF)(VLF)(BF)(LSDF)(LBF)(LLDF)(LDDF)(RSDF) = **0.69**

14. Maintained illuminance per luminaire = (initial illuminance per luminaire)(LLF) = (**13.5**)(**0.69**) = **9.3 fc**

15. Required number of luminaires = $\dfrac{(\text{design illuminance level})}{\text{net illuminance per luminaire}} = \dfrac{(\ 50\ )}{(\ 9.3\ )} = $ **5.4** or **6**

16. Luminaire layout:

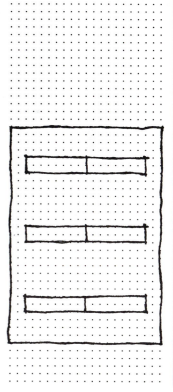

Figure 26.7: Simplified lumen method example worksheet for electric lighting. *(Reproduced from IES Education Committee, 1985, by permission.)*

A candlepower distribution curve (CDC; see Fig. 26.9 for example; also available from luminaire manufacturer's literature) for the luminaire/lamp combination to be used is required in order to determine the illuminance at a point. For example, assume that the luminaire/lamp shown in Fig. 26.10 is used and the reference point is 15 ft away and the angle of incidence (between the light ray and the horizontal workplane) is 30°.

First, determine the luminous intensity (candlepower) from the CDC for the luminaire along the angle toward the reference point (in this case, this is 30°, so the luminous intensity is approximately 7000 cd).

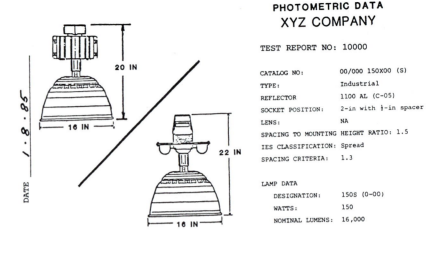

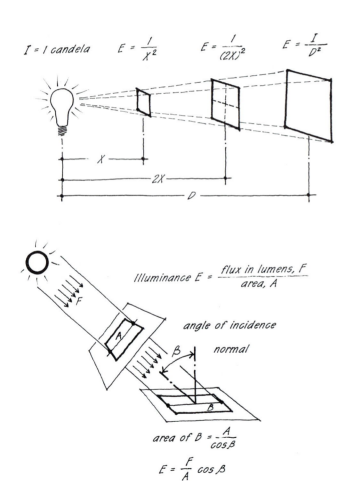

Figure 26.8: (a) Inverse-square effect, and (b) cosine effect. *(Redrawn from Kaufman, 1984, by permission.)*

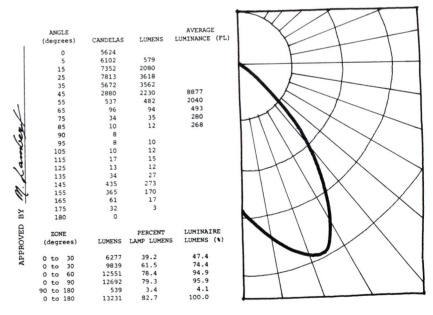

Figure 26.9: Example photometric data sheet. *(Reproduced from IES Education Committee, 1985, by permission.)*

Next, determine the actual "line-of-sight" distance between the light source and the reference point. In this example, that diagonal distance is measured as 15 ft (from an architectural section drawing).

Finally, determine the angle of incidence between the light ray and the reference plane. In this case (where the reference plane is horizontal) the angle of incidence β is identical to the angle leaving the lamp α or 30°. If the reference surface had been vertical (on a wall for example) then the angle of incidence would have been 60°.

Calculate the initial illuminance at point R :

$$E = \frac{I}{d^2} \cos b = \frac{(7000)}{(15)^2} \cos 30° = \frac{(7000)}{(225)} (0.866) = 31.1 \text{ fc}$$

The *light loss factor, LLF*, is computed as in the lumen method (equal to the product of all of the light loss subfactors; see above) and is applied to the initial illuminance to determine the maintained illuminance. In the present example, assume that the LLF is calculated to equal 0.78 for this particular luminaire/lamp combination:

Maintained illuminance = $(I)(\text{LLF}) = (31.1)(0.78) = 24$ fc

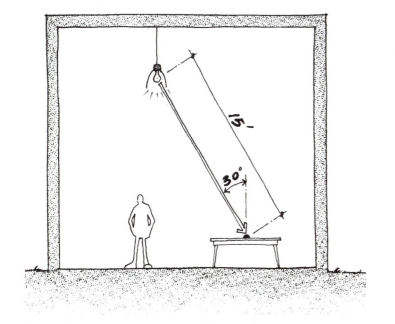

Figure 26.10: Calculating illuminance using the point method.

SUMMARY OF TERMS

Lumen method — a method for calculating the average illuminance in a room on a workplane.

Coefficient of utilization, CU — the percentage of initial lamp lumens that ultimately reach the workplane; it is a function of three factors: room surface reflectances, room size and proportions, and luminaire characteristics.

Initial illuminance — calculated illuminance on a surface based on the initial lumen output of the lamps in combination with the selected luminaire with no allowance for the various light loss factors that reduce this to the maintained illuminance.

Maintained illuminance — the product of the initial illuminance and the light loss factor, LLF.

Light loss factor, LLF — a reduction factor applied to the calculated initial illuminance to determine the maintained illuminance; the product of various light loss subfactors including: luminaire ambient temperature factor, voltage to luminaire factor, ballast factor, luminaire surface depreciation factor, lamp burnout factor, lamp lumen depreciation factor, luminaire dirt depreciation factor, and room surface depreciation factor.

Luminaire ambient temperature factor, LATF — a light loss subfactor applied to the initial illuminance if the ambient temperature of fluorescent lamps is significantly higher or lower than normal room temperature.

Voltage to luminaire factor, VLF — a light loss subfactor applied to the initial illuminance if the service voltage will be predictably high or low.

Luminaire surface depreciation factor, LSDF — a light loss subfactor applied to the initial illuminance due to the depreciation of luminaire surfaces.

Lamp burnout factor, LBF — a light loss subfactor applied to the initial illuminance due to the percentage of lamps allowed to burn out before relamping.

Lamp lumen depreciation factor, LLDF — a light loss subfactor applied to the initial illuminance due to the lumen output gradually and predictably decreasing throughout the life of the lamp.

Ballast factor, BF— a light loss subfactor applied to the initial illuminance due to the ballast.

Luminaire dirt depreciation factor, LDDF— a light loss subfactor applied to the initial illuminance due to the accumulation of dirt on the lamp and luminaire.

Room surface depreciation factor, RSDF— a light loss subfactor applied to the initial illuminance due to the reduction of the amount of light reflected to the workplane due to accumulation of dirt on room surfaces.

Point method — a method for calculating the illuminance at a point.

Angle of incidence, β — the angle between light rays and the perpendicular of the illuminated plane.

STUDY QUESTIONS

1. Compare the two fundamental approaches for calculating illuminance due to electric lighting.

2. What is a coefficient of utilization and of what is it a function?

3. What is a light loss factor (LLF)?

4. Rework the example in Figure 26.7 with the following changes: room length = 40 ft; room width = 30 ft; room cavity height = 8 ft; LLF = 0.72 (blank worksheet available in Appendix F).

5. Using the luminaire in Fig. 26.9, rework the problem shown in Fig. 26.10 except assume that the workplane reference point is 25 ft away, the angle of incidence to the horizontal workplane is 35°, and the light loss factor is 0.62.

27

COMMERCIAL BUILDINGS

The most common error in designing energy-efficient commercial buildings involves choosing and solving the wrong energy problem — usually a residential-scale problem.

— Steve Ternoey (1982)

Buildings (especially continuously occupied residential structures) with thermal loads primarily dominated by the envelope are comparatively simple and straightforward to analyze and to adapt to climate. "Commercial" (in other words, large nonresidential) buildings are much more complex to analyze and to design with a high degree of energy efficiency. The reasons for this complexity are numerous.

Commercial buildings typically have large internal loads (from equipment, lighting, and people). Even in northern climates, for example, cooling is the dominant thermal load in large office buildings. They often are not operated continuously, but on schedules that vary throughout the day and week (and in the case of schools, the year). Because occupants may be restricted to certain locations (a desk, for example), thermal and visual comfort requirements are typically more stringent than for residences. Because occupants (and operations staff) are often not financially responsible for energy costs, energy-efficient operation may be neglected. In the case of buildings built for lease where the tenant will pay for energy costs, the owner's objective of minimizing construction cost discourages investing in any energy-efficient improvements.

In the case of companies building for their own occupancy, the capital costs of upgrading construction quality for the purpose of energy efficiency offer less tax benefit than the alternative of higher utility costs which may be deducted directly as a cost of business operation. Furthermore, when a commercial corporation considers investing in energy-efficient building features, the rate of return on this investment is compared with other investment alternatives (for example, improvements in manufacturing operations); typically, only energy-efficient strategies with a simple payback period of less than two years will compare favorably with competing corporate investment alternatives.

EFFECT OF UTILITY RATE STRUCTURE

One of the greatest differences between residential and commercial buildings is the difference in electric utility rate structure which applies to each. Once the distribution network is in place, electric utilities incur two types of costs in order to deliver energy to a customer: one is the cost directly associated with actually producing the energy (for example, the costs of fuel and plant operation); the other is the cost of building the generating plant capacity (because it is impractical to store large quantities of electrical energy, the plant must be sized to generate electricity at the maximum rate demanded by its customers during the heaviest use period).

Power is the *rate* of energy usage (or generation). Because of this necessity of building adequate capacity to meet peak power demand, the ideal utility customer would be one that consumes power at a consistent rate continuously; this would fully utilize the plant's generating capacity, resulting in a large amount of energy generated (and sold) for a small generating capacity. The worst utility customers are those which consume large amounts of electrical energy at a high rate for a comparatively short period followed by small demands the remainder of the billing period. This requires the utility to build a large generating plant (to cover this peak demand) which remains comparatively idle (and thus inefficient) most of the time (Bryan, 1983).

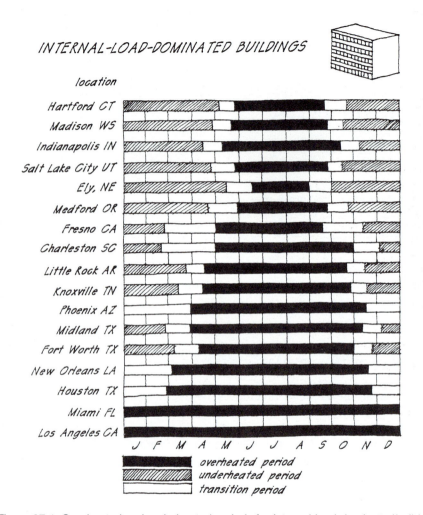

Figure 27.1: Overheated and underheated periods for *internal-load-dominated* buildings for different climatic regions. Assumes a well-constructed internal-load-dominated building with balance point temperature of 50°F; overheated period = average daily temperature > 60°F; underheated = average daily temperature < 50°F. *(Redrawn from Lechner, 1991, by permission.)*

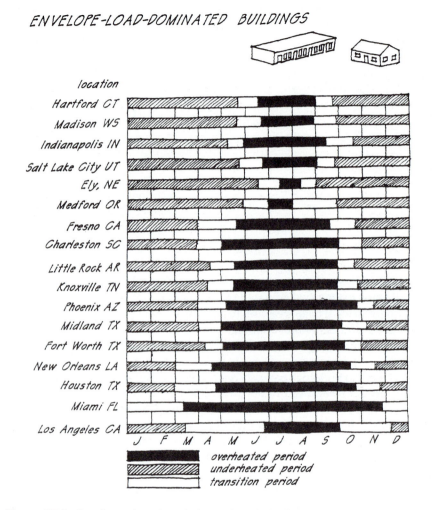

Figure 27.2: Overheated and underheated periods for *envelope-load-dominated* buildings for different climatic regions. Assumes a well-constructed envelope-load-dominated building with balance point temperature of 60°F; overheated period = average daily temperature > 70°F; underheated = average daily temperature < 60°F. *(Redrawn from Lechner, 1991, by permission.)*

In residential buildings, the demand for electric energy is comparatively continuous throughout the day and (depending on climate) throughout the year. Thus, a simple billing rate is used for residential customers based solely on the total quantity of electrical energy consumed throughout the billing period. Because the rate of consumption is fairly constant, this consumption

charge fairly compensates the utility for both the cost of generating the consumed energy but also the long-term cost of building the generating capacity.

In commercial buildings, occupancy is not continuous and typical daily operation causes a sharp peak in power consumption (typically during midafternoon when the maximum lighting, cooling, and equipment loads coincide). Thus, in addition to a consumption charge (based on actual energy consumed), commercial customers are charged an additional "demand" charge based on the peak *rate* of energy use (power demand). This is, in effect, a penalty charge designed to compensate the utility for the costs of building the additional generating capacity necessary to meet infrequent but high power demands. These charges can be quite substantial and typically represent the largest part of commercial building energy costs. Typically, the monthly demand charge is based on the peak power demand occurring any time throughout the billing period — even though that period was brief and much higher than the next highest demand during the billing period. In some cases, the demand charge is based on the peak demand during the last several billing periods; in other words, a single brief heavy consumption period can determine the demand charge for several months (up to a year for some utilities).

Because of the way that demand charges heavily penalize power consumption peaks, there is a great incentive to spread the various loads out so that they do not occur simultaneously. In fact, in commercial buildings, reducing *peak demand* (rather than reducing consumption) becomes the predominant strategy for reducing energy costs. *Load shifting* becomes economically more important than *load reduction.*

Because of the greater number and complexity of the factors that affect commercial buildings (occupancy schedule, internal and ventilation loads, heavy lighting requirements, utility rate schedules, cost/benefit economic considerations, occupant behavior, sophisticated control strategies, maintenance, security), it is important to realize that the relatively simple design strategies and analysis techniques that apply to residences are inadequate or inappropriate to commercial buildings. Today, this complexity necessitates the use of a computer in the design of even comparatively simple commercial buildings, and it is difficult to generalize about their design. However, the emphasis on passive solar heating that applies to residential design in most regions of the United States is replaced by concern for lighting and cooling in commercial buildings.

Commercial building case study: the Bateson Building

The Gregory Bateson Building (Sacramento, California; Van der Ryn Calthorpe and Partners, architects) was the first contemporary climate-adapted commercial building. It was designed in the mid-1970s when most designers associated energy conservation in large commercial buildings with delamping and more insulation. According to architect Scott Matthews, "at this time there were some signs of distaste for the 'bunker' school of energy-conserving design. Many of the early buildings had compact forms and minimum glass area. In ignorance of what was, and what was not, possible,

we turned in the opposite direction — exploiting 'big building-ness' to introduce features that would not only reduce energy consumption, but also contribute to a simulating work environment" (Ternoey et al., 1985).

Figure 27.3: Gregory Bateson Building (Sacramento, California; Van der Ryn Calthorpe and Partners, architects). *(Photo courtesy of Dale Brentrup.)*

The Bateson building was the first contemporary large office building that broke with the tradition of climatic isolation as the means to conserve energy. As such this project represents a major milestone in the history of environmental-control systems for commercial buildings.

The four-story, 267,000-ft^2 government office building was intended as the first of a series of new state facilities to be built in California. In addition to the budget constraints inherent in government construction, the two primary design goals in this building were to establish a humanistic approach to design for institutional buildings and to conserve nonrenewable resources. It is a tribute to the designers that it is often difficult to distinguish which of these two goals was more central to any individual design innovation.

Figure 27.4: Gregory Bateson Building interior of atrium showing south-facing clerestories and colorful suspended fabric destratification fan ducts. *(Photo courtesy of Dale Brentrup.)*

Access to view was a primary determinant of the form of the building, with the designer placing a priority on providing the occupants with a view to improve their well-being and increase their productivity. Access to view requires a narrow building section; this was achieved by adding a large 144-by-150-by-75-ft-high atrium to the center of the square building footprint. This configuration ensured that the maximum distance between occupied space and window is 40 ft, with the average distance about 15 ft.

The atrium is the major energy-related innovation that distinguishes this building from other similar building types of the time. It serves as a source of heating, cooling, and lighting, as well as a protective buffer space for the surrounding large expanse of building. The space is covered with a sawtooth roof with extensive south-facing glazing to capture winter solar radiation. This winter direct gain, diffused by movable fabric banners hung from the ceiling, floods the atrium with light and heat. Because the atrium is connected to the building's air-handling system, excess heat can be passed to the rest of the building or stored in two rock beds located beneath the atrium floor.

In the summer, the south-facing glazing in the sawtooth roof is shaded. North-facing skylights permit the penetration of diffuse light from the north sky. Since the summer nighttime ambient air temperature in Sacramento falls about 25°F below the daytime high, the atrium and rock beds are flushed with this night air to precool the thermal mass. The air-cooled rock beds offset 20 percent of the cooling load of the office spaces.

Unlike the Larkin building (Frank Lloyd Wright, architect) where office space opened directly into the atrium resulting in one large volume for thermal conditioning, the Bateson building (like most contemporary atrium designs) utilizes a windowed partition to separate the office spaces from the atrium. This allows the atrium to act as a thermal buffer space; atrium temperatures are allowed to float, conditioned only by selective exposure to climate and proximity to the conditioned offices. In operation the atrium temperature stabilizes at a temperature halfway between the conditioned office spaces and the outside.

By locating spaces that serve transient functions to the atrium, the volume of the building conditioned to normal standards was reduced. Energy is also conserved because the office walls are exposed to the benign environment of the buffer. With the thermal breaks provided by the surrounding partitions, the sole use of natural space conditioning, and extended comfort limits, this space becomes the architectural equivalent of an HVAC system deadband control strategy. Properly designed, such spaces can stay within bracketed comfort conditions without mechanical assistance.

Properly oriented glass, shading devices, and exposed internal thermal mass are incorporated for natural heating, cooling, and lighting. Extensive use is made of nighttime air to cool the building's thermal mass in the summer. A variable-volume ventilation system is used to purge heat from the mass surfaces during unoccupied hours. This system permits the exposed structure to absorb the radiant and convective heat gains of people, lights, and office machinery during the following day. About 75 percent of the building's cooling load is offset by this direct night venting of office space thermal mass.

The Bateson building is a good example of the potential of a climate-adapted building to add volume and quality to design while achieving both humanistic and energy-related design goals. Its construction cost was comparable to the conventional office buildings that the state was previously leasing from private developers. The building proves that adding volume to a building for both qualitative and energy-related purposes does not necessarily mean that a building will cost more.

THE DOE COMMERCIAL BUILDINGS PROGRAM*

Prior to the 1980s most attempts at climate-responsive buildings were almost entirely residential in scale, and directed at certain highly motivated pioneers — those who would tolerate large temperature swings and peculiar-looking buildings in return for the direct financial savings and the satisfaction for publicly demonstrating their commitment to a resource-conservative philosophy and life-style. Nonresidential buildings were assumed to be unlikely candidates for energy-efficient or passive solar technologies because of their high internal heat gains, large volume, and rigid environmental conditions. Solar heating and daylighting were expected to increase cooling loads which were considerable. Thus the design approaches for residential design were considered inappropriate for larger, more complex buildings.

One reason was a concern about building performance under the demanding and relatively inflexible programmatic requirements of the work environment (for example, stringent requirements for a narrow comfort zone, and fixed working hours and workstation locations). Another was uncertainty about how building users would respond to climate-responsive building in which they had no direct "stake" (that is, no direct financial payoff, no philosophical commitment, and no "pioneer" spirit). The questions became, "Can people who do not stand to benefit directly from financial or philosophical rewards be satisfied in energy-efficient, passive solar buildings and can these users successfully learn to operate these dynamic, flexible buildings to optimize energy savings?"

In order to examine the potential of energy-efficient nonresidential buildings through a process of careful design, construction, and field testing, in 1979, the U.S. Department of Energy (DOE) instituted a large design development and field test program. The program, the Nonresidential Experimental Buildings Program, was intended to build a body of practical information on the design, construction, and performance of nonresidential energy-efficient buildings and to investigate the potential of passive solar technologies to meet commercial building energy requirements. The program is the largest known attempt to guide design and simultaneously evaluate construction and operational costs, actual energy use, occupancy effects, and reactions in climate-responsive, nonresidential buildings.

There were three phases in the DOE program: design, construction, and performance evaluation. Over 300 building owner/design teams applied to participate in the program, but only the best 35 were selected. Of these, 22 buildings located across the country completed design; 19 completed construction.

THE DESIGN PROCESS

In the design phase, each project team first designed a "base case" building, a nonsolar building which the owner would ordinarily build. Team members calculated the building's energy requirements for heating, cooling, lighting, and equipment (taking into account internal loads, building occupancy, schedules, climate, and construction practices). Then the teams developed an alternative design using passive solar approaches to heat, cool, and light the building. They then calculated the design's performance using a variety of energy- and cost-prediction tools. These ranged from complex mainframe energy-simulation programs like BLAST (Building Loads Analysis and System Thermodynamics) to simpler, hand-calculated procedures. The designs were reviewed by technical experts in a series of meetings, ensuring that the designs effectively integrated passive cooling, lighting, and heating strategies.

CONSTRUCTION AND PERFORMANCE EVALUATION

In the construction phase, incremental costs associated with the energy systems were identified. A portion of the redesign and analysis costs were reimbursed by DOE. In each project, energy performance and costs were monitored for one year.

THE BUILDINGS

The 19 completed buildings include varied responses to a wide range of design constraints and opportunities. Each design team faced a different

---

* Excerpted from Burt Hill Kosar Rittelmann (1987) by permission of Van Nostrand Reinhold.

climate, program, client, budget, and site. Yet all utilized passive solar and advanced energy conservation techniques to meet a significant proportion of the heating, cooling, and lighting loads. The following buildings were included in the study (the parenthetical initials provide a reference code for Figs. 28.6 and 28.7):

RPI Visitor Center (RP), a 5,200-ft² office and police headquarters in Troy, New York, relies on a south-facing sunspace with mass walls and floor to supply warm air to the building through a system of plenums. Skylights with reflectors provide daylight and direct-gain heating.

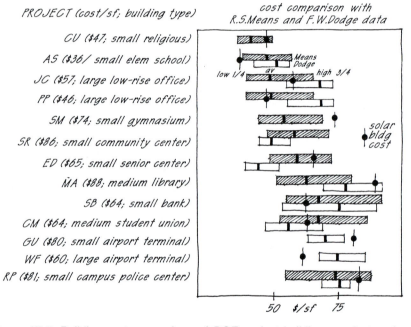

Figure 27.5: Building cost comparison of DOE project buildings against national averages (dollars per square foot for floor area). Comparisons are to a range of typical building costs for similar building types based on data from either R.S. Means, F.W. Dodge, or both. The projects include: RPI Visitor Center (RP), Mt. Airy Public Library (MA), St. Mary's School Gymnasium (SM), Security State Bank (SB), Essex-Dorsey Senior Center (ED), Shelly Ridge Girl Scout Center (SR), Two Rivers School (AS), Blake Avenue College Center (CM), Princeton School of Architecture (PS), Johnson Controls Branch Office Building (JC), Community United Methodist Church (CU), Princeton Professional Park (PP), Kieffer Store (KS), Comal County Mental Health Center (CC), Gunnison County Airport (GU), Philadelphia Municipal Auto Shop (PM), Walker Field Terminal (WF), Touiatos Greenhouse (TG), and Abrams Primary School (AS). *(After Burt Hill Kosar Rittelmann, 1987.)*

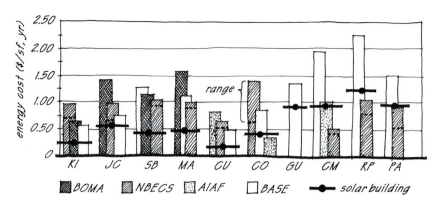

Figure 27.6: Annual utility cost comparison of DOE project buildings against national averages (dollars per square foot of floor area per year). Comparisons of the buildings' actual energy costs were made to: Nonresidential Building Energy Consumption Survey (NBECS) — a survey of over 5,000 nonresidential buildings done in 1979; Building Owners and Managers Association (BOMA) exchange report summarizing office building operating costs for specific cities in the United States; American Institute of Architects Foundation (AIAF) summary of available data on energy cost in public schools; and the base case analysis for the project building based on performance predictions. *(After Burt Hill Kosar Rittelmann, 1987.)*

Mt. Airy Public Library (MA), a 13,500-ft² community library in Mt. Airy, North Carolina, utilizes a set of south-facing, sawtooth clerestories and light baffles to provide diffused daylight to the central areas of the building (see Chapter 23).

St. Mary's School Gymnasium (SM), a 9,000-ft² addition school in Alexandria, Virginia, delivers passive solar heat phased by a concrete Trombe wall in three different thicknesses.

Security State Bank (SB), an 11,000-ft² bank in Wells, Minnesota, uses direct gain and daylighting through south-facing clerestory with a baffle diffusion system.

Essex-Dorsey Senior Center (ED), a 13,000-ft² multipurpose senior center renovation in Baltimore uses a south-facing clerestory on the new wing to provide daylighting and aid natural ventilation.

Shelly Ridge Girl Scout Center (SR), a 5,700-ft² two-story, open-plan community education facility located near Philadelphia uses direct gain and a Trombe wall in a compact, high-mass building (see Chapter 9).

Two Rivers School (AS), a 15,750-ft² elementary school outside Fairbanks, Alaska, includes an experimental passive solar classroom designed to be a prototype of a small rural schoolhouse equipped with a special thermal system over much of the south-facing triple glazing.

Blake Avenue College Center (CM), a 31,900-ft² community college building in Glenwood Springs, Colorado, includes a three-story central atrium that unifies the functions and collects solar heat, acts as a plenum for the cooling system, and is a central lighting core from which adjacent offices and classrooms borrow light.

Princeton School of Architecture (PS) building, a retrofit project of a 13,700-ft² architecture school building in Princeton, New Jersey, integrates new conservation and solar features in an existing building by utilizing existing skylight openings for direct-gain heating and lighting roof monitors.

Johnson Controls Branch Office Building (JC), a 15,000-ft² office located in Salt Lake City, combines a sophisticated computer control system with relatively straightforward passive solar design using a combination of features for direct solar gain and enhanced distribution of daylight.

Community United Methodist Church (CU), a 5,500-ft² educational addition to a community church in Columbia, Missouri, features clerestories with overhangs and insulating shades and thermal mass.

Princeton Professional Park (PP), a 64,000-ft² speculative office building located in Princeton, New Jersey, utilizes a central atrium designed to function as a part of the heating, cooling, and lighting schemes, as well as part of the circulation between offices (see Chapter 17).

Kieffer Store (KS), a 3,200-ft² addition to a retail store in Wausau, Wisconsin, uses a direct-gain sunspace and roof monitors for heating and daylighting.

Comal County Mental Health Center (CC), a retrofit of a 4,800-ft² 1930s school in New Braunfels, Texas, includes a variety of defensive cooling strategies including an evaporative roof spray system.

Gunnison County Airport (GU), a 9,700-ft² airport terminal building in Gunnison, Colorado, uses a large and automatic night insulation.

Philadelphia Municipal Auto Shop (PM), a retrofit of a 57,000-ft² warehouse-like auto maintenance facility in downtown Philadelphia, uses a solar window heater module.

Walker Field Terminal (WF), a 66,700-ft² airport terminal building in Grand Junction, Colorado, uses a series of stepped, south-facing clerestories.

Touiatos Greenhouse (TG), a 6,000-ft² commercial greenhouse building in Memphis, uses vaulted skylights and windows and biomass decomposition for auxiliary heat.

Abrams Primary School (AS), a 27,400-ft² elementary school located in Bessemer, Alabama, features water-filled PVC tubes to store heat as well as to diffuse sunlight.

PERFORMANCE MONITORING

Performance monitoring indicated that actual building use exceeded projections by about 20 percent on an area-weighted average (only one of the projects actually exceeded energy savings). Most of the discrepancy was in heating energy: 31 percent higher than the original estates, despite warmer-than-usual weather. The discrepancies between the actual and projected consumption resulted from at least two factors: unanticipated building-use patterns and design tool limitations. Of these, unanticipated use patterns was identified as the primary factor. For example, building operation hours were extended because of the popularity of the building. Because building-use patterns are so difficult to predict, designers of climate-responsive buildings should anticipate postoccupancy changes by analyzing their designs under a wide range of use patterns.

LESSONS FROM THE DOE PROGRAM

- Vertical glazing was found generally superior to sloped glazing and definitely superior to horizontal skylights in internal-load-dominated buildings. Glazing sloped toward the sun admitted too much direct-beam sunlight and was difficult to shade with overhangs.

- Core daylighting was best achieved using roof monitors. These should face south whenever there is even a modest heating load. They work best as small, distributed apertures instead of a single large opening.

- Well-controlled daylighting will reduce cooling since, lumen for lumen, daylight generates less heat than does artificial light. The designer's objective is to admit modest amounts of light distributed over large areas.

Excessive daylight will generate excessive heat gains, and poor distribution will require more electric illumination in interior areas than is otherwise necessary.

- Daylight distribution to core areas is necessary for good perimeter lighting because light distributed evenly across the room reduces bothersome brightness contrast caused by unilateral exposure.

- Manual light control can be more energy conserving than automated dimming or switching controls. This was particularly true in buildings where users perceived they had a greater level of control over the interior environment. Occupants were found to be often willing to work at lower lighting levels than those recommended by industry standards. This voluntary action is apparently connected to the high degree of personal control that users perceived in those buildings.

- The best cooling strategies are defensive: shading and insulation.

- The next best cooling strategy is natural ventilation and night flushing (in massive construction).

- Ventilation airflow must be direct; convoluted paths that wind through a building are a designer's fantasy.

- Operable windows should not be used for night-flushing ventilation in buildings which are not occupied at night. (For reasons of security and precipitation, building staff will not leave windows open when the building is not occupied.) Instead, use screened louvered openings with weatherstripped interior shutters.

- Venetian blinds effectively obstruct natural ventilation when in the closed position.

- Nonresidential-quality movable insulation is not generally available; consider low-E glazing or selective surface alternatives. In the DOE program, while project designers worked hard to develop custom movable insulation systems, the end results were mixed. In five case, there were either delays in the original installation, problems with operation once installed, or such poor performance that the original system had to be replaced.

- Occupants enjoy and appreciate climate-responsive buildings. In several of the projects, there was a significant increase over anticipated building use. Owners claim that employee productivity is up because employees like the spaces in which they work. Occupant surveys leave no doubt that most occupants enjoy these buildings better than comparable conventional alternatives.

- The "bottom line" is that climate-responsive buildings can reduce energy consumption and costs; those participating in the DOE program used 47 percent less energy than their conventional "base case" counterparts.

- Passive devices must be simple to install and both the function and operation must be intuitively obvious. In the project buildings, devices that were difficult to install or seemed counterintuitive to construction personnel were usually built incorrectly, and (in some cases) were sabotaged by construction personnel. In one case, the auxiliary electric resistance spaceheaters were wired to operate continually because the electrical contractor did not believe the passive techniques would provide sufficient heating; the problem was discovered during the performance monitoring phase and easily corrected.

High-mass vs. low-mass buildings

Both high-mass and low-mass buildings work well but each must be carefully examined with respect to climate, building use and occupancy schedules.

High-mass buildings work well under the following conditions:
- Where there is extended evening and weekend use; such schedules can take advantage of stored heat.

- In sunny climates; solar energy can charge the mass.

- In high-cooling-load buildings, where high mass absorbs gains during the day and allows discharge at night by "night flushing" ventilation.

- In climates with large diurnal temperature swings; mass allows storing up heat during the day for release at night. In the heating season, this release is to the interior; in the cooling season, it is to the outside.

Low-mass buildings work well under the following conditions:
- Where building hours follow typical 40-hour-per-week schedules (for more continuous operating schedules, night and weekend setback may contribute higher savings than will thermal mass, which dampens temperature setback savings). In general, setback is difficult in high-mass

buildings because heating systems must recharge the mass before the building opens; occupants feel cold with cool walls and floors even though the air temperature is sufficiently high.

- In cloudy climates; solar energy should meet the immediate (instantaneous) heating load before being stored in thermal mass. This makes storage less important with limited solar energy.

- In buildings with large internal volume; high ceilings can be used to collect heat for redistribution to areas needing heat.

- In buildings with relatively small solar collection apertures (compared with the heat loss); all of the available solar energy goes to meeting the immediate heating load, and little is left over for storage.

THE IMPORTANCE OF DAYLIGHTING DISTRIBUTION

Daylighting resulted in significant cost and energy savings while contributing to user comfort; approximately 55 percent of the savings over the base case lighting energy was achieved through these daylighting strategies. Successful daylight designs shared a number of characteristics. The most important of these was distribution. If daylight was well distributed, a visually comfortable and largely glare-free environment was attained. The most successful design solutions had the following characteristics:

- Glare and contrast was controlled.

- Direct sunlight was not allowed to enter an occupied space; instead, baffles, diffusing reflecting surfaces, and/or diffusing glazing were used to break up beam lighting.

- Occupants were not able to see the light source directly from the spaces they usually occupied.

- Light was admitted high on the wall plane or at the ceiling plane.

- The view was retained.

- A number of smaller roof apertures (clerestories and monitors) were used rather than fewer larger openings.

- Roof monitors and clerestories were oriented south with vertical glazing.

CONCLUSION: BIG BUILDINGS DEFY INTUITION

The most common error in designing energy-efficient commercial buildings involves choosing and solving the wrong energy problem — usually a residential-scale problem (Ternoey, 1982). It has been said that intuition is internalized experience used in unfamiliar situations. The failure of designers to understand intuitively the energy needs of large buildings is likely based in their lack of broad experience. Commercial buildings have simultaneous, interconnected energy needs. Lowering the lighting load is usually the easiest way to cut the cooling load. Changing the ventilation rate can shift the dominant energy challenge from cooling to heating or vice versa. As a group, designers will certainly gain more detailed experience with this type of energy problem during the coming years. Until they have gained that experience gained as a profession, they must restrain their intuition and use analysis instead to define exactly what energy needs they will address.

SUMMARY OF TERMS

Envelope-dominated building — one with an energy-use pattern that is dominated by heat loss and gain through the building envelope.

Internal-load-dominated building — one with an energy-use pattern that is dominated by internal heat gains from lighting, equipment, and people.

Power — the rate of energy usage (or generation).

Residential electric utility rate — a simple billing rate used for residential customers based solely on the total quantity of electrical energy consumed throughout the billing period.

Commercial electric utility rate — a compound rate consisting of a consumption charge (based on actual energy consumed), plus a demand charge (based on the peak rate of energy use — power demand).

Load-shifting — a strategy of staggering peak electric loads (due to lighting, cooling, and equipment) in order to reduce demand costs in commercial electric utility rates.

REFERENCES

Abrams, D., 1986, *Low Energy Cooling.* New York: Van Nostrand Reinhold.

AIA Research Corporation, 1978, Regional Guidelines for Building Passive Energy Conserving Homes. HUD-PDR-355, Washington, D.C.: U.S. Department of Housing and Urban Development.

ASHRAE, 1981, *Thermal Environmental Conditions for Human Occupancy (Standard 55-1981).* Atlanta, Georgia: American Society of Heating, Air-Conditioning, and Refrigerating Engineers.

————, 1985, *ASHRAE Handbook 1985 Fundamentals.* Atlanta, Georgia: American Society of Heating, Air-Conditioning, and Refrigerating Engineers.

————, 1989, *ASHRAE Handbook 1989 Fundamentals.* Atlanta, Georgia: American Society of Heating, Air-Conditioning, and Refrigerating Engineers.

Aho, A., 1981, *Neo-Dogtrot: Mississippi.* Starkville, Mississippi: Mississippi State University.

Akhenaton, 1984, "The hymn to the sun," *3000 Years of Black Poetry,* Lomax, A., and Abdul, R. (eds.). New York: Dodd and Mead.

Akridge, J., 1982, *Investigation of Passive Cooling Techniques for Hot-Humid Climates - Final Report,* USDOE contract DE-AC02-79CS30238. Atlanta, GA: College of Architecture, Georgia Institute of Technology, as cited by Labs, 1990, op. cit.

Allen, E., and Iano, J., 1989, *The Architect's Studio Companion.* New York: John Wiley and Sons.

American Institute of Architects, 1949-1952, "Regional climatic analyses and design data," *AIA Bulletins,* reprint; Ann Arbor, Michigan: University Microfilms.

————, 1981, *Energy in Architecture: Level 3a Applications.* Washington, D.C.: American Institute of Architects, as cited by Franta, G., 1990, "Thermal energy distribution in building interiors," in Cook, J. (ed.), *Passive Cooling,* Cambridge, Massachusetts: MIT Press.

————, 1982, "HVAC systems," *Architects Handbook of Energy Practice.* Washington, D.C.: American Institute of Architects.

Anderson, B., and Wells, M., 1981, *Passive Solar Energy: The Homeowner's Guide to Natural Heating and Cooling.* Andover, Massachusetts: Brick House.

Arends, E., Gonzalez, R., Bergland, L., McNall, P., and Zeren, L., 1980, "A new bioclimatic chart for passive solar design," *Proceedings of the Fifth National Passive Solar Conference.* Boulder, Colorado: American Solar Energy Society, pp. 1202-1206.

Arnold, F., Bartow, R., and Collier, R., 1980, "Design considerations for solar dehumidifiers," *Proceedings of the Fifth National Passive Solar Conference.* Boulder, Colorado: American Solar Energy Society, pp. 712-716.

Baer, S., 1975, *Sunspots.* Albuquerque, New Mexico: Zomeworks.

————, 1986, "Zomeworks manufacturers reflector/shade," *DNNA Newsletter,* vol. 1, no. 1, p. 6.

Bahadori, M., 1978, "Passive cooling systems in Iranian architecture," *Scientific*

American, vol. 238, no. 2, pp. 145-154.

Balcomb, J., Jones, R., McFarland, R., and Wray, W., 1984, *Passive Solar Heating Analysis: A Design Manual.* Atlanta: American Society of Heating, Refrigerating, and Air-Conditioning Engineers.

Banham, R., 1966, "Frank Lloyd Wright as environmentalist," *Arts and Architecture.* September, pp. 26-30.

———, 1969, *The Architecture of the Well-Tempered Environment.* Chicago: University of Chicago Press.

Bednar, M., 1986, *The New Atrium.* New York: McGraw-Hill.

Beir, J., 1979, "Performance of a low-cost owner-built home using vertical solar louvers," *Proceedings of the Third National Passive Solar Conference.* Boulder, Colorado: American Solar Energy Society, pp. 643-647.

Benedikt, M., 1976, *The Prose Poem.* New York: Dell Publishing Co., p. 380.

Berry, P., 1961, "Effect of colored illumination on perceived temperature," *Journal of Applied Psychology,* vol. 45, pp. 248-250, as cited by ASHRAE, 1985, op. cit.

Bliss, S., 1984, "Vapor Barriers and Condensation," *Solar Age.* February, pp. 53-54.

Bowen, A., 1981, "Classification of air motion systems and patterns," *Proceedings of the International Passive and Hybrid Cooling Conference.* Boulder, Colorado: American Solar Energy Society, pp. 743-763.

Boyer, L., and Johnston, T., 1981, "Organization of interior spaces for earth cooling," *Proceeding of the International Passive and Hybrid Cooling Conference.* Boulder, Colorado: American Solar Energy Society, pp. 121-125.

Brett, C., and Schaetzle, W., 1982, "Experiences with unconfined aquifer chilled water storage," *ASHRAE Transactions* 90(2B)189, as cited by Clark, 1990, op. cit.

Brown, G., 1985, *Sun Wind and Light: Architectural Design Strategies.* New York: John Wiley and Sons, by permission.

Bruemmer, F., 1981, "Eskimos are warm people," *Natural History,* vol. 90, no. 10, pp. 43-48.

Bryan, H., 1983, "Power Play," *Progressive Architecture.* April, pp. 102-105.

———, and Carlsberg, D., 1982, "Daylight protractors: for calculating the effects of clear skies," *Progress in Passive Solar Energy Systems.* Boulder, Colorado: American Solar Energy Society, pp. 399-404.

———, Moore, J., Kwartler, M., and Jones, T., 1981, "The utilization of daylighting as an urban design strategy," in Kroner, W., Bryan, H., and Leslie, R. (eds.), *Daylighting Resourcebook,* Washington, D.C.: Association of Collegiate Schools of Architecture.

Buerhrer, H., 1978, "Estimating energy usage," (developed for AIA Energy Audit Seminars), as cited by Stein and Reynolds, 1992, op. cit.

Burnette, C., and Legerton, J., 1981, "Solar in the City," *Solar Age,* vol. 6, no. 5, May, pp. 38-42, as cited by Ridley, 1990, op. cit.

Burt Hill Kosar and Rittelmann Associates and Min Kantrowitz Associates, 1987, *Commercial Building Design: Integrating Climate, Comfort, and Cost.* New York: Van Nostrand Reinhold.

Butler, L. P., 1978, "Using natural energy in architectural design," *Proceedings of the Second National Passive Solar Conference.* Boulder, Colorado: American Solar Energy Society, pp. 169-172.

Carey, C., and Marsh, R., 1981, "Shivering Finches," *Natural History.* vol. 90, October, pp. 58-63.

Cartwright, V., and Reynolds, J., 1991, "Daylight, energy conservation, and comfort in an office building," *Proceeding of the Biennial Congress of the International Solar Energy Society.* New York: Pergamon Press, pp. 2703-2708.

Chandra, S., Fairey, P., and Houston, M., 1983, *A Handbook for Designing Ventilated Buildings.* FSEC-CR-93-83. Cape Canaveral, Florida: Florida Solar Energy Center.

Chandra, S., Fairey, P., Houston, M., and Kerestecioglu, A., 1983, "Outdoor testing of small scale naturally ventilated models." *Building and Environment*

18(1/2):45-53. London: Pergamon Press.

Chandra, S., Fairey, P., and Houston, M., 1984, "Residential cooling strategies for hot humid climates," draft report to SERI, Cape Canaveral: Florida Solar Energy Center, as cited by Clark, G., 1990, "Passive Cooling Systems," in Cook, J. (ed.), *Passive Cooling*, Cambridge, Massachusetts: MIT Press, pp. pp. 347-548.

Chandra, S., Fairey, P., and Houston, M., 1986, *Cooling with Ventilation.* Springfield, Virginia: National Technical Information Center.

Chardra, S., 1990, "Ventilative cooling," in Cook, J. (ed.), *Passive Cooling*, Cambridge, Massachusetts: MIT Press, pp. 42-84.

Clark, G., and Blanpied, M., 1979, "The effect of IR-transparent windscreens on net nocturnal cooling from horizontal surfaces," in Franta, G. (ed.), *Proceedings, Fourth National Passive Solar Conference.*Boulder, Colorado: American Solar Energy Society, pp. 509-513.

Clark, G., Loxsom, F., Haves, P., and Doderer, E., 1983, "Results of validated simulations of roof pond cooled residences," *Proceedings of the Eighth National Passive Solar Conference.* Boulder, Colorado: American Solar Energy Society.

Collins, K., and Hoinville, E., 1980, "Temperature requirements in old age," *Building Services Engineering Research and Technology*, vol. 1, pp. 165-172, as cited by ASHRAE, 1989, op. cit.

Cook, J., 1982, "Prophetic Presence in downtown Portland," *AIA Journal*, July, pp. 84-89, as cited by Watson, 1989, op. cit.

———, 1984, *Award-Winning Passive Solar Designs.* New York: McGraw-Hill.

———, 1985, "Zomehouse," *Fine Homebuilding*, April/May, pp. 52-57.

———, 1990, "Introduction," in Cook, J. (ed.), *Passive Cooling*, Cambridge, Massachusetts: MIT Press, pp. 1-42.

Crowther, K., 1979, "Cooling from an evaporating, thermosiphoning roof pond," *Proceedings of the Fourth National Passive Solar Conference.* Boulder, Colorado: American Solar Energy Society, pp. 499-503.

Crowther, K., and Melzer, B., 1979, "The thermosiphoning cool pool: a natural cooling system," *Proceedings of the Third National Passive Solar Conference.* Boulder, Colorado: American Solar Energy Society, pp. 448-451.

Dannies, J., 1959, "Solar air-conditioning and solar refrigeration," *Solar Energy*, vol. 3, no. 1, pp. 34-39.

Davenport, A., 1965, "The relationship of wind structure to wind loading," *Proceedings of the Conference of Wind Effects on Structures*, vol. I, pp. 53-102, National Physics Laboratory, London: H. M. Stationery Office, as cited by Landsburg, 1981, op. cit.

Davis, P., 1976, "To air is human: some humanistic principles in the design of thermosiphon air heaters," *Proceedings of the Passive Solar Heating and Cooling Conference* (First National Passive Solar Conference). Boulder, Colorado: American Solar Energy Society, pp. 40-46.

———, 1977, "To air is human," *Solar Age*, February, pp. 24-27.

Dufton, A. F., 1946, "Protractors for the computation of daylight factors," D.S.I.R. Building Research Technical Paper No. 28, London: Her Majesty's Stationery Office, as cited by Bryan, H., and Carlsberg, D., 1982, "Daylight protractors: for calculating the effects of clear skies," *Progress in Passive Solar Energy Systems*. Boulder, Colorado: American Solar Energy Society, pp. 399-404.

Dunkle, R., 1966, "Regenerative evaporative cooling systems," *Aus. Refrig., Air Cond. Heating* 20(1):22-26, as cited by Yellott, 1990, op. cit.

Edholm, O., 1978, *Man — Hot and Cold.* London: Edward Arnold Limited.

Editor, 1974, "A breakaway house that's heated by the sun," *House and Garden*, January, pp. 72-73.

———, 1979a, "Kelbaugh house," *Progressive Architecture*, April, pp. 116-117.

———, 1979b, "Unit One First Village," *Progressive Architecture*, April, pp. 111-112.

———, 1981, "Milford Reservation Environmental Center," *Progressive Architecture*, April, pp. 118-121.

———, 1982, "Mastin double-envelope house: performance results," *Solar*

Age, July, pp. 48-49.

———, 1983a, "Mount Airy's Library: a runaway best-seller," *Solar Age.* February, pp. 20-21.

———, 1983b, "New Hampshire Conservation Center," *Progressive Architecture,* April, pp. 86-89.

———, 1983c, "Mercer County Library," *Progressive Architecture*, April, p. 39.

———, 1983d, "New Canaan Horticultural Education Center," *Progressive Architecture*, April, pp. 94-97.

———, 1983e, "Princeton Professional Park," *Progressive Architecture,* April, pp. 94-97.

Eichna, L., Park, C., Nelson, N., Horvath, S., and Palmes, E., 1950, "Thermal regulation during acclimization in a hot, dry environment," *American Journal of Physiology,* 163: 585-597, as cited by Fanger, 1982, op. cit.

Evans, B., 1957, *Natural Air Flow Around Buildings.* RR-59, College Stations, Texas: Texas A&M University, Texas Engineering Experiment Station.

———, 1979, "Energy conservation with natural air flow through windows." *ASHRAE Transactions,* 85(2), pp. 641-650.

———, 1989, "Letting fresh air back into buidlings," *Architecture,* 73(3), March, pp. 72-77.

Fairey, P., 1986, "Radiant energy transfer and radiant barrier systems in buildings," FSEC-DN-6-86, Cape Canaveral, Florida: Florida Solar Energy Center.

Fanchiotti, A., and Scudo, G., 1981, "Large scale underground cooling system in Italian 16th century Palladian villas," *Proceeding of the International Passive and Hybrid Cooling Conference.* Boulder, Colorado: American Solar Energy Society, pp. 179-182.

Fanger, P. O., and Langkilde, G., 1975, "Individual differences in ambient temperature preferred by seated persons," *ASHRAE Transactions* 81(2):140-147, as cited by ASHRAE, 1989, op. cit.

———, 1982, *Thermal Comfort.* Malabar, Florida: Robert E. Krieger Company.

Fathy, H., 1973, *Architecture for the Poor.* Chicago: University of Chicago Press.

Felts, D., 1985, "Daylighting with skylights and reflectors," *Proceedings of the Tenth National Passive Solar Conference.* Boulder, Colorado: American Solar Energy Society, pp. 594-598.

Fisher, T., 1983, "Post-industrial architecture," *Progressive Architecture.* April, pp. 109-113.

———, 1984, "The well-tempered tropics," *Progressive Architecture.* April, pp. 98-102.

———, 1985, "An energy education: Florida A&M Architecture School," *Progressive Architecture*, April, pp. 74-7.

Fitch, J., and Branch, D., 1960, "Primitive architecture and climate," *Scientific American,* vol. 203, pp.134-145.

Fleischhacker, P., Clark, G., and Gioloma, P., 1983, "Geographic limits for comfort in unassisted roof pond cooled residences," *Proceedings of the Eighth National Passive Solar Conference.* Boulder, Colorado: American Solar Energy Society, pp. 835-838.

Flynn, J., and Segil, A., 1970, *Architectural Interior Systems.* New York: Van Nostrand Reinhold.

Ford, R., 1982, *Mississippi Houses: Yesterday Toward Tomorrow.* Starkville, Mississippi: Robert Ford.

Fraker, H., 1984, "Formal speculations on thermal diagrams," *Progressive Architecture,* April, pp. 104-108.

Francis, C., 1981a, "A dual-bed solid desiccant dehumidifier for use with passive hybrid cooling systems," *Proceeding of the International Passive and Hybrid Cooling Conference.* Boulder, Colorado: American Solar Energy Society, pp. 292-295.

———, 1981b, "Earth cooling tubes: case studies of three midwest installations," *Proceeding of the International Passive and Hybrid Cooling Conference.* Boulder, Colorado: American Solar Energy Society, pp. 171-175.

Franklin Research Center, 1979, *The First Passive Solar Home Awards.* Washington, D.C.: U.S. Government Printing Office, pp. 140-145.

Gagge, A. P., et al., 1941, "A practical system of units for the description of the heat exchange of man with his environment," *Science*, vol. 94: 428-430, as cited by ASHRAE, 1989, op. cit.

Gardner, J., 1984, "Daylighting cuts energy use to 19,600 Btu per sq ft per year," *Architectural Record*. January, pp. 139-143.

Geiger, R., 1950, *The Climate Near the Ground*. Cambridge, Massachusetts: Harvard University Press.

Germer, J., 1983, "A public role for the Conservation Center," *Solar Age*, February, pp. 19-20.

———, 1986a, "Phase-change drywall," *Solar Age*. April, pp. 24-27.

———, 1986b, "The four-inch Trombe wall," *Solar Age*, July, pp. 27-28.

Givoni, B., 1969, *Man, Climate, and Architecture*. London: Applied Science Publishers.

———, 1977, "Solar heating and night radiation cooling by a roof radiation trap," *Energy and Buildings* 1: 141-145, as cited by Martin, 1990, op. cit.

———, 1980, "Earth integrated buildings, an overview," *Proceedings of the International Expert Group Meeting on Passive and Low Energy Cooling, Heating, and Dehumidification*, Bowen, A., editor. Coral Gables, Florida: University of Miami.

———, 1981, "Experimental studies on radiant and evaporative cooling of roofs," *Proceeding of the International Passive and Hybrid Cooling Conference*. Boulder, Colorado: American Solar Energy Society, pp. 279-283.

Gougeon, M., and Gougeon, J., 1988, *The Gougeon Brothers on Boat Construction*. Bay City, MI: Gougeon Brothers, Inc., P. O. Box X908, Bay City, Michigan 48707.

Grundfeld, F., 1975, "Houses that just grew," *Horizon*, vol. 17, no. 2, pp. 97-101.

Guerin, D., 1979, "Fabrics and passive solar design," *Solar Age*, July, p. 45.

Hancocks, D., 1973, *Master Builders of the Animal World*. London: Hugh Evelyn. Hansen, J., 1981, "Clothing for Cold Climes," *Natural History*, vol. 90, no. 10, pp. 90-96.

Harrison, D., 1976, "Beadwalls," *Proceedings of the Passive Solar Heating and Cooling Conference* (First National Passive Solar Conference). Boulder, Colorado: American Solar Energy Society, pp. 283-287.

Hay, H., 1976, "Atascadero residence," *Proceedings of the Passive Solar Heating and Cooling Conference* (First National Passive Solar Conference). Boulder, Colorado: American Solar Energy Society, pp. 101-107.

———, and Yellott, J., 1970, "A naturally air-conditioned building," *Mechanical Engineering*, vol. 32, no. 1, pp. 19-23.

Heschong, L., 1979, *Thermal Delight in Architecture*. Cambridge, Massachusetts: MIT Press.

Hewitt, P., 1977, *Conceptual Physics*. Boston: Little, Brown and Company.

Holleman, T., 1951, *Air Flow Through Conventional Window Openings*. RR-33, College Station, Texas: Texas A&M University, Texas Engineering Experiment Station.

Hopkinson, R. G., 1963, *Architectural Physics: Lighting*. London: Her Majesty's Stationery Office.

———, and Kay, J. D., 1969, *The Lighting of Buildings*. London: Farber and Farber.

———, Petherbridge, P., and Longmore, J., 1966, *Daylighting*. London: Heinemann.

Howard, B., and Fraker, H., 1990, "Thermal energy storage in building interiors," in Anderson, B. (ed.), *Solar Building Architecture*, Cambridge, MA: MIT Press, pp. 147-256.

Huber, H., 1982, "A step beyond the envelope house," *Solar Age*, June, pp. 24-28.

Illuminating Engineering Society, 1924, *Illuminating Engineering Society Handbook*. New York: Illuminating Engineering Society, as cited by Robbins, C., 1986, *Daylighting Design and Analysis*. New York: Van

Nostrand Reinhold.

IES Education Committee, 1985, *Introductory Lighting.* ED-100.1, IES Education Series, Atlanta: Illuminating Engineering Society.

Jackson Mac Low, 1962, "7th Light poem, for John Cage — June 17th, 1962," *Open Poetry: 4 Anthologies of Expanded Poems.*

Jaffe, M., and Dunkan, E., 1980, *Site Planning for Solar Access.* For the United States Department of Housing and Urban Development, Chicago: American Planning Council, as cited by Ridley, 1990, op. cit.

Johnson, T., 1978, "Preliminary performance of the MIT Solar Building 5," *Proceedings of the Second National Passive Solar Conference.* Boulder, Colorado: American Solar Energy Society, pp. 610-615.

Jones, M., and Morris, W. S., 1980, "Two innovative passive air thermosiphon houses in Santa Fe," *Proceedings of the Fifth National Passive Solar Conference.* Boulder, Colorado: American Solar Energy Society, pp. 1051-1055.

Kantrowitz, M., 1983, "Occupant effects and interactions in passive solar commercial buildings: preliminary findings from the U.S. DOE passive solar commercial buildings program," *Proceedings of the Eighth National Passive Solar Conference.* Boulder, Colorado: American Solar Energy Society, pp. 433-438.

Kaufman, J., editor, 1981, *IES Lighting Handbook, 1981 Reference Volume.* New York: Illuminating Engineering Society of North America.

———, editor, 1984, *IES Lighting Handbook 1984 Reference Volume.* New York: Illuminating Engineering Society of North America.

———, editor, 1987, *IES Lighting Handbook 1987 Application Volume.* New York: Illuminating Engineering Society of North America.

———, editor, 1987, *IES Lighting Handbook 1987 Reference Volume.* New York: Illuminating Engineering Society of North America.

Kelbaugh, D., 1976a, "Solar home in New Jersey," *A.D.* November, pp. 653-656.

———, 1976b, "Kelbaugh house," *Proceedings of the Passive Solar Heating and*

Cooling Conference (First National Passive Solar Conference). Boulder, Colorado: American Solar Energy Society, pp. 119-128.

———, 1976c, "The Kelbaugh house," *Solar Age.* July, pp. 18-23.

———, 1978, "Kelbaugh House: Recent Performance," *Proceedings of the Second National Passive Solar Conference.* Boulder, Colorado: American Solar Energy Society, pp. 69-75.

———, 1983, "A thermal history of the Kelbaugh house," *Proceedings of the Eighth National Passive Solar Conference.* Boulder, Colorado: American Solar Energy Society, pp. 925-930.

Knowles, R., 1974, *Energy and Form.* Cambridge, Massachusetts: MIT Press.

———, and Berry, R., 1980, *Solar Energy Concepts.* Golden, Colorado: Solar Energy Research Institute.

Knutson, R., 1981, "Flowers that make heat while the sun shines," *Natural History,* vol. 90, October, pp. 75-80.

Koenigsberger, O., Ingersoll, T., Mayhew, A., and Szokalay, S., 1974, *Manual of Tropical Housing and Building: Climatic Design.* London: Longman.

Kukreja, C., 1978, *Tropical Architecture.* New York: McGraw-Hill.

Labs, K., 1981, "Direct-coupled ground cooling: issues and opportunities," *Proceeding of the International Passive and Hybrid Cooling Conference.* Boulder, Colorado: American Solar Energy Society, pp. 131-135.

———, 1990, "Earth coupling," in Cook, J. (ed.), *Passive Cooling,* Cambridge, Massachusetts: MIT Press, pp. 197-346.

Landsberg, H., 1950, "Microclimatic research in relation to building construction," BRAB Conference Report No. 1, Weather and the Building Industry, Washington, DC, January, as cited by Olgyay, V., 1963, *Design With Climate.* Princeton, New Jersey: Princeton University Press.

———, 1981, *The Urban Climate.* New York: Academic Press.

Langdon, W., 1980, *Movable Insulation.* Emmaus, Pennsylvania: Rodale.

Laubin, R., and Laubin, G., 1977, *The Indian Tipi: Its History, Construction and*

Use. Norman, Oklahoma: University of Oklahoma Press.

Lebens, R., 1979, "Determining the optimum design for the Solar Modulator," *Proceedings of the Third National Passive Solar Conference.* Boulder, Colorado: American Solar Energy Society, pp. 100-106.

Lechner, N., 1991, *Heating, Cooling, Lighting: Design Methods for Architects.* New York: John Wiley and Sons.

Lewis, D., Kohler, J., and Reno, V., 1982, "Passive principles: rockbeds," *Solar Age,* March, pp. 44-48.

Lewis, S., 1982, "Radiant floors," *Solar Age.* May, pp. 42 - 44.

Libbey-Owens-Ford, 1974, *Libbey-Owens-Ford Sun Angle Calculator.* Toledo, Ohio: Marketing Department, Libbey-Owens-Ford.

Lind, A. R., and Bass, D. E., 1963, "The optimal exposure time for the developement of acclimatization to heat." *Federal Proceedings* 22: 704., as cited by ASHRAE, 1989, op. cit.

Longmore, J., 1967, "BRS daylight protractors," Building Research Station, London: Her Majesty's Stationery Office.

Los Angeles, 1982, *Solar Envelope Zoning: Application to the City Planning Process.* Golden, Colorado: Solar Energy Research Institute, as cited by Ridley, 1990, op. cit.

Lovett, D., 1980, "Sensitivity of the appreciation of passive solar construction to selected economic parameters," Report for Natural Bureau of Standards, as cited by Ridley, 1990, op. cit.

Lynes, J., Burt, W., Jackson, G., and Cuttle, C., 1966, "The flow of light into buildings," *Transactions of Illuminating Engineering Society (London),* Vol. 31, No. 3, pp. 65—91, as cited by Stein et al., 1986, op. cit.

Malt, H., and Ripoll, J., 1981, "A contemporary naturally cooled residence in Coconut Grove, south Florida," *Proceedings of the International Passive and Hybrid Cooling Conference.* Boulder, Colorado: American Solar Energy Society, pp. 105-109.

Marlatt, W., Murray, K., and Squier, S., 1984, *Roof Pond Systems.* NTIS report DE84016401, Springfield, VA: National Technical Information Center.

Marquez, G. G., 1970, *One Hundred Years of Solitude.* New York: Avon Books, pp. 231-232.

Martin, M., 1990, "Radiative cooling," in Cook, J. (ed.), *Passive Cooling,* Cambridge, Massachusetts: MIT Press, pp. 138-196.

———, and Berdahl, P., 1984, "Summary of results for the Spectral and Angular Sky Radiation Measurement Program," *Solar Energy* 33(3/4):241-252, as cited by Martin, 1990, op. cit.

Mathews, S., and Calthorp, 1979, "Daylight as a central determinant of design," *AIA Journal,* September, pp. 86-93.

Mazria, E., 1979, *The Passive Solar Energy Book.* Emmaus, Pennsylvania: Rodale.

McFarland, R., 1978, "PASOLE: a general simulation program for passive solar energy," Los Alamos National Laboratory report LA-7433MS, Springfield, Virginia: National Technical Informantion Center.

Melody, I., 1987, "Radiant barriers," FSEC-EN-15-87, Cape Canaveral, Florida: Florida Solar Energy Center.

Middleton, W., and Millar, F., 1936, "Temperature profiles in Toronto," *Journal of the Royal Astronomical Society of Canada,* vol. 30, pp. 265-272, as cited by Landsberg, H., 1981, *The Urban Climate.* New York: Academic Press.

Milne, M., and Givoni, B., 1979, "Architectural design based on climate," in Watson, D. (ed.), *Energy Conservation Through Building Design,* New York: McGraw-Hill, pp. 96-113.

Moore, F., 1980a, "Thermal layering: a passive solar design strategy," *Proceedings of the Fifth National Passive Solar Conference.* Boulder, Colorado: American Solar Energy Society, pp. 1234-1238.

———, 1980b, "Solargreen and Patoka Nature Center," *Proceedings of the Internationale Sonnenforum 3,* Hamburg, Germany, pp. 546-553.

———, 1982, "Passive Solar Test Modules," *Passive Solar Journal,* vol. 1, no. 2, Spring, pp. 91-108.

———, 1983, "Monitored performance of Patoka Nature Center: a direct-gain building with Beadwall night insulation in southern Indiana," *Proceedings of the Eighth National Passive Solar Conference.* Boulder, Colorado: American Solar Energy Society, pp. 387-390.

————, 1984, "Dot charts for estimating daylight illumination in buildings," *Proceedings of the Ninth National Passive Solar Conference.* Boulder, Colorado: American Solar Energy Society, September, pp. 280-285.

————, 1985, *Concepts and Practice of Architectural Daylighting.* New York: Van Nostrand Reinhold.

————, 1992, "The Society of Building Science Educators," *Proceedings of the Sixteenth National Passive Solar Conference.* Boulder, Colorado: American Solar Energy Society, at press.

————, and May, H., 1983, "Daylighting performance of four daylighted libraries in Europe designed by Alvar Aalto," *Proceedings of the 1983 International Daylighting Conference.* Washington, D.C.: AIA Service Corporation, pp. 187-204.

Morgan, L., 1965, *Houses and House-life of the American Aborigines.* Chicago: University of Chicago Press.

Morris, W. S., 1981, "A thermosiphon floor heating system: design considerations and performance data," *Proceedings of the Sixth National Passive Solar Conference.* Boulder, Colorado: American Solar Energy Society, pp. 102-106.

Morse, E. S., 1885, *Abstracts of the Society of Arts.* Massachusetts Institute of Technology Meeting 331, Cambridge, Massachusetts: Massachusetts Institute of Technology, pp. 115-120.

Morse, R., 1968, "A rock bed regenerative building cooling system," *Mech. and Chem. Eng. Trans. Institute of Engineers, Australia* MC4(1):23-30, as cited by Yellott, 1990, op. cit.

Munsell, A. H., 1941, *A Color Notation.* Baltimore, Maryland: Munsell Color Company.

Murphy, J., 1983, "Yankee independence," *Progressive Architecture,* April, pp. 86-89.

National Oceanic and Atmospheric Administration, 1978, *Climates of the States.* Detroit: Gale Research Corporation.

Naval Facilities Engineering Command, 1983, *Earth Sheltered Buildings Design Manual 1.4.* Washington, D.C.: U.S. Government Printing Office.

Ne'eman, E., and Longmore, J., 1973, "The integration of daylight with artificial light," paper presented at CIE Symposium, Istanbul, as cited by Stein, B., et al, 1986, op. cit.

Nevins, R., Rohles, F., Springer, W., and Feyerherm, A., 1966, "Temperature-humidity chart for thermal comfort of seated persons," *ASHRAE Transactions,* vol. 72, p. 283, as cited by ASHRAE, 1989, op. cit.

Nichols, W., 1976, "Unit 1, First Village," *Proceedings of the Passive Solar Heating and Cooling Conference* (First National Passive Solar Conference). Boulder, Colorado: American Solar Energy Society, pp. 137-149.

Northeast Solar Energy Center, 1980, "Energy efficient building and rebuilding: the profit opportunities," *Proceedings of the Builders' and Remodelers' Conference.* Boston: Northeast Solar Energy Center, as cited by Levy, E., 1983, *The Passive Solar Construction Handbook.* Emmaus, Pennsylvania: Rodale Press.

Novitski, B., 1989, "Northwest office building breaks through the clouds to successful daylighting," *Architectural Lighting.* August.

Olgyay, V., 1963, *Design With Climate.* Princeton, New Jersey: Princeton University Press.

————, and Olgyay, A., 1953, *Application of Climatic Data to House Design,* vols. I and II, Washington, D.C.: U.S. Housing and Home Finance Agency.

————, and Olgyay, A., 1957, *Solar Control and Shading Devices.* Princeton, New Jersey: Princeton University Press.

Owings-Corning, 1981, "Tenth Annual Owens-Corning Figerglass Energy Conservation Awards," publication number 5-GL-10902, Toledo, Ohio: Owens-Corning Corporation.

Passive Division of the American Solar Energy Society, 1975 through 1991, *Proceedings of National Passive Solar Conferences,* volumes 1 through 15, Boulder, Colorado: American Solar Energy Society.

Patel, A., 1981, "Air Handling Equipment Room and Air Cleaners," *Architectural Graphic Standards,* American Institute of Architects, New York: John

Wiley and Sons.

Perry, J., 1980, "Rockbed behavior and reverse thermosiphon effects," *Proceedings of the Fifth National Passive Solar Conference.* Boulder, Colorado: American Solar Energy Society, pp. 106-110.

Pleijel, G., 1954, "The computation of natural radiation in architecture and town planning," Meddelande (bulletin) #25, Stockholm: Statens Namnd for Byggnadsforskning, p. 364, as cited by Hopkinson, R. G., Petherbridge, P., and Longmore, J., 1966, *Daylighting.* London: Heinemann.

Powell, J., 1980, "Economic evaluation of passive design for urban environments," *Proceedings of the Fourth National Passive Solar Conference.* Boulder, Colorado: American Solar Energy Society, pp. 581-585, as cited by Ridley, 1990, op. cit.

Prowler, D., and Fraker, H., 1981, *Project Journal: Teaching Passive Design in Architecture.* Philadelphia: Graduate School of Fine Arts, University of Pennsylvania.

Prowler, D., and Kelbaugh, D., 1990, "Building envelopes," in Anderson B., (ed.), *Solar Building Architecture.* Cambridge, Massachusetts: MIT Press.

Rapoport, A., 1969, *House Form and Culture.* Englewood Cliffs, New Jersey: Prentice-Hall.

Reaves, F., and Reaves, J., 1981, "Evaporative cooling on the roof," *Proceeding of the International Passive and Hybrid Cooling Conference.* Boulder, Colorado: American Solar Energy Society, pp. 240-243.

Reed, R., 1953, *Design for Natural Ventilation in Hot Humid Weather.* Washington, D.C.: Building Research Institute, National Research Council.

Reno, V., 1980, "Shakedown for the envelope house," *Solar Age,* November, pp. 14-21.

Reynolds, J., 1984, "Passive rooling, rules of thumb, and historic precedent," *Proceedings of the 9th National Passive Solar Conference.* Boulder, Colorado: American Solar Energy Society, pp. 4-9.

———, Blassel, J., and Papers, G., 1983, "The courtyard: passive cooling performance and shading variables," *Proceedings of the Eighth National Passive Solar Conference.* Boulder, Colorado: American Solar Energy Society, pp. 843-849.

Ridley, L., 1990, "Site, community, and urban planning," in Anderson, B., (ed.), *Solar Building Architecture,* Cambridge, Massachusetts: MIT Press, pp. 36-76.

Robbins, C., and Hunter, K., 1982, "A method for predicting energy savings attributed to daylighting," SERI report TR-254-1687, Golden Colorado: Solar Energy Research Institute; this method is also described in Moore, 1985, op. cit., and in Robbins, 1986, op. cit.

Robbins, C., 1986, *Daylighting: Design and Analysis.* New York: Van Nostrand Reinhold.

Robinette, G., 1977, *Landscape Planning for Energy Conservation.* Reston, Virginia: Environmental Design Press.

Rogers, L., 1981, "A bear in its lair," *Natural History,* vol. 90, October, pp. 64-70.

Rohles, F., and Johnson, M., 1972, "Thermal comfort in the elderly," *ASHRAE Transactions,* vol. 78, p. 131, as cited by ASHRAE, 1989, op. cit.

Rohles, F., Nevins, R., and Springer, W., 1966, "The physiological effects of subject crowding during exposure to high thermal stress," *Report No. 1,* Kansas State University, as cited by ASHRAE, 1989, op. cit.

Rosen, J., 1982, "Natural daylighting and energy conservation: innovative solutions for office buildings." Master of Architecture Thesis, Cambridge: Massachusetts Institute of Technology.

———, 1981, "Heat mirror coatings for internal load dominated buildings," in Hayes, J., and Kolar, W. (eds.), *Proceedings, Sixth National Passive Solar Conference.* Boulder, Colorado: American Solar Energy Society, pp. 626-630.

Ruberg, K., 1980, "Passive solar potential for urban environments," *Proceedings of the Fifth National Passive Solar Conference.* Boulder, Colorado: American Solar Energy Society, pp. 836-840, as cited by Ridley, 1990, op. cit.

Rubinstein, F., 1983, "Photo-electric control of equi-illumination lighting systems," *Proceedings of the International Daylighting Conference.* Washington, D.C.: American Institute of Architects Service Corporation, pp. 373-376.

Rudofsky, B., 1964, *Architecture without Architects*. Garden City, New York: Doubleday.

Sain, A. M., 1983, "Daylighting and artificial lighting control," *Proceedings of the International Daylighting Conference*. Washington, D.C.: American Institute of Architects Service Corporation, pp. 363-365.

Schiler, M., 1987, *Simulating Daylight with Architectural Models*. Los Angeles: University of Southern California.

Schubert, R., and Hahn, P., 1983, "The design and testing of a high-performance ventilator cowl," *Proceedings of the Eighth National Passive Solar Conference*. Boulder, Colorado: American Solar Energy Society, pp. 867-872.

Schwolsky, R., 1980a, "Moisture control in buildings: vapor barriers," *Solar Age*. November, pp. 49-50.

———, 1980b, "Moisture control in buildings: ventilation," *Solar Age*. December, pp. 57-58.

Scott, L., and Scott, M., 1980, "Indoor air pollution in passive solar structures," *Proceedings of the Fifth National Passive Solar Conference*. Boulder, Colorado: American Solar Energy Society, pp. 960-963.

Scott, W. T., 1962, "North Light," *Collected Poems: 1937-1962*. New York: Macmillan.

Selkowitz, S., 1979, "Transparent heat mirrors for passive solar heating applications," Report LBL-7829, Berkeley, California: Lawrence Berkeley Laboratory.

———, and Gabel, M., 1983, "LBL daylighting nomographs," report LBL-13534 W-113, Berkeley, California: Lawrence Berkeley Laboratory, Energy Efficient Buildings Program.; also see Moore, 1985, op. cit.

Skurka, N., and Naar, J., 1976, *Design for a Limited Planet*. New York: Ballantine.

Shurcliff, W., 1980, *Superinsulated Houses and Double-Envelope Houses*.

Cambridge, Massachusetts: W. Shurcliff, 19 Appleton Street.

———, 1981, *Air-to-Air Heat Exchangers for Houses*. Cambridge, Massachusetts: Wm. Shurcliff, 19 Appleton Street, 02138.

———, 1982a, "An amazing furnace-free house," *Solar Age*. November, pp. 33-35.

———, 1982b, "Air-to-air heat exchangers for houses," *Solar Age*. March, pp. 19-22.

Simon, M. (ed.), 1947, *Your Solar Home*. New York: Simon & Schuster.

Society of Building Science Educators, c/o Fuller Moore, Architecture Department, Miami University, Oxford, Ohio, 45056.

Stein, B., Reynolds, J., and McGuiness, W., 1986, *Mechanical and Electrical Equipment for Buildings*, 7th ed, New York: John Wiley and Sons.

Stein, B., and Reynolds, J., 1992, *Mechanical and Electrical Equipment for Buildings*. 8th edition, New York: John Wiley and Sons.

Stein, R., and Serber, D., 1979, "Energy required for building construction," in Watson, D. (ed.), *Energy Conservation Through Building Design*. New York: McGraw-Hill, pp. 182-203.

Stromberg, R., and Woodall, 1977, *Passive Solar Buildings: A Compilation of Results*. SAND77-1204. Springfield, VA: National Technical Information Service, as cited by Prowler, D., and Kelbaugh, D., 1990, "Building envelopes," in Anderson, B., (ed.), *Solar Building Architecture*, Massachusetts: MIT Press, pp. 77-146.

Sun, T., and Park, K., 1981, "Electric heating systems," *Architectural Graphic Standards*, American Institute of Architects, New York: John Wiley and Sons.

Talib, K., 1984, *Shelter in Saudi Arabia*. New York: St. Martin's Press.

Ternoey, S., 1982, "Don't trust your instincts: big building design defies intuition," *Solar Age*. April, p. 96.

———, Bickle, L., Robbins, C., Busch, R., McCord, K., 1985, *The Design of Energy-Responsive Buildings*. New York: John Wiley and Sons.

Trombe, F., 1967, "Perspectives sur l'utilisation des rayonnements solaires et terrestres dans certaines regions du monde," *Rev. Gen. Thermique* 6(70):1285-1314, as cited by Martin, 1990, op. cit.

———, Robert, J., Cabanat, M., Sesolis, B., 1976, "Some performance characteristics of the CNRS solar house collectors," *Proceedings of the Passive Solar Heating and Cooling Conference*(First National Passive Solar Conference). Boulder, Colorado: American Solar Energy Society, pp. 201-222.

———, Robert, J., Cabanat, M., Sesolis, B., 1977, "Concrete walls to collect and hold heat," *Solar Age.* August, pp. 14-19.

Turner, D. P., ed., 1971, *Windows and Environment.* London: Architectural Press.

Ubbelohde, S., 1986, "The new School of Architecture Building at Florida A&M University," *Proceedings of the Eleventh National Passive Solar Conference.* Boulder, Colorado: American Solar Energy Society, pp. 38-41.

Underground Space Center, 1979, *Earth Sheltered Housing Design.* Minneapolis, Minnesota: University of Minnesota.

———, 1983, *Earth Sheltered Residential Design Manual.* New York: Van Nostrand Reinhold.

United States Department of Commerce, 1978, *Climatic Atlas of the United States.* Washington, D.C.: United States Government Printing Office.

Urban Land Institute, 1980, *Focus on Energy Conservation: A Second Project List.* Washington, D.C.: Urban Land Institute, as cited by Ridley, 1990, op. cit.

Vieira, R., and Sheinkopf, K., 1988, *Energy-Efficient Florida Home Building.* Cape Canaveral, Florida: Florida Solar Energy Center.

Villecco, M., Selkowitz, S., and Griffith, J., 1979, "Strategies of daylight design," *AIA Journal.* September, pp. 68-75.

Vine, E., 1981, "Solarizing America: the Davis experience," *Conference on Alternative State and Local Policies,* Washington, D.C., as cited by Ridley, 1990, op. cit.

Walker, L., 1981, *American Shelter.* Woodstock, New York: Overlook Press.

Watson, D., 1989, "Bioclimatic design research," in Boer, K. (ed.), *Advances in Solar Energy,* vol. 5, Boulder, Colorado: American Solar Energy Society, pp. 404-438, excerpted by permission.

White, R., 1953, "Effects of landscape development on the natural ventilation of buildings and their adjacent area," Texas Engineering Experiment Station, Research Report 45, March, as cited by Robinette, 1977, op. cit.

Winter, S., and Associates, 1983, *The Passive Solar Construction Handbook.* Emmaus, Pennsylvania: Rodale Press.

Wright, D., 1976, "Adobe: designing for passive solar heat in the Southwest," *Solar Age,* July. pp. 10-15.

———, 1978, *Natural Solar Architecture.* New York: Van Nostrand Reinhold.

Yaglou, C., and Drinker, P., 1928, "The summer comfort zone: climate and clothing," *Journal of Industrial Hygiene,* vol. 9, pp. 297-309, as cited by Fanger, 1982, op. cit.

Yellott, J., 1990, "Evaporative cooling," in Cook, J. (ed.), *Passive Cooling,* Cambridge, Massachusetts: MIT Press, pp. 85-137.

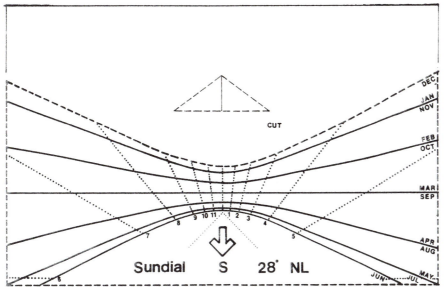

Figure A.1: Sundial for 28°N latitude. *(Reproduced from Moore, 1986, by permission.)*

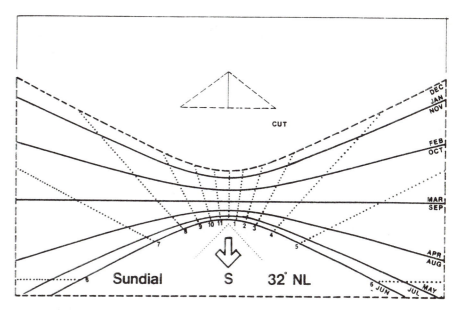

Figure A.2: Sundial for 32°N latitude. *(Reproduced from Moore, 1986, by permission.)*

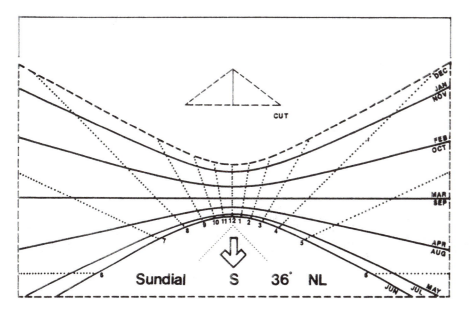

Figure A.3: Sundial for 36°N latitude. *(Reproduced from Moore, 1986, by permission.)*

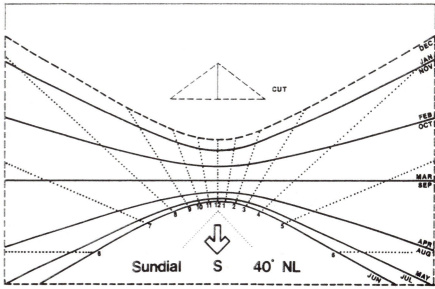

Figure A.4: Sundial for 40°N latitude. *(Reproduced from Moore, 1986, by permission.)*

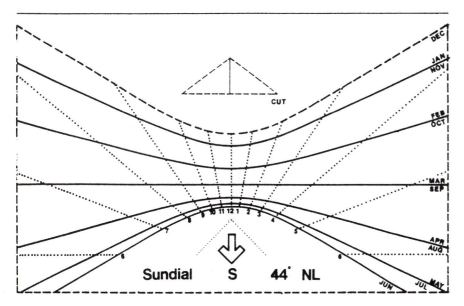

Figure A.5: Sundial for 44°N latitude. *(Reproduced from Moore, 1986, by permission.)*

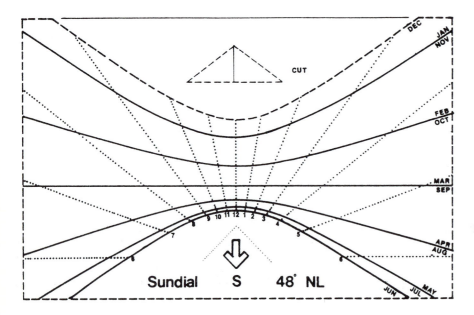

Figure A.6: Sundial for 48°N latitude. *(Reproduced from Moore, 1986, by permission.)*

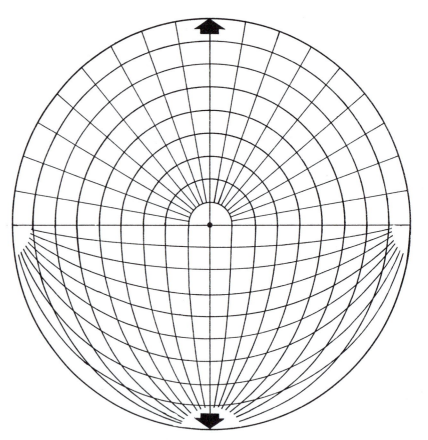

Figure A.7: Shading mask protractor. *(Reproduced from Moore, 1986, by permission.)*

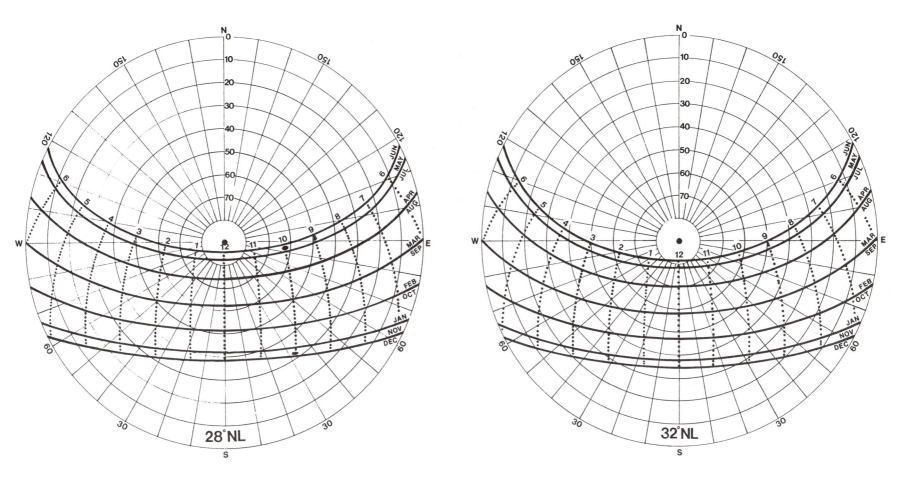

Figure A.8: Sun path diagram for 28°N latitude. *(Reproduced from Moore, 1986, by permission.)*

Figure A.9: Sun path diagram for 32°N latitude. *(Reproduced from Moore, 1986, by permission.)*

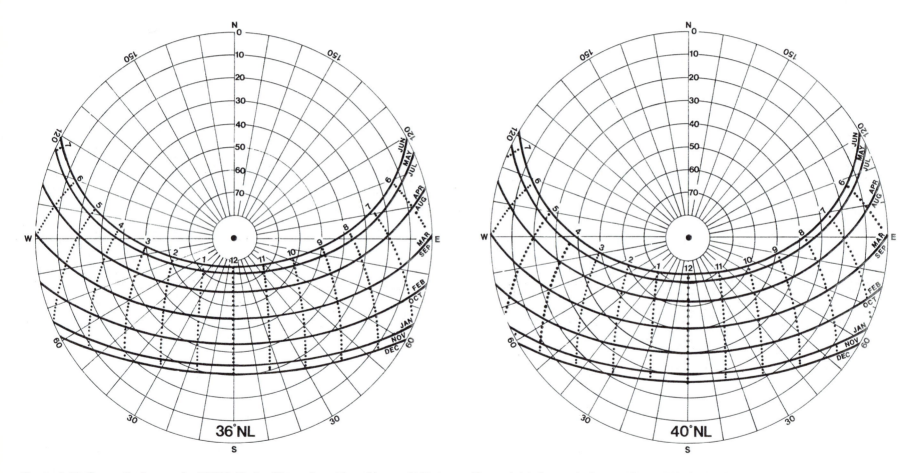

Figure A.10: Sun path diagram for 36°N latitude. *(Reproduced from Moore, 1986, by permission.)*

Figure A.11: Sun path diagram for 40°N latitude. *(Reproduced from Moore, 1986, by permission.)*

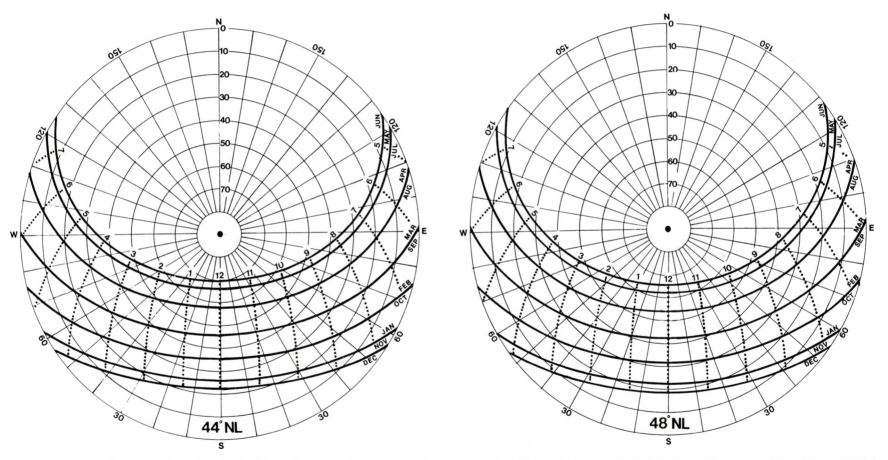

Figure A.12: Sun path diagram for 44°N latitude. *(Reproduced from Moore, 1986, by permission.)*

Figure A.13: Sun path diagram for 48°N latitude. *(Reproduced from Moore, 1986, by permission.)*

Table B.1: Direct Gain Reference Designs
(Reproduced from Balcomb et al., 1984, by permission.)

Designation	Thermal Storage Capacity* (Btu/ft$^2 \cdot$ °F)	Nominal Mass Thickness (in.)**	Mass-to-Glazing-Area Ratio	Number of Glazings	Night Insulation	$U_{collector}$
DGA3	30	2	6	2	yes	0.26
DGC1	60	4	6	2	no	0.50
DGC2	60	4	6	3	no	0.31
DGC3	60	4	6	2	yes	0.26

*Per unit of projected area, A_p.　　** For the particular case of $\rho c = 30$ Btu/ft$^3 \cdot$ °F .

Table B.2: Vented*** Trombe Wall Reference Designs
(Reproduced from Balcomb et al., 1984, by permission.)

Designation	Thermal Storage Capacity* (Btu/ft$^2 \cdot$ °F)	Nominal Wall Thickness (in.)**	Number of Glazings	Wall Surface	Night Insulation	$U_{collector}$
TWA2	22.5	9	2	normal	no	0.25
TWA3	30	12	2	normal	no	0.24
TWE1	30	12	1	selective	no	0.23
TWE2	30	12	2	selective	no	0.20

*Per unit of projected area, A_p.　** For the particular case of $\rho c = 30$ Btu/ft$^3 \cdot$ °F (concrete with density of 150 lb/ft^3).　*** total vent area = 6% A_p, 8 ft height between vents, and no reverse thermocirculation.

Table B.3: Unvented Trombe Wall Reference Designs
(Reproduced from Balcomb et al., 1984, by permission.)

Designation	Thermal Storage Capacity* (Btu/ft$^2 \cdot$ °F)	Nominal Wall Thickness (in.)**	Number of Glazings	Wall Surface	Night Insulation	$U_{collector}$
TWF2	22.5	9	2	normal	no	0.25
TWF3	30	12	2	normal	no	0.24
TWJ1	30	12	1	selective	no	0.23
TWJ2	30	12	2	selective	no	0.20

*Per unit of projected area, A_p.

** For the particular case of $\rho c = 30$ Btu/ft$^3 \cdot$ °F (concrete with density of 150 lb/ft^3).

Table B.4: Water Wall Reference Designs
(Reproduced from Balcomb et al., 1984, by permission.)

Designation	Thermal Storage Capacity* (Btu/ft$^2 \cdot$ °F)	Wall Thickness (in.)	Number of Glazings	Wall Surface	Night Insulation	$U_{collector}$
WWA2	31.2	6	2	normal	no	0.31
WWA3	46.8	9	2	normal	no	0.31
WWB4	46.8	9	2	normal	yes	0.18
WWC2	46.8	9	2	selective	no	0.24

*Per unit of projected area, A_p.

Table B-5: Sunspace* Reference Designs
(Reproduced from Balcomb et al., 1984, by permission.)

Designation	Type	Tilt (degrees)	Common Wall	End Walls	Night Insulation	$U_{collector}$
SSA2	attached	50	masonry	opaque	yes	0.21
SSA6	attached	50	insulated	opaque	yes	0.04
SSA8	attached	50	insulated	glazed	yes	0.04
SSB1	attached	90/30	masonry	opaque	no	0.26
SSB5	attached	90/30	insulated	opaque	no	0.04
SSB7	attached	90/30	insulated	glazed	no	0.04
SSC2	semienclosed	90	masonry	common	yes	0.28
SSC4	semienclosed	90	insulated	common	yes	0.08
SSD2	semienclosed	50	masonry	common	yes	0.26
SSD4	semienclosed	50	insulated	common	yes	0.07
SSE1	semienclosed	90/30	masonry	common	no	0.41
SSE4	semienclosed	90/30	insulated	common	yes	0.08

*All are double-glazed.

Reference Design Common Characteristics
(Reproduced from Balcomb et al., 1984, by permission.)

Masonry properties
thermal conductivity, direct gain and sunspace	1.0 Btu/h $\cdot$ °F
density	150 lb / ft^3
specific heat	0.2 Btu / lb $\cdot$ °F
infrared emittance of normal surface	0.9
infrared emittance of selective surface	0.1

Solar absorptances
water wall	0.95
masonry:	
Trombe wall	0.95
direct gain and sunspace	0.8
sunspace:	
water containers	0.9
lightweight common wall	0.7
other lightweight surfaces	0.3

Control range
room temperature	65°F to 75°F
sunspace temperature	45°F to 95°F
internal heat generation	0

Night insulation (when used)
added thermal resistance	R-9
in place, solar time	5:30 p.m. to 7:30 a.m.

Solar radiation assumptions
shading	none
ground diffuse reflectance	0.3
lightweight absorption fraction	0.2

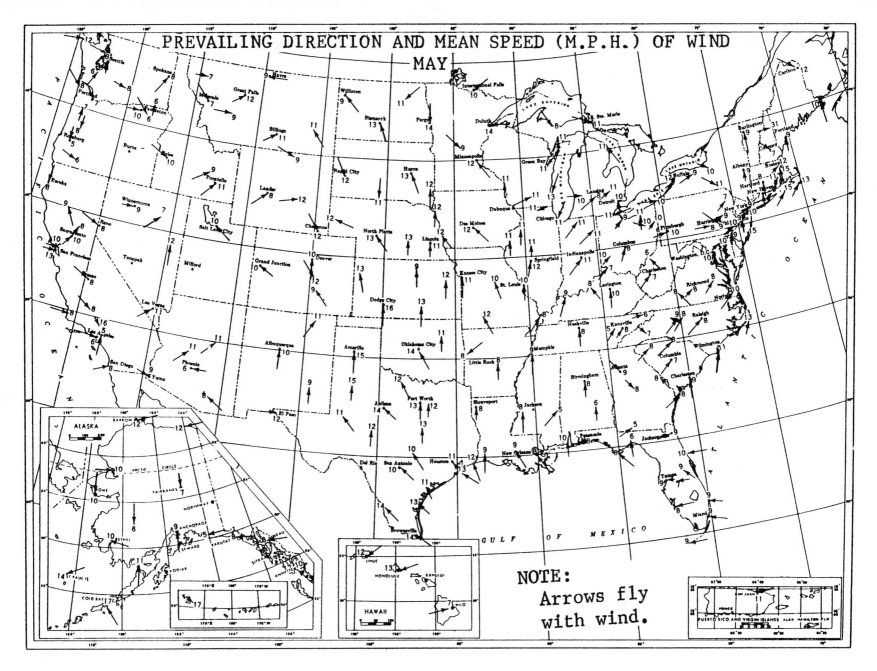

Prevailing direction and mean wind speed, May. (Reproduced from U.S. Department of Commerce, 1978).

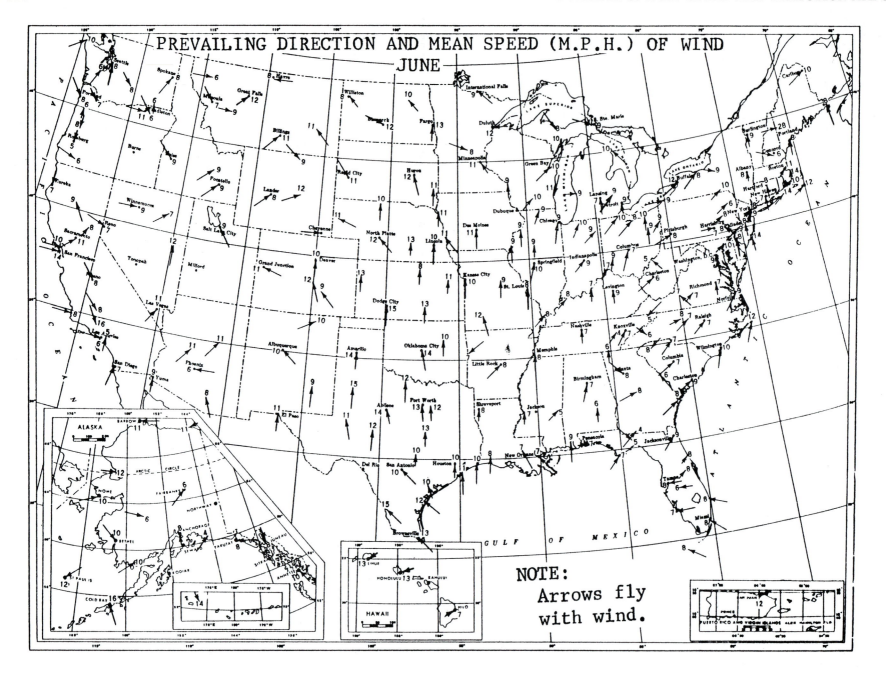

Prevailing direction and mean wind speed, June. (Reproduced from U.S. Department of Commerce, 1978).

Phoenix AZ

Elev: 1112; ADR: 0.95; Lat: 33 ; Jan VT: 1243
Cooling DD: 3334; Winter Design Dry-Bulb (°F): 34
Summer Design Dry-Bulb/Co-Incid WB: 107/71
Design guidelines*:
  low fuel cost: CF = 0.70; LCR = 123; SSF = 53%
  high fuel cost: CF = 0.83; LCR = 66; SSF = 74%

Passive Heating Solar Savings Fraction Table*

LCR	|SSF (%; DD base = 55°F)| 100	70	50	40	30	25	20	15	|SSF (%; DD base = 65°F)| 100	70	50	40	30	25	20	15
DGA1	63	85	92	95	96	97	97	97	29	51	64	75	81	87	91	93
DGA2	71	91	96	98	98	98	98	98	31	54	68	79	85	90	93	95
DGA3	69	91	96	99	99	99	99	99	30	54	68	80	86	92	95	97
DGB1	72	93	97	98	98	98	98	98	33	59	74	85	90	95	96	98
DGB2	58	79	88	94	97	99	99	99	29	46	56	67	74	82	87	91
DGB3	61	82	90	96	98	99	99	99	29	49	59	70	77	85	89	93
DGC1	72	91	96	99	99	99	99	99	38	60	72	82	88	93	96	98
DGC2	71	90	96	99	99	99	99	99	36	59	71	82	88	93	96	98
DGC3	56	77	87	94	98	99	99	99	26	43	54	65	72	81	85	90
TWA2	57	79	88	95	97	99	99	99	26	44	55	67	74	82	87	92
TWA3	69	89	95	99	99	99	99	99	35	57	70	80	86	92	95	98
TWA4	68	88	95	98	99	99	99	99	33	56	68	79	85	92	95	97
TWD1	63	84	92	97	98	99	99	99	32	50	62	72	79	87	90	94
TWD2	67	87	94	98	99	99	99	99	33	54	66	77	83	90	93	96
TWD3	75	93	98	99	99	99	99	99	39	64	76	86	91	96	98	99
TWD4	74	93	97	99	99	99	99	99	39	63	75	85	90	95	97	99
TWE1	72	90	96	99	99	99	99	99	41	62	73	83	88	93	96	98
TWE2	72	90	96	99	99	99	99	99	41	62	73	83	88	93	96	98
TWF2	71	89	95	98	99	99	99	99	40	61	72	81	87	92	95	97
TWF3	57	78	87	94	96	99	99	99	29	46	56	67	73	81	86	90
TWF4	51	71	81	89	93	97	98	99	27	41	50	60	66	75	80	85
TWI1	47	67	77	86	91	95	97	99	25	37	46	55	62	70	75	81
TWI2	68	88	95	98	99	99	99	99	34	56	68	79	85	91	94	97
TWI3	62	83	92	96	98	99	99	99	30	50	62	73	79	87	91	95
TWI4	80	95	98	99	99	99	99	99	47	70	81	89	93	97	98	99
TWJ1	78	94	98	99	99	99	99	99	46	68	79	88	92	96	98	99
TWJ2	68	87	94	99	99	99	99	99	36	56	67	77	83	90	93	96
WWA2	71	90	96	99	99	99	99	99	39	60	71	81	87	93	95	98

Weather Data

	Jan	Feb	Mar	Apr	May	Jun	Jul	Aug	Sep	Oct	Nov	Dec	Year
Daily Max Temp (°F)**	65	69	75	84	93	102	105	102	98	88	75	66	85
Daily MinTemp (°F)**	38	41	45	52	60	68	78	76	69	57	45	39	56
Daily Temp Range (°F)**	27	28	30	32	33	34	27	26	29	31	30	27	30
Heating DD (base 65°F)*	431	292	185	60	0	0	0	0	0	17	182	389	1556
Heating DD (base 55°F)*	162	100	25	5	0	0	0	0	0	0	29	115	436
Normal Precip (in.)**	0.7	0.6	0.8	0.3	0.1	0.1	0.7	1.2	0.7	0.5	0.5	0.8	7
Daily Max Rel Hum (%)**	67	58	58	43	36	36	46	54	53	54	62	69	53
Daily Min Rel Hum (%)**	30	25	23	15	12	13	20	24	23	22	29	35	23
Mean Dewpoint (°F)***	33	33	33	35	36	42	58	60	53	44	36	33	41
Prevailing Wind (from)**	E	E	E	E	E	E	W	E	E	E	E	E	
Mean Wind Spd (mph)**	5	5	6	7	7	7	7	6	6	6	5	5	6
Hor Solar Rad (lang'ys)***	301	409	526	638	724	739	658	613	566	449	344	281	521

Little Rock AR

Elev: 257; ADR: 0.99 ; Lat: 35 ; Jan VT: 805
Cooling DD: 1925; Winter Design Dry-Bulb (°F): 20
Summer Design Dry-Bulb/Co-Incid WB: 96/77
Design Guidelines*:
  low fuel cost: CF = 1.04; LCR = 97; SSF = 31%
  high fuel cost: CF = 1.30; LCR = 34; SSF = 59%

Passive Heating Solar Savings Fraction Table*

LCR	|SSF (%; DD base = 55°F)| 100	70	50	40	30	25	20	15	|SSF (%; DD base = 65°F)| 100	70	50	40	30	25	20	15
DGA1	17	32	42	54	62	71	76	82	11	20	27	36	43	52	58	65
DGA2	17	30	41	52	60	70	75	80	10	17	23	30	35	43	48	54
DGA3	17	30	43	55	64	74	80	85	11	20	26	35	41	51	57	65
DGB1	20	36	49	63	72	82	87	92	13	24	32	42	50	61	69	77
DGB2	18	29	37	46	53	62	67	74	12	19	24	30	35	42	47	53
DGB3	18	30	39	49	56	65	71	78	11	19	25	32	37	45	50	56
DGC1	23	40	51	62	70	79	84	89	13	26	34	44	50	60	66	73
DGC2	21	39	50	62	70	79	84	89	12	25	34	43	50	60	66	74
DGC3	16	27	35	44	50	59	65	72	10	17	22	28	33	39	44	50
TWA2	15	27	35	45	52	61	67	74	8	16	22	28	33	41	46	52
TWA3	20	37	48	60	67	77	82	88	11	23	32	41	48	57	64	71
TWA4	19	36	47	59	67	75	82	88	10	22	31	40	47	57	63	71
TWD1	20	32	41	51	58	67	72	79	12	21	26	33	38	46	51	58
TWD2	20	34	44	55	62	71	77	83	11	21	28	36	41	50	55	62
TWD3	22	42	55	67	75	83	88	93	11	26	37	48	55	66	72	79
TWD4	22	42	54	68	73	82	87	92	12	26	36	46	54	64	70	78
TWE1	26	43	54	65	72	80	85	90	18	31	39	48	55	64	69	76
TWE2	26	43	54	64	71	80	85	90	18	30	39	48	54	63	69	75
TWF2	26	42	52	63	70	78	83	88	18	30	37	46	52	61	67	73
TWF3	19	30	38	47	53	62	67	71	13	21	26	32	37	44	48	54
TWF4	18	27	33	41	47	55	60	66	13	19	23	28	32	38	42	47
TWI1	17	24	30	37	42	50	55	61	13	17	21	25	29	34	37	42
TWI2	20	36	46	58	65	75	80	86	11	22	30	39	48	55	61	68
TWI3	18	32	41	52	59	68	74	81	11	20	27	35	41	49	55	62
TWI4	30	50	62	73	80	87	91	95	19	35	45	56	63	72	78	84
TWJ1	29	48	60	71	78	86	90	94	19	34	44	54	61	70	76	82
TWJ2	22	37	46	57	64	72	78	84	14	24	31	38	44	52	57	64
WWA2	24	41	52	63	70	79	83	89	15	28	36	45	52	61	66	73

Weather Data

	Jan	Feb	Mar	Apr	May	Jun	Jul	Aug	Sep	Oct	Nov	Dec	Year
Daily Max Temp (°F)**	50	54	62	74	81	89	93	93	86	76	62	52	73
Daily MinTemp (°F)**	29	32	39	50	58	67	70	69	61	49	38	31	49
Daily Temp Range (°F)**	21	22	23	24	23	22	23	24	25	27	24	21	23
Heating DD (base 65°F)*	791	620	470	139	21	0	0	0	5	143	442	726	3357
Heating DD (base 55°F)*	487	350	224	15	0	0	0	0	0	20	169	422	1687
Normal Precip (in.)**	4.2	4.4	4.9	5.3	5.3	3.5	3.4	3.0	3.5	3.0	3.9	4.1	49
Daily Max Rel Hum (%)**	82	79	78	82	87	87	88	88	89	86	83	81	84
Daily Min Rel Hum (%)**	62	57	54	56	56	54	58	56	60	52	57	63	57
Mean Dewpoint (°F)***	32	34	39	49	60	67	70	69	62	52	40	34	51
Prevailing Wind (from)**	S	SW	NW	S	S	SW	SW	SW	NE	SW	SW	SW	SW
Mean Wind Spd (mph)**	9	9	10	10	8	8	7	7	7	7	8	9	8
Hor Solar Rad (lang'ys)***	188	260	353	446	523	559	556	518	439	343	244	187	385

Data sources: *Balcomb et al., (1984); **National Oceanic and Atmospheric Administration, 1978; ***U.S. Department of Commerce (1978).

Fresno CA

Elev: 328; ADR: 0.99; Lat: 37; Jan VT: 753
Cooling DD: 1671; Winter Design Dry-Bulb (°F): 30
Summer Design Dry-Bulb/Co-Incid WB: 102/70
Design guidelines*:
   low fuel cost: CF = 0.91; LCR = 158; SSF = 39%
   high fuel cost: CF = 1.12; LCR = 47; SSF = 60%

Passive Heating Solar Savings Fraction Table*

LCR	SSF (%; DD base = 55°F)								SSF (%; DD base = 65°F)							
	100	70	50	40	30	25	20	15	100	70	50	40	30	25	20	15
DGA1	31	49	60	70	76	83	86	90	17	30	39	49	56	65	70	76
DGA2	33	50	60	71	77	84	87	91	16	28	37	46	52	60	64	70
DGA3	33	51	62	73	80	87	90	94	17	30	39	49	58	65	71	77
DGB1	35	55	66	78	85	91	94	96	19	34	45	54	64	74	79	85
DGB2	30	45	54	63	69	77	81	86	18	28	35	42	48	55	60	67
DGB3	31	47	57	66	72	79	84	89	17	28	36	44	50	58	64	70
DGC1	38	57	67	77	82	89	92	95	21	37	46	57	63	72	77	83
DGC2	37	56	67	77	82	89	92	95	20	36	46	56	63	73	77	83
DGC3	28	43	52	61	67	75	80	85	15	25	32	40	45	53	58	64
TWA2	27	43	53	63	69	77	81	86	14	25	32	40	47	55	60	66
TWA3	35	55	65	75	81	88	91	95	19	34	44	54	61	70	75	81
TWA4	34	54	64	74	80	87	91	94	17	33	43	53	60	69	75	81
TWD1	33	49	53	68	74	81	85	90	19	30	38	46	52	60	65	71
TWD2	34	52	62	71	77	84	88	92	18	31	40	49	56	64	69	75
TWD3	39	60	71	80	86	92	95	97	20	38	49	61	68	77	82	87
TWD4	39	59	70	80	85	91	94	97	20	38	49	60	67	76	81	86
TWE1	40	58	68	77	82	88	92	95	26	41	50	59	65	73	78	83
TWE2	40	58	98	76	82	88	92	95	26	41	50	59	65	73	78	83
TWF2	39	57	66	75	81	87	91	94	26	40	48	57	63	71	76	81
TWF3	30	49	53	62	68	75	80	85	19	29	36	43	49	56	61	66
TWF4	28	40	48	56	62	69	73	79	18	27	32	39	43	50	54	60
TWI1	25	37	45	52	58	65	69	75	17	24	29	35	39	45	49	55
TWI2	35	53	64	73	79	86	90	94	18	33	42	52	59	68	73	79
TWI3	31	49	59	68	74	82	86	90	17	30	38	47	53	62	67	74
TWI4	45	65	75	83	88	93	96	98	29	46	57	67	73	80	85	89
TWJ1	44	63	73	82	87	92	95	97	28	45	55	65	71	79	83	88
TWJ2	36	53	62	71	77	84	88	92	22	34	42	51	57	64	69	75
WWA2	38	56	66	75	81	88	91	95	23	38	47	57	63	71	76	82

Weather Data

	Jan	Feb	Mar	Apr	May	Jun	Jul	Aug	Sep	Oct	Nov	Dec	Year
Daily Max Temp (°F)**	55	61	67	74	83	90	98	96	91	80	66	55	76
Daily MinTemp (°F)**	36	39	41	46	52	58	63	61	57	49	41	37	48
Daily Temp Range (°F)**	19	22	26	28	31	32	35	35	34	31	25	18	28
Heating DD (base 65°F)*	612	424	436	182	51	9	0	0	0	90	348	595	2747
Heating DD (base 55°F)*	314	164	88	35	0	0	0	0	0	5	102	292	1000
Normal Precip. (in.)**	1.8	1.7	1.6	1.2	0.3	0.1	0.0	0.0	0.1	0.4	1.2	1.7	10
Daily Max Rel Hum (%)**	92	91	87	82	73	68	63	68	75	79	88	94	80
Daily Min Rel Hum (%)**	68	55	45	35	25	24	23	25	27	34	57	73	41
Mean Dewpoint (°F)***	38	41	41	44	45	48	51	52	51	46	42	40	45
Prevailing Wind (from)**	SE	NW	NW	NW	NW	NW	NW	NW	NW	NW	NW	SE	NW
Mean Wind Spd (mph)**	5	6	7	7	8	8	7	7	6	5	5	5	6
Hor Solar Rad (lang'ys)***	184	289	427	552	647	702	682	621	510	376	250	161	450

Data sources: *Balcomb et al., (1984); **National Oceanic and Atmospheric Administration, 1978; ***U.S. Department of Commerce (1978).

Denver CO

Elev: 5331; ADR: 0.83; Lat: 39.7; Jan VT: 1245
Cooling DD: 630; Winter Design Dry-Bulb (°F): 1
Summer Design Dry-Bulb/Co-Incid WB: 91/59
Design guidelines*:
   low fuel cost: CF = 1.27; LCR = 36; SSF = 57%
   high fuel cost: CF = 1.52; LCR = 19; SSF = 76%

Passive Heating Solar Savings Fraction Table*

LCR	SSF (%; DD base = 55°F)								SSF (%; DD base = 65°F)							
	100	70	50	40	30	25	20	15	100	70	50	40	30	25	20	15
DGA1	29	39	50	58	68	74	80	87	20	28	37	44	54	61	68	76
DGA2	27	36	47	55	66	72	78	84	17	24	31	37	46	52	59	66
DGA3	29	39	51	60	71	77	83	90	20	27	36	43	53	60	68	77
DGB1	33	44	58	68	80	85	91	95	24	33	43	52	64	72	80	88
DGB2	27	34	43	49	58	64	71	80	19	253	31	36	44	49	55	64
DGB3	28	36	45	52	61	67	75	83	19	26	33	39	47	52	59	69
DGC1	37	47	59	66	76	82	88	93	26	35	45	53	62	69	76	84
DGC2	36	47	58	66	76	82	88	94	26	35	45	52	62	69	76	85
DGC3	24	32	40	47	55	61	69	78	17	22	29	34	41	46	53	62
TWA2	24	32	41	48	57	64	71	80	16	22	29	35	42	48	55	65
TWA3	34	45	56	64	74	80	86	92	24	33	43	50	60	66	74	83
TWA4	33	44	55	63	73	79	86	92	23	32	42	49	59	66	74	83
TWD1	30	38	47	54	63	69	76	85	21	27	35	40	48	54	61	70
TWD2	31	41	51	58	68	74	81	88	21	29	37	43	52	58	66	75
TWD3	39	51	63	72	81	86	92	96	27	38	50	58	68	75	82	89
TWD4	38	50	62	70	80	85	91	96	27	37	48	56	67	73	80	88
TWE1	39	49	60	67	76	81	87	93	31	40	49	56	65	71	77	85
TWE2	39	49	60	67	76	81	87	93	31	39	49	56	64	70	77	85
TWF2	38	47	58	65	74	79	85	91	30	38	47	53	62	68	74	82
TWF3	27	34	42	48	57	62	69	78	21	26	33	38	45	50	56	65
TWF4	24	30	37	42	50	55	61	70	19	24	29	33	39	43	48	56
TWI1	22	27	33	38	45	49	55	64	17	21	26	29	34	38	43	50
TWI2	33	43	54	62	72	78	84	91	23	31	41	48	57	63	71	80
TWI3	29	38	48	55	65	71	78	86	20	28	36	42	51	57	64	74
TWI4	45	57	69	76	84	89	93	97	36	46	57	64	74	79	85	92
TWJ1	44	55	66	74	82	87	92	96	34	45	55	62	72	77	83	90
TWJ2	33	42	51	58	67	73	80	87	24	31	39	45	54	59	66	74
WWA2	37	47	58	65	74	80	86	92	28	37	46	53	62	68	75	83

Weather Data

	Jan	Feb	Mar	Apr	May	Jun	Jul	Aug	Sep	Oct	Nov	Dec	Year
Daily Max Temp (°F)**	44	46	50	61	70	80	87	86	78	67	53	46	64
Daily MinTemp (°F)**	16	19	24	34	44	52	59	57	48	57	25	19	38
Daily Temp Range (°F)**	28	27	26	27	26	28	28	29	30	10	28	27	26
Heating DD (base 65°F)*	1089	902	869	528	253	80	0	0	120	408	769	1004	6022
Heating DD (base 55°F)*	781	626	565	256	41	7	0	0	12	153	473	695	3609
Normal Precip. (in.)**	0.6	0.7	1.2	1.9	2.6	1.9	1.8	1.3	1.1	1.1	0.8	0.4	15
Daily Max Rel Hum (%)**	63	67	69	68	70	72	72	70	72	66	70	66	69
Daily Min Rel Hum (%)**	45	44	41	38	38	37	36	35	37	36	44	45	40
Mean Dewpoint (°F)***	12	16	17	24	35	42	47	46	37	27	19	14	28
Prevailing Wind (from)**	S	S	S	S	S	S	S	S	S	S	S	S	S
Mean Wind Spd (mph)**	9	9	10	10	9	9	9	8	8	8	9	9	9
Hor Solar Rad (lang'ys)***	201	268	401	460	460	525	520	439	412	310	222	182	367

Miami FL

Elev: 7; ADR: 1.00; Lat: 26 ; Jan VT: 953
Cooling DD: 4038; Winter Design Dry-Bulb (°F): 47
Summer Design Dry-Bulb/Co-Incid WB: 90/77
Design guidelines*:
 low fuel cost: CF = 0.32; LCR = 714; SSF = 45%
 high fuel cost: CF = 0..37; LCR = 348; SSF = 69%

Indianapolis, IN

Elev: 807; ADR: 0.97; Lat: 39.7 ; Jan VT: 574
Cooling DD: 902; Winter Design Dry-Bulb (°F): + 2
Summer Design Dry-Bulb/Co-Incid WB: 92/74
Design guidelines*:
 low fuel cost: CF = 1.33; LCR = 158; SSF = 12%
 high fuel cost: CF = 1.76; LCR = 40; SSF = 30%

Passive Heating Solar Savings Fraction Table* (Miami FL)

LCR	*SSF (%; DD base = 55°F)* 100	70	50	40	30	25	20	15	*SSF (%; DD base = 65°F)* 100	70	50	40	30	25	20	15
DGA1	97	97	97	97	97	97	97	97	79	93	96	97	97	97	97	97
DGA2	99	99	99	99	99	99	98	98	88	97	98	99	99	99	98	98
DGA3	100	100	100	100	100	100	100	100	86	98	99	100	100	100	100	100
DGB1	99	99	99	99	99	99	98	98	88	98	98	99	99	99	98	98
DGB2	100	100	100	100	100	100	100	100	73	91	96	99	100	100	100	100
DGB3	100	100	100	100	100	100	100	100	76	93	97	99	100	100	100	100
DGC1	100	100	100	100	100	100	100	100	86	98	99	100	100	100	100	100
DGC2	100	100	100	100	100	100	100	100	85	97	99	100	100	100	100	100
DGC3	100	100	100	100	100	100	100	100	71	90	96	99	99	100	100	100
TWA2	100	100	100	100	100	100	100	100	72	91	96	99	100	100	100	100
TWA3	100	100	100	100	100	100	100	100	84	97	99	100	100	100	100	100
TWA4	100	100	100	100	100	100	100	100	83	96	99	100	100	100	100	100
TWD1	100	100	100	100	100	100	100	100	78	94	98	99	100	100	100	100
TWD2	100	100	100	100	100	100	100	100	82	96	99	100	100	100	100	100
TWD3	100	100	100	100	100	100	100	100	89	98	100	100	100	100	100	100
TWD4	100	100	100	100	100	100	100	100	88	98	100	100	100	100	100	100
TWE1	100	100	100	100	100	100	100	100	89	98	100	100	100	100	100	100
TWE2	100	100	100	100	100	100	100	100	89	99	100	100	100	100	100	100
TWF2	100	100	100	100	100	100	100	100	89	98	100	100	100	100	100	100
TWF3	100	100	100	100	100	100	100	100	75	92	97	99	100	100	100	100
TWF4	100	100	100	100	100	100	100	100	68	87	94	98	99	100	100	100
TWI1	100	100	100	100	100	100	100	100	64	85	92	97	99	100	100	100
TWI2	100	100	100	100	100	100	100	100	83	96	99	100	100	100	100	100
TWI3	100	100	100	100	100	100	100	100	77	94	98	99	100	100	100	100
TWI4	100	100	100	100	100	100	100	100	94	100	100	100	100	100	100	100
TWJ1	100	100	100	100	100	100	100	100	93	99	100	100	100	100	100	100
TWJ2	100	100	100	100	100	100	100	100	ß	97	99	100	100	100	100	100
WWA2	100	100	100	100	100	100	100	100	88	98	100	100	100	100	100	100

Passive Heating Solar Savings Fraction Table* (Indianapolis, IN)

LCR	*SSF (%; DD base = 55°F)* 100	70	50	40	30	25	20	15	*SSF (%; DD base = 65°F)* 100	70	50	40	30	25	20	15
DGA1	5	6	8	8	9	10	10	9	9	12	16	19	22	25	29	34
DGA2	8	11	14	16	20	22	25	29	8	12	16	19	23	26	30	36
DGA3	11	15	20	24	30	34	40	47	7	8	9	10	11	11	11	11
DGB1	5	6	8	9	10	10	11	11	9	13	18	22	28	32	37	44
DGB2	8	11	14	17	20	23	26	31	11	17	23	28	34	39	45	53
DGB3	12	16	21	25	31	36	42	51	11	18	25	31	39	45	52	61
DGC1	7	9	11	13	15	16	17	19	13	19	25	30	37	42	49	57
DGC2	10	13	17	21	25	28	33	39	11	18	25	30	37	43	49	58
DGC3	13	18	24	29	36	41	48	57	15	18	21	24	27	30	33	38
TWA2	10	13	15	17	20	22	25	29	18	23	29	34	40	44	50	57
TWA3	9	12	15	18	21	24	27	31	15	18	20	22	25	27	29	33
TWA4	12	16	21	25	31	34	40	47	18	23	28	33	39	43	48	56
TWD1	6	7	8	9	10	10	11	12	12	15	17	20	23	25	28	32
TWD2	10	14	18	21	26	30	34	40	15	20	26	30	36	40	46	53
TWD3	10	14	19	23	28	32	37	44	12	14	16	18	20	22	24	27
TWD4	11	17	23	28	35	40	46	55	15	19	25	29	34	38	44	51
TWE1	13	17	23	27	34	38	44	51	8	10	13	15	18	20	23	27
TWE2	12	17	23	28	35	39	46	54	10	14	19	23	29	33	38	45
TWF2	8	10	13	15	18	20	23	26	9	11	13	14	17	18	20	23
TWF3	6	9	12	14	18	20	23	28	10	13	18	21	26	29	34	40
TWF4	5	7	11	13	17	20	23	28	15	19	24	27	31	34	38	43
TWI1	4	5	6	7	8	9	9	10	19	26	33	39	46	51	58	66
TWI2	7	11	15	18	23	26	31	37	16	19	22	25	29	31	34	39
TWI3	8	12	17	20	26	30	35	42	19	25	32	37	45	49	56	64
TWI4	9	14	20	25	32	37	43	52	12	15	18	21	24	27	30	34
TWJ1	10	15	21	25	32	36	42	50	15	21	27	32	38	43	49	56
TWJ2	10	15	21	26	32	37	43	52	12	15	17	19	22	24	26	30
WWA2	10	13	16	18	21	23	26	30	15	20	25	30	36	40	45	52

Weather Data (Miami FL)

	Jan	Feb	Mar	Apr	May	Jun	Jul	Aug	Sep	Oct	Nov	Dec	Year
Daily Max Temp (°F)**	76	77	80	83	85	88	89	90	88	85	80	77	83
Daily MinTemp (°F)**	59	59	63	67	71	74	76	76	75	71	65	60	68
Daily Temp Range (°F)**	17	18	17	16	14	14	13	14	13	14	15	17	15
Heating DD (base 65°F)*	53	67	17	0	0	0	0	0	0	0	13	56	206
Heating DD (base 55°F)*	0	8	0	0	0	0	0	0	0	0	0	5	13
Normal Precip (in.)**	2.2	2.0	2.1	3.6	6.1	9.0	6.9	6.7	8.7	8.2	2.7	1.6	60
Daily Max Rel Hum (%)**	84	82	82	80	82	87	86	86	89	87	84	83	84
Daily Min Rel Hum (%)**	61	56	56	55	60	67	65	66	67	65	60	59	61
Mean Dewpoint (°F)***	57	59	61	63	68	72	73	74	74	69	63	58	66
Prevailing Wind (from)**	NW	SE	SE	SE	SE	SE	SE	SE	SE	NE	N	N	SE
Mean Wind Spd (mph)**	9	10	10	11	10	8	8	8	8	8	9	9	9
Hor Solar Rad (lang'ys)***	349	415	489	540	553	532	532	505	440	384	353	316	451

Weather Data (Indianapolis, IN)

	Jan	Feb	Mar	Apr	May	Jun	Jul	Aug	Sep	Oct	Nov	Dec	Year
Daily Max Temp (°F)**	39	40	50	62	73	83	87	85	78	68	52	38	63
Daily MinTemp (°F)**	22	23	30	40	51	61	64	63	55	44	33	24	43
Daily Temp Range (°F)**	17	17	20	22	22	22	23	22	23	24	21	14	20
Heating DD (base 65°F)*	1151	961	789	387	159	11	0	5	63	302	699	1058	5585
Heating DD (base 55°F)*	842	682	496	144	29	0	0	0	0	92	403	752	3440
Normal Precip (in.)**	3	2.5	3.4	3.7	4.2	4.8	3.4	3	3	3.8	3	2.5	40
Daily Max Rel Hum (%)**	83	82	81	80	81	83	84	85	86	87	86	84	84
Daily Min Rel Hum (%)**	72	68	62	57	56	55	55	55	54	53	59	66	59
Mean Dewpoint (°F)***	23	24	31	38	49	60	63	63	55	44	33	25	42
Prevailing Wind (from)**	NW	NW	NW	SW	SW	SW	SW	SW	SW	SW	SW	SW	SW
Mean Wind Spd (mph)**	12	12	13	13	11	9	8	8	9	10	12	11	11
Hor Solar Rad (lang'ys)***	144	213	316	369	488	543	541	490	405	293	177	132	343

Data sources: *Balcomb et al., (1984); **National Oceanic and Atmospheric Administration, 1978; ***U.S. Department of Commerce (1978).

New Orleans LA

Elev: 10; ADR: 1.0; Lat: 30.0 ; Jan VT: 808
Cooling DD: 2706; Winter Design Dry-Bulb (°F): 33
Summer Design Dry-Bulb/Co-Incid WB: 92/78
Design guidelines*:
  low fuel cost: CF = 0.70; LCR = 176; SSF = 36%
  high fuel cost: CF = 0.85; LCR = 71; SSF = 64%

Passive Heating Solar Savings Fraction Table*

LCR	\	SSF (%; DD base = 55°F)						\	\	SSF (%; DD base = 65°F)					
	100	70	50	40	30	25	20	15	100	70	50	40	30	25	20	15
DGA1	43	67	78	87	91	94	95	96	21	38	50	62	69	78	83	87
DGA2	47	73	84	91	94	96	97	98	21	38	50	62	70	79	83	87
DGA3	46	72	84	92	95	98	99	99	22	39	51	65	73	82	87	91
DGB1	49	77	88	94	96	98	98	98	24	44	57	72	80	88	92	95
DGB2	41	61	72	81	87	93	95	97	22	35	44	54	60	70	75	81
DGB3	43	64	75	84	89	94	97	98	22	36	46	57	64	73	79	85
DGC1	53	75	85	92	96	98	99	100	28	47	59	70	77	85	90	94
DGC2	52	75	85	92	95	98	99	100	27	46	58	69	77	85	89	94
DGC3	39	59	70	80	86	92	95	97	20	33	41	51	58	67	73	80
TWA2	39	60	71	81	87	93	95	98	19	33	42	53	60	69	75	82
TWA3	50	73	84	91	95	98	99	100	25	44	56	68	75	84	88	93
TWA4	48	72	83	91	94	98	99	100	24	43	55	66	74	83	88	92
TWD1	45	66	77	86	91	95	97	99	24	39	48	59	66	75	80	86
TWD2	48	70	81	89	93	97	98	99	24	41	52	63	70	79	84	89
TWD3	55	79	88	95	97	99	100	100	28	50	63	74	81	89	93	96
TWD4	55	78	88	94	97	99	99	100	28	49	62	73	80	88	92	95
TWE1	56	78	87	93	96	99	99	100	33	52	63	74	80	88	91	95
TWE2	56	78	87	93	96	99	99	100	33	52	63	74	80	87	91	95
TWF2	56	77	86	93	96	98	99	100	33	51	62	73	79	87	90	94
TWF3	42	62	73	82	87	93	95	98	24	37	46	56	63	72	77	83
TWF4	38	56	66	76	82	88	92	95	22	33	41	49	56	64	69	76
TWI1	35	52	62	72	78	85	89	93	20	30	37	45	51	59	65	71
TWI2	49	72	82	90	94	97	99	99	25	43	54	66	73	82	87	91
TWI3	44	66	77	86	91	95	97	99	22	38	48	59	67	76	81	87
TWI4	64	85	92	97	99	100	100	100	38	60	72	82	87	93	96	98
TWJ1	62	83	91	96	98	99	100	100	36	58	70	80	86	92	95	97
TWJ2	52	73	83	91	94	97	99	99	28	45	56	67	74	82	86	91
WWA2	54	76	86	93	96	98	99	100	30	49	61	72	79	86	90	94

Weather Data

	Jan	Feb	Mar	Apr	May	Jun	Jul	Aug	Sep	Oct	Nov	Dec	Year
Daily Max Temp (°F)**	62	65	70	78	85	90	90	91	87	80	70	64	78
Daily Min Temp (°F)**	44	46	51	59	65	71	73	73	70	60	50	45	59
Daily Temp Range (°F)**	18	19	19	19	20	19	17	18	17	20	20	19	19
Heating DD (base 65°F)*	403	299	188	29	0	0	0	0	0	40	179	327	1465
Heating DD (base 55°F)*	189	126	41	0	0	0	0	0	0	0	30	106	492
Normal Precip (in.)**	4.3	4.8	5.5	4.2	4.2	4.7	6.7	5.3	5.6	2.3	3.9	5.1	57
Daily Max Rel Hum (%)**	86	84	84	89	89	90	90	91	89	88	86	86	88
Daily Min Rel Hum (%)**	67	62	60	60	60	62	66	66	66	59	60	67	63
Mean Dewpoint (°F)***	46	48	52	59	66	72	73	73	70	60	52	47	60
Prevailing Wind (from)**	N	E	SE	SE	SE	SE	SW	SE	NE	NE	NE	NE	SE
Mean Wind Spd (mph)**	10	10	10	10	9	8	7	6	6	8	8	9	8
Hor Solar Rad (lang'ys)***	214	259	335	412	449	443	417	416	383	357	278	198	347

Data sources: *Balcomb et al., (1984); **National Oceanic and Atmospheric Administration, 1978; ***U.S. Department of Commerce (1978).

Minneapolis MN

Elev: 837; ADR: 0.97; Lat: 44.9 ; Jan VT: 653
Cooling DD: 585; Winter Design Dry-Bulb (°F): -12
Summer Design Dry-Bulb/Co-Incid WB: 88/72
Design guidelines*:
  low fuel cost: CF = 1.60; LCR = 126; SSF = 11%
  high fuel cost: CF = 2.13; LCR = 39; SSF = 23%

Passive Heating Solar Savings Fraction Table*

LCR	\	SSF (%; DD base = 55°F)						\	\	SSF (%; DD base = 65°F)					
	100	70	50	40	30	25	20	15	100	70	50	40	30	25	20	15
DGA1	9	12	16	19	23	25	29	34	7	9	12	14	17	19	21	24
DGA2	13	19	25	30	37	42	48	57	10	15	21	25	31	35	41	48
DGA3	12	18	25	30	38	43	49	58	9	14	20	25	32	36	42	50
DGB1	15	23	33	40	49	56	64	73	12	19	28	35	44	53	57	67
DGB2	11	13	16	18	21	23	25	29	9	11	13	14	16	18	19	21
DGB3	9	12	15	18	21	24	27	32	7	10	12	14	16	18	20	23
DGC1	13	18	23	30	33	38	43	51	10	14	19	23	28	32	36	43
DGC2	12	18	24	28	35	40	46	54	10	14	20	24	29	34	39	46
DGC3	8	11	13	15	18	20	23	26	7	8	10	12	14	15	17	19
TWA2	7	9	12	15	18	20	24	28	5	7	9	11	13	15	17	20
TWA3	11	15	21	25	31	36	42	49	8	12	17	21	26	30	35	41
TWA4	10	15	21	26	33	37	43	52	7	12	17	21	27	31	37	44
TWD1	10	13	16	18	21	24	26	30	8	10	12	14	16	18	19	22
TWD2	9	12	16	19	23	25	29	34	7	9	12	14	17	19	21	24
TWD3	12	18	26	31	39	45	52	61	9	14	21	26	33	38	45	54
TWD4	12	18	25	30	38	43	49	58	9	14	20	25	32	36	42	50
TWE1	17	22	27	31	37	41	47	54	15	19	24	28	33	37	42	48
TWE2	16	21	26	30	36	40	45	52	15	19	24	27	32	35	40	46
TWF2	16	20	24	28	33	37	41	47	14	18	22	25	29	32	36	41
TWF3	11	13	16	18	21	23	25	29	10	12	14	16	18	19	21	23
TWF4	12	13	15	17	19	20	22	24	11	12	13	14	16	17	18	19
TWI1	11	12	13	14	15	16	17	19	10	11	12	12	13	14	14	14
TWI2	10	14	19	23	29	33	38	45	8	11	15	19	23	27	31	37
TWI3	10	14	18	21	26	29	34	40	8	11	15	17	21	24	28	33
TWI4	17	24	31	36	43	48	54	63	15	21	27	32	38	43	48	56
TWJ1	17	23	30	35	42	46	52	60	15	21	26	31	37	41	47	54
TWJ2	11	13	16	19	22	24	26	30	9	11	13	15	17	18	20	21
WWA2	14	18	23	27	33	37	42	49	12	16	20	24	29	32	36	42

Weather Data

	Jan	Feb	Mar	Apr	May	Jun	Jul	Aug	Sep	Oct	Nov	Dec	Year
Daily Max Temp (°F)**	21	26	37	56	68	77	82	81	71	61	41	27	54
Daily MinTemp (°F)**	3	7	20	35	46	57	61	60	49	39	24	11	34
Daily Temp Range (°F)**	18	19	17	21	22	20	21	21	22	22	17	16	20
Heating DD (base 65°F)*	1637	1358	1140	600	271	65	11	21	173	472	978	1439	8165
Heating DD (base 55°F)*	1327	1078	836	321	83	5	0	0	23	211	680	1129	5693
Normal Precip (in.)**	0.7	0.8	1.7	2.0	3.4	3.9	3.7	3.1	2.7	1.8	1.2	0.9	26
Daily Max Rel Hum (%)**	73	74	77	76	77	80	82	85	87	83	82	79	80
Daily Min Rel Hum (%)**	67	65	63	54	52	53	54	56	60	60	67	72	60
Mean Dewpoint (°F)***	6	10	20	32	43	55	60	59	50	40	25	13	34
Prevailing Wind (from)**	NW	NW	NW	NW	SE	SE	S	SE	S	SE	NW	NW	NW
Mean Wind Spd (mph)**	10	11	11	12	12	11	9	9	10	11	11	10	11
Hor Solar Rad (lang'ys)***	168	260	368	426	496	535	557	486	366	237	146	124	347

Portland OR

Elev: 39; ADR: 1.00; Lat: 45.6; Jan VT: 375
Cooling DD: 300; Winter Design Dry-Bulb (°F): 23
Summer Design Dry-Bulb/Co-Incid WB: 85/67
Design guidelines*:
   low fuel cost: CF = 1.21; LCR = 120; SSF = 21%
   high fuel cost: CF = 1.55; LCR = 46; SSF = 36%

Passive Heating Solar Savings Fraction Table*

	SSF (%; DD base = 55°F)								SSF (%; DD base = 65°F)							
LCR	100	70	50	40	30	25	20	15	100	70	50	40	30	25	20	15
DGA1	23	30	37	43	50	55	61	68	16	21	28	32	39	43	48	55
DGA2	20	26	31	35	41	44	48	52	13	16	20	22	26	28	31	33
DGA3	23	29	36	42	49	53	59	66	15	20	25	30	35	39	44	50
DGB1	26	34	43	49	58	63	70	78	19	25	32	28	45	50	57	65
DGB2	21	26	32	36	41	45	50	56	15	18	22	25	29	32	35	39
DGB3	21	27	33	37	43	47	52	59	14	18	22	26	30	33	37	42
DGC1	27	35	43	49	56	61	67	74	19	25	31	36	43	47	53	60
DGC2	27	35	43	49	57	62	68	76	18	25	32	37	44	48	54	62
DGC3	19	24	29	33	39	43	47	54	13	16	20	23	27	29	33	37
TWA2	18	23	29	34	40	44	49	56	11	15	19	22	27	30	34	39
TWA3	25	32	41	46	54	59	65	73	17	23	29	34	41	45	51	58
TWA4	24	32	40	46	54	60	66	74	16	22	29	34	41	45	52	60
TWD1	23	28	34	38	44	48	53	59	15	19	23	26	31	33	37	41
TWD2	23	29	36	41	47	51	57	63	15	19	24	28	32	36	40	45
TWD3	28	37	46	53	62	67	73	81	18	26	34	40	48	53	60	68
TWD4	28	36	45	52	60	65	72	79	18	25	33	39	47	52	58	66
TWE1	30	37	45	50	57	62	68	75	24	30	36	41	47	51	56	63
TWE2	30	37	44	50	57	61	67	74	24	30	36	40	46	50	55	62
TWF2	29	36	43	48	54	59	64	71	23	29	34	38	44	48	52	58
TWF3	22	27	32	36	41	44	49	55	17	20	24	27	31	34	37	41
TWF4	21	24	29	32	36	39	43	48	16	19	22	25	28	30	32	36
TWI1	19	22	26	29	33	35	39	43	15	18	20	22	25	26	28	31
TWI2	24	31	39	44	52	57	63	70	16	21	27	32	38	42	47	54
TWI3	22	28	35	40	47	52	58	65	15	20	25	29	35	38	43	50
TWI4	34	42	51	57	64	69	75	82	26	33	41	46	53	58	63	70
TWJ1	33	41	49	55	63	67	73	80	26	32	40	45	52	56	61	68
TWJ2	25	30	36	40	46	50	54	60	18	22	27	30	34	36	39	43
WWA2	28	35	42	48	55	60	65	72	21	27	33	38	44	48	53	59

Weather Data

	Jan	Feb	Mar	Apr	May	Jun	Jul	Aug	Sep	Oct	Nov	Dec	Year
Daily Max Temp (°F)**	44	50	54	60	67	72	79	78	74	63	52	46	62
Daily MinTemp (°F)**	33	36	37	41	46	52	55	55	51	45	39	35	44
Daily Temp Range (°F)**	11	14	17	19	21	20	24	23	23	18	13	11	18
Heating DD (base 65°F)*	837	622	598	433	264	128	48	56	119	349	591	753	4798
Heating DD (base 55°F)*	538	346	292	153	53	11	0	0	8	94	296	444	2235
Normal Precip (in.)**	5.9	4.1	3.6	2.2	2.1	1.6	0.5	0.8	1.6	3.6	5.6	6.0	38
Daily Max Rel Hum (%)**	86	76	86	86	85	84	83	84	87	90	88	87	85
Daily Min Rel Hum (%)**	76	68	60	55	53	49	45	46	49	64	74	79	60
Mean Dewpoint (°F)***	33	36	37	41	46	50	53	54	51	47	40	36	44
Prevailing Wind (from)**	SE	SE	SE	NW	NW	NW	NW	NW	NW	SE	SE	SE	NW
Mean Wind Spd (mph)**	10	9	8	7	7	7	7	7	6	6	8	10	8
Hor Solar Rad (lang'ys)***	90	162	270	375	492	469	539	461	354	209	111	79	301

Charleston SC

Elev: 39; ADR: 1.00; Lat: 32.9; Jan VT: 768
Cooling DD: 2078; Winter Design Dry-Bulb (°F): 28
Summer Design Dry-Bulb/Co-Incid WB: 92/78
Design guidelines*:
   low fuel cost: CF = 0.84; LCR = 129; SSF = 35%
   high fuel cost: CF = 1.03; LCR = 51; SSF = 62%

Passive Heating Solar Savings Fraction Table*

	SSF (%; DD base = 55°F)								SSF (%; DD base = 65°F)							
LCR	100	70	50	40	30	25	20	15	100	70	50	40	30	25	20	15
DGA1	33	50	60	70	77	85	89	93	20	31	39	47	53	61	66	73
DGA2	30	49	61	71	78	86	90	94	16	28	36	45	51	60	66	73
DGA3	34	56	68	79	85	91	95	97	18	32	42	53	60	70	76	82
DGB1	24	39	49	60	67	75	81	86	14	23	29	36	42	49	55	61
DGB2	29	46	56	67	74	82	87	91	17	27	34	42	48	57	62	69
DGB3	30	48	59	70	77	85	89	94	16	28	36	45	51	60	66	73
DGC1	38	60	72	82	88	94	96	98	21	36	47	58	65	74	80	86
DGC2	37	59	71	82	88	93	96	98	19	38	46	57	65	74	80	86
DGC3	26	54	54	65	72	80	85	90	14	25	32	40	46	54	60	67
TWA2	26	44	55	66	74	82	87	92	13	24	32	41	47	56	62	69
TWA3	35	57	69	80	86	92	95	98	18	34	44	55	63	72	78	84
TWA4	33	56	68	79	86	92	95	97	17	37	43	54	62	72	77	84
TWD1	32	50	61	72	79	87	91	94	18	30	38	46	53	62	67	74
TWD2	33	54	66	76	83	90	93	96	18	31	40	50	57	66	72	79
TWD3	39	63	76	86	91	96	98	99	19	38	50	62	70	79	85	90
TWD4	39	63	75	85	90	95	97	99	20	38	49	61	69	78	84	89
TWE1	41	63	74	83	89	94	96	98	25	41	51	62	69	77	82	88
TWE2	41	63	74	83	89	94	96	98	25	41	51	61	68	77	82	87
TWF2	41	62	73	82	88	93	96	98	25	40	50	60	67	76	81	86
TWF3	30	47	57	67	74	82	87	91	18	29	36	44	50	58	64	70
TWF4	27	41	51	60	67	75	80	86	17	26	32	39	44	51	56	63
TWI1	25	38	47	56	63	71	76	82	16	24	29	35	40	47	51	57
TWI2	34	56	68	79	85	91	95	97	18	32	42	53	60	70	76	82
TWI3	30	50	61	72	79	87	91	95	16	29	38	47	54	64	70	76
TWI4	48	71	82	90	94	97	99	99	28	47	59	70	77	85	89	93
TWJ1	46	69	80	88	93	97	98	99	27	46	57	68	75	83	88	92
TWJ2	37	57	68	78	84	91	94	97	21	34	43	53	60	69	74	80
WWA2	39	61	72	82	88	93	96	98	23	38	48	59	66	75	81	86

Weather Data

	Jan	Feb	Mar	Apr	May	Jun	Jul	Aug	Sep	Oct	Nov	Dec	Year
Daily Max Temp (°F)**	60	62	68	76	83	88	89	89	85	77	68	61	76
Daily MinTemp (°F)**	37	39	45	53	61	68	71	71	66	55	44	38	54
Daily Temp Range (°F)**	23	23	23	23	22	20	18	18	19	22	24	23	22
Heating DD (base 65°F)*	521	419	300	69	5	0	0	0	0	74	271	491	2150
Heating DD (base 55°F)*	264	199	113	0	0	0	0	0	0	5	69	219	869
Normal Precip (in.)**	2.9	3.3	4.8	3.0	3.8	6.3	8.2	6.4	5.2	3.1	2.1	3.1	52
Daily Max Rel Hum (%)**	85	82	83	84	88	90	91	92	91	89	87	84	87
Daily Min Rel Hum (%)**	56	52	50	50	54	59	63	63	63	55	51	54	56
Mean Dewpoint (°F)***	40	41	44	53	62	69	72	71	68	57	47	39	55
Prevailing Wind (from)**	SW	NE	SW	SW	S	S	SW	SW	NE	NE	N	NE	NW
Mean Wind Spd (mph)**	9	10	10	10	9	8	8	7	8	8	8	9	9
Hor Solar Rad (lang'ys)***	252	314	388	512	551	564	520	501	404	338	286	225	405

Data sources: *Balcomb et al., (1984); **National Oceanic and Atmospheric Administration, 1978; ***U.S. Department of Commerce (1978).

Knoxville TN

Elev: 981; ADR: 0.96; Lat: 35.8 ; Jan VT: 667
Cooling DD: 1569; Winter Design Dry-Bulb (°F): 19
Summer Design Dry-Bulb/Co-Incid WB: 92/73
Design guidelines*:
   low fuel cost: CF = 1.06; LCR = 118; SSF = 25%
   high fuel cost: CF = 1.35; LCR = 37; SSF = 51%

Passive Heating Solar Savings Fraction Table*

LCR	|SSF (%; DD base = 55°F)| 100	70	50	40	30	25	20	15	|SSF (%; DD base = 65°F)| 100	70	50	40	30	25	20	15
DGA1	15	27	37	47	55	65	70	77	10	18	25	32	38	47	53	60
DGA2	14	25	34	44	51	60	66	72	8	15	20	25	29	36	40	45
DGA3	15	27	37	47	56	66	72	79	9	18	24	31	26	44	50	57
DGB1	17	32	43	55	64	75	81	87	12	22	29	38	45	55	62	71
DGB2	17	26	33	41	46	55	60	67	11	17	22	27	31	37	41	47
DGB3	16	26	34	43	49	58	64	71	10	17	22	28	33	39	44	50
DGC1	20	35	45	56	63	73	78	84	12	23	30	39	45	54	60	67
DGC2	19	34	44	55	63	73	78	84	11	22	30	39	46	55	60	68
DGC3	14	23	30	38	44	52	58	65	9	15	19	25	29	35	39	44
TWA2	13	23	30	39	45	54	60	67	7	14	19	25	29	36	40	46
TWA3	17	32	42	53	61	70	76	83	9	20	28	37	43	52	58	65
TWA4	16	31	41	52	60	70	76	82	8	19	27	36	43	52	58	65
TWD1	17	29	38	48	55	64	70	77	10	18	24	31	36	44	49	55
TWD2	16	30	40	50	57	66	72	79	9	18	25	32	38	46	51	58
TWD3	18	36	48	60	68	78	83	89	9	23	32	43	50	60	66	74
TWD4	19	36	47	59	67	76	82	88	10	23	32	42	49	58	65	72
TWE1	23	38	48	59	66	74	80	85	17	28	36	44	50	58	64	71
TWE2	23	38	48	58	65	74	79	85	17	28	35	43	50	58	63	70
TWF2	23	37	47	57	64	72	78	83	16	27	34	42	48	50	61	68
TWF3	17	27	33	44	47	55	61	67	12	19	24	29	33	39	43	49
TWF4	17	24	30	36	41	48	53	60	13	18	22	26	29	34	38	42
TWI1	15	22	27	33	37	44	48	54	12	16	19	23	26	30	33	37
TWI2	17	31	41	51	58	68	74	81	9	19	27	35	41	49	55	62
TWI3	16	28	36	46	52	62	68	75	9	18	24	31	36	44	49	56
TWI4	26	44	56	67	74	82	87	92	17	32	41	51	58	67	73	79
TWJ1	25	43	54	65	72	80	85	90	17	31	39	49	56	65	70	77
TWJ2	19	32	41	50	57	65	71	77	13	21	27	34	39	46	51	57
WWA2	21	36	46	56	63	72	78	84	14	25	32	41	47	55	61	68

Weather Data

	Jan	Feb	Mar	Apr	May	Jun	Jul	Aug	Sep	Oct	Nov	Dec	Year
Daily Max Temp (°F)**	49	52	60	72	80	86	88	87	82	72	59	50	70
Daily MinTemp (°F)**	32	34	39	49	57	65	68	67	61	50	39	33	50
Daily Temp Range (°F)**	17	18	21	23	23	21	20	20	21	22	20	17	20
Heating DD (base 65°F)*	761	630	484	173	47	0	0	0	10	175	475	731	3486
Heating DD (base 55°F)*	470	377	239	27	0	0	0	0	0	32	197	433	1775
Normal Precip (in.)**	4.7	4.7	4.9	3.6	3.3	3.6	4.7	3.2	2.8	2.7	3.6	4.5	46
Daily Max Rel Hum (%)**	80	77	78	78	83	87	90	92	91	88	82	81	84
Daily Min Rel Hum (%)**	64	59	54	51	54	59	62	61	59	54	59	65	58
Mean Dewpoint (°F)***	32	32	36	45	55	63	66	66	59	49	38	31	48
Prevailing Wind (from)**	NE	NE	NE	SW	SW	SW	SW	SW	NE	NE	NE	NE	NE
Mean Wind Spd (mph)**	8	9	9	9	7	7	6	6	6	6	7	8	7
Hor Solar Rad (lang'ys)***	161	239	331	450	518	551	526	478	416	318	213	163	364

Data sources: *Balcomb et al., (1984); **National Oceanic and Atmospheric Administration, 1978; ***U.S. Department of Commerce (1978).

Fort Worth TX

Elev: 538; ADR: 0.98; Lat: 32.8; Jan VT: 574
Cooling DD: 2587; Winter Design Dry-Bulb (°F): 22
Summer Design Dry-Bulb/Co-Incid WB: 99/74
Design guidelines*:
   low fuel cost: CF = 0.88; LCR = 115; SSF = 35%
   high fuel cost: CF = 1.08; LCR = 45; SSF = 63%

Passive Heating Solar Savings Fraction Table*

LCR	|SSF (%; DD base = 55°F)| 100	70	50	40	30	25	20	15	|SSF (%; DD base = 65°F)| 100	70	50	40	30	25	20	15
DGA1	28	49	61	73	79	86	89	92	15	27	36	47	55	65	70	77
DGA2	29	51	64	76	82	88	91	94	14	25	33	43	51	60	66	73
DGA3	29	51	65	77	84	90	93	98	15	27	36	47	55	66	72	79
DGB1	32	56	71	83	89	94	96	97	17	31	42	55	64	76	82	88
DGB2	28	44	54	65	72	80	85	90	16	25	32	40	46	54	60	67
DGB3	28	46	57	68	75	83	87	92	15	26	34	42	49	58	64	71
DGC1	36	58	70	80	86	92	95	97	19	34	45	56	63	73	78	85
DGC2	35	57	69	80	86	92	95	97	18	34	44	55	63	73	78	85
DGC3	25	41	52	63	70	78	83	89	13	23	30	38	44	52	58	65
TWA2	25	42	53	64	71	80	85	90	12	23	30	38	45	54	60	67
TWA3	33	55	67	78	84	91	94	97	16	32	42	53	61	70	76	83
TWA4	32	54	66	77	84	90	94	97	15	30	41	52	60	70	76	83
TWD1	30	48	59	70	77	85	89	93	17	28	35	44	51	59	65	72
TWD2	32	52	63	74	81	88	92	95	16	29	38	48	55	64	70	77
TWD3	37	61	74	84	89	95	97	98	17	36	48	60	68	78	83	89
TWD4	37	60	73	83	89	94	96	98	18	36	47	59	67	77	82	88
TWE1	40	61	72	81	87	93	95	97	24	39	49	60	67	76	81	86
TWE2	40	61	72	81	87	92	95	97	24	39	49	59	66	75	80	85
TWF2	39	60	71	80	86	92	94	97	23	38	48	58	65	74	79	85
TWF3	28	45	55	65	72	80	85	90	17	27	34	42	48	56	62	68
TWF4	26	40	49	58	65	73	78	84	16	24	30	37	42	49	54	60
TWI1	24	36	45	54	60	69	74	80	15	22	27	33	38	44	49	55
TWI2	32	54	66	76	83	90	93	96	16	30	40	51	58	68	74	81
TWI3	29	48	59	70	77	85	89	93	15	27	36	45	52	62	68	75
TWI4	46	69	80	88	92	96	98	99	26	45	57	68	75	84	88	92
TWJ1	44	67	78	87	91	96	97	99	26	44	55	66	73	82	86	91
TWJ2	35	55	66	76	82	89	92	95	19	32	41	51	57	66	72	78
WWA2	37	59	70	80	86	92	95	97	21	36	46	57	64	73	79	85

Weather Data

	Jan	Feb	Mar	Apr	May	Jun	Jul	Aug	Sep	Oct	Nov	Dec	Year
Daily Max Temp (°F)**	56	60	67	76	83	91	96	96	89	79	68	59	77
Daily MinTemp (°F)**	34	38	43	54	62	70	74	74	67	56	44	37	54
Daily Temp Range (°F)**	22	22	24	22	21	21	22	22	22	23	24	22	22
Heating DD (base 65°F)*	629	459	335	88	0	0	0	0	0	60	287	532	2390
Heating DD (base 55°F)*	337	206	130	7	0	0	0	0	0	5	83	244	1012
Normal Precip (in.)**	1.8	2.4	2.5	4.3	4.5	3.0	1.8	2.3	3.2	2.7	2.0	1.8	32
Daily Max Rel Hum (%)**	82	79	81	85	88	86	81	83	89	86	83	81	84
Daily Min Rel Hum (%)**	59	52	51	54	59	52	45	48	60	56	56	60	54
Mean Dewpoint (°F)***	33	36	39	51	61	66	67	66	61	53	41	35	51
Prevailing Wind (from)**	S	S	S	S	S	S	S	S	S	S	S	S	S
Mean Wind Spd (mph)**	12	12	13	13	12	11	10	9	10	10	11	11	11
Hor Solar Rad (lang'ys)***	250	320	420	488	562	651	613	593	503	403	306	245	446

Houston TX

Elev: 108; ADR: 1.00; Lat: 30.0 ; Jan VT: 724
Cooling DD: 2889; Winter Design Dry-Bulb (°F): 32
Summer Design Dry-Bulb/Co-Incid WB: 94/77
Design guidelines*:
  low fuel cost: CF = 0.72; LCR = 216; SSF = 28%
  high fuel cost: CF = 0.87; LCR = 74; SSF = 58%

Passive Heating Solar Savings Fraction Table*

LCR	|SSF (%; DD base = 55°F) 100	70	50	40	30	25	20	15	|SSF (%; DD base = 65°F) 100	70	50	40	30	25	20	15
DGA1	41	65	76	85	89	93	95	96	19	34	45	57	64	74	79	84
DGA2	44	70	82	90	93	96	97	97	18	33	44	56	64	73	78	83
DGA3	43	69	82	90	94	97	98	99	19	34	46	59	67	77	82	88
DGB1	46	74	86	93	96	97	98	98	21	39	52	66	75	84	89	93
DGB2	39	58	69	79	85	91	94	97	20	32	40	49	56	65	70	77
DGB3	40	61	72	82	88	93	96	98	20	33	42	52	59	68	74	80
DGC1	50	73	83	91	95	98	99	100	25	43	54	65	73	81	86	91
DGC2	49	72	83	91	94	98	99	99	24	42	53	65	72	81	86	91
DGC3	36	56	67	77	84	90	93	96	17	29	37	46	53	62	68	75
TWA2	36	57	69	79	85	91	94	97	16	29	38	48	55	64	70	77
TWA3	47	70	81	90	94	97	98	99	22	40	51	63	70	79	85	90
TWA4	46	69	80	89	93	97	98	99	21	38	50	62	69	79	84	89
TWD1	43	63	74	84	89	94	96	98	21	35	44	54	61	70	75	82
TWD2	45	67	78	87	92	96	98	98	21	37	47	58	65	74	80	86
TWD3	52	76	87	93	96	99	99	100	24	45	58	70	77	86	90	94
TWD4	52	76	86	93	96	98	99	100	24	44	57	69	76	85	89	93
TWE1	54	75	85	92	95	98	99	100	30	48	59	70	76	84	88	93
TWE2	54	75	85	92	95	98	99	100	30	48	59	70	76	84	88	93
TWF2	53	75	84	92	95	98	99	100	29	47	58	68	75	83	87	92
TWF3	40	60	70	80	86	92	94	97	21	34	42	52	58	67	72	79
TWF4	36	53	63	73	79	87	90	94	20	30	37	45	51	59	65	71
TWI1	33	50	60	69	76	83	88	92	19	28	34	41	47	55	60	67
TWI2	46	69	80	89	93	97	98	99	22	38	49	61	68	77	83	88
TWI3	41	63	74	84	89	94	96	98	20	34	44	55	62	71	77	83
TWI4	61	83	91	96	98	99	100	100	34	55	67	78	84	91	94	97
TWJ1	59	81	90	95	98	100	100	100	33	53	65	76	82	89	93	96
TWJ2	49	70	81	89	93	97	98	99	25	41	51	62	69	77	82	88
WWA2	52	74	84	91	95	98	99	100	27	45	56	67	74	83	87	92

Weather Data

	Jan	Feb	Mar	Apr	May	Jun	Jul	Aug	Sep	Oct	Nov	Dec	Year
Daily Max Temp (°F)**	63	66	72	79	86	91	94	94	90	84	73	66	80
Daily MinTemp (°F)**	42	45	50	59	66	71	73	72	68	58	49	43	58
Daily Temp Range (°F)**	21	21	22	20	20	20	21	22	22	26	24	23	22
Heating DD (base 65°F)*	416	294	189	23	0	0	0	0	0	24	155	333	1434
Heating DD (base 55°F)*	184	111	43	0	0	0	0	0	0	0	5	44	387
Normal Precip (in.)**	3.6	3.5	2.7	3.5	5.1	4.5	4.1	4.4	4.7	4.0	4.0	4.0	48
Daily Max Rel Hum (%)**	89	86	89	90	93	92	93	95	95	95	89	89	91
Daily Min Rel Hum (%)**	68	56	60	59	60	58	58	62	68	61	59	63	61
Mean Dewpoint (°F)***	45	48	51	60	66	72	73	73	69	60	51	47	60
Prevailing Wind (from)**	NW	SE	SE	SE	SE	SE	S	SE	SE	SE	SE	SE	SE
Mean Wind Spd (mph)**	8	8	9	9	8	7	6	5	7	6	8	8	7
Hor Solar Rad (lang'ys)***	261	320	421	451	532	610	587	562	461	407	291	264	431

Midland TX

Elev: 2858; ADR: 0.88; Lat: 31.9 ; Jan VT: 1265
Cooling DD: 2250; Winter Design Dry-Bulb (°F): 21
Summer Design Dry-Bulb/Co-Incid WB: 98/69
Design guidelines*:
  low fuel cost: CF = 0.88; LCR = 77; SSF = 55%
  high fuel cost: CF = 1.04; LCR = 41; SSF = 75%

Passive Heating Solar Savings Fraction Table*

LCR	|SSF (%; DD base = 55°F) 100	70	50	40	30	25	20	15	|SSF (%; DD base = 65°F) 100	70	50	40	30	25	20	15
DGA1	34	58	70	81	86	91	93	95	18	34	45	58	65	75	80	85
DGA2	36	62	76	85	90	94	95	97	18	33	44	57	66	75	80	85
DGA3	36	62	76	85	91	95	97	99	19	34	46	60	69	79	84	89
DGB1	39	67	81	90	94	97	98	98	21	39	53	67	77	86	90	94
DGB2	33	51	63	73	80	87	91	95	19	31	40	49	56	66	71	78
DGB3	34	54	66	77	83	90	93	96	19	33	42	52	60	69	75	82
DGC1	43	67	78	87	92	96	98	99	24	43	55	66	74	83	87	92
DGC2	42	66	78	87	92	96	98	99	23	42	54	66	73	82	87	92
DGC3	30	49	61	71	78	86	90	94	17	29	37	47	54	63	69	76
TWA2	30	50	62	73	80	88	91	95	16	29	38	48	56	65	71	78
TWA3	40	64	76	86	91	95	97	99	22	40	52	64	71	81	86	91
TWA4	39	62	75	85	90	95	97	99	20	39	50	62	70	80	85	91
TWD1	36	57	68	79	85	91	94	97	21	35	44	54	62	71	77	83
TWD2	38	61	72	83	88	94	96	98	21	37	48	59	66	76	81	87
TWD3	45	70	82	90	94	98	99	99	24	45	58	71	78	87	91	95
TWD4	45	69	81	90	94	97	99	99	24	45	57	70	77	86	90	94
TWE1	46	68	79	88	92	96	98	99	29	47	58	69	76	84	89	93
TWE2	46	68	79	88	92	96	98	99	29	47	58	69	76	84	88	93
TWF2	45	67	78	87	91	96	97	99	29	46	57	67	74	83	87	92
TWF3	33	52	63	73	80	87	91	94	20	33	41	51	57	66	72	79
TWF4	30	46	56	66	73	81	85	90	19	29	36	44	50	59	64	71
TWI1	27	42	51	61	68	77	81	87	18	27	33	40	46	54	59	66
TWI2	39	62	74	84	90	95	97	99	21	39	50	61	69	79	84	89
TWI3	35	56	68	79	85	91	94	97	19	34	44	55	63	72	78	85
TWI4	53	77	86	93	96	99	99	99	33	55	67	78	84	91	94	97
TWJ1	52	75	85	92	95	98	99	99	32	53	65	76	82	89	93	96
TWJ2	41	63	74	83	89	94	96	98	25	40	51	61	68	77	82	88
WWA2	44	66	76	87	91	96	98	99	26	44	56	67	74	83	87	92

Weather Data

	Jan	Feb	Mar	Apr	May	Jun	Jul	Aug	Sep	Oct	Nov	Dec	Year
Daily Max Temp (°F)**	58	62	69	79	87	93	95	94	88	79	68	61	78
Daily MinTemp (°F)**	29	34	39	49	58	67	70	69	63	52	39	32	50
Daily Temp Range (°F)**	29	28	30	30	29	26	25	25	25	27	29	29	28
Heating DD (base 65°F)*	666	484	349	98	0	0	0	0	0	81	356	593	2627
Heating DD (base 55°F)*	373	228	133	8	0	0	0	0	0	6	120	291	1159
Normal Precip (in.)**	0.6	0.6	0.6	0.9	2.2	1.5	1.8	1.5	1.5	1.4	0.5	0.5	14
Daily Max Rel Hum (%)**	69	73	67	65	74	75	69	74	83	81	77	71	73
Daily Min Rel Hum (%)**	39	35	28	26	30	30	31	37	47	42	44	42	36
Mean Dewpoint (°F)***	25	29	29	37	49	58	60	58	56	47	36	30	43
Prevailing Wind (from)**	S	SW	S	S	SE	SE	SE	SE	SE	S	S	SW	SE
Mean Wind Spd (mph)**	10	11	12	13	12	12	10	10	10	10	10	10	11
Hor Solar Rad (lang'ys)***	253	358	476	550	611	617	608	574	522	396	325	275	464

Data sources: *Balcomb et al., (1984); **National Oceanic and Atmospheric Administration, 1978; ***U.S. Department of Commerce (1978).

Salt Lake City UT

Elev: 4226; ADR: 0.85; Lat: 40.8; Jan VT: 864
Cooling DD: 927; Winter Design Temp (°F): 8
Summer Design Dry-Bulb/Co-Incid WB: 95/62
Design guidelines*:
  low fuel cost: CF = 1.31; LCR = 50; SSF = 41%
  high fuel cost: CF = 1.64; LCR = 22; SSF = 61%

Passive Heating Solar Savings Fraction Table*

LCR	|	SSF (%; DD base = 55°F)								|	SSF (%; DD base = 65°F)							
	|	100	70	50	40	30	25	20	15	|	100	70	50	40	30	25	20	15
DGA1	|	25	33	43	50	59	64	71	78	|	19	25	33	39	47	53	60	68
DGA2	|	23	30	38	44	52	57	62	69	|	15	20	26	31	37	41	46	52
DGA3	|	25	33	43	49	59	65	71	79	|	18	24	31	37	45	51	58	66
DGB1	|	29	39	50	58	68	74	81	88	|	22	29	38	46	56	62	70	79
DGB2	|	24	30	37	42	49	54	60	68	|	18	22	28	32	38	42	47	54
DGB3	|	24	31	38	44	52	57	64	72	|	17	22	29	33	40	44	50	58
DGC1	|	31	41	50	57	66	71	78	85	|	23	31	39	46	54	60	67	75
DGC2	|	31	40	50	57	66	72	78	86	|	23	31	39	46	55	61	68	76
DGC3	|	21	27	34	39	47	52	58	66	|	15	20	25	29	35	39	45	52
TWA2	|	21	27	35	40	48	53	60	68	|	14	19	25	30	36	41	46	54
TWA3	|	29	38	48	55	64	69	76	84	|	21	28	37	43	52	58	65	73
TWA4	|	28	37	47	54	64	69	76	84	|	20	28	37	43	52	58	65	74
TWD1	|	26	32	40	46	53	58	65	73	|	19	24	30	34	41	45	51	59
TWD2	|	27	34	43	49	57	63	69	77	|	19	25	32	37	44	49	55	64
TWD3	|	33	43	54	62	72	77	83	90	|	23	33	43	50	60	66	73	82
TWD4	|	32	43	53	61	70	76	82	89	|	23	32	42	49	59	65	72	80
TWE1	|	34	43	52	58	66	72	78	85	|	28	36	44	49	57	62	69	76
TWE2	|	34	43	51	58	66	71	77	84	|	28	35	43	49	57	62	68	75
TWF2	|	33	41	49	55	63	68	75	82	|	27	34	41	47	54	59	65	72
TWF3	|	24	30	36	41	48	53	59	66	|	19	24	29	33	39	43	48	55
TWF4	|	22	27	32	36	42	46	51	59	|	18	22	26	29	34	37	41	47
TWI1	|	20	24	29	33	38	42	46	53	|	16	20	23	26	30	33	36	42
TWI2	|	28	37	46	53	62	67	74	82	|	20	27	35	41	49	55	62	70
TWI3	|	25	33	41	47	56	61	68	76	|	18	24	31	37	44	49	56	64
TWI4	|	39	49	59	66	74	79	85	91	|	32	41	50	56	65	70	76	84
TWJ1	|	38	47	57	64	72	77	83	89	|	31	39	48	55	63	68	75	82
TWJ2	|	34	43	53	60	69	74	80	87	|	27	35	44	50	58	63	70	78
WWA2	|	33	40	49	56	64	70	76	83	|	25	32	40	46	54	59	66	74

Weather Data

	Jan	Feb	Mar	Apr	May	Jun	Jul	Aug	Sep	Oct	Nov	Dec	Year
Daily Max Temp (°F)**	37	43	51	62	72	81	93	90	80	66	50	39	64
Daily MinTemp (°F)**	19	23	28	37	44	51	61	59	49	38	28	22	38
Daily Temp Range (°F)**	18	20	23	25	28	30	32	31	31	28	22	17	25
Heating DD (base 65°F)*	1147	885	788	478	237	88	0	5	105	407	777	1076	5993
Heating DD (base 55°F)*	839	603	481	216	62	10	0	0	13	165	482	766	3637
Normal Precip (in.)**	1.3	1.2	1.6	2.1	1.5	1.3	0.7	0.9	0.7	1.2	1.3	1.4	15
Daily Max Rel Hum (%)**	76	76	69	69	63	60	51	54	61	68	73	78	67
Daily Min Rel Hum (%)**	67	58	44	39	30	27	19	22	28	40	58	71	42
Mean Dewpoint (°F)***	20	23	26	31	36	40	44	45	38	34	28	24	32
Prevailing Wind (from)**	SE	SE	SE	SE	SE	SE	SE	SE	SE	SE	SE	SE	SE
Mean Wind Spd (mph)**	8	8	9	10	9	9	9	10	9	9	8	8	9
Hor Solar Rad (lang'ys)***	163	256	364	479	570	621	620	551	446	316	204	146	395

Burlington VT

Elev: 341; ADR: 0.99; Lat: 44.5; Jan VT: 486
Cooling DD: 396; Winter Design Dry-Bulb (°F): -7
Summer Design Dry-Bulb/Co-Incid WB: 85/70
Design guidelines*:
  low fuel cost: CF = 1.56; LCR = 229; SSF = 7%
  high fuel cost: CF = 2.08; LCR = 64; SSF = 15%

Passive Heating Solar Savings Fraction Table*

LCR	|	SSF (%; DD base = 55°F)								|	SSF (%; DD base = 65°F)							
	|	100	70	50	40	30	25	20	15	|	100	70	50	40	30	25	20	15
DGA1	|	10	13	17	21	25	29	34	40	|	8	11	15	17	22	25	29	34
DGA2	|	5	6	8	8	9	9	10	9	|	3	4	4	5	4	3	2
DGA3	|	8	11	14	17	20	23	26	30	|	7	9	11	13	16	18	20	23
DGB1	|	12	16	21	25	30	35	41	49	|	10	13	18	21	26	30	35	42
DGB2	|	9	10	12	14	15	17	18	20	|	7	8	9	10	11	12	12	13
DGB3	|	7	9	12	13	16	17	19	22	|	6	7	8	10	11	12	13	14
DGC1	|	10	14	18	22	27	30	35	41	|	8	11	14	17	21	24	28	33
DGC2	|	10	14	19	23	29	32	38	45	|	7	11	15	18	23	26	31	37
DGC3	|	6	8	10	11	13	14	16	18	|	5	6	7	8	9	9	10	10
TWA2	|	5	7	9	10	13	14	16	19	|	3	4	6	7	8	9	10	11
TWA3	|	8	12	16	20	25	29	33	40	|	6	9	13	16	20	23	27	32
TWA4	|	7	12	17	21	26	30	36	43	|	5	9	13	16	21	25	29	35
TWD1	|	8	10	12	13	15	17	18	20	|	6	8	9	9	10	11	11	11
TWD2	|	7	9	11	13	16	18	20	22	|	4	6	8	9	10	11	12	13
TWD3	|	8	14	20	25	32	37	44	52	|	6	10	16	20	26	31	36	44
TWD4	|	9	14	20	24	31	35	41	49	|	6	10	15	19	25	29	34	41
TWE1	|	15	19	24	27	33	36	41	47	|	13	17	21	24	29	32	36	41
TWE2	|	14	18	23	26	31	35	39	45	|	13	16	20	23	27	30	34	39
TWF2	|	14	17	21	24	29	31	35	40	|	12	15	19	21	25	27	30	34
TWF3	|	10	12	14	15	17	19	20	22	|	9	10	11	13	14	15	16	17
TWF4	|	10	12	13	14	16	16	17	18	|	10	11	11	12	13	13	14	14
TWI1	|	10	10	11	12	13	13	14	14	|	9	9	10	10	10	10	10	9
TWI2	|	7	11	15	18	22	25	30	35	|	5	8	11	14	17	19	22	27
TWI3	|	8	11	14	17	21	23	27	32	|	6	8	11	13	16	18	21	24
TWI4	|	15	20	27	31	37	42	47	55	|	13	18	23	27	33	37	41	48
TWJ1	|	15	20	26	30	36	40	46	53	|	13	17	22	26	32	35	40	46
TWJ2	|	9	11	13	14	16	17	19	20	|	7	8	10	11	12	12	12	11
WWA2	|	12	15	20	23	28	31	36	42	|	10	13	17	20	24	26	30	35

Weather Data

	Jan	Feb	Mar	Apr	May	Jun	Jul	Aug	Sep	Oct	Nov	Dec	Year
Daily Max Temp (°F)**	26	28	38	53	66	76	81	78	70	59	44	30	54
Daily MinTemp (°F)**	8	9	20	33	43	54	58	56	49	39	30	15	35
Daily Temp Range (°F)**	18	19	18	20	23	22	23	22	21	20	14	15	20
Heating DD (base 65°F)*	1494	1299	1113	660	331	63	20	49	191	503	840	1315	7878
Heating DD (base 55°F)*	1185	1019	804	366	115	0	0	0	29	210	541	1005	5274
Normal Precip (in.)**	1.7	1.7	1.9	2.6	3.0	3.5	3.5	3.7	3.0	2.7	2.9	2.2	32
Daily Max Rel Hum (%)**	68	70	71	75	78	83	85	86	89	82	82	78	79
Daily Min Rel Hum (%)**	62	60	57	53	52	58	55	58	63	62	71	72	60
Mean Dewpoint (°F)***	12	12	20	32	43	54	59	58	51	40	30	17	36
Prevailing Wind (from)**	10	9	9	9	9	8	8	8	8	9	10	10	9
Mean Wind Spd (mph)**	S	S	N	S	S	S	S	S	S	S	S	S	S
Hor Solar Rad (lang'ys)***	117	218	238	403	462	512	501	462	307	223	146	96	307

Data sources: *Balcomb et al., (1984); **National Oceanic and Atmospheric Administration, 1978; ***U.S. Department of Commerce (1978).

Typical Luminaire	Typical Intensity Distribution and Per Cent Lamp Lumens		$\rho_{CC} \rightarrow$	80			70			50			30			10			0	WDRC
			$\rho_W \rightarrow$	50	30	10	50	30	10	50	30	10	50	30	10	50	30	10	0	
	Maint. Cat.	SC	RCR ↓	Coefficients of Utilization for 20 Per Cent Effective Floor Cavity Reflectance ($\rho_{FC} = 20$)																
1 Pendant diffusing sphere with incandescent lamp	V 35½%↑ 45%↓	1.5	0	.87	.87	.87	.81	.81	.81	.70	.70	.70	.59	.59	.59	.49	.49	.49	.45	
			1	.71	.66	.62	.65	.61	.58	.55	.52	.49	.46	.44	.42	.38	.36	.34	.30	.368
			2	.60	.53	.48	.55	.50	.45	.47	.42	.38	.39	.35	.32	.31	.29	.26	.23	.279
			3	.52	.44	.38	.48	.41	.36	.40	.35	.31	.33	.29	.26	.27	.24	.21	.18	.227
			4	.45	.37	.32	.42	.35	.29	.35	.30	.25	.29	.25	.21	.23	.20	.17	.14	.192
			5	.40	.32	.27	.37	.30	.25	.31	.25	.21	.26	.21	.18	.21	.17	.14	.12	.166
			6	.35	.28	.23	.33	.26	.21	.28	.22	.18	.23	.19	.15	.19	.15	.12	.10	.146
			7	.32	.25	.19	.29	.23	.18	.25	.20	.16	.21	.16	.13	.17	.13	.11	.09	.130
			8	.29	.22	.17	.27	.20	.16	.23	.17	.14	.19	.15	.12	.15	.12	.09	.07	.117
			9	.26	.19	.15	.24	.18	.14	.21	.16	.12	.17	.13	.10	.14	.11	.08	.07	.107
			10	.24	.17	.13	.22	.16	.12	.19	.14	.11	.16	.12	.09	.13	.10	.08	.06	.098
2 Concentric ring unit with incandescent silvered-bowl lamp	II 83%↑ 3½%↓	N.A.	0	.83	.83	.83	.72	.72	.72	.50	.50	.50	.30	.30	.30	.12	.12	.12	.03	
			1	.72	.69	.66	.62	.60	.57	.43	.42	.40	.26	.25	.25	.10	.10	.10	.03	.018
			2	.63	.58	.54	.54	.50	.47	.38	.35	.33	.23	.22	.20	.09	.09	.08	.02	.015
			3	.55	.49	.45	.47	.43	.39	.33	.30	.28	.20	.19	.17	.08	.07	.07	.02	.013
			4	.48	.42	.37	.42	.37	.33	.29	.26	.23	.18	.16	.15	.07	.06	.06	.02	.012
			5	.43	.36	.32	.37	.32	.28	.26	.23	.20	.16	.14	.12	.06	.06	.05	.01	.011
			6	.38	.32	.27	.33	.28	.24	.23	.20	.17	.14	.12	.11	.06	.05	.04	.01	.010
			7	.34	.28	.23	.30	.24	.21	.21	.17	.15	.13	.11	.09	.05	.04	.04	.01	.009
			8	.31	.25	.20	.27	.21	.18	.19	.15	.13	.12	.10	.08	.05	.04	.03	.01	.008
			9	.28	.22	.18	.24	.19	.16	.17	.14	.11	.10	.09	.07	.04	.03	.03	.01	.008
			10	.25	.20	.16	.22	.17	.14	.16	.12	.10	.10	.08	.06	.04	.03	.03	.01	.007
3 Porcelain-enameled ventilated standard dome with incandescent lamp	IV 0%↑ 83½%↓	1.3	0	.99	.99	.99	.97	.97	.97	.93	.93	.93	.89	.89	.89	.85	.85	.85	.83	
			1	.87	.84	.81	.85	.82	.79	.82	.79	.77	.79	.76	.74	.76	.74	.72	.71	.323
			2	.76	.70	.65	.74	.69	.65	.71	.67	.63	.69	.65	.62	.66	.63	.60	.59	.311
			3	.66	.59	.54	.65	.59	.53	.62	.57	.53	.60	.56	.52	.58	.54	.51	.49	.288
			4	.58	.51	.45	.57	.50	.45	.55	.49	.44	.53	.48	.44	.51	.47	.43	.41	.264
			5	.52	.44	.39	.51	.44	.38	.49	.43	.38	.47	.42	.37	.46	.41	.37	.35	.241
			6	.46	.39	.33	.46	.38	.33	.44	.38	.33	.43	.37	.33	.41	.36	.32	.31	.221
			7	.42	.34	.29	.41	.34	.29	.40	.33	.29	.39	.33	.29	.38	.32	.28	.27	.203
			8	.38	.31	.26	.37	.31	.26	.36	.30	.26	.35	.30	.25	.34	.29	.25	.24	.187
			9	.35	.28	.23	.34	.28	.23	.33	.27	.23	.32	.27	.23	.32	.26	.23	.21	.173
			10	.32	.25	.21	.32	.25	.21	.31	.25	.21	.30	.24	.21	.29	.24	.20	.19	.161

Typical Luminaire	Typical Intensity Distribution and Per Cent Lamp Lumens		$\rho_{CC} \rightarrow$	80			70			50			30			10			0	WDRC
			$\rho_W \rightarrow$	50	30	10	50	30	10	50	30	10	50	30	10	50	30	10	0	
	Maint. Cat.	SC	RCR ↓	Coefficients of Utilization for 20 Per Cent Effective Floor Cavity Reflectance ($\rho_{FC} = 20$)																
7	IV	0.7	0	.52	.52	.52	.51	.51	.51	.48	.48	.48	.46	.46	.46	.45	.45	.45	.44	
	0% ↑		1	.49	.48	.47	.48	.47	.46	.46	.45	.45	.44	.44	.43	.43	.43	.42	.41	.055
			2	.46	.44	.43	.45	.44	.43	.44	.43	.42	.43	.42	.41	.41	.41	.40	.39	.054
			3	.43	.41	.40	.43	.41	.40	.42	.40	.39	.41	.39	.38	.40	.39	.38	.37	.053
			4	.41	.39	.37	.41	.39	.37	.40	.38	.37	.39	.37	.36	.38	.37	.36	.35	.052
			5	.39	.37	.35	.39	.37	.35	.38	.36	.35	.37	.36	.34	.36	.35	.34	.34	.051
	43½% ↓		6	.37	.35	.33	.37	.35	.33	.36	.34	.33	.35	.34	.33	.35	.34	.32	.32	.049
EAR-38 lamp above 51 mm (2″) diameter aperture (increase efficiency to 54½% for 76 mm (3″) diameter aperture)*			7	.35	.33	.31	.35	.33	.31	.34	.33	.31	.34	.32	.31	.33	.32	.31	.30	.048
			8	.34	.31	.30	.33	.31	.30	.33	.31	.30	.32	.31	.29	.32	.31	.29	.29	.046
			9	.32	.30	.28	.32	.30	.28	.31	.30	.28	.31	.29	.28	.31	.29	.28	.28	.045
			10	.31	.28	.27	.31	.28	.27	.30	.28	.27	.30	.28	.27	.30	.28	.27	.26	.043
8	V	1.0	0	.65	.65	.65	.63	.63	.63	.60	.60	.60	.58	.58	.58	.55	.55	.55	.54	
	0% ↑		1	.59	.57	.56	.58	.56	.55	.56	.54	.53	.53	.52	.52	.52	.51	.50	.49	.133
			2	.54	.51	.49	.53	.50	.48	.51	.49	.47	.49	.47	.46	.48	.46	.45	.44	.130
			3	.49	.46	.43	.48	.45	.43	.47	.44	.42	.45	.43	.41	.44	.42	.41	.40	.123
			4	.45	.41	.38	.44	.41	.38	.43	.40	.38	.42	.39	.37	.41	.39	.37	.36	.116
			5	.41	.37	.35	.41	.37	.34	.40	.36	.34	.39	.36	.34	.38	.35	.33	.32	.109
	54½% ↓		6	.38	.34	.31	.38	.34	.31	.37	.33	.31	.36	.33	.31	.35	.33	.31	.30	.103
			7	.35	.31	.29	.35	.31	.29	.34	.31	.28	.33	.30	.28	.33	.30	.28	.27	.097
			8	.33	.29	.26	.32	.29	.26	.32	.28	.26	.31	.28	.26	.31	.28	.26	.25	.092
Medium distribution unit with lens plate and inside frost lamp			9	.31	.27	.24	.30	.27	.24	.30	.26	.24	.29	.26	.24	.29	.26	.24	.23	.087
			10	.29	.25	.22	.28	.25	.22	.28	.25	.22	.27	.24	.22	.27	.24	.22	.21	.082
9	IV	0.5	0	.82	.82	.82	.80	.80	.80	.76	.76	.76	.73	.73	.73	.70	.70	.70	.69	
	0% ↑		1	.78	.77	.75	.76	.75	.74	.74	.73	.72	.71	.70	.70	.69	.68	.68	.67	.051
			2	.74	.72	.71	.73	.71	.70	.71	.70	.68	.69	.68	.67	.67	.66	.66	.65	.050
			3	.71	.69	.67	.71	.68	.67	.69	.67	.66	.67	.66	.65	.66	.65	.64	.63	.049
			4	.69	.66	.64	.68	.66	.64	.67	.65	.63	.66	.64	.63	.64	.63	.62	.61	.048
			5	.67	.64	.62	.66	.63	.62	.65	.63	.61	.64	.62	.61	.63	.61	.60	.59	.047
	68½% ↓		6	.64	.62	.60	.64	.61	.60	.63	.61	.59	.62	.60	.59	.61	.60	.59	.58	.045
			7	.63	.60	.58	.62	.60	.58	.61	.59	.57	.61	.59	.57	.60	.58	.57	.56	.044
Recessed baffled downlight, 140 mm (5 ½″) diameter aperture—150-PAR/FL lamp			8	.61	.58	.56	.60	.58	.56	.60	.58	.56	.59	.57	.56	.59	.57	.56	.55	.043
			9	.59	.56	.55	.59	.56	.55	.58	.56	.54	.58	.56	.54	.57	.55	.54	.54	.042
			10	.58	.55	.53	.57	.55	.53	.57	.55	.53	.56	.54	.53	.56	.54	.53	.52	.041

Typical Luminaire	Typical Intensity Distribution and Per Cent Lamp Lumens			ρcc →	80			70			50			30			10			0	WDRC
				ρw →	50	30	10	50	30	10	50	30	10	50	30	10	50	30	10	0	
	Maint. Cat.	SC	RCR ↓		Coefficients of Utilization for 20 Per Cent Effective Floor Cavity Reflectance (ρFC = 20)																
37 2-lamp diffuse wraparound—see note 7	V (8%↑ 37½%↓)	1.3	0		.52	.52	.52	.50	.50	.50	.46	.46	.46	.43	.43	.43	.39	.39	.39	.38	
			1		.44	.42	.40	.42	.40	.39	.39	.37	.36	.36	.35	.33	.33	.32	.31	.30	.201
			2		.38	.35	.32	.37	.33	.31	.34	.31	.29	.31	.29	.27	.28	.27	.25	.24	.171
			3		.33	.29	.26	.32	.28	.25	.29	.26	.24	.27	.25	.22	.25	.23	.21	.20	.149
			4		.29	.25	.22	.28	.24	.21	.26	.23	.20	.24	.21	.19	.22	.20	.18	.17	.132
			5		.26	.22	.19	.25	.21	.18	.23	.20	.17	.21	.18	.16	.20	.17	.15	.14	.117
			6		.23	.19	.16	.22	.18	.16	.21	.17	.15	.19	.16	.14	.18	.15	.13	.12	.106
			7		.21	.17	.14	.20	.16	.14	.19	.15	.13	.17	.15	.12	.16	.14	.12	.11	.096
			8		.19	.15	.12	.18	.15	.12	.17	.14	.12	.16	.13	.11	.15	.12	.11	.10	.088
			9		.17	.14	.11	.17	.13	.11	.16	.13	.10	.15	.12	.10	.14	.11	.09	.09	.081
			10		.16	.12	.10	.15	.12	.10	.14	.11	.09	.14	.11	.09	.13	.10	.09	.08	.075
38 4-lamp, 610 mm (2') wide troffer with 45° plastic louver—see note 7	IV (0%↑ 50%↓)	1.0	0		.60	.60	.60	.58	.58	.58	.56	.56	.56	.53	.53	.53	.51	.51	.51	.50	
			1		.53	.51	.49	.52	.50	.49	.50	.48	.47	.48	.47	.46	.46	.45	.44	.43	.168
			2		.47	.44	.42	.46	.43	.41	.44	.42	.40	.43	.41	.39	.41	.40	.38	.37	.159
			3		.42	.38	.36	.41	.38	.35	.40	.37	.35	.39	.36	.34	.37	.35	.34	.32	.146
			4		.38	.34	.31	.37	.34	.31	.36	.33	.30	.35	.32	.30	.34	.32	.30	.29	.135
			5		.34	.30	.27	.34	.30	.27	.33	.29	.27	.32	.29	.27	.31	.28	.26	.25	.124
			6		.31	.27	.24	.31	.27	.24	.30	.27	.24	.29	.26	.24	.28	.26	.24	.23	.114
			7		.29	.25	.22	.28	.24	.22	.28	.24	.22	.27	.24	.21	.26	.23	.21	.20	.106
			8		.26	.22	.20	.26	.22	.20	.25	.22	.20	.25	.22	.20	.24	.21	.19	.19	.099
			9		.24	.21	.18	.24	.21	.18	.24	.20	.18	.23	.20	.18	.23	.20	.18	.17	.092
			10		.23	.19	.17	.22	.19	.17	.22	.19	.16	.22	.19	.16	.21	.18	.16	.16	.086
40 Fluorescent unit dropped diffuser, 4-lamp 610 mm (2') wide—see note 7	V (1%↑ 60½%↓)	1.2	0		.73	.73	.73	.71	.71	.71	.68	.68	.68	.65	.65	.65	.62	.62	.62	.60	
			1		.63	.60	.58	.62	.59	.57	.59	.57	.55	.56	.55	.53	.54	.53	.51	.50	.259
			2		.55	.51	.47	.54	.50	.46	.51	.48	.45	.49	.46	.44	.47	.45	.43	.42	.236
			3		.48	.43	.39	.47	.42	.39	.45	.41	.38	.43	.40	.37	.42	.39	.36	.35	.212
			4		.43	.37	.33	.42	.37	.33	.40	.36	.32	.39	.35	.32	.37	.34	.31	.30	.191
			5		.38	.33	.29	.37	.32	.28	.36	.31	.28	.35	.31	.28	.33	.30	.27	.26	.173
			6		.34	.29	.25	.34	.29	.25	.33	.28	.24	.31	.27	.24	.30	.27	.24	.23	.158
			7		.31	.26	.22	.31	.26	.22	.30	.25	.22	.29	.25	.21	.28	.24	.21	.20	.144
			8		.28	.23	.20	.28	.23	.20	.27	.23	.19	.26	.22	.19	.25	.22	.19	.18	.133
			9		.26	.21	.18	.26	.21	.18	.25	.21	.17	.24	.20	.17	.24	.20	.17	.16	.123
			10		.24	.19	.16	.24	.19	.16	.23	.19	.16	.22	.19	.16	.22	.18	.16	.15	.115

Typical Luminaire	Maint. Cat.	SC	RCR ↓	ρcc → 80			70			50			30			10			0	WDRC
				ρw → 50	30	10	50	30	10	50	30	10	50	30	10	50	30	10	0	
19 "High bay" intermediate distribution ventilated reflector with phosphor coated HID lamp	III	1.0	0	.96	.96	.96	.93	.93	.93	.88	.88	.88	.83	.83	.83	.78	.78	.78	.76	
		6½% ↑	1	.88	.86	.83	.86	.83	.81	.81	.79	.78	.77	.75	.74	.73	.72	.71	.69	.167
			2	.80	.76	.73	.78	.74	.71	.74	.71	.69	.71	.68	.66	.68	.66	.64	.62	.168
			3	.73	.68	.64	.71	.67	.63	.68	.64	.61	.65	.62	.60	.63	.60	.58	.56	.162
			4	.67	.61	.57	.65	.60	.57	.63	.59	.55	.60	.57	.54	.58	.55	.52	.51	.155
		75½% ↓	5	.61	.56	.52	.60	.55	.51	.58	.53	.50	.56	.52	.49	.54	.50	.48	.46	.147
			6	.57	.51	.47	.56	.50	.46	.54	.49	.45	.52	.48	.45	.50	.46	.44	.42	.139
			7	.52	.47	.43	.51	.46	.42	.50	.45	.42	.48	.44	.41	.47	.43	.40	.39	.132
			8	.49	.43	.39	.48	.42	.39	.46	.42	.38	.45	.41	.38	.44	.40	.37	.36	.125
			9	.45	.40	.36	.45	.39	.36	.43	.39	.35	.42	.38	.35	.41	.37	.34	.33	.118
			10	.42	.37	.33	.42	.37	.33	.41	.36	.33	.39	.35	.32	.38	.35	.32	.31	.112
20 "High bay" wide distribution ventilated reflector with phosphor coated HID lamp	III	1.5	0	.93	.93	.93	.90	.90	.90	.83	.83	.83	.77	.77	.77	.72	.72	.72	.69	
		12% ↑	1	.85	.82	.80	.82	.79	.77	.76	.74	.73	.71	.70	.69	.66	.65	.65	.62	.168
			2	.76	.72	.69	.74	.70	.67	.69	.66	.64	.65	.63	.61	.61	.59	.58	.56	.168
			3	.69	.64	.60	.67	.62	.59	.63	.59	.56	.59	.56	.54	.56	.54	.51	.49	.163
		69% ↓	4	.62	.57	.52	.61	.55	.51	.57	.53	.50	.54	.51	.48	.51	.48	.46	.44	.156
			5	.57	.51	.46	.55	.50	.46	.52	.48	.44	.49	.46	.43	.47	.44	.41	.39	.148
			6	.52	.45	.41	.50	.45	.40	.48	.43	.39	.45	.41	.38	.43	.40	.37	.35	.141
			7	.47	.41	.37	.46	.40	.36	.44	.39	.35	.42	.37	.34	.40	.36	.33	.32	.133
			8	.43	.37	.33	.42	.36	.33	.40	.35	.32	.38	.34	.31	.37	.33	.30	.29	.126
			9	.40	.34	.30	.39	.33	.29	.37	.32	.29	.35	.31	.28	.34	.30	.27	.26	.120
			10	.37	.31	.27	.36	.30	.27	.34	.29	.26	.33	.28	.25	.31	.28	.25	.23	.114
21 "Low bay" rectangular pattern, lensed bottom reflector unit with clear HID lamp	V	1.8	0	.82	.82	.82	.80	.80	.80	.76	.76	.76	.73	.73	.73	.70	.70	.70	.68	
		0° ↑	1	.73	.70	.68	.71	.69	.67	.68	.66	.64	.65	.64	.62	.63	.62	.61	.59	.231
			2	.64	.60	.56	.63	.59	.55	.60	.57	.54	.58	.55	.53	.56	.54	.52	.50	.227
			3	.56	.51	.47	.55	.51	.47	.53	.49	.46	.52	.48	.45	.50	.47	.44	.43	.213
		45°	4	.50	.44	.40	.49	.44	.40	.48	.43	.39	.46	.42	.39	.44	.41	.38	.37	.199
			5	.45	.39	.34	.44	.38	.34	.42	.38	.34	.41	.37	.33	.40	.36	.33	.32	.184
		68½% ↓	6	.40	.34	.30	.39	.34	.30	.38	.33	.29	.37	.33	.29	.36	.32	.29	.28	.171
			7	.36	.30	.26	.36	.30	.26	.35	.29	.26	.34	.29	.26	.33	.29	.25	.24	.159
			8	.33	.27	.23	.32	.27	.23	.31	.26	.23	.31	.26	.23	.30	.26	.23	.21	.148
			9	.30	.24	.20	.29	.24	.20	.29	.24	.20	.28	.23	.20	.27	.23	.20	.19	.138
			10	.27	.22	.18	.27	.22	.18	.26	.22	.18	.26	.21	.18	.25	.21	.18	.17	.129

Coefficients of Utilization for 20 Per Cent Effective Floor Cavity Reflectance (ρFC = 20)

BUILDING LOAD WORKSHEET 1

Project _____   Date _____   Analyst _____   Location _____

Part I: PROJECT DATA (site data from Appendix D)

Annual heating DD $_{65}$ _____ ; Annual heating DD $_{55}$ _____ ; Annual cooling DD _____ ; Winter OD design temp _____ °F

Winter thermostat setpoint _____ °F; Summer OD design temp (2.5%) _____ °F; Summer thermostat setting _____ °F

Vertical solar radiation, VT _____ Btu/h•ft^2; Heating fuel cost, F_{cost} $ _____ per _____ ; Fuel cost : low /high

Heat value of fuel (Table 6.1), HV _____ per _____ ; Shading coefficient, SC for south-glass (from Table 5.1) _____

Heating equipment efficiency factor (Table 6.7), k = _____ ; Recommended conservation factor, CF = _____

Cooling equipment coefficient of performance, COP $_{cooling}$ = _____ ; No. of hrs building is occupied per day = _____ hrs.

Part II: RECOMMENDED CONSERVATION DESIGN GUIDELINES

Recommended wall total R-value: R_{wall} = 14 × CF   = _____

Recommended ceiling total R-value: $R_{ceiling}$ = 22 × CF   = _____

Recommended insulation R-value to be added to slab perimeter: $R_{perimeter}$ = (13 × CF) − 5   = _____

Recommended floor (over vented space) total R-value: R_{floor} = 14 × CF   = _____

Recommended insulation R-value to be added to basement wall: $R_{basement}$ = (16 × CF) − 8   = _____

Recommended number of glazing layers on windows: N_{glass} = 1.7 × CF   = _____

Recommended number of air changes per hour: ACH   = 0.42 ÷ CF   = _____

Part III: HEATING LOAD CALCULATIONS (based on proposed design)

Building element: load formula (fill in blanks and calculate)   = **Load, UA**

Walls: $(UA)_{wall}$ = A_{wall} ÷ R_{wall} = _____ ÷ _____   = _____

Ceiling: $(UA)_{ceiling}$ = $A_{ceiling}$ ÷ $R_{ceiling}$ = _____ ÷ _____   = _____

Slab-on-grade: $(UA)_{perim}$ = 4.17 × P_{perim} ÷ (R_{perim} + 5) = 4.17 × _____ ÷ (_____ + 5)   = _____

Floor : $(UA)_{floor}$ = A_{floor} ÷ R_{floor} = _____ ÷ _____   = _____

Basement: $(UA)_{base}$ = 10.7 × P_{base} ÷ (R_{base} + 8) = 10.7 × _____ ÷ (_____ + 8)   = _____

Glass: $(UA)_{glass}$ = 1.1 × A_{glass} ÷ number of glazings = 1.1 × _____ ft^2 ÷ _____   = _____

Infiltration: $(UA)_{Infilt}$ = 0.018 × VOL × ACH × ADR = 0.018 × _____ × _____ × _____   = _____

Sum of UA = _____

Heating total load coefficient: TLC $_{heating}$ = 24 × sum of UA = _____ Btu/DD $_{heating}$

Design temperature difference: Δt_{winter} = winter thermostat setpoint − winter OD design temp = _____ °F

Design heating load: q_H = sum of UA × $\Delta t_{heating}$ = _____ × _____ = _____ Btu/h

BUILDING LOAD WORKSHEET 2

Part IV: COOLING LOAD CALCULATIONS (based on proposed design)

A. External sensible gain through envelope:

1. Walls: $(UA)_{wall}$ x factor (from Table 6.6, part A1) ÷ total floor area:

_____ x _____ ÷ _____ = _____ Btu/h•ft²

2. Roof: $(UA)_{ceiling}$ x factor (from Table 6.6, part A2) ÷ total floor area:

_____ x _____ ÷ _____ = _____ Btu/h•ft²

3. Shaded window area x factor (from Table 6.6, part A3) ÷ total floor area:

_____ x _____ ÷ _____ = _____ Btu/h•ft²

4. Unshaded window and skylight area x GLF (from Table 6.5) ÷ total floor area:

Orientation _____ : _____ x _____ ÷ _____ = _____ Btu/h•ft²

Orientation _____ : _____ x _____ ÷ _____ = _____ Btu/h•ft²

Orientation _____ : _____ x _____ ÷ _____ = _____ Btu/h•ft²

B. External sensible gain from infiltration or ventilation:

EITHER Infiltration: (window area + opaque wall area) x (Table 6.6, part D1) ÷ total floor area:

$q_{infiltration}$ = (_____ + _____) x _____ ÷ _____ = _____ Btu/h•ft²

OR Ventilation: VOL x ACH x ADR x factor (from Table 6.6, part D 2) ÷ total floor area:

$q_{ventilation}$ = _____ x _____ x _____ x _____ ÷ _____ = _____ Btu/h•ft²

C. Internal sensible gains — People and Equipment:

People factor (from Table 6.6, part C): q_{people} = _____ Btu/h•ft²

Equipment factor (from Table 6.6, part C): $q_{equipment}$ = _____ Btu/h•ft²

D. Internal sensible gains — Lighting:

Lighting (daylighting and electric) factor (from Table 6.6, part D): q_{light} = _____ Btu/h•ft²

Total sensible heat gains, q_t = sum sensible gains from above = (A + B + C + D) = _____ Btu/h•ft²

Design sensible cooling load: q_{sc} = total sensible gains x tot. flr. area = _____ x _____ = _____ Btu/h

Design total cooling load (including latent load): q_c = 1.3 x q_{sc} = 1.3 x _____ = _____ Btu/h

Design temperature difference: Δt_{summer} = summer OD design temp. – summer thermostat setpoint = _____ °F

Cooling load coefficient: CLC = q_c x 24 ÷ Δt_{summer} = _____ x 24 ÷ _____ °F = _____ Btu/DD cooling

Required cooling equipment capacity: C_c = q_c ÷ 12,000 Btu/ton = _____ ÷ 12,000 = _____ tons

Part V: BALANCE POINT

Winter solar gain: Q_s = VT (from Part I) x (area of south glass) x SC (from Part I) ÷ 24 =

_____ x _____ x _____ ÷ 24 = _____ Btu/h

Internal heat gain: Q_i = (q_{people} + $q_{equipment}$ + q_{light}) x (hrs occupied per day) x (floor area) ÷ 24 =

(_____ + _____ + _____) x _____ x _____ ÷ 24 = _____ Btu/h

Balance point: T_b = winter thermostat setpoint temperature – [(Q_s + Q_i) ÷ sum UA from Part III] =

_____ – [(_____ + _____) ÷ _____] = _____ °F

Part VI: HEATING and COOLING ENERGY ESTIMATE (based on proposed design)

Annual heating energy required: $Q_{heating}$ = TLC x DD $_{heating}$ = _____ x _____ = _____ x 10⁶ Btu/yr

Annual heating energy consumed: E_H = $Q_{heating}$ ÷ k = _____ x 10⁶ ÷ _____ = _____ x 10⁶ Btu /yr

Annual heating fuel consumed: F_{heat} = E_H ÷ HV = _____ x 10⁶ ÷ _____ = _____ /yr

Annual heating cost: Cost $_{heat}$ = F_{heat} x F_{cost} = _____ x _____ = $ _____ /yr

Annual cooling energy required: $Q_{cooling}$ = CLC x DD $_{cooling}$ = _____ x _____ = _____ x 10⁶ Btu /yr

Annual cool'g energy cons'd: E_c = 0.000293 x $Q_{cooling}$ ÷ COP = 0.000293 x _____ x 10⁶ ÷ _____ = _____ kWh/yr

Annual cooling cost: Cost $_{cool}$ = E_c x F_{cost} = _____ x _____ = $ _____ /yr

PASSIVE SOLAR WORKSHEET

Project _____   Date _____   Analyst _____   Location _____   Fuel cost (circle one): low/high

Part I: RECOMMENDED DESIGN GUIDELINES (for this location and fuel cost)

Recommended CF (Appendix D) = ____ ; recommended LCR (Appendix D) = ____ ; target SSF (Appendix D) = ____%.

Recommended wall total R-value:	R_{wall} = 14 x CF	= ____
Recommended ceiling total R-value:	$R_{ceiling}$ = 22 x CF	= ____
Recommended R-value to be added to slab perimeter:	$R_{perimeter}$ = (13 x CF) − 5	= ____
Recommended floor (over vented space) total R-value:	R_{floor} = 14 x CF	= ____
Recommended R-value to be added to basement wall:	$R_{basement}$ = (16 x CF) − 8	= ____
Recommended number of glazing layers on E, W, N walls:	$N_{E,W,N}$ = 1.7 x CF	= ____
Recommended number of air changes per hour:	ACH = 0.42 ÷ CF	= ____

Part II: PERFORMANCE CALCULATIONS BASED ON PROPOSED DESIGN

Building element: load formula (fill in blanks and calculate) **= Load, UA**

Walls:	$(UA)_{wall}$ = A_{wall} ÷ R_{wall} = ____ ÷ ____	= ____
Ceiling:	$(UA)_{ceiling}$ = $A_{ceiling}$ ÷ $R_{ceiling}$ = ____ ÷ ____	= ____
E, W, N glass:	$(UA)_{glass}$ = 1.1 x $A_{E,W,N}$ ÷ number of glazings = 1.1 x ____ ft² ÷ ____	= ____
Floor :	$(UA)_{floor}$ = A_{floor} x R_{floor} x ____ ÷ ____	= ____
Slab-on-grade:	$(UA)_{perim}$ = 4.17 x P_{perim} ÷ (R_{perim} + 5) = 4.17 x ____ ÷ (____ + 5)	= ____
Basement:	$(UA)_{base}$ = 10.7 x P_{base} ÷ (R_{base} + 8) = 10.7 x ____ ÷ (____ + 8)	= ____
Infiltration:	$(UA)_{Infil}$ = 0.018 x VOL x ACH x ADR = 0.018 x ____ x ____ x ____	= ____

Sum of UA = ____ Btu/h°F

Net load coefficient NLC = 24 x Sum of UA = 24 x Sum of UA = ____ Btu/DD

Recommended projected area: A_p = NLC ÷ recommended LCR = ____ ÷ ____ = ____ ft²

Design A_p (based on recommended A_p and construction considerations) = ____ ft²

Load collector ratio: LCR = NLC ÷ Design A_p = ____ ÷ ____ = ____ Btu/DD·ft²

Name of reference design	Design Projected Area, A_p	Fraction of Projected Area		SSF for each ref. design	Product of SSF x Fraction	A_p x U_{col} (Appx. B) = $(UA)_{collector}$
_____	____ ft²	x	____	= ____		A_p x ____ = ____
_____	____ ft²	x	____	= ____		A_p x ____ = ____
_____	____ ft²	x	____	= ____		A_p x ____ = ____
total design A_p =	____ ft²		**combined (sum) SSF** = ____			**Total $(UA)_{col}$** = ____

Total load coefficient (for sizing auxiliary heating equipment), TLC = NLC + [24 x $(UA)_{collector}$] = ____ Btu/DD

Auxiliary heat, Q_{aux} = NLC x DD (1 − SSF) = ____ x ____ x (1 − ____) ÷ 10^6 = ____ M Btu/year

Worksheet for Calculating Window Areas of Naturally Ventilated Houses

Project _____   Analyst _____

1. Building conditioned floor area = _____ (1) ft²

2. Average ceiling height = _____ (2) ft

3. House volume = (step 1) x (step 2) = _____ (3) ft³

4. Design air change rate / hour (recommended value is 30) = _____ (4) ACH

5. Required airflow rate, cfm = (step 3) x (step 4) ÷ 60 = _____ (5) cfm

6. Design month (recommended: May for Florida and Gulf Coast; June elsewhere) = _____ (6)

7. Name of nearest city = _____ (7)

8. From maps in Appendix C, determine windspeed (WS) and direction (WD) for the design month: WS = _____ (8a) ; WD = _____ (8b) mph

9. From prevailing direction, determine the incidence angle on the *windward* wall having the *largest* area of window (0° = perpendicular to wall) = _____ (9) deg.

10. From Table 15.1, determine inlet-to-site 10-meter windspeed ratio = _____ (10)

11. Determine windspeed correction factors:

11a. For house location and ventilation strategy, determine terrain correction factor from Table 15.2 = _____ (11a)

11b. For neighboring buildings, assume neighborhood convection factor = 0.77; no surrounding buildings = 1.0 = _____ (11b)

11c. For windows for the second floor (or for house on stilts), use a correction factor of 1.15 (otherwise, use 1.0). Correction factor = _____ (11c)

12. Calculate windspeed correction factor = (step 11a) x (step 11b) x (step 11c) = _____ (12)

13. Calculate site windspeed in ft/min = (step 8a) x (step 12) x 88 = _____ (13) ft/min

14. Calculate window inlet airspeed = (step 13) x (step 10) = _____ (14) ft/min

15. Calculate net aperture inlet area = (step 5) ÷ (step 14) = _____ (15) ft²

16. Determine total effective inlet + outlet effective area (screened) = 3.33 x (step 15) = _____ (16) ft²

17. Determine total effective area as % of floor area = (step 16) ÷ (step 1) x 100 = _____ (17) %

18. This total effective area requirement can be met by the same area of net opening. If windows or doors are used, then this area must be increased to allow for their effective area by applying the following effective opening factor: single- or double-hung window = 0.45; single- or double-sliding window = 0.45; hopper = 0.45; awning window = 0.75; casement window = 0.9; jalousie windows = 0.75; sliding door = 0.45; hinged door = 0.95.

19. Select openings and calculate their total effective area:

Opening type: frame opening area (ft²) x effective opening factor (step 18) x no. of this opening type =

.... _____   x _____   = _____ ft²

.... _____   x _____   = _____ ft²

.... _____   x _____   = _____ ft²

.... _____   x _____   = _____ ft²

.... _____   x _____   = _____ ft²

.... _____   x _____   = _____ ft²

.... _____   x _____   = _____ ft²

.... _____   x _____   = _____ ft²

20. Total effective area as designed and installed (should equal or exceed step 16) = _____ ft²

BRS DAYLIGHTING PROTRACTOR WORKSHEET

Project _____   Analyst _____   Conditions _____

PART I: SKY COMPONENT

Reading on primary sky component scale	upper reading = _____	1
	lower reading = _____	2
Primary sky component for window of infinite length (step 1 − step 2)	_____	3
Angles of elevation of visible sky	upper reading = _____ °	4
	lower reading = _____ °	5
	_____ °	6
Average angle of elevation: (step 4 − step 5) x 2		
Readings from auxiliary scale:	left reading = _____	7
	right reading = _____	8
Correction factor for window width: (step 7 ± step 8)	= _____	9
Sky component for window of finite length (step 3 x step 9)	= _____	10
Factor for glazing material (1.0 for single glazing)	= _____	11
Factor for window mullions and frames (0.75 is typical)	= _____	12
Factor for dirt on glazing (0.9 for clean, 0.6 for very dirty)	= _____	13
Combined factors (step 11 x step 12 x step 13)	= _____	14
Corrected sky component (step 10 x step 14)	= _____	15

PART II: EXTERNALLY REFLECTED COMPONENT

Readings on primary sky component scale:	upper reading = _____	16
	lower reading = _____	17
Primary sky component for window of infinite length (step 16 − step 17)	= _____	18
Angles of elevation of visible sky	upper reading = _____ °	19
	lower reading = _____ °	20
	_____ °	21
Average angle of elevation: (step 19 − step 20) x 2		
Readings from auxiliary scale:	left reading = _____	22
	right reading = _____	23
Correction factor for window width: (step 22 ± step 23)	= _____	24
External reflected component for window of finite length (step 18 x step 24)	= _____	25
Correction factor for relative luminance of external obstruction (0.2 typically)	= _____	26
Corrected externally reflected component (step 25 x step 26 x step 14)	= _____	27

PART III: INTERNAL REFLECTED COMPONENT

Internal reflected component (from Table 24.2)	= _____	28

PART IV: DAYLIGHT FACTOR

Daylight factor (step 15 + step 27 + step 28)	= _____	29

comments:

SIDELIGHTING DAYLIGHT ILLUMINANCE WORKSHEET (Lumen Method)

Project _____ Analyst _____ Location _____ .

Date to be analyzed (circle one): Jun 21, Mar/Sep 21, Dec 21; Time (circle one): 8 a.m. 10 a.m. noon 2 p.m. 4 p.m.

Room Length (parallel to window) = _____; Room Width = _____; Ceiling Height = _____; Wall Reflectance = _____%

Latitude = _____; Predominant sky condition (circle one): clear / overcast; Window facing direction (N, E, S, W) _____ .

1. Enter the vertical illuminance from the sky on the glazing surface for the predominant sky condition for the above date and time (either clear diffuse from Table 24.4, or overcast from Table 24.5; do not include direct sun) _____ kilolux x 100 fc/kilolux = E_s = _____ fc

2. Determine the ground reflectance, (typically 0.2; 0.6 for snow) = ρ_g = _____

3. Determine the total horizontal illuminance on the ground for the predominant sky condition (due to both sun and sky; from Table 24.6) _____ kilolux x 100 fc/kilolux = E_h = _____ fc

4. Calculate vertical illuminance due to ground = $E_h \times \rho_g \times 0.5$ = (_____) (_____) = E_g = _____ fc

5. Enter the gross window area A_w above the 30 in. workplane height = E_h = _____ ft²

6. Estimate the mullion factor, MF = reduction factor applied to gross window area to allow for mullions and other obstructions in the window plane (0.75 is typical; that is 25% of the window is obstructed by mullions, 75% is glass area). MF = _____

7. Calculate net glazing area = (A_w) (MF) = (_____) (_____) = A_g = _____ ft²

8. Determine the net transmittance, T_{net} (less than 1.0, it is the product of such light loss factors as glazing transmittance, dirt factor, drapery transmittance, etc.; for example, double-glazed clear glass in an office building with no draperies has a net transmittance of about 0.65; single-glazed clear glass in a factory with no draperies has a net transmittance of about 0.55). T_{net} = _____ .

9. From Table 24.7 a or b, look-up C_{max}, C_{mid}, C_{min}, K_{max}, K_{mid}, and K_{min} sky-contributed coefficients of utilization:

   Sky-contributed: C_{max} = _____ ; C_{mid} = _____ ; C_{min} = _____ ; K_{max} = _____ ; K_{mid} = _____ ; and K_{min} = _____

10. From Table 24.7 c or d, look-up C_{max}, C_{mid}, C_{min}, K_{max}, K_{mid}, and K_{min} ground-contributed coefficients of utilization.

    Ground-contributed: C_{max} = _____ ; C_{mid} = _____ ; C_{min} = _____ ; K_{max} = _____ ; K_{mid} = _____ ; and K_{min} = _____

11. Sky-contributed $E_{int, sky}$ at Max = $(E_s)(A_g)(T_{net})(C)(K)$ = (_____)(_____)(_____)(_____)(_____) = _____ fc

    Ground-contributed $E_{int, gnd}$ at Max = $(E_g)(A_g)(T_{net})(C)(K)$ = (_____)(_____)(_____)(_____)(_____) = _____ fc

    Total interior illuminance E_{int} at Max = $(E_{int, sky})$ + $(E_{int, gnd})$ = _____ fc

12. Sky-contributed $E_{int, sky}$ at Mid = $(E_s)(A_g)(T_{net})(C)(K)$ = (_____)(_____)(_____)(_____)(_____) = _____ fc

    Ground-contributed $E_{int, gnd}$ at Mid= $(E_g)(A_g)(T_{net})(C)(K)$ =(_____)(_____)(_____)(_____)(_____) = _____ fc

    Total interior illuminance E_{int} at Mid = $(E_{int, sky})$ + $(E_{int, gnd})$ = _____ fc

13. Sky-contributed $E_{int, sky}$ at Min = $(E_s)(A_g)(T_{net})(C)(K)$ = (_____)(_____)(_____)(_____)(_____) = _____ fc

    Ground-contributed $E_{int, gnd}$ at Min= $(E_g)(A_g)(T_{net})(C)(K)$ = (_____)(_____)(_____)(_____)(_____) = _____ fc

    Total interior illuminance E_{int} at Min = $(E_{int, sky})$ + $(E_{int, gnd})$ = _____ fc

TOPLIGHTING DAYLIGHT ILLUMINANCE WORKSHEET (Lumen Method)

Project _____ Analyst _____ Latitude = _____ ; Sky condition (circle one): clear / overcast

Date to be analyzed (circle one): Jun 21, Mar/Sep 21, Dec 21; Time (circle one): 8 a.m. 10 a.m. noon 2 p.m. 4 p.m.

Room length = _____ ft; Room width = _____ ft; Ceiling height = _____ ft; Wall reflectance = _____ %

Ceiling reflectance = _____ % ; Number of skylights _____ ; Skylight gross area (each) _____ ft^2; Skylight well height _____ ft

Skylight well width, _____ ft; Skylight well length _____ ft; Skylight well reflectance _____ %

1. Determine the exterior horizontal illuminance, E_h (use total of direct sun plus sky for clear conditions; from Table 24.6) _____ kilolux x 100 fc/kilolux = E_h = _____ fc

2. Calculate total gross area of skylights, A_t = (gross area of one skylight)(# of skylights) = A_t = _____ ft^2

3. Determine the T_g = transmittance of the glazing medium (from manufacturer's literature, or assume 0.85 for clear double domes and 0.44 for translucent double domes) = T_g = _____

4. Calculate the skylight well index, WI = $\dfrac{\text{(height)(width+height)}}{2\text{(width)(length)}} = \dfrac{(\quad)(\quad + \quad)}{2(\quad)(\quad)}$ = WI = _____

5. Determine the well efficiency, N_w (from Fig. 24.11) N_w = _____

6. Estimate the mullion factor, MF = reduction factor applied to gross window area to allow for mullions and other obstructions in the skylight (0.75 is typical; that is 25% of the window is obstructed by mullions, 75% is glass area). MF = _____

7. Determine the transmittance of any controls, T_c (louvers, for example; 1.0 if none) = T_c = _____

8. Determine the net transmittance, $T_{net} = (T_g)(N_w)(MF)(T_c) = (\underline{\quad})(\underline{\quad})(\underline{\quad})(\underline{\quad}) = T_{net}$ = _____

9. Calculate RCR = $\dfrac{5\text{(room height} - \text{workplane height)(room width} + \text{room length)}}{\text{(room length)(room width)}}$

$= \dfrac{5(\quad - \quad)(\quad + \quad)}{(\quad)(\quad)}$ = RCR = _____

10. Look-up the room coefficient of utilization, RCU (Table 24.3) = RCU = _____

11. Calculate the utilization coefficient, $K_u = (RCU)(T_{net}) = (\underline{\quad})(\underline{\quad})$ = K_u = _____

12. Calculate the light loss factor: K_m = skylight and room wall dirt depreciation factors (typically between 0.4 for factories and 0.8 for offices) = K_m = _____

13. Workplane average illuminance:

$E_{wp} = \dfrac{(E_h)(A_t)(K_u)(K_m)}{\text{(room length)(room width)}} = \dfrac{(\quad)(\quad)(\quad)(\quad)}{(\quad)(\quad)}$ = E_{wp} = _____ fc

comments:

AVERAGE ILLUMINANCE WORKSHEET - ELECTRIC LIGHTING

1. Project name _____ Room _____ Designer _____

2. Illuminance category (from Table 21.1 recommendations or other) _____ Design illumination _____ fc

3. Luminaire manufacturer _____

   4. Luminaire mfg'rs. catalog no. _____

5. Lamps: type and color _____

   6. Initial lumen output (per lamp) _____

7. Number of lamps per luminaire _____

   8. Total lumens per luminaire _____

9. Fill in sketch:

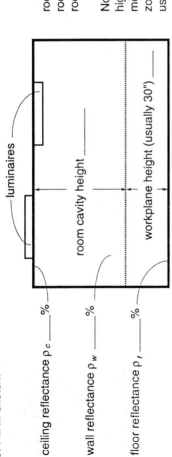

luminaires

room cavity height

workplane height (usually 30")

room length _____
room width _____
room area _____

Note: If ceiling is substantially higher than the luminaire mounting height, the general zonal cavity method must be used (see Kaufman, 1987).

ceiling reflectance ρ_c ___ %

wall reflectance ρ_w ___ %

floor reflectance ρ_f ___ %

10. Calculate the room cavity ratio, RCR:

$$RCR = \frac{5(\text{room cavity height})(\text{room length} + \text{room width})}{(\text{room length})(\text{room width})} = \frac{5(\quad)(\quad + \quad)}{(\quad)(\quad)} = \underline{\qquad}$$

11. Coefficient of utilization, CU (from manufacturer's literature or Kaufman, 1984) = _____

12. Initial av. illuminance per luminaire $= \dfrac{(\text{lumens per lamp})(\text{\# lamps per luminaire})(CU)}{\text{floor area}} = \dfrac{(\quad)(\quad)(\quad)}{(\quad)} = \underline{\qquad}$

13. Determine light loss subfactors:

    Luminaire ambient temperature factor, LATF _____   Voltage to luminaire factor, VLF _____
    Ballast factor, BF _____   Luminaire surface depreciation factor, LSDF _____
    Lamp burnout factor, LBF _____   Lamp lumen depreciation factor, LLDF _____
    Luminaire dirt depreciation factor, LDDF _____   Room surface depreciation factor, RSDF _____

    Light loss factor, LLF = (LATF)(VLF)(BF)(LSDF)(LBF)(LLDF)(LDDF)(RSDF) = _____

14. Maintained illuminance per luminaire = (initial illuminance per luminaire)(LLF) = (___)(___) = _____

15. Required number of luminaires $= \dfrac{(\text{design illuminance level})}{\text{net illuminance per luminaire}} = \dfrac{(\quad)}{(\quad)} = \underline{\qquad}$ or _____

16. Luminaire layout:

Multiply	By	To Get
acres	4047	square meters
Btu (British thermal unit; energy)	0.252	kilocalories
Btu (energy)	1.055	kilojoules
Btu (energy)	200	lumens
Btu/h (power)	0.2928	watts
Btu/h•ft	3.152	watts per square meter
Btu•°F (heat capacity)	4.182	kilojoules per kelvin
Btu/lb•°F (specific heat)	1.897	kilojoules per kilogram per kelvin
Btu/h•°F•in (conductivity)	0.144	watts per kelvin per meter
Btu/h•°F•ft^2 (conductance)	5.673	watts per kelvin per square meter
Btu/°F•day•ft^2 (load-collector ratio)	5.673	watts per kelvin
°C (Celcius degree)	1.8	plus 32 = degree Fahrenheit
cd (candela)	0.00146	watts per steradian
cd (candela)	1	lumen per steradian
degree (angular)	0.1745	radians
degree (solid angle)	0.0003	steradian
°F (degree; first subtract 32)	0.5555	degrees Celsius
ft^3 (cubic feet)	0.028	cubic meters
ft (feet)	0.305	meters
ft/sec (feet per second)	0.305	meters per second
ft•lb/sec	1.356	watts
fc (footcandle)	1	lumen per square foot
fc (footcandle)	0.0014	langleys per hour
fc (footcandle)	10.76	lux
fL (footlambert)	0.3184	candelas per square foot
fL (footlambert)	3.426	candelas per square meter
gal (gallon)	3.785	liters
gal/h (gallons per hour)	0.00152	liters per second
g (grams)	0.035	ounces (avoirdupois)
hp (horsepower)	0.746	watts
in (inches)	25.4	millimeters
in Hg (inches of mercury)	0.033	atmospheres
in^3 (cubic inches)	16.39	cubic centimeters

Multiply	By	To Get
kcal (kilocalories)	3.968	British thermal units
kcal (kilocalories)	4190	joules
kg (kilograms)	2.205	pounds
kg/m^3 (kilograms per cubic meter)	1.686	pounds per cubic yard
kg/m^2 (kilograms per square meter)	0.205	pounds per square foot
kJ (kilojoules)	0.948	British thermal units
km/h (kilometers per hour)	0.621	miles per hour
kWh (kilowatt-hours)	3,142	British thermal units
lb (pounds)	0.454	kilograms
lb/ft^2 (pounds per square foot)	4.882	kilograms per square meter
L (liters)	0.03532	cubic feet
langley	1.0	calories per square centimeter
langley	3.69	Btu per square foot
langleys/min (langleys per minute)	0.0698	watts per square centimeter
lumen	0.005	British thermal units per hour
lumen	0.00146	watts
lx (lux)	1	lumen per square meter
lx (lux)	0.093	footcandles
MJ (megajoules)	0.278	kilowatt-hours
m (meters)	3.281	feet
m^3 (cubic meters)	35.32	cubic feet
m/s (meters per second)	196.86	feet per minute
mph (miles per hour)	1.609	kilometers per hour
mL (mililiters)	0.061	cubic inches
mm (milimeters)	0.039	inches
steradian	3283	solid degrees
tons (of refrigeration)	12,000	Btu per hour
therm	1 x 10^5	British thermal units
W (watts)	3.412	British thermal units per hour
W (watts)	683	lumens
W (watts)	683	candelas per steradian
W/m^2 (watts per square meter)	0.317	Btu per square foot
yards	0.914	meters